Expert Consolidation in Oracle Database 12c

T0183683

Martin Bach

Apress

Expert Consolidation in Oracle Database 12c

ISBN-13 (pbk): 978-1-4302-4428-8

ISBN-13 (electronic): 978-1-4302-4429-5

President and Publisher: Paul Manning
Lead Editor: Jonathan Gennick
Technical Reviewer: Frits Hoogland
Editorial Board: Steve Anglin, Ewan Buckingham, Gary Cornell, Louise Corrigan, Morgan Ertel,
    Jonathan Gennick, Jonathan Hassell, Robert Hutchinson, Michelle Lowman, James Markham,
    Matthew Moodie, Jeff Olson, Jeffrey Pepper, Douglas Pundick, Ben Renow-Clarke, Dominic Shakeshaft,
    Gwenan Spearing, Matt Wade, Tom Welsh
Coordinating Editor: Kevin Shea
Copy Editor: Lori Cavanaugh
Compositor: SPi Global
Indexer: SPi Global
Artist: SPi Global
Cover Designer: Anna Ishchenko

Distributed to the book trade worldwide by Springer Science+Business Media New York, 233 Spring Street, 6th Floor, New York, NY 10013. Phone 1-800-SPRINGER, fax (201) 348-4505, e-mail orders-ny@springer-sbm.com, or visit www.springeronline.com.

For information on translations, please e-mail rights@apress.com, or visit www.apress.com.

Apress and friends of ED books may be purchased in bulk for academic, corporate, or promotional use. eBook versions and licenses are also available for most titles. For more information, reference our Special Bulk Sales–eBook Licensing web page at www.apress.com/bulk-sales.

Any source code or other supplementary materials referenced by the author in this text is available to readers at www.apress.com. For detailed information about how to locate your book's source code, go to www.apress.com/source-code.

Contents at a Glance

Contents

About the Author

Martin Bach is an enthusiastic Oracle database administrator and co-author of *Pro Oracle Database 11g RAC on Linux*, also with Apress. He has specialized in the Oracle Database Management System since 2001. His main interests are high availability and disaster recovery solutions for mission-critical 24x7 systems.

Martin is a proud member of the Oracle Certified Master community as well as an Oracle Ace, an accreditation which has been awarded based on his significant contribution and activity in the Oracle technical community. The greatest honor of all is to be a part of the Oak Table Network. The Oak Table is an informal network for the Oracle scientist, who believes in better ways of administering and developing Oracle-based systems.

Martin maintains a successful weblog at martincarstenbach.wordpress.com in addition to his written publications, which is regularly updated with his latest research results and additional information about this book.

About the Technical Reviewer

Frits Hoogland is an IT professional specializing in Oracle database performance and internals. Frits frequently presents on Oracle technical topics at conferences around the world. In 2009 he received an Oracle ACE award from the Oracle Technology Network and a year later became an Oracle ACE Director. In 2010 he joined the OakTable Network. In addition to developing his Oracle expertise, Frits works with MySQL, PostgreSQL, and modern operating systems. Frits currently works at Enkitec LP.

Acknowledgments

A book such as this one you are reading right now is never the sole effort of one single person—nobody is an island after all. Therefore I would like to thank the people who assisted in all stages of the researching, testing, writing, reviewing, and publication of this book. Fist I would like to thank the Apress team of Lead Editor Jonathan Gennick and coordinating Editor Kevin Shea for their patience, advice, and support, but also their input in getting this project started. For the technical review, I would like to thank Frits Hoogland for his time in reading, commenting, and improving the contents of the book. The technical reviewer too often does not get enough credit when you read a book as his name is not on the front cover. Frits however has been outstanding in thoroughness and dedication when it came to reviewing the contents of the book you are holding in your hands. I am very grateful for his contributions.

At this place it is time for me to thank the people who also helped with research and ideas. Steve Shaw—the lead author of Pro Oracle Database RAC 11g on Linux—has been inspirational in many ways and it was a great pleasure to have worked with him on the previous book we wrote. I tried to take his example when writing this book.

I would also like to thank the following people, and they are listed in no particular order: Kevin Closson, Chris Buckel, Matt Morris, Alex Gorbachev, Yury Velikanov, Doug Burns, The Oak Table Network, Martin Nash, Jerry Pride, Simon Haslam, Ronny Egner, Shirish Jamthe, and Kunal Vasavada. I had so many great conversations with people I worked for—and with—that cannot all be named here individually. I am sure those who remember a joint project will know who is meant. I also won't ever forget the great atmosphere during after-work conversations with friends in London. I still remember how thrilled I was when I was first invited along. And last but certainly not at all least Kerry Osborne, Andy Colvin, Randy Johnson, Hank Tullis, Karl Arao, Tanel Poder, and everyone else at Enkitec that I don't have space to list individually. It has been a fantastic journey.

Thinking back it has been a very long way from the humble beginning to where I am now. Invaluable support at the university was provided by Prof. Dr. Steinbuß, who first started my enthusiasm for the Oracle Database. I can't forget Jens Schweizer, Timo Philipps, Harald Ferber Axel Biesdorf, and Thorsten Häs for countless good hours in H105, and discussing more than just the most obvious solution to a problem. Furthermore I would also like to thank everyone at the "old" e-DBA for a lot of support during my first years in England.

It is important to me to point out that it is not only about the help of the Oracle community. I have been able to draw a lot of inspiration and passion from my supportive family. Without your help and understanding of the countless hours of research it would certainly not have been possible to finish this book at all.

Introduction

Ever since I have started looking at the Oracle database engine a little more than a decade ago, I have been fascinated by its features and the way it integrates with the underlying platforms it runs on. Before studying Oracle at the university as part of my degree I was exposed to MySQL (still independent then, and version 3.23) and thought that Oracle couldn't be so different. After all, it's about insert, delete, update, and commit, right? It is almost ironic how wrong I was! Over the years there was only one thing that became clearer and clearer: the more I learned about the product, the less I thought I understood. Although that isn't really the case, one can't help escaping that feeling sometimes. Add in the constant change of the software to meet Oracle's customer needs then you get the picture. What makes it difficult to keep up to date is the fact that you can find a lot of information—sometimes conflicting—on the Internet about our favorite database engine.

I personally think that all DBAs have to keep an open mind and try to do the best we can to keep up with new releases to provide an ultimately great service to our end users who should be happy to be able to use a well-maintained database estate. I hope the book you are about to read helps you on this mission: instead of having to dissect the available information "out there" I went through it and analyzed it to the best of my abilities so you don't have to spend the same time and effort.

Note: Oracle as a company has acquired an enormous number of smaller and not-so-small companies during the last few years. When speaking of "Oracle" in this book you can safely assume the database engine is being referred to, unless otherwise stated.

In this introduction the general structure of the book is presented, my motivation for writing it and a guide on how to approach the material. Don't be intimidated by the page count, the chapters follow what I think is a logical structure.

How This Book Is Structured

This book has been written with one goal in mind: to help technical and managerial staff alike to make best use of the most current Oracle database release in order to build a consolidated database environment. The book follows what could be a potential path to adopting a consolidation strategy for your company or a project. Although the focus clearly is with Linux and the x86-64 platforms, I have no intention of making this the platform of *your* choice for your consolidation project. Even though I think that you would be a very good value for the money out of this platform, it is by far not ideal to introduce an unknown platform to the already complex equation dealing with database consolidation. Many companies have a preferred hardware platform for which trained and experienced staff is available. Consolidation projects can be challenging, and do not need additional challenges by the introduction of an unfamiliar platform to the hardware estate.

If a new hardware platform is well maintained by the vendor though, who provides a balanced, well-engineered system right from the start then there is great value in such a product. Rather than going over a certification and validation cycle yourself you rely on the vendor to ensure that the components of the system are compatible, and that drivers as well as firmware combinations have been tried and tested. Oracle's own Engineered Systems are a great example for this hardware category.

The book you are about to read tries to help you along the various stages of the consolidation project, from planning to implementation. In my opinion consolidation projects using Oracle 12c will need to provide answers to the following key questions:

- Which Operating System should be chosen?

- How should the database instance be protected from failure?

- How can I increase availability for the solution?

- How much automation can be put into the provisioning of the stack?

- How can I make use of the new Pluggable Databases Feature?

- How should I monitor the environment?

- How do I protect the database from site failure, and how can it be backed up and recovered?

It begins with background material about some of the current challenges in IT and ways users have already started coping with them. First of all it's important to understand the importance of consolidation in the IT industry, and which technical evolutions in the x86-world made them possible. Another section in the same chapter describes the Cloud Computing hype, which every reader probably has heard about.

The next chapter introduces Oracle 12c: which features are new with the obvious focus on database consolidation but some other interesting ones as well. Other additional and noteworthy features making the DBA's life easier will be introduced as well. Since there is a lot of uncertainty about Oracle Automatic Storage Management (ASM) in the field, a section has been dedicated to it.

The next chapters are dedicated to supporting infrastructure. Chapters 3 and 4 introduce different infrastructure options followed by various methods for protecting the consolidated database and offers other suggestions to the deployment of the database. The last thing anyone wants to see is a database containing a lot of critical information from multiple applications that crashes and creates an unnecessary and avoidable outage. Depending on how you want to play it and how much budget is available different ways for protecting the database instance are available. The chapters assume that you are building your own system rather than using one available.

Before one can install the Oracle software you have to install the underlying operating system. Although Oracle still exists for a large number of platforms I decided to present the installation of Linux. The probability that Linux will be used for your consolidation project is quite high and I am hoping to provide you with some benefit about the installation of the operating system.

Installing the Oracle software is the next logical step after the operating system has been configured properly. This again is demonstrated on the Linux platform. Following the Oracle installation you can read a chapter about Pluggable Databases, the exciting new consolidation features of Oracle 12c.

The following chapter is dedicated to monitoring Oracle 12c. A great number of monitoring tools are available for the Oracle database, but since Oracle themselves own their Enterprise Manager which has undergone substantial redevelopment for version 12 this tool has been chosen as the monitoring solution of choice.

No important production database deployment is complete without a disaster recovery solution. Chapters 9 and 10 cover Data Guard—one way of protecting the database from environment hazards and other catastrophes, small and large.

Similarly, deployments are not complete without a backup and recovery strategy. A dedicated chapter explores which tools are available for backup and recovery, and how to integrate them into the enterprise-wide solution.

The final chapter explains possible ways to upgrade to Oracle 12.1.

A word about print screens

One of the comments I read about the previous book project I was involved in is related to print screens. An advanced Oracle user complained about the print screens, essentially saying that the use of print screens artificially inflated the contents of the book. Although I sympathize with the writer of the comment there are a few points I would like to add.

First of all, not everyone will have firsthand knowledge of Oracle 12c. DBAs who are about to install the new release for the first time might enjoy seeing the various screens in print when reading the book. I certainly would have! The same goes for screen output. You will find a lot of output from running commands in the book for the same reason: if you are about to perform a certain task you might find it comforting to see a little more output than just the command with the supplied command line arguments. In addition to providing more detail for the reader who can compare his to the book's output I hope to also demonstrate that the contents of this book are based on true research. But please bear in mind that patches can alter the output of commands.

Please be careful with Licenses

This book is not a license guide. Please bear this in mind when reading about features and check with the Oracle website or your sales representative if a feature mentioned in the book is licensable separately. Notice that Oracle can change the license model over the time this book is available. You should double-check if a particular feature you would like to use requires a separate license or database pack.

Conventions

Throughout the book, I have tried to keep a consistent style for presenting commands and their results. Where a piece of code is presented in the text, it is presented in fixed-width font, such as this example. Where it made sense to display it you should see the context in which a command has been executed in the SQL*Plus SQLPROMPT variable.

```
SYS@CDB$ROOT> select name, cdb from v$database;
```

The syntax of the command is most often provided for reference, the preceding paragraphs should already have provided background information about the command.

A similar approach has been chosen for operating system commands. Normally you should see commands shown as in this example:

```
[oracle@server1 ~]> df -h /u01
```

The shell's PS1 variable follows the conventions set on Oracle Linux 6.x and many other popular Linux distributions using the Bourne Again Shell (BASH) as their default command line interpreter. It shows the account name followed by the @-sign and the server name on which the command has been executed. The standard accounts you will see throughout the book are root, oracle, and grid.

You will notice that most of the shell-scripts are written for BASH as found on Oracle Linux 6.x. Shell scripts are not necessarily compatible between interpreters, and care should be used to evaluate and test scripts first before using them on actual systems.

Critical thinking welcome!

The book is written from my point of view, and opinions are my own. To loosely quote Jonathan Lewis: "just because it is written does not mean it is right." If you disagree with passages of the book, I would like to know. Email me your questions and constructive remarks and I will be happy to reply. Since a book is a static object once in print I intend to provide errata and updates on my own and Apress's website.

Downloading the code

The code for the examples shown in this book is available on the Apress web site, `www.apress.com`. A link can be found on the book's information page under the Source Code/Downloads tab. This tab is located underneath the Related Titles section of the page.

CHAPTER 1

▓ ▓ ▓

Consolidation as an industry trend

Welcome to chapter one! In this chapter you will be introduced to many of the concepts important in the context of database consolidation. Unlike the chapters that follow, this chapter will specifically focus on the theoretical foundations rather than technical implementation.

Let's begin the discussion with an overview of consolidation, automation, and database standards as I see them. Consider Figure 1-1, which describes the roadmap ahead for a possible consolidation project. The figure depicts a situation where the current IT landscape has grown organically and become unstructured over time, which is termed "legacy IT landscape." Most likely there is a wealth of platforms supported and a rich ecosystem of applications for each. Due to current business and budget constraints imposed by management and additional reasons explained shortly (bear with me!), the number of architectures can be reduced to meet the goals set by management. At the same time the IT organization should aim to improve quality and reusability of solutions rolled out by using consolidation, automation, and a largely standardized set of environments, leading up to what is meant by the future architecture shown in Figure 1-1.

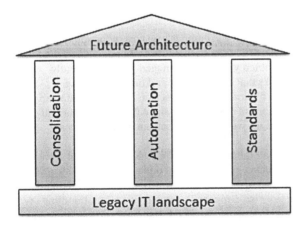

***Figure 1-1.** The three pillars of the future architecture proposition*

Each of the future architecture's three pillars will be explained in detail in the course of this chapter. Further sections detail additional concepts often heard in the context of database consolidation, such as virtualization and cloud computing. They are covered here to give the reader a more complete overview of the subject. I think that without an explanation of the virtualization trend and cloud computing it is difficult to follow the path set by Oracle 12.1, which allows you to implement virtualization inside the database.

Finishing the chapter you are presented with an appetizer to Chapter 3 which explains a little more about hardware changes and platform trends. The chapter will focus on the Intel architecture before giving you an insight into developments of the other relevant platforms for the Oracle database. Hopefully, at the end of the chapter you should have a better understanding about the motivation behind this book, and why the Linux on x86-64 proposition is a valuable one.

Consolidation

You, dear reader, are probably using this book because a team somewhere in your organization decided that it was time to consolidate databases and servers. Such a decision may have been made for many reasons, but most likely somewhere cost is involved. When this book was written, the economic outlook for the immediate future was not great. The Eurozone was in financial trouble, and the United States was not much better off. Few economies in the world grew, and even less so by more than one percent.

As a direct consequence many companies downsized support teams looking after the essential business applications, increasing the burden on the remaining production support staff. What was not reduced, or at least not in the same proportion, was the workload. This factor plays considerably into the steadily increasing number of tasks to be juggled by the reduced workforce.

As another consequence engineering departments or local production support teams need to come up with ideas on how to streamline their efforts, and to make it as easy as possible for new starters to become productive sooner.

■ **Note** "Engineering" in this context refers to the team responsible for developing and certifying new (Oracle) releases, documenting processes, and performing third-line support. This is in contrast to the operational team which keeps the databases running.

Additionally, companies review their existing hardware estate with special emphasis on cost reduction. The buzzwords associated with this situation are the ones heard often, and they are discussed in this book: *automation* and *consolidation*. If the workload cannot be reduced, then it undoubtedly has to be managed (more) efficiently. For example, database administrators should not spend time on tasks that are repetitive and time consuming. Provisioning a database used to be a long process when you run the dictionary creation scripts. While the DBA can simply kick off the `create database` statement followed by invocations of `catalog.sql` and `catproc.sql` manually, it would be better if the DBA could simply call a procedure that does the work on his behalf and simply returns a success/error message back while he does other work.

However, this automated procedure needs to be created and maintained, and if you envision a wealth of server platforms such as AIX, HP-UX, Solaris, and Linux in use the maintenance of any generic code applicable for all quickly becomes very difficult. If it was instead possible to reduce the number of platforms many variables could be cut out of the equation, and there would be less (parallel) code to maintain. Also, supporting patch instructions, bundling up releases and other work performed in the engineering world would be greatly simplified. Database consolidation was not the easiest of tasks before Oracle 12.1. The most stringent requirement was to have non-colliding namespaces. For example, two users named "SCOTT" could not coexist in a consolidated database. Additionally, database links proved tricky business and any reference and grant to PUBLIC could potentially cause unwanted side effects in the consolidated environment. Luckily, Oracle 12c addresses these shortcomings of the previous release in a way so elegant one is asking oneself why this has not yet been implemented before.

Now cost is not the only contributing factor to consolidation. There are other environmental aspects that could contribute to the initiation of a project. Let's look at these in more detail.

End of life announcements-Hardware

During the past few decades administrators and casual spectators have seen the demise of many platforms. Only very few, of which Linux is the most notable, have been able to step in the void and fill a gap. What almost looks like a zoo of platforms supported with Oracle 8i Release 3 from 1999 boiled down to a very modest few supported platforms with Oracle 12.1. Most platforms died silently without too much of an outcry in the user community.

However the biggest waves in recent times were caused by Oracle's announcement to stop development for the HP-UX/Itanium platform. This announcement came at a time when HP was trying to (re-)define itself and the threat of the loss of a big revenue spinning platform was certainly not what the company expected. On their corporate website, Oracle states the following:

> *After multiple conversations with Intel senior management Oracle has decided to discontinue all software development on the Intel Itanium microprocessor. Intel management made it clear that their strategic focus is on their x86 microprocessor and that Itanium was nearing the end of its life.*

> — http://www.oracle.com/us/corporate/press/346696

Ever since the announcement was made, the press had a real interest in the outcome of the story. What has been forgotten in this discussion was that Microsoft (and Red Hat somewhat more unnoticed) stopped their development for Itanium ports, which Oracle also acknowledges. This is a real shame since the processor design offered many interesting features, although in the end the Itanium range of processors proved to be exotic and not widely used. As any Oracle database administrator knows, the more widely used a platform, the less likely one runs into platform-specific problems. However, it should be made clear that an end-of-life announcement does not mean that Oracle abandons the platform completely, but rather that planning considerations on how to replace the platform should start sooner rather than later. In the above-mentioned, high-profile case with Itanium, Oracle issued a statement on September 2012 stating it was continuing to port the database to the platform.

From a planning point of view, although unpleasant, the de-support notice from the vendor for a certain platform might be suited to free up budget for a technology refresh of the database estate. Even though the effort might not encompass everything, the most critical systems at least need to be migrated before support for the current database release ceases.

High-profile Oracle customers might be lucky in prolonging support for an ageing hardware estate, but in general terms not acting when the time has come is going to introduce more problems later. Also, it should be noted that migration projects take a certain amount of time and planning, especially when the destination platform uses a different endian format. The author's advice is not to delay the necessary until it is too late. Time pressure is known to introduce human mistakes!

In summary, end-of-life announcements provide the perfect occasion to get budget for a technology refresh, also affectionately referred to as "tech-refresh." Even the tightest budget owner cannot ignore the fact that operations require supported platforms and hardware. Quite often, the platform to be replaced has outlived its useful life anyway, and (some) "big iron" can be replaced by industry standard hardware.

Support policy for Oracle Software

Hardware is not the only thing affected by end-of-life announcements. Oracle introduced their lifetime support policy with Oracle database 10g. The associated document, available from the Internet at: http://www.oracle.com/us/support/lifetime-support/index.html, details the Oracle product roadmap as well as the support matrix for not-so-current releases.

■ **Note** The lifetime support policy encompasses far more than just the database, which is covered here. Please refer to the URL provided for other Oracle products and divisions. It may also have been updated in the meantime.

Think of the Oracle lifetime support policy as Oracle's own product matrix, dividing the support Oracle sells into the following categories:

Premier Support: This is essentially the support model you get with the current release of the database. Current is defined as five years from the time the database version was generally available. With Premier Support you are entitled to technical support and certification, all within the limits of the product and further defined in the lifetime support PDF. However, be careful t to stay with the current point-release of the database or you might not benefit from the provision of Patch Set Updates! My Oracle Support note 742060.1 is a good reference to be considered.

Extended Support: After the expiration of Premier Support, you can apply for Extended Support. Oracle somewhat euphemistically states that as a way to give the database user the freedom to upgrade in his own time. But that freedom obviously comes at a cost. The duration of the Extended Support agreement is three years. Extended Support however will allow you to request new fixes for newly discovered problems, and you also get Critical Patch Updates as well as Patch Set Updates. This is very important for operation teams as it allows security vulnerabilities to be fixed.

Sustaining Support: After the expiration of the Extended Support (or as an alternative to it) users can apply for Sustaining Support. Sustaining Support never ends and is valid for as long as you pay Oracle licenses. However, you will not get new fixes, updates, and Critical Patch Updates (CPUs). Certification with any new product, supplied by Oracle or a third party will not be available.

Link to online content: There is a hint at the end of the lifetime support policy document referring to content online at oracle.com/support/policies.html, which contains some more fine print to read.

There is more to the lifetime support policy than can be covered in this short section, the reader should make sure to review the current document available from the Oracle website through the link provided in the introduction to this section. Additionally the reader should refer to the online resource as well to get a clear understanding of the situation. In summary, the lifetime policy offers peace of mind in situations where Premier Support ended. Nevertheless it is strongly recommended to upgrade wherever possible to avoid the monetary penalties.

At the time of this writing, the most widely used Oracle database releases have dates set for Premier, Extended, and Sustained support as shown in Table 1-1.

Table 1-1. *Oracle Support Levels*

Oracle Release	Available from	End of Premier Support	End of Extended Support
10.2	07/2005	07/2010	07/2013
11.1	08/2007	08/2012	08/2015
11.2	09/2009	01/2015	01/2018

As stated above, and therefore not in this table, Sustaining Support does not expire until you stop paying licenses to Oracle. Although the options of staying on your current Oracle release may sound tempting, you are ultimately going to pay a higher price than necessary. I recommend implementing a policy in your company's technology roadmap which moves ageing releases into the de-supported stage soon enough to guarantee a smooth transition. Chapter 12 will explain how to upgrade your current environment to Oracle 12.1.

Different kinds of consolidation

So far in the introduction you did not find specific information about the different ways to consolidate. Since that is important for the understanding of this book, I would like to introduce a systematic overview of the various aspects of consolidation. Depending on your point of view there are different forms of classification, such as:

- Hardware consolidation

- Operating system consolidation

- Storage consolidation

- Platform consolidation

When speaking of hardware consolidation most people associate it with a move towards standard hardware. In many cases today this implies a move to blade servers or blades for short. Primarily based on the x86-64 platform, a blade server is a small somewhat naked looking device with the bare minimum required to function as a computer. Blades are not exclusively made for the x86 architecture. Apart from the mainstream there are enterprise blades for IBM Power and Oracle SPARC processors as well. If your IT department is absolutely sure it does not want to consider x86, then there is no need to move away from their favorite platform.

Multiple blades are combined in a so-called blade enclosure. The enclosure is mandatory and provides the power, cooling, and outward connectivity to the users of the whole system. Blade vendors have of course read the signs of the times already and add interesting management capabilities into their products. Chapter 3 describes blades in more detail.

Operating System consolidation is a term coined for those users who want to consolidate as many of their environments as possible under a common operating system. It is not to be confused with operating system virtualization, although the latter is often used in facilitating such a move! You have by now read a number of times that increased efficiency, a lowered license footprint, and a better support are the main drivers behind operating system consolidation.

Storage consolidation is another form of consolidation discussed in the media. Often Storage consolidation is initiated to counter the sprawl of storage systems in an enterprise. Due to cost constraints, absence of site-wide storage agreements, lack of oversight, or other reasons projects and product groups may have bought storage for their project on their own. These insular solutions are ineffective in the long run since a lot of time and energy has to be invested to keep the storage stack current. Additionally, storage technology is as complex as many other technologies, requiring in investment in talent to manage and operate it. The overhead of managing many different storage products becomes even more apparent during upgrades of components involved. Instead of repeating the certification and test process for controllers and firmware for each combination of storage array, fiber channel switch and host bus adapter synergies can be achieved by reducing the complexity of the stack.

Additionally, the move away from small or low-end storage may improve storage performance overall. One has to be careful though no to apply the rule without exception: storage is a complex topic, and the rule of thumb that one size fits all does not apply to all systems. High-end decision support systems and OLTP systems should probably not reside on the same storage array! The term storage consolidation is also applied when low-end systems move data from internal disk to a storage array.

As you may have already guessed, this book is about all of these aspects, something which is referred to as platform consolidation. Storage consolidation however will not be dealt with in more detail because many mid-sized and large enterprises are very likely to have an agreement with one of the major storage vendors to consolidate storage with them. This has the big advantage that storage sprawl is under (better) control, and also removes a lot of work from the storage engineers. Whoever has worked on a certified storage stack from storage array firmware to firmware version of the switches in the storage network to finally the host bus adapter will appreciate the reduction in moving parts.

Virtualization

Very few subjects have been discussed as extensively in the last decade as virtualization. Unfortunately the hype around virtualization makes it difficult to fully understand what it *actually* is. A multitude of terms exist, describing different aspects of the same subject. Some examples include platform virtualization, operating system virtualization, network virtualization, storage virtualization, server virtualization, and many more. Not all of these technologies are relevant from a database administration point of view. This is why the following section will primarily focus on platform virtualization. Platform virtualization is probably the best understood of all virtualization technologies. Even if you have not used enterprise-grade virtualization software you may be familiar with desktop virtualization products.

Why has virtualization received so much attention? This requires a little bit of travel back in time. Virtualization has been with IT professionals for a long time, and made its first appearance on IBM hardware in the 1960s. In the next 50 years it did not receive widespread adoption. Before virtualization became a truly mainstream subject around 2005, many servers were oversized to deal with sudden peaks and expected workload growth. Administrators looking at top, glance, nmon, and other utilities often showed that the systems were badly underutilized. Underutilized systems are not only used inefficiently, but they still cost almost as much as fully utilized machines. Power, cooling, and rack space are still required even if a server is running at 10–20% capacity.

When the IT industry became a lot more cost conscious it didn't take long for engineers to think of better ways of utilizing machines and, as mentioned previously, platform virtualization received a lot of attention. Instead of just one instance of an operating system to run on a physical server, engineers developed an abstraction layer, called a virtual machine monitor or hypervisor. You see this layer in Figure 1-2.

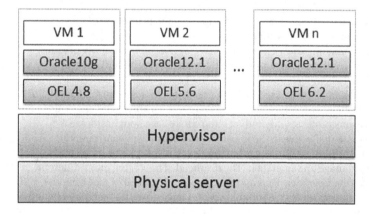

Figure 1-2. *Simplified view on a virtualized system*

■ **Note**   This section discusses enterprise-class virtualization only!

Platform virtualization is sometimes also referred to as hardware virtualization. The hypervisor is the only software on the server with direct access to the hardware-processor, storage, and memory. It is responsible for presenting virtual hardware to the virtual machines, or "guests," executing on the server.

The hypervisor has to translate system calls issued by the guest operating system and executes them in a safe way so as to ensure the guests can operate safely side-by-side on the same hardware. Early x86-64 hypervisors struggled since many functions in the i386 instruction set were not easy to virtualize. As a result many instructions had to be translated in software. This led to an overhead for fully virtualized hosts. The main x86-processor vendors tried to address this problem by adding hardware support for virtualization. The Intel chips use an extension called VT-d while AMD called their extension AMD-V. Although the two are implemented differently, the idea is the same: certain expensive operations which have previously been executed in software should be hardware assisted.

Benefits of virtualization

The major vendors for virtualization products are keen to point out the advantages of platform virtualization. There are for example:

- Reducing cost (there it is again!) by better utilizing servers and all in all reduce the footprint in the data center

- Increase manageability

- Better ability to address a change in demand for resources

- Easier planning for disaster recovery

- Enhanced security

The cost aspect does not require a lot of explanation. It should immediately become apparent that by reducing the number of servers drawing power, there is less of a requirement for cooling, energy, and rack space. By better utilizing the existing servers less capacity is wasted idly.

Manageability is increased, and common "reference" templates make it very easy to get started with a new technology. "Standard" operating system images can be used as templates from which new virtual machines are rolled out very quickly. Oracle provides a wealth of pre-created templates for Oracle VM—the company's premier enterprise virtualization product for the x86-architecture. Oracle's competitors in the market, such as VMWare, use the same concept. In their language the getting-you-started-quickly Virtual Machines are called virtual appliances. Most commercial virtualization solutions feature a management interface for the administrator allowing him to see the state of his virtualized server farm. The better these management interfaces, the more likely the adoption of the product in the enterprise.

Another key element in virtualization is the potential to react to changed user demand. Many virtualization products allow the dynamic addition and removal of operating system resources at the virtual machine's runtime. Imagine that the virtual machine requires more virtual CPU power for an important batch run. The administrator can grant a few more cores to the VM at runtime or otherwise increase computer resources. Live migration of a virtual machine has its main use in maintenance operations, but the flexibility to shuffle virtual machines around in the farm is very useful.

Finally, executing a workload on a virtualized platform offers more mobility in planned and unplanned downtime scenarios. For example, if the underlying physical hardware does not provide enough computing power then a live migration to another host can keep the users connected while the guest is moved to another server in the same farm. Similarly, disaster recovery solutions can be developed so that the impact on the service is minimized. If a virtualization vendor does not provide a product for the Disaster Recovery (DR) case, then it is usually possible to create one's own.

More virtualization options

Apart from platform virtualization, there are other forms of virtualization to explore. From an Oracle DBA's point of view the most important virtualization strategy is the use of operating system virtualization. The term is again somewhat loosely defined, but consensus seems to exist around the fact that an operating system can execute multiple isolated instances of itself. Good examples for operating system virtualization are Solaris Containers, and to a degree IBM Logical Partitions (LPARs).

Take a Solaris zone for example. Unlike hardware virtualization, a Solaris container cannot execute another operating system. This slight disadvantage is more than made up by the fact that the overhead with this virtualization method is very low. Solaris containers or zones are a very popular way to make better use of existing hardware, especially for development and user acceptance test environments. The whole storage presented to a zone can be block-level replicated to a remote data center, and with clever DNS changes make failover a simple operation. A simplified deployment, as opposed to unneeded complexity, is a target worth aiming for. The downside to the Solaris container approach is the relative high cost for the hardware. This is somewhat alleviated by the next generation SPARC chip, called T5. Initial benchmarking suggests that the single-thread performance has improved a lot from its predecessors.

A stepping stone on the way to the cloud

Readers with a bit of background of cloud computing will instantly recognize that many virtues of virtualization have made their way into the cloud paradigm. Especially the decoupling of location and user session is important, and virtualization vendors are integrating their own products into the public cloud.

Virtualization is of course used a lot in the cloud. For example, Enterprise Manager 12c "Cloud Control" has a built-in feature to manage Oracle VM server farms to provide cloud-like functionality inside the (private) data center, a deployment technique often referred to as "private" cloud. Cloud computing is yet another one of these overloaded terms requiring a little explanation, so let's cover it next.

Cloud computing

Cloud computing has certainly had a big impact on the IT industry over the past years. Similar in concept to consolidation, cloud computing offers the promise to be more flexible, start small and grow big, and only pay for the resources you use. Cloud computing is a top level term used for many things, each of which will be discussed in its own section below. A possible taxonomy of cloud computing is shown in Figure 1-3.

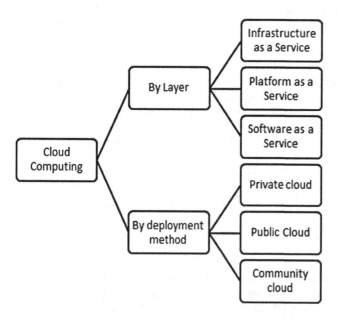

***Figure 1-3.** Relevant taxonomy of cloud computing for this discussion*

There are other attributes and characteristics associated with the "cloud" but they are mainly marketing terms and won't be listed here. Cloud computing is nothing really new, and Oracle admitted that in a much-quoted investor relations meeting available online: `http://blogs.reuters.com/mediafile/2008/09/25/what-on-earth-is-cloud-computing/`. Despite the characteristic way Mr. Ellison voiced his concerns he is correct, and there is a lot of confusion about what this cloud computing paradigm really is. Sometimes products and services are used synonymously with cloud computing, like Amazon's EC2 which is going to be covered in the Infrastructure as a service section below. Oftentimes though cloud computing is used to describe very different offerings. The classic cloud computing model uses the layers as shown in Figure 1-4.

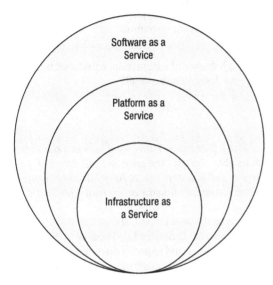

Figure 1-4. The different layers in cloud computing

Why is cloud computing part of this introduction chapter to database consolidation? The simple answer is: because it is very relevant! This section will show why for certain industries such as insurances and financial services it is impossible for many factors, soft *and* hard, to move data outside their own data center.

■ **Note**   You are right to object now that there are financial institutions who have already outsourced some of their processing to a service provider, but these agreements tend to be a lot more secure.

Various deployment methods for the "cloud" exist, out of which the so-called private cloud is probably the most appropriate for in-house consolidation projects involving sensitive data. Other cloud deployment options are out of the scope of this chapter, but can be found online, for example at `http://en.wikipedia.org/wiki/Cloud_computing`.

Regardless of the cloud deployment method and layer, all cloud computing lives by the following promises and characteristics:

- *A reduction in cost*: since an upfront investment in hardware ("capital expenditure") is not needed. However, the cost of running the cloud infrastructure can be higher initially, there is most certainly a tradeoff of capital versus operational expenditure

- *Added flexibility*: the ability to add computer resources on demand.

- *Network-based provisioning*: the cloud is usually accessed via (hopefully) secure channels through the public Internet. Actually the cloud in many cases really is just another company's data center.

- *Multi Tenancy*: Due to the nature of cloud systems it is likely that you are sharing an environment with someone else in a certain way. Although environments are isolated from one another, workload peaks may still filter through.

- *Self-management*: The cloud infrastructure provided should allow users to tweak their configuration. Public clouds especially allow the user to choose from a variety of virtual machines, ranging from very small to really, really big. Additionally many cloud providers expose management options such as starting, stopping, and cloning cloud systems to customers.

Cloud computing, making use of consolidated environments with a high degree of automation, could well be the future for the majority of computing needs. Let's continue by discussing each layer in more detail.

Infrastructure as a Service

My first contact with the cloud was by using Infrastructure as a Service (IaaS). Since then I have used IaaS in a number of projects. Opting for IaaS as opposed to other cloud deployment options gives the user the greatest flexibility, but also most responsibility for the environment. The option to install software on the system and to have full control over it gives the user said flexibility but it comes at a price. At the same time the system administrator is responsible for its security and for keeping it current in terms of patching.

The value proposition by the industry heavyweights (Amazon AWS maybe the best known) shows that the upfront investment in hardware can be costly. The initial deployment could also be undersized and unable to deal with unexpected peaks in the workload. Infrastructure as a service allows the user to add capacity on demand within very little time. In an IaaS environment the user gets a virtualized environment, often termed an instance. The user has full control, is able to install software, and modify the storage layout and any other parameter in the environment. Cost for operating such an instance is most often calculated depending on the type of the instance and its characteristics such as memory capacity, isolation from other users, and CPU power. Similar in a way to the popular root server which offers even more flexibility in regards of the software installation, a virtual instance needs to be maintained and hardened by its user to prevent security breaches.

Software as a Service

Software as a service (SaaS) is the most common touch-point to the cloud for non-infrastructure providers or developers. The model behind Software as a Service goes back a while, and in its basic form presents an application via the Internet. The application can be simpler (it wouldn't really be simple) such as a web mail interface, or rather complex such as Sales Force.

SaaS as a concept probably does not need much introduction as it has been around for so long and many of us have already used it in some form. The first web clients appeared in the early half of the last decade, and since then there has been a consolidation of providers. Some of them, like Google, have successively enhanced their offering from the original core capability to web-based office suites. Established "fat client" vendors also offer an increasing number of web-based services to supplement their established revenue streams. A little while ago a hardware device was released by Google which is based entirely on the services provided over the Internet. Although such a class of devices is appealing in certain situations, the biggest drawback to them is their limited functionality when in offline mode. Who knows, we might see more of these in the future when true mobile broadband becomes a reality at a reasonable cost.

Platform as a Service

The final of the classic cloud computing layers to be discussed in this context is Platform as a Service (PaaS). This layer is a hybrid between full access as it is granted with an instance in an IaaS environment, and the ready-made web application available to you in the SaaS world. From the offerings available on the Internet, it appears as if PaaS is mainly targeted at developers, and it is aimed at making deploying applications easier. In addition to the developer focus, some PaaS providers have developed their own frameworks promising the user to deploy applications in very little time without being a hardcore coder.

Most providers of PaaS will allow access based on an API (Application Programming Interface) to the deployment environment. The benefit in such a scenario is again the limited cost of upfront development. A small startup company does not have to pay licenses to access Enterprise-grade software to get started with the implementation. The fee to be paid includes access to the hosted environment-specialist skill to maintain a few servers with databases and web server is often not required immediately. Previously, before the advent of a PaaS offering, the start-up fee presented substantial up-front cost before any revenue was generated.

The Public Cloud

When thinking about the Cloud as such, most users I spoke to immediately think about the public cloud. For example, your webmail client's interface uses an external facing HTML 5 application hosted in a data center somewhere in the world. For most use cases this is not a big deal. Users of webmail clients and other services to synchronize files with multiple private computers do not worry where their date is stored. The security-conscious user thinks a bit differently and installs software to encrypt traffic to and from the cloud, and maybe the data that has been permanently stored in the cloud as well.

Commercial use of the public cloud requires a different approach. Many countries have very strict rules about data protection and privacy. While this is a great democratic achievement for the citizen, it imposes barriers to the use of the public cloud. If for example no personal data may be stored outside the country, then it is next to impossible to legally make use of external data centers.

Additionally the Internet infrastructure becomes very important: while most users enjoy a lot of bandwidth downstream, equal upstream capacity is either very expensive or simply not available. Anyone who uploaded data over the Internet will notice that immediately. Also a failure of the Internet connection will cut off the users from the service. Realistically speaking this should be a rare occurrence, but it can happen. Frequent travelers will know the problem of being disconnected during the time on an airplane, and roaming fees while travelling abroad naturally impose limits on bandwidth usage.

The Private Cloud

The private cloud takes the ideas already implemented outside the company's data center in the public cloud inside the data center. There are many reasons for this: accessibility, connection quality, bandwidth, and security are just a few to mention. By "private cloud" I refer to a cloud-like deployment of applications and services which are not accessible to the public.

Private cloud is an oxymoron to the purist, and here is why. The Cloud Computing movement has advocated the shift of paradigm from capital expenditure (capex) to operational expenditure (opex). As you saw before, using for example Amazon's EC2 offering you don't need to invest upfront in dedicated hardware and storage (=capital expenditure), but pay for when you use it (=operational expenditure). So when using the in-house data center, clearly capex are not reduced.

When the benefits of automation, consolidation, and standards were discussed in this chapter, I implicitly assumed that they were implemented locally, in the company's own, or alternatively outsourced, data center rather than with a third party.

In many ways application deployment in the private cloud is easier, mainly because the security, regulation, and other legal requirements are under tighter control. This of course can become a moot point if security is not properly implemented in the data center. Nevertheless tight security checks and measures should be implemented early during the product deployment stage to prevent frantic activity should audit points be discovered. This has become even more important after recent successful attacks on many high-profile services.

Security in the cloud

One aspect has not been discussed yet: security. Security is a big complex, and sometimes a psychological barrier more than a technical one. And when it comes to storing sensitive information in the cloud the mere thought of that rings the alarm bells with many. Who, for example, would want his mortgage data or other sensitive information to be stored in the public cloud? Even if such a storage option was one hundred percent secure from a technical point of view, it would be very hard to communicate that fact to customers.

For these reasons it would appear very unlikely for large enterprises with sensitive data to make use of the public cloud. And coincidentally this aspect is key in a design choice! The cloud hype has impacted the way infrastructure projects are managed in many ways and potentially changed the IT landscape profoundly. Management especially is keen to leverage the benefits the cloud computing paradigm offers, and this plays into the hands of the consolidation expert.

Use for the cloud hype

With many aspects of cloud computing hype, it is difficult to differentiate between plain wrong and correct information. I am hoping to have made the main aspects clearer for the reader, and especially why I think consolidation, automation, and the most suitable concepts taken from the cloud computing revolution fit into a bigger picture. Combining these properly we are well suited to fulfill the goals upper management sets to operations and engineering to help cut cost and streamline operations.

Automation

Another major keyword heard quite often in recent times is "automation." Most often it goes hand-in-hand with consolidation, and each greatly benefits from the other. Automation is a very important concept, and many routine maintenance tasks will undoubtedly be automated in the near future. The introduction to this book already stated the fact that many production teams are more than busy trying to keep production systems ticking over. Additionally the time spent by a team on mundane tasks such as unlocking user accounts or extending tablespaces is enormous.

To counter the trend many large enterprises try to hire labor in less cost-intensive countries. But even these decisions are now questioned, and an automated task sounds like the answer to the problem. However, automation needs to be done properly, which applies to every aspect of business life. Many large companies have especially stringent audit requirements, and an automated process needs to leave information in an audit trail which must be machine-readable and stored for as long as the regulating body requires it.

Processes with the potential for automation

There are a large number of database administration processes that can potentially be automated. When considering whether or not a process can be automated, audit requirements are to be taken into consideration as well. In recent times auditors have asked much more pertinent questions, and security problems have moved into focus. As an example, the following processes could be automated:

- Extension of a tablespace
- Taking a hot backup
- Unlocking a user

- Provisioning of a database

- Resetting a user password

- Creating a user

- Running an export of a schema

- And many more…

More fundamental tasks such as installing an operating system for the Oracle database server or deploying the Oracle database software are not listed here since they should already be automated. You can read more about these tasks in Chapters 5 and 6 covering the Linux installation and Oracle deployment.

It would appear logical not to allow any operation that could negatively affect the availability of the service to be automated. Not only could that cause much unwanted disruption, security problems with the code could also lead to malicious denial of service attacks. Shutting down or otherwise restarting a database or database service should probably not be in scope of a project to automate. Consider the simplified example in Figure 1-5.

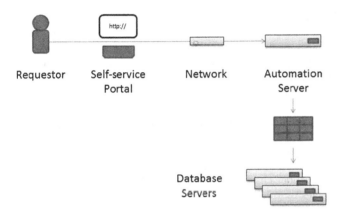

Figure 1-5. *Greatly simplified automation architecture with sample workflow*

Figure 1-5 describes one possible way to set up an automation gateway. A dedicated automation server, which has been specifically security hardened and equipped with an intrusion detection system (IDS) will accept communication from users via a self-service portal. The communication between the portal and automation server can be in many forms. In the past XML messages proved to be a popular means of communication, if sent securely. After verification of the validity of the message, to prevent illegal command injection, the request will be inserted into a workload queue. In addition to the syntax check there should also be a query against the enterprise trouble-ticket system to ensure that the raised request has been duly approved. The FIFO (first in first out) queuing mechanism can be configured either to execute the incoming requests immediately or delayed, depending on the request's urgency. A one-time password should be generated for access to the database system, either from a local system or the enterprise standard authentication system. Access to the database server itself could be granted via SSH keys. And it goes without saying that all operations must be logged, ideally in a central location that cannot be tampered with.

The actual execution of the management task is most likely trivial in comparison. In the most basic form a shell script calls sqlplus with the verified and validated parameters and executes the task. Another possibility is the use of the Enterprise Manager command line interface to perform a task, but as with any development-related task there is more than one way to do it.

Auditing and securing automated processes

Many of the just-described operations require elevated privileges in the database. To facilitate a secure execution of automated change requests special precaution has to be taken. First, the scope of the change request has to be set. Many organizations may refrain from the idea of automating database administration tasks in a production environment. Although user acceptance tests (UAT) and development databases were traditionally attributed with a lower status than production, their importance for many applications ranks equally with production. It is very costly to incur downtime with a development database as developers cannot compile/test their code against it! Any automation should only go ahead after careful testing and an evaluation of the benefits against risks.

If appropriate coding, due diligence, and reviews of the automation process have taken place, logging and auditing have to be watertight to convince the auditors about the security of the implemented solution. In this context it is very important to ensure that the audit data is immutable. One way to secure the auditing information is to direct the information logged by the application and operating system to a trustworthy, central destination. If the implemented automation solution supports logging to the UNIX Syslog facility it is relatively straightforward to secure the audit trail. Modern Syslog daemons are capable of sending messages to a remote service.

The importance of standards for support

In addition to consolidation and automation, many companies choose the introduction of consolidated environments to extend on the use of their operational standards. A globally consistent set of standards is not only essential for a follow-the-sun support model, but it can also greatly reduce cost. Only a standard way of deploying software allows for viable automated procedures. If all environments were unique, then it is impossible to cater to all permutations of the environments and roll out consistent database images.

To give that claim a little more background, consider this: a major problem faced by many newly employed database administrators in large organizations is the complexity and large number of environments. With the reduction in head-count of product-aligned database administrators more and more support staff need to take responsibility of the global database estate. The idea of a follow-the-sun-approach takes shape in many global companies, and where the regulating body supports such a model, chances are high that it will eventually be adopted. On paper, a follow-the-sun approach offers many advantages, of which the following are probably most noteworthy:

- More efficient use of DBA time since all environments are identical.

- A problem can be worked on longer until it is resolved.

- Database administrators can hand problems over after a shift and are less exhausted the next morning.

- Ultimately there should be better service.

In real life the ideal world as shown in the bulleted list above does not always apply. Cultural differences and communication problems can often hamper efforts to turn the follow-the-sun approach into a success. More than anything this is a management challenge that needs to be addressed at the appropriate level.

However it would be too simple to reduce problems of a global support team to the above-described difficulties. More often than not, systems in different regions, and/or under different product groups were set up and configured without respect to any consistency. This is a very big inhibitor to the global support model. Where possible, a global standard should be developed to unify the deployments.

Integrating acquisitions and mergers

Acquisitions form a special kind of challenge to the global support model. Although one can probably compare the IT estate of a company taken over with a previously independent business unit or a different region, acquired companies may use an entirely different approach to running Oracle. It is also possible that the newly integrated business uses a different set of hardware. In that case the systems are great candidates for consolidation, and we have come full circle to the first sections in this chapter. Whichever way the future direction of the common IT department goes, any change should be introduced gently so as not to alienate the "other" team!

However, an acquisition does not necessarily imply a negative challenge from a technical point of view. Sometimes companies are too successful, however paradoxical that might sound. Business units in such companies are very likely too busy adapting to the rapid requirements of customers to deliver new functionality in their software products that there is simply no time to develop a standards framework. And quite often there is not even time to consider how the estate should be managed when a "steady phase" is eventually reached. In such circumstances the acquisition of another company that has reached a healthy balance between the requirement to produce new features and the need to develop a corporate standard is most likely a great opportunity. Instead of having to reinvent the wheel, an existing standard model can be used as a baseline and refined to match the growing company's needs.

How much standardization is needed?

Defining the scope of the standards set to be implemented is a difficult task. You read in the introduction to the standards section that very few business units use engineered builds right from the outset of their existence. As a direct result, very few Oracle installations look alike. And as you also read before, this makes it difficult for someone who is not familiar with an environment to support it efficiently. But often, as soon as efforts are set underfoot to align the configurations, difficulties are not far down the line.

The first logical choice is to set up a central body responsible for the definition of the standards. In large companies, this usually ends up in the hands of the engineering department. After this transition of "power," it is possible that regional or product-aligned representatives, who in the past decided about deployments, versions, and other details feel sidelined.

Again, a gentle approach by the engineering department is needed, and as you can imagine regional representatives might need gentle nudging from time to time to move in unison. Where appropriate, regional "best practices" should be considered for inclusion in the standards document, and certainly not brushed aside. In the same way as concessions need to be considered, it also has to be made clear that the owner of the standards has the final say in how a specific feature is to be implemented. Therefore it is very important that the engineering department or whichever other team performs the task has full backing from management.

New environments brought into the organization, for example appliances which offer little (or less) possibility to fine-tune the setup pose a challenge. Should the appliance be "pressed" to fit the corporate standards, or should it remain outside? This question can only be answered individually. Very often, vendors claim their appliance is specifically built to make it easier to support. This may be true for the vendor, but not necessarily for the customer. If your vendor is flexible, it should hopefully be less of a problem to integrate standards into the product, but you might have to take initial teething problems into account. On the upside, however, management of the environment can be greatly simplified, and another application-specific siloed team of DDAs is avoided.

Another challenge is the evolution of standards. As business requirements change, and companies adopt new technologies, existing standard documents have to be reviewed periodically to ensure the current standard document is not holding the teams back. Such a review is more or less unavoidable when a new Oracle database release is adopted for production use. In this case though there should not be any problem to incorporate a new feature into the standard since it cannot collide with anything in the standards document. If the document structure permits it you could simply add a section pertaining to the new release. The standards-owner needs to discuss whether or not fundamental changes to the standard are retrofitted into existing environments or not. If it is decided to only build new systems to the current specification, environments could become fragmented again. On the other hand, changing environments to match the standards can be a very time-consuming process and most likely requires an outage, especially of the operating system or Oracle directory structure is touched upon. It is to hope that the standard document is suitably mature before modification to prevent said fragmentation and to preserve a common set of commands and directory structures. A newly developed consolidation platform is a great opportunity to test and implement the latest edition of the standards, and to ensure they are suitable for this kind of environment. Before going into detail as to which elements of the software stack could be standardized, a little discussion of the different aspects is necessary.

Standardization of the full stack

From a high level, multiple aspects to standardization can be made out. When thinking of standardization and certification you need to consider the full stack relevant to database deployments. To keep it in scope with this book, the discussion begins with storage, continues with hardware and the operating system and ends with Oracle software. The full stack encompasses even more: middle tier, the network layer and finally the clients. Since this book is about the database I will not discuss the higher tiers in the stack.

In large organizations, there are often separate engineering teams responsible for each of them:

- Storage engineering

- Operating system engineering

- Database Engineering

These teams can further be subdivided, adding complexity to the task of coordination of standards. It is not uncommon that these teams to work as if they were isolated from one another. Rarely are interfaces between the teams defined, which is unfortunate. These interfaces are very important for automation and consolidation. If, for example, the operating system team changes vital parameters of the Linux build, it may result in additional overhead for the database team to ensure all prerequisites for a database installation are in place.

In an ideal world the individual team would detail the current build on an internal website including external (to the team) interfaces and their change history. Everyone interested in a specific interface could subscribe to changes in the documentation and act accordingly well in advance. This is far more preferable than having to find out the hard way via failed builds and installations that an interface has changed. Unfortunately the benefit to the team is not immediately visible, which can cause such documentation tasks to be put on to the list of low-priority tasks.

Potential storage standards

The group responsible for storage backend system engineering is typically responsible for tasks such as these:

- Liaise with the storage vendors.

- Develop and support backup and recovery technologies.

- Certify storage technology for use with operating systems.

- Manage maintenance of non-Oracle file systems and volume managers if the UNIX engineers do not already take care of them.

- Develop and maintain block-level replication best practices and recommendations.

There are obviously many more tasks performed by the team, but from an Oracle DBA point of view the ones mentioned above are the most important. The third bullet point mentions certification of storage technology for use with operating systems. In this respect, storage engineering researches and evaluates new storage technology such as the use of Enterprise Flash Drives (EFDs) in traditional storage arrays, flash-based storage solutions inside and outside of the database server, new versions of backup and recovery software, and many more. The aim is the provision of a uniform solution internal customers can choose from.

In an environment where strict separation of duties is enforced the storage layer is often transparent to the database administrator. The introduction of Oracle Automatic Storage Management (ASM) with Oracle 10g Release 1 brought big changes for the storage team. Most of these changes are process related. The design and operation of ASM is fundamentally different from the way file systems have traditionally been used. As a consequence the storage engineer and administrator needs to develop an understanding of ASM, especially in the context of Real Application Cluster databases if they continue to be responsible for this part in the stack.

Standards developed by the storage team do not normally clash with the needs of the database administrator. Depending on the level of adoption of Oracle technologies in your organization, discussions will arise around the deployment of Oracle Automatic Storage Management and replication. Many storage engineers favor block-level replication on the storage level over application-level replication such as Data Guard. Unfortunately, the debate often becomes a religious one without a lot of reasoning to the arguments. To aid you to formulate an opinion, the pros and cons of block-level and application-level replication will be discussed in Chapter 9 which explains techniques for setting up disaster recovery solutions for Oracle databases.

Potential operating system standards

The Operating System engineers oversee the general direction of supported operating systems for use within the organization. Common tasks performed by the OS engineers include:

- Creating automated standard builds for the supported platforms.
- Maintaining a lifecycle matrix.
- Reacting to security vulnerability reports.
- Providing tested hot fixes.
- Evaluating (new) hardware for mass-rollout.
- Third-line support.

The most important aspect is certainly the building and maintenance of the standard operating system image for use by other consumers. One could envisage a tiered set of packages and configuration provided—a bare metal, an application server-specific set of packages and settings, or a database server package for example.

Changes to the operating system build for the Oracle database are critical to consistently deploying databases successfully. From a standards point of view it is very important to keep in touch with the operating system engineer. The standards defined in the operating system document touching the database installation are related to everything listed in the Oracle installation guide in the preinstallation requirements section. In other words the Oracle-specific package must define parameters in /etc/sysctl.conf as well as user shell limits and other relevant parameters. You can learn more about these requirements and how to automate them in Chapter 5. Ultimately the efforts of the engineers for creating operating system images need to be documented and then automated and regression tested for their respective use.

Potential database standards

Finally, we will address the standards the Oracle database administrator is most concerned about. After it has been ensured by means of open communication that the storage layer and operating system meet the requirements laid out by Oracle to install the database software, further detail can be cast in stone. Database standards can be roughly subdivided into two groups:

1. Operating system related
2. Database related

The first set of rules should be set around the operating system build, and ideally it is consistent across platforms. Items which certainly require standardization are the mount points for the database home and Grid Infrastructure (if applicable). Also, a generous use of space should be made for these mount points. Oracle homes grow and grow with every release, and many upgrades cannot be installed in place. Personal experience shows that the actual path to the Oracle binaries is not so important, as long as it is consistent. Paths such as /oracle, /u01/app/oracle etc. are all perfectly valid paths, if you decide to use one of them consistently.

The origin of the space needed for the mount points can either be on the storage area network or alternatively come from a set of local disk. If stateless computing as propagated for example by the Cisco UCS is used, then placement of Oracle binaries on the storage array is a big advantage.

Additionally the numeric group IDs and user IDs for the Oracle account and any supporting groups and users should be defined. This ensures that cluster installations succeed, which requires identically configured accounts. Even if you are not planning any cluster installation right now, you could be asked to do so in the future.

Difficulties with the current operational model

As with any theory, it is easier to talk about it than to implement it. Until Oracle 10g, the strict separation of duties between storage administrator, operating system administrator, and database administrator worked nicely. The storage administrator provided LUNs from a large machine in the data center. The storage administrator or the OS administrator then created physical volumes for use with the proprietary volume manager, and added file systems and other attributes the DBAs did not get involved with. Only then was the mount point information sent over to the database administrator. By and large, the infrastructure was out of scope for the 8i/9i DBA.

Then Oracle started to incorporate more and more infrastructure elements into its product. For example, beginning with 10.1, Automatic Storage Management has been introduced. This takes a little chunk out of the operating system administrator's role. No longer does the DBA have to worry about mount options, concurrent I/O, direct I/O, and whether the file system can do asynchronous I/O or not. The storage model across all supported platforms can technically be unified. Similarly, for Real Application Clusters there is no more need for non-Oracle cluster software. Oracle Clusterware is perfectly capable of performing this task, especially now with IPMI support for proper fencing. Most organizations I know of delegate the administration of the cluster stack to the Oracle DBA, again widening the DBAs activities and narrowing the scope of the Unix administrator. And there are many more examples like this.

Coming back to the classical separation of duties that worked so well, taking care of this new set of responsibilities has quite drastic consequences. The DBA is asked to do more and more, but the tools and privileges he has at his disposal have not kept up with the times. For security and audit reasons the oracle account does not normally have the privilege to sudo to the root account. Elevated privileges however are very often required to do the job. For example, if you want to start the Oracle Restart software stack after troubleshooting a problem, root privileges are required. Similarly, certain diagnostic commands require root privileges and patching.

Forward thinking is required to overcome these difficulties. An appropriate communication structure, encompassing mitigating controls around procedures needs to be put in place to prevent DBAs from waiting unnecessarily for required privileges. When it comes to the standards documents, this needs to be clearly reflected. Initial problems with the process can be overcome if all parties involved work towards a resolution, instead of blocking it and insisting on their own position.

Or maybe it is time to reflect about the operations model? Maybe there is place for a new job title, a person who primarily deals with the infrastructure required to run an Oracle database—the title "Oracle Platform Operator" has been suggested for this. The OPA deals with storage, clustering, patching, and whatever else is appropriate in your organization. The Database Administrator can then finally go back and focus on application support. The time is near where the title Oracle Database Administrator does not reflect the actual daily work carried out.

Changes in the hardware world

Over the last few years the hardware landscape has changed at an ever-increasing pace. Computing power provided by industry standard hardware has exploded at an unprecedented rate. Even consumer computers sport a power that would rival a high-end server from a decade ago at a fraction of the price. And there it sneaked in again: the cost element!

In the following sections a little bit of history describes how the popular high-end platforms at the beginning of the century, such as SPARC, Power, and Itanium, slowly but steadily lost ground against the x86-64 platform. But changes did not only happen to the processors powering mission critical x86-64 systems, other peripheral components improved as well. Oracle successfully crammed 4 terabytes of memory into an x86-64 server in early 2012 which should be enough to run workloads almost entirely in memory. Although this server is not currently listed on the Oracle website, its successor now is.

The storage backend in the form of classic storage arrays is also changing the way it operates. The proliferation of Solid State Disks finally makes Moore's law applicable to storage vendors. Non-spinning storage appears in PCI Express (PCIe) cards, Infiniband-connected to database servers and as special storage devices either in their own right or embedded in classic storage arrays connected via Fibre Chanel. Alternative deployments to Fiber Channel appear more and more thanks to ever-increasing bandwidth of Ethernet and a robust direct NFS implementation in the Oracle kernel.

The world of the application architect was easier a decade ago: high-end servers with the need to run Oracle were mostly using either Solaris SPARC or IBM Power systems, with a strong presence of HP-UX and True64. All of which are great platforms! Designing a system for high-transactional throughput and optimal performance in the Oracle world quite often meant going for one of these. Since the mid-2000s things have changed. Certain processor architectures such as PA-RISC and Alpha were approaching the end of their life, and the vendors of these processors were replacing them with systems based on Intel architecture. However, instead of choosing the now dominant Xeon series of processors, decision was taken to use Itanium instead, which at the time promised to be the true high-end Intel processor. Intel initially planned to use the Itaniums as their true 64-bit processors for heavy-duty workloads and the Xeons for the lower end of the server spectrum. That was back in the day; however, interestingly the Xeons caught up with Itanium and when it comes to raw performance, Intel is confident that the Xeon series of processors, most notably the E5 series, can outperform the Itanium series.

Oracle and other vendors recognized the potential of the new hardware class. Cheaper to produce and run, the industry standard (oftentimes referred to as commodity) hardware has a very good value for money proposition. Oracle aggressively marketed the idea of joining many small servers to form single entities rather than purchasing one expensive server. Similar to the energy grids, the compute grid should provide computing as a utility—a promise which took a few years to mature. Thinking back to the Oracle database, you could clearly see that the vendor made use of this change in paradigm. Real Application Clusters was heavily promoted, and Oracle also dropped the "i" suffix from Oracle 9i in favor of the new "g" for grid in 10g. The Oracle proposition was to use cheaper hardware to build resilient systems that could scale with user demand. For instance, if a compute cluster consisting of four nodes could not deal with the workload it was asked to deal with, one could simply add another node and scale horizontally that way. Oracle thought that using hardware this new way would make expensive mainframe-like hardware obsolete while making it easier to adopt RAC in the enterprise. This concept has been adopted by many of Oracle's customers over the years, and research shows that a large proportion of RAC deployments in the late 2000s was indeed implemented on x86-64 hardware running predominantly the Linux operating system.

Other more recent developments also favor the x86-platform. Take the PCI Express flash cards for example. Vendors such as Virident and Fusion IO created PCI Express cards that provide huge amounts of NAND flash memory available to the server. Suitable database workloads can theoretically be stored entirely on flash, outperforming most other storage solutions. These cards are most likely best tested and supported on the Linux and Windows platforms although vendor data sheets list other operating systems as supported as well. The third generation of PCI Express has been made available for server hardware commercially with the E5 series of Xeon processors, and the ever more bandwidth-hungry flash cards, next-generation Infiniband cards, and other devices certainly will benefit from the performance gain offered. Again, PCIe v3 has first been available on the Intel x86-64 platform.

Memory—and lots of it—has always been a domain of the high-end platforms. The data sheet for high-end RISC platforms still exceeds multiple terabyte and the largest RISC servers still take more than the largest E7-based systems. But again, the x86 platform is fast catching up with systems available commercially with up to 4 TB based on Sandy Bridge Xeons. By the time this book will be published the next-generation Xeons, based on Ivy Bridge will get a little closer again.

Most industry standard hardware cannot match the Reliability, Availability, and Serviceability (RAS) features of mainframes however, and hardware vendors are trying to address this problem with tolerant systems. Oracle especially markets its own version of a versatile, highly available platform for computing as a utility.

The mainframes these systems are targeted to replace are still out there, and dealing with very demanding workloads. If it came to datasheet comparisons with their commodity-cousins, mainframes probably would find it hard to justify their existence. However, because of the RAS features mentioned before, they deserve their place. In addition, there are countless business applications designed to run on the now slightly unfashionable operating systems HP-UX, IBM z Series, and others that are difficult to port to commodity hardware (and probably should not be ported!). Some hardware is almost fault-tolerant, and that is quintessential for some critical workloads. IBM mainframes for example provide very high reliability

In summary, specialized hardware has its place in the IT landscape, and it would not be wise trying to replace these. There is only so much evangelism to be done, and anyone who tells you that your special requirement can be processed with another system should be challenged to prove the assumption. On the other hand, purchasing a mainframe system just to virtualize apache instances does not seem to be the best value for the money. Most of today's workloads can be processed by the dual-socket server based on Intel's x86-64 architecture, and there seems to be a clear trend towards that platform.

The Linux operating (eco-) system

The choice of operating system for the consolidation platform is very relevant, and has a great many implications. Most companies already have an existing set of supported platforms, and it takes a while for them to change. While Linux has almost immediately taken off with smaller, dynamic companies right from the start, it had a hard time getting into larger organizations, and it took longer to find widespread adoption. This certainly changed when the big players in the Linux market started to provide customers with Enterprise distributions and good support models. This countered the uncertainty, partly supported by the established UNIX vendors, whether or not Linux installations were actually fit for enterprise use. Also, large vendors of business-relevant software started to port applications to Linux; most notably IBM, Informix, and Oracle among many others. This sent a signal to the world: if these heavyweights support Linux, then it must have reached a state of maturity justifying further investigation into it.

When Linux was in its early days, different ideas about software started to become more visible. Eric S. Raymond famously brought the ideas of Open Source to the wider public's attention when publishing his essay "The Cathedral and the Bazaar." Since then, Linux has come a long way and some of the ideals appear to have been lost over time. Let's look at Linux, how it started, and why it has become so popular.

A little bit of (UNIX) history

Speaking in greatly simplified terms, Linux is the result of a computer science student's experiment, which has been continuously improved by a large number of mostly nonpaid volunteers. Most people consider a Linux distribution as "Linux," but there is a subtle distinction to be made. Linux is only really the operating system's kernel. The kernel includes the low-level drivers to address the hardware, and presents an operating environment to the rest of the ecosystem. Most of the utilities we like, such as bash, tar, and most other GNU tools were ported. Since it is impossible to explain the success of Linux without going even further back in time to its cousin, Unix, a little wider explanation needs to be made.

UNIX was written when operating systems were still in their infancy. Multi-user and multi-tasking support, which are taken for granted today, were certainly not the norm. UNIX meant to change this when Ken Thompson and many others developed it in 1969 as members of the Bell Laboratories. A child of its time, UNIX was entirely written in assembly code. This changed a few years later when it was ported to the C language. This was a great step ahead since it allowed the code to be ported to a larger number of platforms.

One particularly notable element of UNIX was that it (including the sources) was easily available to universities. This not only included the right to use it, but also the kernel and utilities. Like Linux today, that made for an excellent academic research object. For a nominal fee, tapes containing the operating system could be obtained and used. This unique feat is owed to the fact that AT&T, owning Bell Labs at the time, was not allowed to commercially engage businesses other than telecommunication. Many universities made use of the early UNIX and some even created their own derivative. A notable example is the Berkeley Software Distribution (BSD) of the University of California, Berkeley.

The legal requirement not to distribute UNIX commercially was lifted for AT&T when Bell was removed from the AT&T world in the early 1980s in what will turn out to be a very fortunate event for the UNIX community. This sounds paradox, but the commercialization as System V (SysV) of the UNIX code prompted researchers to think about freedom of information. One of the most prominent is Richard Stallman who started the GNU project in the same year: 1983. GNU is a recursive acronym and stands for GNU. It is not UNIX. The aim of the GNU project was to create a free version of the UNIX operating system, including a kernel as well as the necessary command line utilities. While the latter effort was successful, the endeavor to create a kernel was severely impacted by the release of Linux-but I am getting ahead of myself. Freedom in the GNU-context means that anyone should be able to use the software without paying a fee or license charge, and the source code had to be provided as well for modification or study. While this sounds radical to many vendors, it goes even further. The most interesting aspect of the free software ideal was the license under which the software was distributed. The GNU General Public License implements a "copyleft," instead of "copyright." Instead of keeping all the power in the software producer's hand, the GPL as it is generally known reverses this concept. Software based on the GPL *also* has to be placed under the GPL, which prompted some observers to call it viral. It has however not prevented some of the most advanced and widely spread applications to be written and distributed under the GPL.

But before that could happen some other important events took place. In the early 1980s UNIX had split into many different ports, but all had in common that they were either BSD-based or based on the original sources from AT&T/Bell. Commercial versions of UNIX also began to appear throughout the 1980s: SunOS, Xenix OS, and others were based on BSD, while Solaris, HP-UX, AIX and IRIX were by and large descendants of SysV. The BSD Unix variant went through a difficult phase, when AT&T sued the University for copyright infringement. The claim was based on the fact that BSD was initially based on the free Unix sources from AT&T. The lawsuit prevented wider adoption of the Berkeley Software Distribution.

An attempt to merge the BSD-base provided by SunOS and the SysV branch of UNIX in System V Release 4 caused enough aggravation between vendors not part of the deal to form a counter-coalition. The to-ing and fro-ing would result in what is today referred to as the UNIX wars. Fractionalism between various vendor-coalitions lasted until the mid-1990s when the Open Group was formed. This consortium, which is very active still today, has published the Single Unix Specification and holds the UNIX trademark. Only systems meeting the requirements are allowed to be called UNIX systems. All others are UNIX-like operating systems.

Most UNIX systems discussed so far require special hardware to run which made them inaccessible for most outside of universities. With the proliferation of the personal computer and its increasing capabilities towards the mid-1990s users had the technical requirements to run Unix systems on their hardware, except that there were very few ports to the Intel IA32 architecture. This would change soon.

Enter Linus

With all of this background information, most notably about System V Unix, the Berkeley Software distribution and the GNU/free software movement it is possible to explain the Linux phenomenon. Linus Torvalds, at the time a student at the University of Helsinki, started developing an operating system to exploit his Intel 80386 hardware. Making use of the now almost forgotten Usenet, he posted his ideas to the Minix user group asking for opinions about his project and he got plenty. Interestingly the software was developed in a very distributed, de-centralized way by lots of interested individuals around the world. Linus was, and for most aspects still is, the maintainer of the kernel code. He incorporated a lot of these ideas to the kernel and over time the project got a lot of momentum. The code was eventually released on an FTP server, at a time where a full operating system code tree wasn't available.

When early versions of Linux were developed, they greatly benefited from the work done by the GNU project initiated by Richard Stallman. Linux was the missing piece in the puzzle: when the GNU project set out, not only did they want to write the essential utilities, but also a free kernel, codenamed "Hurd." The first few Linux versions saw a lot of the GNU utilities ported to them, which was essential in making Linux more user accessible. This is also the reason Linux really should be called GNU/Linux.

Initially Linux was developed under Torvalds' own license, but was eventually put under the GPL. That move to the GPL was a great benefit to the free software movement. Very much like the Internet in its early days, there was a purist approach to Linux and commercial interest was not the driving factor behind development. In fact, it took a long time before companies could start to make money off of Linux. Most of them do this by bundling up software in what's referred to as Linux distribution. To overcome skepticism in the industry, today's commercially successful pioneers Red Hat and SUSE created their Enterprise Distributions. Whereas Red Hat is going from strength to strength, the same cannot be said about SuSE. Nevertheless their distributions are both widely spread, with Red Hat Enterprise Linux 6 and SuSE 11 being the current distributions. Another noteworthy distribution for Oracle, Asianux, is less widely spread in the English-speaking world but focuses on Asia, as the name implies.

Thanks to the copyleft clause in most free software, any distribution has to distribute the source code as well. This allows "clones" of popular distributions to appear. For an Oracle administrator, distributions based on the Red Hat Package Manager (RPM) are most relevant since only these are supported. Of all these, Red Hat is probably the most important one due to its market share. There are a number of clones for Red Hat: Scientific Linux and CentOS are the most popular. A more recent Red Hat derivative is Oracle Linux, which started off as a near identical clone without the copyrighted material such as logos. Additionally, Oracle has developed its own kernel which is shipped in parallel with the Red Hat kernel, while otherwise maintaining capability with Red Hat.

The non RPM-based distributions like Debian, Ubuntu, and their derivatives may have wider adoption, especially on the netbook and laptop class of hardware than Red Hat clones. However, they do not play a role for Oracle database deployments.

Despite the initial skepticism and aggressive marketing efforts trying to diminish its importance Linux is powering lots of business-critical applications and managed to get into even the most conservative industries. It has more than challenged traditional UNIX variants, for two main reasons: it compares to them in terms of scalability and stability, but it can also be deployed on industry standard hardware, significantly lowering the cost of entry for businesses.

The Linux Kernel

The Linux kernel alongside the C-library and compilers (and of course other tools) forms the core of the Linux system. It has been continuously developed, and at quite a rapid pace. The kernel release cycles adhere to the open source motto: test and release often! Thanks to the efforts of so many individuals, the kernel runs on more hardware platforms than any other system in the world. This is very remarkable, especially since Linus Torvalds didn't envisage portability of his code outside the 80386 processor world.

What is confusing to many new Linux users is the naming of the kernel, and the difference between the mainline kernel and the kernel used in Red Hat, SuSE Linux and Oracle Linux. For a long time, the kernel development was divided into a stable and development tree. For example, kernel 2.4.x represented the stable tree while the kernel-in-development version was 2.5. This led to the problem that 2.5 was considered unstable, yet it provided support for current hardware. Users of kernel 2.4 lagged significantly behind the unstable tree. When kernel 2.6 was introduced the development model changed, and there was no more odd/even branch.

The confusion starts when comparing the mainline kernel developed by Linus Torvalds and the other kernel maintainers with the one used in the distributions. Red Hat 6.x for example used a kernel named 2.6.32.x. Kernel-2.6.32 dates back to December 2009 according to the kernel.org website. What you need to know is that the actual kernel shipped with the distribution but is merely based on 2.6.32.x. It includes many patches that have been added into it. Most of these patches are taken from upstream development, either to add features or bug fixes, or to add support for hardware that was not yet available when the base kernel was released. So when dealing with the Red Hat kernel, bear in mind that it is not necessarily the version you think it is.

The Unbreakable Enterprise Kernel or Kernel-UEK

When Oracle announced Enterprise Linux it was a nearly identical clone of Red Hat's Enterprise Linux with only a few exceptions that did not impact the way the system operated. This was only the first step though, and after a little while when RHEL 6 was still in development, Oracle introduced their Enterprise Kernel to the user community. Like Red Hat's kernel it was based on 2.6.32, but it could be used for Oracle Linux/Red Hat Enterprise Linux 5. As a sign of confidence, the Unbreakable Kernel is installed by default starting with Enterprise Linux 5.6. The Red Hat compatible kernel is still shipped, and is installed in parallel but is not selected as the default in the boot loader.

Where previously Enterprise distributions were careful not to advance the version numbers too quickly, Oracle now seems to pursue a middle ground between the community and the Enterprise distributions. Principal engineers within Oracle have proposed that a modern kernel must keep up with hardware innovations, and they make that argument probably having the Exa-series of offerings in mind.

The information available around the kernel states that the Unbreakable Enterprise Kernel is based on 2.6.32-46 stable, and includes performance enhancements around IRQ management, virtual memory management, better network performance, and finally improvements in the RDS stack. RDS is short for Reliable Datagram Socket which is a part of the Infiniband family of protocols and is used in Exadata.

Since the release of kernel UEK Oracle has released a second iteration, named UEK 2. Although the uname command in Linux will tell you it is version 2.6.39, the initial release of the kernel is based on 3.0.16. The choice to keep a 2.6.x name was mainly made for compatibility reasons. Kernel UEK 2 can be installed on Oracle Linux 5.8 and newer and 6.2 or newer. Oracle recommends users to switch to UEK2 where possible to benefit from new features and development.

Why is Linux so popular?

The answer to this question has two dimensions for the author: the first one is personal, the second expands on the first and shifts the focus to a business point of view. When I started to have a more serious interest in computing and the needs of data processing, it was next to impossible to get hands-on experience with the relevant commercial packages used in enterprises at the time. This includes databases such as DB2, Oracle, Informix, Adabas D, and others which required platforms not available to me . What this meant was that the interested student of computer science needed to go to a university to get access to the previously mentioned systems. The hardware platforms to run Solaris, Tru64, HP-UX, or AIX were simply unaffordable to a student.

Linux changed all that inaccessibility. In the late 1990s many relevant applications had been ported or porting efforts to Linux were underway. Thanks to its flexibility Linux ran on almost any student's hardware, and allowed instant access to the Oracle database for example. Whenever you had an idea and wanted to try something out (maybe LDAP integration with the database), you didn't have to dial in to the university campus network (those of us were the lucky ones) or physically get to the campus. Instead you started your PC, selected Linux from the boot menu, and began experimenting. This was taken further in the last few years where memory and disk space became cheaper commodities, allowing users to use virtualization to build lab environments to be used with Oracle clustering and RAC databases. Linux was the catalytic element by significantly lowering the entry hurdle to high tech. We have come a long way since the initial ports of Oracle to Linux. No longer is it necessary to buy extensions to an operating system to build a cluster. No proprietary interconnect technology had to be purchased, no expensive clustering software was needed, no additional cluster logical volume manager, and so on.

Of course this trend is a double-edged sword, and vendors of specific clustering technology are under pressure. And so are the traditional Unix vendors: some have disappeared altogether; others were bought. But the common problem all of them face is the diminishing market share. The Intel/AMD platform certainly has played a major role. Where Unix lost ground, Windows and Linux gained. Due to the nature of the Open Source model it is difficult to get real numbers of Linux deployments. Oracle Linux is free to download and use, and I assume a great number of deployments will never be counted. Any figure comparing Linux market penetration with other operating systems therefore is to be viewed with this in mind.

The only serious alternatives to Linux on i386 at the time I started a serious interest in computing were SCO Unix and UnixWare and Solaris. Sun, still independent at the time, had a few attempts at porting Solaris to the Intel platforms but could not enjoy the same level of success as Linux. This does not do the Solaris Intel port any justice: Solaris 11/Intel is a mature operating system despite its slow adoption.

If one considers that many students of computer science had exposure to Linux at university, and assuming that experience did not put them off, this helps explain the success of Linux in the commercial world. A large number of graduates are likely to prefer Linux over other operating systems leading to a generational change in corporations. This again shows why Linux is gaining ground, and the lower initial cost of deploying Linux helps the proliferation.

Another reason Linux is a desirable platform comes from Oracle Corporation. When the development/reference platform for the database and some other products changed to Linux the Linux support from Oracle became a lot better. Rather than having to wait for a port from the reference platform, Oracle Support can coordinate the release of corrections a lot more efficiently.

Summary

This chapter has introduced the key ideas and my motivation to write the rest of the book. With economic problems weighing heavily on the world, companies are either in the process or starting to reduce head count in what they perceive as "expensive labor" countries. The remaining staff quite often faces a high workload requiring a high degree of efficiency to deal with it.

Efficiency can be increased by standardizing the database environments to the highest degree possible. Standardization cries for automation! Rolling out software in exactly the same way every single time is challenging at best. Most likely the human factor will play in, creating subtle differences between environments which are difficult to diagnose and troubleshoot. A scripted deployment is more deterministic than any human could ever be. It also relieves the DBAs from mundane tasks.

Cloud computing is a quickly evolving subject, and companies can make good use of its concepts where they fit the organization. Many sites might decide that the principles of the public cloud can equally be applied in their own data centers. Similar to the rollout of the Oracle binaries, the creation of a database does not necessarily have to involve a DBA. Self-service portals with automatic chargeback workflows have the potential to transition to a "Database as a Service" environment.

The final aspect in this chapter mentioned the Linux operating environment. Thanks to its flexibility and wide industry support based on standard components the Linux platform excels as a consolidation target for many workloads. This is not to say that every single workload in the world should be moved to the Linux platform. There are many applications out there requiring mission critical platforms.

The following chapters will develop these ideas and show you possible ways to achieve these goals with the latest-generation Oracle database.

## CHAPTER 2

Oracle 12c New Features

In this chapter you can learn more about some the new features of Oracle 12c in general, but with special emphasis to database consolidation, the main theme of this book. Some new features will not be covered in this chapter but in other chapters instead to give them the space they need. This is especially true for one of the most interesting new features introduced in 12c: Pluggable Databases. Other interesting new features can be found Chapters 9 and 10 on disaster recovery, and in Chapter 11 on backup and recovery. Changes in the migration process can be found in Chapter 12. To make it easier to use this chapter as a reference, new features are grouped into their respective scope:

- Interesting changes for developers
- Changes relevant to the database availability
- Enhanced support for Information Life Cycle Management
- Other infrastructure changes

The chapter will begin with the noteworthy changes for Oracle database developers.

Changes for Developers

As with every release there are interesting new features for developers. There are too many new features to cover in this space so I will mention only the most interesting ones. Most of these new features should directly be related to consolidating Oracle applications. Some features however were so interesting that they deserved to be mentioned. If you want to see all of the new features in all their glory you need to refer to the official Oracle New Features Guide, which lists them all briefly and refers to the relevant guides.

Security is rapidly becoming a key feature in the database and securing the environment is very often left to the database administrator. Security however begins with the application, and the developers should be the first ones to implement the provided interfaces in their code. Security is therefore listed here as a developer feature, not as an administrator feature.

The Quest for Security and Least Privilege

Unfortunately security is an all-too-often neglected topic, not only in consolidation but elsewhere as well. Several exploits of security vulnerabilities have reached the evening news, and it appears as if the bad guys are always a step ahead. Knowing about the dangers of the Internet age is one thing, securing the database environment is another. Using the least-privilege approach as opposed to granting a schema owner the DBA role is what should be done moving forward. Many applications though started their life on Oracle 7 or 8 in what the author likes to call the age of innocence. One could use FTP and the telnet protocol on a day-to-day basis and clear-text authentication was the standard. And thus the application schema owner was granted the DBA role out of the same laziness instead of granting only the required privileges. Changing such an application will be difficult but is well worth the time.

Although some problems are addressed with the introduction of the self-contained Pluggable Databases, security was and is very relevant. Imagine what would happen if someone broke out of this environment and had access to a much larger number of databases and their data! Thankfully Oracle has done a lot to limit damage that can be done. A hardened audit administration, the ability to restrict privilege inheritance for procedures with invoker rights, and many more are aimed at reducing the possibility of an exploit.

Roles and PL/SQL Units

The security model in Oracle 12c knows of two different sets of privileges. Either a procedure was invoked with all the rights and privileges of the definer or alternatively with the rights of the invoker of the procedure. The documentation stack refers to the model as "definer" vs. "invoker" rights. There are two significant changes to the invoker rights model: the first one is explained in this section and deals with the ability to grant roles to a PL/SQL unit. The second one will be detailed in the next section and allows you to restrict the rights of the invoker.

The Oracle SQL language now allows you to grant roles to PL/SQL units, that is, to a stored procedure, function, or package. Note the absence of a trigger here! This allows the developer to create an invoker rights procedure in the schema of the application owner which should be well protected by means of a secure password and a strict non-interactive use policy. By granting the necessary rights to the role necessary for the execution on the stored PL/SQL unit it is possible to create low-privileged accounts accessing the application. More importantly, there are no direct grants to the underlying tables within the application owner's schema.

Figure 2-1 demonstrates how the combined rights of the invoker and the role allow for the execution of the PL/SQL unit.

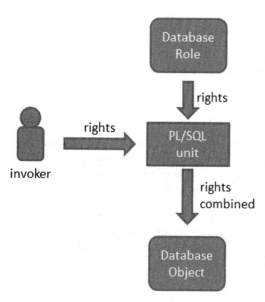

Figure 2-1. *Access privileges granted to a user and a role allow for the execution of an invoker rights procedure*

Consider the following simplified example for a demonstration of the concept.

- An application owner, named APPOWNER owns the tables for the application.

- A user account, named LOWPRIVS accesses the application via a well-defined API.

The LOWPRIVS account has merely been granted the right to connect to the database. The API is owned by the APPOWNER schema. The following procedure is part of the API and allows any application owner to enter data into the system. Crucially the LOWPRIVS account does not have any grants to objects in the application owner's schema.

```
SQL> CREATE OR REPLACE PROCEDURE appowner.insert_critical_data(
  2    pi_id appowner.critical_table.id%type,
  3    pi_secret appowner.critical_table.secretData%type)
  4  authid current_user
  5  as
  6  begin
  7    insert into appowner.critical_table (
  8        id, secretData)
  9    values (
 10      pi_id,
 11      pi_secret);
 12* end;
SQL>
```

Notice that the procedure is an invoker rights procedure. The next step is to create a role that allows the execution of this stored procedure. In order to insert into a table the select and insert privileges are needed.

```
SQL> create role critical_table_role;

Role created.

SQL> grant insert on appowner.critical_table to critical_table_role;

Grant succeeded.

SQL> grant select on appowner.critical_table to critical_table_role;

Grant succeeded.
```

With the grants sorted the role can be granted to the procedure as shown:

```
SQL> grant critical_table_role to procedure insert_critical_data;

Grant succeeded.
```

With the execute privilege on the stored procedure granted to the LOWPRIVS user either directly or better via another role, the low privileged user can make use of the API:

```
SQL> exec appowner.insert_critical_data(1, 'test')

PL/SQL procedure successfully completed.

SQL> commit;

Commit complete.
```

As soon as the role grant is revoked from the stored procedure, its invocation fails:

```
SQL> exec appowner.insert_critical_data(2, 'test 2')
BEGIN appowner.insert_critical_data(2, 'test '); END;

*
ERROR at line 1:
ORA-00942: table or view does not exist
ORA-06512: at "APPOWNER.INSERT_CRITICAL_DATA", line 7
ORA-06512: at line 1
```

The new way of granting roles to PL/SQL units allows for much finer granularity in the implementation of the API. Whereas in 11g and before it was necessary to either grant privileges on the application schema directly to users to allow them to execute code or alternatively use definer rights procedures. Security auditors might find that definer rights procedures are dangerous since many application schemas have more privileges granted to them than needed. Using roles allows the developer to only grant the privileges needed to stored code and nothing more.

Inheritance in Invoker's Rights Procedures

The second change to the invoker rights security model when calling PL/SQL units was already alluded to in the previous section. The change allows you to prevent exploits in situations where a user with high privileges executes a procedure with invoker rights. The invoker's set of privileges can potentially be higher than what is needed.

In normal circumstances executing stored code using the invoker's privileges does not need to be a problem, there is trust in the developers not to add malicious code into the system but stricter security rules require more control. Imagine for a second that a developer replaces the stored procedure harmless() with something malicious, and therefore highjacks the higher-privileged account which performs an undesired operation. Consider this scenario:

- According to the security guidelines application, programming interface is grouped into a schema with low privileges. In this scenario the schema is named LOWPRIVS, and it contains—among other code—a procedure named harmless to perform a harmless operation.

- All application data is defined and stored in its own schema, named APPOWNER in the example.

- Sometimes an account with higher privileges than those granted to LOWPRIVS needs to execute the procedure harmless() as part of a different workflow. The account-HIGHPRIVS-is granted the DBA role as an extreme example.

The procedure harmless() is used to insert data into a table. Following is the definition:

```
CREATE OR REPLACE PROCEDURE lowprivs.harmless(
  pi_id appowner.critical_table.id%type,
  pi_secret appowner.critical_table.secretData%type)
authid current_user
as
begin
  insert into appowner.critical_table (
    id, secretData)
  values (
```

```
        pi_id,
        pi_secret);

end;
/
```

The LOWPRIVS account has a direct grant to select and insert into the table APPOWNER.critical_table. Now if LOWPRIVS executes the procedure everything is fine. However if someone changes the code to perform some undesired operation things can go wrong. For example:

```
SQL> CREATE OR REPLACE PROCEDURE lowprivs.harmless(
  2    pi_id appowner.critical_table.id%type,
  3    pi_secret appowner.critical_table.secretData%type)
  4  authid current_user
  5  as
  6  begin
  7    execute immediate 'truncate table appowner.critical_table';
  8  end;
  9  /
Procedure created.
```

Thanks to the execute immediate statement privilege checks are deferred to run time and the procedure compiles normally. If LOWPRIVS executes the procedure nothing happens; the malicious developer has to wait for someone with higher privileges to execute the code.

```
LOWPRIVS> exec lowprivs.harmless(3, 'evil lowprivs')
BEGIN lowprivs.harmless(3, 'evil lowprivs'); END;

*
ERROR at line 1:
ORA-01031: insufficient privileges
ORA-06512: at "LOWPRIVS.HARMLESS", line 7
ORA-06512: at line 1
```

Disaster will strike when the higher privileged user—HIGHPRIVS—executes the procedure!

```
HIGHPRIVS> exec lowprivs.harmless (4, 'test highprivs #2')

PL/SQL procedure successfully completed.

APPOWNER> select count(1) from appowner.critical_table;

  COUNT(1)
----------
         0


APPOWNER>
```

This is definitely not what you want. To prevent such code from performing undesired operations by exploiting the higher privileges of the invoking user Oracle designed an additional security layer around invoker rights: inheritance of privileges. In order for an invoker with higher privileges to grant those to the called procedure the caller must have granted the "inherit privileges" system privilege to the owner of the stored code. Alternatively the "inherit any privileges" system privilege must be granted to the owner of the invoker rights code. If the owner of the stored code has neither of these two the runtime engine will raise an ORA-06598 "insufficient INHERIT PRIVILEGES privilege" error.

It appears that "inherit privileges" is granted to public in order not to break any existing applications. Post-migration you might want to review these grants and perhaps remove the grant from public:

```
SYS AS SYSDBA> revoke inherit privileges on user highprivs from public;

Revoke succeeded.
```

Subsequent calls to the procedure will cause the error mentioned above:

```
HIGHPRIVS> exec lowprivs.harmless(2, user)
BEGIN lowprivs.harmless(2, user); END;

*
ERROR at line 1:
ORA-06598: insufficient INHERIT PRIVILEGES privilege
ORA-06512: at "LOWPRIVS.HARMLESS", line 1
ORA-06512: at line 1
```

White Lists to Restrict PL/SQL Program Unit References

Oracle 12c introduces a finer level of granularity for calls to PL/SQL stored units, named white lists. This allows the developer to create stored code which can only be invoked by other PL/SQL units which are on the calling unit's white list. Imagine a procedure that performs debugging operations. To prevent the procedure from being invoked outside the context of your code you can add the new accessible by clause.

Before Oracle 12c it was really difficult to implement a list of calls that was permissible from within an application. At best a list of privileges granted to roles and/or multiple users was necessary to facilitate more fine-grained access.

Consider for example an Application Programming Interface (API) which defines access to the tables of an application. The API could be defined in a way similar to the Java interface, providing just a stub that must be implemented elsewhere. The implementation can then be "private" to the application, in other words cannot be invoked outside the context of the calling API.

To demonstrate how easy it is consider a function which helps write debugging information into a log table.

```
SQL> create or replace procedure debug_proc( pi_message varchar2 )
  2  accessible by (input_api_interface_pkg)
  3  as
  4  pragma autonomous_transaction;
  5  begin
  6    insert into debug_tab (
  7          t, vc)
  8    values (
  9          systimestamp,
 10          pi_message
 11    );
```

```
12  commit;
13  end;
14  /
```

Procedure created.

The important new information is in line 2: the new accessible-by clause defines that only stored units within the package input_api_interface_pkg can invoke the procedure debug_proc. Failing to do so will cause a runtime error:

```
SQL> exec debug_proc('test')
BEGIN debug_proc('test'); END;

      *
ERROR at line 1:
ORA-06550: line 1, column 7:
PLS-00904: insufficient privilege to access object DEBUG_PROC
ORA-06550: line 1, column 7:
PL/SQL: Statement ignored
```

This is quite clear: you do not have the rights to invoke debug_proc from outside the package. You can of course reference more than one possible invoker in the accessible by clause separated by comma.

```
SQL> create or replace procedure debug_proc
  2    accessible by (f_1,p_2,pkg_3,pkg_4)
  3  as
  4  begin
  5    dbms_output.put_line('invoker() has been called');
  6  end;
  7  /
```

The stored units referenced in the accessible by clause do not need to exist at the time of the object's creation. You cannot however define white lists within packages. Trying to do so will result in an error:

```
SQL> create or replace package pkg_3 as
  2    procedure pkg_3_p1 accessible by (pkg_4);
  3  end;
  4  /
```

Warning: Package created with compilation errors.

```
SQL> show err
Errors for PACKAGE PKG_3:

LINE/COL ERROR
-------- ------------------------------------------------------------------
0/0      PLS-00157: Only schema-level programs allow ACCESSIBLE BY
```

The error message actually indicates that this works in both directions: you cannot reference individual procedures or functions within a package either. If you try to reference a specific procedure in the package in another stored unit of code you are going to receive an error:

```
SQL> create or replace function ANSWER return number
  2    accessible by (pkg_5.pkg5_p1)
  3  as
  4  begin
  5    return 42;
  6  end;
  7  /

Function created.
```

Notice how procedure pkg5_p1 of package pkg_5 is (theoretically) allowed to execute the function. In reality, it is not (the package header is deliberately not shown).

```
SQL> CREATE OR REPLACE PACKAGE BODY PKG_5 as
  2      procedure pkg5_p1 (pi_vc varchar2) as
  3        the_answer number;
  4      begin
  5        the_answer := answer;
  6      end pkg5_p1;
  7      procedure pkg5_p2 (pi_n number) as begin null; end;
  8      procedure pkg5_p3 as begin null; end;
  9  end;
 10  /

Warning: Package Body created with compilation errors.

SQL> show err
Errors for PACKAGE BODY PKG_5:

LINE/COL ERROR
-------- ------------------------------------------------------------------
5/5      PL/SQL: Statement ignored
5/19     PLS-00904: insufficient privilege to access object ANSWER
SQL>
```

So if you want to restrict access to a function to a specific piece of code you need to create this independently and not within a package.

Other Improvements

There are many more improvements for developing Oracle database applications in the new release. Although they are not directly related to consolidation they are noteworthy features . There is no particular order to these features, the one thing they have in common is their usefulness.

As with every new feature it is just this one that makes you long for a migration to the current release. But this has always been the case. The current problem one is working on is always solved, or at least less of an issue, with a future version of the database you cannot currently use.

Sequence Values as Default Values in Tables

One of the most dearly missing features from the author's point of view was the possibility to define the next value of a sequence as the default value for a table. Quite often a developer finds himself in the situation that it was necessary to populate an artificial key with a sequence value. A classic example is the use of an Oracle replication technology. Some of Oracle's replication technologies require you to add a unique key constraint where there was none before.

When running prior versions, the developer is faced with a number of problems. Obviously, it is not possible to insert a null value into the table as the application's code currently would. Not many applications have a PL/SQL API to populate values in tables. If that was the case the addition of the new column would not cause any issues because you could simply modify the API. For the more realistic case where a multitude of interfaces exist to populate table data-external applications, SQL*Loader, a user interface written in APEX or similar you cannot guarantee that the key will always be populated. A common solution to this kind of problem is the use of a before insert trigger. This way you can guarantee that there will always be a key value! A trigger however always means overhead. Consider this simple example: a table that requires a new key to be added using an ID column.

```
SQL> > desc t1
 Name                                     Null?    Type
 -------------------------------- -------- --------------------------
 VC                                                VARCHAR2(100)
 T                                                 TIMESTAMP(6)

SQL> alter table t1 add id number;

Table altered.

SQL> alter table t1 add constraint
  2  pk_t1 primary key(id);

Table altered.

SQL> create sequence s_t1 cache 1000;

Sequence created.

SQL> create or replace trigger bit_t1 before insert on t1
  2  for each row
  3  begin
  4    if :new.id is null then
  5      :new.id := s_t1.nextval;
  6    end if;
  7  end;
  8  /

Trigger created.
```

With the trigger in place the application is not broken and the addition of the primary key has been added completely transparently. However, there is a downside: performance will take a hit. Especially if you perform this operation for many tables! Inserting a mere 100,000 rows into the table with the trigger enabled takes 8 seconds on a test system.

```
SQL> begin
  2  for i in 1..100000 loop
  3    insert into t1 (vc, t) values (i,systimestamp);
  4  end loop;
  5  end;
  6  /
```

PL/SQL procedure successfully completed.

Elapsed: 00:00:08.00

Beginning with Oracle 12c it is possible to add a sequence as the default value for a column. The code example shown earlier changes to this:

```
SQL> alter table t1 modify id default s_t1.nextval;
```

Table altered.

The before insert trigger is disabled next. The same code block to insert 100,000 rows now takes a lot less time:

```
SQL> begin
  2  for i in 1..100000 loop
  3    insert into t1 (vc, t) values (i,systimestamp);
  4  end loop;
  5  end;
  6  /
```

PL/SQL procedure successfully completed.

Elapsed: 00:00:04.26

So not only does the code look cleaner, but it also executes a lot faster and there is a lot less maintenance to be done. You can see the new default value in the user_tab_columns view for example:

```
SQL> select column_name,data_default
  2    from user_tab_columns
  3  where table_name = 'T1'
  4    and column_name = 'ID';
```

```
COLUMN_NAME                      DATA_DEFAULT
-------------------------------- --------------------------------
ID                               "MARTIN"."S_T1"."NEXTVAL"
```

Increased varchar2 Limit

An interesting change has been made to the maximum length of the familiar varchar2 and some related data types. Instead of the previous limit of 4000 bytes for this field it is now possible to store up to 32 kilobytes. The initialization parameter in charge of changing the behavior is max_string_size. It is a static parameter, and changing it requires an instance restart. In addition, changing from the default standard string width to the extended string width requires starting the database or PDB in UPGRADE mode and executing the script $ORACLE_HOME/rdbms/admin/utl32k.sql.

The easiest way to change to 32k varchar2 fields is to apply the change in a PDB. The initialization parameter in the PDB is independent of the value in the root, so you can make the change—maybe on a clone of the PDB—and test the changed behavior. Here is an example of how the parameter has been changed in a Pluggable Database, PDB1:

```
[oracle@server1 ~]$ sqlplus sys/***@server1/pdb1 as sysdba

[...]

SQL> alter pluggable database PDB1 close immediate;

Pluggable database altered.

SQL> alter pluggable database pdb1 open upgrade;

Pluggable database altered.

SQL> show parameter max_string_size

NAME                                 TYPE        VALUE
------------------------------------ ----------- ------------------------------
max_string_size                      string      EXTENDED

SQL> @?/rdbms/admin/utl32k
```

After the script terminates you should restart the PDB in NORMAL mode before you can make use of the extended length as this example shows:

```
SQL> create table t2 (vc varchar2(32767));

Table created.

SQL> desc t2
 Name                                   Null?    Type
 -------------------------------------- -------- -------------------------
 VC                                              VARCHAR2(32767)
```

Be warned though that you need a different tool other than SQL*Plus to insert that much data into the vc column. The inherent limit of SQL*Plus is 2500 characters for a column.

Enhanced Support for Top-N Queries

Before Oracle 12c one had to perform a few tricks to get the top-n rows of a query, or to perform pagination of a result set. It has been said many times that users entering a query are unlikely to move beyond the first few pages of results. Fetching the complete result set of a query for a user interface usually does not yield much benefit. Oracle's own SQLDeveloper for example fetches a limited subset of the query result set in the grid first. Only if the users scroll further down in the result set are more records fetched. This approach keeps resource consumption low and results in a better user experience.

Before explaining how the new support can benefit your application, let's briefly review how applications are currently written in order to paginate a result set, such as displaying a search result in a web page. The following example shows some code slightly adapted from an excellent example Tom Kyte gave in 2006. This example shows objects owned by the user MARTIN. The objects are listed five at a time.

```
SQL> select *
  2    from ( select /*+ FIRST_ROWS(n) */
  3    a.*, ROWNUM rnum
  4        from ( select object_name, object_type, subobject_name from t3
  5                where owner = 'MARTIN'
  6                order by object_name, subobject_name ) a
  7        where ROWNUM <= :last_row_in_set )
  8  where rnum  >= :first_row_in_set
  9 /
```

The bind variables here constitute the clever bit of the query. In the initial query execution first_row_in_set is set to 1 while last_row_in_set is set to 5. The bind variables are then changed with every execution of the query allowing for a rolling window.

The complete result set for the user MARTIN is important for the rest of this section. Querying table T3 for all objects owned by MARTIN, and ordering the results by object_name and subobject_name, the following result is displayed:

```
SQL select object_name,object_type,subobject_name
  2  from t3 where owner = 'MARTIN'
  3  order by object_name,subobject_name;


OBJECT_NAME          OBJECT_TYPE      SUBOBJECT_NAME
-------------------- -------------------- --------------------
ANSWER               FUNCTION
DEBUG_PROC           PROCEDURE
DEBUG_TAB            TABLE
I_PARTTAB            INDEX PARTITION      P1
I_PARTTAB            INDEX PARTITION      P2
I_PARTTAB            INDEX PARTITION      P3
I_PARTTAB            INDEX PARTITION      PMAX
I_PARTTAB            INDEX
PARTTAB              TABLE PARTITION      P1
PARTTAB              TABLE PARTITION      P2
PARTTAB              TABLE PARTITION      P3
PARTTAB              TABLE PARTITION      P4
PARTTAB              TABLE PARTITION      P5
PARTTAB              TABLE PARTITION      PMAX
PARTTAB              TABLE
PKG_3                PACKAGE
PKG_5                PACKAGE
PKG_5                PACKAGE BODY
PK_T1                INDEX
S                    SEQUENCE
SEQTEST              TABLE
SYS_C009851          INDEX
S_T1                 SEQUENCE
T1                   TABLE
T3                   TABLE

25 rows selected.
```

Now, getting back to the pagination query, it indeed returns the first 5 rows:

```
OBJECT_NAME          OBJECT_TYPE          SUBOBJECT_NAME          RNUM
-------------------- -------------------- --------------------- -----------
ANSWER               FUNCTION                                       1
DEBUG_PROC           PROCEDURE                                       2
DEBUG_TAB            TABLE                                           3
I_PARTTAB            INDEX PARTITION      P1                        4
I_PARTTAB            INDEX PARTITION      P2                        5
```

The next 5 records where then fetched by changing the where clause in lines 6 and 7 of the query. This whole query can now be greatly simplified thanks to the new "row limiting clause" in the select statement. Two options exist: using an offset and either a number of rows or a percentage of the result set can be returned. Returning to the above example, the offset is useful when a certain number of rows in the result set have to be skipped. Skipping the first five rows in the result set is achieved using this query:

```
SQL> select object_name, object_type, subobject_name from t3
  2  where owner = 'MARTIN' order by object_name, subobject_name
  3  offset 5 rows;

OBJECT_NAME          OBJECT_TYPE     SUBOBJECT_NAME
-------------------- --------------- ---------------------
I_PARTTAB            INDEX PARTITION      P3
I_PARTTAB            INDEX PARTITION      PMAX
I_PARTTAB            INDEX
PARTTAB              TABLE PARTITION      P1
[...]
T1                   TABLE
T3                   TABLE

20 rows selected.
```

As you would expect, the first 5 objects are not part of the result set. The query however does not limit the result set. Keep the execution plan of this query in mind, which is as follows:

```
SQL> select * from table(dbms_xplan.display_cursor);

PLAN_TABLE_OUTPUT
--------------------------------------------------------------------------------
SQL_ID  fyrpmgskxx073, child number 0
-------------------------------------
 select object_name, object_type, subobject_name from t3  where owner =
'MARTIN' order by object_name, subobject_name  offset 5 rows

Plan hash value: 3729804300
```

```
--------------------------------------------------------------------------
| Id  | Operation          | Name | Rows  | Bytes | Cost (%CPU)| Time     |
--------------------------------------------------------------------------
|   0 | SELECT STATEMENT   |      |       |       | 425  (100)|           |
|*  1 |   VIEW             |      |    25 |  7250 | 425    (1)| 00:00:01 |
|   2 |    WINDOW SORT     |      |    25 |  1050 | 425    (1)| 00:00:01 |
|*  3 |     TABLE ACCESS FULL| T3 |    25 |  1050 | 425    (1)| 00:00:01 |
--------------------------------------------------------------------------

Predicate Information (identified by operation id):
---------------------------------------------------

   1 - filter("from$_subquery$_002"."rowlimit_$$_rownumber">5)
   3 - filter("OWNER"='MARTIN')
```

22 rows selected.

Pagination of the result set is achieved by adding the limit clause to the query. In order to display rows 6 through 10 in the result set, the query can be changed as follows:

```
select /*+ gather_plan_statistics */
  object_name, object_type, subobject_name from t3
  where owner = 'MARTIN' order by object_name, subobject_name
  offset :a rows
  fetch next :a rows only;
```

```
OBJECT_NAME          OBJECT_TYPE      SUBOBJECT_NAME
-------------------- ---------------- --------------------
I_PARTTAB            INDEX PARTITION     P3
I_PARTTAB            INDEX PARTITION     PMAX
I_PARTTAB            INDEX
PARTTAB              TABLE PARTITION     P1
PARTTAB              TABLE PARTITION     P2
```

Pagination is working nicely here. However, the explain plan becomes slightly more difficult to read:

```
SQL> select * from table(dbms_xplan.display_cursor(format=>'TYPICAL'));

PLAN_TABLE_OUTPUT
-----------------------------------------------------------------------------
SQL_ID  czwjx2jkxcj2t, child number 0
-------------------------------------
 select /*+ gather_plan_statistics */    object_name, object_type,
subobject_name from t3    where owner = 'MARTIN' order by object_name,
subobject_name    offset :a rows    fetch next :a rows only

Plan hash value: 171896480
```

```
---------------------------------------------------------------------------
| Id  | Operation                   | Name | Rows  | Bytes | Cost (%CPU)| Time     |
---------------------------------------------------------------------------
|   0 | SELECT STATEMENT            |      |       |       | 425 (100)|          |
|*  1 |  VIEW                       |      |    25 |  7250 | 425   (1)| 00:00:01 |
|*  2 |   WINDOW SORT PUSHED RANK   |      |    25 |  1050 | 425   (1)| 00:00:01 |
|*  3 |    FILTER                   |      |       |       |          |          |
|*  4 |     TABLE ACCESS FULL       | T3   |    25 |  1050 | 425   (1)| 00:00:01 |
---------------------------------------------------------------------------
```

```
Predicate Information (identified by operation id):
---------------------------------------------------

   1 - filter(("from$_subquery$_002"."rowlimit_$$_rownumber"<=CASE  WHEN
              (:A>=0) THEN FLOOR(TO_NUMBER(TO_CHAR(:A))) ELSE 0 END +:A AND
              "from$_subquery$_002"."rowlimit_$$_rownumber">:A))
   2 - filter(ROW_NUMBER() OVER ( ORDER BY
              "OBJECT_NAME","SUBOBJECT_NAME")<=CASE  WHEN (:A>=0) THEN
              FLOOR(TO_NUMBER(TO_CHAR(:A))) ELSE 0 END +:A)
   3 - filter(:A<CASE  WHEN (:A>=0) THEN FLOOR(TO_NUMBER(TO_CHAR(:A)))
              ELSE 0 END +:A)
   4 - filter("OWNER"='MARTIN')

31 rows selected.
```

The approach well since the offset thankfully accepts a value of 0 rows as well. Your web frontend could simply keep track of the number of records already displayed and passes the bind variables :first_row_to_fetch as well as a constant for the :number_of_rows to fetch.

Changes Relevant to Database Availability

Oracle has always been one at the forefront when it came to supporting a highly available infrastructure for its database product. Broadly speaking you can categorize the high availability options into two categories. The first is all about protecting a single instance database. A database instance in Oracle's terminology broadly speaking is what you find in memory on a database server or within a virtual machine. An instance is gone as soon as the power is turned off, as it does not have a persistent part. The persistent information, or in other words the database, is separate from the instance. A single instance database has a one-to-one mapping with the database, and is most likely the predominant deployment method of an Oracle database. It is also by far the easiest to manage. A multi-instance database is called a Real Application Clusters (RAC) Database. In RAC the strict mapping of instance to database is lifted, and you can have n-to-1 mappings between instances and databases. Bear in mind that with RAC you always get only one copy of the database; it therefore does not qualify as a disaster recovery (DR) solution!

Among the options for protecting your single instance database you can choose from are:

- Virtualization

- Active/Passive Clusters

The loss of the instance even for the briefest of moments always means a loss of connectivity to the database. This connectivity loss is going to be noticed by the user. Depending on how well your application has been written the end-users will either see the ORA-03113 "end of file on communication channel" or a friendlier variant of the same. Loss of the instance can be completely acceptable, for as long as the service can be restored in a reasonable recovery period. If all goes well then all there is to do is for the SMON process to perform instance recovery. Worse cases involve restarting the middle-tier since it was never written to deal with loss of database connectivity in mind. If such an interruption is not possible then you need to become more resourceful and invest in the previously mentioned Real Application Cluster. The active-active configuration allows the application to continue despite the fact that an instance was lost although there might be a brief period where the system seems to "hang" due to resource remastering. Of course, RAC cannot prevent you from a brown-out in the data center: if all the servers go down so will your RAC database and you might have to invoke your disaster recovery scenario.

Since not every database administrator is familiar with RAC and the supporting technology the following sections will introduce the most important aspects you need to know before you can appreciate the 12c new features for RAC. Please note that virtualization and active/passive clusters will be explained in much more depth in Chapter 4.

Brief Introduction to Real Application Clusters

Oracle RAC is a cost option on top of Oracle Enterprise Edition. Using a shared-everything approach each database instance "sees" all the changes made by its peers. Operating the database on multiple instances offers resilience and more fault-tolerance compared to single instance deployments, if the applications are appropriately written and tested. RAC pays tribute to the fact that many enterprise deployments moved from what accountants consider expensive hardware to industry standard equipment. These enterprise deployments have often been on hardware that supported extensive Reliability, Availability and Serviceability (RAS) features built-in. Although hugely beneficial to the stability of the platform, these features come at a cost. Although RAS features exist in the high-end x86-64 platform as well to a degree, a server failure can still happen with the previously mentioned problems associated with it. The RAC value proposition includes:

- High Availability: thanks to the multi-instance database a server crash can be mitigated by cleverly architected applications.

- Scalability: a Real Application Cluster can be extended should the need for new processing power arise.

- Manageability: Multiple databases can be consolidated into a Real Application Cluster.

- Reduced Cost of Ownership: Combining Pluggable Databases and RAC can potentially reduce the number of database servers, cutting cost for electricity, cooling, and real estate in the data center.

From a technical point of view RAC is based on Oracle Grid Infrastructure. Grid Infrastructure combines Oracle's cluster-aware logical volume manager, named Automatic Storage Management (ASM) with a high-availability framework-Oracle Clusterware. Oracle Clusterware serves one main purpose: to hide the fact that multiple physical machines are connected to form a cluster from the user. As such Clusterware performs all tasks you would expect from a cluster framework:

- Cluster membership management: Every cluster framework must manage which hosts are considered healthy members of the cluster. Under no circumstances must the cluster find itself in a split-brain situation. In such a catastrophic state communication between cluster members is interrupted while the cluster nodes are still running. Adhering to its programming, the cluster software in each of the cluster halves will try to fail over resources of the nodes it considers crashed. The danger of data corruption looms here: if the application communicates with effectively unsynchronized cluster halves, different data can be written to disk. Oracle Clusterware uses a network and disk heartbeat to prevent a split brain scenario.

- Fencing: If Clusterware detects that a node or set of nodes in the cluster is unresponsive then it will evict members from the cluster to prevent corruption. This process is called node fencing. Beginning with Oracle 11.2 fencing has been greatly improved using the Intelligent Platform Management Interface (IPMI) effectively allowing a cluster member to evict an unhealthy member using a hardware command.

- Inter-node connectivity: RAC employs a shared-everything approach. A cluster database has one global SGA that spans all the nodes on which the database is up and running. For various reasons such as the transfer of database blocks over the network or the exchange of cluster-wide enqueue information database instances must communicate with one another.

- Resource management: Everything Clusterware manages is referred to as a resource. The ASM instance, network, database, services—literally everything in a RAC environment is a resource. Each resource has an associated profile, stating on which node to execute the resource, how to monitor the resource's health, and what to do if a resource has stopped working. Local resources by definition exist on one node only and cannot be failed over to another cluster node. Cluster resources however can be moved within the cluster.

Figure 2-2 shows a typical configuration for a Real Application Cluster consisting of two nodes. Note that the figure does not take any of the new 12c features into account. The management interface used for out-of-band management is not shown in order to simplify the diagram.

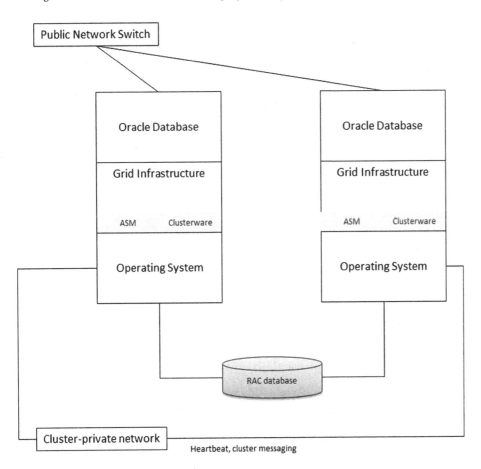

Figure 2-2. *Conceptual design of a RAC environment*

You can see from Figure 2-2 that the RAC database is concurrently mounted by all instances. It is supported to use a third-party file system for this purpose. For quite some time now Oracle has tried to deliver all the required technology to run a clustered system, and its chosen technology—ASM—has matured and is more than adequate for the purpose.

Usually access to shared storage is provided by Fiber Channel Host Base Adapters; however, other possibilities exist as well. The inter-node communication mentioned earlier in this chapter is made possible by a dedicated, cluster-private network. Most sites employ either multiple aggregated Gbit Ethernet ports or a couple of 10 Gbit Ethernet ports for the purpose. More sophisticated deployments such as Exadata make use of Infiniband for the cluster interconnect.

Once the operating system is configured for RAC the database administrator begins the installation of Grid Infrastructure which is a mandatory component when installing RAC.

The final step is to install the database binaries over the Grid Infrastructure layer. The installer will detect that you are trying to deploy the database binaries on a cluster and offer you a list of nodes to deploy the binaries to.

Brief Introduction to Automatic Storage Management

Automatic Storage Management (ASM) is a feature that was introduced in Oracle 10g Release 1. Among the primary design goals is the intention to simplify storage administration by automating disk and file management tasks. As with many new features introduced with the Oracle database, another aim is to reduce management overhead and deployment costs. ASM is a generic alternative to a clustered file system (CFS)/cluster logical volume manager that works on all supported platforms. The implementation of ASM differs greatly from other file systems which you normally install on the operating system in form of kernel loadable modules and a user-mode part for the administration. ASM on the other hand is an additional lightweight Oracle instance on each server. ASM provides similar functionality to a classic CFS but includes volume management capabilities, such as disk balancing and redundancy.

With the introduction of Oracle 10.2, ASM has become a popular choice for storage management, especially for RAC. As a sign of its maturity, documentation and functionality have increased with each release since its inception, and while initially documentation consisted of a chapter in the Administrator's Guide in 10g, it has now got a manual of its own.

ASM is built on Oracle Managed Files (OMF), a feature that was first introduced in Oracle 9i. OMF greatly simplifies the management of database files. Oracle ASM is by no means restricted to RAC as its position in this chapter suggests. ASM is a great choice if you are looking for standardization of the storage layer.

Conceptually, ASM resembles the classical logical volume manager (LVM) known from Linux and AIX, but it can do a lot more and—most importantly—it is cluster aware. Individual physical volumes, called ASM disks, are aggregated into volume groups. Instead of volume groups these entities are referred to as ASM disk groups. In a RAC environment, the ASM disks have to be located on shared storage accessible from all nodes in the cluster. Just like all other cluster resources, disk groups are managed internally via Clusterware. Unlike for example Linux LVM, there are no logical volumes created on top of a volume group. Instead, the disk group as a whole can be used to create and store database files. Following the logic of the Oracle Managed File, all you need to do is define the disk group on which your database should be created.

One of the striking beauties of Oracle ASM is the online-almost-everything approach. Adding and removing ASM disks from an ASM Disk Group is an online operation. After an addition or removal of a disk, a so-called rebalance operation ensues. Following a "Stripe-And-Mirror-Everything" (SAME) principle Oracle tries very hard to evenly distribute information on ASM disks. Figure 2-3 compares the classic LVM approach with ASM.

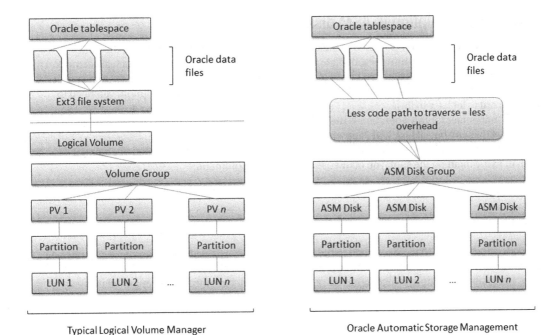

Figure 2-3. Comparing a typical logical volume manager with Oracle ASM

Very often you find discussions around ASM to be of a political nature. With the deployment of ASM the database administrator enters the world of the storage or—depending on your company—the system administrator's realm. Since they are most likely not aware of ASM or what it can do and how to use it, a lot of resistance will likely be faced. The factor of job security also plays an important role in the discussions. You read before that ASM is implemented as an Oracle instance which is radically different from the way the storage or operating system administrator worked before. Instead of entering commands on the shell prompt the storage administrator will have to log in to the ASM instance and perform the maintenance from there. The alternative way of administering ASM is by using Oracle Enterprise Manager. Either way, the implementation of ASM resembles a paradigm shift. Beginning with Oracle 11.1 however it is possible to separate the administration of the storage and cluster layer to a dedicated account on the operating system which is different from the oracle account. If needed the separation of duties that has worked so well for Oracle 9i can be carried over into the cloud age.

Enhancements in the Cluster Layer

Oracle Clusterware and Automatic Storage Management together make up the cluster layer in Oracle RAC. It includes the High Availability framework and the storage management. For quite a while now it has been possible to run Oracle RAC without any third-party Clusterware at all. For those users, who probably form the majority of Oracle's RAC customers the following sections are of interest: The limit of 63 ASM disk groups has been increased. This could be potentially interesting for consolidated environments where for some reason each database has its own disk group.

Oracle also allows you now to store the ASM password file in a shared ASM disk group. This new ability is not only useful, but also a prerequisite for using Flex ASM.

Checking for Logical Corruption in ASM disk groups

The alter diskgroup command has been extended to include the scrub clause. This clause allows the ASM administrator to check ASM diskgroups, individual disks in a disk group, or a single ASM files for logical corruption in cases where ASM is responsible for protecting the data. If logical corruption is detected during the scrubbing process ASM can try to repair it using mirror copies of the extent. By default ASM will only report corruption, you need to specify the repair keyword to let it try to fix it.

The final relevant parameter for this operation is the power level. Unlike some other ASM commands you do not specify an integer, but rather any one of low, high, and max.

If you suspect a problem with the diskgroup "RECO" of your system, and want to be reported of potential problems rather than fixing them on the spot, you could use the following command:

```
SQL> alter diskgroup reco scrub power high;

Diskgroup altered.
```

No further information was found to be returned to the prompt, but it is expected that a summary of errors will be returned if there are any. Just like the check diskgroup clause additional information is recorded in the ASM instances alert.log. In the above example, which found no problem the alert.log information contained these few lines:

```
2013 10-10 08:59:42.373000 +01:00
SQL> alter diskgroup reco scrub power high
NOTE: Start scrubbing diskgroup RECO
Starting background process SCRB
SCRB started with pid=34, OS id=7934
SUCCESS: alter diskgroup reco scrub power high
```

Scrubbing will be prevented if the I/O load of the ASM instance is currently considered too high. You can view the progress of the scrubbing operation in v$asm_operation as usual.

ASM Becomes More Flexible

Before Oracle 12c every node in the cluster needed to have its own ASM instance. This collection of ASM instances is generically referred to as an ASM cluster. Instances within the cluster communicated with each other with the goal to present shared storage to all users. Up until Oracle 11.2 this included databases only, but with the introduction of the general purpose file system based on ASM, named ASM Cluster File System or ACFS for short Oracle offers a complete stack of a cluster aware storage solution.

Up until 12c it has been the case that a failed ASM instance meant all the databases on the host were to fail as well. Oracle Flex ASM, as the new set of features has been named, addresses this situation by removing the strict requirement to have one ASM instance per cluster node. The default configuration of ASM up to version 12c is shown in Figure 2-4.

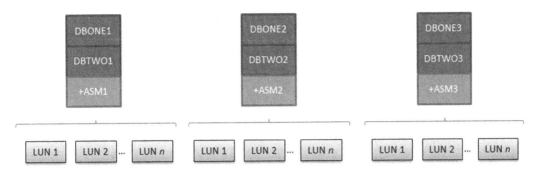

Figure 2-4. *The pre-12c ASM configuration with one ASM instance per cluster node*

Flex ASM removes the strict requirement to have one, and only one ASM instance per cluster node. Instead, with Flex ASM enabled, Oracle will create three ASM instances in the cluster, regardless of cluster size. The number of ASM instances can of course be configured, most importantly when non 12c databases are supposed to be hosted on the 12c Grid Infrastructure deployment. In such situations you will need to operate Flex ASM in the same way ASM operated in the earlier release. Figure 2-5 shows a four-node RAC with Flex ASM enabled. All databases have already been migrated to 12c.

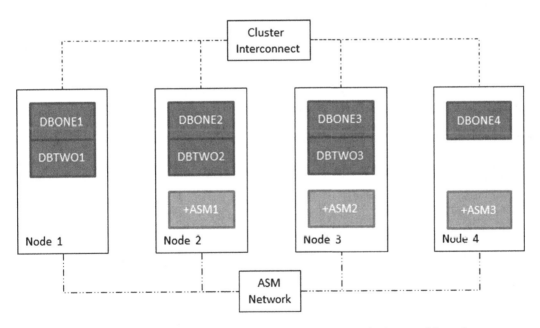

Figure 2-5. *Schematic display of a Flex ASM configuration in a four-node cluster, public and management network are not shown*

Flex ASM can be configured from the start during the installation of Grid Infrastructure and is mandatory if you are planning on using a Flex Cluster (another new RAC 12c feature). Alternatively an existing configuration can be changed to Flex ASM using the ASM Configuration Assistant after the ASM spfile, password file, and the OCR and voting disks are all stored in a disk group within ASM.

ASM traffic can be sent over the private network but might collide with existing workloads. Thankfully there is an option to allow the ASM traffic to use a dedicated network, as shown in Figure 2-5. If a dedicated network is used, a new cluster resource of type ora.ASMNET1LSNR_ASM.lsnr will be created for the network. As you can imagine Oracle will create multiple listeners if you specify multiple networks to be of type "ASM". It is visible using the crsctl utility as shown here:

```
[root@rac12node1 ~]# crsctl stat res -t
--------------------------------------------------------------------------
Name            Target  State         Server              State details
--------------------------------------------------------------------------
Local Resources
--------------------------------------------------------------------------
ora.ASMNET1LSNR_ASM.lsnr
                ONLINE  ONLINE        rac12node1          STABLE
                ONLINE  ONLINE        rac12node2          STABLE
                ONLINE  ONLINE        rac12node3          STABLE
```

The idea is strikingly simple: should an ASM instance to which databases are connected fail, the database will dynamically reconnect to another ASM instance in the cluster. The following example demonstrates the new principle in a three-node test cluster with the default cardinality reduced to two:

```
[grid@rac12node1 ~]$ srvctl modify asm -count 2
[grid@rac12node1 ~]$ srvctl status asm
ASM is running on rac12node3,rac12node1
```

The database started on node 2 will now not have its own ASM instance. It dutifully reports the fact in the alert.log:

```
NOTE: ASMB registering with ASM instance as client 0xffffffffffffffff (reg:89854640)
NOTE: ASMB connected to ASM instance +ASM1 (Flex mode; client id 0x10007)
```

And it is also shown in the v$asm_client view. Here is the example of the first ASM instance:

```
SQL> select dg.name,c.instance_name,c.db_name,c.status
  2  from v$asm_diskgroup dg, v$asm_client c
  3  where dg.group_number = c.group_number
  4 and c.db_name = 'RCDB1'
  5 /

NAME        INSTANCE_N DB_NAME  STATUS
----------  ---------- -------- ------------
DATA        RCDB12     RCDB1    CONNECTED
DATA        RCDB11     RCDB1    CONNECTED
```

If an ASM instance such as the instance on node 3 crashes, the client will migrate to the surviving instance for the time it takes to restart the other instance:

```
NAME        INSTANCE_N DB_NAME  STATUS
----------  ---------- -------- ------------
DATA        RCDB11     RCDB1    CONNECTED
DATA        RCDB13     RCDB1    CONNECTED
DATA        RCDB12     RCDB1    CONNECTED
```

After a little while you see the third database instance connect back to the second ASM instance on node 3.

To see if Flex ASM is configured you can use the showclustermode command for the ASM command line utility:

```
[grid@rac12node3 ~]$ asmcmd showclustermode
ASM cluster : Flex mode enabled
```

The configuration of your ASM cluster can be queried as well as shown next.

```
[root@rac12node1 usr]# srvctl config asm
ASM home: /u01/app/12.1.0.1/grid
Password file: +OCR/orapwASM
ASM listener: LISTENER
ASM instance count: 3
Cluster ASM listener: ASMNET1LSNR_ASM
```

Flex ASM also supports ACFS operations, but these are out of the scope of this section.

■ **Note**   You may have also read about Flex Clusters allowing the administrator to create a more loosely coupled RAC system. In my opinion this feature—although nice—will not be part of a Database as a Service platform.

Evaluating Commands Before Execution

An interesting new feature for the database as well as Cluster layer is the option to evaluate commands before they are executed. The lower-level crsctl command as well as the everyday application srvctl has a new option named -eval to give administrators more peace of mind.

The targets of your evaluation commands are a database instance, the cluster database, services, and server pools for policy managed databases. You can evaluate valid combinations of the target with the start, stop, remove, relocate, modify, and add commands.

The eval option works only for policy managed databases. If you try to use it with an administrator managed RAC database then you will get the following error:

```
[oracle@rac12node1 ~]$ srvctl start database -db cdb1 -eval
PRKO-2712 : Administrator-managed database cdb1 is not supported with -eval option
```

If your cluster deployments feature policy managed databases then the command can potentially be very useful, especially when you are dealing with server pools since there can be interactions between the current and all the other server pools and their associated databases.

Non-RAC Options to Increase Availability

The previous sections have mainly dealt with cluster enhancements which allow better resilience to instance failure. But even with a multi-instance RAC system you can still incur outages when changing code in your application. For example, library cache lock on a login trigger can have devastating consequences. Edition-Based Redefinition (EBR) can alleviate many of these problems but EBR is a new feature that has not yet resonated the way it should have with developers.

Some of the enhancements you will read about below do not require the use of Editions. This should not prevent you from having a look at EBR because it is beautiful! Do you remember when an index could be rebuilt online for the first time? No more requirements for a change window to rebuild indexes! The list of online operations available to the database administrator has increased with Oracle 12c and you should know about them.

Moving a Partition without Blocking

Partitioning has seen quite a lot of improvement over the past releases. If you consider the new options allowing you to combine partitioning schemes, interval partitioning, and referencing then you can see why Partitioning is such an important option.

Oracle 12c has added many more enhancements, including the possibility to move a partition online. In versions before Oracle 12c you had to wait for a compatible lock to move a partition. Consider the following example. A simulated batch job is continuously inserting information into a partitioned table created as follows:

```
SQL> create table part_demo
  2  partition by range (creation_date) (
  3  partition p_2013      values less than (to_date('01.01.2013','dd.mm.yyyy')),
  4  partition p_jan_2013 values less than (to_date('01.02.2013','dd.mm.yyyy')),
  5  partition p_feb_2013 values less than (to_date('01.03.2013','dd.mm.yyyy')),
  6  partition p_mar_2013 values less than (to_date('01.04.2013','dd.mm.yyyy')),
  7  partition p_apr_2013 values less than (to_date('01.05.2013','dd.mm.yyyy')),
  8  partition p_may_2013 values less than (to_date('01.06.2013','dd.mm.yyyy')),
  9  partition p_jun_2013 values less than (to_date('01.07.2013','dd.mm.yyyy')),
 10  partition p_jul_2013 values less than (to_date('01.08.2013','dd.mm.yyyy')),
 11  partition p_aug_2013 values less than (to_date('01.09.2013','dd.mm.yyyy')),
 12  partition p_sep_2013 values less than (to_date('01.10.2013','dd.mm.yyyy')),
 13  partition p_oct_2013 values less than (to_date('01.11.2013','dd.mm.yyyy')),
 14  partition p_nov_2013 values less than (to_date('01.12.2013','dd.mm.yyyy')),
 15  partition p_dec_2013 values less than (to_date('01.01.2014','dd.mm.yyyy')),
 16  partition p_def values less than (maxvalue))
 17  enable row movement
 18  as select sysdate+dbms_random.normal*100 as creation_date,
 19* object_id, object_name from dba_objects
SQL> /

Table created.

SQL> exec dbms_stats.gather_table_stats(user,'PART_DEMO')
```

Referential integrity constraints are then defined on the table. Simulating the batch job, the following little snippet of code is executed.

```
SQL> begin
  2   for i in 1..10000 loop
  3    insert into part_demo (
  4     creation_date,
  5     object_name
  6    ) values (
  7     (to_date('02.05.2013','dd.mm.yyyy')+i/1440),
  8     'test ' || i
  9    );
```

```
 10     end loop;
 11* end;
SQL> /

PL/SQL procedure successfully completed.

SQL>
```

At the same time the DBA wants to move the August partition from fast storage to slow storage. Here is the outcome of that exercise in up to and including 11.2. It is also the default for 12c:

```
SQL> alter table part_demo move partition p_may_2013 tablespace tbs_arch_01;
alter table part_demo move partition p_may_2013 tablespace tbs_arch_01
              *
ERROR at line 1:
ORA-00054: resource busy and acquire with NOWAIT specified or timeout expired
```

The new syntax to perform the same operation online is shown here:

```
SQL> alter table part_demo move partition P_MAY_2013 tablespace tbs_arch_01 online;

Table altered.
```

The operation takes a little longer but it is an online operation! Only when all the locks on the partition are removed will the operation complete.

Moving Data Files While They Are Accessed

Moving data files from one location to another has most often been an operation that required downtime or otherwise impacted the availability of your application. Moving a database from one file system to another—perhaps during a SAN replacement—commonly required the database administrator to shut the database down, using operating system utilities to copy the data files to the new location, start the database into mount mode followed by a call to `alter tablespace rename datafile ....`

This task has now been greatly simplified by the introduction of the `alter database move datafile` command. Using the new command it is very simple to move data and temp files (but not online redo log files) from a file system into ASM while they are in use. In this context it is possible to move an Oracle Managed File (OMF) to another location managed as an Oracle Managed File, allowing you to move OMF files from a file system into ASM. Oracle will briefly create a copy of the data file so ensure that there is enough space for the copy and the original file.

After the move is completed, the old file will automatically be removed unless you specify the keep keyword. If your old file was not an Oracle Managed file you can specify that you want to keep the old file. Here is an example for moving a data file into ASM which has accidentally been created on the file system for tablespace tbs_arch_01:

```
SQL> select file_name from dba_data_files
  2  where tablespace_name = 'TBS_ARCH_01';

FILE_NAME
--------------------------------------------------------------------------
/u01/oradata/cdb1/tbs_arch_01.dbf
```

The file is now moved to the correct location:

```
SQL> alter database move datafile '/u01/oradata/cdb1/tbs_arch_01.dbf'
  2  to '+DATA';

Database altered.
```

After the move the data file is in the correct location. The database stayed available all the time while the data file has been moved. Notice that this was executed in a Pluggable Database. Chapter 7 explains file names in PDBs in more detail.

```
SQL> select file_name from dba_data_files
  2  where tablespace_name = 'TBS_ARCH_01';

FILE_NAME
--------------------------------------------------------------------------------
+DATA/CDB1/E025A74226115F1CE0436538A8C0FDF9/DATAFILE/tbs_arch_01.274.821486701
```

Notice that the move data file command creates a copy of the data file you are moving. In most cases this is not a problem, but if you are short on space you should not execute multiple commands in parallel.

Data and Information Lifecycle Management

Many vendors are spending a lot of time and effort in educating users on how important it is to use Information Life Cycle Management (ILM) on a grand scale to cut costs and become more efficient. The vendors' value propositions are sound of course: there are many applications that do not use any kind of life cycle management at all, wasting premium storage at high cost for all data. Since a lot of data is related to time in one way or another it would make sense to put older—less frequently accessed data—on lower performance (read: cost) storage while keeping the other storage on higher storage tiers.

Storage vendors of course know about that problem, and try to address it with clever software on the storage array. Since most enterprise arrays have some sort of storage tiering built-in algorithms in software try to move the most frequently accessed data to the fastest storage tier while keeping "cold" data on slower storage. This happens automatically.

Storage Tiers

Storage engineers and vendors often refer to a storage tier when discussing persistent storage. The classic division of storage in an enterprise array consists of the following tiers, sorted by performance in descending order.

- Flash memory

- High performance Fibre Channel disks

- High capacity Fibre Channel disks

- High capacity "near-line" disks

The actual implementation is of course dependent on the array vendor but most implement a high IOPS/low latency technology for very demanding applications to very high capacity disks which are slow but cheap for data that the business cannot decide to archive differently.

Partitioning

Partitioning is one of the most important tools for Information Lifecycle Management (ILM) in the Oracle database as it allows the administrator and application developer to group data in a heap table into more manageable, smaller pieces. Implemented correctly the effect of using partitioning can be felt immediately, and is usually a very positive one. A lot of the data in transactional systems is time based in one way or another. Usually, the most recently inserted data is what the application needs to access most. In trading systems for example this would be the current hour, day, or week depending on the granularity and volume of data to store and process. Recent data is often accessed and modified, therefore having the highest demand for high quality storage. This low latency/high bandwidth storage comes at premium cost, which is why older data that has cooled off a little is moved to lower-cost storage. Depending on the age of the data and retention period mandated by the auditors this process could be repeated a number of times until the data is on tertiary storage, maybe even in a platform-neutral format for really long-term archiving.

Many developers have already made good use of the Oracle Partitioning option to partition large tables into range partitions stretching the before mentioned intervals. For administrators though moving partitions to lower tier storage required the implementation of the change during a maintenance window, where partitions for a table have been moved (and optionally compressed) to a different storage tier.

Automatic Data Optimization in Oracle 12c

Automatic Data Optimization (ADO) is based on access tracking on different segments of the database (the feature requires a separate license). A segment in this context can be a table, or a (sub)partition.

■ **Note** ADO is not supported for pluggable databases. But ADO is so incredibly useful that you should know about it anyway.

The alter table and create table statements have been enhanced with new syntax allowing you to define ILM policies once the tracking has been enabled. The initialization parameter heat_map controls the access tracking and it has to be set system wide. Once the heat map tracking is enabled information about segment access is recorded in the dictionary. Live tracking information is found in v$heat_map_segment. That view provides information about reads and writes as well about as full- and lookup scans. A number of DBA%-views exist as well which can be queried for access to segments.

One common use case of data lifecycle management is to compress "cold" data. The next example does exactly this. The implemented strategy is as follows:

1. Access tracking is globally enabled by setting heat_map to "on."

2. A new ILM policy is attached to the table, stating that the cold data should be compressed.

Thinking about the technology ADO makes the most sense with range-partitioned data based on a date column in the context of Information Life Cycle Management. Hopefully the application has been designed with that in mind allowing the optimizer to perform runtime partition pruning. Partitioning for performance and manageability sometimes are conflicting goals.

To demonstrate the new lifecycle management technology the following demo has been created. A table containing 100,000 is range partitioned on a date.

```
create table t1 (
  d    date,
  vc1  varchar2(100),
```

```
  vc2   varchar2(100),
  n1    number
)
partition by range (d)
interval (NUMTODSINTERVAL(7, 'day'))
(
  partition p_start values less than (to_date('01.01.2008','dd.mm.yyyy'))
);
```

The interval portioning algorithm created 53 partitions in addition to the initial one. The table is populated with random dates and some padding for a year in the future. A small PL/SQL procedure executed every second by ten scheduler jobs should bring the table to the attention of the access tracking algorithm:

```
CREATE PROCEDURE p
IS
  CURSOR c
  IS
    SELECT d, vc1
    FROM t1
    WHERE d = TRUNC(to_date('23.07.2014', 'dd.mm.yyyy') - DBMS_RANDOM.value(0,128));
  TYPE t IS TABLE OF c%rowtype INDEX BY pls_integer;
  v_t t;
BEGIN
  OPEN c;
  LOOP
    FETCH c bulk collect INTO v_t limit 500;
    EXIT
  WHEN v_t.count < 500;
  END LOOP;
END;
```

Notice that the code deliberately leaves out half the data created to satisfy the "no access" criteria for the ILM process. After a little while individual partitions of T1 appeared in V$HEAT_MAP_SEGMENT:

```
SQL> select object_name, subobject_name, segment_write, segment_read,
  2    full_scan,lookup_scan
  3  from v$heat_map_segment where object_name = 'T1'

OBJECT_NAM SUBOBJECT_ SEG SEG FUL LOO
---------- ---------- --- --- --- ---
T1         SYS_P623   NO  NO  YES YES
T1         SYS_P641   NO  NO  YES YES
[...]
T1         SYS_P635   NO  NO  YES YES
T1         SYS_P660   NO  NO  YES NO

53 rows selected.
```

Implementing the ILM policy is done by invoking the alter table command for table T1:

```
SQL> alter table martin.t1
  2  ilm add policy
  3  row store compress basic segment
  4  after 3 months of no access;

Table altered.
```

The criteria to apply the ILM policy can be based on access, modification, or creation. In this example the policy is applicable to the table partition. The interval can be any number of days, months, or years. In the above example the data in segments (=partitions) with no access will be compressed using BASIC compression. If you are lucky enough to be on an Exadata system you can request Hybrid Columnar Compression as well. You can view policies attached to a table in the view dba_ilmpolicies. More detail for a policy is available in the view dba_ilmdatamovepolicies.

Fast forward three months and you can see that the ILM processes in the database start reviewing the access to the segments more closely. The view dba_ilmevaluationdetails lists the outcome of the evaluation. The system periodically checks ILM policies against the heat map. This process is externalized in dba_ilmtasks. You could join dba_ilmtasks to dba_ilmevaluationdetails for more detail about when a given task has been executed. In the above example the following evaluation results have been made available by the ILM engine:

```
SQL> select task_id,policy_name,object_name,subobject_name,
  2     selected_for_execution, job_name
  3  from dba_ilmevaluationdetails
  4  order by policy_name,selected_for_execution;

  TASK_ID POLICY_NAM OBJEC SUBOBJECT_ SELECTED_FOR_EXECUTION                     JOB_NAME
---------- ---------- ----- ---------- ------------------------------------------ ------------
        2 P1         T1    SYS_P658   PRECONDITION NOT SATISFIED
[...]
        2 P1         T1    SYS_P650   SELECTED FOR EXECUTION                     ILMJOB190
        2 P1         T1    SYS_P648   SELECTED FOR EXECUTION                     ILMJOB192
```

These jobs are executed by the database scheduler, and you can find out about them in dba_ilmresults. The outcome of the operation is visible in the dba_tab_partitions

```
SQL> r
  1  select partition_name, compression, compress_for
  2  from DBA_TAB_PARTITIONS
  3* where table_name = 'T1'

PARTITION_NAME                  COMPRESS COMPRESS_FOR
------------------------------- -------- ------------------------------
SYS_P621                        DISABLED
[...]
SYS_P632                        ENABLED  BASIC
SYS_P660                        ENABLED  BASIC
SYS_P670                        ENABLED  BASIC
[...]

54 rows selected.

SQL>
```

As requested the data has been compressed with basic compression.

Automatic storage tiering is the second option you have in ADO. It works slightly differently as it is not based on access but rather on the amount of free space on the tablespace. The ILM engine reviews a tablespace and compares the free space with what it finds in dba_ilmparameters. If the tablespace on which the segment is stored falls below the free space threshold a job will be started moving the data from the higher tier storage to the storage defined in the ILM policy. An example for an ILM policy to change the storage tier is shown here:

```
SQL> alter table t1
  2  ilm add policy
  3  tier to ARCH segment;

Table altered.
```

During the next maintenance window—the time when the ILM policies are evaluated—jobs will be started to move the partitions to the low cost storage. As with the compression you can see the results of the operation in dba_ilmresults.

Infrastructure Changes

Changes to the way the Oracle database interacts or touches the infrastructure it executes on are of particular interest to the consolidation project. Some features in the 12c release are very relevant, and have been moved into their respective chapters. One of the best features added has been semi-officially introduced with 11.2.0.2 as "clonedb." But there are others you should know about.

Database Resident Connection Pool Exposed to Middle Tier

The usefulness of exposing the connection pool to the middle tier is not immediately visible to everyone, including the author when he first read about it. Why would anyone create a (Database Resident) connection pool for another connection pool (in the middle tier)? Before explaining the finer details of the feature lets recap on what the Database Resident Connection Pool (DRCP) was intended for. When it was introduced in Oracle 11.2, DRCP allowed programming languages without support for connection pooling in the middle-tier to reduce the cost of establishing connections. At the time DRCP was introduced the popular programming language was PHP, a HyperText Preprocessor. Perl Common Gateway Interface scripts using the popular DBI module could equally have benefitted from the feature but Perl's importance as a web development language at the time was diminishing quickly.

In short, all (web) applications that are not really modular do not use connection pools, and instead establish a session to the Oracle database as the first thing in their code. These applications were ideal candidates for the DRCP. The idea was to create a connection pool in the database, rather than in the middle tier where such a feature did not exist. The DRCP is somewhere in between a shared server and a dedicated server, but with a lot less code path to go through than MTS. More importantly it is a database feature, unlike the traditional connection pool which exists on the middleware exclusively.

With Oracle 12c the DRCP has been opened up for Java Database Connectivity JDBC. The immediate question that comes to mind is:

> *JDBC allows you to use connection pooling already in form of the Universal Connection Pool (UCP). Why then should you add a connection pool for the connection pool?*

The answer is: scalability! Many connection pools are (inappropriately) designed to use a minimum number of connections set to a value less than the maximum pool size. This is a bad idea since sudden plan changes can cause real havoc or even downtime with the application. Imagine a configuration when 10 middle-tier servers establish 10 sessions each, initially. The increment is another 10 sessions until the maximum size of 100 sessions per pool

(=per server) is reached. Now if for some reason an execution plan changes and response times for queries increase it is likely that the application servers will start spawning new sessions to compensate. But instead of 10 times 10 sessions the database now has to deal with potentially 10 times 100 sessions which is a much higher workload. And many of these sessions will actually be busy executing code, further reducing latency and so own. If the DBAs cannot quickly rectify this problem a downward spiral that can even lead to the complete overloading of the database server as shown in Figure 2-6.

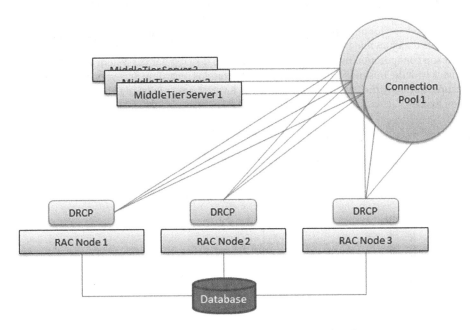

Figure 2-6. *Structural view on the DRCP exposure for JDBC applications*

When using a DRCP on the database host this effect can potentially limit the impact of spikes of activity on the underlying infrastructure. As you can see from Figure 2-6, the middle-tier remains the owner of their own connection pools. In addition, each RAC node has its own DRCP to which the connection pools connect. Just as with "plain" DRCP, the effect of connection storms can potentially be better contained.

The correct solution to the problem however would be to reduce the number of processes working on the database and to set the minimum pool size equal to the maximum pool size to avoid unpleasant surprises.

Copy-on-Write for Cloning Databases

One of the problems frequently encountered for the database administrator is the exponential growth in storage requirements. Imagine for a moment that one of your operational databases is 10 TB in size. If the business requires five different test environments for different streams of work than those 10 TB quickly become 60 TB which can no longer be considered a small footprint. The fact that storage is considered cheap can no longer be considered true for everyone. Enterprise class storage is expensive, especially when you need lots. Some companies have long-term agreements with the large storage providers, rendering them less flexible when it comes to offering discounts to internal customers. The high price tag for additional storage has made requisition of additional terabytes or even gigabytes a lengthy process with a lot of red tape around it.

Thankfully there is a way to reduce the storage requirement for test environments, and it is built in with the Oracle database. The benefit of the new technology increases with every additional copy of the live environment. The underlying technology is called copy-on-write. Instead of requiring full copies of the database for each test environment, only one full copy is required. Additional environments are then created based on the clone, but with independent data files. These data files contain only the changes made during testing. Experience shows that test environments rarely change a large portion of the operational database. To benefit from the new method of cloning databases you need to use character based storage: the network file system (NFS). This works hand in hand with many organizations' desire to make use of cheaper storage tiers for non-critical workloads. You should not be fooled by the lower price though, and perform testing to ensure that the new method of cloning database environments matches your performance expectations. Figure 2-7 shows the minimum setup needed for using clonedb. The production and development server are both connected to an NFS filer using dual 10GBit Ethernet. The NFS filer exports two file systems. The export /m/backups is used for the production database image copy. The other export /m/CLONE will be used for the clone database's data files and is mounted to the development host. The infrastructure is likely supplemental to an existing backup configuration but it is of course possible to take regular file system backups from the NFS mount. You should check with the business users about their expectations regarding Recovery Time Objects and other details around backups. Normally the hosting platform will use RMAN backups directly, the clonedb infrastructure exists in addition to it.

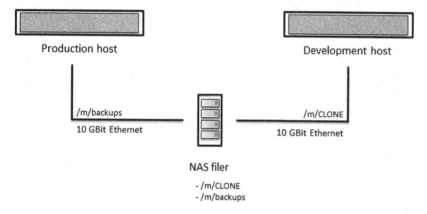

Figure 2-7. *The minimum architectural components for copy-on-write cloning*

Note the key feature of direct NFS here. Oracle's direct NFS client—available as part of the 11g release—is entirely written in user mode, potentially allowing environments to benefit from less overhead compared to kernel-NFS. Another great advantage is the availability of direct NFS on Windows, a platform that does not otherwise benefit from NFS.

■ **Note**   The use of the clonedb feature requires the use of direct NFS. The setup of directNFS is out of the scope of this chapter but is available from the author's website.

Overview

The process to be followed for the new feature is remarkably simple and comprises these steps:

1.   Create an image copy of your life database

2.   Make this backup available on the test server using direct NFS

3. Prepare the test database

   a. Create a controlfile

   b. Use DBMS_DNFS to rename the data files

4. Open the database

The following sections provide more detail about the process. You may have seen reference to the above process on My Oracle Support and the Internet before Oracle 12c has been released. However this is the first time that the clonedb feature is in the official documentation set and therefore more generally available. Some of these steps need to be executed each time a clone is needed, others are a one-time setup. Let's review the process in more detail.

Preparation

Creating an image copy of the database can be done in many ways, beginning with a cold backup which has been taken using the well-known combination of tar and gzip or a simple Unix "cp" command to an RMAN image copy. Below is an example for such a copy command using RMAN. The example assumes that appropriate settings have been made in the RMAN catalog database such as parallelism and destination. The necessary image copy of the database is created on the production host and stored in an NFS mount, namely /m/backups/ which in turn is mounted to /u01/oraback on the production host.

```
RMAN> backup as copy database format '/u01/oraback/NCDB/%u';
```

As always it is a good idea to take backups of the database during quieter periods. If you are not using NFS you need to make the backup available on your test database server. To say it in the words of a perl developer: "there is more than one way to do it". Unlike with the RMAN duplication the location of the backup on the test server does not matter.

Next you will need to prepare the `create controlfile` statement for the clone database. The controlfile can be created in a number of ways. You either create the controlfile using the command `backup controlfile to trace at '/path/to/script.sql'`, or you use the Oracle-provided script clonedb.pl in `$ORACLE_HOME/rdbms/install`. The use of clonedb.pl requires you to set a few environment variables, and you can execute the script on the production host or the destination server. The following example demonstrates its use. The environment variables in the below output are required and need to reflect the directory structure on the clone database's host. The MASTER_COPY_DIR indicates the NFS mount with the production database backup, CLONE_FILE_CREATE_DEST points to the location where you'd like to store the clone database's data files (which must be NFS mounted to the development host) and finally the database name for the clone database.

```
[oracle@server2 install]$ perl clonedb.pl
usage: perl clonedb.pl <init.ora> [crtdb.sql] [rename.sql]
[oracle@server2 install]$ export MASTER_COPY_DIR=/media/backup/NCDB
[oracle@server2 install]$ export CLONE_FILE_CREATE_DEST=/u01/oradata/CLONE
[oracle@server2 install]$ export CLONEDB_NAME=CLONE
[oracle@server2 install]$ perl clonedb.pl /tmp/initNCDB.ora /tmp/crtdb.sql /tmp/rename.sql
```

Review the files created and amend them to suit your needs. The initNCDB.ora file in the above output is the production database's initialization file. In addition to the two SQL scripts the perl script will create an initialization file for the clone database in the directory indicated by the environment variable CLONE_FILE_CREATE_DEST. The parameter file will also need amending to suit your needs. Following along the example the following parameter file was used:

```
*.audit_file_dest='/u01/app/oracle/admin/CLONE/adump'
*.audit_trail='db'
```

```
*.compatible='12.1.0.0.0'
*.db_block_size=8192
*.db_domain=''
*.db_name=CLONE
*.db_recovery_file_dest='/u01/fra'
*.db_recovery_file_dest_size=4800m
*.dispatchers='(PROTOCOL=TCP) (SERVICE=CLONEXDB)'
*.open_cursors=300
*.pga_aggregate_target=256m
*.processes=300
*.remote_login_passwordfile='EXCLUSIVE'
*.sga_target=768m
*.undo_tablespace='UNDOTBS1'
#*.db_create_file_dest=/u01/oradata
*.clonedb=TRUE
*.control_files='/u01/oradata/CLONE/ctrl01.ctl','/u01/oradata/CLONE/ctrl02.ctl'
```

Please ensure that all the required directories exist, especially the audit file destination. The parameter clonedb must be set to true. If you intend to connect to the database as SYS please create a password file as well. You should also update the oratab file and add the new clone database to it.

Creating the Clone Database

With the parameter file in place connect to the database and execute the crtdb.sql script. For example:

```
SQL> @crtdb
SQL> SET FEEDBACK 1
SQL> SET NUMWIDTH 10
SQL> SET LINESIZE 80
SQL> SET TRIMSPOOL ON
SQL> SET TAB OFF
SQL> SET PAGESIZE 100
SQL>
SQL> STARTUP NOMOUNT
ORACLE instance started.

Total System Global Area  801701888 bytes
Fixed Size                  2293496 bytes
Variable Size             318767368 bytes
Database Buffers          478150656 bytes
Redo Buffers                2490368 bytes
SQL> CREATE CONTROLFILE REUSE SET DATABASE CLONE RESETLOGS
  2       MAXLOGFILES 32
  3       MAXLOGMEMBERS 2
  4       MAXINSTANCES 1
  5       MAXLOGHISTORY 908
  6   LOGFILE
  7     GROUP 1 '/u01/oradata/CLONE/CLONE_log1.log' SIZE 100M BLOCKSIZE 512,
  8     GROUP 2 '/u01/oradata/CLONE/CLONE_log2.log' SIZE 100M BLOCKSIZE 512
  9   DATAFILE
 10   '/media/backup/NCDB/NCDB/system01.dbf' ,
```

```
11  '/media/backup/NCDB/NCDB/sysaux01.dbf' ,
12  '/media/backup/NCDB/NCDB/undotbs01.dbf' ,
13  '/media/backup/NCDB/NCDB/users01.dbf'
14  CHARACTER SET WE8ISO8869P15;
```

Control file created.

Notice how the create controlfile statement references the image copies made available to the development server via NFS. Following this step you need to execute the rename.sql script. It will rename the files pointing them to the NFS mount. The directory /m/CLONE—exported from the NFS appliance—is mounted to /u01/oradata/CLONE on the development server.

```
begin
 DBMS_DNFS.CLONEDB_RENAMEFILE(
    '/media/backup/NCDB/system01.dbf', '/u01/oradata/CLONE/system01.dbf');
 DBMS_DNFS.CLONEDB_RENAMEFILE(
    '/media/backup/NCDB/sysaux01.dbf', '/u01/oradata/CLONE/sysaux01.dbf');
 DBMS_DNFS.CLONEDB_RENAMEFILE(
    '/media/backup/NCDB/undotbs01.dbf', '/u01/oradata/CLONE/undotbs01.dbf');
 DBMS_DNFS.CLONEDB_RENAMEFILE(
    '/media/backup/NCDB/users01.dbf', '/u01/oradata/CLONE/users01.dbf');
end;
/
```

This step will only succeed if the destination location is an NFS mount. Although it is theoretically not needed to recreate the create controlfile script every time, you should still develop a habit to do so. If someone added a data file to the production system in the meantime this data file will not be in the controlfile and you have to start over. After completion of this step you can open the database with the resetlogs option. Don't forget to add temp-files and other auxiliary structures you may need! If you verify the database files now using the "sparse" flag, you will see that they really take little or no space on disk:

```
[oracle@server2 ~]$ ls -lsh /u01/oradata/CLONE/*.dbf
total 220K
92K -rw-r-----. 1 oracle oinstall 551M Nov 13 22:45 sysaux01.dbf
16K -rw-r-----. 1 oracle oinstall 211M Nov 13 22:45 system01.dbf
16K -rw-r-----. 1 oracle oinstall 1.6G Nov 13 22:45 undotbs01.dbf
16K -rw-r-----. 1 oracle oinstall 5.1M Nov 13 22:45 users01.dbf
```

The first column indicates the actual space used, and the familiar figures in the middle of the output show the size the file would occupy if this was a full-sized copy. The space savings are immediately visible.

Deprecation of OEM DB Console

Oracle has removed the Database Console which it introduced with Oracle 10g with immediate effect. There is no further warning: it is gone with Oracle 12c. Although unexpected, this step should not cause trouble to most organizations that rely on centralized monitoring solutions such as OEM 12c Cloud Control. The replacement however is very neat and deserves a closer look, even though it requires Flash for it to operate.

During the database creation the Database Creation Assistant will assign an unused port for DB Express, on most systems this will be 5500. The documentation states that this port is also the HTTPS Port for XML DB, which is no longer an optional component of the database.

■ **Note**   You can get the HTTPS port by issuing the following statement: "select dbms_xdb_config.gethttsport from dual."

As an interesting side note you can see the port registered with the listener:

```
[oracle@server1 ~]$ lsnrctl status

LSNRCTL for Linux: Version 12.1.0.1.0 - Production on 25-JUL-2013 20:36:31

Copyright (c) 1991, 2013, Oracle.  All rights reserved.

Connecting to (ADDRESS=(PROTOCOL=tcp)(HOST=)(PORT=1521))
STATUS of the LISTENER
------------------------
Alias                     LISTENER
Version                   TNSLSNR for Linux: Version 12.1.0.1.0 - Production
Start Date                25-JUL-2013 20:24:19
Uptime                    0 days 0 hr. 12 min. 11 sec
Trace Level               off
Security                  ON: Local OS Authentication
SNMP                      OFF
Listener Parameter File   /u01/app/grid/product/12.1.0.1/grid/network/admin/listener.ora
Listener Log File         /u01/app/grid/diag/tnslsnr/ol64/listener/alert/log.xml
Listening Endpoints Summary...
  (DESCRIPTION=(ADDRESS=(PROTOCOL=ipc)(KEY=EXTPROC1521)))
  (DESCRIPTION=(ADDRESS=(PROTOCOL=tcp)(HOST=server1.example.com)(PORT=1521)))
  (DESCRIPTION=(ADDRESS=(PROTOCOL=tcps)(HOST=server1.example.com)(PORT=5500))
  (Security=
    (my_wallet_directory=/u01/app/oracle/product/12.1.0.1/dbhome_1/admin/CDB1/xdb_wallet))
  (Presentation=HTTP)(Session=RAW))
```

Point your web browser to the HTTPS port just detected and wait a few seconds for the interface to load. You are presented with the user interface shown in Figure 2-8.

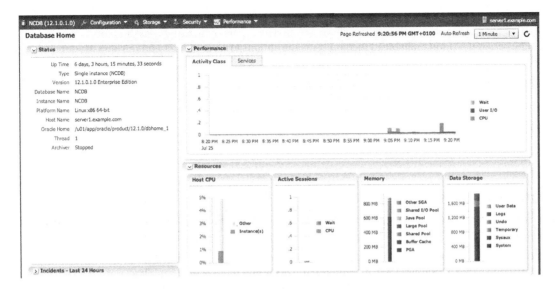

Figure 2-8. *DB Express after the initial login*

The dashboard is a nice overview of the software's potential. A lot of the information you can get and set pales in importance when comparing with the "Performance Hub."

The Performance Hub

The Performance Hub screen, which is available from the Performance drop-down menu on top end of the screen, certainly is the best bit of DB. You need to be appropriately licensed to use the feature. Its overview page is shown in Figure 2-9.

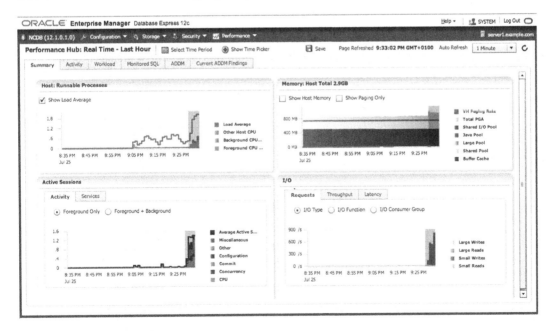

Figure 2-9. *DB Express Performance Hub*

As you can see the summary screen is divided into a number of areas. In this example the time picker has been hidden to free up some more space. When shown it allows you to select an interval over the last hour or alternatively use a historic time period if it is still available. It then presents the options to enter different other views of your system, namely:

- RAC if applicable

- (Top) Activity

- Workload

- Monitored SQL

- ADDM

- Current ADDM findings

We will cover the most interesting ones of these a little later. Continuing the discussion of the summary screen you can see the following panes:

- *Host runnable processes*, indicating the load on the server. The contributors of the load are broken down into background and foreground processes plus all the other non-Oracle processes contributing to the current state of the operating system's run queue.

- *Host memory:* shows the database's SGA and its components relative to the total memory on the system. This is a useful view to show automatic memory operations of individual SGA components.

- *Active Sessions:* this panel gives you an overview of the current activity in total or broken down into services and—in case of RAC—instances.

- *I/O:* The final pane on this page shows you I/O Requests, Throughput, and Latency.

Hover the mouse over these panes and you will notice they are all interactive.

Top Activity

This screen is like a combination of ASH Analytics you already know from Oracle Enterprise Manager Cloud Control and the Top Activity screen we know from pre-Enterprise Manager 12c. The Top Activity page is shown in Figure 2-10:

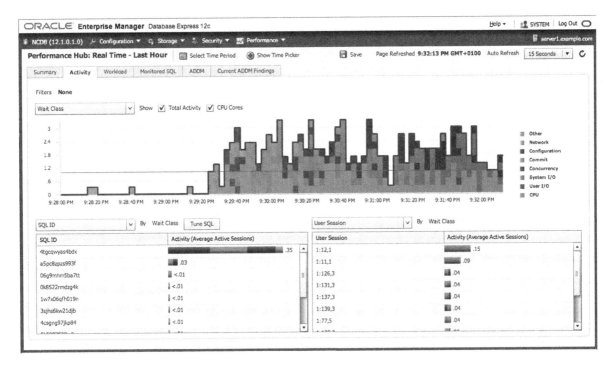

Figure 2-10. *DB Express Performance Hub: ASH Analytics and Top Activity*

If you have already worked with ASH Analytics you will immediately feel comfortable with this screen. It allows you to analyze your database's workload by combining the available dimensions. One possibility is to review a time period on the coarse level, for example using the wait class. Upon identifying a particular wait class consuming more resources than expected you can click on the wait class, further drilling down. Whenever you drill down a level you can see a filter indicating what you are currently looking at. The number of statements in the lower half is also reduced to those contributing mostly to the metric you are looking at.

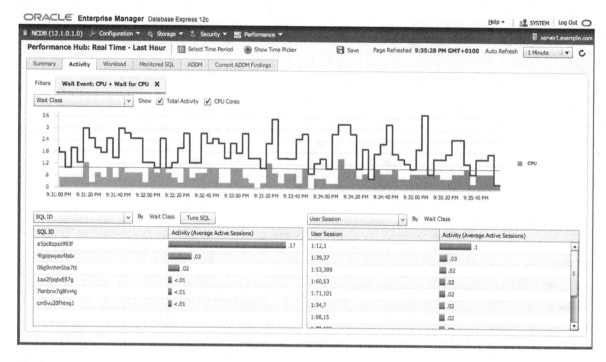

Figure 2-11. DB Express Performance Hub: Drilling down into wait events

You can finally investigate individual SQL statements: use SQL Monitoring, schedule a Tuning Advisor task and so on. Although not ground-breakingly new the Activity page in the Performance Hub is a great tool, visualizing you workloads and—thanks to ASH Analytics—point out performance problems quite easily.

Workload

The final page to be discussed in this section is the Workload page, shown below in Figure 2-12:

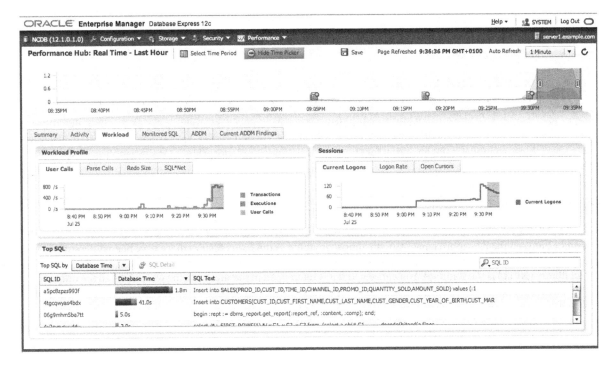

Figure 2-12. *DB Express Performance Hub: Workload*

The Workload page allows you to view the application's workload profile in a very elegant way. The top-left panel shows the user calls, parse calls, redo size, and network traffic. The Sessions panel shows you the rate of logins, number of currently connected users, and number of open cursors.

Shaping of Network Traffic

Another interesting feature affecting the infrastructure services required to run the Oracle database are related to network compression and a change in the maximum size of the Session Data Unit (SDU) size. New parameters in the sqlnet.ora file allow you enable or disable compression. You need to set sqlnet.compression to "on" to enable compression if you have the correct license for this feature. Data Guard streaming redo is exempt from this parameter by the way, but that has little relevance: Data Guard has been able to compress archived logs for gap resolution since 11.1. Oracle 11.2 extended the scope of the compression to redo transmission.

If network compression is enabled via sqlnet.ora then you have the option to further define the aggressiveness of the compression. The parameter sqlnet.compression_levels can take two values: low and high. It is needless to say that a higher compression ratio comes at the cost of increased CPU consumption. To alleviate that effect it is possible to define a threshold in bytes for data compression. Only if the size of the data sent over the wire exceeds the threshold will the database server enable its compression algorithms. The default is to leave anything at less than 1024 bytes alone.

Threaded Architecture

There have been only two major forms of implementation in Oracle's recent releases. One was the all-threaded model for the Windows platform, and the other one was the process architecture for the UNIX world. Beginning with 12c the UNIX world can benefit from a multi-threaded architecture as well. This is a dramatic change that requires the revision of a popular interview question about the Oracle architecture. Looking back the Oracle architecture has always distinguished between the major process types:

- The foreground process
- The background process
- Potential slave processes

The new threaded architecture allows the administrator to create most background processes as threads within a process. User processes in the dedicated server model will also be created as threads. It should also be stated clearly that the new threaded model is not an option for Oracle on the Windows platform since Oracle has always used that threaded approach on this platform.

The Reason for Threads

Before explaining how the thread architecture is different from the process model it is important to review the actual difference between the two approaches. As with almost anything in the Linux history there have been different implementations for threads. Since kernel 2.6 (its release date now seems like an eternity ago) the native POSIX thread library (NPTL) is the standard. You can see that it is referenced in the make.log file which lists all the output of the linking phase. Search for -lpthread to see which binaries are linked against it. The main executable certainly links against it:

```
[oracle@server1 ~]$ ldd $(which oracle) | grep thread
        libpthread.so.0 => /lib64/libpthread.so.0 (0x000000314f600000)
```

This library is part of the standard C library on Linux and therefore is available by default. But why has Oracle gone to the great length to implement the background processes using threads? First, a thread is an independent execution unit within a process. In the most basic case there will be a one-to-one mapping between processes and threads. Such an implementation however would not make much sense. Instead most models—including the one described here—use multiple threads per process. Threads share the address space and are not as independent as processes, but on the other hand allow for faster context switching. Using a threaded model of execution could help with scalability as you can see later.

The Process Model

The default mode of operation in 12c on Unix is still the process model. The main background processes are listed in the dynamic performance view v$bgprocess. Reviewing the process model allows me to remind you of the many background processes that have been added with every release! On a typical system you will find the background processes using the following query:

```
SQL> select name,description
  2  from v$bgprocess
  3  where paddr <> '00';
```

Each of the processes you will see when executing the query on your system corresponds to exactly one process on the operating system. Oracle uses column SPID in view v$process to pair a process in the database to its corresponding process on the operating system. To change from the process model to the threaded model you need to change an initialization parameter:

```
SQL> alter system set threaded_execution=true scope=spfile;

System altered.
```

This parameter is not dynamic and you have to restart the instance for it to take effect. There is one caveat though: operating system authentication no longer works with the threaded model.

Preparing for Threaded Execution

When you simply restart the instance after changing the initialization parameter you will be in for a surprise after you issue the "startup" command:

```
[oracle@server1 ~]$ $ORACLE_HOME/bin/sqlplus / as sysdba
[...]
Connected to an idle instance.
SQL> startup
ORA-01017: invalid username/password; logon denied
```

You cannot mount or open the database by using the bequeath protocol. Instead, you must use a password file and connect over the network. Continuing from the previous output:

```
SQL> conn sys as sysdba
Enter password:
Connected.
SQL> alter database mount;

Database altered.

SQL> alter database open;

Database altered.
```

If you have not yet created a password file you definitely should do so if you want to use the threaded execution mode. Additionally you should consider statically registering your databases with the listener. Statically registered databases allow you to connect to the database using a net*8 connection and still start an instance even if there was no pmon process to register with the listener.

Administrative connections to the database are not the only area where changes have occurred. Using the threaded model the architecture changes; you still have the same background processes as before, but they look very different. Using the ps command to view the processes you will be interested to find that most of them have been combined:

```
[oracle@server1 ~]$ ps -ef | grep -i cdb1
oracle   22107     1  0 10:11 ?        00:00:00 ora_pmon_CDB1
oracle   22109     1  0 10:11 ?        00:00:00 ora_psp0_CDB1
oracle   22114     1 17 10:11 ?        00:00:58 ora_vktm_CDB1
oracle   22118     1  1 10:11 ?        00:00:04 ora_u004_CDB1
oracle   22124     1 12 10:11 ?        00:00:42 ora_u005_CDB1
oracle   22130     1  0 10:11 ?        00:00:00 ora_dbw0_CDB1
```

Instead of a one-to-one mapping of entries in v$bgprocess to operating system processes, there is now a mapping between the thread and the process. To see what's hiding under the ora_u004_CDB1 process you can use a custom report format when invoking the ps command:

```
[oracle@server1~]$ ps -eLo user,pid,tid,nlwp,class,rtprio,comm:30  | grep 22118
USER       PID   TID NLWP CLS RTPRIO COMMAND
oracle   22118 22118   13 TS       - ora_scmn_cdb1
```

```
oracle    22118 22119    13 TS       - oracle
oracle    22118 22120    13 TS       - ora_gen0_cdb1
oracle    22118 22121    13 TS       - ora_mman_cdb1
oracle    22118 22127    13 TS       - ora_dbrm_cdb1
oracle    22118 22131    13 TS       - ora_lgwr_cdb1
oracle    22118 22132    13 TS       - ora_ckpt_cdb1
oracle    22118 22133    13 TS       - ora_lg00_cdb1
oracle    22118 22134    13 TS       - ora_lg01_cdb1
oracle    22118 22135    13 TS       - ora_smon_cdb1
oracle    22118 22140    13 TS       - ora_lreg_cdb1
oracle    22118 22141    13 TS       - ora_rbal_cdb1
oracle    22118 22142    13 TS       - ora_asmb_cdb1
[oracle@server1 ~]$
```

The output shows that the process with OSPID 22118 has 13 lightweight processes (column NLWP), and their lightweight process IDs are shown in column TID which stands for Thread ID. The "traditional" process names are still available in the "command" column. If you examine the output of the first ps command can see from the above listings there are still some processes left.

```
[oracle@server1 ~]$ ps -eLf | egrep  -i "uid|cdb1" | \
> awk ' { if ($6 == 1 || $1=="UID")  print}'
UID       PID PPID    LWP  C NLWP STIME TTY           TIME CMD
oracle   22107    1 22107  0    1 10:11 ?         00:00:00 ora_pmon_CDB1
oracle   22109    1 22109  0    1 10:11 ?         00:00:01 ora_psp0_CDB1
oracle   22114    1 22114 17    1 10:11 ?         00:01:52 ora_vktm_CDB1
oracle   22130    1 22130  0    1 10:11 ?         00:00:00 ora_dbw0_CDB1
 [oracle@server1 ~]$
```

Process monitor (PMON), the virtual keeper of time (VKTM), process spawner (PSP0), and database writer (DBW0) processes are still implemented as traditional UNIX processes. Notice the absence of the SMON process! The view v$process has been changed slightly to cater to the new execution model. Comparing Oracle's view on its processes with the operating system yields the following result:

```
SQL> select pid,sosid,spid,stid,execution_type,pname
  2  from v$process
  3  where background = 1
  4    and spid = 22118
  5  order by execution_type;
```

PID	SOSID	SPID	STID	EXECUTION_	PNAME
5	22118_22120	22118	22120	THREAD	GEN0
6	22118_22118	22118	22118	THREAD	SCMN
7	22118_22121	22118	22121	THREAD	MMAN
11	22118_22127	22118	22127	THREAD	DBRM
14	22118_22131	22118	22131	THREAD	LGWR
22	22118_22142	22118	22142	THREAD	ASMB
16	22118_22133	22118	22133	THREAD	LG00
17	22118_22134	22118	22134	THREAD	LG01

18	22118_22135	22118	22135	THREAD	SMON
20	22118_22140	22118	22140	THREAD	LREG
21	22118_22141	22118	22141	THREAD	RBAL
15	22118_22132	22118	22132	THREAD	CKPT

```
12 rows selected.
```

The output of the above command has to be interpreted depending on the execution type. For a "PROCESS" nothing changes from the way previous Oracle releases handled processes on UNIX. If an entry in v$process has an execution type of "THREAD" then the output has to be read as follows:

- The column SPID still references the process on the operating system level with the exception that such a process can and will have multiple sub-processes

- STID is the thread number as shown in the output of ps -eLf, column LWP

- SOSID is simply the concatenation of the OSPID with the STID

Thankfully Oracle still provides us with the process name in the view as well. The use of the threaded execution model reduces the overhead of process attaching to the SGA. In a very simple example the same database is started with threaded_execution set to false, and then with the parameter set to true. Without any user connecting, the IPC statistics after the startup command completed showed the following:

```
[oracle@server1 ~]$ ipcs -m

------ Shared Memory Segments --------
key        shmid       owner    perms     bytes       nattch     status
0x74464570 1451851778 oracle    640       35651584    50
0x00000000 1451884547 oracle    640       3204448256  25

[oracle@server1 ~]$
```

The number of attached processes to the shared memory segments (=SGA) was 105. Restarting the database with the threaded model enabled shows a different picture.

```
[oracle@server1 ~]$ ipcs -m

------ Shared Memory Segments --------
key        shmid       owner    perms     bytes       nattch     status
0x74464570 1221394434 oracle    640       35651584    14
0x00000000 1221427203 oracle    640       3204448256  7
```

The number of attached processes is down to 21. This can have a positive effect on consolidated environments. In addition to the benefits of using threads such as simplified memory management and faster context switching there has been significant work on the Linux kernel scheduler to allow scalability to hundreds of thousands of threads since NPTL became mainstream.

Summary

There are many really interesting new features in Oracle 12c. Some have made their way into this chapter; others could not to keep the page count in check. As with every new database release it is easiest to get started with the new features guide. This document will introduce the new features by functional area and point you to further information in the respective guide. Every document in the documentation has a "what is new ... " section at the beginning. This section provides more information than the new features guide and again points you to the relevant chapter.

Of all the available new features this chapter presented a taste for what you can expect with the latest version of the database. Some of the contents here will be referenced in other chapters, especially the threaded execution model and Automatic Storage Management. In the author's opinion ASM is a great, simple, and most importantly unified storage mechanism the DBA can employ on any platform currently supported. By implementing ASM the agility of provisioning storage will improve, and thanks to the online (almost) everything, stripe-and-mirror approach ASM is well suited for large deployments, be it single instance or a Real Application Cluster.

CHAPTER 3

■ ■ ■

Supporting Hardware

After a quick introduction to some of the most noteworthy Oracle 12.1 New Features, it is time to get back to the core theme of this book: consolidation. What you need to consider as important for any new project is even more true for consolidation projects: defining the right infrastructure for the task ahead. Consolidation projects most likely differ from other projects in that the infrastructure platform—once decided upon—is to be used in many deployments in exactly the same way. A successful consolidation project has the potential of replacing a lot of hardware. But only if done right! And this is exactly the reason why you are finding such a large chapter dedicated to the matter of selecting hardware.

But hardware is not the only important subject to consider. Once the hardware platform has been agreed upon by all parties, the next step is to think about the deployment for Oracle databases. The next chapter is written with that in mind. You read about the author's preference for the Linux platform on x86-64 hardware in previous chapters, and you will find this thread throughout the rest of the book. Although many believe that Linux on x86-64 is the future mainstream platform, there is, of course, no obligation for you to follow the same path. This is another of the key elements you will find throughout the book: use what your staff is comfortable with. If you would like to transition to new systems, or to new processes and tasks, please do so only after appropriate change management has been implemented. Getting buy-in from the engineers and operational team supporting your systems is important, not only because it is needed for smooth operations and internal support, but also because it adds extra motivation to the team if you are proud of what you do.

This chapter aims at evaluating and introducing options related to the consolidation hardware platform, taking into account the developments in terms of CPU, operating system, and storage. When evaluating these, it is important not to focus on individual components but rather adhere to the big picture. You can read about enabling software in the following chapter. Again, there is a wealth of options here, and the fact that the ones you read about made it into the book doesn't mean they are the best options for all tasks out there. The chapter is not about comparing and ranking: It is about introducing and familiarizing you with some of the available products.

Enabling Hardware

This chapter will explore some of the potential hardware choices for the consolidation platform. As you just read in the introduction, the choice of hardware should be made after careful consideration. The impact of selecting an inappropriate platform can be felt painfully if it turns out that some factors have not been taken into account. Once budget is allocated for a specific iteration of the consolidated service, it might be difficult to arrange for major changes. After all, it's economies of scale your company is after!

The focus of the chapter is going to be on the Linux operating system running on the x86-64 platform. The main reason lies in the platform's great current and future potential. The mantra of commodity computing has always been to use easy-to-replace standard building blocks.

The established vendors in the server market offer a comprehensive suite of support products around these industry standard servers, and making use of them allows you to benefit from economies of scale. First of all, there is a benefit of reducing the platform footprint. Training and employing staff capable of supporting multiple platforms to a high degree of professionalism is expensive. Especially in large organizations where all major platforms are in use, a great deal of time has to be spent to certify a given platform with storage, the operating system, and software stack. Naturally some of this work can be reduced by limiting the number of supported platforms. The number of supported platforms depends on the strategic direction of the company and also on the budget available. Certain vendors, however, may not be able to comply with the platform strategy, but that is not a problem either. Support arrangements can be put in place between the vendor and the application team to cover the nonstandard platform as an exception. The vendor should then be persuaded to adjust its product to be in line with the corporate strategy.

One often-heard argument against limiting the number of supported platforms is that of the vendor lock-in. Being supplied by only one or very few parties for mission critical systems can be either a big advantage (as the vendor marketing will tell you) or a disadvantage (what the other vendors will tell you). There is no clear-cut answer to the question of vendor diversity. This again is often down to managerial decisions and relationships with vendors, but the Linux-operating environment at least gives you a lot of choice.

However, despite the strong favor of Linux in this book, you should not feel motivated to rush and replace your existing estate with x86-64 servers. During many site visits it has become apparent that the staff responsible for "their" operating system (and the servers running it) often have strong feelings towards that platform. In addition to the necessary skill that the administrators must possess to manage a platform, it is important to use adequate change management when introducing something new. The concerns and worries of staff should be taken into consideration, and the budget forecast should include training or new hiring as well.

After so much theory it is time to get back to the real matter: hardware! This section will start off with a question of whether or not blades make sense and whether rack-mounted systems fit into your organization better. It will then discuss the changes in the hardware space that happened in the past two years before exploring more advanced aspects of the x86-64 platform.

Blades or Rack-Mounted?

Blades have established themselves as suitable alternatives to the classical 19-inch rack-mounted server for many workloads. Blades are usually smaller than rack-mounted servers, but they also have fewer components and fewer possibilities for expansion. Some of the components you would normally find inside a rack-mounted server will be in the so-called blade enclosure. The small form factor for blades will allow a very high density, and when they were first introduced, blades seemed ideal to reduce the space required in the data center. However, with the high density comes a heightened requirement to cool the blades and enclosure to prevent them from overheating. With the introduction of chips capable of adjusting their clock rate depending on workload, cooling becomes even more important. Often the chips need to be in their comfort zone when it comes to their Thermal Design Power (TDP). As soon as the processor temperature rises too high, it will clock down and run at reduced speed to prevent damage to its components. Sufficient cooling of modern CPUs is therefore essential to stable CPU performance! Luckily the ever shrinking manufacturing process for processors allows for a reduction of cooling requirements. Processor vendors have realized that a power-efficient processor is a real necessity in the drive to cut cost in data centers.

There is no general industry standard blade enclosure, but you can expect most blade enclosures to contain power supply units, networking equipment to support storage and client connectivity, and other shared infrastructure. The introduction of Data Center Ethernet or Converged Ethernet allows vendors to use high speed Ethernet switches for network and storage traffic, potentially reducing the number of cables in the data center. The matured graphical management interfaces allow the administrator to perform lights-out management of his blades. Graphical representations of the blade enclosure tell the administrator to see which slots are free and which ones are occupied. Often warnings and alerts can be sent via SNMP (Simple Network Management Protocol) traps to monitoring solutions.

A blade enclosure would be of little use if it were not for the blades. The little, yet powerful computers can either be horizontally or vertically added into the enclosure. Depending on the model, they can either occupy a full slot or half a slot. The terms full-width and half-width (or height) have been coined for these. Blades are highly versatile and configurable. If your data center can accommodate them, they are definitely worth evaluating.

Rack-mounted servers have been the predominant form of servers and probably still are. The typical rack-mounted server is measured in unit height; the width is predetermined by the rack you are mounting the server to. The industry currently uses mainly 19-inch- and occasionally 23-inch-wide racks. The rack unit corresponds to 1.75 inches, and a typical 19-inch rack has support for 42 units. With the basic parameters set, the IT department is free to choose whatever hardware is 19-inch-wide and otherwise fits inside the rack. The benefit of rack-mounted servers is that you can mix and match hardware from different vendors in the same cage. Rack-mounted servers can usually take more memory and processors than their blade counterparts. Recent benchmark results available from the TPC website refer to high-end x86-64 servers with 5 and up to 7 unit height, taking a massive two to four terabyte of memory. The next generation of Xeon processors to be released in 2013/2014 will push that limit even further.

Blades seem well suited for clustered applications, especially if individual blades can boot from the SAN and generally have little static configuration on internal storage or the blade itself. Some systems allow the administrator to define a personality of the blade, such as network cards and their associated hardware addresses, the LUN(s) where the operating system is stored on, and other metadata defining the role of the blade. Should a particular blade in a chassis fail, the blade's metadata can be transferred to another one, which can be powered up and resume the failed blade's role. Total outage time, therefore, can be reduced, and a technician has a little more time to replace the failed unit.

Rack-mounted servers are very useful when it comes to consolidating older, more power-hungry hardware on the same platform. They also generally allow for better extension in form of available PCIe slots compared to a blade. To harness the full power of a 5U or even 7U server requires advanced features from the operating systems, such as support for the Non-Uniform Memory Architecture (NUMA) in modern hardware. You can read more about making best use of your new hardware in Chapter 4.

Regardless of which solution you decide to invest in for your future consolidation platform, you should consider answering the following questions about your data center:

- How much does the data center management charge you for space?

- How well can the existing air conditioning system cope with the heat?

- Is the raised floor strong enough to withstand the weight of another fully populated rack?

- Is there enough power to deal with peaks in demand?

- Can your new hardware be efficiently cooled within the rack?

- Is your supporting infrastructure, especially networking and fiber channel switches, capable of connecting the new systems the best possible way? You definitely do not want to end up in a situation where you bought 10Gbps Ethernet adapters, for example, and your switches cannot support more than 1 GBps.

- Does your network infrastructure allow for a sufficiently large pool of IP addresses to connect the system to its users?

There are many more questions to be asked, and the physical deployment of hardware is an art on its own. All vendors provide planning and deployment guides, and surely you can get vendor technicians and consultants to advise you on the future deployment of their hardware. You might even get the luxury of a site survey wherein a vendor technician inspects corridors, elevators, raised flooring, and power, among other things, to ensure that the new hardware fits physically when it is shipped.

Let's not forget at this stage that the overall goal of the consolidation efforts is to reduce cost. If the evaluation of hardware is successful, it should be possible to benefit from economies of scale by limiting yourself to one hardware platform, possibly in a few different configurations to cater to the different demands of applications. The more standardized the environment, the easier it is to deliver new applications with a quick turnaround.

With the basic building block in sight, the next question is: what should be added as peripheral hardware? Which options do you have in terms of CPU, memory, and expansion cards? What storage option should you use, etc.? The following sections introduce some changes in the hardware world which have happened over the last few years.

Changes in the Hardware World

The world of hardware is changing at a very rapid pace. The core areas where most technological advance is visible are processor architecture, the explosion of available memory, storage, and networking infrastructure. Combined these changes present unique challenges not only to the operating system but also to the software running on it. Until not too long ago it was unthinkable to have 160 CPU threads exposed to the operating system in the x86-64 world, and scheduler algorithms had to be developed to deal with this large number. In addition to the explosion of the number of CPU cores and threads you also have the possibility of vast amounts of memory at your disposal. Commercial x86-64 servers can now address up to four terabytes. Non-uniform memory access (NUMA) has also become more important on x86-64 platforms. Although the NUMA factor is most relevant in systems with four NUMA nodes and more, understanding NUMA in Linux will soon become crucial when working with large servers.

Exadata was the first platform widely available running Oracle workloads and moving Remote Direct Memory Access into the focus. Most of us associate Infiniband with RDMA, but there are other noteworthy applications, such as iWARP and RoCEE (RDBMA over Converged Enhanced Ethernet), for example. Also, Infiniband is a lot more than you might think: it is a whole series of protocols for various different use cases, ranging from carrier for classic IP ("IP over IB") to the low-latency Exadata protocol based on RDS or Reliable Datagram Sockets to transporting SCSI ("SRP," the SCSI RDMA Protocol).

Changes to storage are so fundamental that they deserve a whole section of their own. Classic fiber channel arrays are getting more and more competition in form of PCI Express Flash Cards, as well as small-form factor flash-arrays connected via Infiniband, allowing for ultra-low latency. New vendors are challenging the established storage companies with new and interesting concepts that do not fit the model in which many vendors placed their products over the last decade. This trend can only be beneficial for the whole industry. Even if the new storage startups are quickly swallowed by the established players in the storage market their dynamics, products and ideas will live on. No one can ignore the changes flash memory brought to the way enterprises store data anymore.

Thoughts About the Storage Backend

Oak Table member James Morle has written a great paper titled "Sane SAN 2010." He has also predicated changes to the way enterprise storage arrays are going to be built. With his statements he alluded to the flash revolution in the data center. Over the last decade the use of NAND flash has become prolific, and that for a reason. Flash storage can offer a lot more I/O operations per second in a single unit, while at the same time requiring a lot less space and cooling. Given the right transport protocol, it can also boost performance massively. The pace of development of flash memory outpaced the development for magnetic disk in the relatively short time it has existed. Advances in capacity for magnetic disks have been made consistently in the past, but the performance data of the disks have not increased at the same speed. Before starting a discussion about storage tiering and the flash revolution, a little bit of terminology must be explained.

> *Bandwidth/throughput:* these figures indicate how much data you can transmit between your storage backend and the database host per unit of time. Most decision support systems are highly bandwidth hungry.

> *Response time/latency: the quicker the I/O request can be satisfied, the better.* Response time is the time it takes from issuing an I/O request to its completion. Online transaction processing systems are usually sensitive to changes in response times.

What are typical ball-park figures to expect from your storage array? In terms of latency you should expect 6–8 milliseconds for single block random reads and 1 or 2 milliseconds for small sequential writes such as log writes. These figures are most likely not reads from physical disk, but rather are those reads affected by the caches in the arrays. With the wide variety of existing storage solutions and the progress made on an almost monthly basis, it is next to impossible to give a valid figure for expected throughput, which is why you do not find one here.

Storage Tiering

Storage tiers have been common in the storage array for quite some time. Storage engineering maps different classes of storage to tiers, often with the help of the storage array's vendor. The different classes of storage are taken from a matrix of storage types such as DRAM, flash memory, spinning disk, and performance attributes such as RAID levels. A third dimension to the matrix is the transport protocol. Current mainstream transport media include Fiber Channel, Fiber Channel over Ethernet and iSCSI as well as Network File System. As you can imagine, the number of permutations of these are large, and it requires careful planning for which combination should be made available as a storage tier. One approach to storage tiering relying solely on hard disks could resemble the following:

1.   15k RPM Fiber Channel disks in a RAID 10

2.   15k RPM Fiber Channel disks in a RAID 5

3.   10k RPM Fiber Channel disks in RAID 5

4.   Direct NFS with dedicated appliances

In the above list, the lowest number should be the "best" storage tier. Storage tiering has often been used to enable organizations to implement data life-cycle models. Frequently accessed, or "hot," data was placed on the better-quality storage tiers, and cold, or very infrequently used, data was placed on lower-end storage. In the Oracle world, that often meant placing objects on tablespaces defined within a storage tier. Moving data from one tier to another required either the use of "alter table ... move" commands or alternatively the implementation of calls to the database package DBMS_REDEFINITION. Needless to say, this was a non-automated task that had to be performed during maintenance windows. High-end enterprise arrays nowadays try to perform the same task automatically in the background. Predictable performance is more important than stellar performance on day one, followed by abysmal performance on day two. Time will tell if the automated models are sophisticated and stable enough to guarantee consistent execution times and adherence to the agreed service levels.

The commoditization of flash storage has changed the classic storage tier model presented in the preceding list. The introduction of flash memory, or what some call *solid state disk*, has fundamentally changed the storage industry.

The Flash Revolution

The proliferation of NAND flash memory, colloquially referred to as solid state disk or SSD, has changed the storage industry profoundly. Where it has been previously necessary to short-stroke many 15k RPM fiber-channel disks to achieve a high number of I/O operations per second, the same performance characteristics, plus potentially lower- access time and less congestion on disk, make flash memory a very attractive solution. Very high I/O performance can now be achieved in smaller, less power-hungry, and easier-to-cool solutions either inside the database host or externally connected.

Interestingly, consumers benefit from flash storage in a similar way to enterprise customers, although the way the storage is actually presented to the hardware differs greatly between the two customer groups. Most enterprise offerings for flash-based memory, which in reality is NAND flash, fall into the following categories:

- Connected internally to the server or blade
  - As 2.5-inch or 3.5-inch solid state disk
  - As a PCI Express card
- Externally attached
  - Fiber Channel
  - Via PCIe card
  - Infiniband

Internally attached 2.5-inch SSD do not play a major role in enterprise computing: the majority of these disks use a SATA 6G interface and are made for high-end consumer desktops and graphic workstations. The next category of internally attached flash memory is more interesting. Recent processors feature PCI Express version 3, offering a lot more bandwidth at a reduced overhead compared to the previous PCI Express version 2.x.

A WORD ABOUT PCI EXPRESS

PCI Express, short for Peripheral Component Interconnect Express (PCIe), is the x86 world's standard way to add functionality to a server which isn't already available on the mainboard. Examples for such PCIe cards are 10 Gigabit Ethernet cards, Fiber Channel Host Bus Adapters, Infiniband cards, and the like. PCIe has been designed to replace older standards such as the Accelerated Graphics Port and the older PCI-X and PCI standards. Unlike some of the standards it replaces, PCIe is a high-speed point to point serial I/O bus.

When considering PCIe bandwidth server, vendors often specify the number of lanes to a card slot. These lanes, broadly speaking, equate to bandwidth. Industry standard servers use PCIe x4, x8, and x16 lanes for slots, most of which are version 2. Every processor or mainboard supports a certain maximum number of PCIe lanes. The exact number is usually available from the vendor website.

PCI Express is currently is available in version 3. Thanks to more efficient encoding, the protocol overhead could be reduced compared to PCI version 2.x, and the net bitrate could be doubled.

PCIe 3.0 has a transfer rate of eight giga-transfers per second (GT/s). Compared to 250 MB/s per PCI lane in the initial PCIe 1.0, PCIe 3.0 has a bandwidth of 1 GB/s. With a PCIe 3.0 x16 slot, a theoretical bandwidth of 16 GB/s is possible, which should be plenty for even the most demanding workloads. Most systems currently deployed, however, still use PCIe 2.x with exactly half the bandwidth of PCIe 3.0: 500 MB/s per lane. The number of cards supporting PCIe 3.0 has yet to increase although that is almost certainly going to happen while this book is in print.

PCIe is possibly the best way to connect the current ultra-fast flash solutions so they are least slowed down by hardware and additional protocol bottlenecks. Such cards use single-level cells (SLC) for best performance or multi-level cells (MLC) for best storage capacity. According to vendor specifications, such devices have low micro-second response times and offer hundreds of thousands of I/O operations per second. When it comes to the fastest available storage, then PCIe x4 or x8 cards are hard to beat. The PCIe cards will show up as a storage device under Linux and other supported operating systems, just like a LUN from a storage array making it simple to either add it into an ASM disk group as an ASM disk or alternatively create a suitable file system, such as XFS on top of the LUN. The downside to the use of PCIe flash memory is the fact that a number of these cards cannot easily be configured for redundancy in hardware. PCIe cards are also not hot-swappable, requiring the server to be powered off if a card needs to be replaced. Nor can they be shared between hosts (yet?), making them unsuitable for Oracle configurations requiring shared storage.

Another use case for PCIe flash memory is to use a second-level buffer cache, a feature known as Database Smart Flash Cache. With today's hardware taking terabytes of DRAM this solution should be carefully evaluated to assess its use in applications and the new hardware platform to see if there is any benefit. Finally, some vendors allow you to use the PCIe flash device as a write-through cache between database host and Fiber Channel attached array. PCIe flash devices used in this way can speed up reads because those reads do not need to use the fiber channel protocol to access data on the array. Since the flash device is write-through, failure of the card does not impact data integrity.

External flash based storage solutions can be connected in a number of ways, with Fiber Channel probably the most common option. Most established vendors of storage arrays offer a new storage tier inside the array based on flash memory. For most customers, that approach is very easy to implement because it does not require investment into new network infrastructure. It also integrates seamlessly into the existing fabrics, and the skillset of the storage team does not need to be extended either. In short, Fiber Channel is a great solution for established data centers to quickly get some of the benefits of flash memory. Using Fiber Channel to address "SSD" inside an array is a bit slower, though—the Sane SAN 2010 paper explains the difference in great detail. Essentially the round trip time of Fiber Channel is higher than the blazing fast Remote Direct Memory Access available with Infiniband's SCSI RDMA Protocol (SRP).

Some vendors exploit the capabilities of PCIe and allow the external array to be connected via PCIe card plugged into the database server to the array instead of Fiber Chanel. All storage communication has to use that wire, and the storage system behaves as if it were directly plugged into a PCIe slot. Thus the storage system benefits greatly from PCIe's high bandwidth and low latency properties. Although again a very fast solution, this design does not allow the array to be shared between hosts, the same limitation as with directly attached PCIe cards. The best, although probably most expensive, way to attach an external array to the database hosts is to use Infiniband and the previously mentioned SCSI RDMA Protocol or SRP.

USING INFINIBAND TO TRANSPORT SCSI COMMANDS

The Small Computer System Interface has proven remarkably versatile over the many years of its existence. SCSI has mostly been used in expensive enterprise hardware initially to address hard disks or tape drives when it came out in the 1980s. Like so many protocols it started out as a parallel bus but has been replaced by a serial version, which is known as Serially Attached SCSI, or SAS for short.

SAS has emerged as the de-facto standard for enterprise-class direct attached storage, in which the stricter rules about signaling and cable-length do not matter as much. The current implementations of the SCSI protocol do not allow for more than 10-20m cable length.

The cable-length limitations have been addressed with the introduction of Fiber Channel. FC is a networking protocol, and despite being capable of transporting many workloads, it has found its niche as the predominant form of transporting SCSI commands over a distance. Almost every single modern database server is "SAN-connected," which means it has its storage provided by an external array. Fiber Channel is divided into a number of protocol layers that remind you of the ISO/OSI layers; the upper level layer is primarily concerned with mapping SCSI to the new method of transportation.

Fiber Channel has evolved over time from Gigabit Fiber Channel in 1997 to 16 GB Fiber Channel available in 2011. Since changing from one generation to another requires investment in supporting infrastructure, it is expected that 8 GB FC will remain mainstream for a few more years.

Some users thought that the evolution of Fiber Channel as the method of choice for transporting SCSI commands did not happen quickly enough. Alternative approaches to the lower level protocols of Fiber Channel are Fiber Channel over Ethernet, Internet SCSI (iSCSI), and other less widely used ones. Most of these additional protocols use layers of the TCP/IP stack. The idea behind that approach is to be able to make use of existing know-how and potentially infrastructure—Ethernet is well understood.

One of the fastest (but also most expensive) ways to transport SCSI commands today is by using Remote Direct Memory Access, RDMA. RDMA is often implemented as Infiniband, which has seen a lot more widespread use since the introduction of Oracle's Exadata. RDMA allows zero-copy networking between hosts, bypassing many parts of the operating system, taking load off the CPUs, and considerably benefitting the latency of operations. Of the many uses Infiniband permits, the SCSI RDMA Protocol is one and is most useful for general purpose storage solutions.

Infiniband is so much faster than Fiber Channel because of its incredibly low latencies, the high bandwidth, and the zero-copy feature. Quad Data Rate (QDR) has been available since 2008 and is in use in Oracle's Exadata. It offers up to 10 Gb/s per link, and Exadata, just like most Infiniband systems, has four-lane ports accumulating to 40 Gb/s, which is referred to as "Quad Data Rate". The next evolution is already available today, called Fourteen Data Rate Infiniband. FDR increases the link speed to 14 Gb/s per link. It is to be expected that most IB ports will be QDR ports again, offering a total of 56 Gb/s. A new encoding method also promises less overhead, but you are well advised to use FDR with PCIe version 3 to make use of the enormous bandwidth on offer if you do not want to bottleneck on the 2nd generation PCIe express cards currently in use. Infiniband is a new technology for most of us, for which your organization needs to start acquiring hardware as well as operational know-how. This can be a significant investment.

In an attempt to categorize flash-based storage irrespective of the way it is attached to the server and to put it into perspective, you can refer to Hennessy and Patterson's *Computer Architecture: A Quantitative Approach*. There you find a Memory Hierarchy ranging from super-fast access to registers within the processor to very slow access to external storage such as tape. Sources vary in terms of access times, but the general dimensions are undisputed. Consider the following shortened memory hierarchy in Table 3-1:

Table 3-1. *An Attempt to Define the Memory Hierarchy with a Select Few Examples*

Storage tier	Approximate latency	Comment
Processor register	Picosecond	Processor registers store information retrieved from higher-tier caches such as the processor L1 cache
Level 1 cache	Less than 1 nanosecond	Usually implemented as Static RAM (SRAM) as opposed to DRAM
Level 2 cache	A few nanoseconds	Can be slower if implemented off the chip but usually found on-die
DRAM	~30-50 nanoseconds, depending on locality	Dynamic Random Access Memory is otherwise referred to as main memory. A typical server would use DDR3 modules
Flash memory read	microseconds	Not taking the time into account to send the data to the host, i.e., no round-trip time. For that time you need to consider the Fiber Channel roundtrip time or alternatively Infiniband roundtrips.
Flash memory write	Usually longer than flash memory read but still within microseconds	Writes take longer on the physical layer; some solutions use caches to mitigate the write penalty
15k Hard disk read	Few milliseconds	

Hennessy and Patterson also graphically plotted the access time for DRAM, which is used for "main memory" in servers and hard disk in a logarithmic scale on the horizontal axis of a chart. The vertical axis denoted the cost per gigabyte. As you can imagine, the access time for DRAM is very, very low; however, that comes at the expense of an exorbitant cost per GB for DRAM. According to the graph a DRAM module provided approximately 50 nanoseconds response time at the cost of roughly 100 dollars per GB. The same year the cost per GB magnetic storage was a lot lower than 1 dollar per GB; however, the access time in nanoseconds could be around 8,000,000 nanoseconds, which is the equivalent of 8 milliseconds. The costs are obviously relevant to when the graph has been created and does not reflect current prices.

■ **Note** Let's not forget that this is an academic comparison. You currently will not be able to build a system with enough DRAM and backup batteries to compete for capacity in a cost-effective way with a multiple-shelf, enterprise storage array.

What is striking, though, by looking at the numbers is what is called the access time gap: less than 100 nanoseconds to access DRAM compared to 8,000,000 nanoseconds for magnetic storage is quite a difference.

You can also see from the above table that the latency for flash memory access is a lot lower than for hard disks, but before you start to base your whole storage estate on SSD, you need to know a little more. Let's approach the complex topic of SSDs using the categorization in Figure 3-1 as our basis.

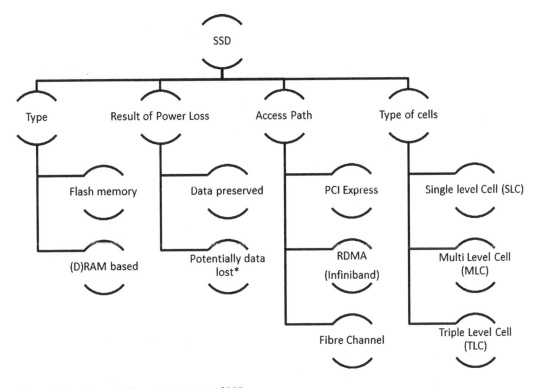

Figure 3-1. *Attempt of a categorization of SSD*

The type of SSD is important, but there is little to say other than that (D)RAM-based SSDs do not have a significant market share anymore. Practically all SSDs today are NAND-flash based. This leads to the next item in the list: DRAM is volatile memory, which means that if there is a power cut, then all the data is potentially lost. Vendors realized that early on and added batteries to their DRAM-based solutions. NAND-based flash memory does not exhibit the same behavior. Please note that the following sections focus on NAND-based flash memory.

You already read about the access paths to the NAND storage; they are listed again for the sake of completeness. What you need to remember is that accessing SSD via PCIe is the quickest path to the storage. This is followed by Remote Direct Memory Access and finally by Fiber Channel.

The type of memory cell bubble denotes how many bits a cell in a NAND-based SSD can store. To better understand the significance of that sentence you need to know that the SSD's base memory unit is a cell. In other words, information is stored in a non-volatile way in an array of cells. It is the amount of information that can be stored in a cell that is significant to this discussion: a single level cell stores one bit in each cell, which leads to fast transfer speeds. As an added advantage, SLC last longer than their counterparts. Fast and reliable—there has to be a downside, and that is cost. The higher cost associated with SLC means that such cells are almost exclusively found in enterprise class solutions. You also expect high-performance flash memory to be based on Single-Level Cells.

Multi-Level Cells store two bits per cell. Most MLCs, therefore, are slower due to the way the data is accessed. For the same reason individual MLC cells wear out more quickly than SLCs. However, the MLC-based SSDs allow for larger capacity. As a rule of thumb, you would buy SLC for performance and MLC for capacity. But let's not forget that both SLC and MLC are still a lot faster than magnetic storage.

Triple-Level Cells are not really new, but they do not seem to make commercial sense yet in the enterprise segment. TLC SSDs exist for the consumer market. The advantage of storing three bit per cell is higher capacity, but similar to the step from SLC to MLC, you get even more wear and slower performance.

Another term often heard in the context of SSD is wear leveling. You read in the previous paragraphs that individual cells can wear out over the usage time of the device. The wearing of the cell is caused by writes. The controller managing the device therefore tries to spread the write load over as many cells as possible, completely transparently. The fewer writes a cell has to endure, the longer it will potentially last.

Multiple cells are organized in pages which in turn are grouped into blocks. Most enterprise-type SSD use a page size of 4 KB and a block size of 512 KB. These blocks are addressed much like any other block device, i.e., hard disk, making 1:1 replacements easy and straightforward. For the same reason you could set the sector size of the SSD in Linux and other operating systems to 4k. Read and write operations allow you to access random pages. Erase (delete) operations, however, require a modification of the whole block. In the worst case, if you need to erase a single page (usually 4 KB), then you have to delete the entire block. The storage controller obviously preserves the non-affected memory, writing it back together with the modified data. Such an operation is undesirable simply because it adds latency. Additionally, the write operation adds to the individual cell's wear factor. If possible, instead of modifying existing cells, the controller will try to write to unused cells, which is a lot faster. Most SSDs, therefore, reserve a sizeable chunk of space, which is not accessible from the operating system. Delete operations can then either be completed in the background after the operation has completed or alternatively be deferred until space pressure arises. The more data is stored on the SSD, the more difficult it is for the controller to find free space. While performance of SSD, therefore, is generally very good, sometimes you might see certain outliers in write performance. All of a sudden, some writes have up to 50 milliseconds additional latency. Such outliers are called a write cliff, caused by the above phenomenon. When getting a SSD on loan, it is important to check how full the device is, a function which is often available from the driver.

When measuring the performance of SSD with Oracle, it is important to use direct I/O. Using direct I/O allows Oracle to bypass the file system cache, making performance numbers a lot more realistic. Without direct I/O a request to read from the storage layer might as well be satisfied from the operating system file system cache. A blazingly fast millisecond response time in an extended trace file cannot be attributed to a very well-functioning I/O storage subsystem, for there is no extra information as to where the requested block was found. When you instruct Oracle to bypass the file system cache, the reported times in the Active Session History or other performance-related information is more likely to reflect the true nature of the I/O request.

When testing a flash memory solution, you might also want to consider the use of a very small Oracle SGA to ensure that I/Os generally are not satisfied from the buffer cache. This is easier said than done since Oracle allocates certain memory areas based, for example, on the number of CPUs as reported in the initialization parameter cpu_count. If you want to set your buffer cache to 48 MB, which is among the lowest possible values, you probably have to lower your cpu_count to 2 and use manual SGA management to size the various pools accordingly.

Putting it Together

So far, you have read a lot about different ways to attach storage to your consolidated platform. Why all that detail? In the author's experience the DBA (or database engineer) is the best person to consult when it comes to rolling out an Oracle database solution. Why? It's a simple answer: the database administrator knows how storage, client, and internal facing networking matter to his or her database. The operating system, storage, networking, and every other solution only serve the purpose to allow the database to execute. You will find congenial storage administrators,

Unix gurus from the days of Dennis Ritchie, Brian Kernighan, and Ken Thompson, but ultimately their view is focused on their specific area of expertise. Therefore it is more often than not the database administrator or engineer who can provide the big picture! Hopefully after you read these sections of the book, this can be you!

Besides the organizational difficulties just described, there is another reason all the different technologies have been laid out. When you are thinking about the future hosting platform, it is beneficial to roll out a uniform hardware platform. Storage tiering is certainly going to stay with us for the foreseeable future. Its main uses will be information lifecycle management and offering a different cost structure to internal clients. Whether moving data from one tier to another is going to be an automatic process or manual depends largely on the maturity of the automatic solution and the comfort level of engineering to release that feature into production.

Flash storage is going to be increasingly used, and there is a potential to design different hardware classes as the consolidation target. One could think of the platform arrangement described in Table 3-2.

Table 3-2. *Potential Hardware Platforms*

Platform designation	Characteristics
Gold	Rack-mounted servers, using multiple rack units (≥ 4U) with lots of DRAM for data intensive processing. Many fast CPU cores with latest generation processors.
	Flash storage could be provided externally via Infiniband or, more traditionally via 8 or 16 GB/s Fiber Channel. Magnetic disk is available in form of Fiber Channel attached storage array(s).
	This platform should primarily be used to more critical production databases with high I/O demands. If high availability is a concern, then the database might be clustered with the Real Application Clusters option, hence the requirement to use flash storage outside the server itself.
Silver	This could be the mainstream consolidation platform. The server could use two to four sockets with reasonably fast CPU cores or dual socket with very fast cores. Total memory capacity is less than for the gold platform for architectural reasons.
	High I/O requirements could be satisfied by PCIe-based SSD as an option. A PCIe SSD can either store data in a way a directly attached block device does, or it act as a write-through cache.
	In addition to the "bread and butter" production workloads, such a platform could be used as integration testing platform for the gold servers to save cost. If possible, it should not be used as a UAT platform for gold servers. Using different architecture and hardware has never been a great recipe to ensure a smooth testing period—and more importantly—a smooth production rollout.
Bronze	The bronze platform could be aimed at development and integration systems. These are early in the development cycle, and rapid provisioning of a production clone to debug a serious issue is more important than the latest and greatest technology, memory, etc. Another use case for these systems is as repositories for slowly growing data.
	There would most likely be no flash storage due to cost considerations.

Table 3-2's matrix has only taken storage and CPUs into account. There are, of course, many more factors influencing the final offering from the engineers. The purpose of this section was to encourage you to think out of the box and include more than the immediately obvious aspect into the mix. The preceding table has deliberately been kept short. Offering too many options could confuse less technical users of the hosting service, leading to lots of questions that could be avoided.

Finally, you should be aware of specific hardware solutions for running Oracle workloads. Exadata has already been mentioned in the sections above. The other option you have from Oracle is the Oracle Database Appliance (ODA). Both of these are part of the Engineered Systems initiative by Oracle, that aims at giving customers a balanced platform for database processing. Both Exadata and the ODA benefit from the fact that their hardware and software stacks are standardized. Over and above that standardization, Oracle will provide you with patches to the whole system. In the case of Exadata, the storage tier as well as the database servers will be supplied with regular patches. Patches to the database running on top of these are also closely related and specifically provided by Oracle. The benefit of such a combination is a further reduced effort in certifying the whole stack by the engineering department. In the ideal case, only the patch application needs to be thoroughly tested before it is rolled out. It's also possible to create your own platform. You can read more about that approach in the following sections.

Consolidation Features in Linux

The Linux platform appears to the author as one of the most dynamic operating systems currently available for enterprise use. This can be a blessing and a curse at the same time. Engineering departments usually need to spend time to certify the operating system with the various components that are required to convert industry-standard hardware into a platform suitable for mass rollout. As you can imagine, this certification requires time, and the time needed for a certification is exactly proportional to the resources available. You read in the introduction chapter that resources in all departments, but especially for engineering, are becoming scarce. Quick-release cycles for Linux kernels do seem counterproductive in this context. This might be a reason why you see enterprise distributions seemingly using the same kernel (like 2.6.18.x for Red Hat 5.x) even though the change logs indicate hundreds of backports from the mainline kernel.

One of the open-source ideals, however, is "release small, but release often," and that will not change. New features in enterprise-class hardware are often well supported by the Linux distributions. While the mainline kernel as maintained by Linus Torvalds and other subsystem maintainers moves quickly, the enterprise distributions are careful not to release too often. Oracle Linux appears to become an exception as the Unbreakable Enterprise Kernel ("UEK") is updated at a faster pace. Each new kernel potentially provides new functionality and support for hardware, which makes it advisable to check for release notes. The following sections explain some interesting features in Linux that appeared with Oracle Linux/Red Hat Enterprise Linux 6.

Non-Uniform Memory Architecture with Intel X86–64

The Non-Uniform Memory architecture has been mentioned in a number of places in this book, and this section is finally providing more information about it. You read earlier that x86-64-based servers have the capability to address huge amounts of memory compared to systems a few years ago. So what does that mean? In the days of the classic Symmetrical Multiprocessor (SMP) systems, memory access had to be shared by all processors on a common bus. The memory controller was located on the Front Side Bus, or FSB. Main memory was attached to a chip called the Northbridge on the mainboard. Needless to say, this approach did not scale well with increasing numbers of CPUs and their cores. Additionally, high speed I/O PCI cards could also be attached to the Northbridge, further adding to the scalability problem.

The memory-access-problem was addressed by moving the memory closer to the processor. New, modern CPUs have memory controllers on the chip, allowing them to address their local memory at very high speeds. Furthermore, there is no shared bus between CPUs; all CPU-to-CPU connections in the x86-64-architecture are point-to-point. In some configurations, however ,an additional hop is required to access remote memory. In such systems, which are not in scope of this section, CPU 1, for example, can only directly talk to CPU 2. If it needs to communicate with CPU 3, then it has to ask CPU 2 first, adding more latency. A typical dual-socket system is shown in Figure 3-2:

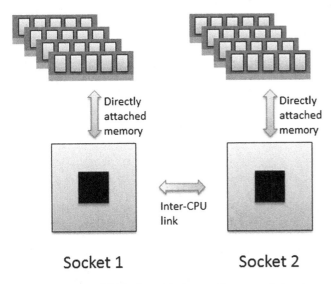

Figure 3-2. Simplified schematic design of a two-socket system

Current x86–64 processors have multiple DDR3-memory channels—individual memory channels, however, are not shown in this figure. The operating system has the task of masking the location of memory from its processes. The goal is to allow applications not having to be NUMA-aware to execute on NUMA hardware. However, they should be to take advantage of the local memory! Remember for the rest of the section that local memory access is faster, hence preferred. If local memory cannot be used, then remote memory needs to be used instead. This can happen if a process migrates (or has to migrate) from one CPU to another, in which case local and remote memory are reversed. The previously mentioned point-to-point protocols allow the CPU to access remote memory. This is where the most common NUMA-related problem lies. With every Oracle database it is important to have predictable performance. There are a number of reports from users who have experimented with NUMA: some processes executed a lot faster than without NUMA, but some others did not. The reason was eventually determined to be caused by access to remote memory in a memory-sensitive application. This had the following consequences:

- Oracle's "oracle-validated" and "oracle-rdbms-server-12cR1-preinstall" RPMs disable NUMA entirely by adding numa=off to the boot loader command line.

- Multiple notes on My Oracle Support do not openly discourage the use of NUMA but make it very clear that enabling NUMA can cause performance changes. A change can be positive or negative; you are also told to test the impact of enabling NUMA first, but that almost goes without saying.

So how can you make use of NUMA? First you have to enable it—check if your boot loader doesn't have the numa=off line appended as shown here:

```
kernel /boot/vmlinuz-2.6.xxx ro root=... rhgb quiet numa=off
```

It might additionally be necessary to enable NUMA in the BIOS or EFI of your machine. After a reboot your server is potentially NUMA aware. Linux uses the numactl package, among other software, to control NUMA. To list your NUMA nodes in the server, you use the following command:

```
[oracle@server1 ~]$ numactl --hardware
available: 4 nodes (0-3)
node 0 cpus: 0 1 2 3 4 5
```

```
node 0 size: 8190 MB
node 0 free: 1622 MB
node 1 cpus: 6 7 8 9 10 11
node 1 size: 8192 MB
node 1 free: 41 MB
node 2 cpus: 12 13 14 15 16 17
node 2 size: 8192 MB
node 2 free: 1534 MB
node 3 cpus: 18 19 20 21 22 23
node 3 size: 8176 MB
node 3 free: 1652 MB
node distances:
node   0   1   2   3
  0:  10  16  16  16
  1:  16  10  16  16
  2:  16  16  10  16
  3:  16  16  16  10
[oracle@server1 ~]$
```

In this example, you see a small system with four memory sockets. For each NUMA node, the number of its CPUs is reported, which are in fact cores. In addition to the cores per NUMA node, you get the size and utilization of the node's memory. The previously shown server has 32GB available in total, with about 8 GB available per NUMA node. The node distance map is based on the ACPI SLIT—the Advanced Configuration and Power Interface's System Locality Information Table. Don't worry about the names and technology. What matters is that the numbers in the table show the relative latency to access memory from a particular node, normalized to a base value of 10. Additional information, similar to the /proc/meminfo output per NUMA node, can be found in /sys/devices/system/node/*/meminfo and related files in the same directory. If you have allocated large pages, then you will find more information about these in /sys/devices/system/node/*/hugepages/.

The numactl utility is not only used to expose the hardware configuration, but it can also actively influence how processes and their memory access are handled by applying what is called the NUMA policy. By default, the NUMA policy matches the one shown here:

```
[oracle@server1 ~]$ numactl --show
policy: default
preferred node: current
physcpubind: 0 1 2 3 4 5 6 7 8 9 10 11 12 13 14 15 16 17 18 19 20 21 22 23
cpubind: 0 1 2 3
nodebind: 0 1 2 3
membind: 0 1 2 3
```

The default NUMA policy sets the current node as the preferred one and does not enforce binding processes to memory nodes or CPUs. If, for example, you want to override the default policy, you have plenty of options:

```
[root@server1 ~]# numactl
usage: numactl [--interleave=nodes] [--preferred=node]
               [--physcpubind=cpus] [--cpunodebind=nodes]
               [--membind=nodes] [--localalloc] command args ...
       numactl [--show]
       numactl [--hardware]
       numactl [--length length] [--offset offset] [--shmmode shmmode]
               [--strict]
```

```
        [--shmid id] --shm shmkeyfile | --file tmpfsfile
        [--huge] [--touch]
        memory policy | --dump | --dump-nodes

memory policy is --interleave, --preferred, --membind, --localalloc
nodes is a comma delimited list of node numbers or A-B ranges or all.
cpus is a comma delimited list of cpu numbers or A-B ranges or all
all ranges can be inverted with !
all numbers and ranges can be made cpuset-relative with +
the old --cpubind argument is deprecated.
use --cpunodebind or --physcpubind instead
length can have g (GB), m (MB) or k (KB) suffixes
```

The meaning of all these are well described in the manual page for numactl. However, there is a better way to control memory and process allocation described in the next section. Although the Oracle database has supported NUMA for quite a while, you should be very careful to set the necessary NUMA initialization parameters in an instance. I would like to encourage you to resort to Control Groups instead, unless you are on Oracle Linux 5 without the Unbreakable Enterprise Kernel. But even then it is important, just as the My Oracle Support notes say, to thoroughly test the implication of enabling NUMA support.

Control Groups

Control Groups, or cgroups for short, are an interesting new feature that made it into the latest enterprise Linux kernels. Control groups are available with Oracle's Kernel UEK in Oracle Linux 5 or with Oracle Linux 6, where it does not matter which kernel you use. Control Groups are a great way to divide a powerful multi-core, NUMA-enabled server into smaller, more manageable logical entities. Some of the concepts you will read about in this section sound similar to Solaris projects, which is part of the Solaris resource management framework.

■ **Note**   You can read more about Solaris Zones in Chapter 4.

The current Linux implementation is not quite as advanced as its Solaris counterpart yet. But who knows, maybe the Linux community will get a very similar feature: development on LXC or Linux Containers has already started to be more serious.

You read in the previous section that modern computer systems have local and remote memory in a non-uniform memory architecture. Depending on your system's micro architecture, accessing remote memory can be more costly, or a lot more costly than accessing local memory. It is a good idea to access local memory if possible, as you have seen in the previous section. Very large multi-processor systems with more than four sockets can easily be divided vertically into logical units matching a socket. In such a situation it is crucial to have enough local memory available! Assuming that your system has four NUMA nodes and 64 GB of memory, you would expect to see each NUMA node to have approximately 16 GB RAM.

Control Groups are based on grouping processes into subsystems, such as memory and CPU. All children of processes belonging to a control group will also automatically be associated with that cgroup. Cgroups are not limited to managing CPU and memory: further subsystems have been added to the framework. You can query your system to learn more about which subsystem is available and in use:

```
[root@server1 cgroup]# lssubsys -am
cpuset /cgroup/cpuset
cpu /cgroup/cpu
cpuacct /cgroup/cpuacct
```

```
memory /cgroup/memory
devices /cgroup/devices
freezer /cgroup/freezer
net_cls /cgroup/net_cls
blkio /cgroup/blkio
```

■ **Note**   This section is about the cpuset subsystem only. The complete reference to Control Groups can be found in the Oracle Linux Administrator's Solution Guide for Release 6 in Chapter 8. You are encouraged to review it to get a better understanding about all the interesting features available in the other systems!

The preceding output shows the default configuration from a recent Oracle Linux 6 system with package libcgroup installed. If enabled, the cgconfig service, which is part of the package, will read the configuration file in /etc/cgconfig.conf and mount the subsystems accordingly. Interestingly, the control group hierarchy is not exposed in the output of the mount command but rather in /proc/mounts.

From a consolidation point of view, it makes sense to limit processes to CPU socket(s). The aim of this section is to create two databases and bind all their respective processes to an individual socket and its memory. Control Groups are externalized in userland similar to the sys file system sysfs in Linux by a set of virtual files. Figure 3-3 demonstrates the relationship between the different subsystems and Control Groups.

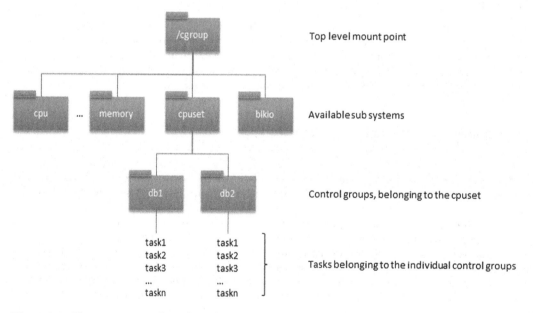

Figure 3-3. *The cgroup example explained*

Thankfully for the administrator, the first step of defining mount points for each subsystem is already done for us with the installation of the libcgroup package. You read earlier that the cgroup mount point resembles the SYSFS mount, following the UNIX paradigm that everything is a file. The contents of the top level cpuset directory are shown here:

```
[root@server1 ~]# ls /cgroup/cpuset/
cgroup.clone_children  cpuset.memory_migrate      cpuset.sched_relax_domain_level
cgroup.event_control   cpuset.memory_pressure     notify_on_release
```

```
cgroup.procs              cpuset.memory_pressure_enabled   release_agent
cpuset.cpu_exclusive      cpuset.memory_spread_page        tasks
cpuset.cpus               cpuset.memory_spread_slab
cpuset.mem_exclusive      cpuset.mems
cpuset.mem_hardwall       cpuset.sched_load_balance
[root@server1 ~]#
```

This is the top-level hierarchy, or the hierarchy's root. Some of the properties in this directory are read-write, but most are read-only. If you make changes to a property here, the change will be inherited by its siblings. The siblings are the actual control groups which need to be created next:

```
[root@server1 cgroup]# cgcreate -t oracle:dba -a oracle:dba -g cpuset:/db1
[root@server1 cgroup]# cgcreate -t oracle:dba -a oracle:dba -g cpuset:/db2
```

It is indeed that simple! The cgcreate command will create control groups db1 and db2 for the cpuset controller, as shown by the -g flag. The -a and -t flags allow the oracle account to administer and add tasks to the cpuset. Behind the scenes you will see that it creates two subdirectories in the cpuset directory, each with its own set of virtual configuration files. These control groups will inherit information from their parent, with the exception of the cpuset.memory_pressure_enabled and release_agent fields. From an Oracle point of view, all that remains to be done is to define which CPUs, and memory should be assigned to the cgroup. You use the cgset command to do so. There is a confusingly large number of attributes that can be set, but luckily the documentation is quite comprehensive. Following the example from the previous section, the first six "CPUs," which are cores in reality, are mapped to db1; the other six will be set to db2. The same happens for memory:

```
[root@server1 cpuset]# cgset -r cpuset.cpus=0-5 db1
[root@server1 cpuset]# cgset -r cpuset.mems=0 db1
[root@server1 cpuset]# cgset -r cpuset.cpus=6-11 db2
[root@server1 cpuset]# cgset -r cpuset.mems=2 db2
```

Note that the memory is allocated by NUMA node; the CPU cores are enumerated the same way the operating system sees them. Further enhancements could include a decision on whether the CPUs should exclusively be useable by the processes in a cgroup. In that case, if cpuset.cpu_exclusive is set to 1 and no other processes can utilize the CPU—use this feature with care! The same applies for cpuset.mem_exclusive, but related to memory.

The manual way to start a process in a certain cgroup is called cgexec. Consider this example for starting an Oracle database:

```
[oracle@server1 ~]$ cgexec -g cpuset:db1 /u01/app/oracle/product/12.1.0.1/dbhome_1/bin/sqlplus

SQL*Plus: Release 12.1.0.1.0 Production on Fri Jun 28 13:49:51 2013

Copyright (c) 1982, 2013, Oracle.  All rights reserved.

Enter user-name: / as sysdba
Connected to an idle instance.

SQL> startup
ORACLE instance started.
...
Database opened.
SQL> exit
```

An alternative approach would be to add the PID of your current shell to the tasks pseudo-file in the control group directory. This way all the shell's child processes automatically belong to the control group:

```
[oracle@server1 ~]# echo $$ > /cgroups/oracle_cpuset/db1/tasks
```

Now start the Oracle database as normal. Since the oracle account has been specified as an administrator of the cgroup during its creation, this operation is valid.

In addition to the manual way of adding processes to cgroups, you can make use of the new initialization parameter processor_group available on Linux and Solaris. So instead of using cgexec, you simply set the initialization parameter to point to the existing cgroup:

```
SQL> show parameter processor_group_name

NAME                                    TYPE         VALUE
------------------------------------    -----------  ------------------------------
processor_group_name                    string       db1
```

There are a few ways to validate the cgroup mapping. The most common are probably these:

- The taskset command
- Checking the /proc/pid/cgroup pseudo file
- Using custom options to the ps command

Using the taskset approach, you need the process ID of your database first:

```
[oracle@server1 ~]# ps -ef | grep CDB1
oracle    2149    1  0 14:24 ?        00:00:00 ora_pmon_CDB1
oracle    2151    1  0 14:24 ?        00:00:00 ora_psp0_CDB1
oracle    2153    1  1 14:24 ?        00:00:06 ora_vktm_CDB1

[root@server1 ~]# taskset -cp 2149
pid 2149's current affinity list: 0-5
```

This confirms that the cgroup settings are indeed in place. If you want to know the name associated with the control group as well, check the /proc entry for the process:

```
[oracle@server1 ~]# cat /proc/2149/cgroup | grep cpuset
1:cpuset:/db1
```

And finally, you can view the same information with the ps command as well. Feel free to remove fields you do not need:

```
[oracle@server1 ~]# ps -ax --format uname,pid,cmd,cls,pri,rtprio,cgroup
...
oracle    2149 ora_pmon_CDB1              TS  19      - ... cpuset:/db1
oracle    2151 ora_psp0_CDB1              TS  19      - ... cpuset:/db1
oracle    2153 ora_vktm_CDB1              RR  41      1 ... cpuset:/db1
...
```

With that knowledge it should be relatively simple to track down shared pool and other memory related problems with the database.

Up to this point all the configuration about control groups are transient. In other words, if your server reboots, the control group configuration will all be gone. This will be a serious headache because it might prevent databases from starting if the processorgroup_name parameter is set, but the corresponding control group is not defined at the operating system level. Thankfully you can dump your configuration into a file to be read by the cgconfig service. Use the cgsnapshot utility to write the configuration to standard output and cut/paste the relevant bits into the main configuration file /etc/cgconfig.conf. This time the configuration will be read and applied during the system boot.

In addition to the processor_group_name parameter, a little bit of additional setup work needs to be performed. First of all, it is recommended to set another initialization parameter named use_dedicated_broker to true and also enable the new connection broker in the listener configuration file by setting DEDICATED_THROUGH_BROKER_*listener_name* to on, followed by a reload of the listener. Note that if you are using the new multi-threaded architecture, the use_dedicated_broker parameter is already set to true. You can read more about the multi-threaded architecture in Chapter 2.

Benchmarks

When building a consolidated platform, you might want to consider testing hardware from different vendors to ensure that your choice optimally fits your environment, standard operating procedures, and deployment process. Getting hardware on loan for evaluation is a great way of testing combinations of hardware, software, networking, and storage. From the outset of this testing, you should ensure the following:

- Availability of dedicated resources. For example, if you are evaluating a storage solution, you need resources from storage engineering or whoever is responsible. If necessary, you need operating system support to compile drivers and package them in form of RPMs. If you are resource-constrained, it might be better to postpone the evaluation until more continuous time from the respective teams is available. There is nothing more frustrating than having to return the hardware without having been able to come to a conclusion.

- Define a test plan. Your evaluation should be planned well in advance. Benchmarks, workloads to be run, and (performance) statistics to be gathered need to be defined and documented for each iteration. A minimum number of iterations should be defined as well to minimize statistical outliers.

- Ensure that the hardware can be installed and configured. Your data center needs to have enough rack space, network ports, electricity, etc. The raised floor must support the weight of the hardware, etc. This sounds trivial, but neglecting these factors can lead to significant delay. In reference back to the first bullet point, your data center management also needs to be available to add cables and to configure the essential remote access console for the engineers to take over. If Fiber Channel based storage is required, then the servers need to be connected to the right fabric switches, and initial zoning needs to be performed.

- Vendor support must be secured, at least for the duration of the evaluation. The support you get during the evaluation must be at least adequate. Bear in mind that the vendor ought to be very keen to sell. A poor support quality during the proof-of-concept phase might well be an indication of the things to come. Potential support problems should be treated seriously and put on the critical path if necessary.

- If you are migrating to a different hardware platform such as x86, then you need support from the operational team in case you have any questions about the application after the migration has taken place. This favor can easily be returned to the operational team by scripting the migration process or at least documenting it to a good, detailed standard.

There are a number of benchmarks you can employ, with varying degrees of meaningfulness. The best benchmarks for Oracle workloads are your own applications. No synthetic benchmark, regardless of how well it is written, can represent your workload. If your applications perform well on the new platform, then there is a higher probability of the platform's acceptance and ultimate success. The worst possible outcome for the consolidated platform would be the lack of acceptance!

■ **Caution**   Some of the benchmarks listed and described below can perform destructive testing and/or cause high system load. Always ensure that your benchmark does not have any negative impact on your environment! Do not benchmark outside your controlled and isolated lab environment! Always carefully read the documentation that comes with the benchmark. And be especially careful when it comes to writing benchmarks

---

If you cannot find representative workloads from within the range of applications in use in your organization, you may have to resort to an off-the-shelf benchmark. Large Enterprise Resource Planning systems usually come with a benchmark, but those systems are unlikely candidates for your consolidation platform. If you want to test different components of your system, specialized benchmarks come to mind, but those don't test the platform end-to-end. For storage related testing you could use these benchmarks, for example:

- iozone
- bonnie++
- hdbench
- fio
- And countless others more . . .

Of all the available storage benchmarks, FIO sounds very interesting. It is a very flexible benchmark written by Jens Axboe to test different I/O schedulers in Linux and will be presented in more detail below.

Network-related benchmarks, for example, include the officially Oracle-sanctioned iperf and others. Kevin Closson's Silly Little Benchmark tests memory performance, and so does the University of Virginia's STREAM benchmark. The chips on the mainboard, including the CPU and also cooling, can be tested using the High Performance Linpack benchmark, which is often used in High Performance Computing (HPC).

Each of these benchmarks can be used to get the bigger picture, but none is really suited to assess the system's qualities when used in isolation. More information about the suitability of the platform, especially in respect to storage performance, can be obtained by using Oracle IO Numbers (ORION) or the Silly Little Oracle Benchmark (SLOB) written by Kevin Closson. The below sections are a small selection of available benchmarks.

FIO

FIO is an intelligent I/O testing platform written by Jens Axboe, whom we also have to thank for the Linux I/O schedulers and much more. Out of all the I/O benchmarks, I like FIO because it is very flexible and offers a wealth of output for the performance analyst. As with most of I/O related benchmarks, FIO works best in conjunction with other tools to get a more complete picture.

What is great about the tool is the flexibility, but it requires a little more time to learn all the ins and outs of it. However, if you take the time to learn FIO, you will automatically learn more about Linux as well. FIO benchmark runs are controlled by plain text files with instructions, called a job file. A sample file is shown here; it will be used later in the chapter:

```
[oracle@server1 fio-2.1]# cat rand-read-sync.fio
[random-read-sync]
rw=randread
```

```
size=1024m
bs=8k
directory=/u01/fio/data
ioengine=sync
iodepth=8
direct=1
invalidate=1
ioscheduler=noop
```

In plain English, the job named "random-read-sync" will use the random-read workload, creates a file of 1 GB in size in the directory /u01/fio/data/, and uses a block size of 8 kb, which matches Oracle's standard database block size. A maximum of 8 outstanding I/O requests are allowed, and the Linux I/O scheduler to be used is the noop scheduler since the storage in this case is non-rotational. The use of direct I/O is also requested, and the page cache is invalidated first to avoid file system buffer hits for consistency with the other scripts in the test harness—direct I/O will bypass with buffer cache anyway, so strictly speaking, the directive is redundant.

Linux can use different ways to submit I/O to the storage subsystem—synchronous and asynchronous. Synchronous I/O is also referred to as blocking I/O, since the caller has to wait for the request to finish. Oracle will always use synchronous I/O for single block reads such as index lookups. This is true, for example, even when asynchronous I/O is enabled. The overhead of setting up an asynchronous request is probably not worth it for a single block read.

There are situations wherein synchronous processing of I/O requests does not scale well enough. System designers therefore introduced asynchronous I/O. The name says it all: when you are asynchronously issuing I/O requests, the requestor can continue with other tasks and will "reap" the outstanding I/O request later. This approach greatly enhances concurrency but, at the same time, makes tracing a little more difficult. As you will also see, the latency of individual I/O requests increases with a larger queue depth. Asynchronous I/O is available on Oracle Linux with the libaio package.

Another I/O variant is called direct I/O, which instructs a process to bypass the file system cache. The classic UNIX file system buffer cache is known as the page cache in Linux. This area of memory is the reason why users do not see free memory in Linux. Those portions of memory that are not needed by applications will be used for the page cache instead.

Unless instructed otherwise, the kernel will cache information read from disk in said page cache. This cache is not dedicated to a single process allowing other processes to benefit from it as well. The page cache is a great concept for the many Linux applications but not necessarily beneficial for the Oracle database. Why not? Remember from the preceding introduction that the result of regular file I/O is stored in the page cache in addition to being copied to the user process's buffers. This is wasteful in the context of Oracle since Oracle already employs its own buffer cache for data read from disk. The good intention of a file-system page cache is not needed for the Oracle database since it already has its own cache to counter the relatively slow disk I/O operations.

There are cases in which enabling direct I/O causes performance problems, but those can easily be trapped in test and development environments. However, using direct I/O allows the performance analyst to get more accurate information from performance pages in Oracle. If you see a 1 ms response time from the storage array, you cannot be sure if that is a great response time from the array or rather a cached block from the operating system. If possible, you should consider enabling direct I/O after ensuring that it does not cause performance problems.

To demonstrate the difference between synchronous and asynchronous I/O, consider the following job file for asynchronous I/O.

```
[oracle@server1 fio-2.1]$ cat rand-read-async.fio
[random-read-async]
rw=randread
size=1024m
bs=8k
directory=/u01/fio/data
```

```
ioengine=libaio
iodepth=8
direct=1
invalidate=1
ioscheduler=noop
```

Let's compare the two—some information has been removed in an effort not to clutter the output. First, the synchronous benchmark:

```
[oracle@server1 fio-2.1]$ ./fio rand-read-sync.fio
random-read-sync: (g=0): rw=randread, bs=8K-8K/8K-8K/8K-8K, ioengine=sync, iodepth=8
fio-2.1
Starting 1 process
Jobs: 1 (f=1): [r] [100.0% done] [39240KB/0KB/0KB /s] [4905/0/0 iops] [eta 00m:00s]
random-read-sync: (groupid=0, jobs=1): err= 0: pid=4206: Mon May 27 23:03:22 2013
  read : io=1024.0MB, bw=39012KB/s, iops=4876, runt= 26878msec
    clat (usec): min=71, max=218779, avg=203.77, stdev=605.20
    lat (usec): min=71, max=218780, avg=203.85, stdev=605.20
    clat percentiles (usec):
     |  1.00th=[  189],  5.00th=[  191], 10.00th=[  191], 20.00th=[  193],
     | 30.00th=[  195], 40.00th=[  197], 50.00th=[  205], 60.00th=[  207],
     | 70.00th=[  209], 80.00th=[  211], 90.00th=[  213], 95.00th=[  215],
     | 99.00th=[  225], 99.50th=[  233], 99.90th=[  294], 99.95th=[  318],
     | 99.99th=[  382]
    bw (KB  /s): min=20944, max=39520, per=100.00%, avg=39034.87, stdev=2538.87
    lat (usec) : 100=0.08%, 250=99.63%, 500=0.29%, 750=0.01%, 1000=0.01%
    lat (msec) : 4=0.01%, 20=0.01%, 250=0.01%
  cpu          : usr=0.71%, sys=6.17%, ctx=131107, majf=0, minf=27
  IO depths    : 1=100.0%, 2=0.0%, 4=0.0%, 8=0.0%, 16=0.0%, 32=0.0%, >=64=0.0%
     submit    : 0=0.0%, 4=100.0%, 8=0.0%, 16=0.0%, 32=0.0%, 64=0.0%, >=64=0.0%
     complete  : 0=0.0%, 4=100.0%, 8=0.0%, 16=0.0%, 32=0.0%, 64=0.0%, >=64=0.0%
     issued    : total=r=131072/w=0/d=0, short=r=0/w=0/d=0

Run status group 0 (all jobs):
   READ: io=1024.0MB, aggrb=39012KB/s, minb=39012KB/s, maxb=39012KB/s,
         mint=26878msec, maxt=26878msec

Disk stats (read/write):
  sda: ios=130050/20, merge=0/4, ticks=25188/12, in_queue=25175, util=94.12%
```

The important information here is that the test itself took 26,878 milliseconds to complete, and the storage device completed an average of 4,876 I/O operations per second for an average bandwidth of 39,012KB/s. Latencies are broken down into scheduling latency (not applicable for synchronous I/O— you will see it in the below output) and completion latency. The last number, recorded as "lat" in the output above, is the complete latency and should be the sum of scheduling plus completion latency.

Other important information is that out CPU has not been terribly busy when it executed the benchmark, but this is an average over all cores. The IO depths row shows the IO depth over the duration of the benchmark execution. As you can see, the use of synchronous I/O mandates an I/O depth of 1. The "issued" row lists how many reads and writes have been issued. Finally, the result is repeated again at the bottom of the output. Let's compare this with the asynchronous test:

```
[oracle@server1 fio-2.1]$ ./fio rand-read-async.fio
random-read-async: (g=0): rw=randread, bs=8K-8K/8K-8K/8K-8K, ioengine=libaio, iodepth=8
fio-2.1
Starting 1 process
random-read-async: Laying out IO file(s) (1 file(s) / 1024MB)
Jobs: 1 (f=1): [r] [100.0% done] [151.5MB/0KB/0KB /s] [19.4K/0/0 iops] [eta 00m:00s]
random-read-async: (groupid=0, jobs=1): err= 0: pid=4211: Mon May 27 23:04:28 2013
  read : io=1024.0MB, bw=149030KB/s, iops=18628, runt=   7036msec
    slat (usec): min=5, max=222754, avg= 7.89, stdev=616.46
    clat (usec): min=198, max=14192, avg=408.59, stdev=114.53
     lat (usec): min=228, max=223110, avg=416.61, stdev=626.83
    clat percentiles (usec):
     |  1.00th=[  278], 5.00th=[  306], 10.00th=[  322], 20.00th=[  362],
     | 30.00th=[  398], 40.00th=[  410], 50.00th=[  414], 60.00th=[  422],
     | 70.00th=[  430], 80.00th=[  442], 90.00th=[  470], 95.00th=[  490],
     | 99.00th=[  548], 99.50th=[  580], 99.90th=[  692], 99.95th=[  788],
     | 99.99th=[ 1064]
    bw (KB  /s): min=81328, max=155328, per=100.00%, avg=149248.00, stdev=19559.97
    lat (usec) : 250=0.01%, 500=96.31%, 750=3.61%, 1000=0.06%
    lat (msec) : 2=0.01%, 20=0.01%
  cpu          : usr=3.80%, sys=21.68%, ctx=129656, majf=0, minf=40
  IO depths    : 1=0.1%, 2=0.1%, 4=0.1%, 8=100.0%, 16=0.0%, 32=0.0%, >=64=0.0%
     submit    : 0=0.0%, 4=100.0%, 8=0.0%, 16=0.0%, 32=0.0%, 64=0.0%, >=64=0.0%
     complete  : 0=0.0%, 4=100.0%, 8=0.1%, 16=0.0%, 32=0.0%, 64=0.0%, >=64=0.0%
     issued    : total=r=131072/w=0/d=0, short=r=0/w=0/d=0

Run status group 0 (all jobs):
   READ: io=1024.0MB, aggrb=149030KB/s, minb=149030KB/s, maxb=149030KB/s,
         mint=7036msec, maxt=7036msec

Disk stats (read/write):
  sda: ios=126931/0, merge=0/0, ticks=50572/0, in_queue=50547, util=95.22%
```

Apart from the fact that the test completed a lot faster—7,036msec vs. 26,878msec—you can see that bandwidth is a lot higher. The libaio benchmark provides a lot more IOPS as well: 18,628 vs. 4,876. A doubling of the IO depth yields better bandwidth with the asynchronous case at the expense of the latency of individual requests. You do not need to spend too much time trying to find the maximum I/O depth on your platform, since Oracle will transparently make use of the I/O subsystem, and you should probably not change any potential underscore parameter.

You should also bear in mind that maximizing I/O operations per second is not the only target variable when optimizing storage. A queue depth of 32, for example, will provide a large number of IOPS, but this number means little without the corresponding response time. Compare the output below, which has been generated with the same job file as before but a queue depth of 32 instead of 8:

```
[oracle@server1 fio-2.1]$ ./fio rand-read-async-32.fio
random-read-async: (g=0): rw=randread, bs=8K-8K/8K-8K/8K-8K, ioengine=libaio, iodepth=32
[...]
  read : io=1024.0MB, bw=196768KB/s, iops=24595, runt=   5329msec
```

```
[...]
    lat (usec) : 500=0.01%, 750=0.01%, 1000=0.01%
    lat (msec) : 2=99.84%, 4=0.13%
```

The number of IOPS has increased from 18,628 to 24,595, and the execution time is down to 5,329 milliseconds instead of 7,036, but this has come at a cost. Instead of microseconds, 99.84% of the I/O requests now complete in milliseconds.

When you are working with storage and Linux, FIO is a great tool to help you understand the storage solution as well as the hardware connected against it. FIO has a lot more to offer with regards to workloads. You can read and write sequentially or randomly, and you can mix these as well—even within a single benchmark run! The permutations of I/O type, block sizes, direct, and buffered I/O, combined with the options to run multiple jobs and use differently sized memory pages, etc., make FIO one of the best benchmark tools available. There is a great README as part of FIO, and its author has a HOWTO document, as well, for those who want to know all the detail: http://www.bluestop.org/fio/HOWTO.txt.

Oracle I/O numbers

The ORION tool has been available for quite some time, initially as a separate download from Oracle's website and now as part of the database installation. This, in a way, is a shame since a lot of its attractiveness initially came from the fact that a host did *not* require a database installation. If you can live with a different, lower, version number, then you can still download ORION for almost all platforms from Oracle's OTN website. At the time of this writing, the below URL allowed you to download the binaries: http://www.oracle.com/technetwork/topics/index-089595.html. The above link also allows you to download the ORION user's guide, which is more comprehensive than this section. For 11.2 onwards you find the ORION documentation as part of the official documentation set in the "Performance Tuning Guide". Instead of the 11.1 binaries downloadable as a standalone package, this book will use the ones provided with the Oracle server installation.

ORION works best during the evaluation phase of a new platform, without user-data on your logical unit numbers (LUNs). (As with all I/O benchmarking tools, write testing is **destructive**!) The package will use asynchronous I/O and large pages, where possible, for reads and writes to concurrently submit I/O requests to the operating system. Asynchronous I/O in this context means the use of libaio on Linux or equivalent library as discussed in the FIO benchmark section above. You can quite easily see that the ORION slave processes use io_submit and io_getevents by executing strace on them:

```
[root@server1 ~]# strace -cp 28168
Process 28168 attached - interrupt to quit
^CProcess 28168 detached
% time     seconds  usecs/call     calls    errors syscall
------ ----------- ----------- --------- --------- ----------------
 97.79    0.323254           4     86925           io_submit
  2.11    0.006968           1     12586           io_getevents
  0.10    0.000345           0     25172           times
------ ----------- ----------- --------- --------- ----------------
100.00    0.330567               124683           total
[root@server1 ~]#
```

The process with ID 28168, to which the strace session attached, was a running ORION session.

So what does ORION allow you to do? It's easiest to start off with the way it generates I/O workloads. Internally ORION uses a two-dimensional matrix depicting small I/O and large I/O requests. Columns in the matrix represent small I/O requests; rows are large I/O requests. This matrix approach is illustrated in Table 3-3:

Table 3-3. *The Point Matrix Used Internally by ORION*

Type of I/O	# concurrent small I/Os			
# concurrent large I/Os	0	1	2	. . .
0	Data point	Data point	Data point	. . .
1	Data point	Data point	Data point	. . .
2	Data point	Data point	Data point	. . .
. . .	. . .	. . .	. . .	. . .

Small I/O requests are user-configurable but default to 8k, which equals the default block size of modern Oracle databases and most of the other databases. Large I/O requests can also be defined as an input parameter to the benchmark run; they default to 1MB, which is in line with the default maximum size of a single I/O on most platforms. Benchmarks generate load by increasing the concurrency of outstanding I/O requests, either with or without additional large I/O requests. For each element in the matrix, ORION records information and presents it later in text files. To use ORION, you need to pass an argument to the mandatory parameter "run." It can take the following values:

- Simple: A simple run which tests random small 8k in isolation, i.e., uses row 0 in the above matrix: multiple concurrent small I/Os but no large ones. It then runs tests using multiple concurrent large I/Os, i.e., stays in column 0. It does not combine small and large I/Os.

- Normal: traverses the whole matrix and tests various combinations of small and large I/Os. This run can take a while to complete.

- DSS: Uniquely tests random large I/Os at increasing concurrency, stays in column 0 in the above matrix.

- OLTP: tests only small I/Os, stays in row 0 in the above matrix.

- Advanced: allows you define your own workload by picking rows, columns, or individual data points in the matrix. Advanced testing is out of scope of this chapter.

There are some concerns whether or not ORION really represents a true database workload. One argument against ORION is that it does not have to deal with a buffer cache and its maintenance and some other work an active Oracle instance has to perform. Despite the few downsides to ORION, you should assume that ORION is a good tool, albeit not 100 percent accurate. It certainly is good enough to get a better understanding of your storage subsystem when used as a baseline.

Before you can start a benchmark run with ORION, you need to define a set of targets you want to test against. These are usually LUNs provisioned from the storage array or a directly attached block device, maybe even via PCIe. The LUNs need to be listed in an input file and terminated with a new line. If you were testing a system with 5 LUNs for a future ASM disk group "DATA," the file could have the following contents:

```
/dev/mapper/asm_data_disk001p1
/dev/mapper/asm_data_disk001p2
/dev/mapper/asm_data_disk001p3
/dev/mapper/asm_data_disk001p4
/dev/mapper/asm_data_disk001p5
```

Note that the devices have been partitioned in this setup. This was done to align the partition with the storage array block boundaries, based on a vendor recommendation. Partitioning a LUN also indicates that it is in use and thus prevents it from being accidentally deleted.

■ **Tip** If you are using flash-based storage, then it almost always required to align the partition at a 4k boundary—remember, the page size for NAND flash is usually 4k. You could also review the vendor documentation to update tunables in `/sys/block/sdx/queue/`.

The LUNs need to be saved in a file called `orion.lun`. You can optionally pass a parameter "testname" to ORION, in which case the LUNs need to be saved as *testname*.lun. ORION will make use of large pages by default. If your system does not have large pages configured, ORION will error unless you specify the -hugenotneeded flag. To perform a simple, read-only OLTP-like test named "test1," you need a file test1.lun containing the LUNs to test against. Make sure that the oracle account has access rights to these LUNs. You invoke ORION using its complete path. After the calibration run you can check the output of the "summary" file to get an idea about your storage subsystem:

```
ORION VERSION 12.1.0.1.0

Command line:
-run oltp -testname test1

These options enable these settings:
Test: test1
Small IO size: 8 KB
Large IO size: 1024 KB
IO types: small random IOs, large random IOs
Sequential stream pattern: RAID-0 striping for all streams
Writes: 0%
Cache size: not specified
Duration for each data point: 60 seconds
Small Columns:,      1,      2,      3,      4,      5,      6,      7,      8,      9,
10,     11,     12,     13,     14,     15,     16,     17,     18,     19,     20
Large Columns:,      0
Total Data Points: 21

Name: /dev/sdc  Size: 1073741824
1 files found.

Maximum Small IOPS=9899 @ Small=17 and Large=0
Small Read Latency: avg=1711 us, min=791 us, max=12316 us, std dev=454 us @ Small=17 and Large=0

Minimum Small Latency=123.58 usecs @ Small=1 and Large=0
Small Read Latency: avg=124 us, min=41 us, max=4496 us, std dev=76 us @ Small=1 and Large=0
Small Read / Write Latency Histogram @ Small=17 and Large=0
        Latency:            # of IOs (read)        # of IOs (write)
        0 - 1       us:         0                     0
        2 - 4       us:         0                     0
        4 - 8       us:         0                     0
        8 - 16      us:         0                     0
        16 - 32     us:         0                     0
```

32 - 64	us:	10	0
64 - 128	us:	364355	0
128 - 256	us:	90531	0
256 - 512	us:	4281	0
512 - 1024	us:	2444	0
1024 - 2048	us:	244	0
2048 - 4096	us:	38	0
4096 - 8192	us:	8	0
8192 - 16384	us:	0	0
16384 - 32768	us:	0	0
32768 - 65536	us:	0	0
65536 - 131072	us:	0	0
131072 - 262144	us:	0	0
262144 - 524288	us:	0	0
524288 - 1048576	us:	0	0
1048576 - 2097152	us:	0	0
2097152 - 4194304	us:	0	0
4194304 - 8388608	us:	0	0
8388608 - 16777216	us:	0	0
16777216 - 33554432	us:	0	0
33554432 - 67108864	us:	0	0
67108864 - 134217728	us:	0	0
134217728 - 268435456	us:	0	0a

This output has been produced from a testbed environment; the numbers are not to be used for comparison with a real storage backend.

Large I/Os are random by default but can be defined as sequential if desired. To add write testing to the benchmark, you need to tell ORION to do so. The -write flag indicates how many percent of I/Os should be writes, and according to the documentation the default is 0.

■ **Caution** Write testing WILL DESTROY existing data. Double or triple check that the LUNs you test against do NOT contain data!

At the end of the benchmark, you are presented with a lot of information. All the result files are prefixed with the test name you chose with an added time stamp:

```
[oracle@server1 temp]# ls -l
total 104
-rw-r--r--. 1 oracle oracle 19261 Jul 22 10:13 test1_20130722_0953_hist.txt
-rw-r--r--. 1 oracle oracle   742 Jul 22 10:13 test1_20130722_0953_iops.csv
-rw-r--r--. 1 oracle oracle   761 Jul 22 10:13 test1_20130722_0953_lat.csv
-rw-r--r--. 1 oracle oracle   570 Jul 22 10:13 test1_20130722_0953_mbps.csv
-rw-r--r--. 1 oracle oracle  1859 Jul 22 10:13 test1_20130722_0953_summary.txt
-rw-r--r--. 1 oracle oracle 18394 Jul 22 10:13 test1_20130722_0953_trace.txt
-rw-r--r--. 1 oracle oracle    20 Jul 22 09:46 test1.lun
[oracle@server1 temp]#
```

The summary file is the first one to look at. It shows the command line parameters, I/O sizes, the I/O type among other information. From a storage-backend perspective, the matrix data points are most interesting:

```
Duration for each data point: 60 seconds
Small Columns:,     1,     2,     ...     20
Large Columns:,     0
Total Data Points: 21
```

Here you see that the OLTP test does not use large I/Os at all. The name and size of the LUNs used are also recorded just prior to the performance figures:

```
Maximum Small IOPS=9899 @ Small=17 and Large=0
Small Read Latency: avg=1711 us, min=791 us, max=12316 us, std dev=454 us @ Small=17 and Large=0

Minimum Small Latency=123.58 usecs @ Small=1 and Large=0
Small Read Latency: avg=124 us, min=41 us, max=4496 us, std dev=76 us @ Small=1 and Large=0
Small Read / Write Latency Histogram @ Small=17 and Large=0
```

Following that information, you are shown the same latency histogram you were presented at the end of the ORION run. In the above example, that's the histogram for the data point of 17 small I/Os and 0 large I/Os. All other histograms can be found in the test1_20130722_0953_hist.txt file. The other files contain the information listed in Table 3-4.

Table 3-4. *Files Generated During an ORION Benchmark (taken from the file headers)*

File name	Contents as per file header
*_hist.txt	Contains histograms of the latencies observed for each data point test. Each data point test used a fixed number of outstanding small and large I/Os.
	For each data point, histograms are printed for the latencies of small reads, small writes, large reads, and large writes.
	The value specifies the number of I/Os that were observed within the bucket's latency range.
*_iops.csv	Contains the rates sustained by small I/Os in IOPS. Each value corresponds to a data point test that used a fixed number of outstanding small and large I/Os.
*_lat.csv	Contains the average latency sustained by small I/Os in microseconds. Each value corresponds to a data point test that used a fixed number of outstanding small and large I/Os.
*_mbps.csv	Contains the rates sustained by large I/Os in MBps. Each value corresponds to a data point test that used a fixed number of outstanding small and large I/Os.
*_trace.txt	Raw data

The use of ORION should have given you a better understanding of the capabilities of your storage subsystem. Bear in mind that the figures do not represent a true Oracle workload due to the lack of the synchronization in the Oracle-shared memory structures. Furthermore, ORION does not use the pread/pwrite calls Oracle employs for single block I/O. However, the initial test of your storage subsystem should be a good enough approximation.

There is a lot more to ORION which could not be covered here, especially when it comes to testing I/O performance of multiple LUNs. It is possible to simulate striping and mirroring, and even to simulate log write behavior, by instructing the software to stream data sequentially.

Silly little Oracle Benchmark

Don't be fooled by the name—SLOB is one of the most interesting and hotly discussed Oracle-related storage benchmarks you can get hold of. It has been released by Kevin Closson and has extensively been discussed on social media and weblogs. SLOB is designed to test the Oracle storage backend and is available in source code. It relies on a C-program's control, the execution of the actual benchmark work defined in shell scripts and SQL. Since its initial release SLOB has been enhanced, and a new version of the benchmark has been released as SLOB 2. The following section is about SLOB2 unless stated otherwise.

■ **Caution**   Do NOT run SLOB outside your controlled lab environment! It has the potential to cause serious trouble, such as creating severe queuing delays and a very noticeable performance hit on your shared storage system. The purpose of this section is to give you a tool to **evaluate** storage solutions for your consolidation environment, before the solution is deployed. So again, do not run SLOB outside your lab, especially not on non-lab storage (storage arrays)! Also ensure that you read the accompanying documentation carefully and make yourself comfortable with the implications of running SLOB.

Before you can actually use SLOB, you need to perform some setup work. The first step is to create a database, and then you load the test data. SLOB is made available here:

```
http://kevinclosson.wordpress.com/2013/05/02/slob-2-a-significant-update-links-are-here/
```

At the time of this writing, the May 5 release was current. Download and uncompress the file to a convenient location on the server you want to benchmark. Let's assume you unzipped it to /home/oracle/SLOB.

Creating and Populating the SLOB Database

The first step when working with the tool is to create the database. For the purpose of our testing, the database will be created as a regular database as opposed to a Container Database. You can read more about the various database types available in Oracle 12.1 in Chapter 7. Despite SLOB being developed for databases pre-Oracle 12.1, you can use the supplied init.ora and database creation script. Before you launch them, add the database to the oratab file, for example:

```
SLOB:/u01/app/oracle/product/12.1.0.1/dbhome_1:N
```

Next, review the initialization file to be found in ~/SLOB/misc/create_database_kit. Change the file to match your environment, especially with regards to the Oracle Managed Files (OMF) parameters. You should definitely consider changing the value for compatible to 12.0 at least. You may also need to increase the value for processes. You can optionally create a password file if you would like to connect remotely. Ensure that the directories referenced in the initialization file exist and that the database owner has read-write permissions to them as well. The file used for the below example is shown here for reference. Instead of Automatic Memory Management, as in the original create. ora file, Automatic Shared Memory Management is used.

```
db_create_file_dest = '/u01/oradata/'
db_name = SLOB
compatible=12.1.0.1.0
UNDO_MANAGEMENT=AUTO
db_block_size = 8192
```

```
db_files = 300
processes = 1000
sga_target=10G
filesystemio_options=setall
```

Note that the above initialization file will only be used to create the database. The initialization file for the actual benchmark test runs will be different and is found in the top-level SLOB directory named simple.ora. Nevertheless, once the database is created, keep a note of the control_files parameter to ensure you do not have to dig around looking for them later.

Now create the database by executing cr_db.sql. A few minutes later, a minimalistic database is ready. It is not in archivelog mode, which could be important for your testing.

In the next step the wait kit needs to be compiled. This is not normally a problem with Linux-based systems but can be a bit of a challenge on Solaris and AIX. If you followed the pre-requisites for the database installation on Linux, you should already have a compiler, linker and interpreter for Makefiles. On other platforms you should have everything except for the C-compiler "cc." Regardless of platform, once you have the compiler suite in place, you use the make command in ~/SLOB/wait_kit to compile the code, as shown here on a Linux system:

```
[oracle@server1 SLOB]$ cd wait_kit/
[oracle@server1 wait_kit]$ make
rm -fr *.o mywait trigger create_sem
cc      -c -o mywait.o mywait.c
cc -o mywait mywait.o
cc      -c -o trigger.o trigger.c
cc -o trigger trigger.o
cc      -c -o create_sem.o create_sem.c
cc -o create_sem create_sem.o
cp mywait trigger create_sem ../
rm -fr *.o
[oracle@server1 wait_kit]$
```

The empty database has to be populated with test data next. SLOB works by creating a number of schemas (users) on the tablespace created as part of the cr_db.sql script named IOPS: 128 by default. A new feature of SLOB 2 allows you to scale the data volume per user. Unless defined otherwise, the setup script used to create the test data will create just a single table named CF1 with a unique index in each schema. The table structure is especially prepared for the benchmark so that a block contains a single row only. By default, 10,000 rows are created based on a seed table but in completely random order so that no two users have the same dataset.

If you would like to scale the dataset per user, you need to modify the SLOB configuration script slob.conf and modify the SCALE variable. The default of 10,000 rows equates to approximately 80 MB per user on the lab test system:

```
SQL> select sum(bytes/power(1024,2)) mb,segment_type
  2    from dba_segments
  3   where owner = 'USER1'
  4   group by segment_type
  5  /

        MB SEGMENT_TYPE
---------- ------------------
     .1875 INDEX
        80 TABLE
```

The total space needed for the default 128 users therefore is approximately 10,240 MB. Larger data volumes require a larger value for the SCALE variable. If you are considering increasing the data set by adding more users, then don't. Comments in the setup script indicate that the tested maximum number of users is 128, so instead of increasing their number, you should use the SCALE variable.

The data is loaded into the database by calling the setup.sh script. It takes two parameters: the tablespace to store the data on, and optionally the number of users:

```
[oracle@server1 SLOB]$ ./setup.sh
FATAL: ./setup.sh args
Usage : ./setup.sh: <tablespace name> <optional: number of users>
[oracle@server1 SLOB]$ ./setup.sh IOPS 128

NOTIFY: Load Parameters (slob.conf):

LOAD_PARALLEL_DEGREE == 12
SCALE == 10000
ADMIN_SQLNET_SERVICE == ""
CONNECT_STRING == "/ as sysdba"
NON_ADMIN_CONNECT_STRING ==

NOTIFY: Testing connectivity to the instance to validate slob.conf settings.
NOTIFY: ./setup.sh: Successful test connection: "sqlplus -L / as sysdba"

NOTIFY: Creating and loading seed table.

Table created.

PL/SQL procedure successfully completed.

NOTIFY: Seed table loading procedure has exited.
NOTIFY: Setting up user   1  2  3  4  5  6  7  8  9  10  11  12
[...]
NOTIFY: Setting up user   121  122  123  124  125  126  127  128

Table dropped.

NOTIFY: ./setup.sh: Loading procedure complete (158 seconds). Please check
./cr_tab_and_load.out for any errors

[oracle@server1 SLOB]$
```

Depending on the quality of your storage subsystem, this process can take a little while. You should heed the advice and check the logfile for errors.

Benchmarking Storage with SLOB

The SLOB kit allows you to run three different benchmarks, according to the documentation. Unlike the previously introduced benchmarks, which focused on physical I/O, SLOB also allows you to check how well your architecture can deal with logical I/O. The test cases are categorized in the documentation into focus areas:

Physical I/O on Oracle data files. For this test you need a small buffer cache, ideally less than 100 MB. The test is useful to see how well your storage subsystem is attached to the server and how much physical I/O it can provide.

Logical I/O test. This test case requires a large SGA and especially a large buffer cache. It tests how well your architecture can scale logical I/O. If you think of today's multi-socket systems with their complex memory arrangements in form of level 1, level 2, last-level cache, DRAM remotely and locally attached, then this test suddenly starts to make a lot of sense.

The final test is about redo. Like the previous LIO test, it too requires a large SGA, in such a way that the database writer processes do not have to flush dirty buffers to disk.

Controlling SLOB

Unlike the initial release of the software, SLOB 2 is controlled slightly differently, by means of a configuration file. The slob.conf file controls the aspects of the benchmark such as allowed levels of concurrency as well as the ratio between reads and writes. In the initial SLOB release, you needed to call the main benchmark script-runit.sh-with two parameters. One indicated the number of readers and the other the number of writers. Concurrency was not permitted. SLOB 2 uses a configuration file to define the characteristics of a given benchmark execution. A sample file is shown here:

```
[oracle@server1 SLOB]$ cat slob.conf

UPDATE_PCT=0
RUN_TIME=60
WORK_LOOP=0
SCALE=10000
WORK_UNIT=256
REDO_STRESS=HEAVY
LOAD_PARALLEL_DEGREE=12
SHARED_DATA_MODULUS=0

# Settings for SQL*Net connectivity:
#ADMIN_SQLNET_SERVICE=slob
#SQLNET_SERVICE_BASE=slob
#SQLNET_SERVICE_MAX=2
#SYSDBA_PASSWD="change_on_install"

export UPDATE_PCT RUN_TIME WORK_LOOP SCALE WORK_UNIT LOAD_PARALLEL_DEGREE REDO_STRESS SHARED_DATA_
MODULUS

[oracle@server1 SLOB]$
```

As you can easily see, these are BASH-style variables sourced into the runit.sh script at runtime to provide the configuration. The most important variables for the purpose of evaluating storage are listed here:

> **UPDATE_PCT**. This parameter replaces the explicit number of readers to writers in the initial release. Specify in percent how many statements should be DML. A setting of 0 or 100 is equivalent to a call to runit.sh with 0 readers or writers respectively. The readme states that values between 51 and 99 are non-deterministic.

> **RUN_TIME**. Setting RUN_TIME to a value in seconds allows you to terminate a given benchmark run after a given interval. The documentation recommends that when you decide to use RUN_TIME, please set WORK_LOOP to 0.

> **WORK_LOOP**. Instead of terminating an execution of runit.sh after a fixed amount of time, you could alternatively specify WORK_LOOP to measure how long it takes for your system to complete a given number of iterations of the workload. When doing so, you should set RUN_TIME to a large number to allow for WORK_LOOP iterations to complete.

For a basic set of tests, the other parameters can be left at their defaults. But SLOB 2 does not stop there. SLOB is made for the Oracle researcher, and there are plenty of methods for trying it in different ways.

Executing a Benchmark

The actual benchmark is initiated by the script `runit.sh`. It takes just one parameter: the number of sessions to be spawned. The script performs the following steps for locally executed tests in a single-instance Oracle database environment:

1. Defines a default set of parameters in case those in `slob.conf` are incomplete before it sources the slob.conf file into the currently executing environment.

2. Provides sanity checks to the environment.

3. Performs a log switch in the database.

4. Sets up operating system monitoring using `vmstat`, `iostat`, and `mpstat`.

5. Creates the required number of user sessions. Values from `slob.conf` are passed to the script responsible for the benchmark, named `slob.sql`. The processes do not execute just yet—they are "held in check" by a semaphore.

6. Creates an AWR snapshot and gets the current wall clock time.

7. Starts the execution of all withheld processes.

8. Waits for the execution of all sessions to finish.

9. Calculates the run time, creates another snapshot, and generates AWR reports in text and HTML format.

Notice that the resulting AWR reports are not preserved; subsequent executions of SLOB will overwrite them. Users of SLOB, especially Yury Velikanov, commented that for very long running benchmarks, you should disable automatic AWR snapshots. Depending on your AWR settings, it is perfectly possible to have an automatic snapshot in between your benchmark run. The logic in the `runit.sh` script takes the last two snapshots and generates the AWR report, which causes problems if an automatic snapshot has been taken after the initial one. The automatic snapshot interval should be set to a high enough value, not 0, because this will turn off automatic AWR snapshots.

These concerns about losing the AWR information of previous benchmarks can easily be addressed by writing a small test harness. A sample wrapper script around runit.sh is shown here:

```bash
#!/bin/bash
#
# Martin Bach 2013
#
# runit_wrapper.sh is a wrapper to preserve the output of the supporting files from
# individual SLOB version 2 test runs

# list of files to preserve. Not all are necesarrily generated during a test run.
FILES="awr.txt awr.*html  awr*.gz iostat.out vmstat.out mpstat.out db_stats.out "
FILES="$FILES sqlplus.out slob.conf"

# setting up ...
[[ ! -f $ORACLE_HOME/bin/sqlplus || -z $ORACLE_SID ]] && {
        echo ERR: Your Oracle environment is not set correctly it appears.
        echo ERR: source oraenv into your session and try again
        exit
}

# Two command line parameters are needed
(( $# != 2 )) && {
        echo ERR: wrong number of command line parameters
        echo usage: $0 testname num_sessions
        exit
}

TESTNAME=$1
NUM_SESSIONS=$2

# The script creates a directory to hold the test results. That will fail
# if the directory already exists
[[ -d $TESTNAME ]] && {
        echo ERR: A test with name $TESTNAME has been found already.
        echo ERR: Please double check your parameters
        exit
}

echo INFO: preparing to preserve output for test $TESTNAME
mkdir $TESTNAME || {
        echo ERR: cannot create a directory to store the output for $TESTNAME
        exit
}

# set the automatic gathering of snapshots to a very high value.
# Note that turning it off (interval => 0) means you cannot even
# take manual snapshots.
echo INFO: increasing AWR snapshot interval
```

```
$ORACLE_HOME/bin/sqlplus / as sysdba > /dev/null <<EOF
spool $TESTNAME/awr_config.txt
select systimestamp as now from dual;
select * from DBA_HIST_WR_CONTROL;
exec DBMS_WORKLOAD_REPOSITORY.MODIFY_SNAPSHOT_SETTINGS(interval=>360)
exit
EOF

# finally run the benchmark. Keep the output too
./runit.sh $NUM_SESSIONS 2>&1 | tee ${TESTNAME}/runit.sh.log

# preserve the generated files in $TESTNAME
for FILE in $FILES; do
        [[ -f $FILE ]] && {
                echo INFO: moving file $FILE to directory $TESTNAME
                cp $FILE $TESTNAME 2> /dev/null
        }
done

# create a copy of awr.txt for the use with awr_info.sh
cp ${TESTNAME}/awr.txt ${TESTNAME}/awr.txt.${NUM_SESSIONS}

# finally preserve all initialisation parameters
$ORACLE_HOME/bin/sqlplus / as sysdba 2> /dev/null <<EOF
create pfile='$(pwd)/${TESTNAME}/init.ora' from memory;
exit
EOF

echo INFO: done
```

Notes on SLOB usage

If you intend to run the Physical I/O or PIO test, you need a small SGA—which is easier said than done. With multi-socket/multi-core servers, Oracle will automatically derive default values for initialization parameters, making it difficult to get small buffer caches. Limiting the cpu_count to a low value—2 or 4—is usually a good starting point, and you could also use manual SGA management, as we know it from Oracle 9i. The below is a sample initialization file with manual SGA management, based on the previously mentioned "simple.ora" initialization file which you should review and adapt if needed:

```
db_create_file_dest = '/u01/oradata/'
db_name = SLOB
compatible=12.1.0.1.0
UNDO_MANAGEMENT=AUTO
db_block_size = 8192
db_files = 300
processes = 500
control_files = /u01/oradata/SLOB/controlfile/o1_mf_812m3gj5_.ctl

shared_pool_size = 600M
large_pool_size = 16M
java_pool_size = 0
```

```
streams_pool_size = 0
db_cache_size=48M
cpu_count = 2

filesystemio_options=setall
parallel_max_servers=0
recyclebin=off
pga_aggregate_target=1G
workarea_size_policy=auto
...
```

There are some further options you can set that have been omitted here for brevity. Starting the database with this parameter file allowed the creation of a really small SGA, as you can see from the query below:

```
SQL> select component,current_size/power(1024,2) mb
  2    from v$sga_dynamic_Components
  3   where current_size <> 0
  4  /


COMPONENT                                                            MB
---------------------------------------------------------------- ----------
shared pool                                                         600
large pool                                                           16
DEFAULT buffer cache                                                 48
```

According to the documentation, the limitation of the cpu_count parameter does not influence the benchmark kit to drive I/O. Running SLOB sessions with an increasing number of sessions, you might notice that the throughput increases up to a point at which the CPUs are completely saturated and form the bottleneck. When reviewing the AWR reports, you should pay attention to the I/O latencies and the throughput. The most interesting sections are the "Load Profile," "Top 10 Foreground Events by Total Wait Time," and the "IO profile":

IO Profile	Read+Write/Second	Read/Second	Write/Second
~~	-----------------	---------------	--------------
Total Requests:	22,138.9	22,132.9	6.0
Database Requests:	22,132.8	22,128.0	4.8
Optimized Requests:	0.0	0.0	0.0
Redo Requests:	0.9	0.0	0.9
Total (MB):	173.0	173.0	0.1
Database (MB):	172.9	172.9	0.0
Optimized Total (MB):	0.0	0.0	0.0
Redo (MB):	0.0	0.0	0.0
Database (blocks):	22,133.8	22,128.3	5.5
Via Buffer Cache (blocks):	22,133.8	22,128.3	5.5
Direct (blocks):	0.0	0.0	0.0

The above output shows the AWR report for an execution of runit.sh 16 and a 16MB buffer cache. This observation is confirmed by collectl, too, which has been running in parallel:

```
#<----CPU[HYPER]-----><---------------Disks---------------->
#cpu sys inter  ctxsw KBRead  Reads Size KBWrit Writes Size
   2   1 42236  47425 182168  22771    8      0      0    0
   2   1 43790  47359 182272  22776    8     16      1   16
   2   1 42955  46644 179040  22380    8     24      3    8
```

Which processing lead to those numbers? So far it has not been described what the benchmark does in more detail. The logic is defined in the slob.sql file. The new file combines the application logic, which has been defined in two different files, readers.sql and writers.sql. The new file follows the same model.

For a read-only-workload, in which UPDATE_PCT is set to 0 in slob.conf, you will see select statements exclusively similar to this one taken from the AWR report:

```
SQL> select * from table(dbms_xplan.display_cursor('309mwpa4tk161'))

PLAN_TABLE_OUTPUT
-------------------------------------------------------------------------------
SQL_ID 309mwpa4tk161, child number 0
-------------------------------------
SELECT COUNT(C2) FROM CF1 WHERE CUSTID > ( :B1 - :B2 ) AND (CUSTID <
:B1 )

Plan hash value: 1497866750
```

```
-------------------------------------------------------------------------------
| Id  | Operation                           | Name  | Rows  | Bytes | Cost (%CPU)| Time     |
-------------------------------------------------------------------------------
|   0 | SELECT STATEMENT                    |       |       |       |  259 (100)|          |
|   1 |  SORT AGGREGATE                     |       |     1 |   133 |           |          |
|*  2 |   FILTER                            |       |       |       |           |          |
|   3 |    TABLE ACCESS BY INDEX ROWID BATCHED | CF1 |   256 | 34048 |  259 (0)| 00:00:01 |
|*  4 |     INDEX RANGE SCAN                | I_CF1 |   256 |       |    2 (0)| 00:00:01 |
-------------------------------------------------------------------------------
```

```
Predicate Information (identified by operation id):
---------------------------------------------------

   2 - filter(:B1>:B1-:B2)
   4 - access("CUSTID">:B1-:B2 AND "CUSTID"<:B1)

23 rows selected.
```

As you can see, the reader part of the script will perform an index range scan. It is advisable to tail the database's alert log when creating the data set, as well as when you are running the benchmark, to ensure that you are not running out of space or other system resources, such as processes.

Summary

This chapter has taken you on a journey about possible hardware solutions for your consolidation project. When thinking about the consolidation platform, you should definitely consider the Linux operating system. It is dynamically developed, and many great minds spend a lot of time contributing to it. When this chapter was written, Oracle used Linux as the primary development platform, which gives adopters of the platform early access to bug fixes and enhancements.

As an additional benefit it runs on industry-standard hardware, which has been deployed thousands of times. Also, Oracle has invested a lot of effort in the Linux platform, as well as making it future-proof. It has been said in the introduction, but it should be repeated here: these ideas you just read about should invite you to critically reflect about them! Test, evaluate, and sample until you have come to the conclusion that the platform you have chosen for iteration 1 of the hosting platform is right for your organization.

■ ■ ■

Supporting Software

After introducing new trends in hardware in Chapter 3, you can read more on how to exploit these with appropriate software. Choosing the operating environment for the next generation hosting platform is equal in importance to choosing the hardware. Hardware and software should be certified both from the vendors and in-house. Strong support contracts with defined Service Level Agreements must be put into place to allow the quick turnaround of troubleshooting problems.

You should not underestimate the amount of testing it takes to certify an Oracle stack, even if it is primarily for the database! This certification requires joint efforts by the storage, operating system, and database engineering teams. Effective management of this joint team effort is important to the overall success. This sounds too logical to be added to this introductory section of the chapter, but experience shows that a strict separation of duties, as seen in many large organizations, requires re-learning how to work together.

Enabling Software Solutions

After spending time on evaluating the hardware for the consolidation project, the next step is to think about deployment of the Oracle 12c database. In the author's opinion, there are two different approaches, depending on the importance of the environment. These approaches are virtualization and clustering. They both are centered on the magic terms "high availability" and "disaster recovery." Clustering can be further broken down, resulting in:

- Virtualization-based solutions
- Using active/passive clusters
- Using active/active clusters

What shouldn't be hidden from the discussion is the fact that complexity and cost increase in almost the same way as the protection from failure!

High Availability Considerations

The "high availability" baseline is a single instance Oracle database. The following discussion assumes there are no unnecessary single points of failure in the chosen hardware, which can potentially render the whole solution very vulnerable. If you want high availability, then you should know it will come at a cost.

Using virtualization-based solutions usually involves a single instance Oracle database installation in a virtual machine. The physical location of a virtual machine is often irrelevant, and, rather than mapping a virtual machine to a host, the mapping is on a logical grouping of hosts. Oracle VM Manager calls such a logical group of servers a server pool. Other vendors use different terminology but the same principle. In case a host has an unrecoverable failure and must reboot, it is possible to migrate virtual machines from the failed host to another host in the cluster, capacity permitting. However, there does not have to be a failure: (live) migration of virtual machines is applicable for planned hardware maintenance or to deal with capacity problems on a given host. Almost all visualization solutions try to automate dealing with failure transparently, which plays nicely toward the requirement to not require a lot of hands-on management.

Another popular approach is to use an active-passive cluster. Most active/passive clusters are still easy to manage since the cluster management software takes care of resource management and failover to the passive node. You achieve higher availability than with a single instance database by means of the cluster framework. A lot of cluster frameworks exist for Oracle from all the major vendors, operating off the following simple principles:

- A dedicated active/passive cluster consists of two nodes. More nodes often do not make sense in active/passive configurations. Quite often, such a setup is dedicated to a specific product and does not normally host more than a couple of databases.

- Storage is provided to the active node. There are exceptions when a cluster logical volume manager, such as Oracle's Automatic Storage Management, or alternative is in place.

- Important entities are grouped into cluster resources. From an Oracle point-of-view, these include the OFA and database file systems, the listener process(es) and the database(s), among others. Resources can be logically grouped.

- All resources have metadata associated with them. Among the information stored is a check interval, the command to check for the resource's status, start retries, and a failover process.

- An agent process monitors resources according to the metadata stored.

- In case a resource has been detected as "failed," and it cannot be restarted on the node it was running on, it will be started on the passive node.

Again, most of this processing is automated internally by the aforementioned agents and the cluster framework. There will be an outage to the clients, at least for the duration of the instance recovery. If you are unlucky, you might have to wait for a file system consistency check after the Oracle-related file systems are mounted to the passive node. Cluster file systems can prevent this problem from happening, but, for most, you need to pay an extra license.

The final option you have at your disposal is to cluster your database in an active/active way. The only way to do so is to use the Real Application Clusters option to the Oracle database. RAC takes away the strict 1:1 mapping of the Oracle instance to the database. Remember that the Oracle instance is the transient part of Oracle in memory, whereas the files on hard disk are referred to as the database. In RAC systems, you have multiple instances running on multiple hosts accessing the same database, so RAC is a high-availability solution and does not protect you from disasters or human error. RAC has been designed so the cluster appears as one database to the end user, and sophisticated programming allows for a single SGA across all the cluster nodes. RAC can be hugely beneficial to applications, if written with the special demands of RAC in mind. RAC has many advanced workload management features available to application developers, most of which aim at making instance failure more or less transparent to the application. In case of a RAC instance failure and supporting programming in the application, there is usually very little delay in processing. RAC can also be instructed to recreate failed sessions on another cluster node.

Unfortunately, many RAC features are not fully exploited in application code. This becomes even more apparent when considering an advanced RAC deployment: extended distance clusters. Extended distance clusters split the RAC setup across two data centers that can be a few miles apart. Each data center uses its own storage array to store the database, while Oracle Automatic Storage Management (ASM) keeps the arrays in sync.

In the field, it turns out that deploying a RAC system can be time consuming. Any RAC deployment requires networking, storage, and operating system support teams to work together closer than with the classic single instance database. Storage needs shared between RAC cluster nodes, and a RAC system needs a few more IP addresses. Finally, RAC requires a little more preparation on the operating system to work.

To streamline the RAC rollout process, Oracle developed what it calls Engineered Systems. Following the idea of a pre-packaged and pre-configured deployment, these systems allow for quicker installation and setup.

The Oracle offerings for the relational database include the Oracle Database Appliance (ODA), as well as Exadata. The Database Appliance has recently been upgraded to the X3-2 model and comprises two dual-socket servers with 10GBit/s Ethernet and 256 GB of DRAM each. Storage in the form of spinning hard disk complemented with SSD is directly attached in a bay and connected via the Serial Attached SCSI interface.

Exadata extends the idea of the database appliance and adds intelligent storage. Many workloads benefit from Exadata's unique features, out of which the best-known is the offloading capability to the storage layer and the I/O Resource Manager.

Exadata is a wonderful piece of engineering and, from an application's point of view, is another case of RAC. Exadata does not require any changes to the applications compared to traditional Real Application Cluster deployments. Depending on the configuration, an Exadata rack can have between two and eight cluster nodes in addition to its own specialized and intelligent storage. From a connectivity and high availability point of view, you do not connect any differently to Exadata than you connect to your own cluster.

Oracle is not the only hardware provider who offers such solutions. Other vendors have tightly integrated solutions in their product portfolios. Exadata-like intelligent storage, however, does not exist outside of Oracle.

Unfortunately, most Oracle applications today are not RAC aware. However, with the new concepts of Pluggable Databases Oracle introduced in this release, that problem is mitigated.

Disaster Recovery Considerations

You just read that Real Application Clusters are not a protection from disasters. You might hear the claim that a stretched RAC will protect you from disasters if the data centers are far enough away from each other. Although it is partially true, if your pockets are deep enough, there is still a fundamental problem with having only one database: in case you have to restore, you will incur an outage. And with the trend to larger and larger databases, even the fastest technology may not give you your database back within the service level agreement. The result is a major embarrassment at best.

There are many ways to protect your environment from disaster, and, because of the importance of that subject, Chapter 9 is dedicated to it. This section is just an appetizer.

■ **Note**   There are more replication technologies available. This section is mainly concerned with bitwise identical replication.

In the Oracle world, you have the option to use Data Guard, which, in its standard form, is included with the Enterprise Edition. The simple yet remarkably effective idea is to take the redo generated by the primary database, ship it over the network, and apply it to up to 30 standby databases. The standby databases are merely mounted and cannot be queried while they apply redo. The log shipping can be configured to be synchronous or asynchronously. At the same time, it has many checks to ensure that the data written is not corrupt. With an additional option, called Active Data Guard, you can even query your standby databases while they receive changes from production. Backups from the standby database are possible as well, allowing you to offload those from your production database. Cautious architects configure backup solutions on all data centers, allowing for flexibility should the unthinkable happen and the primary data center blacks out. Data Guard also allows for planned role changes, it can convert a standby to a full read-write clone of your production system to test hot fixes, and last, but not least, it can be used to fail over from production in the event of a catastrophe. Regulatory requirements and/or standard operational procedures often require regular DR tests, especially before a new architecture goes live. Integrating disaster recovery into the architecture right from the start can save you from having to retrofit it later.

■ **Note**   Chapters 9 and 10 cover Data Guard in greater detail.

The alternative to Data Guard is to use block level replication on the storage array, which operates a on a different level. Storage level replication exists for enterprise arrays, and most use a fiber channel fabric to send blocks as they are from the production to the DR array. Other than that, the processes are quite common. The array does not normally need to know (or care) about what data it is shipping. This is an advantage and disadvantage. If done properly, block replication can be the one ticket to happiness when you replicate your entire application stack: application servers, database servers, and other auxiliary components. Then, all you need to do is mount your replicated storage in your DR data center and bring your systems up. Clever management of your corporate Domain Name System can make it simple to swap the old with the new IP addresses.

Virtualization Examples

The next sections are intended to show you some examples for virtualization technologies. The technologies are chosen to provide you an overview of what is possible on different platforms. The selection is by far not complete! The market leader in virtualization—VMware—for example, is not included in the list. It simply does not need to be introduced anymore.

The first technology presented is Oracle Solaris Zones. Zones are examples for operating system virtualization. One image of the operating system is the basis for multiple isolated copies of the same, operating in complete independence. Solaris is available for x86- and SPARC-based systems. Linux Kernel Virtual Machines are conceptually similar, as to an extent IBM's Logical Partitions.

Following the introduction of Oracle Solaris Zones, you are shown another popular x86-virtualization technology based on a so called bare-metal hypervisor: Oracle VM Server for x86. With Oracle VM, you boot into a very minimalistic operating system that runs directly on the "bare" hardware and provides all access to the hardware for virtual machines.

■ **Note** Non-enterprise or desktop virtualization products are not covered in this chapter. They are aimed at end-users to run operating systems in isolation on their desktops, not at data centers.

Let me stress again that the selection of examples is neither exhaustive nor provides the relevant selection of virtualization technologies. All of them serve a purpose, and the listing here does not imply a ranking or measure of quality. Let's start the discussion with an overview of Oracle Solaris Zones.

Oracle Solaris Zones

Solaris zones are an example for operating system virtualization. A Solaris system-x86 and SPARC alike can be subdivided into logical units called zones. Another name for a zone is a container, and the two terms are often used synonymously. The use of Solaris zones is a very easy and attractive way to make use of a large server that offers plenty of resources. A zone is an isolated environment and, in many respects, resembles a virtual machine from desktop virtualization products, although its management requires experience with the command line.

When you install Solaris 10 or 11, you automatically find one zone already created: the so-called global zone. It is then up to you to create additional zones, referred to as "non-global zones." This section uses the simpler term "zone" instead when referring to non-global zones. Just like with Oracle 12c you have the option to not use zones at all in which case your software will be installed in the global zone. You should, however, consider creating a non-global zone to install your software in. This can make many tasks a lot easier.

In most cases, a zone runs a version of Solaris—the same as the global zone. Recent versions of Solaris support what is termed a *Branded Zone*. A Branded Zone or *BrandZ* allows you to run Solaris 8, Solaris 9, and Red Hat Enterprise Linux 3, in addition to Solaris 10. Solaris 11 has reduced the number of supported brands to Solaris 10 only in addition to Solaris 11. The idea of using a Branded Zone is to allow the user to migrate to Solaris 10 but keep applications that cannot possibly be ported to the current Solaris release.

An Introduction to Solaris Zones

Solaris zones have been the weapon of choice for Solaris virtualization, especially on non-SPARC servers where Logical Domains are not available. A first massive wave of consolidation rolled through data centers some years ago, after zones where first introduced. The zone concept is very compelling, elegant, and simple. Instead of having powerful servers sitting idly most of the time when there are no development or test activities, many of these environments could be consolidated into one server. In addition, a zone isolates applications in a way that even root-owned processes in *zone1* cannot view processes in *zone2*. Block level replication on the array level allows for very simple yet effective disaster recovery solutions. As you will, each zone has its own root directory that can reside on block-replicated storage. Application-specific file systems can equally be storage-replicated. Before starting with a discussion of how to set up a zone, a little bit of terminology is explained in Table 4-1.

Table 4-1. *Necessary Terminology for Solaris Zones*

Concept	Explanation
IPS	The Image Packaging System is a framework for managing software in Solaris 11. It replaces the System V Release 4 package management system used in previous versions of Solaris. The SysVR4 package management system is still available for backward compatibility. So, instead of pkgadd, you will from now on have to get familiar with the pkg command and its many options.
ZFS	ZFS is the next generation Solaris file system and supplements UFS in Solaris. It has many advanced features, such as volume management, high storage capacity, integration checking, copy-on-write clones, Access Control Lists, and many more built-in. In ZFS, you aggregate disks or LUNs into storage pools. The storage pool is conceptually similar to the Linux LVM2 volume group. It can be configured as a striped set of LUNs, or a (RAID 1) mirror, or, alternatively, as a RAIDZ, which is similar to RAID 5.
	You create the actual ZFS file systems on top of the storage pool. It is strongly encouraged to create hierarchies of ZFS file systems, grouping similar file systems under a common top level container. The concept behind this hierarchy is very elegant. ZFS file systems inherit metadata properties from their parent container, such as mount points, quotas, caches, and so on.
	A ZFS dataset is a generic name for a clone, an actual file system, or a snapshot. In the context of zones, a dataset is most often a file system.
Global Zone	The initial zone after the operating system has been installed.
Non-Global Zone	Non-global zones are user defined containers, similar in concept to virtual machines, as known from desktop virtualization products.

Zones can have multiple lifecycle states. The important ones from a DBA point of view are "installed" and "running." A zone with the status "installed" is shut down, waiting to be started. The other states are of more interest to the system administrator who creates the zone.

Storage for Solaris zones merits a closer look. For mid- and higher-tier systems (user acceptance testing, production of course), it makes sense to think in terms of disaster recovery, and this is where the isolation aspect of the zones really shines.

■ **Note** By the way, you can apply the same principle subsequently shown to almost any virtualization technology.

You could, for example, use a dedicated storage device to copy the zones to your disaster recovery center via block-level replication. Figure 4-1 demonstrates this.

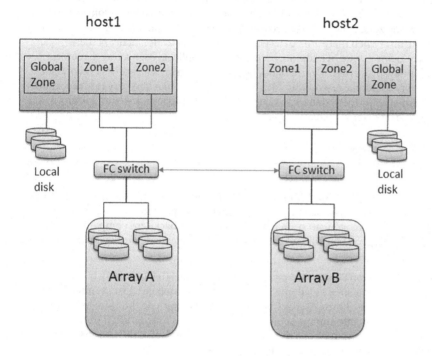

Figure 4-1. *Possible storage setup with SAN replication for zones. This is the same as for the Oracle VM, which is explained in "Oracle VM"*

As you can see in Figure 4-1, the LUNs used for Zones 1 and 2 are provided by a storage array. The use of an ISL (Inter Switch Link) allows the replication of the LUNs' content to a remote data center. The standby LUNs in Array B continuously receive changes from the primary site via the inter-array replication. In the event of a disaster, the zones can be started on the secondary host and resume operations, no more problems with missing configuration items, such as the listener.ora file or different patch levels between primary and standby database. The replication of the Oracle binaries ensures an identical configuration.

Solaris 11 brings a few noteworthy changes to the zone model you may know from Solaris 10. You read previously that the number of supported brands for Branded Zones has been reduced. Only Solaris 10 and 11 are available-migration paths that exist to move Solaris 10 zones to Solaris 11. Solaris 10 zones allowed you to use the loopback device to map certain file systems necessary for the operation of the zone, such as /lib, /platform, /sbin, /usr, as well as others, into the non-global zone, making very efficient use of disk space. The change from the SYSVR4 package system used before Solaris 11 to the new IPS renders this approach unsuitable. For most configurations, a zone is a full-root-zone. Although that might seem disadvantageous at first, it removes a few headaches you could have with Oracle when installing files outside its mount point into /usr, for example. Since /usr was often loopback mounted from the global zone, it was a read only file system. Copying the oraenv related files into /usr was a problem, as was the installation of certain backup software.

Where it was possible to use a non-ZFS file system for the zone root in Solaris 10, the use a ZFS dataset is mandatory in Solaris 11. You can still make use of UFS to store Oracle data files, there is no requirement to only use ZFS in zones. Finally, the package footprint on a newly installed zone is minimal by default. You will see later how to add packages to a zone to support an Oracle database installation.

Creation of a Solaris Zone

A zone can be created using the zonecfg command. When executing zonecfg, you specify which resources you would like to assign to the zone you are creating. Instead of boring you with all the options available, you will walk through the creation of a zone used by an Oracle database. The root file system in the default zone requires only one GB of disk space, but it is recommended to set aside more than that, especially if you are planning to install Oracle. Eight GB should be sufficient for most deployments. In addition to the root file system, an Oracle mount point will be created as well. It is possible to create an oracle installation in the global zone and present that installation to each non-global zone, but this approach has a number of disadvantages. Many users, therefore, decide to create dedicate LUNs for the each zone's Oracle home. If the importance of the environment merits it, these can be added to the replication set. The subsequent example is built to the following requirements:

- Create a virtual machine/zone with name "zone1."

- Assign a root volume of 8 GB storage using the ZFS /zones/zone1/root from the global zone.

- Create a mount point for the database binaries in /u01/app on ZFS /zones/zone1/app of 15 GB.

- Create a mount point for the oracle database files in /u01/oradata on ZFS /zones/zone1/ oradata of 30GB.

- Create a network interface with a dedicated IP address.

- Use the ZFS storage pool zone1pool for all storage requirements of zone1 to allow for block level replication.

The example assumes you are logged into the global zone as root, and it assumes a Solaris 11 installation. The first step in the zone creation is to create the ZFS data sets. It is good practice to create a hierarchy of file systems to make best use of the metadata property inheritance. In the example, the zone's root file system is stored in /zones/zone1, whereas the oracle installation is local to the zone, in a zfs file system called /zones/zone1/app. Finally, the database is created in /zones/zone1/oradata. The data sets are created as follows:

```
root@solaris:~# zfs create -o mountpoint=/zones/zone1 zone1pool/zone1
root@solaris:~# zfs create zone1pool/zone1/root
root@solaris:~# zfs set quota=8G zone1pool/zone1/root
root@solaris:~# zfs create zone1pool/zone1/app
root@solaris:~# zfs set quota=15G zone1pool/zone1/app
root@solaris:~# zfs create zone1pool/zone1/oradata
root@solaris:~# zfs set quota=30G zone1pool/zone1/oradata
```

The mount points for my Oracle database file systems must be set to legacy to allow them to be presented to the zone using the "add fs" command.

```
root@solaris:~# zfs set mountpoint=legacy zone1pool/zone1/app
root@solaris:~# zfs set mountpoint=legacy zone1pool/zone1/oradata
```

This creates all the file systems as required. You can use the zfs list command to view their status. You will also note that the file systems are already mounted, and you do not need to edit the vfstab file at all.

```
root@solaris:~# zfs list | egrep "NAME|zone1"
NAME                 USED  AVAIL  REFER  MOUNTPOINT
zone1pool            377K  24.5G    31K  /zone1pool
zone1pool/zone1      127K  24.5G    34K  /zones/zone1
```

```
zone1pool/zone1/app        31K   15.0G   31K   legacy
zone1pool/zone1/oradata    31K   30.0G   31K   legacy
zone1pool/zone1/root       31K   8.00G   31K   /zones/zone1/root
root@solaris:~#
```

After the storage is provisioned, configure the zone. To do so, start zonecfg and supply the desired zone name as shown:

```
root@solaris:~# zonecfg -z zone1
zone1: No such zone configured
Use 'create' to begin configuring a new zone.
zonecfg:zone1> create
create: Using system default template 'SYSdefault'
zonecfg:zone1> set zonepath=/zones/zone1/root
zonecfg:zone1> set autoboot=true
zonecfg:zone1> set bootargs="-m verbose"
zonecfg:zone1> set limitpriv="default,sys_time"
zonecfg:zone1> set scheduling-class=FSS
zonecfg:zone1> add fs
zonecfg:zone1:fs> set type=zfs
zonecfg:zone1:fs> set special=zone1pool/zone1/app
zonccfg:zone1:fs> set dir=/u01/app
zonecfg:zone1:fs> end
zonecfg:zone1> add fs
zonecfg:zone1:fs> set type=zfs
zonecfg:zone1:fs> set special=zone1pool/zone1/oradata
zonecfg:zone1:fs> set dir=/u01/oradata
zonecfg:zone1:fs> end
zonecfg:zone1> remove anet
Are you sure you want to remove ALL 'anet' resources (y/[n])? Y
zonecfg:zone1> add anet
zonecfg:zone1:anet> set linkname=net0
zonecfg:zone1:anet> set lower-link=auto
zonecfg:zone1:anet> end
zonecfg:zone1> verify
zonecfg:zone1> commit
zonecfg:zone1> exit
```

Although this is a very basic example, it already looks quite complex, but do not despair: it's surprisingly intuitive! The commands you execute create a new zone. Set the zone's "root" file system to the previously created ZFS data store. Then set the scheduler class and a few more attributes to make the zone play nice with others before adding the file systems for Oracle. The anet resource defines the automatic network device and is responsible for dynamically adding the necessary virtual network card when the zone starts. In previous versions of Solaris, you had to pre-create the VNIC before starting the zone—life has been made easier. Once the configuration information is added, verify the settings and, finally, commit it. In the following step, you then install the zone. This requires an Internet connection or a local IPS repository in the network.

```
root@solaris:~# zoneadm -z zone1 install
A ZFS file system has been created for this zone.
Progress being logged to /var/log/zones/zoneadm.20120706T093705Z.zone1.install
       Image: Preparing at /zones/zone1/root/root.
```

```
Install Log: /system/volatile/install.2038/install_log
AI Manifest: /tmp/manifest.xml.iEaG9d
 SC Profile: /usr/share/auto_install/sc_profiles/enable_sci.xml
   Zonename: zone1
Installation: Starting ...

               Creating IPS image
               Installing packages from:
                     solaris
                         origin:  http://pkg.oracle.com/solaris/release/
DOWNLOAD                           PKGS        FILES    XFER (MB)
Completed                         167/167 32062/32062  175.8/175.8

PHASE                                    ACTIONS
Install Phase                          44313/44313

PHASE                                     ITEMS
Package State Update Phase               167/167
Image State Update Phase                   2/2
Installation: Succeeded

       Note: Man pages can be obtained by installing pkg:/system/manual

done.

       Done: Installation completed in 1817.202 seconds.


 Next Steps: Boot the zone, then log into the zone console (zlogin -C)

               to complete the configuration process.

Log saved in non-global zone as /zones/zone1/root/root/var/log/zones/zoneadm.20120706T093705Z.zone1.
install
```

Congratulations! The zone is now installed, but not yet started. Start it using the following command:

```
root@solaris~# zoneadm -z zone1 boot
```

Configuring a Zone

After the prompt returns from the execution of the last command, the zone is ready to log in. Two ways exist to do so, by either your IP address or the zlogin utility. Since the network within the zone is not yet configured, you need to use the zlogin utility.

```
root@solaris:~# zlogin zone1
[Connected to zone 'zone1' pts/2]
Oracle Corporation      SunOS 5.11      11.0     November 2011
```

As you can see, the file systems are present, just as we asked. Notice that the devices allocated to the Oracle mount points on the left hand side refer to the devices in the global zone.

```
root@zone1:~# df -h
Filesystem              Size    Used  Available Capacity  Mounted on
rpool/ROOT/solaris      24G     317M       24G     2%     /
/dev                    0K      0K         0K      0%     /dev
zone1pool/zone1/app     15G     31K        15G     1%     /u01/app
zone1pool/zone1/oradata
                        24G     31K        24G     1%     /u01/oradata
zone1pool/zone1/root/rpool/ROOT/solaris/var
                        24G     25M        24G     1%     /var
proc                    0K      0K         0K      0%     /proc
ctfs                    0K      0K         0K      0%     /system/contract
mnttab                  0K      0K         0K      0%     /etc/mnttab
objfs                   0K      0K         0K      0%     /system/object
swap                    6.1G    248K       6.1G    1%     /system/volatile
sharefs                 0K      0K         0K      0%     /etc/dfs/sharetab
/usr/lib/libc/libc_hwcap2.so.1
                        24G     317M       24G     2%     /lib/libc.so.1
fd                      0K      0K         0K      0%     /dev/fd
swap                    6.1G    0K         6.1G    0%     /tmp
```

However, the system is not yet configured. This is performed using the sysconfig command. Exit your previous session, log into the zone in console mode (using zlogin -Cd zone1), enter sysconfig configure, and then reboot the zone. The console mode does not disconnect you, and, when the zone comes up again, the System Configuration Tool guides you through the setup process. After another reboot, your zone is functional. Since the installation of Oracle binaries is identical to a non-zone installation, it is not shown here.

Monitoring Zones

An invaluable tool for the system administrator or power-DBA is called zonestat. Very often, it is difficult to work out where time is spent on a multi-zone system. All the DBA sees is a high load average, but it is not always apparent where it is caused. Enter zonestat, a great way of monitoring the system. It should be noted, however, that the output of the command, when executed in a non-global zone, will not report individual other zone's resources.

When invoked on the global zone, however, you get an overview of what is happening. When invoked in its most basic form from the global zone, you see the following output:

```
root@solaris:~# zonestat 5 2
Collecting data for first interval...
Interval: 1, Duration: 0:00:05
SUMMARY                   Cpus/Online: 8/8    PhysMem: 8191M   VirtMem: 9.9G
                 ---CPU----  --PhysMem--  --VirtMem--  --PhysNet--
         ZONE   USED %PART  USED %USED   USED %USED  PBYTE %PUSE
      [total]   8.00 100%  1821M 22.2%  2857M 27.9%   278 0.00%
     [system]   0.00 0.00% 1590M 19.4%  2645M 25.8%     -     -
        zone1   8.00 100%  83.1M 1.01%  75.7M 0.73%     0 0.00%
       global   0.01 0.19%  148M 1.80%   136M 1.33%   278 0.00%

Interval: 2, Duration: 0:00:10
SUMMARY                   Cpus/Online: 8/8    PhysMem: 8191M   VirtMem: 9.9G
                 ---CPU----  --PhysMem--  --VirtMem--  --PhysNet--
         ZONE   USED %PART  USED %USED   USED %USED  PBYTE %PUSE
      [total]   7.98 99.8% 1821M 22.2%  2858M 27.9%   940 0.00%
```

```
   [system]   0.00 0.00% 1590M 19.4% 2645M 25.8%     -    -
      zone1   7.97 99.6% 83.1M 1.01% 75.7M 0.73%     0 0.00%
     global   0.01 0.22%  148M 1.80%  136M 1.33%   940 0.00%
```

The previous system has the global zone and a user zone started and running, while a load generator in zone1 stresses all eight CPUs. You have the option to tune in on individual zones, as well as to request more detailed information. In the previous output, you can see that zone1 is fairly busy, the %PART column reports that the system is 96% busy. Physical memory and virtual memory, as well as network traffic, are no reason for concern. What should ring alarm bells is the fact that the total resources are almost 100% in use: in other words, our zone1 consumes all of the host's resources. Time to investigate!

Zonestat can also be used to perform longer-term monitoring and record statistics in the background. To gather statistics over a 12-hour period with data points every 30 seconds and a summary report for high usage every 30 minutes, you could use the following command:

```
root@solaris:~# zonestat -q -R high 30s 12h 30m
```

Deleting a Zone

A zone can be deleted-careful: the subsequent commands do not ask for confirmation and also delete the ZFS data store. In other words, as soon as you hit return, the zone is gone. You should have a valid and tested backup before proceeding. If you built it according to the suggestion provided (all user data on separate datasets), then you won't lose everything, but you do still have to go through a painful recovery of the zone itself.

So if you are absolutely sure that you want to remove the zone, shut it down first, wait a couple of hours to see if anyone complains, and then delete it. It is not unheard of that a zone was officially declared not to be in use when someone actually was using it. The shutdown command can be initiated from within the zone itself, or via the global zone:

```
root@solaris:~# zoneadm -z zone1 shutdown
root@solaris:~# zoneadm list -civ
  ID NAME            STATUS     PATH                          BRAND    IP
   0 global          running    /                             solaris  shared
   - zone1           installed  /zones/zone1                  solaris  excl
```

The zone is now shut down. Last chance to check if the zone is not needed! If you are sure, then proceed by removing the zone data. This must be performed from the global zone as root. Consider this example:

```
root@solaris:~# zoneadm -z zone1 uninstall
Are you sure you want to uninstall zone zone1 (y/[n])? y
Progress being logged to /var/log/zones/zoneadm.20120704T114857Z.zone1.uninstall
root@solaris:~# zoneadm list -civ
  ID NAME            STATUS     PATH                          BRAND    IP
   0 global          running    /                             solaris  shared
   - zone1           configured /zones/zone1                  solaris  excl
```

As you can see, the zone is no longer installed, but rather configured. To really get rid of it, you need to use the zonecfg tool again with the delete option:

```
root@solaris:~# zonecfg -z zone1 delete
Are you sure you want to delete zone zone1 (y/[n])? y
root@solaris:~# zfs list
NAME                    USED   AVAIL  REFER  MOUNTPOINT
rpool                   5.11G  10.5G  39K    /rpool
rpool/ROOT              2.01G  10.5G  31K    legacy
```

```
rpool/ROOT/solaris          2.01G  10.5G  1.54G  /
rpool/ROOT/solaris/var       476M  10.5G   474M  /var
rpool/dump                  2.06G  10.6G  2.00G  -
rpool/export                  98K  10.5G    32K  /export
rpool/export/home             66K  10.5G    32K  /export/home
rpool/export/home/martin      34K  10.5G    34K  /export/home/martin
rpool/swap                  1.03G  10.6G  1.00G  -
```

As you can see, even the ZFS has been removed.

Further Reading

If you are interested in exploring zones in more detail, then you might find the following references useful:

- Oracle® Solaris Administration: Oracle Solaris Zones, OracleSolaris10Zones, and Resource Management

- Oracle® Solaris Administration: ZFS File System

- Oracle® Solaris Administration: Network Interfaces and Network Virtualization

- Solaris 11 manual page: solaris(5)

- Solaris 11 manual page: brands(5)

- Solaris 11 manual page: zones(5)

Oracle VM Server for x86

Oracle has entered relatively late into the virtualization market, but it has since been aggressively promoting and developing its products. One of the company's first virtualization products was Oracle VM, which is today known to us as Oracle VM Server for x86. It is based on the Xen type 1 bare-metal hypervisor and unsurprisingly runs on x86-hardware. Since the inception of Oracle VM, a number of products have been branded Oracle VM, making it important to add more context as to which is meant. At the time of this writing, some of the additional products with Oracle VM in their name were:

- Oracle VM Virtualbox

- Oracle VM Server for SPARC

- Oracle VM Manager

Oracle VM VirtualBox has initially been developed by innotek GmbH, which was acquired by Sun Microsystems in 2008, only to be taken over by Oracle in 2010. VirtualBox is a desktop virtualization product (that is, it runs on top of a desktop operating system). VirtualBox is a popular solution and is available under a liberal license.

Oracle VM Server for SPARC is the new name for Sun Logical Domains or LDOMs. Currently designed mainly for Chip MultiThreading technology such as employed on Oracle's T-Series hardware, the Oracle VM Server for SPARC promises lower overhead since the virtualization technology is already included in the CPU. Logical Domains in this respect are not to be confused with Dynamic Domains, which are only available in M-Series hardware.

Oracle VM is an upcoming competitor in the x 86 virtualization world, but competition in this market segment is tough. The version covered in this section is Oracle VM 3.1.1, which is current at the time of this writing.

Introduction to the Xen Hypervisor

The Xen hypervisor is the result of a research project of the University of Cambridge. As a type 1 hypervisor, it does not require any operating system to run, it rather starts on bare metal. Although available in many commercial offerings, the core of Xen is a true open source solution to run all kinds of workloads, including Amazon's Elastic Compute Cloud. Thanks to a lot of development effort, Xen is able to run a large number of operating systems, including Linux, Solaris, Windows, and even some BSD derivatives.

Xen was different from other virtualization solutions available at the time it was developed. The majority of virtualization solutions at that time used binary translation to execute multiple copies of operating systems on the same hardware. This is termed "full virtualization" in Xen. With full virtualization, guests do not require any modification, and your Windows 2000 CD-ROM could be used to boot virtual hardware almost identically to physical hardware.

Binary translation results in a lot of CPU overhead, since operations of the guest operating system must be translated by the host and implemented in a way that is safe to operate multiple operating systems at the same time. In addition to translating CPU instructions, the virtual machine monitor has to also keep track of the memory used both within the guest and on the host. Finally, some hardware has to be emulated. Before the advent of hardware assisted virtualization technologies, these three were done in very cleverly engineered software. A penalty often applied when running virtualized workloads.

Xen, conversely, used a different approach, called *para-virtualization*, as illustrated in Figure 4-2. In a para-virtualized environment, the guest operating systems are aware that they are being virtualized, allowing for tighter integration with the hypervisor, resulting in better efficiency. For obvious reasons, this requires changes to the operating system, and it is no surprise that Linux was the most significant Xen-deployed platform.

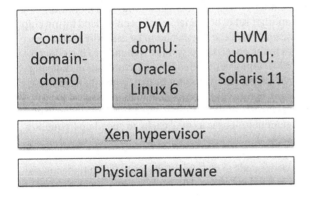

Figure 4-2. *Conceptual view on the Xen architecture with physical- and hardware virtualized machines*

The Xen architecture is built around the hypervisor, the control domain, and the user domains. The hypervisor is a small piece of software governing access to the hardware of the underlying host. The control domain or dom0 in Xen parlance is a para-virtualized Linux that uses the Xen hypervisor to access the hardware and manages the guests.

One of the biggest benefits offered by Xen's para-virtualization, even more so when it was released, is the area of I/O operations. The IO devices ("disks") in a para-virtualized environment merely link to the I/O drivers in the control domain, eliminating the need to I/O virtualization. However, many other important aspects of the operating system also benefit from para-virtualization.

Initially, Xen was not developed as part of the mainline Linux kernel, but that has changed. Two distinct pieces of software are needed to use Xen: the Xen software and changes to the kernel. Before the code merge subsequently described in more detail, the Xen software-including patches to the kernel had to be applied before a Linux system could boot as a dom0. Red Hat Linux 5 supports booting a dom0 kernel based on 2.6.18.x, but has abandoned that approach with the current release, Red Hat Enterprise Linux 6. SuSE Linux has continued to include the patches in their kernels up to SuSE Linux Enterprise 11. The so-modified kernel was said to be "xenified," and it was different from the non-xen kernel. At the same time, efforts were underway to include the Xen patches in the mainline Linux kernel. There were two main lines of work: making Linux work as a guest domain (domU) and allowing it to boot as a control domain (dom0). Both efforts are grouped under the heading "pvops," or para-virtualized ops. The aim of the pvops infrastructure for Xen was to provide a single kernel image for booting into the Xen and non-Xen roles. The rewriting of a lot of code has been necessary to comply with the strict coding quality requirements of the mainline kernel. Starting with Kernel 2.6.24, domU support has been gradually added with each release, and the xen.org wiki states that as of 2.6.32.10 domU support should be fairly stable. It was more problematic to get dom0 support into the upstream kernel, and many times the Xen code was not allowed to exit the staging area. The breakthrough came with kernel 2.6.37, explained in an exciting blog post by Konrad Rzeszutek Wilk: "Linux 3.0 – How did we get initial domain (dom0) support there?" Although 2.6.37 offered very limited support to actually run guests, at least it booted, and without the forward-ported patches from 2.6.18. With Linux kernel 3.0, dom0 support was workable and could be included in Linux distributions.

Although there was a time, shortly after Red Hat announced they would not support a Xen dom0 in Enterprise Linux 6, that the future of Xen looked bleak, thanks to the many talented and enthusiastic individuals, Xen is back. And it did not come a moment too soon: the advances in processor technology made the full-virtualization approach a worthy contender to para-virtualization. Today, it is claimed that the virtualization overhead for fully virtualized guests is less than 10%.

During its development, Xen has incorporated support for what it calls hardware virtualization. You previously read that para-virtualized operating systems are made aware of the fact that they are virtualized. Para-virtualization requires access and modifications of the code. Closed source operating systems, such as Windows, for example, therefore, could initially not be run under Xen, but this has been addressed with Xen version 3.x. Thanks to hardware virtualization support in processors, Xen can now run what it refers to as Hardware Virtualized Machines (HVM). Virtualization support in x86-64 processors is available from Intel and AMD. Intel calls its extensions VT-x, AMD call their support AMD-V, but it is often found as "Secure Virtual Machine," as well in the BIOS settings and literature.

As part of the initiatives to do more work in the processor, another set of bottlenecks has been tackled by the chip vendors. Recall from the previous discussion that the memory structures of the guests had to be carefully shadowed by the hypervisor, causing overhead when modifying page tables in the guest. Luckily, this overhead can be reduced by using Extended Page Tables (EPT) in Intel processors or the AMD equivalent called Rapid Virtualization Indexing (RVI). Both technologies address one of the issues faced by the virtual machine monitor or hypervisor: to keep track of memory. In a native environment, the operating system uses a structure called page table to map physical to virtual addresses. When a request is received to map a logical to physical memory address, a page table walk or traversal of the page tables occurs, which is often slow. The memory management unit uses a small cache to speed up frequently used page lookups, named Translation Lookaside Buffer or TLB.

In the case of virtualization, it is not that simple. Multiple operating systems are executing in parallel on the host, each with their own memory management routines. The hypervisor needs to tread carefully and maintain the image for the guests running on "real" hardware with exclusive access to the page tables. The guest, in turn, believes it has exclusive access to the memory set aside for it in the virtual machine definition. The hypervisor needs to intercept and handle the memory related calls from the guest and map them to the actual physical memory on the host. Keeping the guest's and the hypervisor's memory synchronized can become an overhead for memory intensive workloads.

Extended Page Tables and Rapid Virtualization Indexing try to make the life easier for the hypervisor by speeding up memory management with hardware support. In an ideal situation, the need for a shadow page table is completely eliminated, yielding a very noticeable performance improvement.

The advances in the hardware have led to the interesting situation that Xen HVM guests can perform better under certain workloads than PVM guests, reversing the initial situation. HVM guests can struggle when it comes to accessing drivers. Linux benefits from so called PV-on-HVM drivers, which are para-virtualized drivers, completely bypassing the hardware emulation layer. Less code path to traverse provides better performance for disk and network access. Para-virtualized drivers also exist for Windows and other platforms. This is not to say that you should start using hardware virtualizing all your operating systems, but there might be a workload, especially when the guest's page table is heavily modified where PV-on-HVM can offer a significant performance boost.

Oracle VM Server for x86 Architecture Overview

Oracle VM in its current version, 3.2.2, is based on a server and a management component, plus auxiliary structures, such as external storage. One or more Oracle VM Servers is running Xen 4.1.3 and Oracle's kernel UEK 2. The installation image for Oracle VM Server is very small, only about 220 MB. It installs directly on the bare metal, and, in the interactive installation, asks you only very few questions before transferring the installation image to the hard disk. Each Oracle VM Server has an agent process used to communicate with the central management interface, called Oracle VM Manager.

Multiple Oracle VM Servers can logically be grouped in a server pool. You get most benefit out of a server pool configuration if the server pool makes use of shared storage in the form of Oracle's Cluster File System 2. A cluster file system has been chosen to allow guest domains to be dynamically migrated from one server in the pool to another. Consider Figure 4-3 for a schematic overview of the architecture.

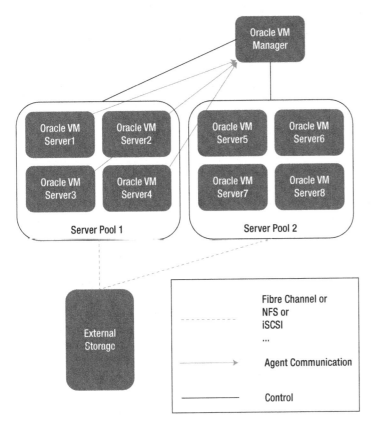

Figure 4-3. *Oracle VM architecture. Agent communication is still used between servers in pool 2 and the management host, but they have been omitted here*

The Oracle VM Manager uses the Application Development Framework (ADF) to render the graphical user interface. The application server is WebLogic 11g, and an Oracle database optionally serves as the repository. The simple installation option provides a MySQL 5.5 database as the repository. Either way, do not forget to include both components into your backup strategy. The Oracle VM Manager is the central tool for managing the entire infrastructure for Oracle VM. From here, you discover the servers, provision storage, configure networks, and so on. It is strongly recommended not to modify the Oracle VM Servers directly, the management interface and the hosts may otherwise get out of sync, leading to errors that are difficult to diagnose.

■ **Note**   Oracle Enterprise Manager Cloud Control 12c has support for Oracle VM as well, but this is out of scope of this chapter.

After the initial installation of Oracle VM Server and Manager, the workflow to create a virtual machine in Oracle VM Manager includes the following steps:

1. Discover Oracle VM Server(s).

2. Create a network to access the virtual machines.

3. Configure storage.

4. Create a new server pool.

5. Create a shareable repository to store installation files and virtual machines.

6. Create the virtual machine.

Let's look at these in more detail. Although the next steps seem quite complex and labor intensive, you have to say, in fairness, that many tasks are one-time setup tasks.

Creating a Virtual Machine

The example to follow assumes that the infrastructure is already in place. In other words, you already have configured SAN storage and networking. Oracle VM defines different types of networks, each of which can be assigned to a network port. Link aggregation is also supported and can be configured in the management interface. In the following example, the following networks have been used:

- 192.168.1.0/24: management network for server management, cluster management, and VM live migration. This is automatically created and tied to bond0 on the Oracle VM Servers. If possible, bond0 should be configured with multiple network ports.

- 192.168.100.0/24: used for iSCSI traffic and bound to bond1.

Shared storage is necessary to create a clustered server pool and to allow for migrations of virtual machines. It is also possible to define server pools with local storage only, but, by doing so, you do not benefit from many advanced features, especially VM migration.

The first step after a fresh installation of Oracle VM Manager and a couple of Oracle VM Servers (at least one must be available) is to connect to the management interface, which is shown in Figure 4-4.

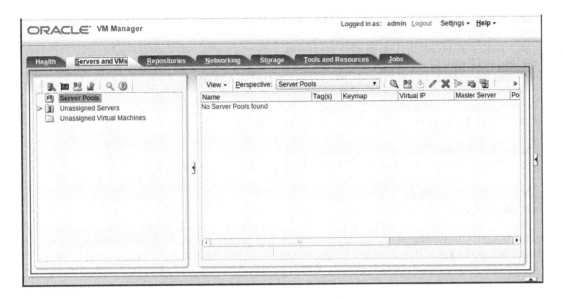

Figure 4-4. *Oracle VM Manager main screen*

You start by discovering a new server, which then is moved to the group "unassigned servers." Let's leave the servers for the moment. You need to make the VM Manager aware of the storage provisioned. In this example, iSCSI is accessible via the storage network on 192.168.100.1. Support for other storage types exists as well. Prominent examples include NFS and Fibre Channel SANs. When using iSCSI, you can create a new network on the "Networking" tab and dedicate it to storage traffic. If you have plenty of Ethernet ports on the physical hardware, you should consider bonding a few of them for resilience and potentially better performance. The option to create a network bond is on the "Servers and VMs" tab. Select the server on which to create a bonded interface, then change the perspective to "Bond Ports". A click on the plus sign allows you to create a new bonded port in a simple to use wizard. The bonded interface must be created before you create the new network. Two new networks have been created in Figure 4-5 matching the initial description.

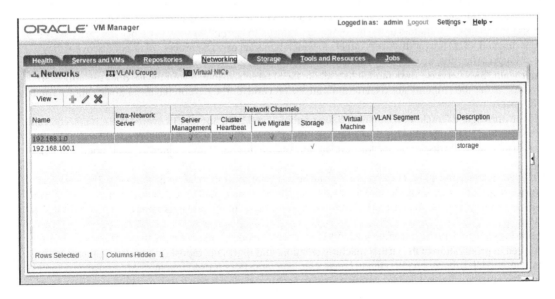

Figure 4-5. *Oracle VM Manager 3 with the new networks in place*

The definition in the management interface is propagated to all VM Servers, visible in the output of ifconfig:

```
[root@oraclevmserver1 ~]# ifconfig | grep ^[0-9a-z] -A1
bond0      Link encap:Ethernet  HWaddr 52:54:00:AC:AA:94
           inet addr:192.168.1.21  Bcast:192.168.1.255  Mask:255.255.255.0
--
eth0       Link encap:Ethernet  HWaddr 52:54:00:AC:AA:94
           UP BROADCAST RUNNING SLAVE MULTICAST  MTU:1500  Metric:1
--
eth1       Link encap:Ethernet  HWaddr 52:54:00:69:E3:E7
           inet addr:192.168.100.21  Bcast:192.168.100.255  Mask:255.255.255.0
--
lo         Link encap:Local Loopback
           inet addr:127.0.0.1  Mask:255.0.0.0
```

In the output, bond0 is the management network and eth1 is the storage network. Most production systems would use bonded devices here. The difference is a simple mouse click when creating the interface for which you can chose to use a single port or an aggregated interface. With the networks in place, you can begin to add storage to the configuration.

Begin by switching to the "Storage" tab and expand the list of "SAN Servers" in the left navigation pane. Then click the "Discover SAN Server" button. Remember, the example assumes a simple setup using iSCSI. Although the documentation makes you believe that iSCSI performs better than NFS, this is too much of a generalization. You should carefully evaluate all types of network storage for performance, resilience, and ease of administration before deploying such a scenario into production. With the advent of 10GBit/s Ethernet, the situation somewhat eases, but iSCSI still remains a protocol with significant overhead. Fibre Channel, conversely, is a well-established alternative and has proven its worth in thousands of installations.

Back to the "SAN discovery wizard," you need to follow a few steps to make use of the iSCSI targets provided by your device. On the first page of the wizard, you need to supply a name and description for the new iSCSI target, and the target type needs changed to iSCSI. On the second page in the wizard, provide the name of the iSCSI host. If you are using a dedicated IP storage network, ensure that the iSCSI targets are exported using it, not via the management interface. In case you are using firewalls on the iSCSI host, ensure that port 3260 is open to allow storage discovery.

In the next step, you define administration servers for the group before you govern access to the iSCSI target. In the example, oraclevmserver1 and oraclevmserver2 both have access to the shared storage. To do so, edit the default access group and add the iSCSI initiators to the list of servers allowed to start iSCSI sessions. Once the "SAN Server" configuration is finished, OVM Server discovers targets to which it has access. The process of target discovery may last a minute or longer. After this, a new entry with the name chosen during the storage discovery appears in the tree structure underneath "SAN Servers." By default, it lists all the iSCSI targets visible. If your device does not appear in the list, ensure that either the authentication credentials are correct and/or the ACL on the iSCSI device allows you to perform the discovery.

Next, add the unassigned Oracle VM Servers to a server pool. If you have not yet discovered the servers, you can do so in the "Servers and VMs" tab. Clicking the "Discover Server" icon opens a wizard that lets you discover servers based on IP address. The newly discovered servers are initially placed into said "unassigned servers" pool before they can be used.

Back in the tab "Servers and VMs," click on the "Create Server Pool" button to begin this process. The wizard is self-explanatory, except for two options. Be sure to tick the "clustered storage pool" check box, and then use "Physical Disk". Click on the magnifying glass to pick a LUN. You discovered storage in the previous steps using the "Storage" tab in the OVM Manager.

In the following step, add all the relevant Oracle VM Servers to the pool. You are nearly there! There is only one more step required in preparation of the virtual machine creation, and that is the repository creation. Change to the "Repositories" tab, and click the green plus sign to create one. The repository is used for your VMs, templates, and ISO files, plus any other auxiliary files needed for running virtual machines. Select a previously detected storage unit, at least 10GB (preferably more), and create the repository. Notice that the repository is shared across virtual machines (that is, using OCFS 2). Fill in the values and present it to all Oracle VM Servers. In the background, you have created two OCFS2 file systems, which are mounted to the Oracle VM Servers in the server pool:

```
[root@oraclevmserver ~]# mount | grep ocfs
ocfs2_dlmfs on /dlm type ocfs2_dlmfs (rw)
/dev/mapper/1IET_00010001 on /poolfsmnt/0...2b4 type ocfs2 (rw,_netdev,heartbeat=global)
/dev/mapper/1IET_00020001 on /OVS/Repositories/0...aa type ocfs2 (rw,_netdev,heartbeat=global)
[root@oraclevmserver ~]#
```

The cluster configuration, including all settings in /etc/ocfs2/cluster.conf, has transparently been applied by Oracle VM Manager. Finally you can create a virtual machine. In the example, a new virtual machine based on Oracle Linux 6 will be created as a para-virtualized guest.

■ **Note** Oracle also offers pre-built templates for many scenarios from http://edelivery.oracle.com/linux.

Switch to the "Servers and VMs" tab and highlight your server pool in the tree on the left side of the screen. Change the perspective to "virtual machines", then right-click the pool and select "Create Virtual Machine". In the appearing wizard, enter the following information provided in Table 4-2.

Table 4-2. *The "Create Virtual Machine" Wizard*

Step	Information to be provided
How do you want to create your Virtual Machine?	Create a new VM (Click "Next" to continue)
Create Virtual Machine	Server: Any
	Repository: your repository name
	Name: OracleLinux6
	Tick the box "Enable High Availability" to allow the VM to migrate to another server in the server pool should the original host fail unexpectedly.
	Description: enter an optional description
	Operating System: Oracle Linux 6
	Keymap: whichever suits your keyboard best
	Domain Type: Xen PVM
	The remaining values can be set, depending on your Oracle VM Server hardware. A minimal installation of Oracle Linux 6 is fine with the defaults.
	Click "Next" to continue to the next step.
Set up Networks	Assign one or more unassigned VNIC (virtual network interface card) to the virtual machine from the drop down labeled "unassigned VNICs". If there are no more VNICs, click "Create VNICs" to create some. Ensure the network is set to the virtual machine network.
Arrange Disks	Select virtual disk from the drop down menu in slot 0. Click the green plus sign in the "Actions" column to create a new disk. It is usually a good idea to name the disk in a way that allows you to identify it as a disk belonging to a certain VM. The size should be at least 4 GB for a minimalistic installation of Oracle Linux 6.

(continued)

Table 12-1. (*continued*)

Step	Information to be provided
Boot Options	Add both network and disk here. Enter a network boot path and point it to the repository location for Oracle Linux 6. This is only possible for para-virtualized guests. See Chapter 5 for more information on how to make the installation tree of Oracle Linux available via the network. HVM guests will require the ISO image of the installation available in the repository.
	Click "Finish" to create the virtual machine description and begin the installation of the virtual machine.

Oracle VM Manager will go off and create the new virtual machine metadata on one of the Oracle VM Servers. This is exactly the same way you would create domUs in Xen from the command line, enriched with some extra information needed by Oracle VM Manager. The configuration files for virtual machines reside in the repository, which is mounted on all servers in the pool under /OVS/Repositories using the numeric repository ID. The subdirectory VirtualMachines contains another ID for each domU. Finally, the vm.cfg file contains the information:

```
vif = ['mac=00:21:f6:00:00:12,bridge=0004fb0010609f0']
OVM_simple_name = 'ol62pvm'
disk = ['file:/OVS/Repositories/0...a/VirtualDisks/0...e.img,xvda,w']
uuid = '0004fb00-0006-0000-5506-fc6915b4897b'
on_reboot = 'restart'
boot = 'c'
cpu_weight = 27500
memory = 1024
cpu_cap = 0
maxvcpus = 1
OVM_high_availability = False
maxmem = 1024
OVM_description = ''
on_poweroff = 'destroy'
on_crash = 'restart'
bootloader = '/usr/bin/pygrub'
name = '0004fb00000600005506fc6915b4897b'
guest_os_type = 'linux'
vfb = ['type=vnc,vncunused=1,vnclisten=127.0.0.1,keymap=en-gb']
vcpus = 1
OVM_os_type = 'Oracle Linux 6'
OVM_cpu_compat_group = ''
OVM_domain_type = 'xen_pvm'
```

Notice the entries beginning with OVM—they are specific to Oracle VM. With the domU definition finished, highlight the domU definition and click "Start." The console button will open a VNC session if you have a VNC viewer installed on the client. From then on, install Linux as you normally would. Again, refer to Chapter 5 for guidance on the Oracle Linux 6 installation.

Further Reading

Xen-based para-virtualization is a very fascinating topic, which is far too encompassing to explain it in its entirety here. Since Oracle VM Server for x86 is based, to a large extent, on the free hypervisor, it makes a lot of sense to understand Xen before diving into Oracle's implementation details. One of the best resources, when it comes to Xen, is the home of Xen: `http://www.xen.org`. The website has a very useful wiki as well, accessible as `wiki.xen.org`. Additional useful resources include:

- Oracle® VM Release Notes for 3.1.1(E27307-05)

- Oracle® VM Getting Started Guide for Release 3.1.1 (E27312-03)

- Xen 4.1.2 release notes: `http://wiki.xen.org/wiki/Xen_4.1_Release_Notes`

- Xen manual pages: `http://wiki.xen.org/wiki/Xen_Man_Pages`

Final Thoughts on Virtualization

The previous sections have given you a high-level overview of different approaches to virtualization. There is most likely a virtualization initiative underway in your company, but most users thus far have only virtualized development and UAT/pre-production environments. The most critical, production and the corresponding disaster recovery environments have most often remained untouched.

During the research for this chapter, a large international company announced that it has completely virtualized their SAP environment, demonstrating that virtualization can work even for production environments. There are some common pitfalls, however. Some users have gone too far with their virtualization strategy. There is a reported case in which one Unix domain containing one Oracle home plus nine databases has been virtualized in nine different virtual machines on x86, each with its own operating system, an own Oracle home and only one database. Although the approach has certainly helped increase isolation between the environments, it has also increased the management overhead. In such a scenario, it is even more important to either not create as many virtual machines or, if that cannot be avoided, have a suitable management strategy for mass-patching operating system and databases. Thankfully, Oracle database 12c and the multi-tenancy option gives administrators similar levels of isolation at reduced overhead of having to maintain too many copies of the operating system.

If done right, virtualization offers tremendous potential and can challenge traditional clustered solutions for uptime and availability. The established companies in the market have very mature and elaborate management frameworks, allowing the administrator to control his environment. It can help contain what the industry refers to as "server sprawl." Recently, vendors are also pushing into the new *yourProductHere* as a service market. Times are interesting!

High Availability Example

You read in the introduction that there are additional ways to protect a single instance Oracle database from failure. We have just thoroughly covered the virtualization aspect, mainly because virtualization is such a big driver of innovation in the industry. In addition to virtualization, you have the option to use more than one physical server to protect the instance from hardware failures. The following section provides more information on how to achieve this goal.

You might want to consider that strict high availability requirements often come down in a way to be compatible with an active/passive cluster. However, if your requirements are such that even the short interruption of service is intolerable then you need to have a look at the Real Application Cluster option. Similar to the previous section, this section presents an example for an active/passive cluster based on Oracle Clusterware. It is assumed that you have some background knowledge about clustering.

Oracle Clusterware HA Framework

Oracle Clusterware is Oracle's cluster manager that allows a group of physically separate servers combine into one logical server. The physical servers are connected together by a dedicated private network and are attached to shared storage. Oracle Clusterware consists of a set of additional operating system processes and daemons that run on each node in the cluster that utilize the private network and shared storage to coordinate activity between the servers. Oracle has renamed the foundation for RAC and the high availability framework from Cluster Ready Services to Clusterware and finally to Grid Infrastructure. Throughout the section, the terms Clusterware and Grid Infrastructure are used interchangeably. This section briefly describes Oracle Clusterware, discussing its components, their functionality, and how to make use of it as a cluster framework. In this context, Clusterware serves the following purposes:

- Monitor each cluster node's health and take corrective action if a node is found to be unhealthy by means of cluster membership management.

- Monitor cluster resources, such as networks, file systems, and databases.

- Automatically restart cluster resources on the surviving node if necessary.

For a high level overview, consider Figure 4-6.

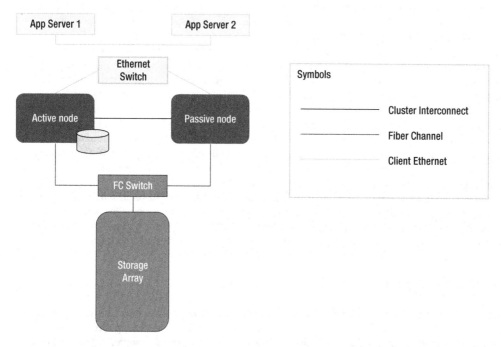

Figure 4-6. *Schematic overview of Clusterware in an active passive configuration*

Figure 4-6 shows the most common setup for Clusterware in an active/passive configuration. Please note that the figure is greatly simplified to focus on the important aspects of the architecture. Beginning from the lower part of the figure and moving up, you see a storage array providing LUNs to boot the servers from, as well as storage for the Oracle installation and the database itself. Connectivity from the servers to the closest fiber channel switches is multipathed to prevent single points of failure.

The file system employed for storing the operating system and Grid Infrastructure does not really matter, it would be JFS, ZFS, or EXT3/4, depending on your flavor of UNIX. What matters, though, is that you should ideally use Oracle's Automatic Storage Management (ASM) for the database binaries and the database files, and you need to perform a clustered installation across both nodes. The simple reason is that, with a shared database home reduces the possibility to miss configuration steps on the passive node. The use of ASM prevents time consuming file system consistency checks when mounting the database files on the passive node, a common problem with clusters that don't use cluster aware file systems.

The database can, by definition, only be started on one node at the same time. For license reasons, it must not be a cluster database. In normal operations, the database is mounted and opened on the active node. Should the Clusterware framework detect that the database on the active node has failed—perhaps caused by a node failure—it will try to restart the database on the same node. Should that fail, the database will be restarted on the passive node. In that time, all user connections will be aborted. Thanks to the cluster logical volume manager (ASM), there is no requirement to forcefully unmount any file system from the failed node and to mount it on the now active node. The failed database can almost instantly be started on the former passive node. As soon as the instance recovery is completed, users can reconnect. Oracle has introduced a very useful feature in Clusterware 10.2, called an application virtual IP address. Such an address can be tied to the database resource in the form of a dependency and migrate with it should the need arise. Application VIPs must be manually created and maintained, adding a little more complexity to the setup.

An easier to implement alternative is available in form of the virtual IP address, which is automatically created during the Clusterware installation. The so-called VIPs exist on every cluster node and have been implemented to avoid waiting for lengthy TCP timeouts. If you try to connect to a net service name and the server has crashed, you may have to wait too long for the operating system to report a timeout. The Clusterware VIP is a cluster resource, meaning it can be started on the passive node in the cluster to return a "this address no longer exists" message to the requestor, speeding up connection requests. Common net service name definitions for an active/passive cluster are:

```
activepassive.example.com =
(DESCRIPTION=
  (ADDRESS_LIST=
    (FAILOVER=YES) (LOAD_BALANCE=NO)
    (ADDRESS=(PROTOCOL=tcp)(HOST=activenode-vip.example.com)(PORT=1521))
    (ADDRESS=(PROTOCOL=tcp)(HOST=passivenode-vip.example.com)(PORT=1521)))
  (CONNECT_DATA=
    (SERVICE_NAME=activepassive.example.com)
  )
)
```

This way, the active node, which should be up and running for most of the time, is the preferred connection target. In case of a node failover, however, the active node's VIP migrates to the passive node and immediately sends the request to try the next node in the address list. This way, no change is required on the application servers in case of a node failure. Once the former active node is repaired, you should relocate the database back to its default location.

Installing a Shared Oracle RDBMS Home

This section assumes that Clusterware is already installed on your servers. The first step in creating the shared Oracle RDBMS home is to create the ASM Cluster File System (ACFS). ACFS is a POSIX compliant file system created on top of an ASM disk group. In many scenarios, it makes sense to create a dedicated disk group for the ACFS file system (the keyword is block-level replication). Once the new ASM disk group is created, you can create a so-called ASM volume on top of it. The volume is managed internally by an entity called ASM Dynamic Volume Manager. Think of ADVM as a logical volume manager. The ASM dynamic volume does not need to be of identical size as the ASM disk group. ADVM volumes can be resized online, allowing for corrections if you are running out of space.

The choice went to ACFS for the simple reason that it guarantees a consistent configuration across nodes. In many active/passive clusters, changes are not properly applied to all nodes, leaving the passive node outdated and unsuitable for role transitions. It is very often the little configuration changes—maybe an update of the local tnsnames.ora file to point to a different host—that can turn a simple role reversal into a troubleshooting nightmare. If there is only one Oracle home, then it is impossible to omit configuration changes on the passive cluster node.

When the ADVM volume is created, you need to create a file system. ADVM supports ext3, but, since this file system will be concurrently mounted on both cluster nodes, it must be a cluster file system. The cluster file system is also provided by Oracle in the form of ACFS—the ASM Cluster File System. First, you need to create the ASM Disk Group for the ASM Cluster File System. Note that you need to set a number of compatibility attributes on the disk group to allow for the creation of an ACFS:

```
SQL> create diskgroup acfs external redundancy
  2  disk 'ORCL:ACFS_001'
  3  attribute 'compatible.asm'='12.1', 'compatible.advm'='12.1';

Diskgroup created.
```

Mount this disk group in all cluster nodes. The easiest way to do so is to use srvctl to start the diskgroup:

```
[grid@rac12node1 ~]$ srvctl start diskgroup -g ACFS
```

Next, create an ACFS volume that will later contain the file system. You can use either the graphical user interface—ASM Configuration Assistant or ASMCA—or the command line. It is easier to use the latter in scripts, so it was chosen here. Instead of asmcmd, the primary tool used in Oracle 11g, you can now make use of ASMCA in silent mode to create the ACFS volume and file system. The command options used are silent and createVolume:

```
[grid@rac12node1 ~]$ asmca -silent -createVolume -volumeName orahomevol \
> -volumeDiskGroup ACFS -volumeSizeGB 8

Volume orahomevol created successfully.
```

The syntax is self-explanatory. ASMCA has been instructed to create a volume with the name "orahomevol" on disk group ACFS with a size of 8 GB. This operation completes quickly. The venerable asmcmd command proves that the volume was indeed created:

```
[grid@rac12node1 ~]$ asmcmd volinfo -G ACFS -a
Diskgroup Name: ACFS

        Volume Name: ORAHOMEVOL
        Volume Device: /dev/asm/orahomevol-137
        State: ENABLED
        Size (MB): 8192
        Resize Unit (MB): 32
        Redundancy: UNPROT
        Stripe Columns: 4
        Stripe Width (K): 128
        Usage:
        Mountpath:
```

With the volume in place, you can create the file system on top. Again, ASMCA is used to perform this task:

```
[grid@rac12node1 ~]$ asmca -silent -createACFS -acfsVolumeDevice /dev/asm/orahomevol-137 \
> -acfsMountPoint /u01/app/oracle
```

ASM Cluster File System created on /dev/asm/orahomevol-137 successfully. Run the generated
ACFS registration script /u01/app/grid/cfgtoollogs/asmca/scripts/acfs_script.sh as
privileged user to register the ACFS with Grid Infrastructure and to mount the ACFS. The
ACFS registration script needs to be run only on this node: rac12node1.

The script creates the ACFS file system, registers it as a resource with Clusterware, and starts it. The final
configuration of the file system is:

```
[grid@rac12node1 ~]$ srvctl config filesystem -d /dev/asm/orahomevol-137
Volume device: /dev/asm/orahomevol-137
Canonical volume device: /dev/asm/orahomevol-137
Mountpoint path: /u01/app/oracle
User:
Type: ACFS
Mount options:
Description:
Nodes:
Server pools:
Application ID:
ACFS file system is enabled
[grid@rac12node1 ~]$
```

Installing the Shared Database Binaries

When you have made sure that the database binaries have been mounted on each host, you need to install the
database binaries. Again, you should install the binaries for a single instance only. This way you are protected from
accidentally starting a database as a cluster database, which would constitute to a license violation. When selecting
the location for the database installation, double-check that you are installing on the newly created ACFS, instead of
a local file system.

The installation of the database binaries is completely identical to an installation to a non-shared file system.
You can read more about installing the database binaries for a single instance Oracle database in Chapter 6.

Creating the Database

With the Oracle Home created on a shared ACFS device, you can now start the Database Configuration Assistant
from it. To make maximum use of the shared file system you should consider placing the diagnostic destination to the
cluster file system as well. All other database related files should be placed into ASM. Remember that the database
must be a single instance Oracle database.

If your engineering department has supplied a database template, the configuration of the database could not be
easier. Here is an example for a single instance database creation in which the default data file location is set to disk
group DATA and the fast recovery area is defined in disk group +RECO. Also note how the audit file destination and
diagnostic destination are explicitly placed on the ACFS file system:

```
[oracle@rac12node1 ~]$ /u01/app/oracle/product/12.1.0.1/dbhome_1/bin/dbca \
> -silent -createDatabase -templateName active_passive.dbc -gdbName apclu \
> -sysPassword sys -createAsContainerDatabase true -numberOfPDBs 1 \
> -pdbName apress -systemPassword sys -storageType ASM -diskGroupName DATA \
> -recoveryGroupName RECO -totalMemory 1536
Enter PDBADMIN User Password:
```

```
Copying database files
1% complete
[...]
74% complete
Creating Pluggable Databases
79% complete
100% complete
Look at the log file "/u01/app/oracle/cfgtoollogs/dbca/apclu/apclu.log" for further details.
[oracle@rac12node1 bin]$
```

■ **Note**   Pluggable Databases (PDBs) are one of the most interesting new features in Oracle 12c. You can read more about the technical details pertaining to PDBs in Chapter 7.

The silent creation of a database is a very powerful command; refer to the online help or the official documentation set for more information about its options.

Registering the Database with Clusterware

As part of its creation, the database will be registered in Clusterware as a single instance database resource. In all normal circumstances that would be a much appreciated service, but in this special case it needs changing. An Oracle single instance database deployed on a multi-node cluster does not have the ability to "move" around in the cluster. When created, the instance sticks to the cluster node where it was created.

To gain some flexibility, a new custom resource needs created. This resource will allow the database to be started on more than one cluster node: in the event of a node failure it will be relocated to the surviving node without user intervention. Since the database files all reside in ASM—a cluster file system concurrently mounted on all nodes—no time consuming file system integrity check is needed. The first step is to remove the database configuration from the Cluster registry:

```
[oracle@rac12node1 ~]$ srvctl stop database -d apclu
[oracle@rac12node1 ~]$ srvctl remove database -d apclu
Remove the database apclu? (y/[n]) y
```

Note that this command cleans the entry from the oratab file as well. The following steps require a little more planning. Recap from the introduction that Clusterware manages resources during their life cycle. The major states the resource can be in are:

- Stopped: the resource is stopped, either intentionally or because it crashed.

- Started: the resource is up and running.

- Intermediate: something went wrong when starting the resource.

The status of each resource managed by Clusterware can be viewed using the crsctl utility, as shown here:

```
[oracle@rac12node1 ~]$ /u01/app/12.1.0.1/grid/bin/crsctl stat res -t
--------------------------------------------------------------------------
Name            Target  State       Server           State details
--------------------------------------------------------------------------
[...]
--------------------------------------------------------------------------
Cluster Resources
--------------------------------------------------------------------------
ora.LISTENER_SCAN1.lsnr
        1       ONLINE  ONLINE      rac12node2       STABLE
ora.LISTENER_SCAN2.lsnr
        1       ONLINE  ONLINE      rac12node1       STABLE
ora.LISTENER_SCAN3.lsnr
        1       ONLINE  ONLINE      rac12node1       STABLE
```

A resource can be either local to a cluster node or a cluster resource. A local resource always stays on the cluster node and does not relocate to other nodes. A cluster resource, however, is aware that it is deployed in a cluster and can react to node failures. Two prerequisites are to be met to register a custom resource. The first is a so-called action script that implements callbacks to start, stop, and check the resource. The action script is referenced in the resource description, called a profile. First, an action script is needed. A very basic script implementing the minimum amount of code is subsequently provided. It lacks elegance and sufficient error checking; you are encouraged to improve as needed.

```
#!/bin/bash

[[ "$TRACE" == "YES" ]] && {
        set -x
}

PATH=/usr/local/bin:$PATH
ORACLE_SID=apclu
ORACLE_HOME=/u01/app/oracle/product/12.1.0.1/dbhome_1
ORACLE_BASE=/u01/app/oracle

export PATH ORACLE_SID ORACLE_HOME ORACLE_BASE

PS=/bin/ps
SU=/bin/su

# avoid "standard in must be a tty" error when executing the script as RDBMS_OWNER
[[ $(whoami) != "$RDBMS_OWNER" ]] && {
        SWITCH_USER="$SU - $RDBMS_OWNER -c"
}

case $1 in
'start')
        $SWITCH_USER $ORACLE_HOME/bin/sqlplus / as sysdba <<EOF
startup
exit
EOF
```

```
        RC=$?
        ;;
'stop')
        $SWITCH_USER $ORACLE_HOME/bin/sqlplus / as sysdba <<EOF
shutdown
exit
EOF
        RC=$?
        ;;
'check')
        $PS -ef | grep -v grep | grep ora_smon_${ORACLE_SID} > /dev/null
        RC=$?
        ;;
*)
        echo "invalid command passed to ${0} - must be one of start, stop or check"
esac

# we are done-return the status code to the caller
if (( RC == 0 )) ; then
        exit 0
else
        # the actual error code from the command does not matter
        exit 1
fi
```

Moving the script to the ACFS file system allows for easier maintenance, and do not forget to make it executable for its owner.

■ **Note** The script assumes that the oratab files on both cluster nodes are properly maintained, otherwise it will fail.

Armed with the script you can create the new resource. The command used for this purpose is crsctl add resource.

```
[oracle@rac12node1 scripts]$ /u01/app/12.1.0.1/grid/bin/crsctl add resource -h
Usage:
  crsctl add resource <resName> -type <typeName> [[-file <filePath>] | [-attr
"<specification>[,...]"]] [-f] [-i]
      <specification>:   {<attrName>=<value> | <attrName>@<scope>=<value>}
          <scope>:   {@SERVERNAME(<server>)[@DEGREEID(<did>)] |
                        @CARDINALITYID(<cid>)[@DEGREEID(<did>)] }
where
      resName         Add named resource
      typeName        Resource type
      filePath        Attribute file
      attrName        Attribute name
      value           Attribute value
      server          Server name
      cid             Resource cardinality ID
      did             Resource degree ID
      -f              Force option
      -i              Fail if request cannot be processed immediately
```

This command allows you freedom in designing your resource profile; for the purpose of a cluster database, however, it is sufficient to add the resource as shown:

```
[oracle@rac12node1 scripts]$ /u01/app/12.1.0.1/grid/bin/crsctl \
> add resource apress.apclu.db -type cluster_resource -file add_res_attr
```

The file referenced in the command contains key/value pairs defining the resource.

```
ACL=owner:oracle:rwx,pgrp:dba:rwx,other::r--
ACTION_SCRIPT=/u01/app/oracle/admin/apclu/scripts/ha_apclu.sh
AUTO_START=restore
CARDINALITY=1
DEGREE=1
DESCRIPTION=Custom resource for database apclu
PLACEMENT=restricted
HOSTING_MEMBERS=rac12node1 rac12node2
RESTART_ATTEMPTS=2
SCRIPT_TIMEOUT=60
START_DEPENDENCIES=
hard(ora.DATA.dg,ora.RECO.dg,ora.acfs.orahomevol.acfs)
weak(type:ora.listener.type,uniform:ora.ons)
pullup(ora.DATA.dg,ora.acfs.orahomevol.acfs)
STOP_DEPENDENCIES=
hard(intermediate:ora.asm,shutdown:ora.DATA.dg,shutdown:ora.RECO.dg,ora.acfs.orahomevol.acfs)
FAILURE_INTERVAL=60
FAILURE_THRESHOLD=1
```

Some of these directives have been taken from the original resource profile, especially those defining the start and stop dependencies. In the example, /u01/app/oracle/ is an ACFS file system. In a nutshell, this profile allows the database to be started on rac12node1 and rac12node2, the "hosting members." For this variable to have an effect, you need to define a placement policy of "restricted." The other variables are internal to Clusterware. If you are interested, you can check their meaning in the Clusterware Administration and Deployment Guide, Appendix B. Do not forget to check that the database is registered in /etc/oratab on both hosts.

Managing the Database

Instead of using the familiar srvctl command or even sqlplus directly, you need to interact with the database using the crsctl utility. Although this might sound daunting, it is not. Starting the database, for example, is accomplished using the following command:

```
[oracle@rac12node1 scripts]$ /u01/app/12.1.0.1/grid/bin/crsctl \
> start resource apress.apclu.db \
> -n preferredHost
CRS-2672: Attempting to start 'apress.apclu.db' on 'rac12node1'
CRS-2676: Start of 'apress.apclu.db' on 'rac12node1' succeeded
```

You should make a habit of specifying the host the database should start on specifically as part of the command. The syntax is very easy to understand. The crsctl command takes a verb and an object to work on. In this case, the verb is to start and the object is the resource with name "apress.apclu.db". The optional parameter "-n" specifies which host the resource should start on.

Conversely, you stop the resource with the "stop" verb:

```
[oracle@rac12node1 scripts]$ /u01/app/12.1.0.1/grid/bin/crsctl \
> stop resource apress.apclu.db
CRS-2673: Attempting to stop 'apress.apclu.db' on 'rac12node1'
CRS-2677: Stop of 'apress.apclu.db' on 'rac12node1' succeeded
```

You can also manually relocate the database if you have to:

```
[oracle@rac12node1 scripts]$ /u01/app/12.1.0.1/grid/bin/crsctl relocate resource \
> apress.apclu.db -s rac12node2 -n rac12node1
CRS-2673: Attempting to stop 'apress.apclu.db' on 'rac12node2'
CRS-2677: Stop of 'apress.apclu.db' on 'rac12node2' succeeded
CRS-2672: Attempting to start 'apress.apclu.db' on 'rac12node1'
CRS-2676: Start of 'apress.apclu.db' on 'rac12node1' succeeded
```

The syntax is straight forward: you specify the source host with the –s and the destination with the –n. Each takes a valid hosting member as an argument. The relocation happens transparently if the current active node experiences an outage, planned and unplanned. The action script will execute the code in the check callback function to see if the resource is available, and issue restart_attempts tries to start the resource on the same host. Since this is impossible—the host went down—it will relocate the resource on the former passive node. Once initiated, the time it takes to fail over to the other node is the same as a recovery from an instance crash on the same server. As a rule of thumb, you can say that the busier the system is then the longer the recovery time will be.

Summary

This chapter discussed possible software solutions for your consolidation project. You first read about virtualization examples using Solaris Zones, followed by an introduction to Oracle VM Server. In the last section you read about creating a single instance database and making it highly available on a clustered ASM configuration with Oracle Clusterware for heartbeat and cluster membership management. This approach is best integrated with Clusterware, different cluster-aware logical volume managers would introduce their own cluster membership stack that could potentially conflict with Oracle's own.

Every vendor currently tries to position his solution as the best suitable technology for consolidation in the (private) cloud. Such solutions are built on top of the respective management frameworks for resilience and high availability. The other approach is to cluster Oracle databases on physical hardware to provide protection from instance failure and to keep applications running. There is no clear winner yet, and times are interesting. Whichever technology you chose, you should spend sufficient time testing it in production-like environments before defining the service and rolling it out to potential users.

■ ■ ■

Installing Oracle Linux

In this chapter you are going to learn how to install and configure Oracle Linux 6 for use with Oracle database release 12c. Oracle Linux 6 has been selected because its installable DVD and CD-ROM images are still freely available. In this respect, Oracle Linux is probably the most accessible supported Linux for use with any Oracle database product. In fact, if you are keen on the "one vendor" approach, Oracle Linux could be your sole operating system for Oracle products besides the database.

For a long time, the differences between Red Hat Linux and Oracle Linux were negligible. This was before Oracle released its own branch of the kernel—the so-called *Unbreakable Enterprise Kernel* (UEK). I use the term *kernel-UEK* to refer to this kernel.

The UEK causes a bit of a dilemma for the system and database administrator. Should you break compatibility with the most widely used Linux distribution and use kernel-UEK? Or should you maintain compatibility instead? Additionally, it might be difficult to get vendor certification for Oracle Linux 6 *and* kernel-UEK. Where one could argue that the use of Oracle Linux with the Red-Hat kernel was more or less like using Red Hat, this is no longer true when you switch to kernel-UEK. However, taking Oracle's aggressive marketing into account, and their ability to set their own timescales for "third party" certification it might be a good idea to go with their favored combination of Oracle Linux 6 plus kernel UEK for future deployments.

■ **Note** The use of Oracle Linux in this book should not be interpreted as a recommendation for this distribution. The choice of Linux distribution should instead be made based on certification with third-party products, in-house experience, and the quality of support.

Installing Oracle Linux 6

The installation of Oracle Linux 6 is not too different from the previous release. Users and administrators of Oracle Linux 5 will quickly find their way around. Since this book is all about minimizing manual (read: administrator) intervention, it will focus on how to automate the installation of Oracle Linux 6 as much as possible. However it is beneficial to get to know the process of the GUI installation first. Kickstart, the RedHat/Oracle Linux mechanism for lights-out installation is much easier to understand once the steps for graphical installation have been shown.

The following sections assume that the operating system is installed on a BIOS-based server. While writing this book the number of servers using Unified Extensible Firmware Interface (UEFI) as a replacement for the BIOS has steadily increased, but the switch to UEFI-only systems has not yet happened. The steps for installing Oracle Linux 6 on an UEFI server are almost identical. Consult your documentation on how to make full use of the UEFI features. Alternatively, many UEFI systems have a BIOS-compatibility switch which can be enabled.

While the transition to UEFI is still outstanding, an important change has happened in that 32-bit systems are dying out. In fact, although you get support for 32- as well as 64-bit Linux, you should not deploy new 32-bit Linux systems. They simply suffer from too many shortcomings, especially when it comes to memory handling. Oracle realized this as well, and stopped shipping the database for 32-bit platforms.

The Oracle Linux installation is performed in stages. In the first stage the server to be installed is powered on and uses a boot medium-the installation DVD or a minimum boot media to start. Alternatively the PXE boot settings can be used to transfer the minimal operating system image to the server. In the following stage, the installation source as defined will be used to guide you through the installation process.

Manual Installation

Before exploring ways to automate the Oracle Linux installation using Kickstart let's have a look at the interactive installation of Oracle Linux 6 first. At the time of this writing, Oracle Linux 6 update 4 was the latest version available for download. The Oracle Linux media can be obtained from Oracle's self-service portal: `http://edelivery.oracle.com/linux`. Before you can access the software you need to supply login information using an account with a validated email address. You also need to agree to the export restrictions and license as is standard with Oracle products. From the list of available Linux releases to download, choose the current release of Oracle Linux 6 and wait for the download to finish.

This section assumes the host you are installing to has a DVD-ROM drive to be used for the installation. (Of course, that DVD_ROM drive can be virtualized). The DVD will be used as the installation source in this section. In the next section, "Automated installation" further options for installing Oracle Linux over the network are presented.

■ **Note**   The advanced installation methods except PXE-booting are out of scope of this book. More details about booting from USB and minimal installation media can be found in Oracle's online documentation.

After downloading and verifying the integrity of the DVD ISO image, proceed by burning it to an empty DVD. Alternatively, make the ISO image available to the virtualized DVD drive on the server. This DVD contains all the required software to install your server, so the need to juggle CD-ROMs as in previous versions has gone. Ensure that you can either have access to a boot menu in your server's BIOS or manually set the boot order to start from CD-ROM/DVD-ROM in the first place. Insert the DVD and power the server on. You should be greeted by the boot menu as shown in Figure 5-1:

Figure 5-1. *The boot menu for Oracle Linux 6*

Most users will chose the default option of installing a new system.

■ **Tip** Even though it is technically possible to upgrade from a previous minor release it is recommended to perform a fresh install instead. Instead of wiping out the existing partitions; however, you could opt for a parallel installation of the new Oracle Linux version. Boot loader entries will allow you to dual-boot the system in case you have to revert back to the earlier release for some reason.

The Oracle Linux installation will begin automatically after a timeout or when you press enter. Before launching the graphical installer "Anaconda," you have the option to perform a check of the installation media. If this is the first time you use the DVD with a server it is recommended to perform the test. You can safely skip it if you have already successfully used the DVD in a previous installation.

Anaconda

Your system will then start Anaconda, the graphical configuration assistant to guide you through the rest of the installation.

■ **Tip**   If your system does not start the X11 session necessary to display Anaconda, you could use its built-in VNC capabilities. Start a VNC server session on a different machine in the build network and specify the boot parameters vnc vncconnect=vncserverHost:vncPort vncpassword=remoteVNCServerPassword at the command line.

The next steps are almost self-explanatory. After acknowledging the welcome screen by clicking next you have the option to select the language to be used during the installation. Alternative languages can always be installed for use with the system later. Once you are happy with the settings click on the "Next" button to select your keyboard layout to be used during the installation. The keyboard setting-just like the language setting made earlier-can be changed after the system has been installed. From a support point of view it is sensible to limit the installation to English. Mixing multiple languages in different regions makes a global support policy difficult. Translating error messages and troubleshooting can become a problem for non-native speakers.

Choice of storage devices

So far the installation process was very similar to the one used in Oracle Linux 5. The next screen though, titled "Storage devices" is new to Oracle Linux 6. It offers two choices:

1.   To use "basic storage devices"

2.   Alternatively use "specialized storage devices"

Specialized storage in this context allows you to install the operating system to a SAN disk or over Fibre Channel over Ethernet or iSCSI. It also (finally!) offers support for installation on hardware RAID and dm-multipathed devices. For all other needs, simply go with the first option.

■ **Note**   The use of specialized storage devices is out of scope of this book. SAN booting however is a very interesting concept that you could implement to quickly replace failed hardware, mainly in blade enclosures.

In the following sections it is assumed that you are installing the operating system to internally attached disks. Most servers will use an internal RAID adapter to present a single view on internal disks. Consult your vendor's manual for more information on how to configure these. In many cases, the array driver is already part of the Linux distribution and you don't need to worry about it once the BIOS setup is completed. If not, then fear not-you have an option to add vendor drivers during the installation process. Whichever way you decide to install the operating system, it is important to have a level of resilience built in. Resilience can come in the form of multiple disks in a RAID 1 configuration, or in the form of multiple paths to the storage to prevent a single point of failure.

Following along the path set out by the example, select the "basic storage devices" click on the "Next" button. You may be prompted with a "storage device warning" before the next screen appears. Oracle Linux tries to read an existing partition table for all detected storage devices made available to the host. The warning is raised whenever no partition table can be found, or alternatively if the detected partition table cannot be read and understood.

If you are certain that the disk for which the warning appears is blank, unpartitioned, and not in use you should click on "Yes, discard my data." Be careful not to check "Apply my choice to all devices with undetected partitions or filesystems!" You can exclude a disk from the further partitioning process by clicking on "No, keep my data" for that disk.

■ **Tip**   The graphical installer allows you to drop into a shell session at any time. Press CTRL-ALT-F2 for a root shell and CTRL-ALT-F3 to view the Anaconda logs. You could try to read the disk header using dd if=/dev/xxx bs=1M count=1 | od -a to ensure that the disk is not in use. CTRL-ALT-F6 brings you back to Anaconda.

For cluster installations in particular you need to be careful at this stage when adding nodes to the cluster. If your system administrator has made the ASM LUNs available to the host you are about to install they must not be touched by the installer, otherwise you lose data! To prevent human errors, it is usually safer to not present the database LUNs to the host at installation time. Linux is very flexible and SAN storage can be made available to the host without rebooting. Be aware that the storage warning dialog will be repeated for each disk with an unknown partition table or file system.

Surprisingly the next screen allows you to configure the network. The storage configuration will be performed later.

Network configuration

You would have expected to be able to review the storage layout now but first you need to define the hostname of your new server. If you are using DHCP, supply the short hostname only, otherwise provide a fully qualified domain name (FQDN). The fully qualified hostname has been used in Figure 5-2. New to Oracle Linux 6 is the ability to define the network properties at this stage. Click on the "Configure Network" button in the lower-left corner of the screen to access the network configuration settings. The following dialog allows you to configure wired, wireless, mobile broadband, VPN, and DSL connections. Most enterprise systems will need to configure wired connections at this stage. Highlight your current network card by clicking on it, then chose "edit" from the right-hand menu. The resulting configuration options are shown in Figure 5-2.

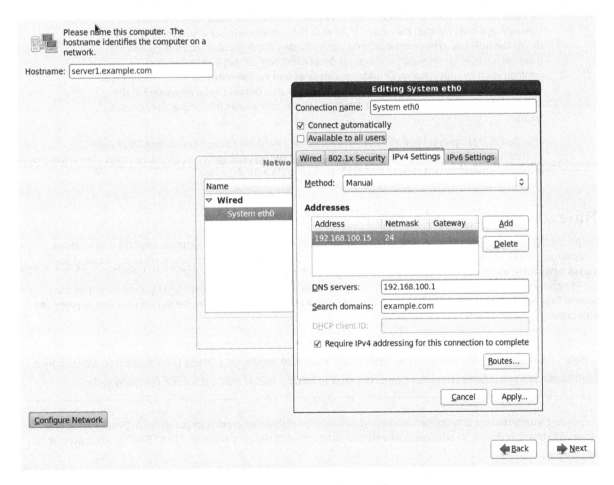

Figure 5-2. *Editing system properties for the first ethernet device discovered*

This network configuration utility uses Network Manager under the covers. Network Manager is the replacement for the network administration tool ("system-config-network") and one of the bigger changes in Oracle Linux 6 over its previous versions. This does not imply that the way network settings were configured in Oracle Linux go away, but you should be aware of the new way of doing things. The system settings for the selected device can be chosen in the tabs "wired," "802.x Security," "IPv4 Settings," and "IPv6 Settings." You have the option to make the following changes on these tabs:

Wired: On this tab you can define the Media Access Control (MAC) address for a specific interface. It is suggested to leave this value blank to use the MAC address of the interface. The MAC address is important when booting-should the network interface card (NIC) return a different MAC address than defined (which can happen during cloning of virtual machines) the network interface will default to a DHCP address and discard its static configuration if used.

802.1x Security: In this tab you can define 802.1.x port-based network access control (PNAC). Normally you would not need to enable 802.1x security-when in doubt leave this option unchecked.

IPv4 Settings: Although the days of the "old" Internet addressing scheme, IPv4 are numbered, it is still the most important way of connecting servers to the local network for the foreseeable future. Therefore the IPv4 protocol plays the most important role in connecting a server within the network. As with the network administration tool you can define the network to be dynamically configured using the dynamic host configuration protocol (DHCP), or manually configured. Most users will probably choose a static configuration by supplying an IP address, netmask, and gateway. Additionally DNS servers can be specified for naming resolution as well as a search domain to be appended in the absence of a FQDN. If necessary you can even set up static routes by clicking the "Routes..." button.

IPv6 Settings: Despite several global IPv6 awareness days there has not been a breakthrough in adoption of the next generation IP protocol inside organizations. Most users therefore will choose to disable IPv6 here ("Method: ignore").

Time zone settings and root password

Following the network configuration you need to set the system's time zone. This setting is important as it allows determining the location of the server. If you are planning on clustering the Oracle system yet to be installed then please ensure that all the cluster nodes share the same time zone.

To pick a time zone you can either use the zoom controls to click on the city depicted by a yellow dot on the map nearest to your location to set the time zone. Another option is to use the dropdown list to find the most appropriate time zone.

■ **Note** The documentation states certain implications when dual-booting your Oracle Linux installation with Windows. A production oracle database server however is not likely to be dual-booted with a non-UNIX operating system.

Before finally making it to the partitioning wizard, you need to set a secure root password to be used with this server. As always, only system administrators should have access to the root account. Click "Next" to proceed with the installation.

Partitioning

An interesting detail of the Oracle Linux installation is the somewhat belated option to choose a partitioning layout. Again this section assumes you have chosen "basic storage devices." The initial screen offers you a number of options to install Oracle Linux exclusively or in conjunction with other operating systems.

Oracle database servers are not normally configured for dual-booting with non-Linux systems. A planned upgrade of Oracle Linux 5 (or another Linux distribution) to Oracle Linux 6 however is a valid reason for a dual-boot configuration. Before beginning the partitioning of your server be sure to create backups of any data you want to preserve. Please bear in mind that mistakes do happen! After the changes you are making on the following screen are written to disk, previously existing partitions may irrevocably be lost!

Whichever option you select from the list of available options, it is recommended to enable the check box labeled "Review and modify partitioning layout" which takes you to the screen shown in Figure 5-3 to fine-tune the setup for a single-boot configuration with Oracle Linux 6.4 as the only installed operating system.

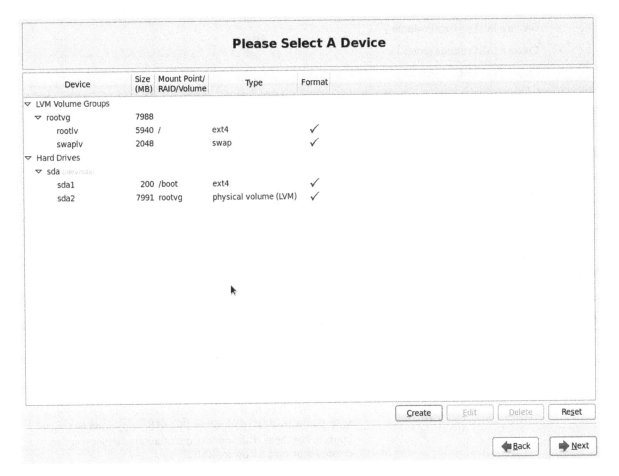

Figure 5-3. *Configuring the storage layout for Oracle Linux 6*

The partitioning screen has a great many options, and a complete description of all possible configuration combinations cannot be provided in this chapter. It is best to align the storage configuration with your current standards. That way you can't really make a mistake. For all the other detail please refer to the online manual. To keep things simple and to prevent mistakes from happening it is often recommended not to present storage to the server, which is not immediately required to install the base operating system at this stage. The commands necessary to create storage mount points for the Oracle accounts will be described in a later section in this chapter.

The partitioning screen resembles the layout used in Oracle Linux 5, but the graphical representation in the top of how full an individual disk is will only appear after clicking on it. The user interface has been uncluttered in comparison with the previous version, but the functionality has remained the same. The "Create" button offers you to create the following entities, disk space permitting:

- Create a standard partition

- Create a (software) RAID partition

- Create a (software) RAID device

- Create a LVM physical volume

- Create a LVM volume group

- Create a LVM logical volume

The "Edit" button allows you to make changes to the highlighted partition, the "Delete" button unsurprisingly removes the selected entity. If you got stuck during the partitioning of your system and want to get back to square one, click on the "Reset" button to undo your changes to the original layout.

Oracle Linux has a wider set of options of file systems available to format your disks. Apart from ext3, which was the standard in Oracle Linux 5.x ext2, ext4, xfs, and Btrfs are available.

■ **Caution**   BTRFs is still considered experimental in the upstream kernel. You should probably not use it for production systems yet.

A possible partitioning scheme in Oracle Linux includes the partitions listed in Table 5-1.

Table 5-1. *Partitioning layout for the operating system*

Mount Point	Size	File System recommendation
/boot	At least 200MiB, up to 2 GiB	Use either an ext2, ext3, or ext4 file system to be on the safe side. The bootloader used in Oracle Linux 6, grub-0.97 has a number of known limitations.
		The boot partition, for example, cannot be in a LVM logical volume, but it can be a software RAID device (with limitations). Most hardware RAID controllers should be supported by Oracle Linux 6, but check with your documentation whether you can create /boot on a hardware RAID.
		The virtual bootloader in Xen-based virtualization might have problems with ext4, ext2 is tested and confirmed to work.

(continued)

Table 5-1. (*continued*)

Mount Point	Size	File System recommendation
swap	See below	The swap partition will be covered in detail in the section "Considerations for swap space" below. Although not a requirement it is strongly recommended to create a swap partition.
/	Minimum 5GiB, better more	The smallest, documented, possible root partition of only 3GiB does not allow the installation of all packages required for an Oracle database installation. If possible, opt for 8GiB or more. This allows for staging Oracle installation media and a sufficiently large /tmp directory.
		If you would like to use storage replication later you should not install the Oracle binaries on local disk. You should definitely not install them in the / file system. Core dumps can quickly lead to a filled-up root partition resulting in serious trouble for Linux. In-line with the advice not to present storage not necessary for the base OS installation the Oracle LUNs are not presented yet.
Others		For many other open-source software additional mount points are suggested, such as /tmp, /home, and others. For an Oracle database server these are usually not needed.

It is strongly recommended not to install the operating system on a single hard disk. Whenever possible make use of a hardware RAID adapter inside the server. Otherwise the failure of a single disk will result in an outage of the server which can easily be prevented. If your server does not use a built-in RAID adapter for the internal disks you have the option to create a software RAID configuration. An example for a software-RAID is shown in Figure 5-4 below. Matching sized partitions are created on the internal disks and mirrored to form RAID 1 pairs. Of course, you have other software RAID levels as well but RAID 1 seems most practical.

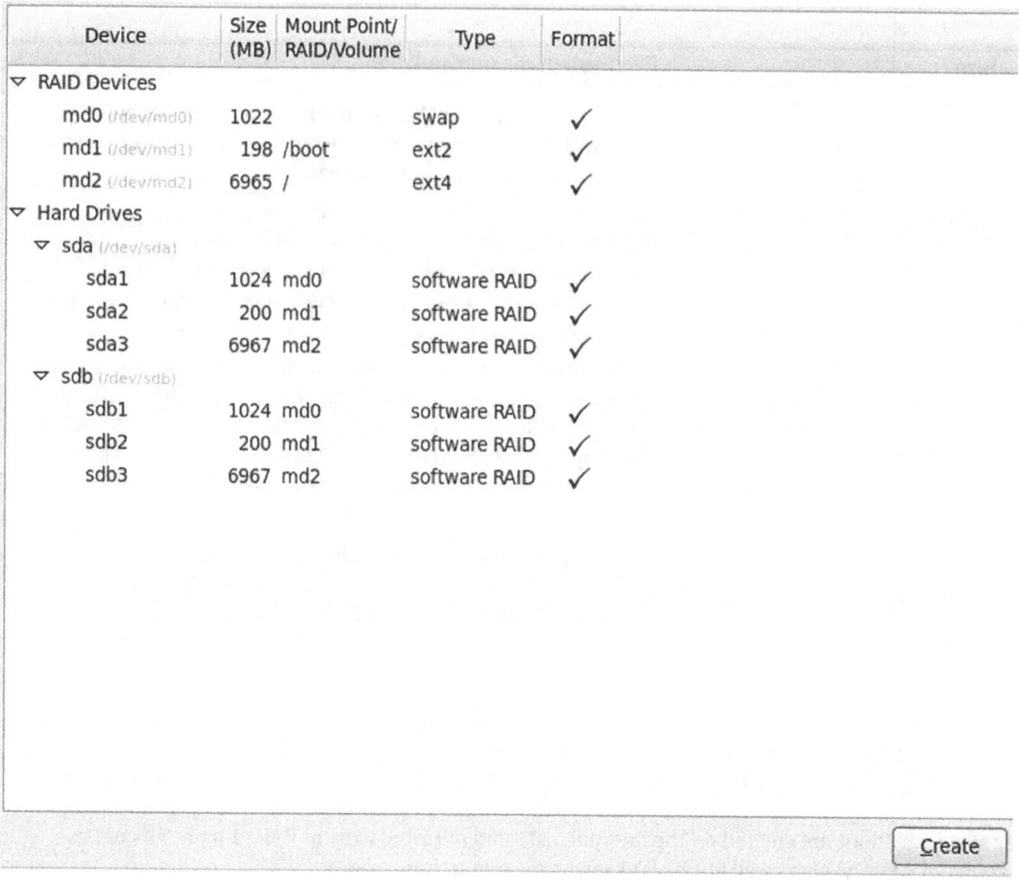

Device	Size (MB)	Mount Point/ RAID/Volume	Type	Format
▽ RAID Devices				
md0 (/dev/md0)	1022		swap	✓
md1 (/dev/md1)	198	/boot	ext2	✓
md2 (/dev/md2)	6965	/	ext4	✓
▽ Hard Drives				
▽ sda (/dev/sda)				
sda1	1024	md0	software RAID	✓
sda2	200	md1	software RAID	✓
sda3	6967	md2	software RAID	✓
▽ sdb (/dev/sdb)				
sdb1	1024	md0	software RAID	✓
sdb2	200	md1	software RAID	✓
sdb3	6967	md2	software RAID	✓

Create

Figure 5-4. *Using Software RAID to protect the operating system*

As you can see the partition layout is symmetrical between the disks: three partitions are created on each device with a partition type of "software RAID" for this small Oracle SE database server. One gigabyte swap in /dev/sda1 and /dev/sdb1 each, 200 MiB boot partition on /dev/sda2 and /dev/sdb2 as well as a root partition spanning the rest of disks /dev/sda and /dev/sdb. In the next step RAID 1 pairs are created, resulting in RAID devices. The boot loader can be installed in the /boot partition. The resulting disk layout is shown here:

```
[root@server1 ~]# df -h
Filesystem      Size  Used Avail Use% Mounted on
/dev/md2        6.7G  787M  5.6G  13% /
tmpfs           497M     0  497M   0% /dev/shm
/dev/md1        194M   39M  146M  21% /boot
```

An alternative approach would be to create two RAID 1 devices /dev/md0 and /dev/md1. The first one has to be a boot partition since the boot loader cannot reside in an LVM logical volume. The other RAID device can be converted into a physical device for use with LVM.

The Linux Logical Volume Manager (LVM) is an excellent choice to add flexibility to your disk layout. LVM is based on physical volumes, or LUNs. For example, a software RAID device can also be a physical volume. Multiple physical volumes can be aggregated into a volume group, which provides the cumulative amount of free space of all underlying physical volumes. You then carve space out of the volume group, creating logical volumes. On top of a logical volume you create the file system and the mount point. You can be guided through all of these steps in the installer, accessible by the "Create" button.

Now why would you use this complex sounding LVM at all? Because it gives you the ability to grow and even shrink your file systems! If you are using partitions it is very difficult, if not impossible, to resize a file system. With LVM all you need to do is extend the logical volume and resize the file system on top. This can be a life saver if you need to upgrade Oracle and OUI complains about a lack of space.

Considerations for /u01-the Oracle mount point

The Oracle mount points have not yet been covered in this discussion. As with anything in life there is more than one way to do it. One approach would be to keep the Oracle binaries on local storage. This means using volume group "rootvg" or an additional, new volume group on the internal RAIDed disks with multiple logical volumes:

- Logical volume "swaplv"

- Logical volume "rootlv" for all Linux binaries, specifically excluding Oracle

- Logical volume "oraclelv" for all Oracle related binaries

In environments where the Automatic Storage Management option is used you could further divide the "oraclelv" volume into "oragridlv" and "orardbmslv" to enforce the concept of separation of duties. This subject will be covered in more detail later in this chapter.

In addition to the local storage approach just described many sites make use of LUNs exported via a storage area network to persist the Oracle binaries in addition to the database. Using that approach is preferred because it allows for greater independence of the hardware. Stateless computing, which has already been mentioned in Chapter 1, is a great way of improving a system's mean time to recovery, especially in Real Application Clusters. All that is needed to be done is to assign the failed node's "personality" (usually an XML file) to a spare node in the chassis and boot it up. Since it looks and feels exactly like the failed node, it can join the cluster in very little time. All of this thanks to intelligent management tools and node-independent storage.

Regardless of whether or not you are planning on using local or SAN storage, you should set plenty of space aside for the Oracle installation. Beginning with Oracle 11.2 the company provided point releases as full releases. The installation process for an 11.1 RAC system begins with the installation of three software homes using the base release 11.1.0.6 software for Clusterware, ASM and the RDBMS home. That is, if you follow the white papers and install ASM into its own software home. It is possible to start the ASM instance out of the RDBMS home as well, but in larger environments every RDBMS patch means an ASM outage on that node too. You next had to patch each of these to the terminal release. In the third step you finally patched all these to the latest Patch Set Update. With the full release you can now skip the middle part and install the full release immediately. However, Oracle strongly discourages in-place upgrades, which drive the space requirements up quite dramatically. Each new point release also seems to be very space-demanding which leads me to the following recommendation:

- Plan for 20GiB+ for Oracle Restart if you would like to use Oracle Automatic Storage Management

- Add an additional 15 GiB for each Oracle RDBMS home

Although this sounds like a lot, it is not. Each upgrade of an Oracle home will require you to store at least another home of the same kind. The above is a conservative recommendation-compare to the Oracle 12.1 documentation which recommends that 100GB should be made available for Grid Infrastructure alone! In addition you can remove the old Oracle home after the successful upgrade and a sufficient grace period. Following the "disk space is cheap" philosophy, do not be tight with disk space for Oracle installation if you can afford it.

Considerations for swap space

Another important consideration for every Oracle installation is the amount of swap space to be provided by the operating system. Discussing virtual memory in Linux easily fills a book on its own; nevertheless I would like to add some information here to allow you to make an informed decision about swap size.

Simply stated, swap allows the operating system to continue running even if all physical memory is exhausted. Technically, swap space is an extension of the virtual memory to hard disk, and can either be a dedicated partition or a file. The use of a dedicated swap partition is recommended over the file-based approach.

For recent Oracle releases, the following formula was used and enforced in Oracle's Universal Installer:

- For physical memory less than 2 GiB Oracle wants 1.5x the physical memory as swap space.

- For systems between 2 and 16 GiB RAM, Oracle recommends a swap partition equal the size of physical memory.

- For servers with more than 16 GiB RAM Oracle suggests 16 GiB of swap space.

Interestingly, there are multiple recommendations made in the Red Hat documentation set about the swap size! This shows that the amount of swap to be provided is not an exact science. Having elaborated on the use of swap for the operating system there is one remark to be made for Oracle: your database processes should not swap. Strategies to control the virtual memory in Linux are described later in this chapter.

Writing changes to disk

So far in the partitioning screen nothing has happened to the data on disk. As soon as you chose to continue with the installation process by clicking on "Next" in the partitioning screen this changes.

A prominent warning pops up stating that when writing the changes to disk all deleted partitions will indeed be erased, and partitions selected to be formatted will be lost. This is the last warning, and final opportunity to abort the installation process without affecting the data on hard disk.

If you are absolutely sure the settings you have chosen are correct, click on "Write Changes to Disk" to proceed.

Boot loader configuration

Oracle Linux continues to use the GRand Unified Bootloader version 0.9x unlike many consumer distributions, which have switched to GRUB 2. The installation screen does not require too much attention if you are not planning on dual-booting the Oracle database server. As pointed out earlier, the main reason to dual-boot a production database server is when you want to perform an operating system upgrade.

If another Oracle Linux distribution is found and correctly detected it will be added to the boot menu.

Software installation

The Oracle Linux software selection screen is not the most user-friendly interface and occasionally can be difficult to use. The software selection screen is shown in Figure 5-5.

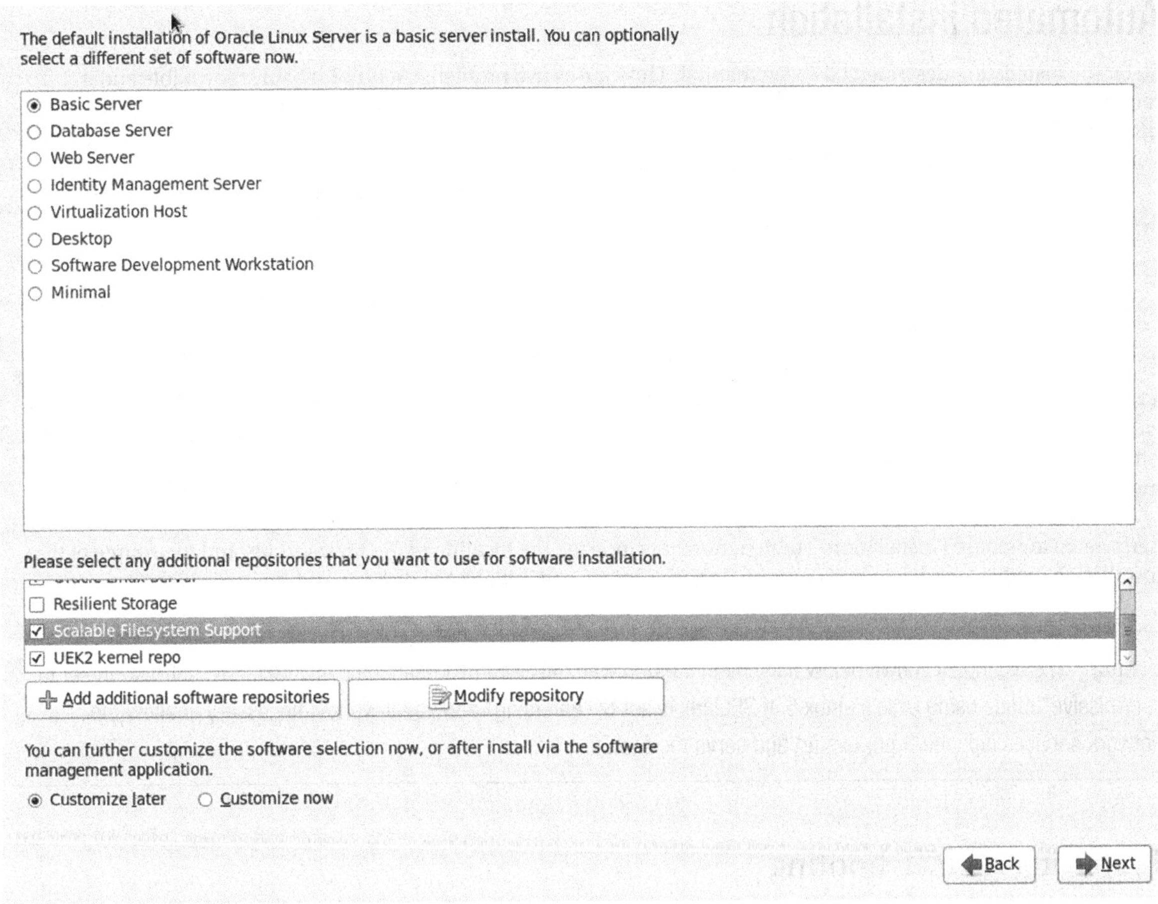

The default installation of Oracle Linux Server is a basic server install. You can optionally
select a different set of software now.

- ◉ Basic Server
- ○ Database Server
- ○ Web Server
- ○ Identity Management Server
- ○ Virtualization Host
- ○ Desktop
- ○ Software Development Workstation
- ○ Minimal

Please select any additional repositories that you want to use for software installation.

- ☐ Resilient Storage
- ☑ Scalable Filesystem Support
- ☑ UEK2 kernel repo

[✛ Add additional software repositories] [📝 Modify repository]

You can further customize the software selection now, or after install via the software
management application.

◉ Customize later   ○ Customize now

[◀ Back]   [➡ Next]

Figure 5-5. *Selecting packages and repositories for an Oracle Linux installation*

For now it is possibly the easiest to select "basic server", which installs a slim variant of the operating system
for use on a server, but without X11. Additional packages can always be added later. Resist the temptation to select
"Database Server"-instead of the packages required by Oracle, this will install MySQL and PostgreSQL instead. What
you should add however is the support for XFS, even if you are not planning on using it right now. To add XFS support,
add an additional repository for the "Scalable Fileystem Support" which adds user land utilities to create and manage
XFS file systems.

The package selection made in the screen shown in Figure 5-5 does not allow you to install the Oracle database
immediately. Additional packages are necessary. In fact it is easier to install the missing packages for an Oracle
installation later from the command line. Upon clicking the "Next" button one more time the installation process
starts by copying the selected packages to the server. Notice that Oracle now boots off the Unbreakable Enterprise
Kernel version 2 by default!

It is now time for a coffee, this process will take a few minutes to complete. After all packages have been
transferred, the Anaconda session congratulates you on your new Oracle Linux installation. After clicking on "Reboot"
the server will restart with the settings you created in the installation process. Please ensure the DVD is no longer in
the drive or virtually mounted to the host.

Automated installation

So far the installation described has been manual. This causes two problems: it is not reliably repeatable and it requires an administrator to sit through it. Surely the administrator can think of more exciting tasks as well. These disadvantages make the manual approach infeasible, especially when a larger number of servers have to be installed. Luckily there are alternatives to this labor-intensive process.

Taking a step back and providing a simplified view of the installation process results in the following steps:

1. Loading the boot loader

2. Fetching the kernel and initial RAM disk

3. Starting the installation process

The boot loader is normally installed in the master boot record of the operating system "disk," from where it picks a kernel and initial RAM disk. On a system that is yet to be installed this is obviously not the case and the boot loader will either be on the installation media or provided via the network using the Preboot Execution Environment (PXE). After the kernel has been loaded, control is transferred to the installer from where it is no different than the manual installation.

Additional boot arguments can be passed on the boot loader command line instructing the installer to perform an automated installation. These parameters indicate the location of the Kickstart file and the source of the installation media. Let's begin by examining how the kernel and initial RAM disk can be obtained via the network.

■ **Note**   The examples shown below have been created with the Security Enhanced Linux (SELinux) subsystem set to "permissive" mode using Oracle Linux 6. If SELinux is set to "enforcing" additional work is necessary to allow the network services (apache/tftpd) to start and serve the files.

Preparing for PXE booting

Booting into the Preboot Execution Environment and then using Kickstart to install the Linux system to match the Unix and Oracle standards is the ultimate form of database server build sophistication. The whole task can be a little bit tricky if a large number of different hardware platforms are used. This is why I suggested standardizing hardware offerings into three different classes matching processing needs in Chapter 1. This allows the engineering team to develop a stable set of installation images.

Before it is possible to spawn new servers or virtual machines using PXE-boot and network installations a little setup work is needed:

1. The Oracle Linux installation files must be made available over the network.

2. A TFTP ("trivial FTP") server must be available to provide a boot environment.

3. A DHCP ("Dynamic Host Configuration Protocol") server must be configured.

Normally you would combine the above points on one server. If provisioning of new Oracle Linux instances-physical or virtual-is a critical task, consider setting up multiple installation servers in your network segment. RSYNC or similar utilities could be used to keep the installation servers in sync.

Making the installation tree available

After the TFTP server is installed and ready, it's time to make the installation sources available. The first task is to provide the installation source. First, you need to decide which way you would like to do this. You have a choice of providing the sources via the FTP, HTTP, NFS, and other protocols. In this example HTTP is used. To export the install source, you need to install a webserver such as apache2 using the yum utility. The example assumes that the yum repository has been configured according to your company's standard. The installation of the webserver is shown here:

```
# yum install httpd
Loaded plugins: security
Setting up Install Process
Resolving Dependencies
--> Running transaction check
---> Package httpd.x86_64 0:2.2.15-15.0.1.el6 will be installed
[...]
--> Finished Dependency Resolution

Dependencies Resolved

================================================================================
 Package              Arch         Version                 Repository Size
================================================================================
Installing:
 httpd                x86_64       2.2.15-15.0.1.el6         cd       808 k
Installing for dependencies:
 apr                  x86_64       1.3.9-3.el6_1.2           cd       123 k
 apr-util             x86_64       1.3.9-3.el6_0.1           cd        87 k
 apr-util-ldap        x86_64       1.3.9-3.el6_0.1           cd        15 k
 httpd-tools          x86_64       2.2.15-15.0.1.el6         cd        69 k

Transaction Summary
================================================================================
Install       5 Package(s)

Total download size: 1.1 M
Installed size: 3.5 M
Is this ok [y/N]: y
Downloading Packages:
--------------------------------------------------------------------------------
Total                                     8.1 MB/s | 1.1 MB        00:00
Running rpm_check_debug
Running Transaction Test
Transaction Test Succeeded
Running Transaction
  Installing : apr-1.3.9-3.el6_1.2.x86_64                           1/5
  Installing : apr-util-1.3.9-3.el6_0.1.x86_64                      2/5
  Installing : httpd-tools-2.2.15-15.0.1.el6.x86_64                 3/5
  Installing : apr-util-ldap-1.3.9-3.el6_0.1.x86_64                 4/5
  Installing : httpd-2.2.15-15.0.1.el6.x86_64                       5/5
```

```
Installed:
  httpd.x86_64 0:2.2.15-15.0.1.el6

Dependency Installed:
  apr.x86_64 0:1.3.9-3.el6_1.2
  apr-util.x86_64 0:1.3.9-3.el6_0.1
  apr-util-ldap.x86_64 0:1.3.9-3.el6_0.1
  httpd-tools.x86_64 0:2.2.15-15.0.1.el6

Complete!
```

You should also enable apache to start at boot time using the familiar chkconfig command:

```
# chkconfig --level 345 httpd on
```

Do not start apache at this stage-a little more setup work is needed. Begin by mounting the Oracle Linux ISO image to your preferred location; this example assumes /media/ol64. The steps necessary to make the software available to apache are shown here (again assuming Oracle Linux 6.4):

```
# mkdir /media/ol64
# mount -o loop /m/downloads/linux/V37084-01.iso /media/ol64
```

Alternatively you could of course copy the contents of the DVD to a directory of your choice. Next apache must be told where to look for the files. Create a file ol64.conf in /etc/httpd/conf.d with the following contents:

```
Alias /ol64/ "/media/ol64/"

<Directory "/media/ol64">
    Options Indexes MultiViews FollowSymLinks
    AllowOverride None
    Order allow,deny
    Allow from 192.168.100.0/255.255.255.0
</Directory>
```

This creates an alias for use with apache, and critically allows the installer to follow symbolic links which is important during the installation. The configuration item also restricts access to the installation tree to the build subnet 192.168.100.0/24.

With all this done, start apache using "service httpd start". When referring to the Oracle Linux install source in a web browser ensure to end the URL with a slash, i.e., http://installServer/ol64/. Otherwise apache will complain that the directory does not exist. Firewalls are another potential source of problems. If you are using firewalls you need to permit access to port 80 on the webserver to access the previously copied files.

Setting up the TFTP server

The TFTP server will contain the initial installation image for Oracle Linux 6. To stay in line with the rest of the book I assumed that your installation server is an Oracle Linux 6 as well. Connect to your installation server and install the tftp-server.x86_64 package using yum as shown here:

```
# yum install tftp-server.x86_64
Loaded plugins: security
Setting up Install Process
```

```
Resolving Dependencies
--> Running transaction check
---> Package tftp-server.x86_64 0:0.49-7.el6 will be installed
--> Finished Dependency Resolution

Dependencies Resolved

================================================================================
 Package          Arch          Version          Repository        Size
================================================================================
Installing:
 tftp-server      x86_64        0.49-7.el6       ol6_u2_base        39 k

Transaction Summary
================================================================================
Install       1 Package(s)

Total download size: 39 k
Installed size: 57 k
Is this ok [y/N]: y
Downloading Packages:
tftp-server-0.49-7.el6.x86_64.rpm                     |  39 kB     00:00
Running rpm_check_debug
Running Transaction Test
Transaction Test Succeeded
Running Transaction
Warning: RPMDB altered outside of yum.
  Installing : tftp-server-0.49-7.el6.x86_64                          1/1

Installed:
  tftp-server.x86_64 0:0.49-7.el6

Complete!
```

TFTP is not the most secure protocol, and therefore should be adequately protected. It is controlled via xinetd and deactivated by default. To enable and start it, execute the following commands:

```
# chkconfig --level 345 xinetd on
# chkconfig --level 345 tftp on
# service xinetd start
Starting xinetd:                                      [  OK  ]
```

The TFTP server supplied with Oracle Linux 6 uses the directory /var/lib/tftpboot to export files. To separate different install images it is a good idea to create a subdirectory per installation source. In the example I am using /var/lib/tftpboot/ol64/. The boot procedure laid out in the following example is based on PXELINUX, a network boot loader similar to SYSLINUX. You may know the latter from installing end-user Linux installations.

Install the syslinux package using YUM. Once the syslinux package has been installed, a few files need to be copied into /var/lib/tftpboot, as shown below:

```
# cp -iv /usr/share/syslinux/pxelinux.0 /var/lib/tftpboot/ol64/
`/usr/share/syslinux/pxelinux.0' -> `/var/lib/tftpboot/ol64/pxelinux.0'
```

```
# cp -iv /usr/share/syslinux/menu.c32 /var/lib/tftpboot/ol64/
`/usr/share/syslinux/menu.c32' -> `/var/lib/tftpboot/ol64/menu.c32'
```

Now the distribution specific files need to be copied from the installation source.

```
# cp -iv /media/ol64/images/pxeboot/* /var/lib/tftpboot/ol64/
`/media/ol64/images/pxeboot/initrd.img' -> `./initrd.img'
`/media/ol64/images/pxeboot/TRANS.TBL' -> `./TRANS.TBL'
`/media/ol64/images/pxeboot/vmlinuz' -> `./vmlinuz'
#
```

Nearly there! A boot menu is now required to allow the user to boot (automatically) into the operating system. The PXELINUX system requires a directory called "pxelinux.cfg" to be present, from where it can access boot configuration. The boot menu is created using the below configuration:

```
# mkdir -p /var/lib/tftpboot/ol64/pxelinux.cfg

# cat /var/lib/tftpboot/ol64/pxelinux.cfg/default
timeout 100
default menu.c32


menu title ------- Boot Menu -------
label 1
menu label ^ 1) ORACLE LINUX 6 KICKSTART
kernel vmlinuz
append initrd=initrd.img ks=http://imageServer/ks/ol64.cfg ksdevice=link

label 2
menu label ^ 2) ORACLE LINUX 6 INTERACTIVE INSTALL
kernel vmlinuz
append initrd=initrd.img
```

The menu defines two items: the first automatically boots after 10 seconds (the timeout is defined in tenths of a second in the configuration file) of inactivity and begins the silent installation of Oracle Linux 6. It achieves this by pointing to the Kickstart file on the webserver just configured and specifying that the first device with an active link should be the Kickstart device. Using ksdevice=link nicely circumvents the problem that the first network card does not necessarily have eth0 assigned to it.

This concludes the TFTP server configuration. Unless you use firewalls again, in which case you need to allow access to port 69, protocol UDP! However it is not yet possible to start the installation-additional information must be passed on to the booting client via DHCP.

Configuring the Dynamic Host Configuration Protocol server

The final step in preparing your build server is to install and configure the DHCP server. A package is available to take care of this task for us, called dhcpd. Install it the usual way using yum:

```
# yum install dhcp
Loaded plugins: security
Setting up Install Process
```

```
Resolving Dependencies
--> Running transaction check
---> Package dhcp.x86_64 12:4.1.1-25.P1.el6 will be installed
--> Finished Dependency Resolution

Dependencies Resolved

================================================================================
 Package        Arch            Version                     Repository   Size
================================================================================
Installing:
 dhcp           x86_64          12:4.1.1-25.P1.el6          cd           815 k

Transaction Summary
================================================================================
Install        1 Package(s)

Total download size: 815 k
Installed size: 1.9 M
Is this ok [y/N]: y
Downloading Packages:
Running rpm_check_debug
Running Transaction Test
Transaction Test Succeeded
Running Transaction
   Installing : 12:dhcp-4.1.1-25.P1.el6.x86_64                        1/1

Installed:
   dhcp.x86_64 12:4.1.1-25.P1.el6

Complete!
```

This version of DHCP is very recent, which is really good for PXE boot environments. DHCP is the magic that sends the configuration information to our new server over the network. Before it can do so however the configuration file /etc/dhcp/dhcpd.conf needs to be amended. The below is an example minimum configuration file needed for PXE clients:

```
allow booting;
allow bootp;
# other global options, such as domain-name, domain-name-servers, routers etc

# build network
subnet 192.168.100.0 netmask 255.255.255.0 {
  range 192.168.100.50    192.168.100.100;
  # further options...

  # specific hosts
  host pxeboot {
    hardware ethernet 08:00:27:62:66:EE;
    fixed-address 192.168.100.51;
  }

}
```

```
# grouping all PXE clients into a class
class "pxeclients" {
  match if substring(option vendor-class-identifier, 0, 9) = "PXEClient";
  next-server 192.168.100.2;
  filename "ol64/pxelinux.0";
}
```

The first two lines instruct DHCP to allow clients to PXE boot, which is the initial requirement followed by other generic configuration options. Next a subnet is defined, which would normally map to the "build" network. The build network is normally out of limits for normal users and specifically designed for software installations such as the one described.

All PXE clients are grouped into their own class "pxeclients." The vendor-class-identifier is an ISC DHCP version 3 directive that lets us identify clients willing to boot via PXE. The "next-server" directive has to point to the tftp-server. The filename directive finally instructs the clients to look for the file ol64/pxelinux.0 which was copied during the TFTP configuration and set up earlier.

■ **Note** You can take this even further by using dynamic DNS updates ("ddns"). DDNS updates in combination with the host {} directive in DHCP allows for true lights out provisioning of servers. You can also use frameworks such as cobbler or spacewalk.

Before the first server can be started, a Kickstart file is required. Remember to add firewall rules for your DHCP server if needed.

Considerations for the Kickstart file

After all the preparations it is time to define how the system is to be installed. Any reputable Linux distribution comes with a lights-out installation mechanism, and Oracle Linux is no exception to that rule. Just like Red Hat Linux, Oracle Linux uses the Kickstart mechanism to perform automated installations. The Kickstart format can be quite daunting at first, and it occupies a lot of space in the installation manual.

It is not as difficult as one might think, mainly because of the following factors:

- Every time you manually install Oracle Linux the installer (called "Anaconda") creates a Kickstart file with the options you chose in /root/anaconda-ks.cfg.

- A GUI tool, system-config-kickstart is available which guides you through the creation of a Kickstart file.

To automate the installation of Oracle Linux it is usually easiest to review the Anaconda-generated Kickstart file and make subtle changes as necessary. Consider the following Kickstart file which you could use as the basis for your own installation. It has been created as a result of the manual installation shown earlier in the chapter.

```
install
url --url http://192.168.100.2/ol64/
lang en_US.UTF-8
keyboard uk
network --device eth0 --bootproto dhcp --noipv6
rootpw -iscrypted a...o
firewall --disabled
```

```
selinux --permissive
authconfig --enableshadow --passalgo=sha512
timezone --utc America/New_York
bootloader --location=mbr --driveorder=sda --append=" rhgb crashkernel=auto quiet"
# The following is the partition information you requested
# Note that any partitions you deleted are not expressed
# here so unless you clear all partitions first, this is
# not guaranteed to work
ignoredisk --only-use=sda
clearpart --initlabel --drives=sda
part /boot --fstype=ext2 --size=200 --ondisk=sda
part pv.008002 --grow --size=200 --ondisk=sda
volgroup rootvg --pesize=4096 pv.008002
logvol swap --name=swaplv --vgname=rootvg --size=2048
logvol / --fstype=ext4 --name=rootlv --vgname=rootvg --size=5940 --grow

%packages
@base
@client-mgmt-tools
@console-internet
@core
@debugging
@directory-client
@hardware-monitoring
@java-platform
@large-systems
@network-file-system-client
@performance
@perl-runtime
@server-platform
@server-policy
@system-admin-tools
pax
python-dmidecode
oddjob
sgpio
certmonger
screen
strace
pam_krb5
krb5-workstation
%end
```

In the above example the Anaconda installer is going to install (instead of upgrade) the software using the HTTP protocol pulling the files from our installation server. Language and keyboard are defined next before the network definition is set to use DHCP for the first Ethernet device. Additional networks can be defined in their own "network --device ethx" section.

The root password used is encrypted; the value is taken from the anaconda-ks.cfg file created during the manual installation. The clear text password has been entered during the initial manual installation performed earlier.

■ **Tip**   Encrypted passwords can be taken from an existing /etc/shadow file.

Specifying an encrypted password is much safer than a clear text password!

The following directives disable the firewall and set the security-enhanced Linux settings to permissive. Be sure to update this section after consulting your IT-security department! The authconfig command enables the use of shadow passwords which implies local user accounts on the machine. Furthermore the shadow passwords should use SHA512 as the password algorithm.

The timezone is then set to America/New_York-this should most definitely be adopted to match the closest location where the server is located. The next few lines are dealing with the boot loader location and the partitioning scheme. The chosen partitioning options can be translated into English as follows:

- *clearpart*: Clear all partitions and initialize the disk label

- *part /boot*: Create a boot partition of 200 MiB using ext4

- *part pv008002:* Create a physical volume and use all remaining space

- *volgroup rootvg:* Create a volume group "rootvg" using the physical volume just created

- *logvol (twice):* Create two logical volumes on volume group rootvg.

The kickstart file explicitly uses disk sda only. The remainder of the file specifies which YUM packages and groups should be installed. If you wonder which groups are available, you can use YUM on a system to execute the following query:

```
# yum grouplist
```

Although it looks intimidating at first-especially the partitioning part-the Kickstart process is logical and easy to master. The Kickstart format is also very well documented in the installation guide. Please refer to it for further information about available options. Once the Kickstart file is ready, move it to a directory on the webserver from where it is accessible to the build network. For security reasons it should not be exposed outside of the build network. To follow the example you need to place it into /var/www/html/ks/.

A final word of warning: please be careful with the file. It absolutely erases everything! As with anything in this book, please adapt the file to your needs and test it thoroughly before deploying it on real systems.

Testing the automated installation

With all the preparation work completed, it is time to put the procedure to test. Connect a machine to the build network and enable PXE booting on the hardware level. Most often you would connect to the lights-out management console before starting the server. After a little while, when the subsystems have initialized, the network card should advertise that it is trying to PXE boot. This triggers a DHCP request on your install server, which should be acknowledged. If you like (still on the install server) start tailing the /var/log/messages file to see what happens. If you are really curious you could start tcpdump on your install server to listen on port 69 to see if the tftp request can be satisfied.

If everything goes well then you will see a (very basic) boot menu which will automatically boot the default operating system. If you are curious you will see the whole installation happening on the lights-out management console. You should do this at least once to ensure that there are no problems with the process. Also bear in mind that you need to be careful where you install the operating system: there is no safety net: all the data on the machine is erased, and you get a fresh Oracle Linux server instead. If you used DDNS you should then have a server, which is correctly configured within DNS and ready for the next steps, the preparation of the OS to install Oracle Database 12.1.

Preparing for the Oracle Database installation

With the operating system in a bootable state, it is time to configure the environment to allow for the installation of a database. This process has not changed from previous releases, and it involves changing kernel parameters, installing additional packages, and creating users and groups. The section assumes a fresh installation of Oracle Linux without any existing Oracle-related accounts in place.

The use of Oracle Automatic Storage Management (ASM) requires an installation of Grid Infrastructure for a standalone server. In this respect there is nothing new to the process. Using ASM even for single instance deployments is worth considering. ASM offers benefits over certain file systems, mainly when it comes to concurrent writes, inode locking, direct IO capabilities, and many more. On the downside, using ASM for storing database files moves these out of the file system and into an Oracle-specific storage area. Although ASM has been enhanced with command-line like access, you still need to connect to the ASM instance implicitly.

Installing additional packages

The first step in the preparation for the Oracle installation involves completing the installation of the required set of packages. A local YUM repository such as the one created earlier can be used to download the packages and resolve any dependencies. To make the repository available to the system create a new file local.repo in /etc/yum.repos.d/ with these lines:

```
[local]
name = local installation tree
baseurl = http://imageServer/ol64/
enabled = 1
gpgcheck = 1
```

Note that the gpgcheck value is set to 1 in the repository configuration. Whenever you are using repositories you must ensure that the packages you download from the repository are signed and match the key! Using the above repository you should be able to install the packages required for the next steps.

```
# yum install compat-libcap1 compat-libstdc++-33 libstdc++-devel gcc-c++ ksh libaio-devel
# yum install xorg-x11-utils xorg-x11-server-utils twm tigervnc-server xterm
```

The preceding list of commands depends on the packages already present on your system. For a complete list of what is needed, please refer to the *Oracle Database Quick Installation Guide 12c Release 1 for Linux x86-64*. See specifically section 6.1, "Supported Oracle Linux 6 and Red Hat Enterprise Linux 6 Distributions for x86-64", for a complete list.

If you are planning the installation of Oracle Restart, you also need to install the package "cvuqdisk," which is part of the Grid Infrastructure installation package. Installing these packages satisfies the Oracle installer.

Creating the operating system users and groups

With all required packages in place it is time to consider the creation of the Oracle user and groups. Whereas this was a simple and straightforward task in releases up to Oracle 11.1, some more thought must now be put into the process if you plan on using ASM or Real Application Clusters. The new process in Oracle 12c even affects the database installation.

The main reason the user and group creation process has become more interesting is the "separation of duties". In the very basic form, one operating system account-usually named "oracle"-owns the binaries for Grid Infrastructure and the database as well. This way whoever logs into the system as oracle has full control over every aspect of database management. While this is acceptable in most smaller companies, larger institutions use different teams for the management of the Oracle stack. In versions leading up to 12.1, the separation in broad terms was between the storage team and DBA team: if so desired, separate accounts were used to install and own Grid Infrastructure and the RDBMS binaries. In addition to the storage aspect, Oracle 12.1 introduced new responsibilities: backup, Data Guard, and encryption key management.

Similar to previous releases, the responsibilities are implemented using internal groups such as OSDBA to which operating system groups are mapped. Operating system accounts can then further be mapped to the groups, inheriting the privileges associated with the role. The mapping between Oracle groups and operating system groups can be found in Table 5-2.

Table 5-2. *Internal groups, operating system groups, and users*

Internal Group	Description	Typical operating system group
OSDBA (RDBMS)	Members of the OSDBA group for the database are granted the SYSDBA privilege. The user can log in using the "/ as sysdba" command on the server and has full control over the database.	dba
OSOPER (optional)	This is an optional privilege. Members of the OSOPER group for the database are allowed to connect to the system as SYSOPER. The SYSOPER role has been used in the past to allow operators to perform certain tasks such as instance management (starting/stopping) and backup-related work without the ability to look at user data. The role is probably superseded by the ones shown below.	oper
OSBACKUPDBA	Allows members to connect using the new SYSBACKUP privilege. The new group has been created to allow non-database administrators to perform backup-related tasks.	backupdba
OSDGDBA	The new SYSDG privilege available to members of this group allows them to perform Data Guard–related tasks.	dgdba
OSKMDBA	This new group is used for users dealing with encryption key management such as for Transparent Data Encryption (TDE) and Oracle wallet.	kmdba
OSASM	Members of the OSASM group are given the SYSASM privilege, which has taken over from SYSDBA as the most elevated privilege in ASM. This is quite often assigned to the owner of the Grid Infrastructure installation.	asmadmin
OSDBA for ASM	Members of the OSDBA have read and write access to files within ASM. If you are opting for a separate owner of Grid Infrastructure, then the binary owner must be part of this group. The owner of the RDBMS binaries must also be included.	asmdba
OSOPER for ASM (optional)	Similar in nature to the OSOPER group for the database, the members of this optional group have the rights to perform a limited set of maintenance commands for the ASM instance. Members of this group have the SYSOPER role granted.	asmoper

Without a policy of separation of duties in place you could map the oracle user to all the above-mentioned groups. In a scenario where storage and database management are separated you could map the ASM-related groups to the grid user, and the rest to oracle. The oracle account also needs the OSDBA for ASM privilege to connect to the ASM instance; without it oracle can't access its storage. Even if you are not planning on using multiple operating system accounts I still recommend creating the operating system groups. This is simply to give you greater flexibility later on, should you decide to allow accounts other than oracle and grid to perform administration tasks with the database.

Up until now, one other very important group has not been mentioned: oinstall. This group owns the Oracle inventory and is required for each account that needs to modify the binaries on the system. Oracle recommends that every Oracle-related operating system account should have oinstall as its primary group.

Scenario 1: one operating system account for all binaries

This is the simplest case-the oracle account will be a member of all the operating system groups mentioned above. To facilitate such a setup, you need to create the operating system groups as shown in the following example. If you are setting your system up for clustering, then the numerical user-IDs and group-IDs need to be consistent across the cluster!

To ensure consistent installations, the numeric user and group-IDs should be part of the standards document covering your build, and the users should ideally be pre-created. For even more consistency you should consider the use of configuration management tools. For a manual installation, you would follow these steps, beginning with the mandatory groups.

■ **Note** In the following examples a hash or "#" indicates commands to be executed as root; a dollar sign denotes a non-root shell.

```
# groupadd -g 4200 oinstall
# groupadd -g 4201 dba
```

Those are the groups you need at least; if you like greater flexibility later on you could also define the other groups mentioned in the above table. Again, it is recommended to use the numeric IDs. Please ensure that the group IDs chosen match those defined in your build standards-the ones shown here are for demonstration only.

```
# groupadd -g 4202 backupdba
# groupadd -g 4203 dgdba
# groupadd -g 4204 kmdba
# groupadd -g 4205 asmdba
# groupadd -g 4206 asmadmin
```

You could also create the "oper" groups for the accounts but they are optional since 11.2. With the groups defined you can create the oracle account as follows:

```
# useradd -u 4200 -g oinstall -G dba,asmdba -m oracle
# passwd oracle
Changing password for user oracle
New password:
Retype new password:
passwd: all authentication tokens updated successfully
```

If you opted for the creation of the supplementary groups, you could add those to the oracle account:

```
# usermod -G dba,backupdba,dgdba,kmdba,asmdba,asmadmin oracle
```

To check how your oracle account is set up, you can use the id command as shown here for the minimum required groups:

```
# id -a oracle
uid=4200(oracle) gid=4200(oinstall) groups=4200(oinstall),4201(dba)
```

Notice that the oracle account must have the new groups assigned to it or they will not be selectable in the OUI session later. Once you are happy with your setup, proceed to the section "Configuring Kernel Parameters."

Scenario 2: separation of duties

If you are planning on installing a Real Application Cluster or want to use ASM, which requires an installation of Oracle Restart, you could separate the storage administration from the database administration. The most common scenario is to create two operating system accounts, oracle and grid. The main reason against such a setup in the past was the problematic support for patching in early Oracle 11.2 releases. These problems have largely been solved, and there are no problems expected with different owners for Grid Infrastructure and the database.

Assuming the above-mentioned groups have already been created, you need to set up the grid owner as well as the oracle owner. Consider the following example for the oracle account:

```
# useradd -u 4200 -g oinstall -G asmdba,dba -m oracle
# passwd oracle
Changing password for user oracle
New password:
Retype new password:
passwd: all authentication tokens updated successfully
```

Conversely, the grid account could be created as follows:

```
# useradd -u 4201 -g oinstall -G asmadmin,asmdba,dba -m grid
# passwd grid
Changing password for user grid
New password:
Retype new password:
passwd: all authentication tokens updated successfully
```

■ **Note** For some strange reason Oracle requires the grid user to be member of the DBA group-failing that you won't be able to install the database software. Optionally, add the oracle user to the kmdba, backupdba and dgdba groups as well.

That concludes the setup of these accounts. If you like you can assign the remaining additional groups to the oracle account before proceeding to the next section to allow for even finer granularity of access.

Checking kernel parameters

The Linux kernel has lots of tunables to affect the way it operates. The Oracle database makes intensive use of these, and you need to modify the standard parameters before you can install the database or Grid Infrastructure software. Many kernel parameters can be changed at runtime by echoing values to files in the /proc file system. To make these changes permanent, you need to modify the /etc/sysctl.conf file which is parsed at every system boot.

Oracle made it somewhat easier by adding an option to the OUI interface allowing you to run a fixup script to correct these values to their minimum required settings. If you are using Oracle Linux 5, you could alternatively install the oracle-validated RPM which helps setting some of the parameters before the installation. There is a similar RPM available for Oracle 12.1, named Oracle RDBMS Server 12cR1 Pre-Install RPM. You should also consult with your system administration team to adjust the values to fit your hardware optimally.

Tables 5-3 and 5-4 list the parameters and provide advice on setting them. Table 5-3 focuses upon semaphore parameters. Table 5-4 lists all the others. It makes sense to check the parameters even after having installed the preinstall RPM!

Table 5-3. *Kernel Parameters relating to semaphores*

Kernel parameter	Recommended (minimum) value	Description
semmsl	250	The maximum number of semaphores in a semaphore set. Applications always request semaphores in sets. The number of sets available is defined by the semmni value, see below. Each of these sets contains semmsl semaphores.
semmns	32000	The total number of semaphores permitted system-wide. The value of 32000 = semmsl * semmni.
semopm	100	Sets a limit for the maximum number of operations in a single semaphore-related operating system call.
semmni	128	The maximum number of semaphore sets.

Table 5-4. *Other kernal parameters and their recommended minimums*

Kernel parameter	Recommended (minimum) value	Description
shmmax	Half the physical memory; set to 4398046511104 byte by Oracle preinstall	Shared Memory Max (size) defines the maximum size of an individual shared memory segment in bytes. When you start an Oracle instance, it tries to allocate the SGA from shared memory. If the total size of the SGA is greater than shmmax then Oracle will create the SGA consisting of multiple smaller segments, which can have implications on NUMA-enabled systems since memory might not be node-local. The Oracle validated RPM uses the maximum size permissible on the 64bit platform: 4TB. That should be enough to fit even the largest SGA!

(continued)

Table 5-3. (continued)

Kernel parameter	Recommended (minimum) value	Description
shmmni	4096	This parameter sets maximum number of shared memory segments permissible. This value comes to play in two different ways: first of all if you set shmmax to a small value and Oracle has to break down the SGA into smaller pieces. Secondly, each time an Oracle instance-ASM and RDBMS-is started, the available number is decremented by one.
		The value of 4096 recommended in the Oracle installation guides guarantees that you will not run out of shared memory segments.
shmall	1073741824	This parameter determines the system-wide limit on the total number of pages of shared memory. It should be set to shmmax/`getconf PAGE_SIZE.
file-max	6815744	This parameter allows you to set a maximum number of open files for all processes, system-wide. The default should be sufficient for most systems.
ip_local_port_range	9000 65500	The local port range to be used for Oracle (dedicated) server processes should be configured to 9000 to prevent a clash with non-oracle operating system services using the port numbers as defined in /etc/services.
		By lowering the boundary to 9000 you should have enough ephemeral ports for your expected workload.
rmem_default	262144	This sets the default receive buffer size (in bytes) for all types of connections-TCP and UDP.
rmem_max	4194304	This sets the maximum receive buffer size (in bytes) for all connections-TCP and UDP.
wmem_default	262144	This sets the default send buffer size (in bytes) for all types of connections-TCP and UDP.
wmem_max	1048576	This sets the max OS send buffer size for all types of connections.
aio-max-nr	1048576	This parameter is related to asynchronous I/O model in Linux as defined by libaio and should be set to 1048576 to prevent processes receiving errors when allocating internal AIO-related memory structures.

The values in Table 5-3 are all listed in /proc/sys/kernel/sem and are responsible for controlling the semaphores in a Linux system. Oracle uses shared memory and semaphores extensively for inter-process communication. In simple terms, semaphores are mainly required by processes to attach to the SGA and to control serialization. The values shown in Table 5-3 should be sufficient for most workloads.

Using the values from Tables 5-3 and 5-4, the resulting /etc/sysctl.conf file contains these lines:

```
kernel.shmall = 1073741824
kernel.shmmax = 4398046511104
kernel.shmmni = 4096
kernel.sem = 250 32000 100 128
fs.file-max = 6815744
net.core.rmem_default = 262144
net.core.wmem_default = 262144
net.core.rmem_max = 4194304
net.core.wmem_max = 1048576
fs.aio-max-nr = 1048576
net.ipv4.ip_local_port_range = 9000 65500
```

You do not need to worry about these though. The Oracle Universal Installer provides a "fixup" option during the installation which can modify the kernel parameters to set the required minimum values. In addition, the Oracle server preinstall RPM ensures that you meet these minimum requirements. You can read more about the preinstall-RPM later in this chapter.

The Oracle mount points

The mount points and file systems suggested for use with the Oracle binaries have been discussed in the section "Considerations for the Oracle mount point". Assuming that the storage has been formatted during the installation, the remaining work is simple: just update the file system table in /etc/fstab with a mount point for the Oracle software and you are done. Most often, the Oracle binaries are installed following the Optimal Flexible Architecture-OFA.

The starting point for mounting the file systems for use with Oracle usually is the /u01 directory and the hierarchy beneath. Alternatively you could use the top-level directory defined in your standards document. The next few paragraphs follow the OFA recommendation.

First, you need to consider the location of the Oracle inventory. The inventory is often owned by the oracle account but more importantly is owned by the operating system group oinstall. This ensures that in the case of separation of duties other operating system accounts have write permissions to the global inventory location. It is also the reason it is so important to define oinstall as the primary group for the oracle and grid user. In many deployments you will find the Oracle inventory in /u01/app/oraInventory, which is also the default.

Before discussing the installation location of Grid Infrastructure it is important to cover the ORACLE_BASE. For the Grid Infrastructure installation, the Oracle base signifies the location where certain diagnostic and other important log files are stored. From a database perspective, the most important subdirectory is the diagnostic destination which has been introduced with Oracle 11.

An important restriction exists for the installation of the Grid Infrastructure for a cluster: the GRID_HOME must not be in the path of any ORACLE_BASE on your system.

The default location for Grid Infrastructure in a cluster configuration is /u01/app/12.1.0/grid, but in the author's opinion you should use one more digit to indicate the version number, i.e. /u01/app/12.1.0.1/grid instead. This will make it easier during patching to identify a software home. Remember that Oracle introduced full releases with the first patch set to 11g Release 2, which are out-of-place upgrades.

To sum it up the following directories are needed for an OFA-compliant installation. You can use these as mount points for the logical volumes defined earlier during the installation:

```
# mkdir -p /u01/app/oraInventory    # Path for the inventory
# mkdir -p /u01/app/oracle          # ORACLE_BASE for the database owner
# mkdir -p /u01/app/grid            # ORACLE_BASE for the grid owner
```

By defining directories with this structure it is ensured that the Oracle Universal Installer (OUI) will pick up the OFA-compliant setup. Assuming a separate oracle and grid user you would continue by setting the permissions as follows:

```
# chown grid:oinstall /u01/app/oraInventory/
# chmod 775 /u01/app/oraInventory/

# chown grid:oinstall /u01/app/
# chmod -R 775 /u01/app/

# chown -R oracle:oinstall /u01/app/oracle
# chmod -R 775 /u01/app/oracle
```

If you are planning on installing the database software only, there is no need for a grid user.

Setting session limits

The Pluggable Authentication Modules or PAM are a flexible way to authenticate users in a Unix environment. PAM itself is "only" a framework-its functionality is implemented via modules. Such modules exist for many authentication methods. When a user requests access to a Linux machine, the login process plays a crucial role in the process. Using the services provided by the PAM library, it assesses that the user requesting a service (bash/ksh or other shell) is actually who he claims to be. To that end, a multitude of authentication methods ranging from password to LDAP can be employed, which are beyond the scope of this chapter. From an Oracle point of view, one property of the login daemon is very important: it can assign limits to an individual user session.

The Oracle installation guide mandates that the following requirements are met:

- The maximum number of open file descriptors must have a soft limit of 1024 and a hard limit of 65536

- The number of processes a user can create must be at least 2047 with a hard limit of 16384

- A stack size (per process) of at least 10240KiB and at maximum of 32768 KiB

These settings are made in the /etc/security/limits.conf file, which unfortunately is still not documented properly in the installation guides. In this file, every line follows this format (see man 5 limits.conf):

```
domain    type    item    value.
```

The relevant domain for the Oracle database installation is a username. The type can be either hard or soft, and the item denotes which attribute is to be changed. To be more precise, we need at least amend the items "nofile," "nproc," and "stack." On the x86-64 platform, the values set by the oracle-rdbms-server-12cR1-preinstall RPM were defined as follows:

```
[root@server1 ~]# cat /etc/security/limits.d/oracle-rdbms-server-12cR1-preinstall.conf \
>| grep ^oracle
oracle    soft    nofile    1024
oracle    hard    nofile    65536
oracle    soft    nproc     16384
oracle    hard    nproc     16384
oracle    soft    stack     10240
oracle    hard    stack     32768
```

You will notice a small variation to the requirements postulated by oracle: the value for the number of processes exceeds the recommendation by Oracle. The settings need to be repeated if you are planning on using the grid user to own the Grid Infrastructure installation:

```
grid    soft    nofile    1024
grid    hard    nofile    65536
grid    soft    nproc     16384
grid    hard    nproc     16384
grid    soft    stack     10240
grid    hard    stack     32768
```

The Oracle Database 11g Release 2 preinstall RPM installed its settings into limits.conf directly. The new version installs its settings into /etc/security/limits.d instead. The next time the oracle or grid user logs in the settings will take effect. The pam_limits.so module is automatically included in the login process via the system-auth module. This way, after traversing the requirements for an interactive shell login, the limits will be set for the oracle and grid user. You can check the limits by using ulimit command. More detailed information about these settings can be found in the man-page "pam_limits" (8).

Configuring large pages

Large pages, also known as "huge pages", are a feature introduced to Linux with the advent of the 2.6 kernel. The use of large pages addresses problems Linux systems can experience managing processes on systems with large amounts of memory. Large amounts of memory at the time when large pages where introduced began with about 16GB of RAM which is not considered large any more. To explain, a little background information about memory management is required.

The Linux kernel on the Intel IA32 architecture (that is not Itanium!) uses a default memory page size of 4kb. All of the physical memory has to be managed by the kernel in tiny chunks of 4kb. Huge pages on the other hand use much larger page sizes of 2MB. It becomes immediately obvious that the kernel benefits from this as there are less memory pages to manage. But it is not only the reduced number of memory pages the kernel needs to keep track of; there is also a higher probability that the part of the CPU responsible for the translation of physical to virtual memory (the translation lookaside buffer, or TLB) will have a page address cached, resulting in faster access.

In earlier Oracle Releases you needed to manually calculate the number of huge pages before starting the Oracle instance. Oracle provides a script as part of a My Oracle Support note, called calc_hugePages.sh. Using it against a started Oracle instance it calculated the number of large pages. Thankfully, you get this information in the Oracle database instance's alert.log now as shown here:

```
**************** Large Pages Information ****************

Total System Global Area in large pages = 0 KB (0%)

Large pages used by this instance: 0 (0 KB)
Large pages unused system wide = 0 (0 KB)
Large pages configured system wide = 0 (0 KB)
Large page size = 2048 KB

RECOMMENDATION:
  Total System Global Area size is 2514 MB. For optimal performance,
  prior to the next instance restart:
  1. Increase the number of unused large pages by
 at least 1257 (page size 2048 KB, total size 2514 MB) system wide to
  get 100% of the System Global Area allocated with large pages
  ********************************************************
```

With the information that another 1257 large pages (of 2048KB) are required you can modify the /etc/sysctl. conf file to ensure these are set aside when the system boots. The value to be entered is the sum of all the huge pages needed for all SGAs on the host plus a few extra ones for safety. Only one database will be used on the server in the following example:

```
vm.nr_hugepages = 1400
```

Memory permitting, you could try to reserve them without reboot: simply echo "1400" into /proc/sys/vm/ nr_hugepages. If your memory is too fragmented this might not work and you have to reboot. The use of huge pages is shown in the /proc/meminfo file. To check if the requested number of huge pages is available, you could grep for HugePages:

```
[root@server1 ~]# grep HugePages /proc/meminfo
HugePages_Total:      1400
HugePages_Free:       1400
HugePages_Rsvd:          0
HugePages_Surp:          0
[root@server1 ~]#
```

The change to /etc/sysctl.conf alone will not allow the oracle (and grid) user to use large pages. Large pages require the memory to be "locked," and large pages cannot be paged out. Since the 12c preinstall RPM does not set the necessary parameter in /etc/security/limit*, you need to do so yourself. Using your favorite text editor, modify /etc/security/limits.conf or its equivalent, and add configuration parameters similar to these:

```
oracle   soft    memlock    60397977
oracle   hard    memlock    60397977

grid     soft    memlock    60397977
grid     hard    memlock    60397977
```

The value to be set is in kilobytes. You could simply take the amount of RAM in your server minus 10 percent and set this in the file. Remember that this is not the allocation; it only defines how much memory the process may lock in theory.

A new session is required for these settings to take effect. If you want to ensure that your database enforces the use of large pages, set "use_large_pages" to "only". Note this is incompatible with Automatic Memory Management! If you have memory_target set in your initialization file, you will get the following error:

```
****************************************************************
Large pages are not compatible with specified SGA memory parameters
use_large_pages = "ONLY" cannot be used with memory_target,
memory_max_target, _db_block_cache_protect or
use_indirect_data_buffers parameters
Large pages are compatible with sga_target and shared_pool_size
****************************************************************
```

If permissions are set correctly, namely the memlock item in /etc/security/limits.conf, and if enough large pages are available you will see a success message in the alert.log:

```
***************** Large Pages Information *****************
Parameter use_large_pages = only
Per process system memlock (soft) limit = 58 GB
```

```
Total System Global Area in large pages = 2514 MB (100%)

Large pages used by this instance: 1257 (2514 MB)
Large pages unused system wide = 143 (286 MB)
Large pages configured system wide = 1400 (2800 MB)
Large page size = 2048 KB
*********************************************************
```

It is possible that only a part of the SGA uses large pages, which is a scenario to be avoided. Setting the initialization parameter "use_large_pages" to "only" as shown in the preceding example ensures that the SGA in its entirety uses large pages. Please do not over-allocate large pages! Large pages affect only the SGA; private memory structures such as the PGA and UGA do not benefit from them. You need to leave enough memory available on the system for user sessions, or otherwise risk problems.

Introducing the oracle-rdbms-server preinstall package

Shortly after Oracle announced support for 11.2.0.3 on Oracle Linux 6 the company also released an updated RPM to simplify the installation of the software for RAC and single instance. Similar to the well-known "oracle-validated" RPM used with Oracle Linux 5, this new package performs many necessary pre-installation steps needed for Oracle database 12c (a separate RPM is available for 11g Release 2). Among those performed is the creation of the oracle account, modifying kernel and session related parameters. The package also modifies the kernel boot loader configuration file. It is a great help when getting started with Oracle, but it is not foolproof. As with any piece of software understanding the changes it makes to the operating system is crucial in configuring a robust system.

The preinstall RPMs are tied to a specific database version at the time of this writing, namely 11.2 and 12.1. During testing it made no difference to the installation of the 12c database and Grid Infrastructure packages whether the 11g Release 2 or 12c Release 1 RPM were installed. This is because the system requirements are very similar for both.

Before adding any of these packages to the default build, ensure that the package matches the build standard. This is especially important with regards to the user and group IDs. If needed, you can always get the source RPM ("SRPM") file and modify the settings in it. In addition, none of the preinstall RPMs create a grid user for a separation of duties, nor do they install the new operating system groups introduced in the earler section "Creating the operating system users and groups".

Configuring storage

In addition to the storage required to host the Oracle binaries, additional space is required for the actual Oracle database. A number of choices exist for the underlying file system, including ASM. For each of them, the starting point will be the logical unit number or LUN(s) to be presented to the host by the storage administrators. Most systems will use multiple paths to the storage for performance and resilience. All major storage vendors have their own proprietary multipathing software-EMC's PowerPath, Hitachi Dynamic Link Manager, and too many more to list here.

In addition to these proprietary drivers, Linux comes has its own generic multipathing package, called dm-multipath. In the following section you will see how that is used in the context of an Oracle database installation.

Partitioning LUNs

Before beginning the multipathing configuration which is covered in the next section it is beneficial to partition the devices at this stage. This prevents unloading and messing with the devices once the multipath configuration is in place. Two utilities exist for partitioning: parted and fdisk. This section focusses on the fdisk utility.

■ **Note** You need `parted` if you need to create LUNs with a size > 2 TB. Such devices cannot be addressed by the Master Boot Record (MBR) format, but rather need a GUID partition (GPT) table. This is a limitation of the addressing scheme of the hard disk, not of the operating system.

Once the LUN you are interested in is discovered on the operating system you can partition it. Most often you will get worldwide IDs from the storage team to use on the new database server. Using the `/dev/disk/by-id` directory it is possible to identify the SAN storage based on these WWIDs and to partition it. Pass the complete path of the disk as an argument to `fdisk`, as shown in this example:

```
# fdisk /dev/disk/by-id/scsi-1IET_00010001
```

Following this, you need to create a partition spanning the whole disk. The steps are shown in the below listing, where the following operations are carried out:

- The LUN is selected

- The display unit it changed to sectors

- A new primary partition is created with an offset. Different vendors require different offsets-check with your storage administrator on how to define the partition to match the requirements stated in the documentation. Also, many advanced formatting devices such as flash based storage are using a 4096 byte sector size instead of the previous 512 byte sectors. For optimal performance, partitions have to be aligned at 4k boundaries on these types of devices.

■ **Note** As you will have noticed the examples presume an iSCSI LUN. Storage provided via Fibre Channel uses a different notation for the WWID, but other than that the steps are identical.

Following is an example. The text in bold are the responses that I typed in while generating the example.

```
# fdisk /dev/disk/by-id/scsi-1IET_00010001

WARNING: DOS-compatible mode is deprecated. It's strongly recommended to
         switch off the mode (command 'c') and change display units to
         sectors (command 'u').

Command (m for help): u
Changing display/entry units to sectors

Command (m for help): c
DOS Compatibility flag is not set

Command (m for help): n
Command action
   e   extended
   p   primary partition (1-4)
p
Partition number (1-4): 1
First sector (2048-4196351, default 2048):
```

```
Using default value 2048
Last sector, +sectors or +size{K,M,G} (2048-4196351, default 4196351):
Using default value 4196351

Command (m for help): w
The partition table has been altered!

Calling ioctl() to re-read partition table.
Syncing disks.
```

This example created a primary partition on a SCSI device. With such a device partitioned, you can start configuring the multipath software.

Configuring dm-multipath

The principle behind any multipathing software is simple. Without the abstraction layer, the operating "sees" each block device once via each path. That means a LUN can be /dev/sdb and additionally /dev/sdk-but still be the same physical device, just using two different paths to the storage. Without a multipath driver the operating system could not easily assess that two devices are logically the same. Thanks to the driver however this becomes possible. Instead of using the native devices a new device is introduced to which the application (read: Oracle) sends I/O requests. The pseudo device is created in a number of different places:

- In the /dev directory such as /dev/dm-35

- Again in the /dev directory, but with /dev/mpath*n* or a WWID

- In the /dev/mapper directory with a user defined alias

In the case of the dm-multipath package, the mapping between block device and pseudo-device is performed in the main configuration file: /etc/multipath.conf. An important aspect is to only use the pseudo-device. Otherwise there would be no protection from path failures or no performance gains!

The installation of Oracle Linux comes with the multipath package installed as part of the standard installation. If the package is not yet available, you should install the package device-mapper-multipath.x86_64 including all its dependencies. When installed, you need to ensure that the multipath process is started at every system boot-this is done via the chkconfig application as shown here:

```
# chkconfig --level 35 multipathd on
# chkconfig --list | grep -i multipath
multipathd      0:off   1:off   2:off   3:on    4:off   5:on    6:off
```

Unlike Oracle Linux 5, there is no example content in /etc/multipath.conf-the file does not exist. A number of example configurations are available in the documentation directory. That directory is named as follows, but replacing version with your own version number:

```
/usr/share/doc/device-mapper-multipath-version.
```

The quickest way to starting with a basic failover scenario is to use the recommendation from the online documentation by using the mpathconf utility as shown here:

```
# mpathconf --enable --with_multipathd y
# echo $?
0
```

The command creates a basic configuration file: /etc/multipath.conf and additionally loads the kernel modules necessary for the correct operation of the package. Querying the mpathconf command you are shown the successful execution:

```
# mpathconf
multipath is enabled
find_multipaths is disabled
user_friendly_names is enabled
dm_multipath module is loaded
multipathd is chkconfiged on
```

The next step is to review the newly created multipath.conf file, which is very similar to the format previously used in Oracle Linux 5. The file still is subdivided into section, using the familiar curly braces. The most important sections are these:

- Blacklist

- Defaults

- Devices

- Multipaths

The first section-blacklist {}-specifically excludes devices from being part of the multipathing configuration. This is necessary for local devices that should not be part of the configuration. A new directive, find_multipaths provides the administrator with some help in regards to blacklisted devices. Unlike the multipathing software in Oracle Linux 5, which tried to create a new pseudo-device for every path it encountered, this behavior can be kept in check without explicit blacklisting, using find_multipaths.

The next sections-defaults and device–are hugely vendor specific. Every storage vendor keeps information about the multipath.conf file and their storage products in their support portals. It is strongly recommended to either raise a call with your vendor or consult his documentation for the defaults and devices section. Interestingly the defaults section does not need to be supplied at all; the package uses built-in variables for any value not specified in the defaults-{} section. These defaults are documented in the /usr/share/doc/device-mapper-multipath-*version*/ multipath.conf file. On an example system, the following values were used:

```
defaults {
        find_multipaths     yes
        user_friendly_names yes
}
```

All other values will be provided from the built-in defaults. This is not true for the devices-{} section, which overrides the defaults for a specific array. For example, the below has been copied from the Oracle Linux 6.4 multipath.conf.defaults file, and can be used for an EMC-Clariion array:

```
devices {
      device {
                vendor "DGC"
                product ".*"
                product_blacklist "LUNZ"
                path_grouping_policy group_by_prio
                getuid_callout "/lib/udev/scsi_id --whitelisted --device=/dev/%n"
                path_selector "round-robin 0"
```

```
                path_checker emc_clariion
                features "1 queue_if_no_path"
                hardware_handler "1 emc"
                prio emc
                failback immediate
                rr_weight uniform
                no_path_retry 60
                rr_min_io 1000
                rr_min_io_rq 1
        }
}
```

Again, this is highly device-specific and should come from the storage vendor.

The last section, multipaths-{} contains specific mapping instructions for individual LUNs. This becomes clearer with an example:

```
multipaths {
        multipath {
                wwid "1IET      00010001"
                alias OCR001
        }
        multipath {
                ...
        }
        ...
}
```

This section is optional; multipath devices will be created even if there are no instructions for mappings between WWID and device name. In the above example, the device with WWID "1IET   00010001" will be configured as /dev/mapper/OCR001. The benefit of adding more human-friendly names is that troubleshooting becomes a lot easier. Instead of having to hunt down the planned purpose for device /dev/mpatha you immediately know why the device has been created. On the other hand there is added overhead involved in maintaining the mapping. Since the device naming can be a little bit confusing, here is a summary of how device names are created when using dm-multipath:

- If user_friendly_names is set to yes, the device will be created in /dev/mapper/mpath*.

- If user_friendly_names is set to no, the device will be created as /dev/mapper/WWID which is very unreadable for humans, making it difficult to find a specific device.

- If a direct mapping exists in the multipaths {} section, the alias name will be used.

- The internal devices (/dev/mpath* and /dev/dm-*) are always created, but should not be used in the context of the Oracle database.

For those who know the device mapper, you might wonder why there is no mention of the gid, uid, and mode settings. These were very useful in Oracle Linux 5.x to set ownership of LUNs when using ASM. Unfortunately this functionality has been deprecated, and once more UDEV rules have to be used instead. A recent alternative is the use of ASMLib. The use of udev and dm-multipath is a little complicated for an Oracle DBA, partly because LVM and the multipath driver share a very similar interface. Thankfully, the device mapper multipath module takes care of half the work. The rest needs to be done in a rules file.

All rules reside in /etc/udev/rules.d. Enter the directory, and create a new file. Name the file as 61-asm.rules for example. It is important that the file ends in ".rules," otherwise it will not be parsed. The following setting allows the disks to be discovered by Oracle later, assuming a separation of duties:

```
KERNEL=="dm-*", PROGRAM="/sbin/scsi_id --page=0x83 --whitelisted --device=/dev/%k",RESULT=="1IET
00010001", OWNER="grid", GROUP="asmdba" MODE="0660"

KERNEL=="sd*", PROGRAM="/sbin/scsi_id --page=0x83 --whitelisted --device=/dev/%k",RESULT=="1IET
00010001", OWNER="grid", GROUP="asmdba" MODE="0660"
```

You have to restart udev to force the changes to take effect. This can be done without a restart, using the "udevadm trigger" command as root. The last example for this chapter demonstrates the correctness of the setting by launching a disk discovery from the command line. For example:

```
[grid@server1 OraInstall2013-08-25_05-22-30PM]$ ./ext/bin/kfod disks=all \
> asm_diskstring='/dev/mapper/*p1'
--------------------------------------------------------------------------
Disk          Size Path                                      User    Group
==========================================================================
   1:         2048 Mb /dev/mapper/OCR001p1                   grid    asmdba
...
```

As you can see, the setting is correct and the disk is discovered. Oracle executes the kfod command whenever it wants to configure ASM disks.

Summary

The groundwork for installing Oracle has been laid in this chapter. In the first half of the chapter the Oracle Linux 6 installation was described in great lengthto help understand the automated installation, which was explained next. Oracle Linux comes with a great method for automating the installation of the operating system which truly helps building many servers quickly. Combined with DHCP and DDNS servers could potentially be rolled out very quickly. Security constraints usually apply and should be taken seriously however, and new servers should be built in a secure network before they can be hardened and made production ready.

After the installation of the operating system, you need to prepare the server for the Oracle database installation. Additional packages are to be installed, users are to be created and kernel parameters need to be adjusted; all pretty much standard Oracle day-to-day operations. Finally storage setup was described using the device-mapper-multipath package and how it changed in Oracle Linux 6. This should give you a solid foundation to proceed with the next tasks: the installation of the Oracle binaries.

■ ■ ■

Installing the Oracle Database

The previous chapter dealt with the installation of Oracle Linux, and its configuration in preparation of the installation of the Oracle binaries. As you have seen there are a number of prerequisites that needed to be met. In this chapter the focus shifts to the Oracle binary installation. In this respect the chapter is divided into two parts. The first one will explain the installation of Oracle Restart or—as it is also known—Grid Infrastructure for a standalone server. You will require such a setup if you would like to make use of ASM, which I recommend as an alternative to older file systems not able to perform concurrent and direct I/O. If you decide to use a file system and don't want to make use of the features offered by Oracle Restart besides ASM, feel free to skip directly to the RDBMS installation in part two. I recommend you read on for arguments in favor of Oracle Restart because there are significant benefits to using it, as described in the section "Installing Oracle Restart".

The second part of the chapter explains the installation of the Oracle RDBMS binaries. Following the overall scheme of the book-automation and consolidation-silent installations of the software will be introduced, as well as an option to install Oracle using the Red Hat Package Manager (RPM). Throughout the chapter, it is assumed that you followed Oracle's advice and use separate accounts for the Grid Infrastructure and RDBMS binaries.

Preparing for the installation

There are a few things that you need to consider before you can start the installation of any Oracle product. First, you obviously need the software, which you can download from OTN or Oracle's edelivery site. Then you need to either configure your graphical user environment to perform an interactive installation, or alternatively prepare for a silent installation.

Beginning with Oracle 11g Release 2 patchset 1 Oracle did a great thing and introduced patch sets as full releases. In other words, instead of having to apply the base release plus all the patches to get to the desired patch level, all you need to do is to download and install the patchset plus any Patch Set Updates. Just as before patches have to be downloaded from My Oracle Support. Using full releases is a great time saver, and especially from an automation point of view this makes life a lot easier by reducing the number of moving parts in your configuration.

The chapter assumes that Grid Infrastructure for a standalone server is owned by the grid account, whereas the Oracle database binaries are owned by Oracle.

Staging the software

When planning for the next-generation Oracle environment, it is the right time to think about the deployment structure. Instead of downloading and staging software and patches for every Oracle installation, you might consider a central location to stage patches, scripts, and other Oracle related data. Consider a global environment with three different locations for the staging servers: the Americas, Europe, and Asia. The locations have been chosen to be equidistant and minimize network-latency between the sites when operating on a global scale. Standard utilities such as rsync can be used to replicate information to each site overnight, keeping the systems in sync with one another.

These servers are very important for day-to-day information and therefore must also be protected locally. This can be achieved by using storage array replication or another rsync process to a local clone of the server for example. Although they should not need mentioning, regular file system backups are of course mandatory.

Once the software is staged, NFS could be used to make the software available for the database servers. In the following example, it is assumed that the software is stored in /media/oracle/x64/12.1.0.1/grid and database.

In order to stage the software, download the latest version of the binaries and use the unzip command to extract the binaries on the staging server, as shown in this example:

```
[root@stagingServer ~] # cd /path/to/nfs/export/oracle/x64/12.1.0.1/
[root@stagingServer ~] # unzip -q V38501-01_1of2.zip
[root@stagingServer ~] # unzip -q V38500-01_1of2.zip
[root@stagingServer ~] # unzip -q V38500-01_2of2.zip
```

Now change permission of the files to match your environment and configuration. You should ensure that you are exporting the file system read only and with maximum security settings enabled to prevent users from tampering with the installation! Standardized (UNIX) user and group IDs work very well toward this goal.

Preparing your environment variables

Whichever way you decided to stage the software—locally or exported via the network—you need to configure the grid user's environment appropriately before continuing. If you followed the suggestions outlined in Chapter 5, you should have an OFA-compliant setup of directories with correct permissions. The most common pitfall is to have incorrect directory permissions for the inventory, usually /u01/app/oraInventory. The grid user must be the directory owner and the oinstall group should have been assigned.

On systems with small root file systems you might run into problems due to a lack of space in the temp directory. By default Oracle Universal installer bootstraps parts of itself to the /tmp directory before launching. If there is insufficient space, this step will fail. Space pressure is added by the fact that unfinished OUI sessions are not cleared up. Additionally, OUI checks for the existence of 1GiB of free space in that same directory and you are doing well to respect that requirement. To circumvent the problem you could create a temporary directory on your oracle mount point, and redirect the TMP and TEMP environment variables at it:

```
[grid@server1 ~]> mkdir /u01/app/grid/temp
[grid@server1 ~]> export TMP=/u01/app/grid/temp
[grid@server1 ~]> export TEMP=/u01/app/grid/temp
```

With these settings the Oracle installer will use $TEMP for its bootstrap process.

Configuring your graphical user interface

Oracle Universal Installer on the UNIX platform requires a graphical user interface to start an interactive session. In the UNIX world, the "GUI" is provided by the X11 software stack. An X-client such as the installer process attaches to an X-server. For most UNIX software this would be a local-to-local connection on a workstation. Very few database systems in the real world however will allow the administrator to use the local console to install the Oracle software! Many even won't have the X11 libraries and binaries which are required for the GUI installed. There are two ways around this:

- Forward X11 via SSH

- Use the VNC server

Let's have a look at these options in detail.

Forwarding an X11 session

Most database administrators will use some variant of the Microsoft Windows operating system on their workstations or desktops. For them to use X11 forwarding, they need to install an X server which has to be started up and accepting connections on their workstations. Free/Open Source X Servers include the Cygwin environment for example. In addition to the Open Source X Servers, commercial products are available as well. It is more a matter of personal taste as to which one to choose. To allow X11 forwarding on the database server you need to modify the SSH server daemon configuration file on the database server.

■ **Note**   Check with your security department if X11-forwarding is allowed in your environment before enabling it.

For an OpenSSH implementation, you need to add/modify the following variable in /etc/ssh/sshd_config and reload the configuration. The below example is for Linux, after the variable X11Forwarding has been uncommented out and set to yes:

```
[root@server1 ~] # grep X11Forwarding /etc/ssh/sshd_config
X11Forwarding yes
[root@server1 ~] # service sshd reload
Reloading sshd:                                          [  OK  ]
[root@server1 ~] #
```

In your putty configuration, ensure to enable X11 forwarding. For putty's new connection dialog, navigate to Connection ➤SSH ➤ X11, tick the checkbox named "Enable X11 Forwarding" before connecting to the server. Unlike port forwarding you can't retrospectively enable X11 forwarding. Your next session will show lines similar to these:

```
login as: grid
grid@server1.example.com's password:
Last login: Fri Sep 6 15:31:29 2013 from jumpbox
/usr/bin/xauth:  creating new authority file /home/grid/.Xauthority
$ echo $DISPLAY
localhost:10.0
```

You can use the xdpyinfo application to check if your terminal session can connect to the X server, which should be the case. This little utility displays information about the X server. Any output different from the below example indicates you can successfully forward your X11 session:

```
xdpyinfo:  unable to open display "".
```

Using the Virtual Network Computing Protocol

An alternative to X-forwarding exists in the form of VNC. It is easiest to picture VNC as an operating system independent equivalent to the Microsoft Terminal Services client. VNC is based on a client/server architecture, and supports many operating systems. It is very common to start a server session on Linux and use a Windows client. The VNC server is slightly easier to configure than X11 forwarding. It does not require a change to the SSH daemon configuration which can be difficult to arrange.

To use VNC you need to install the vnc server on the database server. In Oracle Linux 6, the VNC package to be used is called tigervnc-server. Install it using yum as usual. Once the software is installed, start a VNC server session on the database host. Each of these will create a new display ID, as shown in the example below:

```
[grid@server1 ~]$ vncserver

You will require a password to access your desktops.

Password: <not shown>
Verify: <not shown>

New 'server1.example.com:1 (grid)' desktop is server1.example.com:1

Creating default startup script /home/grid/.vnc/xstartup
Starting applications specified in /home/grid/.vnc/xstartup
Log file is /home/grid/.vnc/server1.example.com:1.log
```

As you can see the VNC server is started on display one. Subsequent VNC server sessions started will increment that counter and start on the next available display. To connect to the VNC server process, start a VNC client on your workstation and provide the connection string, such as server1.example.com:1. The RealVNC client which is probably the most widely spread viewer has not been updated for quite some time, and the free edition is still at version 4.1.3 but works even with tigervnc used in Oracle Linux 6. The viewer does not require an installation and comes as a binary executable of only a few hundred KiB in size.

The neat aspect about the use of VNC is that it does not require a lot of bandwidth to work properly, and a network glitch does not ruin your installer session. Just like a Microsoft Terminal Server session you can resume where you left off.

Installing Oracle Restart

Beginning with 11g Release 2 Oracle has rolled up the installation of Automatic Storage Management (ASM) and Clusterware into one single Oracle home. The new installation type is called Grid Infrastructure, which can be installed either for a standalone host in which it is called "Oracle Restart", or it can be installed for a Real Application Cluster. There are good reasons to install Oracle Restart, even if you are not planning to use RAC. First of all, it gives the administrator a unified interface to his environment: the commands to administer Oracle Restart are identical to the ones the RAC DBA uses. Also, there is no more problem with automatically starting the listener and/or the database when the server reboots; it happens automatically. All these entities are registered in the Oracle Restart metadata from where they can be processed during boot and shutdown. And the best is: Oracle Restart behaves identically regardless of the platform. A server reboot is guaranteed to finish with the start of the database instances and the listener. Oracle Restart works really well in standardizing environments, which is one of the ideas of this book.

Interactive installation of Oracle Restart

The interactive installation is the recommended way to get a "feeling" for the new installer. Interactive installation can also be used to create a response file which is going to be used later for the silent installation. The standard layout of the database servers in terms of file system layout and permissions will make it very easy to perform a silent installation.

Log on to the database server as the grid user. Follow the steps as described earlier in this chapter in section "Configuring your graphical user interface" to create a GUI environment; using your terminal session start the Oracle Universal Installer.

```
[grid@server1 grid]$ ./runInstaller
Starting Oracle Universal Installer...

Checking Temp space: must be greater than 120 MB.   Actual 4789 MB    Passed
Checking swap space: must be greater than 150 MB.   Actual 767 MB    Passed
Checking monitor: must be configured to display at least 256 colors.   Actual 16777216    Passed
Preparing to launch Oracle Universal Installer from /tmp/OraInstall2013-09-06_08-17-48AM.
Please wait ...
```

The installer will bootstrap itself to the /tmp directory by default and a few moments later display the splash screen. Note that the following print screens have been rendered by a forwarded session to my Linux workstation.

Download Software Updates

The software updates screen is the first one you see after the new Oracle 12c logo indicates that you are on the latest release. Figure 6-1 shows this screen.

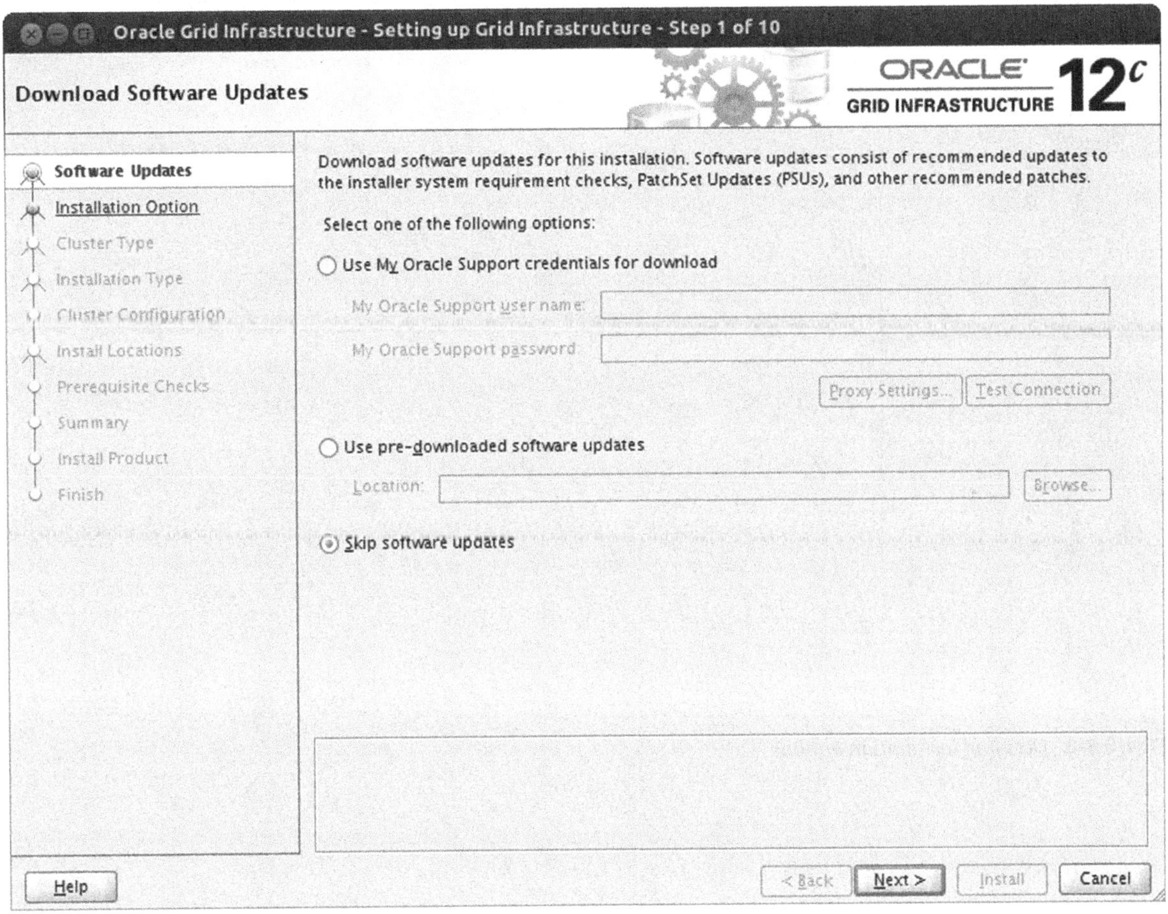

Figure 6-1. Deciding about options for downloading software updates

You have the option to download software updates such as Patch Set Updates and other fixes recommended by Oracle. By selecting the first radio button you allow a connection to My Oracle support to download patches and updates. You can supply proxy connection information to connect to the Internet. In most security conscious environments a direct connection, even facilitated by a proxy server will not be possible or even desirable. Oracle offers the second solution instead, which enables you to make use of previously downloaded patches. OUI has a command line option, called "-downloadUpdates". When you start OUI in this mode on a workstation connected to the Internet, a configuration dialog will guide you through the necessary steps for downloading the patches. These can then be transferred to the staging server and referenced in the location text field. In the above example no patches have been selected for download or application. You can ignore the warning window which pops up in this case for now.

A click on the "next" button advances to the next screen, as shown in Figure 6-2.

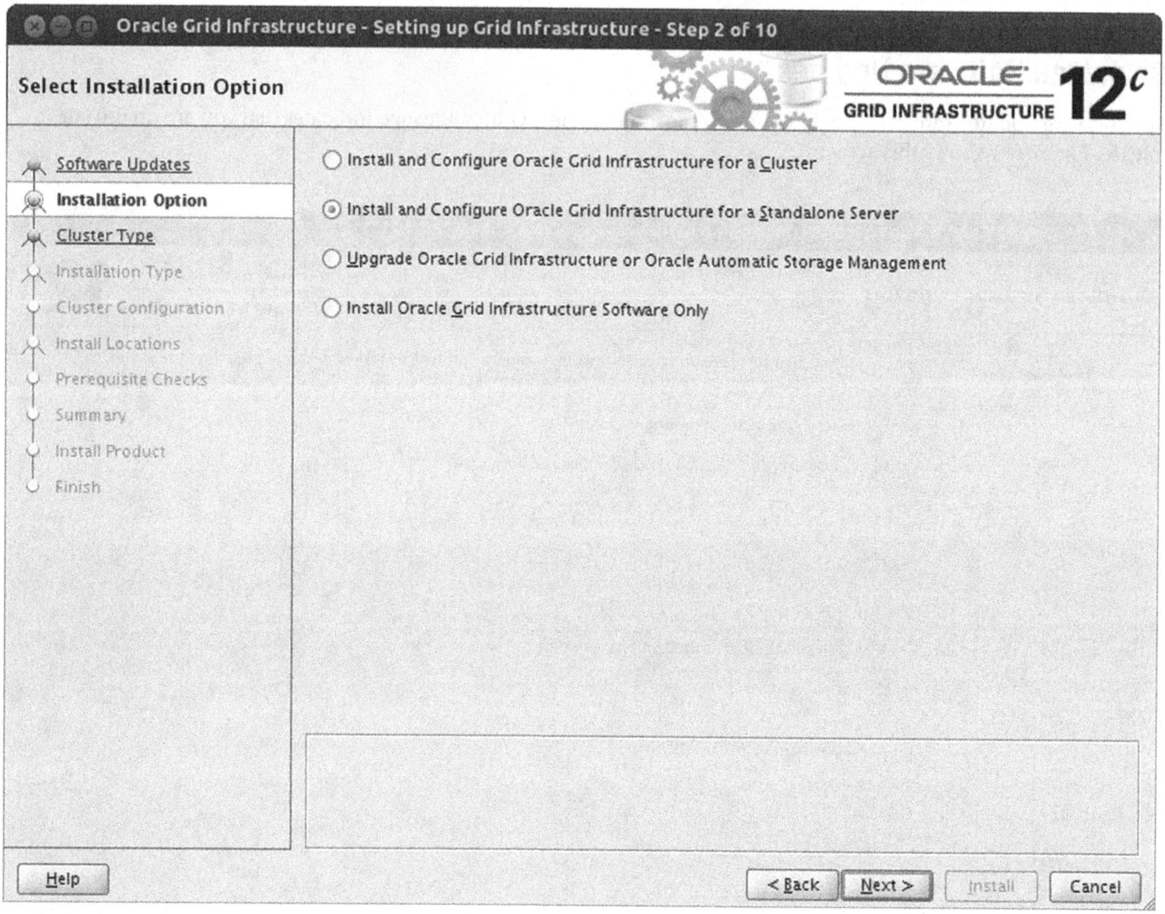

Figure 6-2. Deciding installation options

Select Installation Option

Figure 6-2 shows one of the central screens in the whole installation. On this screen you define the further course of the installation, and the next steps depend on the choice you make here. Not all are applicable to the installation of an Oracle Restart environment.

Your choices in Figure 6-2 include the following:

Install and configure Oracle Grid Infrastructure for a cluster: Select this option to install Grid Infrastructure for a Real Application Cluster. Unfortunately, due to space constraints this cannot be discussed in this chapter.

Install and configure Oracle Grid Infrastructure for a standalone server: This is the option you choose for installing Oracle Restart. It will guide you through a set of screens to define the properties of the new installation. In the course of the chapter I am assuming that you chose this option.

Upgrade Oracle Grid Infrastructure or Oracle Automatic Storage Management: This is the entry point for upgrading an existing Oracle Restart and Real Application Cluster environment. It provides a very convenient way to migrate from a previous release to 12.1. More information about upgrade considerations, the upgrade path and more can be found in Chapter 12.

Install Oracle Grid Infrastructure Software only: This option is appropriate for experienced Oracle administrators without root access to immediately execute the root-scripts during the installation. Unlike the second option, which will run all the configuration assistants after the binaries have been deployed, this installation type requires you to perform manual steps. These include running configuration steps for Oracle Restart, as well as the addition of any resource normally created for you by an automated configuration assistant. On the upside you do not need to wait for any configuration assistant to finish. As soon as the software has been installed it is possible to close the OUI session.

Continue the installation by selecting option 2 "Install and Configure Oracle Grid Infrastructure for a Standalone Server" and click on the "Next" button.

Select Product Language

You can see in Figure 6-3 that Oracle supports a wide range of languages out of the box. The American English language will always be pre-selected, and should not be removed from the selection.

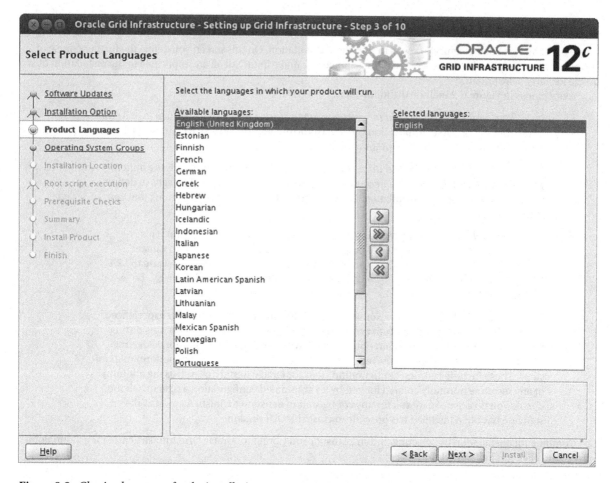

Figure 6-3. *Chosing languages for the installation*

Select any other languages you would like to use with the Oracle Restart installation by highlighting them on the left pane and moving them over to the right pane by clicking the arrow button. Click on "Next" to advance to the ASM disk group creation screen.

Create ASM Disk Group

ASM has been discussed in some detail in chapter 2. At this stage in the installation process you are going to put theory to practice by defining which LUNs are defined in a disk group, using the screen in Figure 6-4. This screen makes use of the fact that the ASM disks have already been defined on the operating system as discussed in Chapter 5.

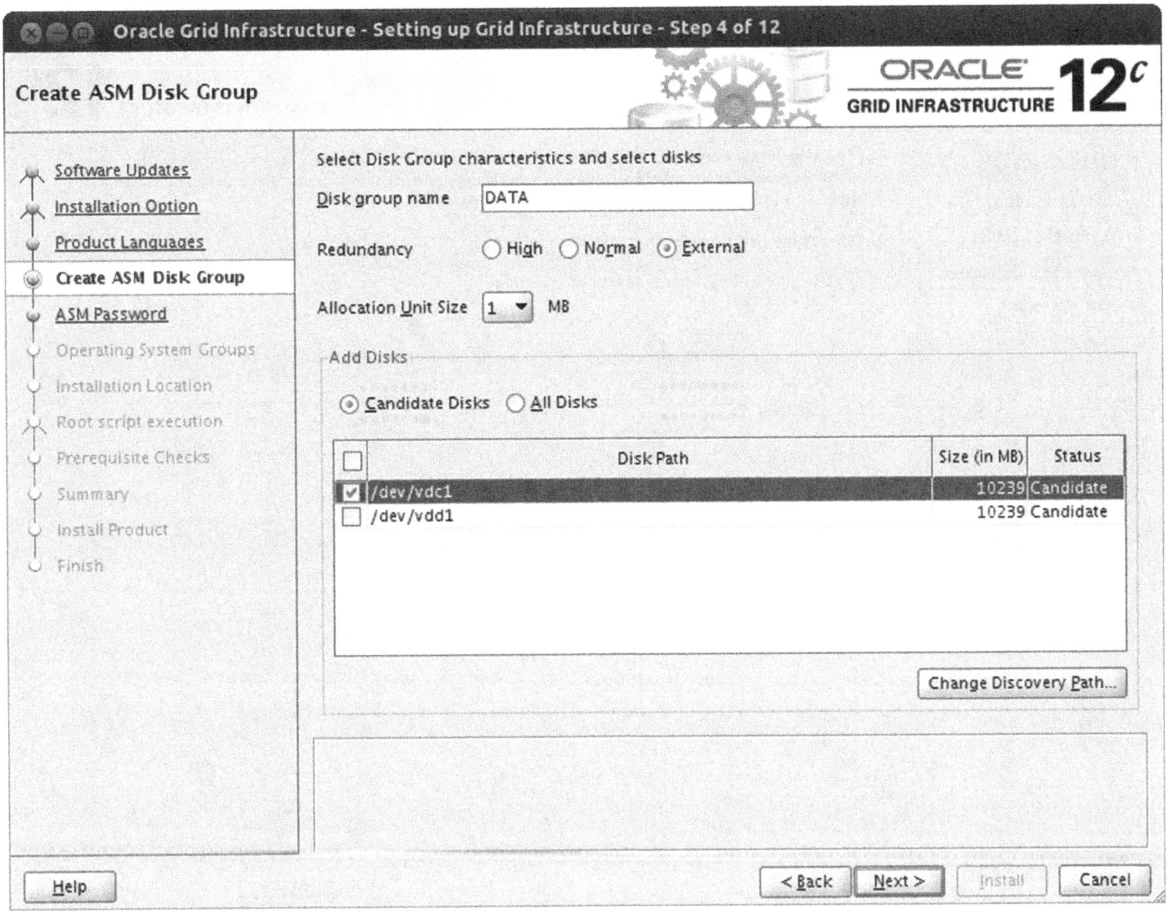

Figure 6-4. *Creating ASM disk groups*

For ASM disks to be accessible by Oracle Restart and the database in this separation-of-duties scenario, they must be owned by the grid user. The group has to be set to asmdba and the permissions on the block device must be set to 0660-otherwise the installer won't be able to attach to the LUNs. If no disks appear, the discovery string could be wrong. In this case, click on the button labeled "Change Discovery Path" and enter an appropriate value. For example, if you are using EMC Power Path on Linux you would use /dev/emcpower* instead. Native Linux device-mapper-multipath devices require a discovery string of /dev/mapper/<some identifier>. Click into the checkboxes in front of the LUNs to select the disks to be added to the disk group. Alternatively, change the default allocation unit if you are expecting the disk group to become very large. The default name of the ASM disk group to be created is named "DATA" (change the name to match your naming standards). When you are happy with the settings continue by clicking on "Next".

Specify ASM Password

On the screen shown in Figure 6-5 you have the choice to enter passwords for the two ASM users: SYS and ASMSNMP.

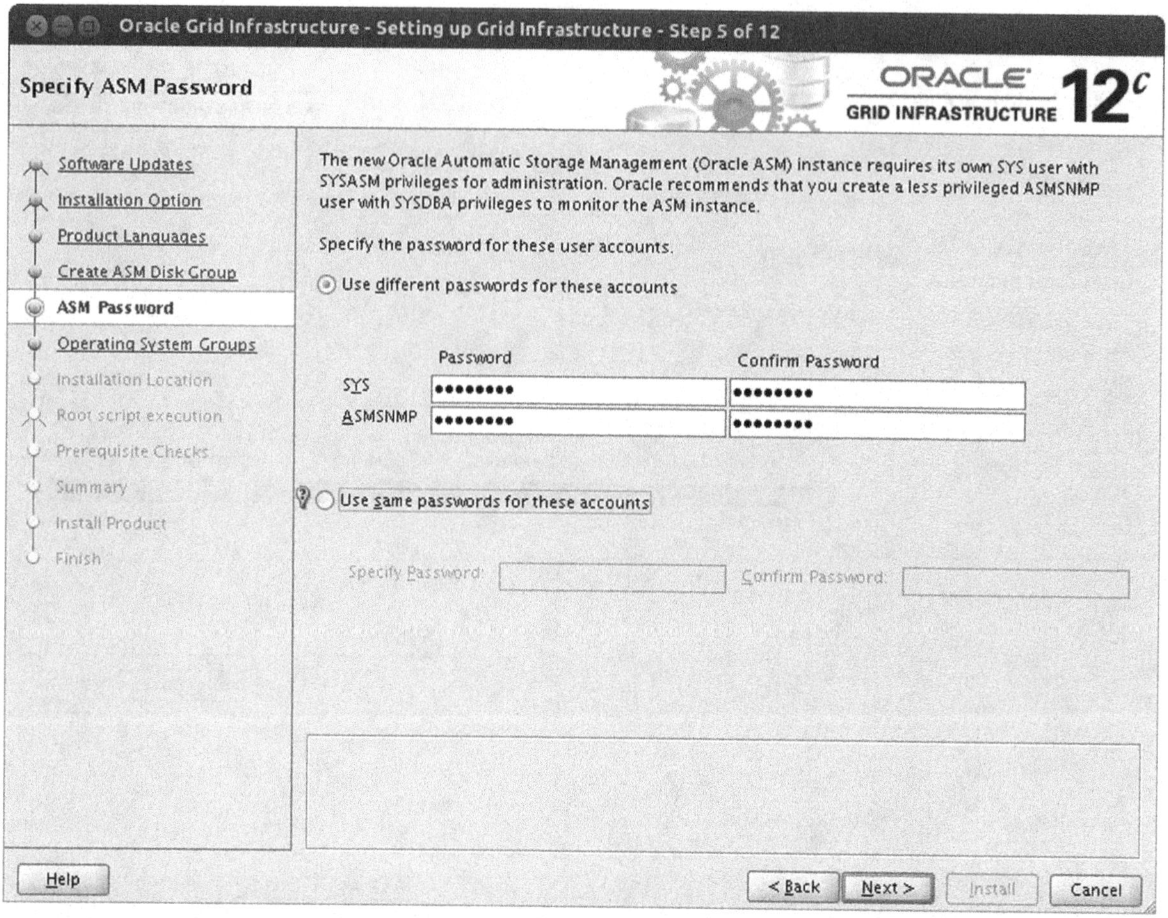

Figure 6-5. *Specifying ASM passwords*

The sys account is the ASM-equivalent of the UNIX root account, and its password should therefore be chosen carefully. The ASMSNMP has been introduced in 11g Release 2 and is primarily used for monitoring the ASM instance from Enterprise Manager. Although the installer offers you to share a common password for both accounts this is strongly discouraged. Press "Next" to continue to the "Privileged Operating System Groups" screen.

Specify Privileged Operating System Groups

On the screen shown in Figure 6-6 you map your previously created operating system groups to privileged groups as defined by Oracle.

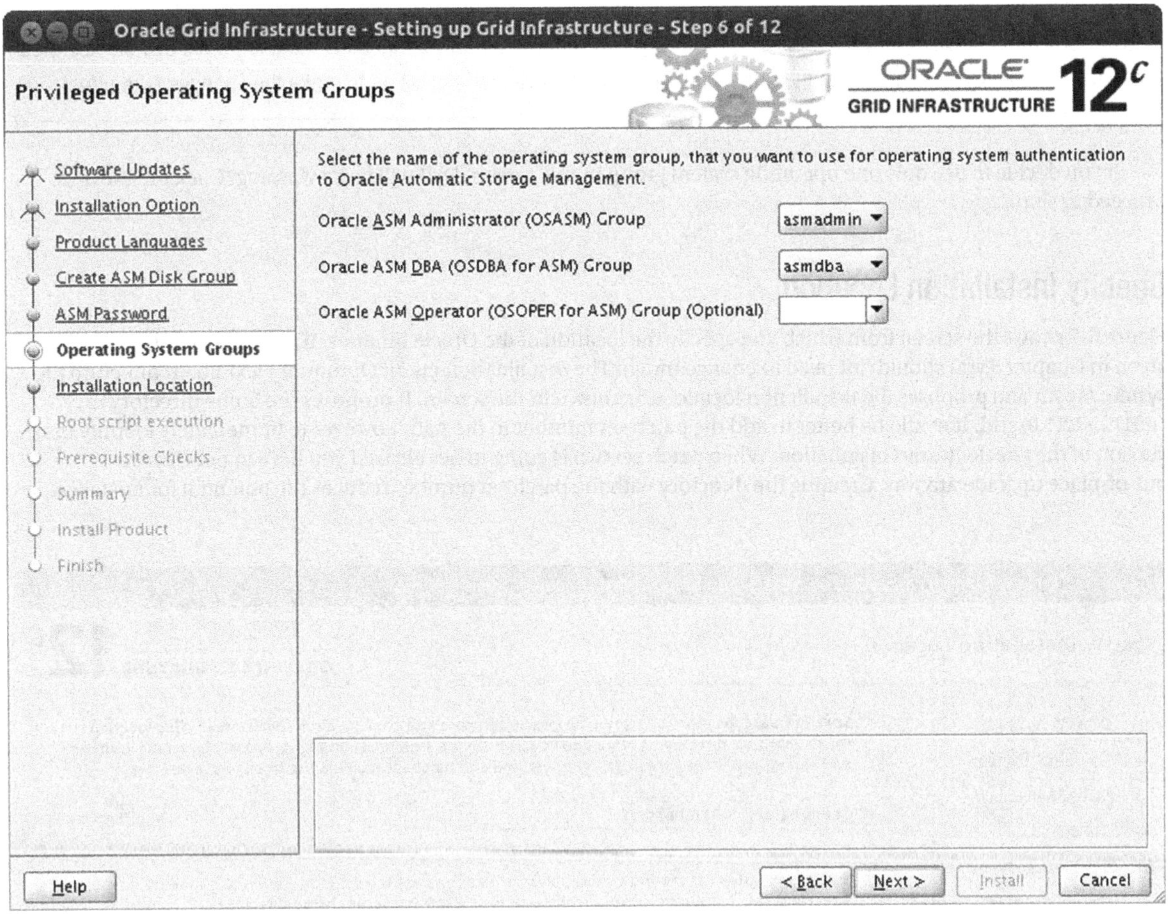

Figure 6-6. *Assigning privileged operating system groups*

The mapping of operating system groups to Oracle's internal groups has been discussed in great detail in Chapter 5. Here is a quick refresher of the discussion:

- Members of the Oracle ASM Administrator Group (OSASM) can connect to the ASM instance using the SYSASM privilege

- Members of the Oracle ASM DBA Group (OSDBA) can connect to the ASM instance using the SYSDBA privilege. The RDBMS owner account (oracle in most cases) must be a member of this group. Otherwise the ASM storage will not be visible to the database

- Members of the optional ASM Operator Group (OSOPER for ASM) can connect using the SYSOPER privilege

Although it is possible to assign the same operating system group to all of the Oracle groups, it is suggested to use the groups as shown in the figure for finer privilege granularity.

> ■ **Note** The drop-down boxes on this screen will only display groups currently assigned to the grid owner. Use the usermod command to add additional groups to the grid owner and log out of your X11-session to make the changes take effect.

If you decide to use only one operating system group in this screen, OUI will flag a warning. Click on "Next" to proceed to step 7.

Specify Installation Location

Figure 6-7 shows the screen from which you specify the location of the Oracle binaries. If you followed the advice given in Chapter 5 you should not need to change much. The installer detects an Optimum Flexible Architecture file system layout and proposes the installation locations as shown in the screen. It proposes the home directory to /u01/.../12.1.0/grid. It would be better to add the patch set number to the path however to immediately identify the version of the Oracle Restart installation. When patch set two is going to be released you have to perform an out-of-place upgrade anyway. Creating the directory with the patch set number reduces the potential for mistakes.

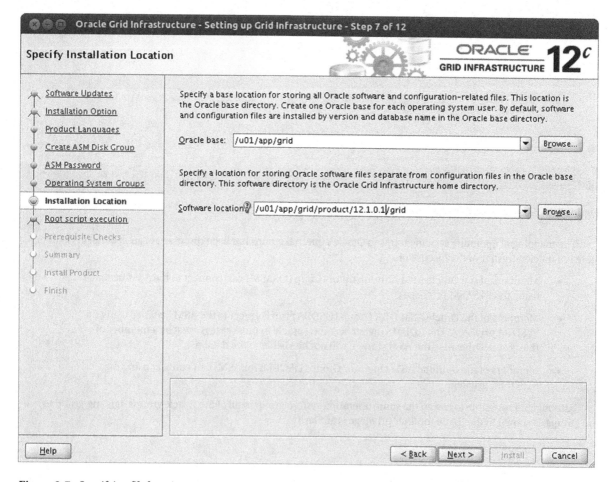

Figure 6-7. *Specifying file locations*

Should you have different requirements adjust the paths to match your standards and click "Next" to proceed to the following screen.

Create Inventory

The Oracle central inventory is an important location for the maintenance of the Oracle software. It stores, among other items, which Oracle home has been installed and where. Figure 6-8 shows the screen from which you define the inventory location. The location should not be inside the ORACLE_BASE; you typically define the inventory location to be one hierarchy above the ORACLE_BASE for the Oracle account.

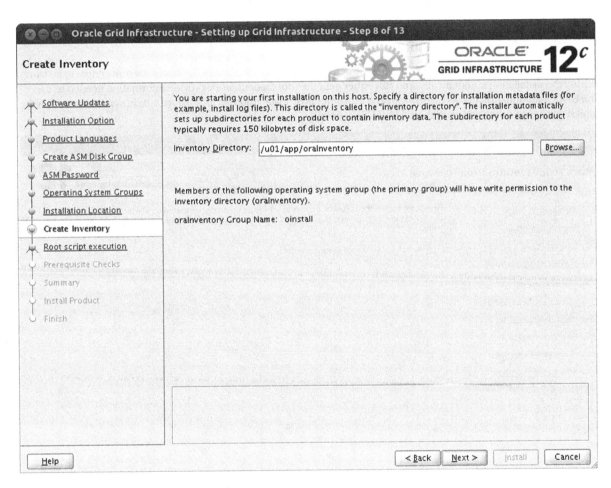

Figure 6-8. Defining the Oracle inventory location

If the inventory location is under ORACLE_BASE, the installer will issue a warning which you should not ignore, especially when using different accounts for Grid Infrastructure and the RDBMS binaries. Although you are prompted to run a script after the transfer of the binaries to the hard disk finished OUI insists that the permissions for the inventory directory are as follows:

- Owner: grid owner-"grid" in this example

- Group: oinstall

- Permissions: 0770

The inventory group is determined by the grid owner's primary group-oinstall. Again click "Next" to advance to the next screen.

Running Root Scripts Automatically

A very nice feature has been added to Grid Infrastructure allowing you to have OUI execute the root scripts to be run during the installation automatically. You can either pass the root credentials or provide information needed to use the UNIX sudo-function to execute the root and any other post-installation scripts. Figure 6-9 shows the screen from which you specific these credentials and other login details.

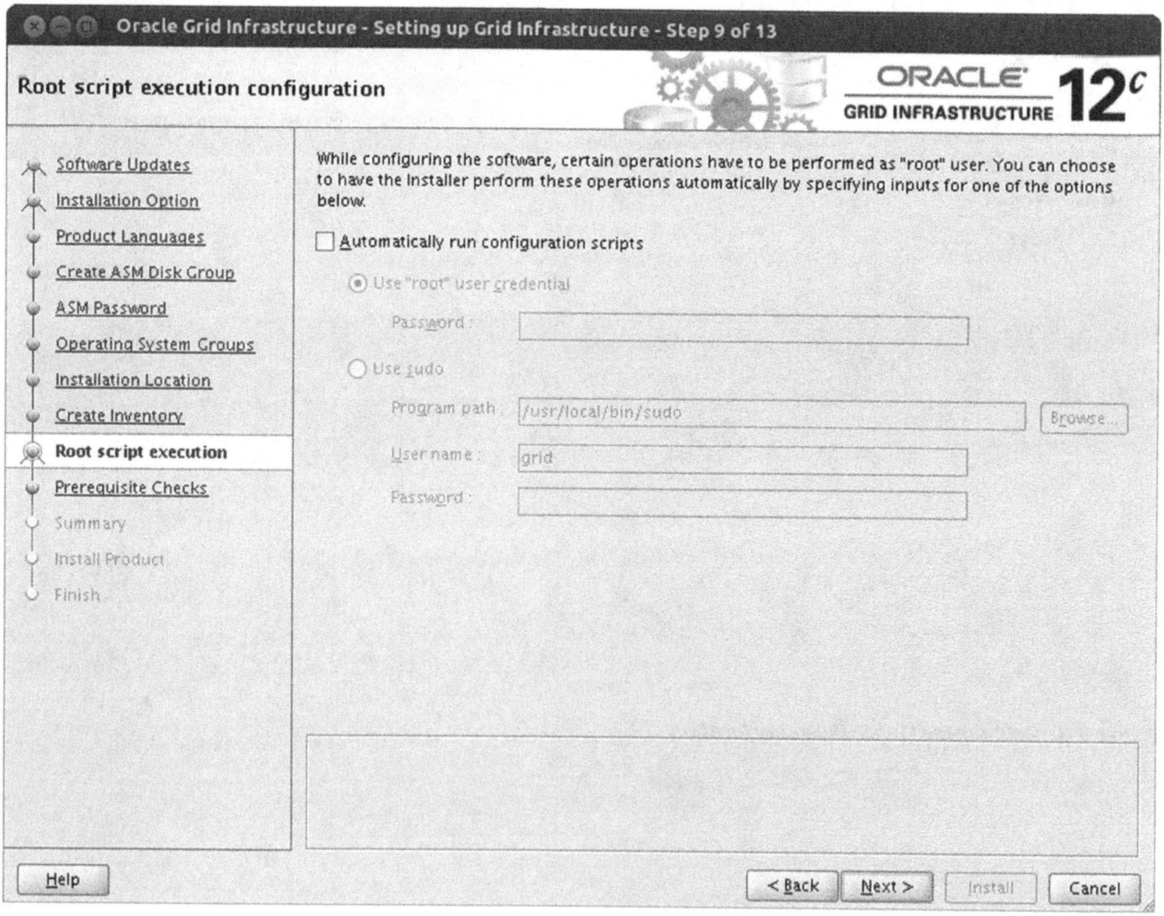

Figure 6-9. *Optionally run root scripts automatically*

Perform Prerequisite checks

You are getting closer to actually transferring the binaries to disk! The installer ensures in this step that the required prerequisites for the installation are met. Depending on your configuration this can take a little while. After the verification has completed, the results are presented to you. If your preparations have been thorough you should not be met with any errors and the installer will proceed straight to the summary screen as shown in Figure 6-11. If you are curious to see the results of the checks anyway you can use the "Back" button to navigate back, the screen will look similar to Figure 6-10.

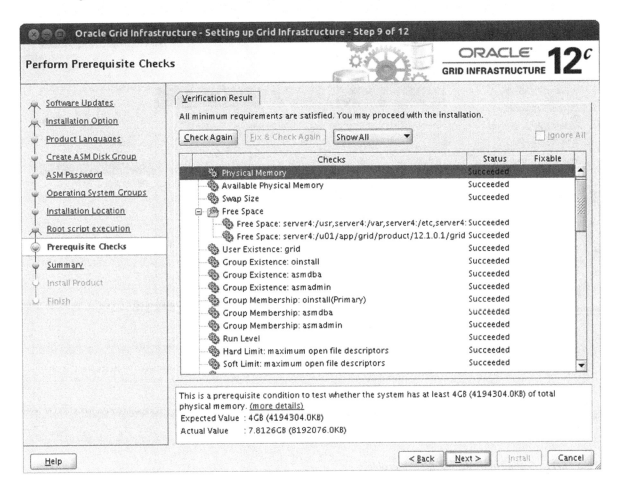

Figure 6-10. *Checking the prerequisites*

In case of errors you can either manually correct the problems by switching to a shell session, or let the installer do the hard work. Beginning with Oracle 11.2 there is an option to let OUI create a so-called fixup script on the server to be executed as root which should correct many common problems with the configuration. If a failed check has "yes" in the fixable column, then OUI can often correct it. Certain issues such as problems with main memory can obviously not be fixed automatically by the installer.

Once you have run the fixup script as root, return to the installer session and acknowledge the script execution. OUI will check the system once more to ensure you are not missing vital configuration steps.

If you opted to modify the system settings yourself, you can use the "Check Again" button to verify the system settings once more. Thankfully you are not left out in the dark with the task of correcting the settings for a failed check.

In the list of problems, click on an entry to display more information, as shown in Figure 6-11. This is the place to get detailed information about the problem by clicking on the hyperlink named "more details". This opens the pop-up box shown. As you can see Oracle expects you to have a maximum limit of open file descriptors for the grid users set to 65536.

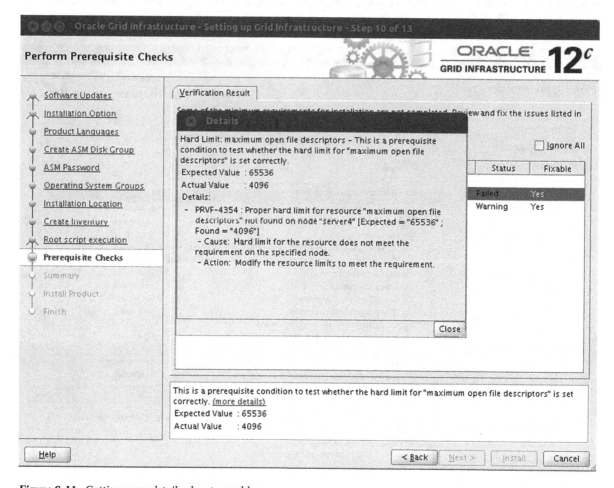

Figure 6-11. *Getting more details about a problem*

The error messages are helpful in most cases, and usually lead you to the source of the error quite quickly. The most common errors to be corrected are related to missing or invalid kernel parameters, swap space, and shell limits.

Once all the problems are fixed click "Next" to proceed to the summary screen.

Review the Installation Summary

The summary screen shown in Figure 6-12 wraps up all the previously made choices in one place. Review your settings and ensure that the choice made reflects your corporate standards. You can always use the "Back" button or click on the [Edit] link to go back to the relevant screen to make any corrections.

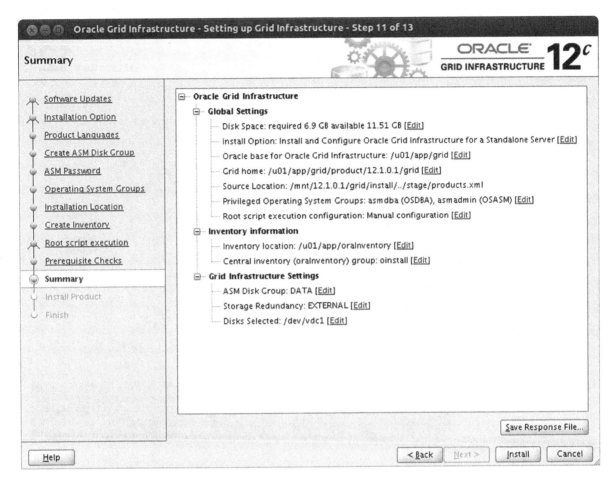

Figure 6-12. *Installation summary*

The greyed-out "Next" button indicates that there are no further screens in the installation wizard. A click on "Install" will initiate the transfer of the software to the defined location. Before doing so, take a moment and consider the creation of the response file. The response file will be needed for a silent install, which will be explained in the next section. The default location OUI offers for the response file is in the grid owner's home directory, and is usually called grid.rsp.

Figure 6-13 shows the progress screen.

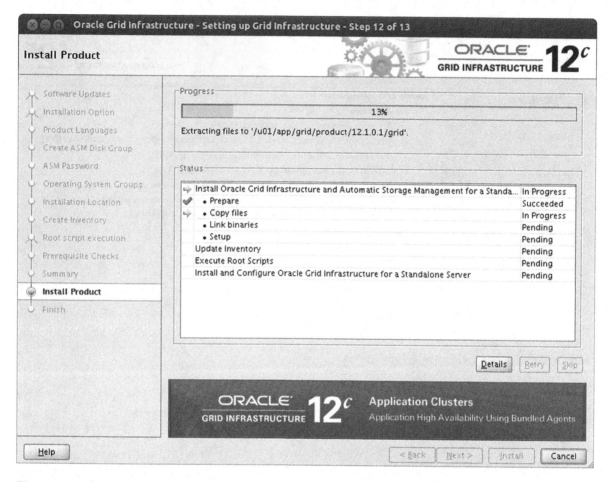

Figure 6-13. *The installation progress screen*

The installation proceeds by preparing, copying, and linking binaries. Once these activities are completed, a window opens as shown in Figure 6-14 and prompts you to run the "root scripts".

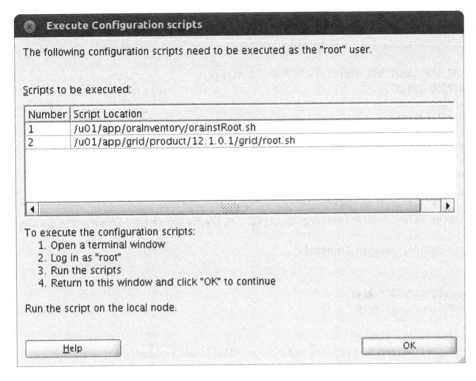

Figure 6-14. *Prompt for root script execution*

Running and troubleshooting configuration scripts

There are two scripts to be executed as root for an Oracle Restart installation:

- orainstRoot.sh

- root.sh

Figure 6-14 shows you the pop-up which prompts for the script execution.

The exact path is indicated in the pop-up window, which can be copied into the clipboard. The first script to run, orainstRoot.sh, ensures that the permissions on the central inventory are set correctly. The output of the script execution is shown here:

```
Changing permissions of /u01/app/oraInventory.
Adding read,write permissions for group.
Removing read,write,execute permissions for world.

Changing groupname of /u01/app/oraInventory to oinstall.
The execution of the script is complete.
```

The next script-root.sh-sets up the foundation for Oracle Restart, and the output from running it is shown below:

```
[root@server1 ~]# /u01/app/grid/product/12.1.0.1/grid/root.sh
Performing root user operation for Oracle 12c
```

The following environment variables are set as:
    ORACLE_OWNER= grid
    ORACLE_HOME= /u01/app/grid/product/12.1.0.1/grid

Enter the full pathname of the local bin directory: [/usr/local/bin]:
    Copying dbhome to /usr/local/bin ...
    Copying oraenv to /usr/local/bin ...
    Copying coraenv to /usr/local/bin ...

Creating /etc/oratab file...
Entries will be added to the /etc/oratab file as needed by
Database Configuration Assistant when a database is created
Finished running generic part of root script.
Now product-specific root actions will be performed.
Using configuration parameter file: /u01/app/grid/product/12.1.0.1/grid/crs/install/crsconfig_params
LOCAL ADD MODE
Creating OCR keys for user 'grid', privgrp 'oinstall'..
Operation successful.
LOCAL ONLY MODE
Successfully accumulated necessary OCR keys.
Creating OCR keys for user 'root', privgrp 'root'..
Operation successful.
CRS-4664: Node server1 successfully pinned.
2013/09/06 18:42:03 CLSRSC-330: Adding Clusterware entries to file 'oracle-ohasd.conf'

Server1   2013/09/06 18:42:32   /u01/app/grid/product/12.1.0.1/grid/cdata/server1/
backup_20130906_184232.olr
2013/09/06 18:43:18 CLSRSC-327: Successfully configured Oracle Grid Infrastructure
for a Standalone Server

If you see the last line "successfully configured Oracle Grid Infrastructure for a Standalone Server", all is well you have successfully executed the root.sh script.

In the past it has been difficult to troubleshoot problems with the root.sh script. These have gradually been addressed with the latest releases. A major improvement is the verbose logging created during the execution of the root.sh script. The file you need to consult is in somewhat hidden in $GRID_HOME/cfgtoollogs/crsconfig/roothas. log. Should you run into problems during the execution of root.sh, begin your investigation there. It shows in great detail which steps are performed on your behalf. Studying the contents of the roothas.log file can greatly improve your understanding of how Grid Infrastructure works internally, but has to be left as an exercise to the reader to do so. Unlike the root.sh for a clustered installation, the script does not seem to be restartable.

If you have adhered to the configuration described in Chapter 5, you should not have any problems with the root.sh script. Common problems encountered in the field are mismatches between /etc/hosts and DNS entries, or ignored prerequisites. Usually the error reported in roothas.log is specific enough to point you to the problem.

Finishing the installation

After the successful execution of the root scripts, click the "OK" button to dismiss the dialog. Control will return to the Oracle Universal Installer session, and the final configuration will complete the installation. This is shown in Figure 6-15.

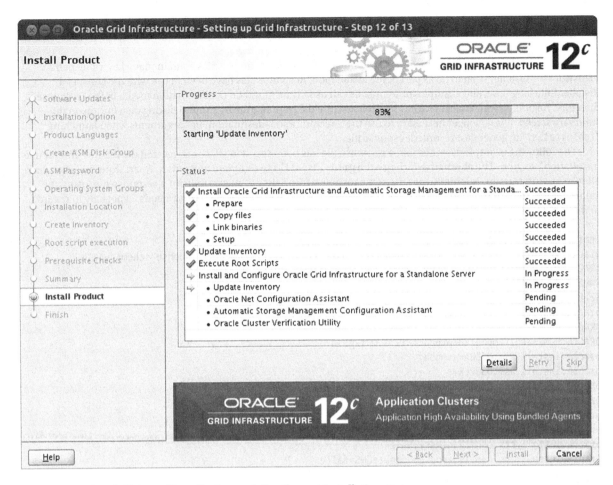

Figure 6-15. *Oracle Universal Installer is completing the post-installation steps*

The following steps are performed:

- Update of the inventory

- Configuration of a basic network configuration

- Creation of the ASM instance

- A final pass of the cluster verification utility

All of these operations are logged in detail in `$GRID_HOME/cfgtoollogs/`. The installer will automatically advance to the next screen and displays a success message. Congratulations! You have installed Oracle ASM! You may proceed by drinking a cup of well-deserved coffee before beginning the installation of the database binaries.

Silent installation of Oracle Restart

A silent installation of Oracle Restart is an elegant way to deploy the software to many hosts using a lights-out approach. The standardized approach to deploying hosts and operating systems should make this task even easier, since you can assume a compliant directory layout. You should also assume that all users have been created with the correct group mappings and so forth. Silent installations also don't need an X11-server anywhere in the network. For secure environments, this is a blessing as it doesn't involve changing the SSH configuration as described earlier in the chapter. Many secure sites do not allow X11 forwarding or port forwarding at all.

The so-called response file is the basis of the silent installation. Response files contain many key-value pairs to instruct the installer what to do as part of the installation. Response files have been in use with the Universal Installer for a long time, and examples or templates can usually be found on the installation media in the "response" directory. Beginning with Oracle 11.2 it is possible to store the response file by simply clicking on a button on the summary screen. It is no longer necessary to use the "-record" and "-destinationFile" arguments when launching "runInstaller" to generate a recorded response file.

The following example assumes that a response file has been saved in OUI as suggested during the "interactive installation" section. The alternative is to use the grid_install.rsp template and edit it. Apart from the passwords all relevant information is initially present in the response file. Below is an example for a response file, using the values defined earlier in the interactive session. Please ensure to adapt the file to your needs, especially in regards to the passwords.

```
[grid@server1 ~]$ sed -e '/^#/d' -e '/^$/d' grid.rsp
oracle.install.responseFileVersion=/oracle/install/rspfmt_crsinstall_response_schema_v12.1.0
ORACLE_HOSTNAME=server1.example.com
INVENTORY_LOCATION=/u01/app/oraInventory
SELECTED_LANGUAGES=en
oracle.install.option=HA_CONFIG
ORACLE_BASE=/u01/app/grid
ORACLE_HOME=/u01/app/grid/product/12.1.0.1/grid
oracle.install.asm.OSDBA=asmdba
oracle.install.asm.OSOPER=
oracle.install.asm.OSASM=asmadmin
oracle.install.crs.config.gpnp.scanName=
oracle.install.crs.config.gpnp.scanPort=
oracle.install.crs.config.ClusterType=STANDARD
oracle.install.crs.config.clusterName=
oracle.install.crs.config.gpnp.configureGNS=false
oracle.install.crs.config.autoConfigureClusterNodeVIP=true
oracle.install.crs.config.gpnp.gnsOption=CREATE_NEW_GNS
oracle.install.crs.config.gpnp.gnsClientDataFile=
oracle.install.crs.config.gpnp.gnsSubDomain=
oracle.install.crs.config.gpnp.gnsVIPAddress=
oracle.install.crs.config.clusterNodes=
oracle.install.crs.config.networkInterfaceList=
oracle.install.crs.managementdb.configure=true
oracle.install.crs.config.storageOption=
oracle.install.crs.config.sharedFileSystemStorage.votingDiskLocations=
oracle.install.crs.config.sharedFileSystemStorage.votingDiskRedundancy=NORMAL
oracle.install.crs.config.sharedFileSystemStorage.ocrLocations=
oracle.install.crs.config.sharedFileSystemStorage.ocrRedundancy=NORMAL
oracle.install.crs.config.useIPMI=false
oracle.install.crs.config.ipmi.bmcUsername=
oracle.install.crs.config.ipmi.bmcPassword=
oracle.install.asm.SYSASMPassword=
oracle.install.asm.diskGroup.name=DATA
oracle.install.asm.diskGroup.redundancy=EXTERNAL
oracle.install.asm.diskGroup.AUSize=1
oracle.install.asm.diskGroup.disks=/dev/vdc1
```

```
oracle.install.asm.diskGroup.diskDiscoveryString=/dev/vd*1
oracle.install.asm.monitorPassword=
oracle.install.crs.config.ignoreDownNodes=false
oracle.installer.autoupdates.option=SKIP_UPDATES
oracle.installer.autoupdates.downloadUpdatesLoc=
AUTOUPDATES_MYORACLESUPPORT_USERNAME=
AUTOUPDATES_MYORACLESUPPORT_PASSWORD=
PROXY_HOST=
PROXY_PORT=0
PROXY_USER=
PROXY_PWD=
PROXY_REALM=
```

For the installation to succeed you need to supply passwords in the response files. Since that is a security problem you can provide the passwords on the command line as well. If you do not choose to provide the passwords on the command line please make sure the response file uses proper operating system security to prevent unauthorized users from gaining access. Better still, change the passwords used during installation as soon as you can during the post-installation steps. This step is so straightforward that it has not been included in the chapter. Do not forget to apply it though!

With a response file in this format you are ready to begin the installation. To start it, use the -silent and -responseFile command line arguments to runInstaller as shown here where passwords are supplied on the command line rather than in the response file. Notice that variables that would normally be supplied in the response file are enclosed in double quotes:

```
$ ./runInstaller -silent -responseFile /home/grid/grid.rsp \
> "oracle.install.asm.SYSASMPassword=randomSysThrowawayPassword" \
> "oracle.install.asm.monitorPassword=randomASMSNMPThrowawayPassword"
Starting Oracle Universal Installer...

Checking Temp space: must be greater than 120 MB.   Actual 4691 MB   Passed
Checking swap space: must be greater than 150 MB.   Actual 8947 MB   Passed
Preparing to launch Oracle Universal Installer from /tmp/OraInstall2013-09-06_07-15-58PM.
Please wait ...
You can find the log of this install session at:
 /u01/app/oraInventory/logs/installActions2013-09-06_07-15-58PM.log
The installation of Oracle Grid Infrastructure 12c was successful.
Please check '/u01/app/oraInventory/logs/silentInstall2013-09-06_07-15-58PM.log' for more details.

As a root user, execute the following script(s):
        1. /u01/app/grid/product/12.1.0.1/grid/root.sh

Successfully Setup Software.
As install user, execute the following script to complete the configuration.
        1. /u01/app/grid/product/12.1.0.1/grid/cfgtoollogs/configToolAllCommands↵
           RESPONSE_FILE=<response_file>

        Note:
        1. This script must be run on the same host from where installer was run.
        2. This script needs a small password properties file for configuration
           assistants that require passwords (refer to install guide documentation).
```

With the setup of the software complete, you should execute the root.sh script as demonstrated in the interactive installation session. The only difference between the two install types is that the root.sh script won't print any output on script, but rather in a log file. The part of the installation requiring some more attention is a script called "configToolAllCommands". It contains commands for all the post-installation configuration assistants to be run. More specifically, it will perform these tasks:

- Update the central inventory.

- Call the network configuration assistant to create a default network configuration.

- Invoke the ASM configuration assistant to start the ASM instance and create the defined disk group.

As the command output from the runInstaller command states, you will need a response file to complete the configToolAllCommands step. Create the response file as shown here, and substitute the values for the passwords (which need to match with the ones specified above):

```
[grid@server1 ~]$ ls -l cfgrsp.properties
-rw-------. 1 grid oinstall 87 Mar  8 23:08 cfgrsp.properties
[grid@server1 ~]$ cat cfgrsp.properties
oracle.assistants.asm|S_ASMPASSWORD=randomSysThrowawayPassword
oracle.assistants.asm|S_ASMMONITORPASSWORD=randomASMSNMPThrowawayPassword
```

Now run the configuration assistant as the installation owner-grid in this case:

```
[grid@server1 ~]$ cd /u01/app/grid/product/12.1.0.1/grid/cfgtoollogs/
[grid@server1 cfgtoollogs]$ ./configToolAllCommands RESPONSE_FILE=~/cfgrsp.properties
```

Once completed, the operation will have produced a log file which indicates success or failure of each component. Should one of the components have failed you can check for logs in the $GRID_HOME/cfgttoollogs/ cfgfw/ directory. Testing showed that the configToolAllCommand execution occasionally can fail if the Oracle environment variables for the Oracle Restart home were not set. If you get strange error messages in the log file review the environment variables and run the script again. When finished you might want to remove the response files now as they might contain sensitive information.

Automatic installation of Oracle Restart using RPM

Most platforms have their proprietary way of deploying software packages, and keeping track of them. Red Hat Linux is based on the Red Hat Package Manager or RPM. Although there are alternatives to RPM, non-RPM Linux distributions such as Debian were never officially supported by Oracle for non-free versions of the database. Attempts to run Oracle on Debian for example have been made, but any success is negated by the lack of support.

Unfortunately Oracle binaries don't lend themselves to installation using RPM. The whole RPM process is more geared toward compiling and installing software from source. Since you can't download and compile Oracle source code a slightly different approach was needed to make Oracle installable with RPM. To do so a post-installation routine is executed calling OUI in silent mode with a response file to perform the installation. The downside to this approach is quickly identified: the RPM containing the Oracle Restart installation code hardly contains a file. System administrators used to verifying the contents of a packages using the --verify option to an RPM query will notice that the files inside the Oracle home are not registered in the RPM database. The examples in this chapter will not include a de-installation section for the RPM, as a hint the reader should consider invoking the $ORACLE_HOME/deinstall/ deinstall tool to remove the software cleanly.

> ■ **Note** There are other methods available to create an Oracle home, such as cloning. In the example shown in this chapter it is assumed that the DBA has control over the application of Patch Set Updates. Cloning the Oracle home seems elegant as well, but the overhead involved in creating a new (tested and validated!) golden image after each release of a PSU is enormous.

The following sections provide a short explanation of how to create the RPM for Grid Infrastructure installation. More details about the RPM building process can be found on the Fedora project's website. Fedora is the "community" distribution made by Red Hat. Red Hat Enterprise Linux is based on an earlier Fedora release.

Preparing the RPM build environment

A few additional packages need to be installed on the host on which you are preparing to install the RPM. On Oracle Linux these are:

- rpmlint
- rpmdevtools
- Plus all their dependencies

It is not recommended to build RPMs as root. Often, the "rpmbuild" account is used, and that is the account used in the following example.

If user rpmbuild does not exist, create it:

```
[root@server1 ~]# useradd -m -g users -G users rpmbuild
[root@server1 ~]# passwd rpmbuild
Changing password for user rpmbuild.
New password:
Retype new password:
passwd: all authentication tokens updated successfully.
```

Now log on as user rpmbuild to complete the process. When building RPMs, a certain directory structure is assumed, such as a top directory ($HOME/rpmbuild) and certain subdirectories:

- BUILD
- BUILDROOT
- RPMS
- SOURCES
- SPECS
- SRPMS

The easiest way to create the required directories is to call the rpmdev-setuptree command in the user's home directory. Thankfully this is all you need to do, as it will also create a small configuration file in ~/ .rpmmacros pointing to the newly created directory tree.

The RPM build process is controlled via a specification or "SPEC" file. Documentation of SPEC files isn't too great, especially since the format has changed over time. The SPEC file describes the steps you would normally follow when compiling a piece of software from a source. The great benefit of the SPEC file is that it puts more structure around the process. Once you understand the SPEC file syntax the process is really powerful, but the initial learning curve is steep. The SPEC file for the Oracle Restart installation has the following content, and resides in the SPEC directory as grid.spec:

```
[rpmbuild@server1 SPECS]$ cat grid.spec
Name:            GridInfrastructure
Version:         12.1.0.1
Release:         1%{?dist}
Summary:         installation of Grid Infrastructure for Enterprise Linux 6.x
Group:           Applications/Databases
License:         Commercial
URL:             http://engineering.example.com/builds/
BuildRoot:       %(mktemp -ud %{_tmppath}/%{name}-%{version}-%{release}-XXXXXX)

Requires:        oracle-rdbms-server-12cR1-preinstall

%description
This RPM checks for the required RPMs on Oracle Linux 6.x and adds them
as dependencies when needed.

Additionally, the RPM deploys the /etc/oraInst.loc file as per the standard
document, with /u01/app/oraInventory as the central inventory.

This RPM is not suitable for a RAC installation, it can only install Oracle
Restart. It will install the software as the grid user.

After deploying the files the Oracle Universal Installer is invoked with the
silent response file from /opt/oracle/grid.rsp, and required configuration
assistants are executed. Be patient!

%install
rm -rf $RPM_BUILD_ROOT
mkdir -p $RPM_BUILD_ROOT/etc
mkdir -p $RPM_BUILD_ROOT/opt/oracle
cp oraInst.loc $RPM_BUILD_ROOT/etc/
cp grid.rsp $RPM_BUILD_ROOT/opt/oracle
cp cfgrsp.properties $RPM_BUILD_ROOT/opt/oracle

%post
GRID_OWNER=grid
GRID_HOME=/u01/app/grid/product/12.1.0.1/grid

# mount the software
umount /mnt
mount -t nfs stagingServer:/export/oracle/x64/ /mnt

if [ $? -ne 0 ]; then
  echo "FATAL error trying to mount the binares from the staging server"
  exit 1
fi
```

```
# Here we invoke the installer. Testing for FATAL errors in the installer
# output. If there is, we abort and say so

su - $GRID_OWNER -c \
"/mnt/12.1.0.1/grid/runInstaller -silent -responseFile /opt/oracle/grid.rsp" \
2>&1 | grep FATAL
if [ $? -eq 0 ]; then
  echo "FATAL error occured-installation NOT completed"
  touch /tmp/gridInstall.failed
  exit 2
fi

# wait 30x30 seconds for OUI to complete. Increase if needed!
cnt=0
while ! test -e $GRID_HOME/root.sh
do
  echo "waiting for the software installation to complete"
  sleep 30
  cnt=$(( $cnt + 1 ))
  if [ $cnt -eq 30 ]; then break ; fi
done

# execute the root.sh script and dependent scripts.
$GRID_HOME/root.sh

su - $GRID_OWNER -c  \
"$GRID_HOME/cfgtoollogs/configToolAllCommands RESPONSE_FILE=/opt/oracle/cfgrsp.properties"

rm /opt/oracle/cfgrsp.properties
rm /opt/oracle/grid.rsp

%clean
rm -rf $RPM_BUILD_ROOT

%files
%defattr(0660, grid, oinstall)
/etc/oraInst.loc
/opt/oracle/grid.rsp
%attr(0600, grid, oinstall) /opt/oracle/cfgrsp.properties
%config /etc/oraInst.loc

%changelog
* Fri Sep 5 2013 Engineering <engineering@example.com>
- initial version
- requires more error checking
```

The SPEC file references three files, which need to be present in the BUILD directory. The grid.rsp file is the same just used for the silent installation and can be used without modification. The oraInst.loc file will be deployed to /etc and contains the pointer to the central inventory. It contains the following familiar lines:

```
[rpmbuild@server1 BUILD]$ cat oraInst.loc
inventory_loc=/u01/app/oraInventory
inst_group=oinstall
```

Finally the cfgrsp.properties file contains the ASM and ASMSNMP passwords, and again is identical to the one used for the silent installation.

Building the RPM

With all preparations in place it is time to build the RPM. Change directory to "SPEC" and execute the rpmbuild executable as shown here:

```
[rpmbuild@server1 SPECS]$ rpmbuild -ba --rebuild grid.spec
Executing(%install): /bin/sh -e /var/tmp/rpm-tmp.gz353e
+ umask 022
+ cd /home/rpmbuild/rpmbuild/BUILD
+ rm -rf /home/rpmbuild/rpmbuild/BUILDROOT/GridInfrastructure-12.1.0.1-0.el6.x86_64
+ mkdir -p /home/rpmbuild/rpmbuild/BUILDROOT/GridInfrastructure-12.1.0.1-0.el6.x86_64/etc
+ mkdir -p /home/rpmbuild/rpmbuild/BUILDROOT/GridInfrastructure-12.1.0.1-0.el6.x86_64/opt/oracle
+ cp oraInst.loc /home/rpmbuild/rpmbuild/BUILDROOT/GridInfrastructure-12.1.0.1-0.el6.x86_64/etc/
+ cp grid.rsp /home/rpmbuild/rpmbuild/BUILDROOT/GridInfrastructure-12.1.0.1-0.el6.x86_64/opt/oracle
+ cp cfgrsp.properties /home/rpmbuild/rpmbuild/BUILDROOT/GridInfrastructure-12.1.0.1-0.el6.x86_64/
opt/oracle
+ /usr/lib/rpm/check-rpaths /usr/lib/rpm/check-buildroot
+ /usr/lib/rpm/brp-compress
+ /usr/lib/rpm/brp-strip
+ /usr/lib/rpm/brp-strip-static-archive
+ /usr/lib/rpm/brp-strip-comment-note
Processing files: GridInfrastructure-12.1.0.1-0.el6.x86_64
warning: File listed twice: /etc/oraInst.loc
Provides: config(GridInfrastructure) = 12.1.0.1-0.el6
Requires(interp): /bin/sh
Requires(rpmlib): rpmlib(CompressedFileNames) <= 3.0.4-1 rpmlib(PayloadFilesHavePrefix)
<= 4.0-1
Requires(post): /bin/sh
Conflicts: Database
Checking for unpackaged file(s): /usr/lib/rpm/check-files /home/rpmbuild/rpmbuild/BUILDROOT/
GridInfrastructure-12.1.0.1-0.el6.x86_64
Wrote: /home/rpmbuild/rpmbuild/SRPMS/GridInfrastructure-12.1.0.1-0.el6.src.rpm
Wrote: /home/rpmbuild/rpmbuild/RPMS/x86_64/GridInfrastructure-12.1.0.1-0.el6.x86_64.rpm
Executing(%clean): /bin/sh -e /var/tmp/rpm-tmp.3aTrRY
+ umask 022
+ cd /home/rpmbuild/rpmbuild/BUILD
+ rm -rf /home/rpmbuild/rpmbuild/BUILDROOT/GridInfrastructure-12.1.0.1-0.el6.x86_64
+ exit 0
```

The exit code of each step was 0, indicating success. Two RPMs have been build: the source RPM as well as the one to be deployed. Check the contents of the RPM/x86-64 directory for the result.

Installing the RPM

With the RPM in place it is time to put the procedure to a test. Transfer GridInfrastructure-12.1.0.1-0.el6.x86_64.rpm to the test yum repository server and install it using YUM as shown in this example:

```
[root@server1 ~]# yum install GridInfrastructure-12.1.0.1-0.el6.x86_64.rpm
```

It will download and install the dependent packages from your repository and install Grid Infrastructure using the silent response file. If anything goes wrong at any phase, warnings are printed on the screen pointing you to the correct log file to check. It is recommended to try the procedure in a (virtual?) test environment first before running live builds.

Installing the Oracle database

After the installation of Oracle Restart has been completed, it is time to focus on the installation of the database binaries. After all, we want to run a database on our server! The installation process will again be divided into the same parts as the Oracle Restart installation.

If you just skipped the Oracle Restart part of the chapter, don't worry there will be references to a filesystem-only database installation in the next chapter. If you have the time please revisit chapter 2 and the first half of this chapter for an explanation of why I like ASM and recommend it to you.

If you followed the advice laid out earlier in this chapter to use a central staging server, ensure that the installation binaries are mounted and accessible to the installation. If not, pick a suitable staging area with enough free space and deploy the downloaded zip files.

Interactive installation of the RDBMS binaries

The same principle already applied to the Oracle Restart installation holds true for the RDBMS installation: the interactive installer is the best way to get a feel for what's new in a release. Even if you plan to use silent installations only, it is still recommended to step through the assistants once to generate the response file.

The installation of the RDBMS binaries is usually owned by the oracle account. You need to log out of the grid account if you still happen to be connected and start the X11 session as explained previously in this chapter. Begin the installation by starting Oracle Universal Installer similar to the call shown here:

```
[oracle@server1 ~]$ /mnt/12.1.0.1/database/runInstaller
```

This command will initiate the bootstrap process and start the graphical user interface.

Security updates

Figure 6-16 shows the security updates screen, which is very similar to the wizard shown with Oracle Restart. The database installer prompts you to enter your My Oracle Support credentials. For some time now you are prompted to provide your email address for Oracle to receive security updates and other information from Oracle. Do this at your own discretion. If you decline the option by unchecking the "I wish to receive security updates via My Oracle Support" you will be prompted once more to confirm you really want to stay uniformed of advisories. You can normally safely ignore the warning. Your enterprise monitoring solution should prompt you for security updates anyway (OEM 12 does this for example).

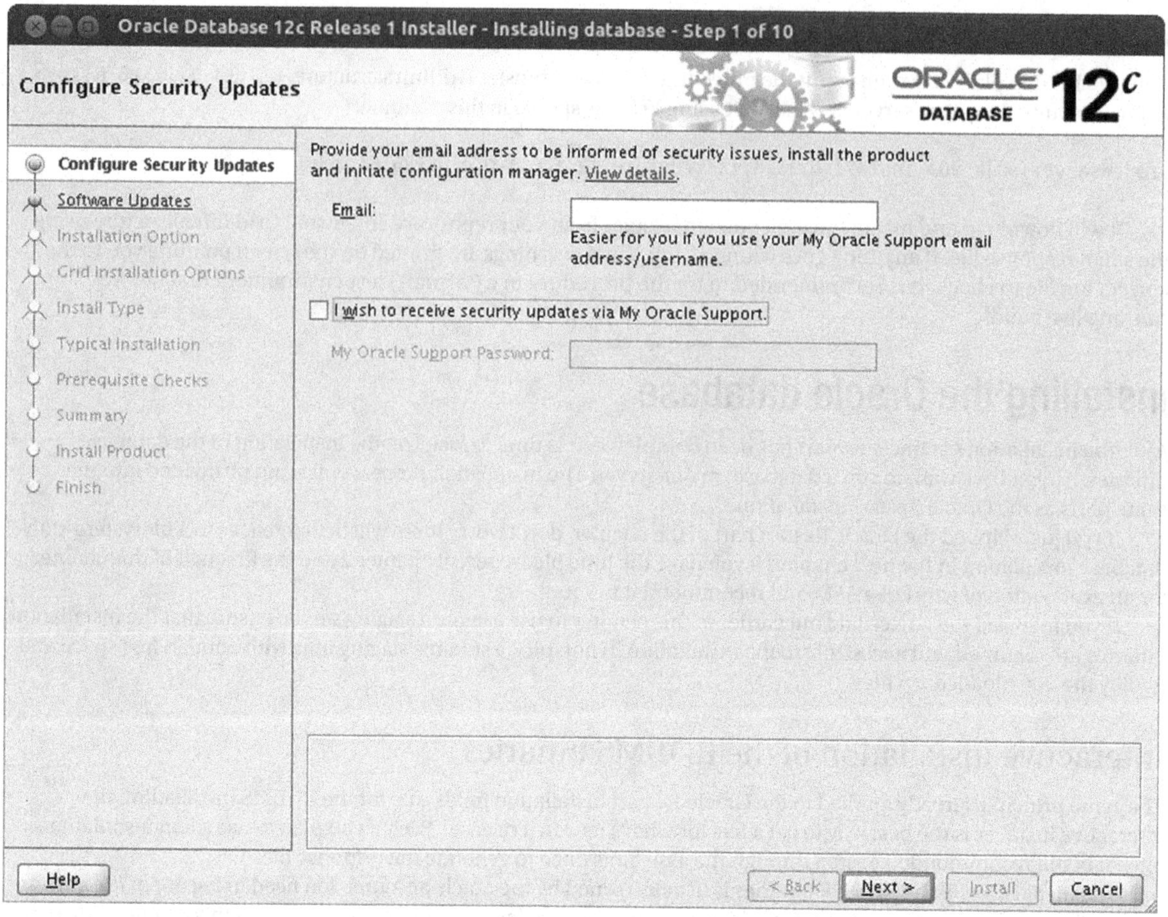

Figure 6-16. *Configuration of security updates*

Proceed to the next screen by clicking the "Next" button.

Downloading updates

As with the Grid Infrastructure installation you are offered the option to download and install updates as part of the installation process. See Figure 6-17.

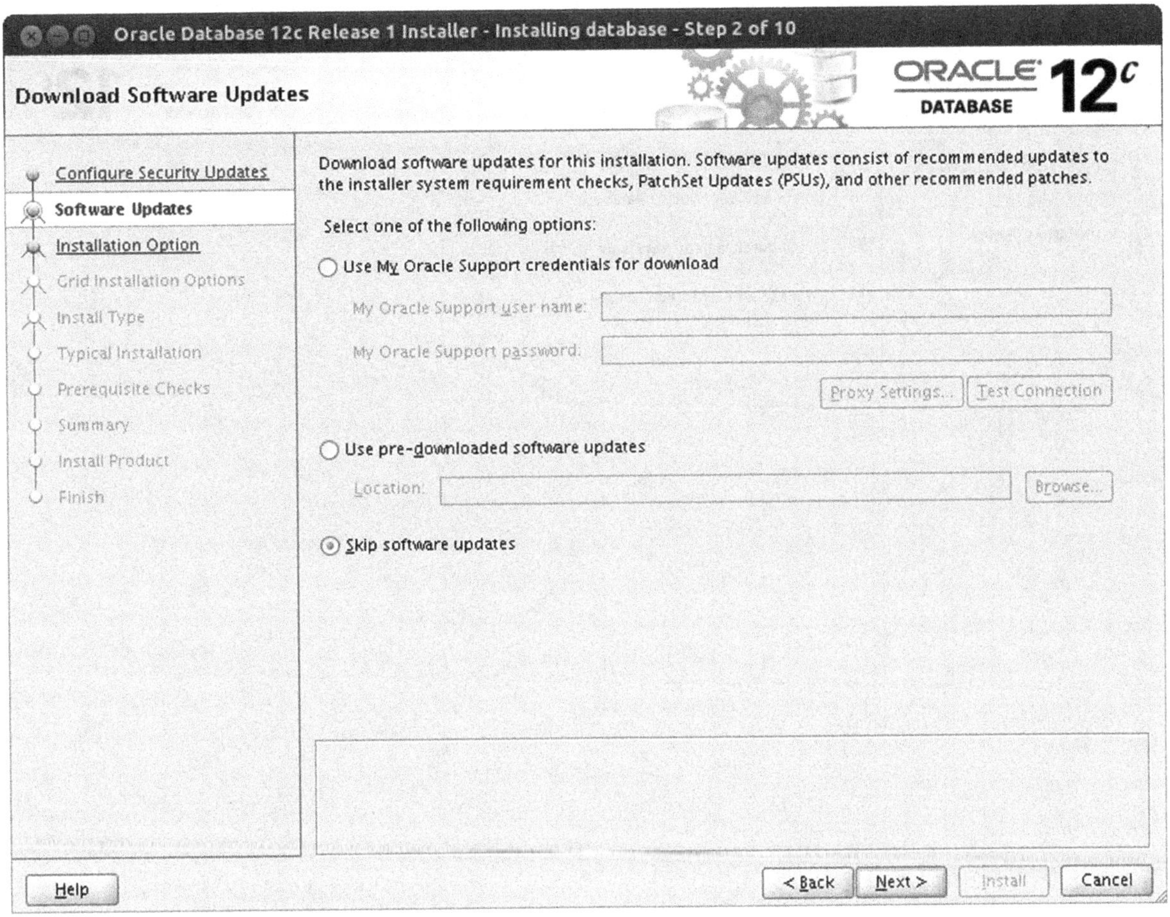

Figure 6-17. *Optionally download and apply updates*

The options are exactly the same as shown earlier in this chapter for Grid Infrastructure. Please refer to section "Download Software Updates" for a more detailed explanation.

Selecting Installation Options

When installing the Oracle database binaries you are offered three options shown in Figure 6-18. The first is to install the binaries and then install a database. The second option, which I recommend, is to install the database software only. The final option is to upgrade an existing database as part of the installation process. It is strongly recommended not to perform that step at this stage! Take your time to plan the installation and upgrade in your own time. Please refer to Chapter 12 which is all about upgrading to Oracle 12c.

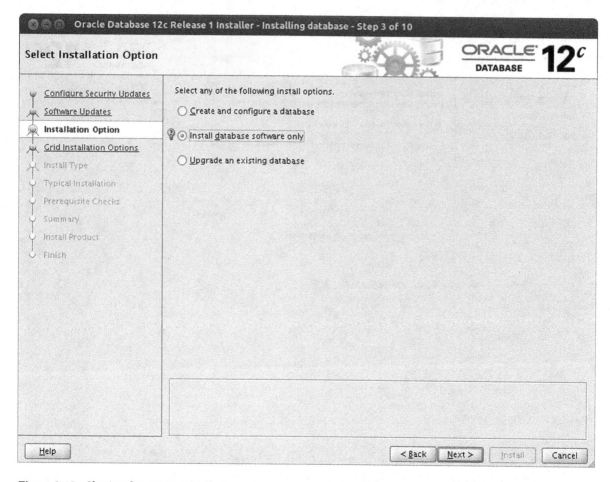

Figure 6-18. *Chosing the various installation options*

A safe way to proceed with the installation is to limit yourself to the installation of the binaries only. This makes patching significantly easier without an existing database. This is especially true in a Grid Infrastructure/RDBMS combination as proposed here. Recommended patches are most often bundled together as Patch Set Updates. These are very easy to install using the automatic detection of Oracle homes and the "opatch auto" feature. If you decided to create a database as part of the installation process you will see a few additional screens presenting a cut-down version of the database configuration assistant (dbca). It is slightly less flexible than invoking dbca directly, which is why I suggest you run it separately after the installation.

To follow the print screens, check the "Install database software only" radio button and click on "Next".

Picking a Grid Installation Option

The screen shown in Figure 6-19 allows you to configure whether you want a single instance database installation, a Real Application Cluster, or alternatively a RAC One Node database installation. All but the single instance database installation option are not applicable unless you have a Grid Infrastructure configuration for RAC.

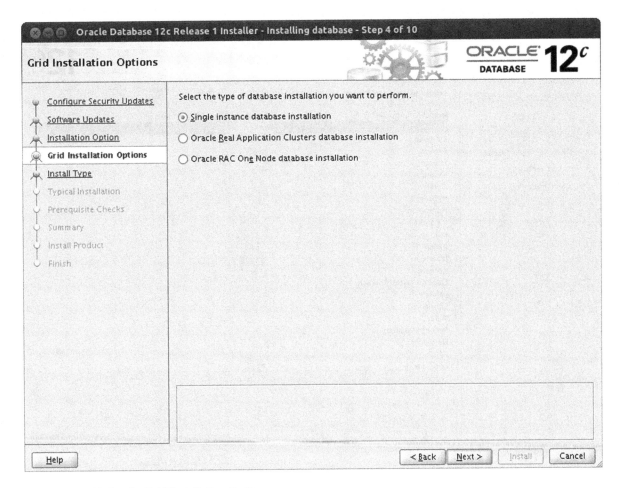

Figure 6-19. *Listing the Grid Installation Options*

Leave the "Single instance database installation" radio button selected and proceed to the next screen by clicking on "Next".

Installing Product Languages

The Oracle database comes with lots of supported languages out of the box, as shown in Figure 6-20. These should make it easy for anyone to get localized messages on the screen. You can select a language from the left-hand side, highlight it by clicking on it, and then use the single arrow to add it to the list of selected languages.

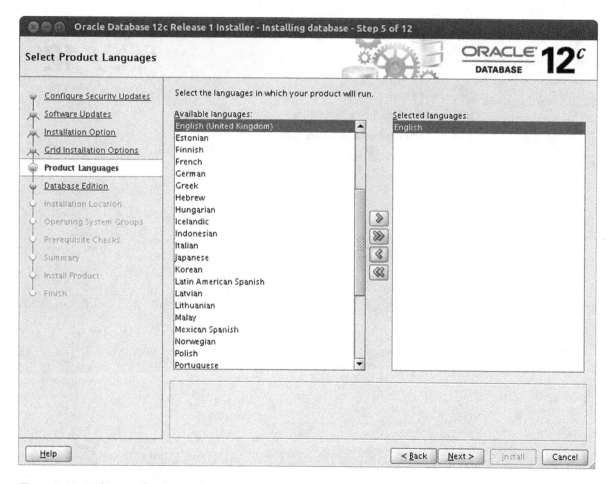

Figure 6-20. *Picking product languages*

It is strongly recommended not to remove English! Once you are happy with your selection, click on "Next" to continue the installation process.

Choosing a Database Edition

The Oracle database can be licensed in many forms. On the screen in Figure 6-21 you have the option to install the Enterprise Edition, Standard Edition, and Standard Edition One. The choice depends directly on your license agreement with Oracle. Don't be tempted to install Enterprise Edition if there is no license for it. Not only is that a breach of your contract with Oracle (which is bound to be noticed), but there is also a lot of work involved in downgrading from Enterprise Edition to Standard Edition.

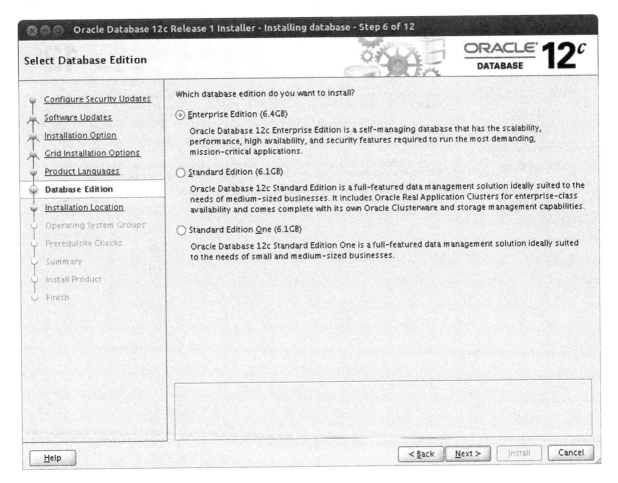

Figure 6-21. *Selecting from the list of available database editions*

In this example Enterprise Edition has been selected.

Defining the Installation Location

Figure 6-22 is the next screen in the installation wizard, and prompts you for the installation locations. You need to pick a suitable location for the Oracle base as well as the software binaries. There is no real restriction to directories, except that the software location should be in the path of the ORACLE_BASE. The Oracle base directory contains many important files, among them the admin directory. It contains the audit trail files per database. By default the Automatic Diagnostic Repository (ADR) is also located underneath the $ORACLE_BASE variable.

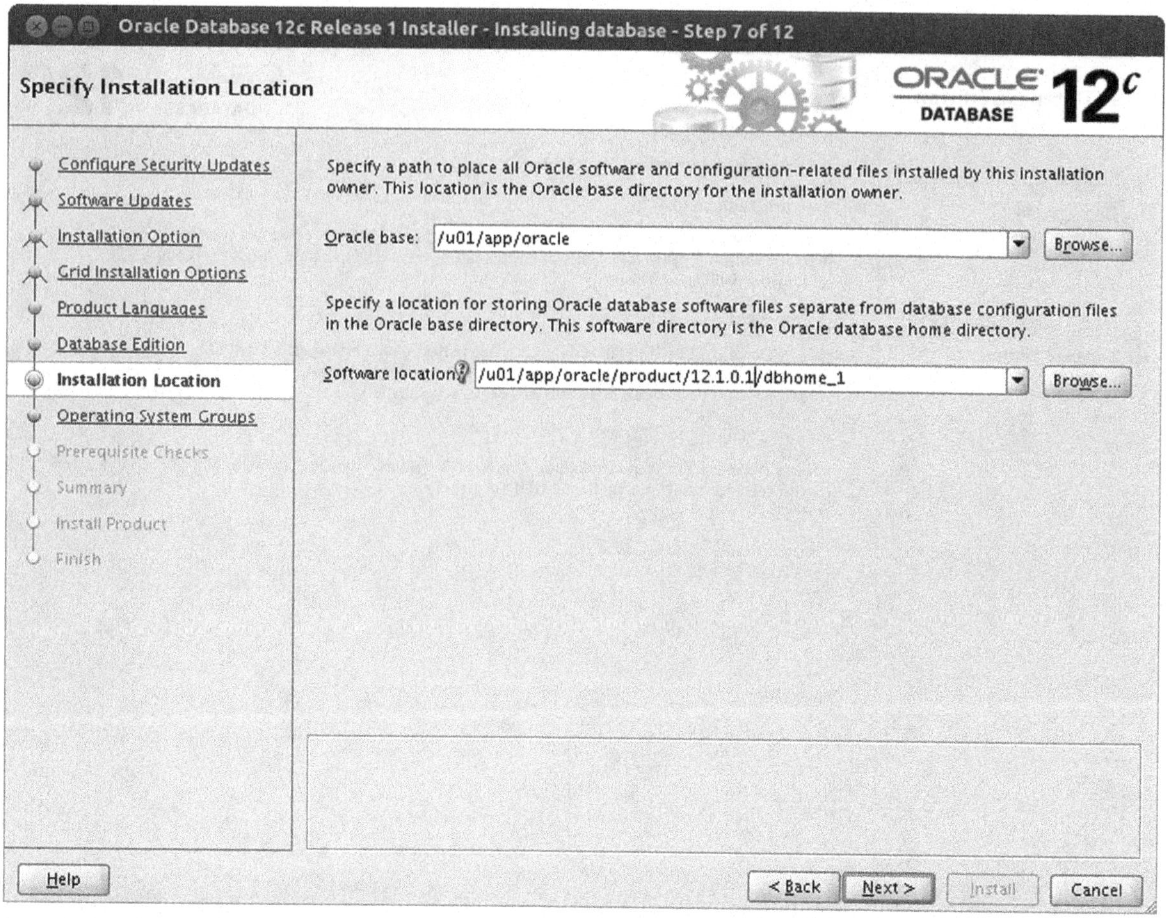

Figure 6-22. *Setting Oracle base and software location*

If you followed the instructions in Chapter 5 about the OFA, then Oracle's installer should have picked up the directories on its own. You should consider changing the software location path to include the patch set number just as with Oracle Restart. At the time of writing only the base release was available. As a result your path should refer to 12.1.0.1 instead of just 12.1.0. Using the patch set number makes it easier to differentiate Oracle homes.

Obviously, you should adhere to your corporate standards if they contradict the OFA. You will notice that the ORACLE_BASE is different from the Grid Infrastructure installation because there was a separate account used to install Oracle Restart. Had you used "oracle" to install Grid Infrastructure and the database, then the ORACLE_BASE would have been /u01/app/oracle for both. By convention, the Oracle base variable is defined as /u01/app/*user*. Review the settings one last time and click on the "Next" button to continue.

■ **Note**   If you did not install Oracle Restart/Grid Infrastructure you will then be prompted to define the central inventory location. You should set this to the $ORACLE_BASE parent directory which is /u01/app/oralnventory by default. Do not place the inventory inside the $ORACLE_BASE!

Mapping Privileged Operating System Groups

The screen shown in Figure 6-23 is one of the few really new screens when comparing Oracle 12c to 11g Release 2. Previous releases only used the OSDBA and OSOPER groups, whereas Oracle 12c adds some new ones to worry about. These groups allow an even finer separation of duties. Refer back to Chapter 5 for a complete discussion of their roles and purposes.

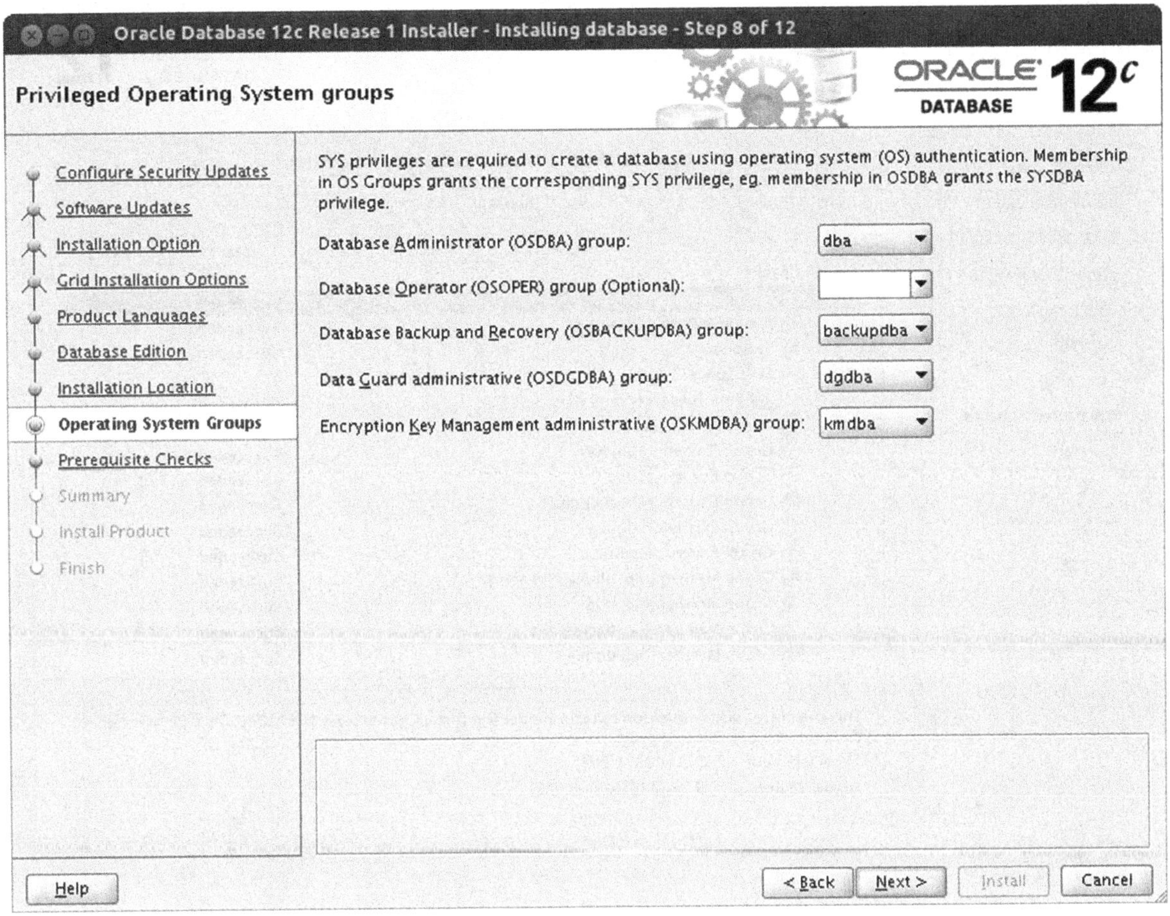

Figure 6-23. *Mapping oracle's groups to privileged groups*

It is of course still possible to use the "dba" operating system group exclusively for all the different groups available in Oracle, but doing so negates the advantages offered by the new system. I recommend the creation of the backupdba, dgdba, and kmdba groups on the operating system, and the Oracle user should have these assigned as its secondary groups. At the risk of repeating myself: you should create the operating system groups and map the Oracle user to them even if you are not planning to use them straight away. Configuring the database software in the new way gives you the flexibility of gradually adding functionality without having to reinstall the binaries. In the screen above the Oracle user had all of the default groups assigned, and the installer picked those up.

Review your settings and click on "Next" to proceed.

Checking the Prerequisites

Oracle will check for the required settings before starting the installation. This step is not new and has been performed in previous releases. If all prerequisites are met, the installer will bypass the screen shown in Figure 6-24 and move to the summary page. If the installer detects any problems, it will report them.

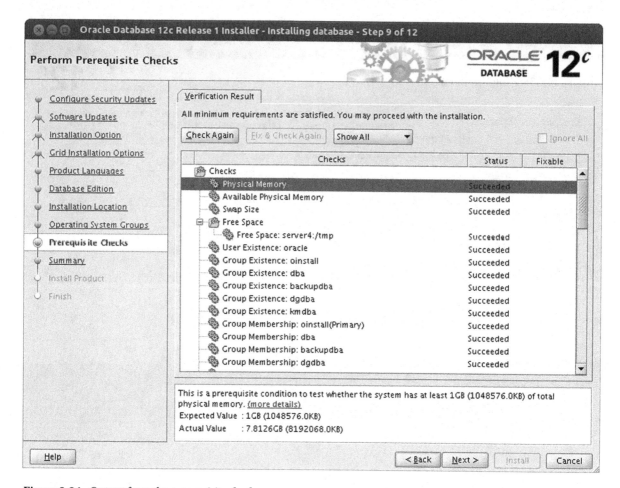

Figure 6-24. *Output from the prerequisite checks*

The process of fixing problems is identical to the Grid Infrastructure installation. Highlight the entry and click on the link labelled "more details" to find out what Oracle expects. If the problem reported is "Fixable", you can make use of the fixup scripts to save yourself some time. Alternatively, correct the problem yourself on the command line, return to the OUI session and click on "Check Again" to instruct the software to reconsider.

Once you are confident that all requirements have been met, click on "Next" to proceed. If the "Next" button is greyed-out you need to check the "Ignore All" checkbox in the top-right corner of the screen after careful consideration of the impact. Be warned that ignoring requirements can lead to installation failures!

Reviewing the Installation Summary

The summary screen in Figure 6-25 presents all your choices made previously on one screen. It also allows you to save the response file, which is recommended. Carefully review all the information presented and check against your corporate standard.

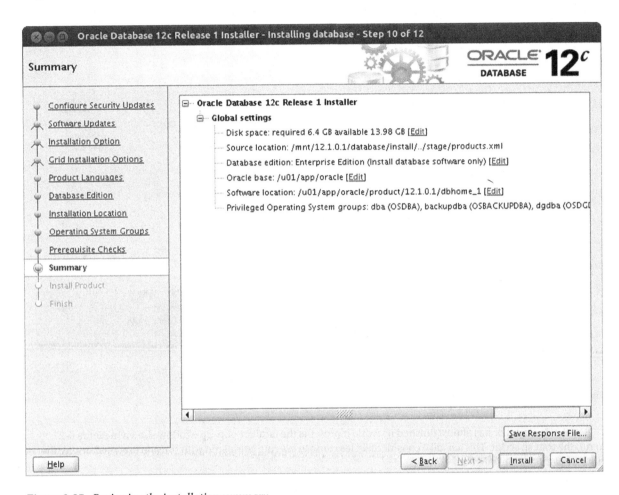

Figure 6-25. *Reviewing the installation summary*

Initiate the software installation by clicking on "Install", or use the "Back" button to go back in the wizard to make any changes to the parameters you provided.

Waiting for the Installation to Complete

Congratulations, you may go and get a cup of coffee while the installation proceeds. Depending on the speed of your NFS mount, DVD drive and hard disks you may have to wait a few minutes for the software to be transferred to the server, linked and ready for use. Figure 6-26 shows the installation status screen that will keep you apprised of progress.

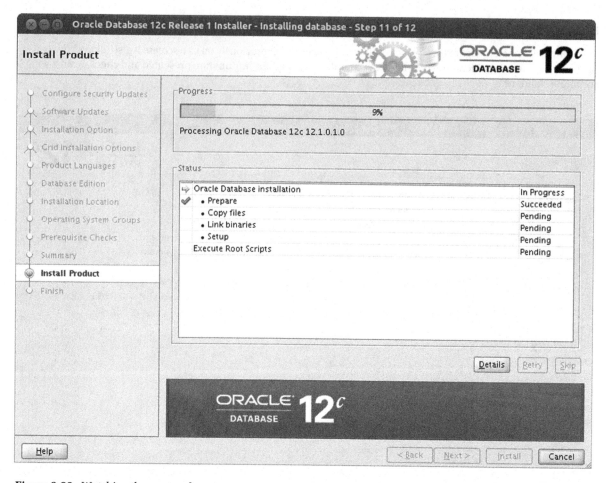

Figure 6-26. *Watching the progress bar*

When the installer has almost finished its work, it presents the familiar pop-up window shown in Figure 6-27 to run the root.sh script. This will take considerably less time to execute compared with the one executed during the Grid Infrastructure installation.

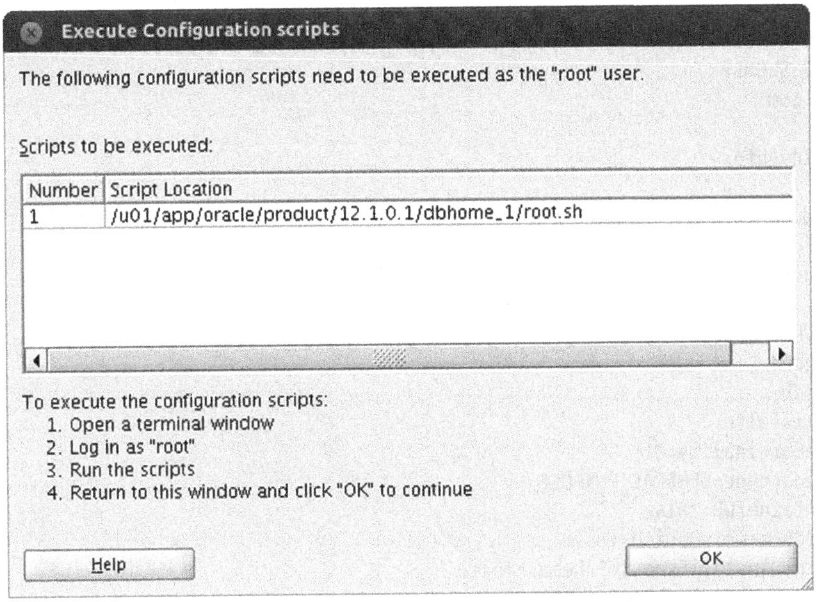

Figure 6-27. *The installer prompts for the execution of the root.sh script*

The output of the root script is shown here for your reference:

```
[root@server1 ~]# /u01/app/oracle/product/12.1.0.1/dbhome_1/root.sh
Performing root user operation for Oracle 12c

The following environment variables are set as:
    ORACLE_OWNER= oracle
    ORACLE_HOME=  /u01/app/oracle/product/12.1.0.1/dbhome_1

Enter the full pathname of the local bin directory: [/usr/local/bin]:
The contents of "dbhome" have not changed. No need to overwrite.
The contents of "oraenv" have not changed. No need to overwrite.
The contents of "coraenv" have not changed. No need to overwrite.

Entries will be added to the /etc/oratab file as needed by
Database Configuration Assistant when a database is created
Finished running generic part of root script.
Now product-specific root actions will be performed.
[root@server1 ~]#
```

This completes the interactive installation of the Oracle database 12c.

Silent Installation of the Database Software

Similar to the Grid Infrastructure installation, a silent installation does not require X11 to be present on the server, making the lights-out installation of the software a lot easier. The following is an example of a response file to install the database. Remember response files are always recorded as part of the installation wizard, and can be saved on the summary screen.

```
[oracle@server1 ~]$ sed -e '/^#/d' -e '/^$/d' -e '/=$/d' db.rsp
oracle.install.responseFileVersion=/oracle/install/rspfmt_dbinstall_response_schema_v12.1.0
oracle.install.option=INSTALL_DB_SWONLY
ORACLE_HOSTNAME=server1.example.com
UNIX_GROUP_NAME=oinstall
INVENTORY_LOCATION=/u01/app/oraInventory
SELECTED_LANGUAGES=en
ORACLE_HOME=/u01/app/oracle/product/12.1.0.1/dbhome_1
ORACLE_BASE=/u01/app/oracle
oracle.install.db.InstallEdition=EE
oracle.install.db.DBA_GROUP=dba
oracle.install.db.BACKUPDBA_GROUP=backupdba
oracle.install.db.DGDBA_GROUP=dgdba
oracle.install.db.KMDBA_GROUP=kmdba
oracle.install.db.isRACOneInstall=false
oracle.install.db.rac.serverpoolCardinality=0
oracle.install.db.config.starterdb.type=GENERAL_PURPOSE
oracle.install.db.ConfigureAsContainerDB=false
oracle.install.db.config.starterdb.memoryOption=false
oracle.install.db.config.starterdb.installExampleSchemas=false
oracle.install.db.config.starterdb.managementOption=DEFAULT
oracle.install.db.config.starterdb.omsPort=0
oracle.install.db.config.starterdb.enableRecovery=false
SECURITY_UPDATES_VIA_MYORACLESUPPORT=false
DECLINE_SECURITY_UPDATES=true
oracle.installer.autoupdates.option=SKIP_UPDATES
[oracle@server1 ~]$
```

It has been generated from the same installation session as shown above in the interactive wizard. As you can see it's fairly lengthy; the examples in db_install.rsp are even longer! The above file has all empty configuration directives and comments removed. Although you find configuration options pertaining to the starter database these are ignored since the installation type is "INSTALL_DB_SWONLY".

With the response file double-checked, you can begin the installation as shown here:

```
[oracle@server1 ~]$ /mnt/12.1.0.1/database/runInstaller -silent \
> -responseFile /home/oracle/db.rsp
Starting Oracle Universal Installer...

Checking Temp space: must be greater than 500 MB.   Actual 4699 MB   Passed
Checking swap space: must be greater than 150 MB.   Actual 8956 MB   Passed
Preparing to launch Oracle Universal Installer from /tmp/OraInstall2013-09-09_12-37-02PM.
Please wait ...
[oracle@server1 ~]$
You can find the log of this install session at:
 /u01/app/oraInventory/logs/installActions2013-09-09_12-37-02PM.log
The installation of Oracle Database 12c was successful.
Please check '/u01/app/oraInventory/logs/silentInstall2013-09-09_12-37-02PM.log' for more details.

As a root user, execute the following script(s):
        1. /u01/app/oracle/product/12.1.0.1/dbhome_1/root.sh


Successfully Setup Software.
```

In case of a database-only installation you would be prompted for the execution of the orainstRoot.sh script in addition to the root.sh script. The root script is "silent", as it creates a log file only:

```
[root@server1 ~]# /u01/app/oracle/product/12.1.0.1/dbhome_1/root.sh
Check /u01/app/oracle/product/12.1.0.1/dbhome_1/install/root_server1.example.com_2013-09-↵
09_12-44-10.log for the output of root script
```

The database installation is complete with the execution of the root script.

Automatic Installation of the Database Software RPM

Creating an RPM for the database is easier than for Grid Infrastructure. The concept will remain the same though: the installer is given the response file to perform a silent installation, and a loop will poll for the completion of the software transfer. Then it is just a matter of executing the root.sh script at the end. If you haven't created the environment to build the RPM yet, refer back to the "Automatic Installation of Oracle Restart" section above. The SPEC file is shown here, it expects the db.rsp and oraInst.loc files to be present in the BUILD directory.

```
Name:           Database
Version:        12.1.0.1
Release:        0%{?dist}
Summary:        installation of the Oracle Database for Enterprise Linux 6.x
Group:          Applications/Databases
License:        Commercial
URL:            http://engineering.example.com/builds/
BuildRoot:      %(mktemp -ud %{_tmppath}/%{name}-%{version}-%{release}-XXXXXX)

Requires:       oracle-rdbms-server-12cR1-preinstall

%description
This RPM checks for the required RPMs for the Oracle database
on Oracle Linux 6.x and adds them as dependencies if necessary.

If necessary, an /etc/oraInst.loc file will be deployed, that is unless a
previous Oracle installation has done so already. The central inventory is
defined as /u01/app/oraInventory as per the standard document

This RPM is not suitable for a RAC installation. An Enterprise Edition database
home will be created.

After deploying the files the Oracle Universal Installer is going to be
invoked with the silent response file from /opt/oracle/db.rsp, and needed
configuration files are executed.

%install
rm -rf $RPM_BUILD_ROOT
mkdir -p $RPM_BUILD_ROOT/etc
mkdir -p $RPM_BUILD_ROOT/opt/oracle

cp oraInst.loc $RPM_BUILD_ROOT/etc/
cp db.rsp $RPM_BUILD_ROOT/opt/oracle
```

```
%post
ORACLE_HOME=/u01/app/oracle/product/12.1.0.1/dbhome_1
ORACLE_OWNER=oracle

# make the software available
umount /mnt
mount -t nfs stagingServer:/m/oracle/linux/x64/ /mnt
if [ $? -ne 0 ]; then
  echo "FATAL error trying to mount the binares from the staging server"
  exit 1
fi

if [ ! -f /mnt/12.1.0.1/database/runInstaller ]; then
  echo "FATAL: cannot find OUI in the install location"
  exit 2
fi

# here we invoke the installer. Testing for FATAL output and won't
# proceed if there is.
su - $ORACLE_OWNER -c \
"/mnt/12.1.0.1/database/runInstaller -silent -responseFile /opt/oracle/db.rsp" \
2>&1 | grep FATAL
if [ $? -eq 0 ]; then
  echo "FATAL error occured-installation NOT completed"
  exit 3
fi

cnt=0
while ! test -e $ORACLE_HOME/root.sh
do
  echo "waiting for the software installation to complete"
  sleep 30
  cnt=$(( $cnt + 1 ))
  if [ $cnt -eq 30 ]; then
   echo "FATAL: timout waiting for the creation of root.sh "
   exit 4
  fi
done

# run the root script.
$ORACLE_HOME/root.sh

%files
%defattr(-,oracle,oinstall)
%config /etc/oraInst.loc
%attr(0660, oracle, oinstall) /etc/oraInst.loc
%attr(0660, oracle, oinstall) /opt/oracle/db.rsp

%changelog
* Mon Sep 9 2013 Engineering <engineering@example.com>
- initial version
- needs more error checking and handling
```

The response file in use is the same as previously described in the silent install section above, and the oraInst.loc file likewise is the same as previously used in the Grid Infrastructure part of the chapter. The RPM can then be built using the rpmbuild command as shown in the below output:

```
[rpmbuild@server1 SPECS]$ rpmbuild -ba --rebuild db.spec
Executing(%install): /bin/sh -e /var/tmp/rpm-tmp.xMaFZt
+ umask 022
+ cd /home/rpmbuild/rpmbuild/BUILD
+ rm -rf /home/rpmbuild/rpmbuild/BUILDROOT/Database-12.1.0.1-0.el6.x86_64
+ mkdir -p /home/rpmbuild/rpmbuild/BUILDROOT/Database-12.1.0.1-0.el6.x86_64/etc
+ mkdir -p /home/rpmbuild/rpmbuild/BUILDROOT/Database-12.1.0.1-0.el6.x86_64/opt/oracle
+ cp oraInst.loc /home/rpmbuild/rpmbuild/BUILDROOT/Database-12.1.0.1-0.el6.x86_64/etc/
+ cp db.rsp /home/rpmbuild/rpmbuild/BUILDROOT/Database-12.1.0.1-0.el6.x86_64/opt/oracle
+ /usr/lib/rpm/check-rpaths /usr/lib/rpm/check-buildroot
+ /usr/lib/rpm/brp-compress
+ /usr/lib/rpm/brp-strip
+ /usr/lib/rpm/brp-strip-static-archive
+ /usr/lib/rpm/brp-strip-comment-note
Processing files: Database-12.1.0.1-0.el6.x86_64
warning: File listed twice: /etc/oraInst.loc
Provides: config(Database) = 12.1.0.1-0.el6
Requires(interp): /bin/sh
Requires(rpmlib): rpmlib(CompressedFileNames) <= 3.0.4-1 rpmlib(PayloadFilesHavePrefix) <= 4.0-1
Requires(post): /bin/sh
Checking for unpackaged file(s): /usr/lib/rpm/check-files /home/rpmbuild/rpmbuild/BUILDROOT/
Database-12.1.0.1-0.el6.x86_64
Wrote: /home/rpmbuild/rpmbuild/SRPMS/Database-12.1.0.1-0.el6.src.rpm
Wrote: /home/rpmbuild/rpmbuild/RPMS/x86_64/Database-12.1.0.1-0.el6.x86_64.rpm
Executing(%clean): /bin/sh -e /var/tmp/rpm-tmp.gkp4kz
+ umask 022
+ cd /home/rpmbuild/rpmbuild/BUILD
+ rm -rf /home/rpmbuild/rpmbuild/BUILDROOT/Database-12.1.0.1-0.el6.x86_64
+ exit 0
```

Once the RPM is built, it is simple to install using the YUM command, referencing the location of the RPM:

```
# yum install Database-12.1.0.1-0.el6.x86_64.rpm
```

After a little while the database software should be installed and ready to assume an operational role.

Summary

In this chapter you learned how to install Oracle Grid Infrastructure and the Oracle database. There are many good reasons for installing Oracle Restart, including the benefit ASM gives over file systems such as ext3. The maintenance overhead you might hear as a counterargument is not as high as in the 10g days. Regardless of the existence of Oracle Restart you will use the same patch command since Oracle Restart and the database are patched together. So instead of having to patch three Oracle homes, the opatch auto option will detect Oracle homes and automatically apply the right patch to the home, as well as any custom scripts that made the application of recommended patches prior to 11.2 so labor intensive a true joy.

The Grid Infrastructure layer provides a common user interface to the database in addition to the Automatic Storage Management instance. The immediate benefit in addition to ASM is the auto-start facility offered by Oracle Restart.

In terms of the installation an interactive, silent, and RPM-based installation has been shown. The examples have been tested on Oracle Linux 6.4 and were correct at the time of writing. Hopefully the code snippets stir your creativity in automating the installation of the database. A consistent, standard compliant setup will be the end result, making future maintenance a lot easier. You might of course say that a clone of an Oracle software home is a better alternative, and there is merit in that argument. Cloning the Oracle home however requires engineering to create a new "golden" image-base release plus PSU or one-off patch even to be created. For each supported release, and each platform. The software must of course be validated and tested, problems in the software release can have far-reaching consequences. If your engineering department can produce such builds: great! But many may struggle to find sufficient time to do so.

■ ■ ■

Pluggable Databases

Pluggable databases, affectionately called PDBs for the remainder of this chapter, are a major new concept in the Oracle database and the outstanding new feature to be aware of in Oracle 12.1. From the author's point of view the introduction of Pluggable Databases into the Oracle kernel is a true major new feature of a magnitude which we have not seen for a long time. In fact, the novelty of this new feature is comparable to the introduction of Automatic Storage Management in 10g Release 1, which radically changed the way we work with Oracle and storage. In comparison, the release of 11g Releases 1 and 2 were moderate improvements of the existing previous release—with new features in certain areas—but nowhere near as novel as Pluggable Databases. The following chapter gives you insight into managing Pluggable Databases in Oracle 12.1, including the new database types available. I hope that by the end of it you will be as excited as I am.

It is important to note that Oracle 12.1 is backward compatible with 11g Release 2. So if you are tight on budget or time it is comforting to know that you do not have to embrace the new feature, but then again you would forfeit many of the benefits of Oracle 12c. Maybe the following sections are enough of a teaser to start experimenting with Pluggable Databases.

Note that the use of Pluggable Databases requires you to be correctly licensed for the feature.

The consolidated hosting platform before Oracle 12.1

Pluggable databases address many of the problems administrators and designers faced with consolidation projects using the previous Oracle releases. Most consolidation projects have used a shared-schema approach where individual suitable applications have been rebased from their current environments, and often into a (RAC) database. The methods used to perform the rebasing included Transportable Tablespaces, and ingenious use of the export/import Data Pump utilities. Some users chose to use replication technologies such as Oracle Streams, Golden Gate, or other third-party products.

The onboarding process for new applications into the hosted environment usually involves some kind of assistance from the DBA team or the service owner. The amount of support that can be made available to users of the hosting service depends greatly on funding. You have to be clear about what the goalposts of the hosting service are: your solution is either fully automated and therefore users get minimal support from the operational DBAs. On the other extreme, a dedicated onboarding team exists taking the user through all stages of the application move, including "intensive care" during the first couple of weeks. Ideally there is a dedicated contact person in the onboarding team answering any questions. In many situations this ideal may be out of reach.

The hosting service using schema-based consolidation as it existed before Oracle 12.1 had to live with a number of limitations. Some of these restrictions are of a technical nature; others are procedural. The restrictions include:

- No two identical users can co-exist in a pre-12.1 database.
- Namespaces must be separate.
- There should not be any grant to the PUBLIC role.
- Use of global database links is ruled out due to security constraints.

- Users with elevated privileges (the DBA role, all privileges with "any" in their name) can read or even modify data in schemas they should not have access to unless special access restrictions are in place.

- Auditing is made difficult as there is no concept of logical partitioning by application—all events are recorded on the database level.

- Restore operations are complicated by the requirement to get approvals from the applications not impacted by the data corruption.

There are of course some more, the ones mentioned above are the most obvious ones. In the past, some users tried to get around the namespace restrictions by using dedicated databases per consolidated application. Although that solved quite a few of the above-mentioned problems, this comes at the cost of a greatly amplified overhead caused by additional background processes and memory requirements. For this reason the database-per-application approach does not scale well.

Another common way of consolidating databases was to create virtual environments with exactly one database in it. This approach is very heavily used in x86-64-based virtualization, but can also be found in the form of Solaris Zones or IBM LPARs. Although there are benefits in terms of isolation of workloads, you should not forget to account for the operating system patching if a full operating system stack is to be maintained. Granted, there is less overhead when using Operating System virtualization such as Solaris Zones, since each virtual copy of the operating system is based on the global operating environment. Figure 7-1 compares the three most popular consolidation approaches before the release of Oracle 12c.

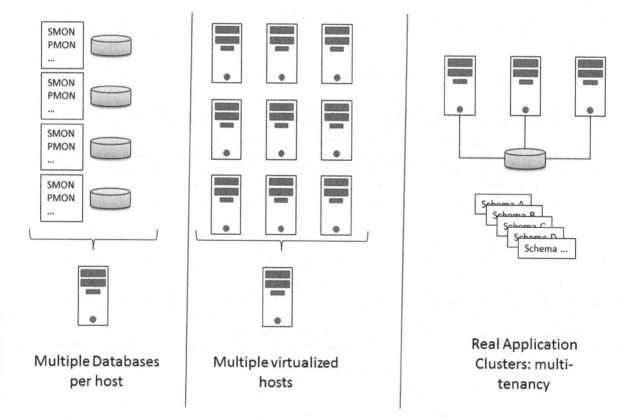

Multiple Databases per host

Multiple virtualized hosts

Real Application Clusters: multi-tenancy

Figure 7-1. Common consolidation methods pre Oracle 12.1

Ideally one would combine the lower memory and lower process footprint of the multi-tenancy RAC database and the application isolation of the single database per host. Well you may have guessed it—that's what the Pluggable Database will offer: horizontal virtualization, but from inside the database. PDBs offer the best of all worlds, and allow you to achieve a much higher consolidation density if your hardware supports it.

Pluggable Databases to the rescue

With Oracle 12.1 a fundamental change has taken place in the architecture. Luckily, as with most technology introduced in the database, you still have the choice not to use it straight away. For those who do, and I hope I can encourage you to do so with this book, you will have the option of using a new database type: the Container Database or CDB.

The main benefit of using the CDB is to allow for horizontal virtualization within the database. A Container Database, as the name implies, contains at least one, and up to 253 user-Pluggable Databases. The Pluggable Database is the consolidation target. From a user's point of view a Pluggable Database (PDB) appears just like any normal database before Oracle 12.1. As such, a PDB is a collection of schemas, tablespaces, and other metadata objects. The Container Database itself is merely a container and does not store user data.

The Container Database serves two purposes. First, it is the container for all these Pluggable Databases you are about to create. Second, it contains what is referred to as the CDB's root. Named CDB$ROOT in the documentation it is the home for information common to the CDB and the PDBs. The CDB has a further component named the seed PDB or PDB$SEED. The seed database is a minimal PDB that you can use like the starter database when creating a database using the Database Configuration Assistant dbca. It cannot be opened or modified.

The Container Database instance type exists alongside the database type as we know it from pre-12.1 days. In the remaining chapters I will refer to this former database type as a "non-CDB" to make a clear distinction between the two. Interestingly the Container Database is not limited to single instance deployments, it can also be created as a Real Application Cluster database. The deployment does not have any impact on the Pluggable Databases for which it provides a home. Consider Figure 7-2, outlining the new database "container database" instance.

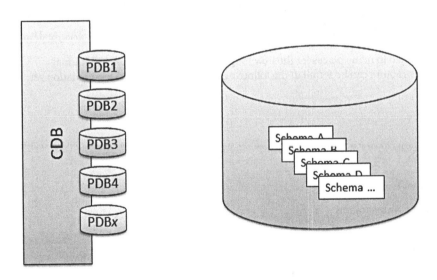

Oracle Container
Database

Conventional
Oracle database

Figure 7-2. *A comparison of CDB vs. non-CDB*

The non-CDB, or any other Oracle database before 12.1 for that matter did not have any facility to separate applications in the same way as a container database has. As you know, the super-users in all releases prior to 12.1 had full visibility of all the data stored in the database. The only way around this was the use of Data Vault or comparable solutions. Although they certainly helped achieve the goal of preserving privacy in realms, they had to be configured and maintenance operations affecting the whole database were somewhat complex to arrange and perform. It is the author's firm belief that complexity is the enemy of successful database operations these days. If something can be simplified, it should be.

The CDB however is a container for multiple Pluggable Databases, without much of the previously required manual configuration. The all-powerful user accounts however can still connect to a PDB quite easily and view data. Without additional configuration however powerful users defined locally in a PDB cannot query information in another PDB. Sensitive environments should still employ additional layers of protection within the Pluggable Database.

Each Pluggable Database is completely self-contained from a user data point-of-view. All user data that makes up a database can safely be stored in a Pluggable Database without the risk of compromising compatibility. The Pluggable Database can easily be moved from one Container Database to another. The PDBs and CDB$ROOT share the data dictionary. Not all dictionary information is duplicated in each PDB—that would be a waste of space. Instead a PDB facilitates pointers to the dictionary of its container database's root. Whether or not an object in the database is shared can be seen in some views, including DBA_OBJECTS. A new column, called SHARING, indicates if the object is a metadata link to an object in the root, or an object link, or none of the two.

This greatly increases flexibility, and is a main differentiator to other consolidation approaches where each application is hosted in a dedicated database—which needs patching of the data dictionary. With a CDB you can potentially patch hundreds of PDBs for the price of one. This chapter will provide you with an overview of how to unplug/plug a PDB from one Container Database to another.

In order to create a Container Database, the DBA has to make a conscious decision at the creation time—the Database Configuration Assistant provides an option to create the new database as a CDB. It is important to note at this point that a non-CDB cannot be converted into a CDB. Instead, it has to be converted to a PDB which in turn can be plugged into an existing CDB. We will see that this is necessary during migrations, which are detailed in Chapter 12.

The CDB creation required an enhancement to the "create database statement," but the scripts to be run to create a custom database have changed in comparison with the non-CDB case. See further down in the section "Creating a CDB using scripts" for more information on how to create a CDB from the command line.

The documentation has been updated in many places for the new Pluggable Databases Feature. Additional information about PDBs and the new structure can be found in the following books of the official documentation set:

- Concepts Guide

- Administrator's Guide

- SQL Language Reference

- Security Guide

- Backup and Recovery User's Guide

- Data Guard Concepts and Administration

- And there are references in many others more

I personally like to keep bookmarks for these in my browser under a special "Oracle 12.1" category. I have been involved in a number of discussions about consolidation projects, and all of these mentioned at one point or another about the difficulties using Oracle before 12.1 to find a consensus between the engineers and the operational DBAs. Great technology is certainly of a lot of academic value, but if the level one and level two support simply cannot support from day one, it is a lot of time and money wasted. It once again comes down to skill, and sadly skill often weighs less than cost per hour. With Oracle 12.1 a good balance can be reached between new technology and operational maintenance procedures.

Guide to rest of chapter

The rest of the chapter will detail Pluggable Databases and all the relevant concepts around them for running a Container Database on your host. It will not try to expand on backup and recovery for such databases. There is a separate chapter covering that topic. It also does not attempt to introduce disaster recovery setup: this is done in a separate chapter as well.

The new features about PDBs are quite rich, and to keep this chapter from being too inflated, the above-mentioned topics have been selected as good candidates for their own chapters.

Implementation details for Pluggable Databases

One of the design goals for Pluggable Databases was to allow for backward compatibility. In other words, anything that was possible with a database pre-12.1 or a non-CDB should be possible with a PDB.

It will soon become apparent that this promise has been fulfilled. One of the restrictions found during the testing was the inability to connect to a PDB using operating system authentication. One could argue either way if this is a serious problem or not, but alternatives are available to fill the void. Local O/S authentication was a neat way to execute jobs on the database server without having to undergo password maintenance on the account.

EXTERNAL AUTHENTICATION

External authentication has been available with Oracle for a long time. Its main function is to allow users to attach to the database to run batch processes or sqlldr instances without having to worry about hard-coding passwords in shell scripts. This is problematic from a security point of view, mainly because it bypasses some settings made in profiles.

On the other hand, not having to worry about password maintenance, password complexity, and storing passwords is an attractive feature. Consider the following example:

A user created using the "create user username identified externally" clause will be able to log in to Oracle after logging in to their respective UNIX account username on the same host. The syntax is simple, a "sqlplus /" will suffice. The same is true for sqlldr and other utilities running on the same host. Since there is no password you do not need to worry about it either. As you can imagine, there is no involvement of the network layer at all. This is no longer possible in 12c. As you will see later, you need to connect to a PDB using a database service.

Bottom line: O/S authentication is a thing of the past and instead of using this type of authentication users should use the secure external password store instead.

Physical structure of a CDB and PDB

The structure of the Container Database is different from the non-CDB or any previous release. Figure 7-3 illustrates the main new concepts in a CDB.

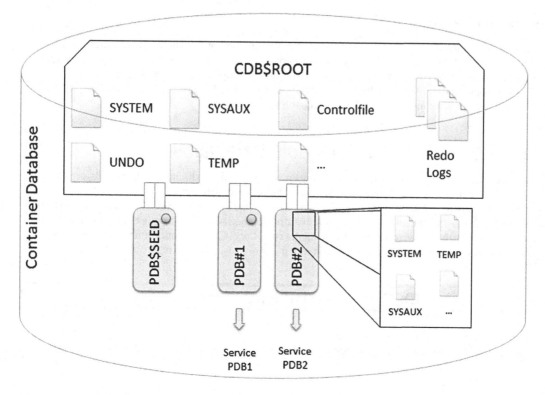

Figure 7-3. *An overview of the Container Database*

To begin with, the main differentiator is the fact that you can see at least one Pluggable Database in addition to the root already. The database you see to the left is a special one, called the seed database. If you decided to create PDBs during the CDB creation then there can be additional PDBs, up to 253 in total for Oracle 12.1.

When thinking about the PDB-CDB relationship one could use the analogy to Solaris zones. Every modern Solaris installation will consist of a global zone. The global zone is what resembles the root-container in the Container Database. The recommendation is not to use the global zone to store applications, and that's exactly the same with the CDB. Storing data in the root zone is as bad as creating applications in the global zone, as it defeats the main purpose of the self-contained unit. You would not store user data in the SYSTEM tablespace either, would you?

Only one listener is required on the database host for single instance Oracle deployments, which will manage connections between applications, ad-hoc query users and generally speaking all other database server to client traffic. When a PDB is opened, a service is started by default which is named after the PDB. Additional services can easily be created to allow for fine-grained charge back models.

Containers

After initial creation of the Container Database, i.e., the top-level container for all components to be stored, you find yourself in a new territory ready to be explored. Since the concept of Pluggable Databases has not existed in Oracle, even from a conceptual point of view it takes a little time to familiarize yourself with the new world.

At first, you need to understand the concept of a container. The container is your namespace, i.e., the scope of the statements you issue. The introduction of the container is not a problem for application owners and developers as you will see shortly, but more of an issue to the database administrator. You need to know which container you are currently connected to. The simple rule to remember: if you used the command "sqlplus / as sysdba" you are in the root container, or CDB$ROOT.

Oracle has once again increased the number of keys available in the USERENV realm to allow you to query which container you are connected to. This can be quite useful in maintenance scripts to work out that you are not accidentally connected to the wrong PDB! You can query the container number as well as the container name you are connected to as shown in this example:

```
SQL> select sys_context('userenv','con_name') from dual;

SYS_CONTEXT('USERENV','CON_NAME')
-----------------------------------------------------------------------
CDB$ROOT

SQL> select sys_context('userenv','con_id') from dual

SYS_CONTEXT('USERENV','CON_ID')
-----------------------------------------------------------------------
1
```

If you were a bit lazy, then you could write a special piece of code in your login.sql to show the container you are connected to:

```
col usr new_value usr
col con new_value con
define con=started
define usr=not
set termout off
select sys_context('userenv','con_name') as con, user usr from dual;
set termout on
set sqlprompt '&&usr.@&&con.> '
```

The root container has a new class of views, called CDB-views. These contain information about the root and all its PDBs. This is useful to get a full overview of the database, but it will not list information for PDBs which are mounted and not open. Additionally, the user executing the query needs to have the privilege to view the PDB. Consider the following example from the Container Database CDB1, executed as SYS in CDB$ROOT:

```
SQL> select con_id,open_mode, name from v$pdbs;

    CON_ID OPEN_MODE  NAME
---------- ---------- -------------------------------
         2 READ ONLY  PDB$SEED
         3 MOUNTED    SWINGBENCH1
         4 MOUNTED    SWINGBENCH2
```

As you can see the only user-PDB, swingbench1, is mounted (closed). A PDB can either be mounted or open. Querying the container data object CDB_DATA_FILES will not show data files belonging to the PDB:

```
SQL> select count(*) from cdb_data_files where con_id=3;

  COUNT(*)
----------
         0
```

Only after the PDB is opened will you see the relevant information:

```
SQL> select count(*) from cdb_data_files where con_id=3;

  COUNT(*)
----------
         3
```

Don't get confused with this when assessing the space usage, and verify which user you are logged in! If you don't get the expected results it is well worth checking the container (available in the sys_context) and your database connection.

When viewing information about containers you should bear in mind that the first 3 container IDs are always fixed:

- Container 0 indicates that the information in the view applies to the whole CDB as such.

- Container ID 1 is reserved for the root: CDB$ROOT

- Container ID 2 is reserved for the seed PDB: PDB$SEED

For queries against the CDB-views you could add a "where" clause to skip the first three containers by requesting a CON_ID > 2.

Common physical structures

The Container Database shares a few components with all PDBs. Some of these are optionally shared, others must be shared. The CDB does not differ much from a non-CDB, except that there are additional files for each Pluggable Database. Each Container Database uniquely owns the following tablespaces:

- SYSTEM

- SYSAUX

- UNDOTBS1 (multiple of those in RAC)

- TEMP

- USERS (if the CDB has been created by dbca)

Don't be misled by the existence of the USERS tablespace in the CDB: its only purpose is to prevent data from accidentally being stored in the SYSTEM tablespace. Remember that user data is stored in the PDBs, not the CDB! Pluggable Databases have their own SYSTEM, SYSAUX, and optionally TEMP tablespaces plus all the user data files. Interestingly the TEMP tablespace is called TEMP in the PDB as well as the CDB, the file names indicate that they are actually different. Additional tablespaces can be added to the PDB just as in any release before Oracle 12.1.

Online redo logs as well as standby redo logs belong to the CDB and are shared with all PDBs. This makes for interesting scenarios when log mining is required. It is suggested you test your favorite log mining based replication technology with a high volume of redo generation before promoting it to production!

The control file is neither CDB nor PDB specific, although it obviously has to keep information pertaining to the PDBs currently plugged into the CDB.

The diagnostic destination used for the Automatic Diagnostic Repository (ADR) is not a physical structure as such, but it is useful to know that the logging facility is based on the CDB. Individual PDBs do not have their own diagnostic destination.

Implications for the Data Dictionary

The data dictionary as we know it needed tweaking, and can now take containers into account. This can be confusing at times, especially when you are used to typing commands quickly and without looking. Before exploring the new data dictionary further, let's step back a little bit and review how the dictionary was used before Pluggable Databases.

When you created a new database using dbca or the scripted method, you were presented with a pristine data dictionary. Pristine in this context means that the only rows stored in the dictionary were Oracle's own metadata. This situation is shown in Figure 7-4

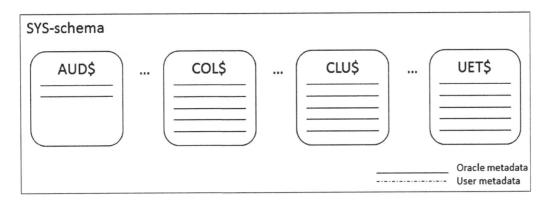

Figure 7-4. *Pristine data dictionary after database creation*

But since the purpose of every database is to store user data, your dictionary (and the underlying tables in the SYS schema) started to become intertwined with user metadata. This applied to data structures within the user table spaces, as well as source code. There is nothing wrong with this by the way, it's the price you pay for using the database! Consider Figure 7-5, which shows the dictionary after it has been populated with user data, such as tables, columns, indexes, and audit information.

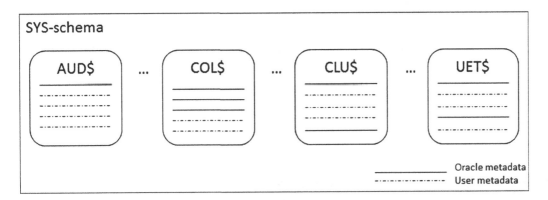

Figure 7-5. *User data and Oracle metadata are now intertwined*

There is an implication to this method of storing metadata, as you will probably recall from your operational experience. Your stored code for example could be invalidated by modifications to the data dictionary as part of patching. It therefore was necessary to recompile dependent code in the database if an Oracle package has been modified by a patch.

The stroke of genius applied for Pluggable Databases is quite simple in theory: instead of allowing user data to "pollute" the Oracle namespace in the CDB$ROOT Database, there is a strict separation of what is stored in the PDB vs. the CDB. Instead of duplicating each row of the data dictionary on each PDB, only the delta is stored within the PDB. The remaining information exists as a pointer from the PDB to the data in the CDB. This not only conserves a lot of space since the PDB's dictionary does not contain redundant information, but it also makes the PDB a lot more independent. This is an important aspect when it comes to unplugging/re-plugging a PDB from one CDB to another.

You already guessed it: the introduction of containers made it necessary to add metadata about them. When researching this book I often found myself selecting from the DBA_% views—those used to contain everything before Oracle 12.1. If you did not find what you were looking for in a DBA% view it probably did not exist. In the current release, such views no longer return all that you might expect. The confusion is quite easily lifted if you consider the following rules:

- The DBA% views list all the information in the current container, but not sub-containers. In other words, you can for example view all the common users in the CDB$ROOT, but it won't show you the users in the seed PDB or any user-defined PDB.

- The same rule applies for the USER% and ALL% views—their scope is the current container.

- Caveat: the new class of CDB% views does not list information about mounted PDBs. To view dictionary information about a PDB it has to be opened read only or read write.

- The V$-type views list information about PDBs as well when you query them from the CDB$ROOT

The following two queries return the same result, but have been executed in different containers. Both queries achieve the same goal: they list all the users for container 3.

First, here is a query executed from the CDB:

```
SYS@CDB$ROOT> select username,authentication_type,common
  2  from cdb_users
  3  where con_id = 3
  4  order by username;

USERNAME                        AUTHENTI COM
------------------------------- -------- ---
ANONYMOUS                       PASSWORD YES
APEX_040200                     PASSWORD YES
APEX_PUBLIC_USER                PASSWORD YES
APPQOSSYS                       PASSWORD YES
[...]

45 rows selected.

SQL>
```

Next is a query executed as SYSTEM while logged on to the PDB:

```
SYSTEM@PDB1> select username,authentication_type,common
  2  from dba_users
  3  order by username;
```

```
USERNAME                          AUTHENTI COM
------------------------------    -------- ---
ANONYMOUS                         PASSWORD YES
APEX_040200                       PASSWORD YES
APEX_PUBLIC_USER                  PASSWORD YES
[...]

45 rows selected.

SQL>
```

The security model obviously had to change as well. You can read more about that subject later in this chapter in section "Users and roles".

The Pluggable Database

After you have created the initial Container Database it is time to consider your options on how to proceed. You will have at least one PDB in your CDB: the seed database. Other Pluggable Databases could have been created as well, but in most cases you may want to keep the CDB lean during creation.

PDBs can be created using ASM and OMF or on the file system. The remainder of the chapter will try to accommodate both of these but sometimes it is necessary to focus on just one. From a manageability point of view using ASM with OMF is the easiest way to administer a CDB with PDBs.

The seed PDB

Every Container Database comes with exactly one seed database, and that fact cannot be changed. The seed database has a fixed container ID of 2, and is opened read only by default. Every user-PDB has started its life a clone of the seed PDB, directly or indirectly. The seed contains the bare minimum Oracle deems necessary to get a PDB cloned and started. For that reason the seed is lightweight and comes with only two tablespaces: SYSTEM and SYSAUX. It also has its own TEMP tablespace.

The seed database should not be modified at all, every attempt to open it will result in" ORA-65017: seed pluggable database may not be dropped or altered". This has an interesting implication: if you were hoping that you could modify the seed to match your organization's database standards, then this is bad news. However, you can have your custom "seed" database from which you clone your user-PDBs as you will see in the section "Managing Pluggable Databases".

The User-Pluggable Database

A User PDB in this book indicates a Pluggable Database that has been cloned from either another user-PDB or the seed database, but is open for business. In other words, the user-PDB is the application object, and responsible for user connections and storing application data. Whenever you read about a PDB in the sections that follow you probably read about a user PDB even if it is not explicitly mentioned.

As you will see shortly, Pluggable Databases are very flexible and can easily be transported between Container Databases.

AN EXAMPLE FOR A BIG WIN

Consider the case of an independent software vendor. As with any support organization working with Oracle databases you need to keep past versions of your application available to reproduce problems and create test cases. Internally, you may have databases named after the current, future, and past releases. Depending on your support policy you may even have to support these databases for different Oracle releases.

When it came to patching—an application of a Patch Set Update for example—a lengthy process starts. First the respective Oracle home is patched out of place, and then all required databases. Patching can become a full Saturday's work to run catupgrade.sql on so many databases.

In this situation, a Pluggable Database would be a great match. Patching the binary home out of place is still required, but doesn't require much application downtime. The team could simply have created a new CDB with the upgraded dictionary, unplugged the PDBs and plugged them into the new CDB.

A Pluggable Database is not automatically opened in Oracle 12.1. This has to do with how the PDBs are treated in RAC, where you are not obliged to open a PDB on every instance. This is vaguely similar to RAC One Node, where you have a multi-node cluster database, which is only ever open on one cluster node. You can save memory and a process footprint by deciding to selectively open PDBs on instances in the cluster. In addition this approach allows for a gentle migration from a single instance to a RAC database, without having to worry about cross-instance messaging and associated potential cluster waits.

Creating a Container Database

Before you can create any Pluggable Database it is necessary to create the container first. This is a very important decision: it is impossible to convert a non-CDB to a CDB database.

■ **Note**   You can always transform a non-Container Database into a Pluggable Database and add it to an existing Container Database. However, you cannot convert a non-Container Database into a Container Database.

There are three popular ways to create a Container Database in Oracle 12.1: using SQL scripts, by invoking the Database Configuration Assistant in silent mode, and finally via dbca's graphical user interface. The scripted method has changed profoundly from the previous way of creating databases. To fully understand the process of a CDB creation it is useful to start the Database Configuration Assistant in GUI mode and let it create the scripts for you. You can see examples of these scripts in the "Creating a CDB using scripts" section below. If you prefer the GUI approach throughout, then there is nothing stopping you from creating your CDB using that tool from end-to-end. An example for the process is shown in the section "Using Database Configuration Assistant to create a CDB" below.

Just like in previous releases you have an option to either run dbca in silent or GUI mode. Silent mode offers you a flexibility, allowing you to run dbca from scripts or in environments where for security reasons you cannot have X11-forwarding or even an X-Server on the machine. Combined with a standard-compliant database template dbca is the tool of choice for rapid standards compliant database creation.

Memory considerations for CDBs

You have seen in Chapter 3 that x86-64 servers are able to take more and more memory and make good use of it. Even a modest dual-socket E5-2600-v2 series Xeon system could potentially address 1.5 TB of memory depending on server model. Memory is readily available most of the time, and in consolidated servers memory should not be scarce: that would be saving at the wrong end.

With that being said, as with any consolidation platform you can expect a lot of consolidated systems—PDBS or otherwise—to be very memory hungry. Interestingly there is no measurable overhead when opening a mounted PDB, however a large number of processes will obviously be a strain on the number of connections the system can serve. To measure the impact of sessions connecting to the Oracle server, a little experiment has been conducted. Consider the PDB "swingbench1", which has extensively been used to benchmark the system performance. How much overhead does a new connection add to the operating system without large pages enabled? A small 8GB SGA will already suffer a huge overhead from a larger number of sessions doing very little actual work when large pages are not configured. Consider the following example of an idle system. With the database started, the PageTables entry in the /proc/meminfo file for Oracle Linux 6.4 will show about 46MB used:

```
[oracle@server1 ~]$ grep -i paget /proc/meminfo
PageTables:       46380 kB
```

Using a little script to generate some XML on the fly will be used as benchmark.

```
[oracle@server1 ~]$ cat xml.sql
declare
  a xmltype;
begin
  a := xmltype('<a>toto</a>');
  dbms_lock.sleep(20);
end;
/

exit;
```

The test consists of 700 different executions of the same script in the current shell:

```
[oracle@server1 ~]$ for i in $(seq 1 700) ; do
>   sqlplus /@swingbench1 @xml &
> done
```

■ **Note** This example uses the secure external password store to connect to a TNS alias without having to provide a password. You can read more about that connectivity method in Chapter 10.

How much overhead does this generate? A lot! Periodically checking the PageTables entries from my system showed that with all 700 sessions connected, the kernel allocated around 750 MB:

```
[oracle@server1 ~]$ grep -i paget /proc/meminfo
PageTables:      750680kB
```

Going back to the initial state of an otherwise idle system, you will find that the number of page tables allocated is a lot lower and nearly back to the initial 46 MB. Let's review the same with large pages enabled. The maximum value registered with large pages enabled is shown here:

```
PageTables:        25228 kb
```

If you needed more persuasion to allocate large pages for your database, then hopefully this should give you another good reason to do so.

Deciding about storing files

The storage options available to the database administrator have not changed with Oracle 12.1. As with previous releases you have the choice of a supported file system or Automatic Storage Management (ASM). With ASM comes a strong encouragement to use Oracle Managed Files. In this respect it does not matter if the storage is local on the host, or provided via a SAN or NFS. Most readers will be familiar with the use of ASM and Oracle Managed Files, if you would like a refresher please refer to Chapter 2 for more information.

If you are not using ASM, you need to think about the location of the seed PDBs file location. Remember from the section "Common physical structures" that the seed is always present in a Container Database and has a SYSTEM, SYSAUX, and a TEMP tablespace. Since the seed database cannot be modified after it has been created some planning is necessary. The seed's data file locations can be configured in the following places:

- Using the "seed file_name_convert" clause in the "create database" command.
- Setting the "db_create_file_dest" initialization parameter to enable Oracle Managed Files.
- Using the "pdb_file_name_convert" initialization parameter.

The easiest way to deal with the seed's and all user PDBs' data files is to use Oracle Managed files. Using it you do not need to worry about any conversion parameters, but this comes at the cost of having slightly less control, especially when using ASM. You give away some command over file names when using OMF. In addition to that ASM is not a traditional file system as such where you can use ls, tar, gzip, and other tools you can use on a different supported file system. Additionally, the data files used by any PDB—seed and user—will include the PDB's globally unique identifier-GUID-in the file name. The system tablespace has the following fully qualified name in ASM:

```
+DATA/CDB1/DD7D8C1D4C234B38E04325AAE80AF577/DATAFILE/system.259.826623817
```

If you are not using OMF, then your approach will be different. You will shortly see that the Oracle by default creates a sub-directory for the seed database:

```
[oracle@server1 ~]$ find /u01/oradata -type d
/u01/oradata/CDB1
/u02/oradata/CDB1/pdbseed
```

This directory structure works well for the initial seed database. To make best use of the Pluggable Databases Feature it can be useful to define the storage location of user-PDBs on SAN attached storage. This way, unplug and plug operations from one database server to another can be much simpler. All it requires is a remount of that mount point to another host, followed by plugging the database in. In this scenario the seed database would still go to /u01/oradata/${ORACLE_SID}/pdbseed, but the user-PDBs could go to /u02/oracle/PDBs/<pdbname>/ for example. Since the seed is never used for anything other than cloning a PDB, its read/write performance can be ignored most of the time if you want to place it on slow storage.

The most convenient way to achieve the goal of ease-of-access of your user-PDBs when not using OMF is to keep the seed file name convert clause in the create database statement as it is, and set the initialization parameter "pdb_file_name_convert" to the appropriate value. Please refer to section "The create pluggable database statement" further down in this chapter for more information about the creation of PDBs and defining their storage location on a file system.

Using Database Configuration Assistant to create a CDB

This is the most basic way to get started with the new database release. Unlike some other Oracle tools which have only seen minor cosmetic change, the dbca looks quite different. Begin by executing $ORACLE_HOME/bin/dbca in order to launch the graphical user interface. The initial page allows you to perform a variety of tasks, including creating and dropping databases. It has a new menu item to manage pluggable databases too. For now, select the "create database option" to get to the next screen.

The utility offers two different ways to create a new database: typical and advanced. The main decision to be taken is shown in Figure 7-6.

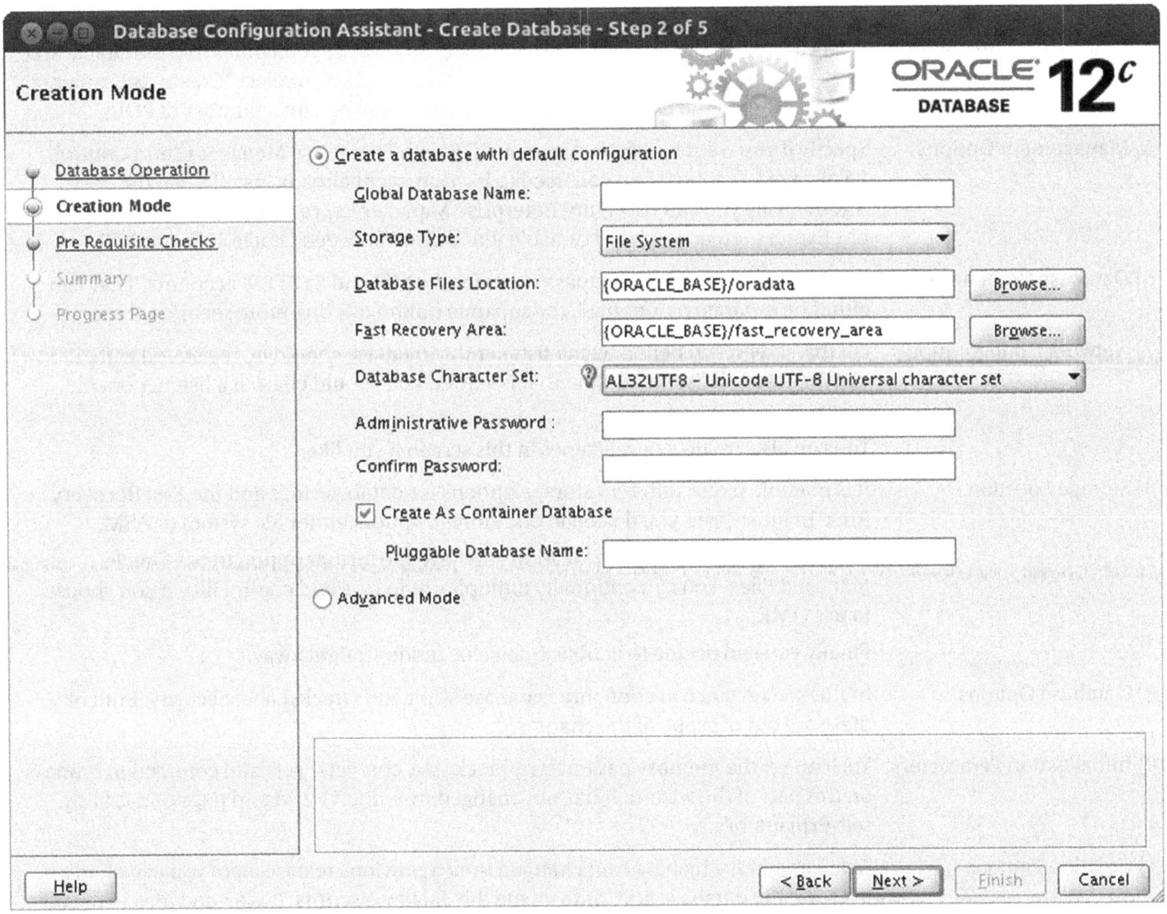

Figure 7-6. Database Creation

The typical options are the ones you see on the screen—they can help you to get started quickly. When opting for the advanced options, you are guided through a few more wizard steps, which are explained in Table 7-1.

Table 7-1. *Wizard Steps and Options*

Step	Action to take for database creation
1) Database Operation	Create a database
2) Creation Mode	Typical or Advanced-select advanced
3) Database Template	Select which template to use for the new database. This has primarily an effect on the database initialization parameters. In the default database software installation you get templates including data files and a custom option. The existence of data files means that dbca will perform an RMAN restore of the data files associated with the template whereas the custom option will create the database based on scripts which takes longer. You can create your own database templates and use them for a standard compliant database creation, possibly the best way to deploy databases at a larger scale.
4) Database Identification	Select a global database name and an Oracle SID. Please remember that the Oracle SID has a maximum length on most platforms. You should also select "Create As Container Database here". You can either create the CDB empty or with a number of PDBs.
5) Management Options	Specify if you want to register the new CDB with Enterprise Manager Cloud Control. If you check that box then you need to have an agent already installed on the host. Alternatively you can configure Enterprise Manager Express, or none of the above. EM Express replaces the DB Console that existed between Oracle 10.1 and 11.2.
6) Database Credentials	On this screen you enter the passwords for the SYS and SYSTEM accounts. They can either be separate or identical, the separate option offering more security of course.
7) Network Configuration	On this screen you define which listener the database should be registered with. If you do not see a listener although it is started you should check if a listener.ora file exists.
	You can also create a new listener in this screen if you like.
8) Storage Location	It is possible to use different storage options for database files and the Fast Recovery Area. In most cases you'd keep to one storage option, either file system or ASM.
	If you are using a file system location you have the further option to use Oracle Managed Files. You can optionally multiplex redo logs and control files if you choose to use OMF.
	Finally you can decide to enable archivelog mode straight away.
9) Database Options	In this screen you can configure Database Vault and Oracle Label Security. Both of these are out of scope of the chapter.
10) Initialization Parameters	You can set the memory parameters, block size, character sets and connection mode on this part of the wizard. It has not changed from the 11.2 wizard page and is fairly self-explanatory.
11) Creation Options	Again a screen which has not changed from a previous release, here you can choose to create the database and/or to create the database scripts. It is a good idea to create the scripts as well to become more familiar with the database creation process in Oracle 12c.

(continued)

Table 7-1. (*continued*)

Step	Action to take for database creation
12) Pre Requisite Checks	The dbca utility validates your choices against the system to ensure that all pre-requisites such as free space to create the database are met. Normally the screen should not be visible: if dbca does not find anything to complain about it moves immediately on to the next screen.
13) Summary	On this page you are presented with the HTML-styled document summarizing the options you chose. It lists the database components you selected and other important information such as Oracle SID and whether or not the database to be created is a CDB.
14) Process	The process page informs you how far into the database creation you have progressed. At the end of the database creation you are presented with account management information in a pop-up window, which you confirm and then exit dbca. The new database is ready for use.

After you have created the database it will be ready to accept user connections. If the database was installed on a system with ASM, it will automatically be registered with Oracle Restart.

Creating a CDB using scripts

The method of creating an Oracle container database has changed with the introduction of the Container Database. It would also appear that the process of creating a CDB from scripts takes longer, but this might be a subjective effect. The below example scripts have been created using the Database Creation Assistant and should be modified for your environment. Some parts of the scripts have already been adjusted. A common location has been chosen for all data files, which could be a problem for production deployments on contended storage use but serves as a good example regarding the location of the PDB files. By default dbca creates the scripts in

```
$ORACLE_BASE/admin/${ORACLE_SID}/scripts/
```

The main script to invoke when creating a database is a shell script named after the database. After creating the supporting directory structure the CDB creation begins with the create database command. While using previously mentioned common location for all data files, the following directories are created by the script, among others:

```
mkdir -p /u01/oradata/CDB1
mkdir -p /u01/oradata/CDB1/pdbseed
```

The shell script ${ORACLE_SID}.sh sets some environment variables for Oracle's perl implementation delivered as part of the RDBMS installation. Before continuing you should heed the advice in the script and add an entry for the new database in the oratab file.

You would expect the CDB$ROOT's files to be stored in /u01/oradata/CDB1, and the seed's files plus in /u01/oradata/CDB1/pdbseed. After all administrative tasks have completed, this slightly modified "create database" statement is executed:

```
CREATE DATABASE "CDB3"
MAXINSTANCES 8
MAXLOGHISTORY 1
MAXLOGFILES 16
```

```
MAXLOGMEMBERS 3
MAXDATAFILES 1024
  DATAFILE '/u01/oradata/CDB3/system01.dbf'
  SIZE 700M REUSE AUTOEXTEND ON NEXT  10240K MAXSIZE UNLIMITED
EXTENT MANAGEMENT LOCAL
  SYSAUX DATAFILE '/u01/oradata/CDB3/sysaux01.dbf'
  SIZE 550M REUSE AUTOEXTEND ON NEXT  10240K MAXSIZE UNLIMITED
SMALLFILE DEFAULT TEMPORARY TABLESPACE TEMP
  TEMPFILE '/u01/oradata/CDB3/temp01.dbf'
  SIZE 20M REUSE AUTOEXTEND ON NEXT  640K MAXSIZE UNLIMITED
SMALLFILE UNDO TABLESPACE "UNDOTBS1"
  DATAFILE  '/u01/oradata/CDB3/undotbs01.dbf'
  SIZE 200M REUSE AUTOEXTEND ON NEXT  5120K MAXSIZE UNLIMITED
CHARACTER SET WE8MSWIN1252
NATIONAL CHARACTER SET AL16UTF16
LOGFILE
  GROUP 1 ('/u01/oradata/CDB3/redo01.log') SIZE 50M,
  GROUP 2 ('/u01/oradata/CDB3/redo02.log') SIZE 50M,
  GROUP 3 ('/u01/oradata/CDB3/redo03.log') SIZE 50M
USER SYS IDENTIFIED BY "&&sysPassword"
USER SYSTEM IDENTIFIED BY "&&systemPassword"
enable pluggable database
seed file_name_convert=(
 '/u01/oradata/CDB3/system01.dbf','/u01/oradata/CDB3/pdbseed/system01.dbf',
 '/u01/oradata/CDB3/sysaux01.dbf','/u01/oradata/CDB3/pdbseed/sysaux01.dbf',
 '/u01/oradata/CDB3/temp01.dbf','/u01/oradata/CDB3/pdbseed/temp01.dbf',
 '/u01/oradata/CDB3/undotbs01.dbf','/u01/oradata/CDB3/pdbseed/undotbs01.dbf'
);
```

The dbca-generated script creates a much longer seed file name convert statement—one for each data file in the CDB. Please bear in mind that the above command is just an example—please review it and modify values appropriately.

TESTING THE FILE_NAME_CONVERT PARAMETERS

The file_name_convert parameters are well known to Oracle DBAs who have cloned databases using RMAN in the past. The parameter seems to be equivalent to the replace() function in SQL. This makes for easy testing. Connect to your database as an administrative user and issue the following query:

```
SQL> select file_name,
  2  replace(file_name,
  3          'string to be matched', 'string to replace match with')
  4    from dba_data_files;
```

The resulting output of the replace function will tell you the location of the data file with the conversion parameter applied.

```
SQL> select replace(file_name,'/u01/','/u02/') from dba_data_files;

REPLACE(FILE_NAME,'/u01/','/u02/')
----------------------------------------------------
/u02/oradata/CDB1/datafiles/system.257.780854341
/u02/oradata/CDB1/datafiles/sysaux.256.780854265
/u02/oradata/CDB1/datafiles/users.258.780854405
/u02/oradata/CDB1/datafiles/undotbs1.259.780854407
```

This technique applies for many Oracle processes, including RMAN database cloning.

The SQL script then executes the scripts necessary to generate the data dictionary, and all the database components you need. What makes these scripts different from previous releases and the non-CDB is the invocation via the catcon.pl script. Consider the following snippet used to create the Oracle Database Catalog Views and Oracle Database Packages and Types (CreateDBCatalog.sql):

```
...
alter session set "_oracle_script"=true;
alter pluggable database pdb$seed close;
alter pluggable database pdb$seed open;
host perl /u01/app/oracle/product/12.1.0.1/dbhome_1/rdbms/admin/catcon.pl↵
 -n 1 -l /u01/app/oracle/admin/CDB3/scripts -b catalog ↵
 /u01/app/oracle/product/12.1.0.1/dbhome_1/rdbms/admin/catalog.sql;
host perl /u01/app/oracle/product/12.1.0.1/dbhome_1/rdbms/admin/catcon.pl↵
 -n 1 -l /u01/app/oracle/admin/CDB3/scripts -b catblock ↵
 /u01/app/oracle/product/12.1.0.1/dbhome_1/rdbms/admin/catblock.sql;
...
```

■ **Note** The scripts creating the dictionary are documented in the Oracle Database Reference 12.1 manual, in Appendix B on "SQL Scripts."

As you can see the scripts we used to run while directly connected to the database have changed and are channeled via the catcon.pl Perl script. This is the reason for setting the perl environment variables in the top-level shell script. The purpose of the script is to execute one or more scripts in a CDB, or within one or more PDBs. The parameters specified in the snippet shown above indicate that:

- The directory /u01/app/oracle/admin/CDB3/scripts should be used for log files
- The log file base name is indicated as the argument to the option "-b" (catalog for example)
- Followed by the file to be executed

The catcon.pl script is often involved when dictionary scripts are executed in a CDB. It is potentially very useful and thankfully Oracle documented it in the Administrator's Guide in Chapter 40 in section "Running Oracle Supplied SQL scripts in a CDB".

The creation process takes a little while depending on the options you need to be present in the Container Database. As with most things in life, less is more, which is especially true with Oracle databases. Not only does the execution of each additional dictionary script take more time, it also opens the door for exploits. If your application does not make use of the InterMedia or Spatial options for example, don't add the options to the database. In releases before Oracle 12.1 one could also argue that any component in the data dictionary that wasn't needed used up precious time during upgrades. But as you have seen in a number of places in this book: that argument does not carry as much weight anymore. Instead of patching the whole database, you may be able to simply unplug your PDB and plug it into an already patched CDB. Bear in mind though that the options need to be compatible with PDBs you intend to plug into your CDB. In some cases you still will have to recompile the PDB-specific parts of the dictionary.

■ **Note**   You can use dbca to create templates of your "golden" image CDB database. Instead of creating the database manually every time which is time consuming and therefore not very efficient you could create the database from the template instead.

Exploring the new CDB

Once the new Container Database is created, it is time to connect to it and explore the new Oracle release. Have a look around; use the CDB% views to query the data dictionary. Create a few PDBs from the seed and see how quickly you can provision a new environment. When querying the data dictionary and you don't see information about a PDB you might have to check the open mode and open the PDB read write or read only. If the PDB is not open in those states the CDB% views won't detect any information about them. Also remember the scope of your commands: when connected to the root (CDB$ROOT) with DBA privileges you should be able to see all the information pertaining to the attached and accessible containers. If you are connected to a PDB, then you will only see the information pertaining to those.

You might also want to familiarize yourself with the physical structure of your CDB. You can check the v$parameter view to see where your control files are located, use cdb_data_files and cdb_temp_files to check where your data and temp files are—all based or sorted on the con_id for each container. You will also see that there is no CDB-view for online redo logs. Online redo logs are not container specific and belong to the Container Database as such. The column CON_ID in V$LOG shows them as member of CON_ID 0. Once you are feeling more comfortable with your database it is time to move on to Pluggable Databases.

Managing Pluggable Databases

Just before I started writing this section I saw a very good discussion on my favorite mailing list: oracle-l@freelist. org about preferred methods used by DBAs created their database. Especially given the fact that the execution of the catalog.sql and catproc.sql plus any ancillary scripts takes a lot of time! I couldn't tell them there and then, but what made me rejoice was that I could have told them: the creation of a new "database" won't take a lot of time at all! That of course depends on your understanding of database. If you consider a database as an entity to give to users in which they can run their applications then a PDB fits the description one hundred percent.

You may recall from the discussion about containers earlier in the chapter that there is always a seed database in a CDB, called PDB$SEED. It can be cloned in almost no time to spin off a new database for users to start working with their new data store. If you don't like to use the rather Spartan way the seed-PDB is set up then there are other ways to address the need to use a PDB as the source for a clone operation. It is even possible to clone a PDB over a database link, although that method requires careful testing due to bandwidth and latency considerations. Before exploring each of these methods in more detail it is necessary to describe an extension to the SQL language: the "pluggable" keyword in the create database statement.

Creating a Pluggable Database

The SQL reference has been extended once again to accommodate the new features available with the new database release. The create/alter database statement has been extended with the "pluggable" attribute. Whenever the "pluggable" keyword is found in any of these examples, you immediately know that the command is aimed at one of the containers. The SQL language reference however has a dedicated section about the "create pluggable database statement"; it is not an extension of the "create database statement".

It almost goes without saying that the user executing any of these statements needs elevated privileges. A new system privilege has been introduced, which unsurprisingly has been called "create pluggable database". Before you can create a new PDB, you need to consider your options:

- Create a new PDB from the seed
- Create a new PDB from another local PDB
- Create a new PDB from a remote PDB
- Plug-in a PDB into a CDB
- Plug a non-CDB into a CDB as a new PDB

The following sections detail all these steps. Regardless of which source you chose to clone the PDB, you have a number of clauses available to fine-tune your new Pluggable Database.

Creating a PDB from the seed database

Creating a PDB from the seed database is the easiest way to get started with Pluggable Databases. By default, the new PDB will consist of a SYSTEM, SYSAUX, UNDO, and TEMP tablespace. It will be accessible by all common users (see section "Users and roles" later in the chapter for an introduction into the new security concept). For now let it suffice that a common user can connect to the root and any container using the same username and password. The other user class is represented by the local users, which you already assumed, can only connect to specific PDBs.

When you create a PDB from the seed, you need to specify a mandatory admin user. This is the only mandatory clause you need to specify if you are using Oracle Managed Files or ASM for that matter. Therefore, the basic statement to create a PDB is as simple as this:

```
SYS@CDB$ROOT> create pluggable database pdb2
  2  admin user pdbdba identified by password;

Pluggable database created.
```

A few seconds later the statement completes and you have your first working PDB! The operation is documented in the alert log of the CDB:

```
create pluggable database pdb2 admin user pdbdba identified by *
2013-09-25 10:35:23.445000 +01:00
********************************************************************
Pluggable Database PDB2 with pdb id - 4 is created as UNUSABLE.
If any errors are encountered before the pdb is marked as NEW,
then the pdb must be dropped
********************************************************************
Deleting old file#5 from file$
Deleting old file#7 from file$
Adding new file#22 to file$(old file#5)
Adding new file#23 to file$(old file#7)
2013-09-25 10:35:24.814000 +01:00
Successfully created internal service pdb2 at open
ALTER SYSTEM: Flushing buffer cache inst=0 container=4 local
********************************************************************
Post plug operations are now complete.
Pluggable database PDB2 with pdb id - 4 is now marked as NEW.
********************************************************************
Completed: create pluggable database pdb2 admin user pdbdba identified by *
```

> ■ **Note** Although the admin user clause is mandatory to create a user-PDB, no one forces you to actually make use of the account. It can be easily locked as part of the database build process after the PDB has been opened.

Further options you can make use of include the definition of a default tablespace in the PDB. Omitting the clause will lead to the new PDB's SYSTEM tablespace to become the default tablespace. Luckily Oracle allows you to create that new tablespace if it does not yet exist, which is the case when you are cloning your PDB from the seed database. The syntax is based on the well-known "create tablespace" command, reusing the same data file name spec and extent management clause. Below is an example for creating a PDB from the seed with a new default tablespace USERS, residing on OMF:

```
SYS@CDB$ROOT> create pluggable database pdb3
  2  admin user pdbdba identified by secret
  3  default tablespace pdb3_default_tbs datafile size 10G
  4  /

Pluggable Database created.
```

If you are implementing a consolidated platform solution, then you certainly appreciate the ability to limit the size of the PDB. This way a user could order a 100 GiB database, and your operations team does not have to limit the size of individual data files. All the settings are implemented at deployment time. The pdb_storage_clause can be used to either set the maximum size to unlimited. Alternatively the clause allows you to limit the amount of shared temp space (for sorting on disk) as well as to set the size of the persistent storage. If the pdb_storage_clause is omitted there is no limit to the size of the PDB, other than the physical storage of course. For example, you could limit the data file growth to 100 G as shown in this example:

```
SYS@CDB$ROOT> create pluggable database pdb4
  2  admin user pdbdba identified by secret
  3  storage (maxsize 100G)
  4  default tablespace pdb4_default_tbs datafile size 10G
  5  autoextend on next 10G;

Pluggable database created.
```

If it should turn out that during the lifetime of the database more space is needed, the database limit can be modified.

The new PDB can of course be placed into a different location. The file_name_convert clause allows you to specify where the new PDB should be located to. Refer back earlier in this chapter to review the basics of the file name conversion in Oracle. Consider for example this CDB which resides on a file system and not on ASM as the ones in the previous examples:

```
SQL> select con_id, file_name from cdb_data_files
  2  order by con_id
  3  /
```

```
   CON_ID FILE_NAME
---------- --------------------------------------------------------
        1 /u01/oradata/CDB2/users01.dbf
        1 /u01/oradata/CDB2/undotbs01.dbf
        1 /u01/oradata/CDB2/sysaux01.dbf
        1 /u01/oradata/CDB2/system01.dbf
        2 /u01/oradata/CDB2/pdbseed/system01.dbf
        2 /u01/oradata/CDB2/pdbseed/sysaux01.dbf
```

This implies the CDB's files are all under /u01/oradata/CDB2/, with the seed database's files in another subdirectory "pdbseed". Since these files are not overly sensitive to I/O requirements, you can store them on lower tier storage. The other PDBs however are a different story and have different I/O requirements from the seed. Assume that the /u01/oradata/CDB2/pdbs/ mount point is the default mount point for PDBs. You could then clone your seed as follows:

```
SQL> create pluggable database fspdb1 admin user pdbdba identified by password
  2  file_name_convert=(
  3    '/u01/oradata/CDB2/pdbseed/','/u01/oradata/CDB2/pdbs/fspdb1/');

Pluggable database created.
```

The file locations are reflected accordingly:

```
SQL> select con_id, file_name
  2  from cdb_data_files
  3  where con_id = 4;

   CON_ID FILE_NAME
---------- -------------------------------------------------------
        4 /u01/oradata/CDB2/pdbs/fspdb1/system01.dbf
        4 /u01/oradata/CDB2/pdbs/fspdb1/sysaux01.dbf
```

The final clause to the "create pluggable database statement" allows you to grant roles to the admin user, but this will be discussed later in the chapter in the section "Users and Roles".

After the PDB has been cloned, it is in mount mode. To access it you need to open it. See further down in the chapter for more information about opening and closing PDBs. The PDB also needs backing up.

Cloning from another PDB

The ability to clone a PDB from another PDB is a very nice feature. As part of it you have a process that handles the copy process as well, which should make the creation of a spin-off PDB a very simple process. As with the creation of a user-PDB you have several options as to where to place the files and to restrict the storage usage of the new PDB.

Cloning a local PDB is the first case to be demonstrated. To that extent the PDB to be cloned is plugged into the current CDB. The source you want to clone from has to be opened in read-only mode. This is very similar to the requirement when exporting metadata for transporting tablespaces. Closing an active PDB is a disruptive process and therefore needs to be carefully coordinated with the business users. To initiate the cloning process, shut down the source PDB in preparation to making it read-only:

```
SQL> alter pluggable database pdb1 close immediate;

Pluggable database altered.
```

Once the PDB has been closed, you can reopen it in read-only mode:

```
SQL> alter pluggable database pdb1 open read only;

Pluggable database altered.
```

The cloning process in its most basic form requires no arguments when OMF is in use, especially not an admin user clause. Consider the following example on a system using Oracle Managed Files:

```
SQL> create pluggable database pdb5 from pdb1;

Pluggable database created.
```

On a regular file system without OMF the command requires the file name conversion parameter. This means that all files belonging to a PDB are always contained under a single directory or mount point. You cannot avoid the file name conversion, and bundle up all the PDBs under a single directory, such as /u01/oradata/pdbs/pdbs. From a deployment perspective you should therefore create mount points for different storage tiers, with sub-directories for each PDB.

The below does not make use of this schema, but rather has a generic mount point "pdbs", under which all the PDBs are created. The user-PDB "fspdb1" has already been created and is now in read-only mode waiting to be cloned:

```
SQL> create pluggable database fspdb2 from fspdb1
  2  file_name_convert = ('/u01/oradata/pdbs/fspdb1','/u01/oradata/pdbs/fspdb2')
  3  /

Pluggable database created.
```

When cloning a PDB you cannot assign a default tablespace in the same command, and you cannot modify or set the roles for the PDB administrator the same way you would as shown in the previous section. You can however make use of the storage clause, and limit the temp and permanent storage used by the PDB. Changes to the physical structure of the PDB need to be completed after the PDB has been created and opened.

Once the PDB is created it needs to be backed up.

Cloning from a remote PDB

Cloning a user-PDB from a remote source requires a very similar syntax as cloning from a local source. In essence, all that is required is a database link between the destination and source. The operation itself is a pull from remote via the database link. There is similar advice to be given concerning the operation compared to RMAN's ability to duplicate an active database: don't overload your network! If you can, you should use tagged VLANs for this kind of operation, or maybe not clone at all.

In the example that follows you find two Container Databases: CDB1 and CDB2. CDB1 currently has a PDB called swingbench1 which needs to be cloned as swingbench2 under CDB2. Before spending time on the clone operation you need to ensure that the CDBs use the same character set. In Oracle 12.1 a clone operation from a remote database requires identical character sets, as does the plug operation as you will see shortly. Additionally, you need to ensure that the database options between the source and destination CDB are identical.

As with any clone operation, the source has to be opened read-only. Again, make sure that all the stakeholders of the application are aware of that operation so that applications can be shut down cleanly prior to the event. Before shutting down the source, create a database link to the CDB$ROOT of your source, then enter the known command "create pluggable database clone *Name* from *sourceName@dblink*.

And you cloned a PDB over the network which opens interesting possibilities.

Moving PDBs between different containers

Another way to add a PDB to a system is to unplug it on the source and plug it into the destination. The best use case for this is the application of a patch on the source CDB. Instead of suffering downtime while the CDB is patched, you could easily unplug/plug the PDB from the database to be patched to another, already patched CDB.

Oracle has developed a procedure to facilitate that process, and it is based on an XML document that travels with the PDB to be moved. The API gives you a great deal of flexibility over the process. Once a PDB is unplugged, it is no longer associated with the CDB it was last plugged into but nevertheless still listed as you will see in a bit. The unplug command is remarkably simple, and the only variables to it are the user-PDB name and the location of the XML file describing it. To export user-PDB pdb5 for example, you can issue this command:

```
SQL> alter pluggable database pdb5 unplug into '/home/oracle/pdb_ddl/pdb5.xml';

Pluggable database altered.
```

For it to succeed the PDB to be exported must be in mount state. When choosing a name for the XML file, you should make it obvious which database it describes. The database (unique) name for example is a great example for a file name. After the XML file has been created, the PDB is not removed from the list of PDBs in v$pdbs. The XML file describing the PDB contains information about the PDB's tablespaces, and some general information required for plugging the database into a CDB. The below is an excerpt from the XML file describing pdb5:

```
<?xml version="1.0" encoding="UTF-8"?>
<PDB>
  <pdbname>PDB5</pdbname>
  <cid>5</cid>
  <byteorder>1</byteorder>
...
  <guid>E732F81E6B640DC7E0436638A8C03EB1</guid>
...
  <tablespace>
    <name>SYSTEM</name>
    <type>0</type>
    <tsn>0</tsn>
    <status>1</status>
    <issft>0</issft>
    <file>
      <path>+DATA/CDB1/E73[...]8C03EB1/DATAFILE/system.275.827060209</path>
      <afn>30</afn>
      <rfn>1</rfn>
      <createscnbas>2390117</createscnbas>
      <createscnwrp>0</createscnwrp>
      <status>1</status>
      <fileblocks>34560</fileblocks>
      <blocksize>8192</blocksize>
      <vsn>202375168</vsn>
      <fdbid>3887550129</fdbid>
      <fcpsw>0</fcpsw>
      <fcpsb>2392086</fcpsb>
      <frlsw>0</frlsw>
```

```
        <frlsb>2256999</frlsb>
        <frlt>826900946</frlt>
      </file>
   </tablespace>
...
   <tablespace>
...
</tablespaces>
```

There are more entries for each tablespace in the PDB as well as all the database options, whether or not Data Vault or Label Security are in use and important initialization parameters. The XML file name is a very important piece of information for the remaining process as you will see next. Before you can plug a PDB into a CDB, the following requirements have to be met in Oracle 12.1:

- The source and destination CDB must have the same endianness (check field "byteorder" in the above XML file). In other words, you cannot directly transport a PDB from a CDB on Solaris SPARC into a PDB on Linux x86-64.

- The PDB must have the same or compatible character set, and also the same national character set. Do you see the value of standardization here?

- The destination CDB must have the same options installed in the data dictionary as the source CDB if the PDB makes use of them. You can view the options used by the PDB in the XML file describing it in the tag <options>. The option is listed alongside its version. Use DBMS_PDB. CHECK_PLUG_COMPATIBILITY() to check for compatibility of PDB and CDB options.

The API for plugging the exported PDB into a CDB gives you a great deal of freedom over the process. The basic command is the now well-known "create pluggable database" statement used previously, with the extension of the "using" clause. Depending on how you stored the unplugged PDB, and whether you want to clone the source or store it in a different location you have many options.

- To create the new user-PDB as a clone. The "as clone" clause to the "create pluggable database" command instructs Oracle to generate new identifiers for the PDB to be plugged in. Most importantly, it will ensure that the new PDB is different from the source PDB from an Oracle point of view.

- If you moved the unplugged PDB physically, or made it available via an NFS mount for example, then the XML file does not represent the file location of the PDB to be plugged in. Instead of editing the XML file manually, you should use the source_file_name_convert option. It is exactly the same as the file_name_convert clause already explained earlier in the chapter.

- If you have already copied or moved the PDB's files to their final location, then you can instruct Oracle not to copy them from the source location indicated in the XML file, which it would be otherwise the default. Alternatively, you can specify the move keyword to move- and not copy- the files to the new location.

- In addition to specifying the source_file_name_convert parameter, you can also tell Oracle where to move files to using the file_name_convert clause as already explained.

As you can see, the number of options available to detail what should happen with an unplugged PDB is quite large. In addition to the ones mentioned here you can also specify the storage clause, which has already been discussed in the section "Create a PDB from the seed database". The options to use depend on your situation. If you are using Oracle Managed Files, then you most likely do not need to consider the file_name_convert clause—the OMF naming convention will take care of the destination location. Years of experience working with Oracle ASM have taught the author that it is often best not trying to outsmart ASM in trying to micro-manage the file names and locations.

You are given great flexibility as to specifying where a file comes from, and where it should be moved to. Assume for example that the data files for the production PDB "vipdb1" is described similar to the one that follows below in the XML document:

...

```
    <path>/u01/oradata/pdbs/vipdb1/system01.dbf</path>
```
...

You could further assume that the files pertaining to the PDB have been copied via sftp to a staging location on the UAT database server: /m/transfer/pdbs/vipdb1/. Both production and UAT server use Linux file systems to store Oracle data files. Using that information, you'd have to use the following syntax to plug the PDB into the UAT CDB:

```
SYS@CDB$ROOT> get create_pdb_plugin.sql
  1  create pluggable database vipdb1uat as clone
  2   using '/home/oracle/vipdb1.xml'
  3  source_file_name_convert=(
  4   '/u01/oradata/pdbs/vipdb1','/m/transfer/pdbs/vipdb1')
  5  file_name_convert=(
  6   '/m/transfer/pdbs/vipdb1','/u01/oradata/CDB1/VIPDB1UAT')
  7* tempfile reuse
SQL> /

Pluggable database created.
```

Another interesting use case could be the migration from file system ASM. This has been a simple operation in the past involving image copies of the data files to which the database was switched over to. With PDBs this has become a slightly different operation as shown here:

```
SQL> create plugable database asmpdb2 using '/m/transfer/pdbs/fspdb1.xml'
  2   copy source_file_name_convert = ...
  3   /
```

The destination CDB has its db_create_file_dest initialization parameter set to '+DATA', allowing the PDB to be copied into ASM-disk group '+DATA'.

Plugging a non-CDB into a CDB

Plugging in a non-CDB is your opportunity to move databases just migrated to Oracle 12.1, or other databases that haven't been created as Container Databases into the consolidation platform. For this scenario you can make use of another package created by Oracle, called DBMS_PDB. The procedure of plugging in a non-CDB into a CDB is very similar to the one just described in the section "Moving PDBs between different containers".

To plug the non-CDB into the container as a Pluggable Database a few steps need to be followed. In the first step you use the DBMS_PDB package's describe() function while connected to the non-CDB to create the XML meta data file. The file can only be created if the non-CDB is opened read-only. Shut the non-CDB database down after the XML file has been created successfully in preparation for the next step.

Connect to the CDB you want to use as the non-CDB's container and use the "create pluggable database" statement to plug the database into the new container. Refrain from opening the new PDB just yet. Connect to the PDB and execute the noncdb_to_pdb.sql script in $ORACLE_HOME/rdbms/admin to complete the conversion to a PDB.

This section has been kept short deliberately: You can read more about plugging in a non-CDB into a CDB in Chapter 12, complete with an example.

Connecting to Pluggable Databases

Connections to PDBs are based on the service created automatically when the PDB is opened. The service name equals the PDB name and is created and registered with the listener. This has two important implications:

1. You need to use net services to connect to the PDB. Operating System authentication (using "ops$-" accounts) is not possible

2. EZConnect will prove really useful

3. If you have two CDBs on your host and both have a PDB named PDB1 then you cannot reliably connect to one or the other. Such a configuration should be avoided

Consider the following example of a listener started out of the Grid Infrastructure home, using the default values:

```
[oracle@server1 ~]$ lsnrctl service

LSNRCTL for Linux: Version 12.1.0.1.0 - Production on 25-SEP-2013 13:50:25

Copyright (c) 1991, 2013, Oracle.  All rights reserved.

Connecting to (ADDRESS=(PROTOCOL=tcp)(HOST=)(PORT=1521))
Services Summary...
[...]
Service "CDB1" has 2 instance(s).
  Instance "CDB1", status UNKNOWN, has 1 handler(s) for this service...
    Handler(s):
      "DEDICATED" established:0 refused:0
        LOCAL SERVER
  Instance "CDB1", status READY, has 1 handler(s) for this service...
    Handler(s):
      "DEDICATED" established:0 refused:0 state:ready
        LOCAL SERVER
[...]
Service "pdb1" has 1 instance(s).
  Instance "CDB1", status READY, has 1 handler(s) for this service...
    Handler(s):
      "DEDICATED" established:0 refused:0 state:ready
        LOCAL SERVER
[...]
The command completed successfully
```

Note the services PDB1 in the above output belonging to CDB1. When you open the PDB either read-only or read write, you will see that the service is automatically created and started for you.

Some output has been removed for the sake of clarity. With this in place it is possible to connect to the PDB as you would to any other service before Oracle 12.1. The obvious choice is to create a net service name for the user-PDB:

```
PDB1 =
  (DESCRIPTION =
    (ADDRESS = (PROTOCOL = TCP)(HOST = server1.example.com)(PORT = 1521))
    (CONNECT_DATA =
      (SERVER = DEDICATED)
      (SERVICE_NAME = pdb1)
    )
  )
```

Now you can connect to the PDB.

In addition to the default service name you can of course create additional services for your PDB. Either use DBMS_SERVICE for this purpose—or if you are on ASM—create the service with srvctl:

```
[oracle@server1 ~]$ srvctl add service -db CDB1 -service soe -pdb swingbench1
```

Note the new "pdb" flag in the above command. When the service is created you can start it to allow user connections.

A CASE FOR EZCONNECT

Many sites I visited over the years were against the use of EZConnect, except perhaps for those running Real Application Clusters 11.2, where the "remote_listener" parameter makes use of the EZConnect syntax.

EZConnect shortens the URL required to connect to a database, and very often becomes a time saver when trying to connect to a database service for which no tnsnames.ora entry exists, and also where change management would prevent a change to the file in time for the project. So instead of using the "connect user@netServiceName syntax, you could use this instead:

```
SQL> connect soe/password@server1.example.com/swingbench1
```

You can even specify a different listener port if needed:

```
SQL> connect soe/password@server1.example.com:1523/swingbench1
```

The reason I heard most often as to why EZConnect was banned was security. However, EZConnect does not add a security problem; it has always been possible to connect to the database service without a service name defined in tnsnames.ora. So instead of using the more convenient statement shown above, you could use this rather long connection string instead:

```
Enter user-name: soe/passwd@(DESCRIPTION=(ADDRESS=(PROTOCOL=TCP) ↵
(HOST=server1.example.com)(PORT=1521)) ↵
(CONNECT_DATA=(SERVER=DEDICATED)(SERVICE_NAME=swingbench1)))
```

As you can see, EZConnect should not pose an additional threat. Nevertheless these discussions need to be had with your security department, the above can only be an example.

Moving within the CDB

During the preparation of this chapter I found myself switching from one PDB to another and back to the CDB$ROOT quite a lot. When using EZConnect this quickly turns into a lot of typing. If you are connected as a common user (see section "Users and Roles" further down in this chapter for more information about common and local users) and possess the "SET CONTAINER" system privilege then you can move vertically within the CDB quite easily. Many DBAs still type the "sqlplus / as sysdba" blindly into their terminal session and end up in the root container. Rather than using the EZConnect syntax "connect system/xxx@localhost:listenerPort/servicename" the easier variant is to set the container appropriately as shown here.

```
SQL> alter session set container = SWINGBENCH1;

Session altered.

SQL> select sys_context('userenv', 'con_name') from dual
  2  /

SYS_CONTEXT('USERENV','CON_NAME')
--------------------------------------------------------------------------
SWINGBENCH1
```

There is an important implication to this command as compared to the network connection: any login trigger defined does not fire after the alter session command has completed (there are workarounds). The container names can be found in V$PDBS.NAME, with the exception of the root, which is referred to as CDB$ROOT.

PDB-specific initialization parameters

Initialization parameters can be set in different places in the Oracle 12c database. Most are applicable for the whole Container Database, but some can be set specifically for a PDB. Most of the session-modifiable parameters can be set at the PDB level, while connected to the PDB. To find out which parameters are specific to a PDB, you can query the system:

```
SQL> SELECT NAME FROM V$PARAMETER WHERE ISPDB_MODIFIABLE='TRUE' ORDER BY NAME;
```

At the time of this writing there were 171 PDB-specific parameters that could be set. They were persistent across lifecycle changes within the PDB. Earlier in this chapter you saw how you could transfer PDB-specific initialization parameters as part of the unplug/plug operation.

Considerations for hosted environments

With all this information you now have in your hands, you can make a lot of practical use in your database consolidation project. Instead of creating individual schemas in a database and live with the limitations of multi-tenancy in Oracle 11.2 and before you can now create new environments very quickly. The below example demonstrates how quickly you can create a new PDB from the seed database residing on ASM:

```
SQL> set timing on time on
22:53:34 SQL> begin
22:53:35    2    for j in 10..20 loop
22:53:37    3      execute immediate 'create pluggable database pdb' || j ||
22:53:39    4        ' admin user pdbadmin identified by secret';
22:53:40    5    end loop;
22:53:42    6  end;
22:53:43    7  /

PL/SQL procedure successfully completed.

Elapsed: 00:02:20.48
```

As you can see from the timing information this anonymous block was completed in a few minutes. The time to deploy a new environment for a requesting business unit in your organization matches the time it takes to execute the request to create a schema in a pre-12.1 database. Even though this process is already fast, it can be further enhanced by using another automated database build procedure.

Assume for example that your build process creates a CDB as described but doesn't stop there. You could have a PDB all set up to match your organization's standards on a shared location in your network exported via NFS. You can clone and plug the reference PDB into the new CDB as a reference for future user (PDBs). Or maybe create a CDB with common users that are required by the database management and monitoring tools. That way you reduce the latency of cloning a PDB over the network and pay the price of over-the-network-cloning only once. Yet you have a fully working reference PDB you can clone locally.

Chapter 3 presents a few considerations about storage classes or tiers. Using the file_name_convert clause in the "create pluggable database" statement you can cater for these as well and create the PDB on premium storage if so requested.

This leaves one concern to the administrators: how can Oracle ensure that a "runaway" PDB does not take all resources of the server and thus starves out everybody else of resources? This question has been anticipated by Oracle in the requirements design phase and as a result Database Resource Manager (DBRM) has been enhanced to deal with inter-PDB resource requirements. Later in this chapter you can read how you could start managing resources within a CDB.

Opening and closing PDBs

You read earlier in the chapter that a PDB is not accessible immediately after its creation. This is how the process has been defined. The lifecycle states for a PDB are:

1. MOUNTED: the Pluggable Database is not accessible for users, and information about it will not be displayed in the CDB% views.

2. OPEN read-only: accessible for queries, and ready to be cloned, but no modifications possible. The PDB must specifically be opened with the "read only" clause to set it into this mode.

3. OPEN read write: the PDB is available for users. This is the default state when opening the PDB.

4. OPEN restricted: opens the PDB read write, but allows only uses with the "restricted session" privilege to connect.

Additionally, after each restart of the CDB, all PDBs currently plugged in will be back in MOUNTED mode irrespectively of their previous open mode. Once the CDB is opened, you can open your PDBs. Luckily the syntax for doing so is straightforward, and it is possible to open all PDBs in a single command.

```
SQL> alter pluggable database all open;
```

You can even instruct Oracle to open all PDBs except for some you don't intend to open. The exception of the rule is the seed database, which will always be open read-only, ready to be cloned.

```
SQL> alter pluggable database all EXCEPT PDB5 open;

Pluggable database altered.
```

The open mode of the PDB has to be compatible with the open mode of the CDB however. In other words, if you opened the CDB in read-only mode, then you cannot open a PDB in read write mode.

Since Oracle won't automatically open PDBs, a little bit of code in combination with a startup trigger can help in this situation. Consider the following sample:

```
SQL> create table pdbtab tablespace users
  2  as select name, 'YES' autostart, 'RW' openmode
  4 from v$pdbs
  3  where name <> 'PDB$SEED';

Table created

SQL> alter table pdbtab add constraint c_autostart
  2  check (autostart in ('YES','NO'));

Table altered

SQL> alter table pdbtab add constraint c_openmode
  2  check (openmode in ('RO','RW'));

Table altered.
```

With the "pdbtab" table in place, it is possible to define a trigger that fires after the database has been started. It is possible to read the list of PDBs in the table "pdbtab", and execute a piece of dynamic SQL to open the PDB according to the requested open mode. A possible trigger could be written like this one:

```
SQL> create or replace trigger autoPDBtrig
  2   after startup on database
  3   declare
  4     v_role v_$database.database_role%type;
  5   begin
  6     select database_role into v_role from v$database;
  7     if v_role = 'PRIMARY' then
  8       for i in (select name,openmode from pdbtab a where exists
  9                 (select 1 from v$pdbs b where b.name = a.name)
 10                 and autostart='YES')
 11       loop
 12         execute immediate 'alter pluggable database ' ||
 13             i.name || ' open ' || case when i.openmode = 'RO'
 14                                   then 'read only' end;
 15       end loop;
 16     end if;
 17* end;
SQL> /

Trigger created.
```

The trigger first checks if the database is in the primary role. If not then PDBs should probably not be opened. Following this verification the code traverses all the entries in PDBTAB for PDBs that exist in the CDB, with the intention of opening them accordingly. This way you have all your PDBs open when the CDB started in a user-defined fashion. You need to add an entry to the pdbtab table after deploying a new PDB or it will not be taken into consideration during the start of the CDB.

The syntax for closing PDBs is very similar. Like with opening PDBs, you can name individual PDBs to be closed. Alternatively you could instruct Oracle to close all of them using the "alter pluggable database all close" command. This will wait for user sessions to disconnect, similar to a "shutdown" command in the non-CDB. To force users to disconnect, specify the "immediate" keyword. This can be useful if you have a short change window and need users to get off the PDB quickly in order to prepare it for cloning.

Users and roles in the context of a PDB

As you can imagine, the introduction of the Container Database brings with it changes in the security model. The most profound change impacts the database user account, and database roles. Users in Oracle 12.1 are either common users, or local users. All Oracle-supplied users are common users. Figure 7-7 shows the relationship between common and local users.

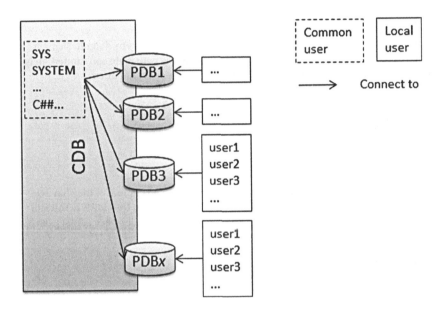

Figure 7-7. Common users and local users compared

Common users are common to the whole CDB, and implicitly to all PDBs currently plugged into the root container. They inherit the same password, and some Oracle-maintained accounts can also execute the "alter session set container" command to quickly change from one container to another without having to reconnect. Non-Oracle maintained common users need to be granted the relevant privileges. Common users will also be created for all future PDBs.

Now that poses an interesting question for your non-Oracle monitoring accounts: will you create them as common users in a dbca-template, or do you create a PDB template with the monitoring account created locally? Many factors favor the common account, which only needs to be maintained once when it has been locked or the password needs to be reset.

Creating common users

To create a common user you need to be connected to the root container, or CDB$ROOT as a common user with appropriate privileges. A new addition to the "create user" and "grant" command, called "container" allows the creation of common users. Common users must be prefixed with c## or otherwise you will receive an error. Take this example for user c##sysbackup:

```
SYS@CDB$ROOT> create user c##sysbackup identified by secret
  2  container = all;

User created.

SYS@CDB$ROOT> grant sysbackup to c##sysbackup;

Grant succeeded.
```

The "container"-clause seems optional, since all users created in the root are common users by default. Using it makes the purpose more visible though, especially in automation where someone reading your code can immediately grasp the intention. Thankfully Oracle prevents the creation of non-common users in the root container:

```
SYS@CDB$ROOT> create user localuser identified by secret container = current;
create user localuser identified by secret container = current
                                               *
ERROR at line 1:
ORA-65049: creation of local user or role is not allowed in CDB$ROOT
```

The newly created user exists in all attached PDBs, and could theoretically connect to all of them, if they have the appropriate permissions. There is no further change to the way that a database user is created in Oracle 12.1. You still assign quotas to users, profiles, default permanent, and temporary tablespaces. Note that the tablespaces must exist in the PDBs or you will get an error similar to this one:

```
SYS@CDB$ROOT> alter user c##donexistinnbcd default tablespace users;
alter user c##donexistinnbcd default tablespace users
*
ERROR at line 1:
ORA-65048: error encountered when processing the current DDL statement in
           pluggable database PDB4
ORA-00959: tablespace 'USERS' does not exist
```

■ **Note**   User profiles, auditing, and security considerations are not in the scope of this chapter. You need to ensure that the relevant standards your information security team comes up with are implemented and enforced.

What was true in Oracle before 12.1 is true for the current release: you cannot simply connect to a container without the "create session" privilege. This is true for the container the user was created in, and any additional containers. The only exception is if a user is granted the very powerful "set container" system privilege. Due to the way common users are organized, there cannot be more than one user with the same name in the database. In this respect common users behave exactly like users in a non-CDB.

Common users can be granted the rights to query information about currently attached PDBs, without actually having to connect to them. This is useful for monitoring accounts where a common user is used by the monitoring software. The "alter user" command has been extended for common users, and it is possible to specify a container_data clause. In this new clause you can specify which objects a common user should have access to. The following example walks you through the creation of such a user. The plan is to grant the user access to v$session without the privilege to connect to PDB1 directly.

```
SYS@CDB$ROOT> create user c##perfuser identified by secret ...

User created.
```

Once the user is created, you can grant it the right to view information in v$session for PDB "pdb1". The CDB has three user-PDBs in total.

```
SYS@CDB$ROOT> alter user c##perfuser
  2   set container_data = (CDB$ROOT, PDB1)
  3   for v_$session container = current;

User altered.
```

The "set container_data" clause allows the user "c##perfuser" to query from v$session for information pertaining to "pdb1". Remember you need to be connected to the root, and you need to limit the command to the current container. Let's assume that the "c##perfuser" has a select privilege on v_$session:

```
SYS@CDB$ROOT> grant create session to c##perfuser;

Grant succeeded.

SYS@CDB$ROOT> grant select on v_$session to c##perfuser;

Grant succeeded.
```

With the above modification the common user can query the view v$session for "pdb1" with con_id of 3.

```
C##PERFUSER@CDB$ROOT> select con_id, username from v$session
  2 where type='USER' and username <> 'SYS';

   CON_ID USERNAME
---------- ------------------------------
        1 C##PERFUSER
        3 USER1
```

The "set container_data" clause is available as part of the alteration of users. The above example has been quite specific: the intention was to only grant the privilege to select from v$session for sessions belonging to "pdb1". You can find this stored in the view DBA_CONTAINER_DATA:

```
SYS@CDB$ROOT> select * from dba_container_data
  2   where username = 'C##PERFUSER';

USERNAME             D OWNER OBJECT_NAME     A CONTAINER_NAME
-------------------- - ----- --------------- - --------------------
C##PERFUSER          N SYS   V_$SESSION      N CDB$ROOT
C##PERFUSER          N SYS   V_$SESSION      N PDB1
```

If you would like to grant the same privilege to all current and future PDBs, then you could have used the following command:

```
SYS@CDB$ROOT> alter user c##perfuser set container_data = all
  2  container = current;
```

User altered.

This allows you to view information for all container object data views across all PDBs. This should be used with care for the obvious reasons. To undo the grant to "all" you have to use the following command:

```
SYS@CDB$ROOT> alter user c##perfuser set container_data = default
  2  container = current;
```

In summary, the use of the "container_data" clause might be more secure then granting access to the PDB as a whole. Think of it as it in the same terms as of a Virtual Private Database. Your deployment process however must ensure that the container data clause includes any new PDBs. You can check which privileges have been granted by querying the DBA_CONTAINER_DATA view.

Creating local users

As the name implies, local users are local to a PDB, and a major consolidation feature within Oracle 12.1. In previous releases it was simply not possible to have multiple users in the same database, but now that is perfectly possible, although these users have to be in different PDBs. What you cannot have however is a global user with the same name as the local user. Each of the local users owns objects independently of any other PDB. A local user must be created in the current container: the "container" clause doesn't take the name of a PDB as an argument.

■ **Note**   Remember that you cannot use operating system authentication for local users in a PDB.

Connect to the PDB as a common user with the DBA role such as SYSTEM or SYS and then create the user as you would in a non-CDB. Again, the same clauses apply to create a user in the PDB as there are in the CDB and discussed before. A more complete example for a user creation is shown below:

```
SQL> create user luser identified by luserpwd
  2  default tablespace users
  3  temporary tablespace temp
  4  quota unlimited on users
  5  profile appSpecificProfile
  6  password expire
  7  account unlock
  8  container = current;
```

User created.

Checking the CDB_USERS view in the CDB root you will see that the user belongs to the container it was created in only.

The PDB admin user is a special kind of local user. It is created as part of the clone from the seed database and is automatically granted the PDB_DBA role. As you will see in the next section, the privileges granted to the role differ between PDBs, the PDB_DBA role is a common role.

```
SYS@CDB$ROOT> select common from dba_roles where role = 'PDB_DBA';

COM
---
YES
```

By default, and in the absence of any dedicated grants, the admin user only has a few privileges. If for example you created the PDB as shown in this example:

```
SYS@CDB$ROOT> create pluggable database pdb1
  2 admin user pdbadmin identified by secretPassword;

Pluggable Database created.
```

The role allows the admin user to connect to the database and perform some administration tasks. Its power is limited by default, if you need more you need to make use of the "roles" clause in the PDB creation to ensure that the admin user really deserves the name. Examples of how to make use of the roles-clause have been provided earlier in this chapter. Please refer back to the section "Create a PDB from the seed database" for more information and examples.

Local users cannot by definition create common roles—they'd have to connect to the CDB$ROOT to do so which they simply cannot. However a local user can grant a common role such as connect to another local or common user if the user has the right privileges to do so.

Common roles

Similar to users, roles can be common or local. When you are connected to the root container and create a role, it is automatically assumed that the role is a common role. Even if you tried to create a local role in CDB$ROOT, you cannot: Oracle prevents you from doing so, with exactly the same ORA-65049 error message as if you tried to create a local user. Just like common users names the common role name must begin with C##.

Many Oracle-supplied roles are common roles, which makes it easy to create common users with a common set of privileges. It also allows you to manage roles centrally in one place. When granting a role to a role or user, it is important to pay attention to the container you are granting the role in. For example, you can grant a common role to a user or role in a PDB, and this grant is valid in the container only. Consider this example. First a common user "C##GUSER" is created in the root container, without any privileges.

```
SYS@CDB$ROOT> create user c##guser identified by secret;

User created.
```

Next, the SYS user that was used to create GUSER in the first place switches his session context to a different container: a PDB named PDB1 and grants the (common) connect role to the new account:

```
SYS@CDB$ROOT> alter session set container=pdb1;

Session altered.

SYS@CDB$ROOT> @$HOME/login
SYS@PDB1> grant connect to c##guser;

Grant succeeded.
```

Another grant is executed in PDB "DB2", this time the DBA role is granted to the C##GUSER account. Note that even though C##GUSER is a common user, it currently cannot connect to any other PDB than PDB1 and PDB2. Neither can it connect to CDB$ROOT. Connecting as C##GUSER to PDB1 you can see that the user really only has the connect role granted by checking the session_privs view:

```
select count(1) from session_privs;

  COUNT(1)
----------
         1
```

Likewise, the granted privileges in the PDB2 database match the DBA role, and the view session_privs returns 221 rows.

Local roles

Local roles are best compared to roles in Oracle before 12.1. In fact, they behave exactly as before. This is mainly thanks to the promise Oracle made of backward compatibility. Local roles have a defined namespace within the PDB they are created in. Similar to the local user, multiple roles with the same names can exist in different PDBs.

Playing nicely with others

One of the major concerns of staff responsible for managing production databases are rogue, or "runaway" queries or databases which can have a severely negative impact on the other users on the same hardware. Oracle addresses the "runaway" session and database over the many database releases now, and 12.1 is no exception to the rule.

There are a number of weapons in the DBA's arsenal to prevent resource starvation. Some are based on the operating system, and others are based on the Oracle kernel. Some operating systems, as well as some virtualization solutions allow you to create lightweight operating system images on to which a database home is installed. Most often you would set resource limits on the virtualized server in the form of memory and CPU. Ideally, this technology integrates with the base operating system to allow for better NUMA-awareness. What Oracle kept telling us users over time was that Operating System scheduling has the downside that it's difficult to quantify, for example by looking at Automatic Workload Repository (AWR) reports. Is the high CPU usage now down to the Oracle instance being extremely busy, or is it down to a resource capping operating system? Like Jonathan Lewis famously said about "know your data," the same principle applies in this situation: know your environment.

The use of Oracle provided technology allows us to benefit from the instrumentation of the kernel in form of the wait interface. Before Oracle 12c it has been possible to use the Database Resource Manager (or DBRM) to manage resource consumption within the same database. The Exadata-only I/O Resource Manager furthermore allows the administrator to regulate I/O bandwidth between databases. Instance Caging allows you to limit the CPU usage of a specific database instance. Let's have a look at these features in the next sections.

■ **Note**   I/O Resource Manager will not be covered in this chapter, for more information about the IORM please refer to *Expert Oracle Exadata*, also from Apress.

Overview of Resource Manager in Oracle 12.1

Before launching into the description of the changes to Resource Manager in 12c, a little bit of background knowledge is necessary. On many site visits I noticed that Resource Manager was not implemented besides the standard deployment by Oracle. This does not do the technology justice, but on the other hand the problem is exactly the way I saw it on site: the business users have to analyze their application and define the usage of Resource Manager in their database. On many occasions "the business" however feels uncomfortable making this decision. Hopefully the following paragraphs allow them to make a more informed decision, based on the facts.

What exactly is that Database Resource Manager (DBRM) then? In the simplest form a definition could be as follows: the Database Resource Manager allows the administrator to use a variety of criteria to logically group users or workloads into a resource consumer group. A resource consumer group defines how many resources in a database can be assigned to users in the form of a resource plan directive. Since Oracle 10, users can be moved into a lower resource consumer group when they cross the threshold for their allowed resource usage. Beginning with Oracle 11, they can also be moved back to the initial consumer group once their downgraded calls are completed. This is especially useful in conjunction with connection pooling and web applications where one session can no longer be directly associated with an individual, as it was in the days of dedicated server connections and Oracle Forms applications. In the connection pooling scenario, the application simply grabs a connection out of the pool of available connections, performs its assigned task, and then returns the connection to the pool. Often these operations are very short in nature. Connection pooling offers a huge advantage over the traditional way of creating a dedicated connection each time a user performs an operation against the database, greatly reducing the overhead associated with establishing a dedicated server process. Before the Resource Manager can become active, it is important to define a mapping between a database user and the corresponding resource consumer group. Once that is established—most often based on the service name the user uses to connect—the resource plan can be created and activated. What you just read was the state-of-play before Oracle 12 and the same principles apply for a 12c non-CDB as well.

Thankfully Oracle extended DBRM to take Pluggable Databases into account. The new DBRM in Oracle 12.1 operates on two different levels, in a Container Database:

- On the CDB level

- On an individual user-PDB level

This allows the administrator to define the potential share of workload available to each PDB first before breaking the CPU quantum down to the individual PDB, where the inter-PDB Resource Manager will work its magic.

Resource Manager for the Container Database

The new extension to the Database Resource Manager in Oracle 12.1 allows the administrator to rank the importance of PDBs within a CDB. The new DBRM makes allowance for the fact that some PDBs are more important than others, or simply to ensure that no individual PDB can starve others for performance. DBRM is essential when it comes to enforcing service levels and predictable performance in the consolidated environment. Depending on the service purchased by the database user you could assign it into the Gold/Silver/Bronze class. Resource Manager is slightly different in a CDB compared with a non CDB. DBRM decisions are made on two levels: first on the CDB level, then on the individual PDB level. You will see a little later in the chapter that the syntax reflects this.

Instead of a Resource Plan you create a CDB plan in DBRM for the multi-tenant database. The CDB plan directives of concern for managing the resource consumption between PDBs are

- Shares

- Utilization limits

- Parallel Execution (PX)

Shares are counters—the more you allocate the resources your PDB gets. Utilization limits are percentages and define how many CPU-percent your application is allowed to consume. Utilization limits are not cumulative for the CDB; each PDB can use up to 100%. Shares and utilization limits currently extend to CPU and parallel query.

To demonstrate the new resource manager features, three very small PDBs will be created for a quick Swingbench run, as shown here:

```
SYS@CDB$ROOT> create pluggable database swingbench1
  2  admin user pdbadmin identified by secret
  3  roles=(dba)
  4  default tablespace soe datafile size 100m
  5   autoextend on next 100m maxsize 10g;

Pluggable Database created.

SYS@CDB$ROOT> alter pluggable database swingbench1 open;

Pluggable Database altered.
```

In the next step the Order Entry schema creation wizard is used to populate the SOE schema in the newly created pluggable database. Once the test data has been created, the PDB is cloned to swingbench2 and swingbench3, using the same technique as demonstrated earlier in this chapter.

```
SQL> create pluggable database swingbench2
  2  from swingbench1;
  3  /

Pluggable database created.
```

■ **Note**   In the absence of specific directives, the following defaults will be applied: each PDB will get exactly one share, and can use 100 percent of CPU and parallel query. That is, unless you decide to change the defaults using the update_cdb_default_directive() procedure in the dbms_resource_manager package.

Creating the CDB plan

With three PDBs in place serving the same purpose the administrator needs to make a choice which one he or she wants to prefer. Let's assume for this scenario that database swingbench1 is twice as important as swingbench2 and swingbench3. The shares will be distributed according to the PDB importance, and parallel query will be forbidden (swingbench is a OLTP-style workload). There is no limit for individual PDB's CPU utilization. To implement this resource plan, the following code has been executed in the root:

```
begin
  DBMS_RESOURCE_MANAGER.CREATE_PENDING_AREA;
  DBMS_RESOURCE_MANAGER.CREATE_CDB_PLAN(
    plan => 'SWINGBENCH_PLAN');

  -- set the shares for PDB swingbench1. Prevent
  -- parallel query
```

```
DBMS_RESOURCE_MANAGER.CREATE_CDB_PLAN_DIRECTIVE(
    plan => 'SWINGBENCH_PLAN',
    PLUGGABLE_DATABASE => 'swingbench1',
    SHARES => 4,
    UTILIZATION_LIMIT => null,
    parallel_server_limit => 0);

-- repeat for swingbench2, reduce the number of
-- shares.
DBMS_RESOURCE_MANAGER.CREATE_CDB_PLAN_DIRECTIVE(
    plan => 'SWINGBENCH_PLAN',
    PLUGGABLE_DATABASE => 'swingbench2',
    SHARES => 2,
    UTILIZATION_LIMIT => null,
    parallel_server_limit => 0);

-- and for swingbench3
DBMS_RESOURCE_MANAGER.CREATE_CDB_PLAN_DIRECTIVE(
    plan => 'SWINGBENCH_PLAN',
    PLUGGABLE_DATABASE => 'swingbench3',
    SHARES => 2,
    UTILIZATION_LIMIT => null,
    PARALLEL_SERVER_LIMIT => 0);
end;
/

PL/SQL procedure successfully completed.
```

Validating and enabling the CDB Plan

With the pending area now created and our directives inside, you need to validate the pending area before you can submit it. This is often performed in two steps:

```
SYS@CDB$ROOT> begin
  2   dbms_resource_manager.validate_pending_area();
  3   end;
  4   /

PL/SQL procedure successfully completed.

SYS@CDB$ROOT> begin
  2   dbms_resource_manager.submit_pending_area;
  3   end;
  4   /

PL/SQL procedure successfully completed.
```

That's one CDB resource plan created. A resource plan is enabled by modifying the initialization parameter resource_manager_plan in the root, as shown here:

```
SYS@CDB$ROOT> select value from v$parameter
  2  where name = 'resource_manager_plan';

VALUE
------------------------------------------------------------------------


SYS@CDB$ROOT> alter system set resource_manager_plan = 'swingbench_plan';

System altered.

SYS@CDB$ROOT> select value from v$parameter
  2  where name = 'resource_manager_plan';

VALUE
------------------------------------------------------------------------
swingbench_plan

SYS@CDB$ROOT>
```

If it should turn out that the effect on your system is catastrophic, you could quickly revert back to the old status by executing a corresponding alter system set resource_manager_plan reverting back to the old one.

Be careful with the automatic maintenance windows and scheduler jobs though. Oracle has resource plans associated with maintenance windows that can enable a different resource plan. The default windows' definition can be obtained from the dba_scheduler_windows dictionary view.

If the resource plan has changed because of a maintenance window you can see output similar to this in the v$parameter view:

```
SYS@CDB$ROOT> select value from v$parameter
  2  where name = 'resource_manager_plan';

VALUE
------------------------------------------------------
SCHEDULER[0x4211]:DEFAULT_MAINTENANCE_PLAN
```

You could do the same and create your own windows and associate a resource manager plan with them or use the "force" keyword to prevent a resource plan from being replaced.

Viewing information about the CDB plans

A new class of views introduced in Oracle 12.1 allows you to view information about the CDB plans. The views all fall into the DBA_CDB% class of views. At the time of this writing the following views existed:

- DBA_CDB_RSRC_PLANS
- DBA_CDB_RSRC_PLAN_DIRECTIVES

You can query both to get more information about the plans defined in the CDB. After the creation of the swingbench plan, I had the following contents in the DBA_CDB_RSRC_PLANS view:

```
SYS@CDB$ROOT> select plan,comments,status
  2  from DBA_CDB_RSRC_PLANS;

PLAN                            COMMENTS                        STATUS
------------------------------- ------------------------------- ----------
DEFAULT_CDB_PLAN                Default CDB plan
DEFAULT_MAINTENANCE_PLAN        Default CDB maintenance plan
SWINGBENCH_PLAN
ORA$QOS_CDB_PLAN                QOS CDB plan
ORA$INTERNAL_CDB_PLAN           Internal CDB plan
```

The plan directives used previously are exported in the DBA_CDB_RSRC_PLAN_DIRECTIVES view:

```
SYS@CDB$ROOT> select pluggable_database, shares, utilization_limit,
  2    parallel_server_limit
  3    from DBA_CDB_RSRC_PLAN_DIRECTIVES
  4    where plan = 'SWINGBENCH_PLAN'
  5    order by PLUGGABLE_DATABASE;

PLUGGABLE_DATABASE          SHARES UTILIZATION_LIMIT PARALLEL_SERVER_LIMIT
--------------------------- ------ ----------------- ---------------------
ORA$AUTOTASK                                      90                   100
ORA$DEFAULT_PDB_DIRECTIVE        1               100                   100
SWINGBENCH1                      4                                       0
SWINGBENCH2                      2                                       0
SWINGBENCH3                      2                                       0
```

You will undoubtedly have noticed the ORA$AUTOTASK and default PDB directive in addition to the explicitly created directives. These two—which are not explicitly covered in detail in this chapter—allow you to grant new PDBs a different default weight in the case of the ORA$DEFAULT_PDB_DIRECTIVE. You change it using the update_cdb_default_directive() function in DBMS_RESOURCE_MANAGER. As you already know, Oracle introduced certain automatic maintenance tasks with 11g Release 1. Since these are also under control of the resource manager they adhere to the same limits. If you'd like to change the priority of the automatic maintenance tasks then you can change the ORA$AUTOTASK directive if you like.

Resource Manager for the Pluggable Database

The DBRM within the PDB is similar to how it used to before Oracle 12.1. Again, it allows the administrator to arrange computing resources for resource consumer groups in the form of mapping of users to plan directives, all wrapped up in resource plans. You can easily expand on the above example, which instructed the Oracle kernel to arrange the available resources between PDBs. Once the individual PDB has received its resource quantum, it is up to the DBRM to decide which users should have priority treatment.

There are some restrictions in the current release of the software, which you need to be aware of. The first restriction is related to sub-plans. The plan_or_subplan argument to the create_plan_directive() function in DBMS_RESOURCE_MANGER allows you to specify a subplan instead of a resource consumer group. The result is a nested resource plan that can be difficult to understand or debug. With the current release you cannot assign subplans. The number of consumer groups is restricted to a maximum of eight.

To enable a resource plan for a PDB, there has to be a resource plan in use in the CDB. This is a similar requirement to Instance Caging (see next section), which also requires a Database Resource Plan to be present.

Creating resource plans for the PDB

Resource plans for PDBs are created while connected to the PDB with an administrative user. Depending on how you created your user-PDB, you might have granted the admin user the necessary privileges already. Alternatively connect as a common user to the PDB directly. The following example makes use of the SYSTEM account to create a simple resource plan.

The Database Resource Manager is a lot more powerful and offers a lot more options than I can reasonably present in this chapter. If you want to learn more about it I recommend you read the relevant sections in the Administrator's Guide. This example focuses on running swingbench in the three PDBs created. The focus for this benchmark is to allow the SOE account, who by default owns the order entry schema, to execute his tasks without being preempted. To that effect, a new resource consumer group "swingbench" is created (note the connection to the PDB!)

```
SYSTEM@SWINGBENCH1> begin
  2    dbms_resource_manager.clear_pending_area;
  3    dbms_resource_manager.create_pending_area;
  4    dbms_resource_manager.create_consumer_group(
  5      consumer_group => 'SWINGBENCH_GROUP',
  6      comment => 'used for the execution of order entry benchmark');
  7    dbms_resource_manager.validate_pending_area;
  8    dbms_resource_manager.submit_pending_area;
  9  end;
 10  /

PL/SQL procedure successfully completed.
```

The mandatory SYS_GROUP and OTHER will be part of the resource plan too. Let's create the plan, using the CPU method of ratio for a simple enough plan:

```
SYSTEM@SWINGBENCH1> begin
  2    -- clear the pending area and create a new one
  3    DBMS_RESOURCE_MANAGER.CLEAR_PENDING_AREA;
  4    DBMS_RESOURCE_MANAGER.CREATE_PENDING_AREA;
  5
  6    -- create the plan-specific to PDB swingbench1. This
  7    -- is a simple example, using RATIOs internally.
  8    -- The goal is to have the following ratios:
  9    -- 1:2:3:5 for low group, other groups, swingbench group
 10    -- and sys group.
 11    DBMS_RESOURCE_MANAGER.CREATE_PLAN(
 12      plan => 'SWINGBENCH_PLAN_SWINGBENCH1',
 13      MGMT_MTH => 'RATIO',
 14      comment => 'running swingbench on first PDB');
 15
 16    -- create a plan directive
 17    DBMS_RESOURCE_MANAGER.CREATE_PLAN_DIRECTIVE(
 18      plan=>'SWINGBENCH_PLAN_SWINGBENCH1',
 19      mgmt_p1 => 1,
 20      GROUP_OR_SUBPLAN => 'LOW_GROUP',
 21      comment => 'low group');
 22
```

```
23    DBMS_RESOURCE_MANAGER.CREATE_PLAN_DIRECTIVE (
24      plan=>'SWINGBENCH_PLAN_SWINGBENCH1',
25      MGMT_P1 => 2,
26      GROUP_OR_SUBPLAN => 'OTHER_GROUPS',
27      comment => 'others group');
28
29    DBMS_RESOURCE_MANAGER.CREATE_PLAN_DIRECTIVE(
30      plan=>'SWINGBENCH_PLAN_SWINGBENCH1',
31      MGMT_P1 => 3,
32      GROUP_OR_SUBPLAN => 'SWINGBENCH_GROUP',
33      comment => 'swingbench group');
34
35    DBMS_RESOURCE_MANAGER.CREATE_PLAN_DIRECTIVE(
36      plan=>'SWINGBENCH_PLAN_SWINGBENCH1',
37      MGMT_P1 => 5,
38      GROUP_OR_SUBPLAN => 'SYS_GROUP',
39      comment => 'sys group');
40
41    DBMS_RESOURCE_MANAGER.SET_CONSUMER_GROUP_MAPPING(
42      attribute => DBMS_RESOURCE_MANAGER.ORACLE_USER,
43      value => 'SOE',
44      CONSUMER_GROUP => 'SWINGBENCH_GROUP');
45  end;
46  /

PL/SQL procedure successfully completed.

SYSTEM@SWINGBENCH1>
```

The code clears and creates a pending area, and then starts off by creating the new resource plan. The following statements assign plan directives to the plan, which indicate the ratio of CPU to be used.

Validating and enabling the PDB resource plan

With the pending area firmly established, you need to validate it for logical errors in the plan description. The procedure is the same as for the CDB plan, namely a call to validate_pending_area():

```
SYSTEM@SWINGBENCH1> begin
  2   dbms_resource_manager.validate_pending_area;
  3   end;
  4   /

PL/SQL procedure successfully completed.
```

If that call doesn't return any errors, you can submit the pending area:

```
SYSTEM@SWINGBENCH1> begin
  2   dbms_resource_manager.submit_pending_area;
  3   end;
  4   /

PL/SQL procedure successfully completed.
```

Great! With the resource plan in place, you can enable it as well.

```
SYSTEM@SWINGBENCH1> alter system set
  2  resource_manager_plan = 'swingbench_plan_swingbench1';

System altered.

SYSTEM@SWINGBENCH1> show parameter resource_manager_plan

NAME                                 TYPE        VALUE               .
------------------------------------ ----------- --------------------------------
resource_manager_plan                string      SWINGBENCH_PLAN_SWINGBENCH1
```

You can view the active resource managers and their settings using the V$RSRC_PLAN dictionary view.

```
SYS@CDB$ROOT> SELECT PDB.name PDB_NAME,
  2     PLN.name PLAN_NAME,
  3     PLN.IS_TOP_PLAN,
  4     PLN.CON_ID,
  5     PLN.PARALLEL_EXECUTION_MANAGED
  6  FROM V$RSRC_PLAN PLN,
  7     V$PDBS PDB
  8  WHERE pln.con_id = pdb.con_id
  9  /
```

PDB_NAME	PLAN_NAME	IS_TO	CON_ID	PARALLEL
PDB$SEED	INTERNAL_PLAN	TRUE	2	FULL
SWINGBENCH1	**SWINGBENCH_PLAN_SWINGBENCH1**	TRUE	5	FULL
SWINGBENCH2	**SWINGBENCH_PLAN_SWINGBENCH2**	TRUE	6	FULL
SWINGBENCH3	**SWINGBENCH_PLAN_SWINGBENCH3**	TRUE	7	FULL

In addition to the dynamic V$-views you will be notified in the alert.log if the plan changes:

```
Sat Sep 28 20:49:56 2013
Setting Resource Manager plan swingbench_plan_swingbench1 at pdb SWINGBENCH1
(5) via parameter
ALTER SYSTEM SET resource_manager_plan='swingbench_plan_swingbench1' SCOPE=BOTH;
```

Continuing with the implementation of the user-PDB plan you should be able to cap resource usage for your PDBs, avoiding conflict with your neighboring databases.

One final step remains: when the user SOE connects to the PDB, then it must be assigned to the appropriate consumer group. There are a number of ways to achieve this goal, the easiest is to map the user to the resource consumer group as shown here:

```
SYSTEM@SWINGBENCH1> begin
  2  dbms_resource_manager.create_pending_area;
  3  dbms_resource_manager.set_consumer_group_mapping(
  4    attribute => DBMS_RESOURCE_MANAGER.ORACLE_USER,
  5    value => 'SOE',
  6    consumer_group => 'SWINGBENCH_GROUP');
```

```
 7   dbms_resource_manager.validate_pending_area;
 8   dbms_resource_manager.submit_pending_area;
 9   end;
10   /
```

PL/SQL procedure successfully completed.

The success of this operation can be seen in the v$session.resource_consumer_group field and in dba_users.initial_rsrc_consumer_group. If for some reason you don't see the correct consumer group in these, then you may need to grant the SOE user the privilege to switch consumer groups, as shown in this example:

```
begin
  DBMS_RESOURCE_MANAGER.CLEAR_PENDING_AREA;
  DBMS_RESOURCE_MANAGER.CREATE_PENDING_AREA;

  -- grant the SOE user the privs to switch his consumer group
  DBMS_RESOURCE_MANAGER_PRIVS.GRANT_SWITCH_CONSUMER_GROUP (
    GRANTEE_NAME => 'SOE',
    CONSUMER_GROUP => 'SWINGBENCH_GROUP',
    GRANT_OPTION => FALSE);

  DBMS_RESOURCE_MANAGER.VALIDATE_PENDING_AREA;
  DBMS_RESOURCE_MANAGER.SUBMIT_PENDING_AREA;
END;
/
```

PL/SQL procedure successfully completed.

Testing the Resource Plan

With all the hard work done it is about time to test and see if the resource manager actually provides a benefit. Unfortunately there was no suitable load generator available to fully exploit the power of the lab server so a slightly different method had to be chosen to saturate the CPU. The lab server has 24 cores and 32 GB RAM available to itself, therefore the load generated has to be substantial. A little script, to be executed on the database server itself helps to achieve this goal:

```
$ cat burn.sh
#!/bin/bash

# check if all parameters have been passed
if [[ -z "$1" || -z "$2" ]] ; then
        echo "usage burn.sh <pdb> <num_sessions>"
        exit 99
else
        PDB=$1
        SESSIONS=$2
fi
```

```
# ramp up some workload
i=1
for i in $(seq 1 $SESSIONS) ; do
        ( sqlplus soe/soe\@localhost/${PDB} @burn > /dev/null 2>&1 ) &
done

# get the start time
STARTTIME=$SECONDS

# wait for the background processes to finish
wait

# calculate how long it took
((DURATION=$SECONDS-$STARTTIME))

# and tell us!
echo "elapsed time in seconds on ${PDB}: ${DURATION}"
```

All it really does is to launch an onslaught of calculations of the square root of an integer:

```
declare
        v number;
begin
        for i in 1..1000000000 loop
                v := sqrt(v);
        end loop;
end;
/
```

Remember that our resource plan was configured for CPU shares! The I/O portion can safely be ignored. You can see the system was suitably under pressure as this output from "top" shows:

```
top - 16:27:31 up 26 min,  7 users,  load average: 26.54, 11.49, 5.69
Tasks: 452 total,  25 running, 427 sleeping,  0 stopped,  0 zombie
Cpu0  : 95.7%us,  0.0%sy,  0.0%ni,  4.3%id,  0.0%wa,  0.0%hi,  0.0%si,  0.0%st
Cpu1  : 94.7%us,  0.0%sy,  0.0%ni,  5.3%id,  0.0%wa,  0.0%hi,  0.0%si,  0.0%st
Cpu2  : 93.7%us,  0.0%sy,  0.0%ni,  6.3%id,  0.0%wa,  0.0%hi,  0.0%si,  0.0%st
[...]
Cpu22 : 95.4%us,  0.0%sy,  0.0%ni,  4.6%id,  0.0%wa,  0.0%hi,  0.0%si,  0.0%st
Cpu23 : 87.4%us,  0.0%sy,  0.0%ni, 12.6%id,  0.0%wa,  0.0%hi,  0.0%si,  0.0%st
Mem:   32994920k total, 26970360k used,  6024560k free,    24028k buffers
Swap:    524284k total,         0k used,   524284k free,   185932k cached
```

Now to answer the question about resource manager: yes it works. Starting three parallel sessions on the database server resulted in these execution times:

- Elapsed time in seconds on swingbench1: 188

- Elapsed time in seconds on swingbench2: 265

- Elapsed time in seconds on swingbench3: 266

Instance Caging

Instance caging has been introduced with Oracle 11g Release 2. It addresses a scenario where multiple databases run on the same physical hardware, and might starve each other out of CPU resources. After you have seen that Database Resource Manager is great to work within the same database (CDB or non-CDB), it does not allow you to manage inter-database resources. Instance Caging to the rescue: in a nutshell, instance caging allows administrators to limit the number of CPUs available to the database instance by setting the initialization parameter cpu_count. In addition, a resource manager plan needs to be active for this feature to work in cases where resource usage is further defined. As you saw in the previous section using a resource plan is very useful anyway, and not at all a high price to pay for the instance caging feature.

To enable instance caging first ensure there is an active resource plan. You could for example query the V$RSRC_PLAN view to find out which resource plan is in use, or alternatively by checking the V$PARAMETER view. When you have made sure that there is a resource manager plan in place, all you need to do is to set the cpu_count parameter. This parameter is dynamic and can easily be changed while the database is up and running. Since cpu_count is the basis for many other derived parameters one should make adjustments carefully. It is best not to change the parameter too drastically. You can either over- or undersubscribe your database server. Oversubscribing in this context means that the sum of all database instances' cpu_count exceeds the value of available CPUs as seen by the operating system. Alternatively you could divide the number of available CPUs and allocate them to the individual databases.

Summary

Pluggable Databases are certainly the most exciting feature of Oracle 12.1. Designers of consolidation platforms have ample use cases to directly embrace the new technology. The ability to create a new namespace in the form of the Pluggable Database allows you to maintain multiple users with the same name in the same Container Database. The same applies for roles of course, and the user concept allows you to have common users with fine-grained access privileges, without having to be granted a "create session" privilege. This should allow for a smooth migration of most enterprise monitoring software.

The many ways to create Pluggable Databases give the architects and designers a lot of flexibility with how they want to provision the golden copy of the Pluggable Database. It can either be NFS exported, ready for cloning. The source file name conversion clause makes it possible.

Another advantage that should not go unmentioned (again) is the fact that the unplug/plug operation can allow the DBAs to upgrade databases very quickly. And even if the databases stay in place, you only patch one database for hundreds potentially. Now that the foundation for the Pluggable Databases has been laid there is more to come. The following chapters will deal with protecting your database from disaster using Data Guard. But the local database has to be protected as well. Even though not really popular, database backups have to be performed regularly. And not only that, you should also regularly restore a random backup to ensure the backups are not corrupted, and can be restored in the worst case. Finally, there will be a chapter dealing with the migration to Oracle 12.1.

CHAPTER 8

■ ■ ■

Monitoring the Hosting Platform

Another very important aspect in the management of the consolidated platform solutions is monitoring. For this purpose many companies have developed their own home-grown monitoring solutions, partly based on existing frameworks, partially written on their own. Very often these solutions have been maintained over a long period of time and have constantly evolved. Although such solutions may work very well for the specific systems for which they were written, there are many potential problems associated with an in-house developed monitoring solution. Consider for example that the main server platform was AIX, with a little Solaris in the mix as it was common for many enterprises. In such environments korn-shell scripts often bore the brunt of the work. The question to ask is: how flexible are your scripts when you change your hardware platform? Has everything been coded so that it is operating system independent? If your new platform is Linux, then there might not be a huge need to rewrite, but if your monitoring solution has to support an altogether different platform—Windows, for example—then you cannot readily make use of any shell scripting. Something more flexible is needed.

Another item to consider is support: who is going to support your home-grown scripts if there is a problem with monitoring? In today's environments, where every DBA looks after a huge number of databases, you cannot readily assume that the primary DBA has intimate knowledge of the system he works on! Being notified by the business users about a problem that the monitoring software has failed to recognize is a major embarrassment at best. But if this happens you need the right people to look into the problem.

Other challenges with home-grown solutions are notification, escalation, and message flood control. Not all systems are equally important, and as an IT department you will have different service-level agreements for development systems compared to live production environments. Nevertheless, if a development system reports a severe problem it still needs fixing. Gentle escalation is important. Flood control is equally important: your monitoring solution should not page you every 5 minutes with the same error. After the page has gone out, there should be an easy way to acknowledge that you have received the alert but have not resolved it yet. One system that is comparatively easy to deploy is Oracle Enterprise Manager 12c Cloud Control, which is the subject of this chapter.

■ **Note**   There is a lot more to Enterprise Manager 12c than it is possible to cover here. Where applicable in this chapter, you will find references to the Oracle documentation set that lead you to even more detail on key topics.

Oracle Enterprise Manager

Oracle Enterprise Manager is designed as a multi-tier application, consisting of agents actively monitoring targets on hosts, a Management Service (OMS) to receive that information and a repository database to persist data. The Enterprise Manager is written entirely using Oracle products. The user interface uses the Java-based Application Development Framework (ADF), which you also know from the My Oracle Support website. The runtime environment is provided by Oracle's WebLogic application server. The management agent is also from Oracle. An advanced deployment of Enterprise Manager is shown in Figure 8-1.

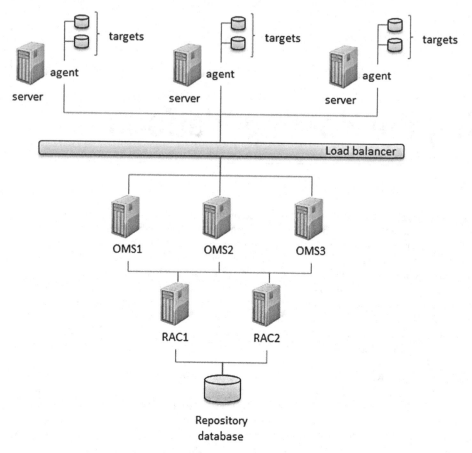

Figure 8-1. *The multi-tier Enterprise Manager architecture*

Starting from the top you see the managed targets: the database servers and the databases. Each monitored server shown in Figure 8-1 has a local agent installed, which in turn communicates with a phalanx of Oracle Management Servers (OMS) via a load balancer. The load balancer is a convenient way to hide an arbitrary number of Management Servers behind a common IP address. In the basic configuration a load balancer will distribute incoming requests in a DNS round-robin fashion to the management hosts. Ideally the load balancer is capable of taking load metrics of the OMSs into account and distributes load to the least loaded server. In a more advanced setup you could use a number of OMSs for agent uploads only while the remaining ones serve users. In addition to the agents that upload their performance metrics to the Management Service, users also connect to it to display the graphical user interface shown in Figure 8-2.

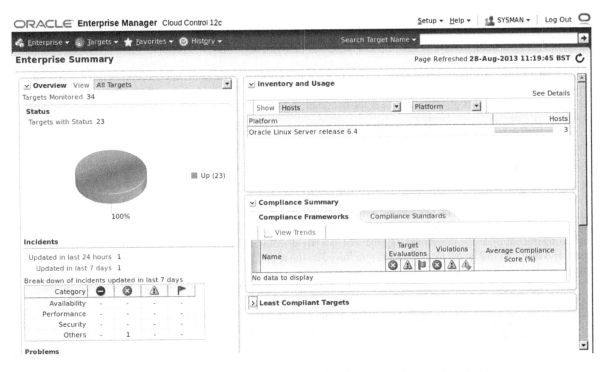

Figure 8-2. *The summary page for Oracle Enterprise Manager Cloud Control after a fresh installation*

The final piece of the architecture is the repository database, which is used to store the metric and performance information as well as the metadata for the Management Service.

Extending Functionality via Plugins

One of the design goals of Oracle Enterprise Manager 12c Cloud Control (the current release at the time of this writing) is to allow Oracle's developers to be more flexible. The previously used framework was quite rigid and made it difficult to change code. It was equally difficult for Oracle to deploy new functionality. The new approach was to make the whole architecture a lot more flexible. In addition to easier development, the new architecture also allows the administrator to deploy a smaller subset of functionality. Instead of deploying all functionality during the installation, the new release starts with a specific number of plugins. Any further functionality or upgrades to an existing plugin can be downloaded and implemented later.

Enterprise Manager relies a lot more on communication with My Oracle Support, and both are tightly integrated. The Management Service will periodically poll Oracle's websites to see if there is new or updated functionality available. This function is called Self Update and will be discussed later in this chapter in greater detail. When new functionality is available the administrator can download it to the so-called software library and apply it during a change window. Plugins are not limited to the Management Service, but also exist for targets and agents. New functionality can equally be added to the agents, allowing for a smaller initial storage footprint.

The Role of the Agent

The Oracle agent is the part of the infrastructure responsible for gathering information about the monitored targets. The agent can be installed via the Enterprise Manager console, or alternatively via the command line. Oracle supplies a response-file based silent installation as well as an RPM for the Linux platform. The latter however proves more trouble than it is worth due to the way it is implemented. When verifying the contents of the RPM you get lots of missing files, which is not a defect but rather how that particular RPM is designed.

The agent has its own package and library prerequisites, which are usually met already when installing it on an Oracle database server. The agent image will require 1 GB free hard disk space. Unlike Oracle Enterprise Manager 11.1 and earlier, you can no longer download the agent from Oracle's website. The agent has become an integral part of Enterprise Manager and as such is internally managed via a new OEM 12c feature named "Self-Update". You always get the agent for your OMS platform as part of the installation. Management agents for other platforms need to be downloaded from My Oracle Support.

■ **Note** You can find more information about how to configure and use Self-Update later in this chapter.

The agent has been specifically created with a less-than-optimal network connectivity to the Management Service in mind. It is able to tolerate network disconnects and poorly performing infrastructure without severely impacting the Enterprise Management deployment as a whole. Although an unreliable communication between an agent and the OMS will be felt for the targets monitored by the agent, it should not cause an effect that can be felt system-wide.

High latencies and disconnects between the repository and Management Service however are poison to the deployment of Enterprise Manager. The impact of poor network quality between the Management Host and the repository database is severe and likely to be felt by every user connecting to the console.

The Oracle Management Service

The Oracle Management Service or OMS is at the heart of the Enterprise Manager infrastructure. Agents upload their metric information to the OMS, and users connect to the Enterprise Manager console. Information, current and historic, is available from the repository database at the application's backend. At its heart, the OMS is a Java application using WebLogic as the execution environment. As such there are considerations about the amount of memory and the number of CPU cycles available for users. Oracle documentation contains a lot of information on the sizing of the OMS, and there is also a section about sizing considerations in the chapter you are reading. Although it tries to list the main points, it cannot replace the official documentation so have a look at that as well.

You are not limited to having only one OMS, Enterprise Manager is built to scale out horizontally by adding more OMSs to the configuration. For larger deployments it might be beneficial to add an optional load balancer into the infrastructure (while at the same time not forgetting to take high availability precautions for the database). Instead of communicating directly with an individual OMS the agents will communicate with the load balancer's IP address. Since the load balancer is a perfect single point of failure, you should ensure with the network department that there is resilience built into the design there too!

A lot of important functionality is available from the Cloud Control console, such as notifications and incident management which are going to be covered later in the chapter.

The Enterprise Manager Repository

The repository database is the place where all the information gathered by agents throughout the estate is stored. Not every database release is certified to act as a management repository. You should check the certification matrix on My Oracle Support first. As a rule of thumb, if your release is still in premium support and Patch Set Updates are produced, then there is a high probability that your database is indeed certified. You may have to wait a little bit though for support of Oracle 12c as a repository database. Unlike some previous versions, the Oracle Universal Installer does not create a database for you, and there is no option to install everything on the same host as in Enterprise Manager 10g. Instead, you have to point the installer to an existing database.

Depending on the number of targets and the amount of history you want to keep you have to set aside quite a bit of storage for the repository. The official Oracle documentation has dedicated a chapter to the maintenance of the repository. You should ensure that the network communication between the repository and the OMS is of low-latency and high-bandwidth quality.

Who Should Look After Enterprise Manager?

Very often the Oracle support team is given the honor of looking after Oracle Enterprise Manager. After all, OEM is an Oracle product so it should naturally fall into the realm of the database administrator, right? This attitude is found in many environments, but it can be counter-productive to a successful deployment. Anyone looking after Enterprise Manager needs knowledge about the architecture, the processes such as the data upload from the agents, maintenance of the repository database and many more. Furthermore debugging problems with the user-visible console require knowledge about WebLogic and ultimately how Java Enterprise Applications are deployed.

Oracle has successfully hidden a lot of the configuration details of the WebLogic applications from the user, but every now and then you still need to know where a specific log-file resides to troubleshoot a problem. For this reason you should invest in the people that look after Enterprise Manager. They could have a DBA background, but a Middleware administrator is likely even better suited. As with any complex multi-tier application procedures need to be developed to define what to do when a problem arises, how to escalate a problem to third line support or—in the worst case—how to fail over to the disaster recovery site.

Sizing Considerations

An installation of Oracle Enterprise Manager has to be well thought through, since it is potentially such an important part of the infrastructure! The sizing exercise for the OEM infrastructure is a crucial part of the deployment process. The following should be taken into account:

- Number of managed targets
- Latency and bandwidth of the network infrastructure leading to the load balancer/Management Service
- Expected number of concurrent connections to the console
- Expected or required availability of the service

The following sections in this chapter assume that repository database and management hosts are physically separate machines.

Considerations for the Oracle Management Service

Elements such as the number of targets, number of agents, and number of concurrent sessions are important and directly influence the hardware purchase requests for the OMS. You need to worry less about the target hosts managed by the agents; you'd hope that they have been sized properly! To be fair they are independent pieces of the overall infrastructure. Special emphasis needs to be placed on memory and CPU power of the Management Services hosts. The Oracle documentation is a bit vague, and you should certainly do your own investigations into what you need. Luckily current CPUs are formidable and offer a lot of processing power per host. Oracle defined three different types of configuration: small, medium, and large.

- *Small configuration*: A small configuration according to Oracle uses no load balancer, a single Management Host, monitors less than 1000 targets from 100 agents and supports a maximum of 10 concurrent sessions. It is quite unlikely that you need to be concerned with such a small environment, even if you wanted to have one per data center.

- *Medium configuration*: This is a bit more realistic featuring 2 Management Hosts, between 1000 and 10,000 targets monitored by a 100 to a maximum of 1000 agents. There are an expected 10–25 concurrent user sessions.

- *Large configuration*: The term "large configuration" is used for anything more than the medium configuration, but does not exceed 50 concurrent users.

Depending on the configuration type you need different hardware. Since the OMS is written mainly in Java and executed in a WebLogic environment, it makes sense to be generous with RAM. The recommendations made by Oracle in the installation guide are probably too conservative. The suggestions are to use 8GB, 12GB, and 20GB RAM for small, medium, and large configurations respectively. The rule of thumb here is that RAM can only be replaced with more RAM! If you can spare the expense to upgrade the host to more than that by all means do it. Remember from the hardware chapter that it is easily possible to add more than half a TB of RAM into a dual-socket Xeon E5 system.

Related to the overall amount of memory available to the system you should consider increasing the amount of memory available to the WebLogic process. Medium-sized deployments should set the heap size of the Java processes on the OMS to 4 GB. Oracle recommends up to 8 GB heap size for large deployments.

Hard disk space is another consideration to be made. If you are planning to patch databases or otherwise download and stage software via the Self-Update functionality, you need to reserve space for the software library. In environments where you are using more than one OMS, the software library has to be in a sharable location. For UNIX that most often means NFS.

Considerations for the Repository Database

The management repository is the other main part of the infrastructure. Depending on the level of availability expected from the Enterprise Manager deployment, the repository database needs to be protected from instance failures. Please refer back to Chapter 4 for more information about possible ways to protect the database. The Maximum-Availability-Architecture (MAA) documents suggest the use of the Real Applications Cluster option for the management repository.

The suggestions for the repository database servers are again conservative by today's industry standards. Using the same classes of configuration as described in the previous section, the recommendation for CPU cores is to use 2/4/8 for small/medium/large configurations and 6/8/16 GB RAM. These can only be the bare minimum; smooth operations of a sizable deployment realistically require more capacity. Luckily even a two-socket x86-64 can support up to 16 cores with Intel or 32 modules with the current AMD processors.

The repository database stores the information sent by the management agents in three tablespaces created during the installation:

- MGMT_ECM_DEPOT_TS

- MGMT_TABLESPACE

- MGMT_AD4J_TS

Depending on how aggressively you decide to purge history, you need to take a considerable amount of space into account for these tablespaces. The minimum recommended space for a large configuration is approximately 400 GB.

Part of the planning for the repository database should be a check of the certification matrix. Not every database release is certified for use as a repository database! Enterprise Manager makes some assumptions about the database initialization parameters in addition to the above-mentioned tablespaces. Recommended initialization parameters and other important information with regards to the repository database are listed in Chapter 11 "Sizing Your Enterprise Manager Deployment" of the "Cloud Control Advanced Installation and Configuration Guide" for Enterprise Manager 12c Release 2.

As you can see from the previous sections it is vital to get the sizing of the hardware for the OMS servers and repository database right. Also don't forget that you might need the same infrastructure in a disaster recovery environment. If OEM really becomes the consolidated monitoring platform then you simply cannot afford if the lights go out and you are not proactively informed about problems with your managed targets. Therefore, before rolling out such a crucial piece of infrastructure the golden rule of IT applies again: test it under production conditions before you rely on it!

More detailed information about sizing considerations than we could cram into this section can be found in the Oracle® Enterprise Manager Cloud Control Advanced Installation and Configuration Guide, Chapter 11: "Sizing Your Enterprise Manager Deployment".

Installing Cloud Control

Oracle Enterprise Manager is installed in two steps. The first step involves the creation of the repository database. Depending on the number of targets and the amount of history to preserve you should allocate sufficient disk space for the management data. If you are planning a large number of targets to be monitored, you should also ensure that the management repository database is hosted on sufficiently powerful hardware.

If resilience to database instance failure is a strict requirement you should consider the Real Application Clusters option for the repository database. Organizations experimenting with the consolidation of monitoring solutions should put special emphasis on the availability of the repository. Consider a high-availability solution for the database. If there are multiple essentially stateless OMSs for resilience, but only a single instance Oracle database you might still be in trouble if that goes down! Losing the repository database means losing availability of the directly attached OMSs, resulting in the undesirable situation of flying blindly. One of the biggest threats to successful database management is not being able to receive alerts proactively.

Choosing the Operating System for the Management Host

The Management host and repository database do not need to have the same operating system, although you cannot really make a mistake using x86-64 Linux. At the time of writing Linux was the development platform for Enterprise Manager, and problem fixing is expected to be quickest and most efficient on the Linux platform. Additionally, as laid out in the chapter about hardware, the performance of the current x86 processors is more than adequate to display the Enterprise Manager console. The Enterprise Manager OMS is certified for Oracle Linux 5 update 2 and later. The OMS is also certified on Oracle Linux 6 after the application of a mandatory patch.

■ **Note** Due to the constraints in regards to addressing RAM you should not use a 32-bit operating system for the management host! This recommendation should actually be extended in most situations to: "you should not use 32-bit operating systems for production."

As with any planned deployment of Oracle products on a specific combination of hardware and software you should check the certification matrix first. Enter the following after logging into My Oracle Support's "Certifications" tab:

- "Enterprise Manager Base Platform - OMS" in the Product field.

- "12.1.0.x.0" as the Release.

- Your target platform in the Platform field.

Ensure you read the additional certification information for your platform by clicking on the link named after your platform to find out more about mandatory patches for the OMS, or the operating system or both. In the remaining chapter Linux x86-64 will be used for the management host and repository database server. For this chapter it is assumed that a suitable and certified database is available for the installation of the repository. Refer back to the section "Sizing considerations" for more information about the repository database.

Whichever operating system you choose, please ensure that you download the software for your platform, and unzip it in a suitable location. This chapter assumes that /mnt has been used to mount the installation media via NFS.

Preparing the Linux Operating System

As with the database, the operating system must be prepared for the installation of the Management Service. Before you begin to be more serious about the installation process you should consider which user account will own the OMS installation. In most situations this will be the Oracle account, which is created similar to a database installation. First, create the inventory group-oinstall, then the oracle account if they have not already been created by the build process. Please consult your standards document to check if there are fixed numeric IDs for these groups, especially if you are using directory services. For any Oracle deployment it is very desirable to use the same user and group IDs throughout the enterprise. Alternatively you could simply use the RDBMS preinstall RPM which will always create the oracle user and groups in the same way.

```
[root@oem12oms1 ~]# groupadd oinstall
[root@oem12oms1 ~]# useradd -g oinstall -G oinstall oracle
[root@oem12oms1 ~]# passwd oracle
```

Note that groups dba and oper are not needed for the installation of a Management Service. In the next step you should review the use of SELinux and iptables for host-based firewalls. Configuration of these is outside the scope of this section, for the sake of simplicity it is assumed that the firewalls are deactivated, and SELinux is in permissive mode. A production system should obviously be better protected, and you have to check with the security team about the correct settings!

You can either go through the list of prerequisites manually or use the prerequisite checker which is part of the installation source. In order to run the prerequisite check, change to the location where you unzipped the installation media. The prerequisite checker resides in the ./install directory, and has to be invoked as in this example:

```
[oracle@oem12oms1 stage]$ ./install/runInstaller -prereqchecker \
> PREREQ_CONFIG_LOCATION=../stage/prereq \
> -entryPoint oracle.sysman.top.em_noseed_Core -prereqLogLoc /tmp  -silent

Starting Oracle Prerequisite Checker...
[...]
Oracle Prerequisite Checker version Version 11.1.0.9.0 Production
Copyright (C) 1999, 2012, Oracle. All rights reserved.

Starting execution of Prerequisites...
Total No of checks: 11

Performing check for CertifiedVersions
S_CHECK_CERTIFIED_VERSIONS
Expected result: One of enterprise-5.6,enterprise-6.2,enterprise-6.0,redhat-6.2,
redhat-6.0,redhat-5.6,enterprise-5.5,enterprise-5.4,enterprise-5.3,enterprise-5.2,
enterprise-5.1,enterprise-5,asianux-3,redhat-5.5,redhat-5.4,redhat-5.3,redhat-5.3,
redhat-5.2,redhat-5.1,redhat-5,SuSE-11,SuSE-10
Actual Result: enterprise-5.6
Check complete. The overall result of this check is: Passed
```

```
Check complete: Passed
========================================================
Performing check for Packages
S_CHECK_PACKAGES
Checking for make-3.81; found make-1:3.81-3.el5-x86_64. Passed
Checking for binutils-2.17.50.0.6; found binutils-2.17.50.0.6-20.el5-x86_64.    Passed
Checking for gcc-4.1.1; found gcc-4.1.2-52.el5-x86_64.  Passed
Checking for libaio-0.3.106; found libaio-0.3.106-5-x86_64.    Passed
Checking for glibc-common-2.3.4; found glibc-common-2.5-81-x86_64.      Passed
Checking for libstdc++-4.1.1; found libstdc++-4.1.2-52.el5-x86_64.      Passed
Checking for setarch-1.6; found setarch-2.0-1.1-x86_64. Passed
Checking for sysstat-5.0.5; found sysstat-7.0.2-11.el5-x86_64.  Passed
Checking for rng-utils-2.0; found rng-utils-1:2.0-5.el5-x86_64. Passed
Checking for glibc-devel-2.5-49-i386; found glibc-devel-2.5-81-i386.    Passed
Checking for glibc-devel-2.5-49-x86_64; found glibc-devel-2.5-81-x86_64.      Passed
Check complete. The overall result of this check is: Passed

[...]

Check complete: Passed
========================================================
PrereqChecks complete
```

If the prerequisite checker returns no failures no further action has to be taken. If the checker does return failures, review which check has failed and correct the problem. If you are planning a graphical installation for the Management Host you should add the necessary packages and their dependencies in order to install via the Virtual Networking Protocol (VNC). You are of course free to use whichever other means to display Oracle Universal Installer, the author has good experience with VNC. Please refer back to Chapters 5 and 6 in this book for more information about VNC and preparations for a graphical installation of the software as well as package management via yum. The reference for packages required for every Linux distribution and release can be found in Chapter 3, "Enterprise Manager Cloud Control Basic Installation Guide". Unlike the database, which requires many modifications of the kernel parameters, only one parameter needs to be changed for the OMS installation: shmmax. Edit /etc/sysctl.conf with your favorite text editor and ensure that the shmmax is set to 4294967295. This unusual value is 1 bit less than 4 GB.

The only change necessary to the per user limits is to increase the maximum number of open files from 1024 to 4096 for the OMS owner in /etc/security/limits.conf:

```
oracle       soft    nofile        4096
oracle       hard    nofile        4096
```

These changes only take effect the next time you log in. If you had a VNC Server session active, you need to kill it and create a new one.

You should have at least 10GB of disk space available for the installation of the OMS on the local host, preferably more. This is purely for the installation of the software required to run the OMS, not the software library. If you can, you should allocate more space for the installation, ideally on a logical volume and an online-resizable file system to be able to deal with space shortages.

Installing Enterprise Manager

Before starting the installation you should ensure that communication between the repository database and the management host is possible. Review any potential firewall rules and make any necessary changes to the configuration in a change window before the OEM installation. If you decided to use VNC for the installation, start a vncserver process as oracle on the Management Host. Connect to your virtual display from your desktop machine to begin the installation.

In this section an advanced OMS installation will be performed. At the end of the installation you will end up with an OMS and an agent on the same host plus a repository schema in a database. Begin the installation by changing to the location where you unzipped the binaries and execute the runInstaller command as usual. After a little while the splash screen appears followed by the first configuration screen shown in Figure 8-3.

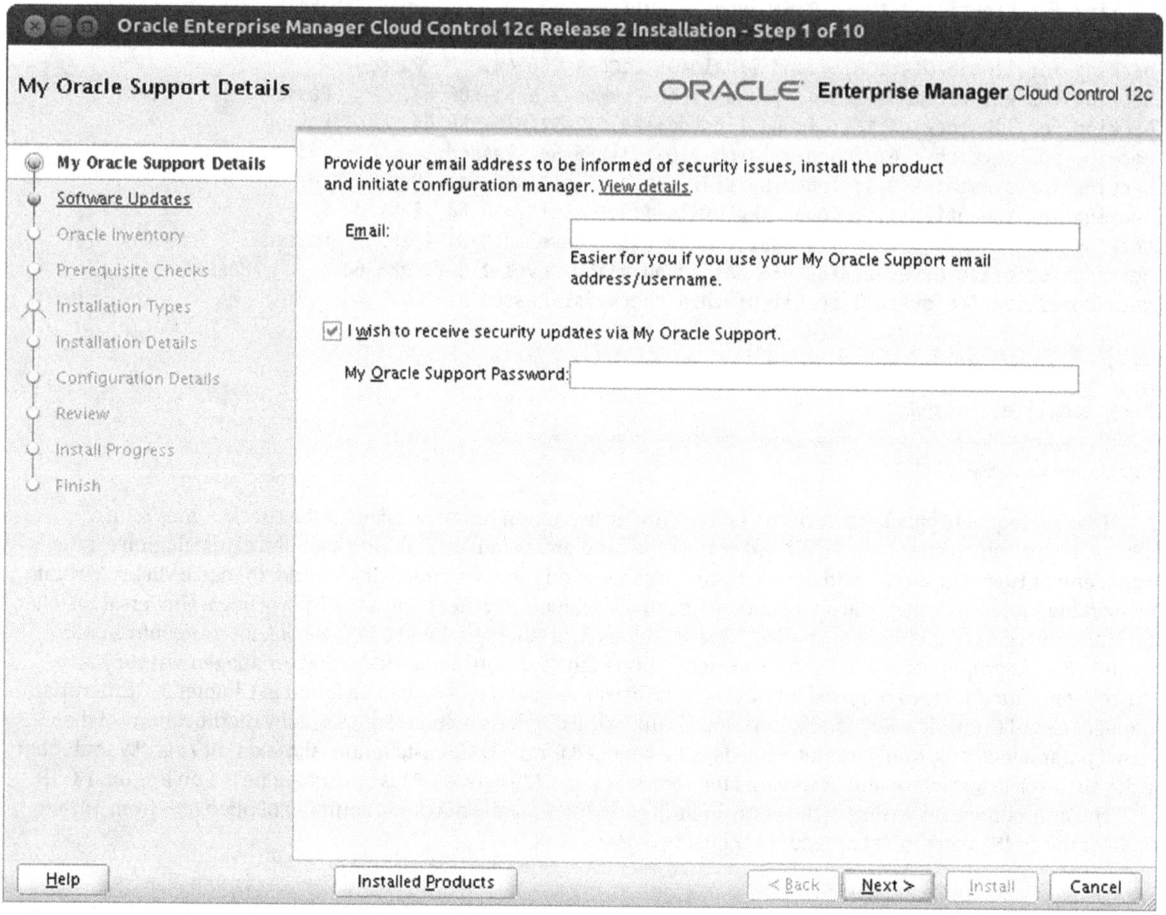

Figure 8-3. *Entering My Oracle Support details*

As with the Oracle database, you have the option to be informed via email of issues with the product. Enter whatever you feel appropriate and click on the "Next" button. You'll be taken to Step 2 in Figure 8-4.

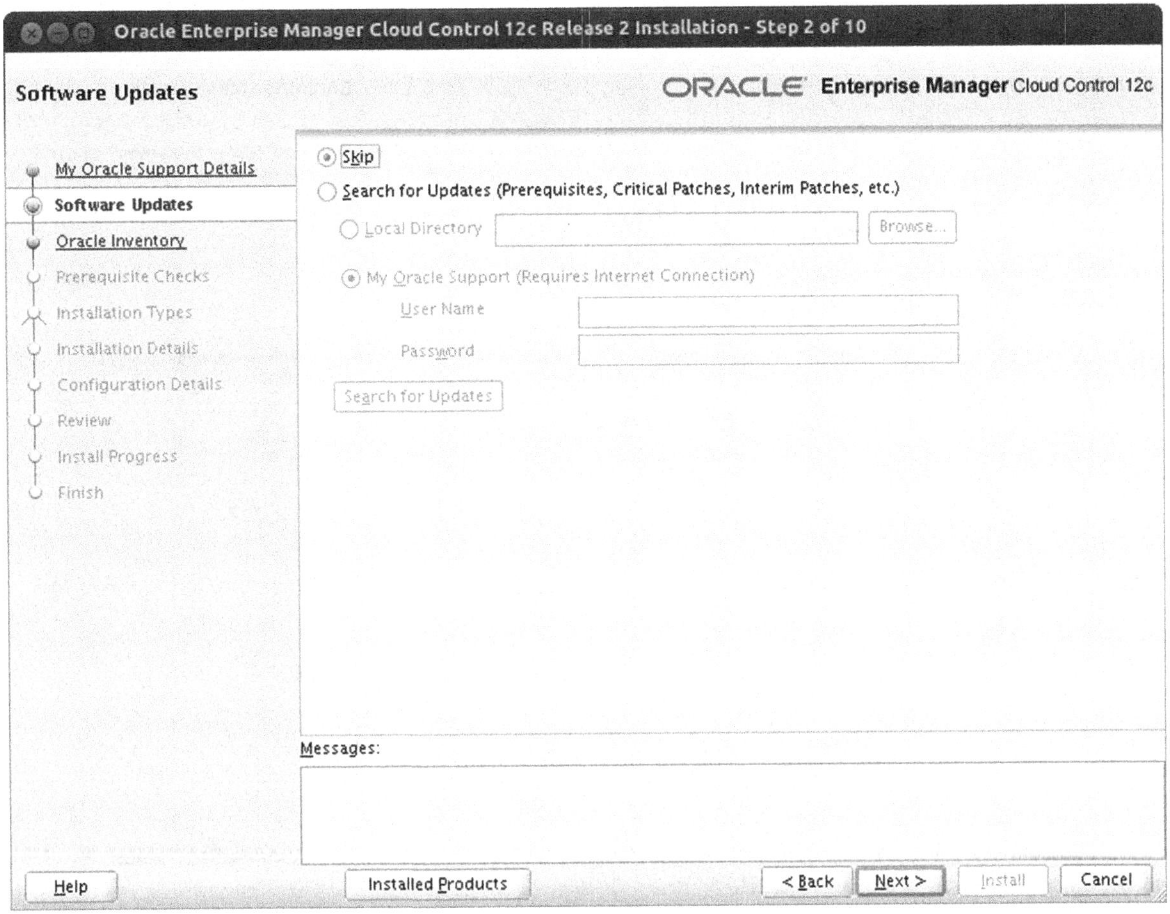

Figure 8-4. *Configuration of software updates*

Figure 8-4 shows another screen which looks similar to one used in the RDBMS installation wizard. If you are installing the software to a host that is connected to the Internet then you could search for updates online by selecting the radio button "My Oracle Support". In this case, enter your username and password in the relevant input fields.

The whole step has been skipped in the example. Skipping the step takes you to Figure 8-5.

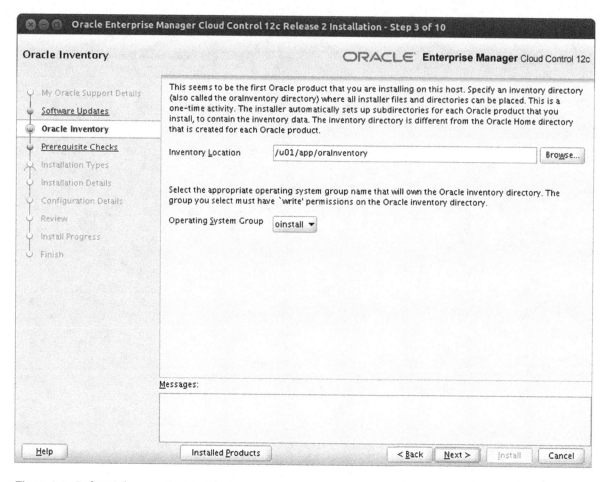

Figure 8-5. *Defining the inventory location*

Figure 8-5 lets you define the inventory location. In this example, the directory /u01/app/oraInventory has been entered to comply with the Oracle Flexible Architecture. If you configured the oracle account in the same way shown earlier in this chapter then your only option is to select oinstall as the inventory group in the drop-down in the center of the screen. Clicking on the "Next" button moves you to step 4 shown in Figure 8-6.

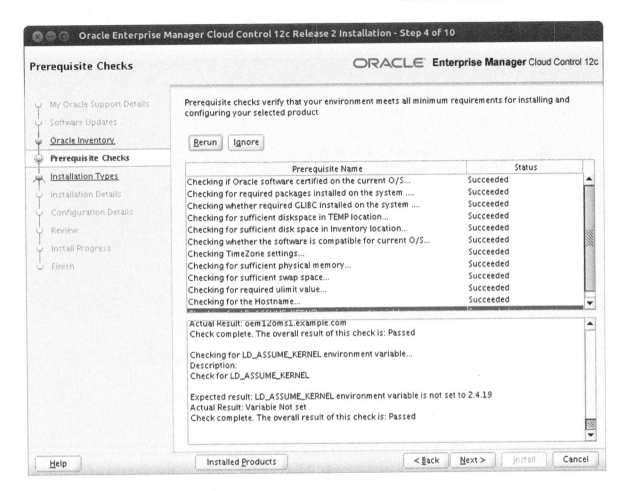

Figure 8-6. *Sample output of the configuration checker*

Figure 8-6 shows the same output from the prerequisite checks that you performed earlier on the command line. Before launching the Oracle Universal installer you should have addressed the problems reported, so you do not expect issues at this stage. If however there are problems reported and a status does not return "Succeeded" please address anything outstanding before proceeding. This is a good time to double-check your firewall and SELinux settings! Once you are confident these settings adhere to the security guidelines and policies while at the same time allowing the installation to proceed, click on the "Next" button to advance to step 5, as shown in Figure 8-7.

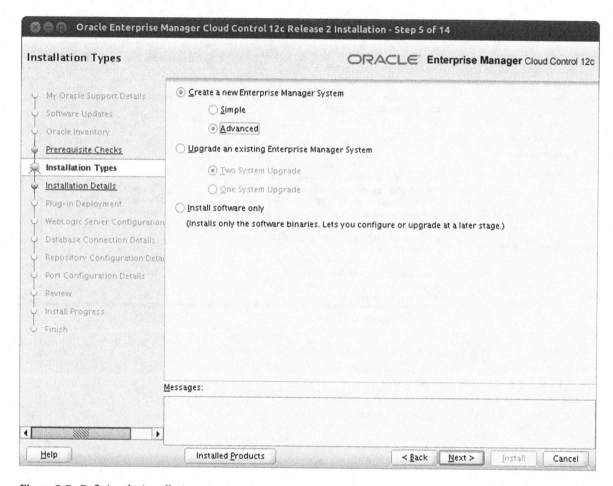

Figure 8-7. *Defining the installation type*

Figure 8-7 shows one of the main screens in the Enterprise Manager installer. It allows you to choose an installation method. You can chose from the following options:

- *Create a new Enterprise Manager System*: This option lets you install a new Oracle Enterprise Manager system. Furthermore you can perform a simple installation or an advanced one. As the names suggest the simple install, which really should have been called simplified installation, does not prompt you for options related to WebLogic and assumes safe default values. The advanced installation gives you a lot more control over the process.

- *Upgrade and Existing system*: Oracle Enterprise Manager greatly enhanced the upgrade method. Whereas in previous versions many users opted to perform a tech refresh and install the new version independently of the existing OMS, an upgrade is a real possibility with Cloud Control. Upgrading OEM is out of the scope of this chapter. If you are interested and want to know more about the difference between a one-system and a two-system upgrade, please refer to the Oracle® Enterprise Manager Cloud Control Upgrade Guide.

- *Install Software only*: This option allows you to install the software only and perform the configuration later. It is clearly aimed at more experienced users and not covered here.

If you would like to follow the example in this chapter, then please select the option to install a new system using the advanced configuration. In the next screen which is not shown here you will need to define a location for the Middleware Home, the Agent Base Directory and a Host Name. The following values have been chosen for this example's installation:

- Middleware Home Location: /u01/app/oracle/oem12c

- Agent base directory: /u01/app/oracle/agent

- Host name: oem12oms1.example.com

Once you've entered the relevant information click on the "Next" button, which leads you to step 7 as depicted in Figure 8-8.

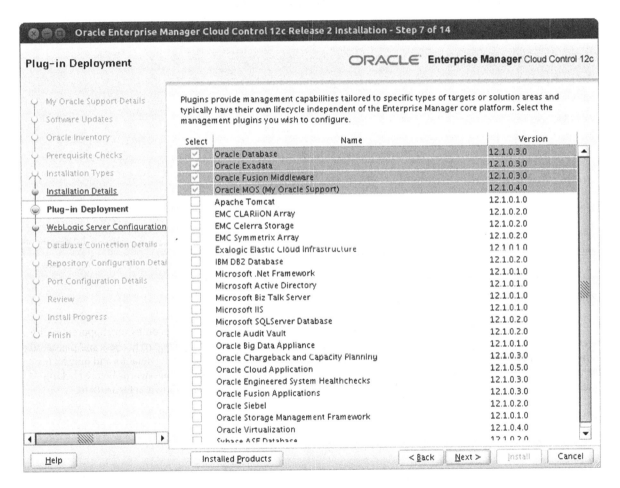

Figure 8-8. *Selecting Plugins*

The plugin selection screen shown in Figure 8-8 allows you to select optional plugins at installation time. Bear in mind that these can always be installed later! Some plugins have dependencies that are automatically resolved when you select them. When you are happy with your selection proceed to the next step where you configure the WebLogic Server, shown in Figure 8-9.

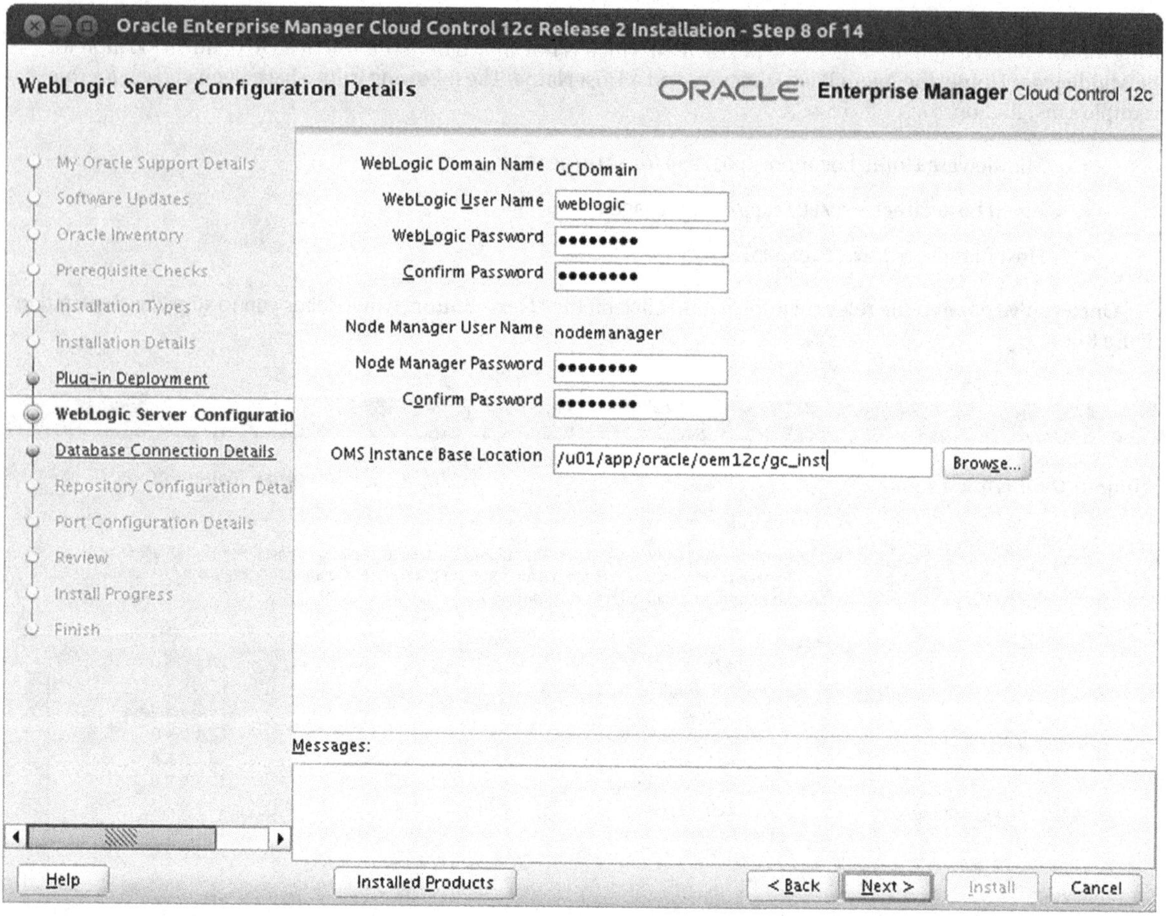

Figure 8-9. *User configuration*

Oracle Enterprise Manager is deployed as a Java application in WebLogic, and this becomes very apparent in the screen in Figure 8-9. Here you get down to the details of the WebLogic deployment with regard to users and passwords in the underlying application server instance. If you are unsure what to fill in here, leave the defaults and only fill in the passwords. The defaults are based on previous input. Remember to only choose safe passwords before clicking "Next". Step 9, which allows you to define the connection to the repository database, is shown in Figure 8-10.

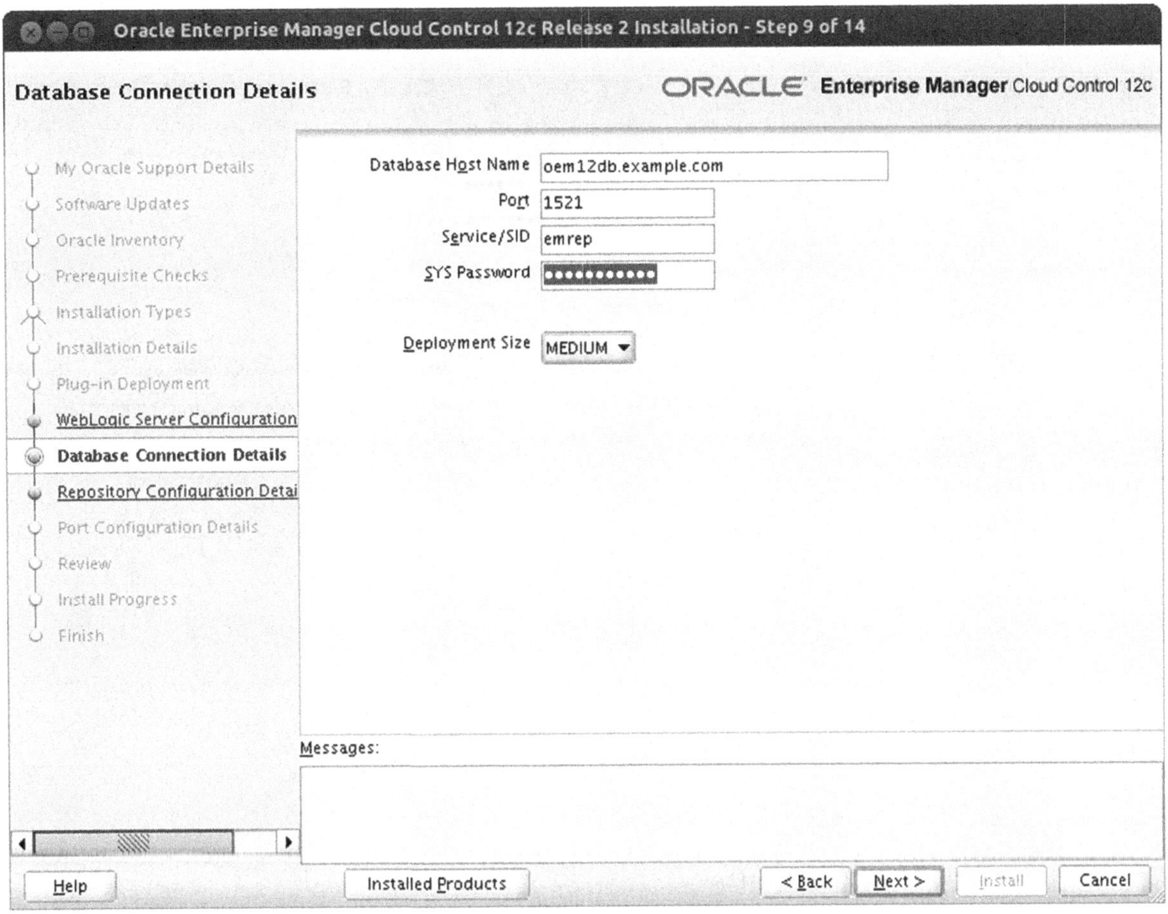

Figure 8-10. *Define the repository database connection*

Enterprise Manager would not be complete without a repository database. In Figure 8-10 this is what you specify. Enter the name of the database server host, the port, Oracle SID or service name, and a sys password. The installer will need this information to create the repository information. One of the few differences between the installation in 12c Release 2 to earlier releases is the drop-down field "deployment size". Here you defined the targeted size of your OEM deployment. You read earlier in this chapter how Oracle defines a small, medium, and large deployment.

You might get a pop-up with warnings if the installer finds that the database does not meet the requirements. OUI needs more information to complete the repository schema creation, and you need to fill the missing values in the next screen, shown in Figure 8-11.

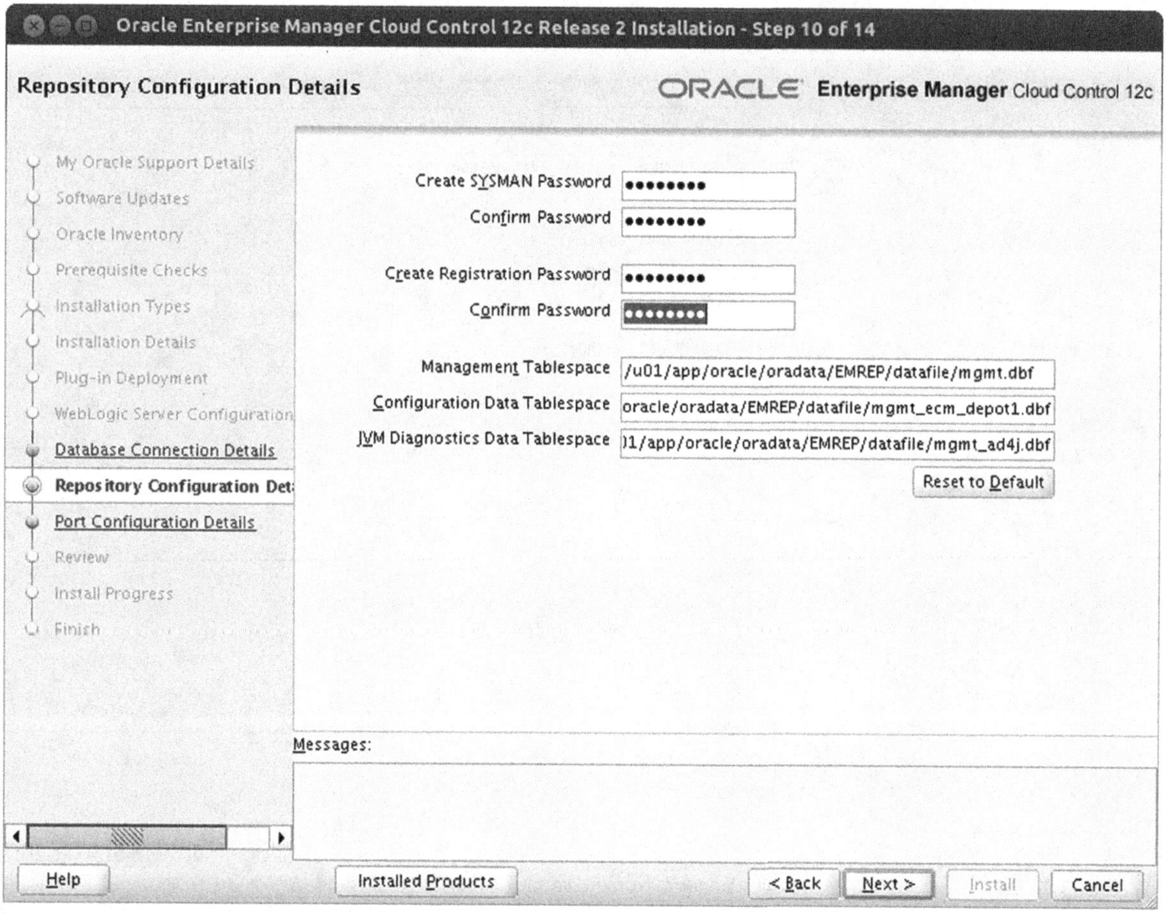

Figure 8-11. *Enter additional repository configuration details*

You are required to supply the following information:

- *SYSMAN password*: The SYSMAN account is the Enterprise Manager super-user. Whoever has control over it has complete control over the whole Enterprise Manager configuration. The SYSMAN password therefore is very sensitive and should not be given out to regular users. Just like the UNIX root account, only qualified and properly trained staff should have the SYSMAN password. Ideally the use of the SYSMAN account is restricted to the initial configuration. For the reasons just outlined the password must be sufficiently complex.

- *Registration password*: In order for agents to initially establish communication with the Oracle Management Service agents need a password. This password is called the registration password which you need to enter here.

- *Tablespace locations*: The Oracle Universal Installer will create three tablespaces in the repository database. Their location can be defined in the last three input fields. Choose appropriate locations and click on "Next" to specify the port ranges in step 11, shown in Figure 8-12.

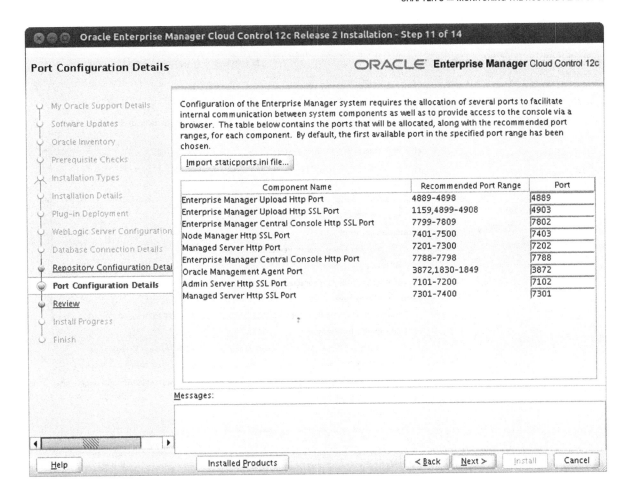

Figure 8-12. *Checking port ranges*

Oracle Enterprise Manager uses network ports for various purposes: the agents need to be able to upload information using the HTTP and HTTPS protocols, there must be free ports for the Enterprise Manager console and so forth. You can normally use the defaults listed in Figure 8-12, unless you have very specific requirements. You are taken to the summary screen, shown in Figure 8-13 after you click on "Next".

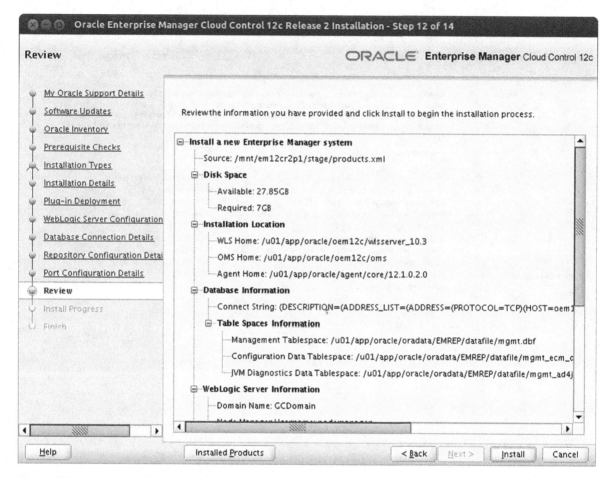

Figure 8-13. *Summary screen*

The summary screen as shown in Figure 8-13 gives you the option to review the choices made. It is the last opportunity to go back and make any changes. If you are happy with the settings click on "Install" to begin the installation and configuration of Enterprise Manager Cloud Control. You can now change your focus to another task since the process is almost certainly going to take a while, even on fast hardware.

You will have to wait for the installation and configuration steps to finish before you can run the root scripts. Eventually the well-known "execute as root" pop-up screen will appear. As usual with Oracle products, open a root shell on the OMS and execute the root scripts as indicated in the pop-up window. If you do not have root access to the host, you will need to ask or ring the friendly Linux administrator on duty to perform that task for you.

Close the pop-up windows after the root scripts completed, and wait for the final screen summarizing the port information and initial access to appear. The information shown in it is important, but thankfully Oracle preserved the text in the Management Services home directory in the setupinfo.txt file. Nevertheless you should take note of the EM console URL, which you need for logging in.

Congratulations, you have successfully installed and configured the initial Enterprise Manager 12 Cloud Control environment! Before you log in for the first time there is one very important step to be performed. The repository is encrypted with a secret key you should back up immediately:

```
[oracle@oem12oms1 bin]$ ./emctl exportconfig oms -dir /path/to/safe/location/
```

Now you are ready to log in for the first time.

The Initial Configuration Steps

The first user account you have available after a fresh installation as just shown is the SYSMAN user. After the OEM welcome screen has loaded, connect as SYSMAN using the password you defined at installation time. You will be asked for a default home screen, a choice that does not require a lot of consideration at this point. The enterprise summary screen seems a good candidate for the default screen, but you can always change your home screen. Figure 8-2 earlier in this chapter showed the summary screen.

Enterprise Manager 12c has a central configuration menu to be used, named "Setup". It can be found near the top-right corner of the screen and will be used extensively throughout the next sections. The example assumes a connection of the OMS to the Internet—either direct or via proxy—which Oracle refers to as the "online" mode. The alternative is named an offline connection and is not covered in this chapter.

Configure My Oracle Support

Enterprise Manager relies heavily on My Oracle Support. Although each user you create in Enterprise Manager can store his own credentials for My Oracle Support access, it might be a good idea to start configuring MOS for the generic SYSMAN account to see if the access works. In order to do so, navigate to Setup ➤ My Oracle Support ➤ Set Credentials. Enter a user name and password for My Oracle Support and click on the "Apply" button. At this stage nothing will happen, since you have not yet configured Enterprise Manager's connection mode. Proceed to configure the connection mode next.

Configure the Connection Mode

Enterprise Manager can be configured to connect directly or indirectly to the Internet. Oracle calls the two modes of operation online and offline. Offline mode has to be chosen if the OMS is securely placed behind firewalls and no proxy is available to connect to the Internet. It is by far the safest operation, but certain features in OEM will not be as easily available. To keep this chapter within a reasonable page count, the example Management Service will be configured so that it can access Oracle's support website via a proxy.

Connection settings are available via Setup ➤ Proxy Settings. The screen you are shown has three tabs: "My Oracle Support and Proxy Connection", "Online and Offline Settings", and "Linux Patching Setup". The default connection mode for Enterprise Manager is "online". You can check the current setting in the tab named "Online and Offline Settings". Please ensure that your system is "online" if you would like to follow the example.

Next please revert back to the "My Oracle Support and Proxy Connection" tab of the Proxy Configuration screen. Take a moment to look at it. You will see that it contains the following sections:

- My Oracle Support

- My Oracle Support Connection Setting

- Agent Connection Setting

You should begin by configuring the proxy under "My Oracle Support Connection Setting". Select the radio button "Manual Proxy Configuration" and enter the proxy information. Depending on how your proxy is configured you may need to enter the realm, and provide authorization and authentication information. If you like you could also tweak the connection settings, the defaults for connection timeouts and retries are usually just fine. Now click on "Apply" to save your changes.

The next item to consider is the Agent Connection setting. Most users choose "No proxy" here if the OMS can directly communicate with the agents. If you made a change, click on "Apply" again.

The URL for My Oracle Support does not normally need to be changed. You can use the "Test" button right next to the "Patch Search URL" to test connectivity with My Oracle Support. If that test fails you most likely did not enter your credentials as described in the previous section. You should also test the agent connectivity right at the bottom of the page. The "Test" button is to the right of the "Test URL" input field.

Both tests should succeed. If not, you need to troubleshoot any issues as there is little point in continuing from this stage. You will notice that there are a couple of jobs Enterprise Manager creates for you that are pending execution. The task of these jobs is to check for the latest information from My Oracle Support. To view these jobs you navigate to Enterprise ➤ Job ➤ Activity. The Enterprise Menu is right beneath the Oracle logo on the top-left corner of the screen. You need to perform an "Advanced Search" for "Target Type" Targetless to view the jobs.

Create a Software Library

The software library is a directory structure used by all the OMSs to store patches and other components. It has to be set up in a way to allow every OMS to access it. Many components within Enterprise Manager will need a software library configured, which is why it has to be set up. Navigate to Setup ➤ Provision and Patching ➤ Software Library. When you first get there you will see no entry in the lists. For the software library to become functional, you need to define at least one "Upload File Location". This location should only be local to the OMS if you do not plan to extend the Enterprise Manager infrastructure to more than just a single Management Service. Since that is rarely the case, you should mount an NFS share to the same location on each OMS in the configuration before creating the first entity.

In the "Software Library: Administration" screen, ensure that you selected the "Upload File Locations" tab and "OMS Shared Filesystem". A click on the plus sign will bring up a pop-up menu allowing you to specify a name and location for your new file system. Provide the settings and click on "OK" to continue. A job will be started in the background to finish the creation of the software library. Oracle will initialize the library and after a little while makes it available to users.

Creating and Managing Enterprise Manager Accounts

Users in Cloud Control are referred to as administrators. The authentication and authorization system provides a wealth of different methods to let users access the Enterprise Manager console. Users can be authenticated outside of Enterprise Manager as well from a variety of other sources, including Microsoft's Active Directory. Covering all of these authentication methods is not possible in this chapter, which is why the default so-called repository-based authentication will be used as one way to identify users. With repository-based authentication every user provisioned in the Enterprise Manager system will be created as a named user in the repository database. The advantage of this approach is that every user password can be maintained with password profiles as any other database account. On the downside EM administrators need to remember yet another username and password combination.

■ **Note** If you have a requirement for authenticating large numbers of users the integration of an existing LDAP-based service should be considered more seriously.

In Enterprise Manager you can create two types of users: administrators and super administrators. Be careful granting the super-administrator role to anyone because real damage can be done with it! The difference between these two classes of users is their scope: the super administrator can create and manage any other administrator and his objects in Cloud Control whereas the administrator is limited to his own objects and therefore more restricted. As is the rule with the root account on UNIX systems, you should limit the use of the super administrator accounts to global setup operations and configuration. You should definitely not use it on a routine basis. Also bear in mind that for auditing purposes it is essential that you use named users rather than generic accounts: another good reason to keep the SYSMAN password very safe.

The privilege system in Enterprise Manager 12c is very flexible, and is a real revelation after the rather strict model in previous generations of the software. Generally speaking the system differentiates between:

- Grants on specific managed targets

- Grants applicable to all targets

- Grants on the Enterprise Manager system itself, so-called resource privileges

To simplify account management, individual privileges can be rolled up into roles. Just as with the database roles can further be granted to other roles, creating nested hierarchies. There are predefined roles available out-of-the-box, but you can of course create your own if you like. The management of users via roles greatly simplifies the management of accounts since changes have to be made only once for the role, not for every individual account. Oracle supplies almost 20 roles for typical tasks, such as patching, target management, deploying and plugins. In addition to these roles you are free to define a set of privileges to the PUBLIC role. This role does not have any privileges by default. But since it is always granted to new users you can define a basic set of privileges every user should have to it, simplifying new user creation. The EM_USER is another essential role, similar to the database's CONNECT role and it allows the user to connect to the Enterprise Manager system.

There are two types of target privileges: those applicable to all targets like "view any target" and those that apply to a named managed target only. There are more than 20 target-specific privileges available that should make it very easy to properly define access to targets. Luckily you do not need to refer to the documentation when reviewing what a privilege can be used for. The Enterprise Manager console does a better job describing what a privilege allows you to do as well as which other privileges are implicitly granted as well.

The final group of privileges refers to the various parts or modules of Enterprise Manager itself. Depending on the plugins deployed—and therefore new functionality—available you can grant privileges for patching, compliance monitoring, the job system and many more.

The creation of a new user follows the process shown in Figure 8-14:

The following sections detail the user creation.

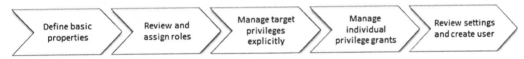

Figure 8-14. *The five-step process to create a new administrator*

Defining Basic User Properties

To begin the creation of a new administrator account, navigate to Setup ➤ Security ➤ Administrators.

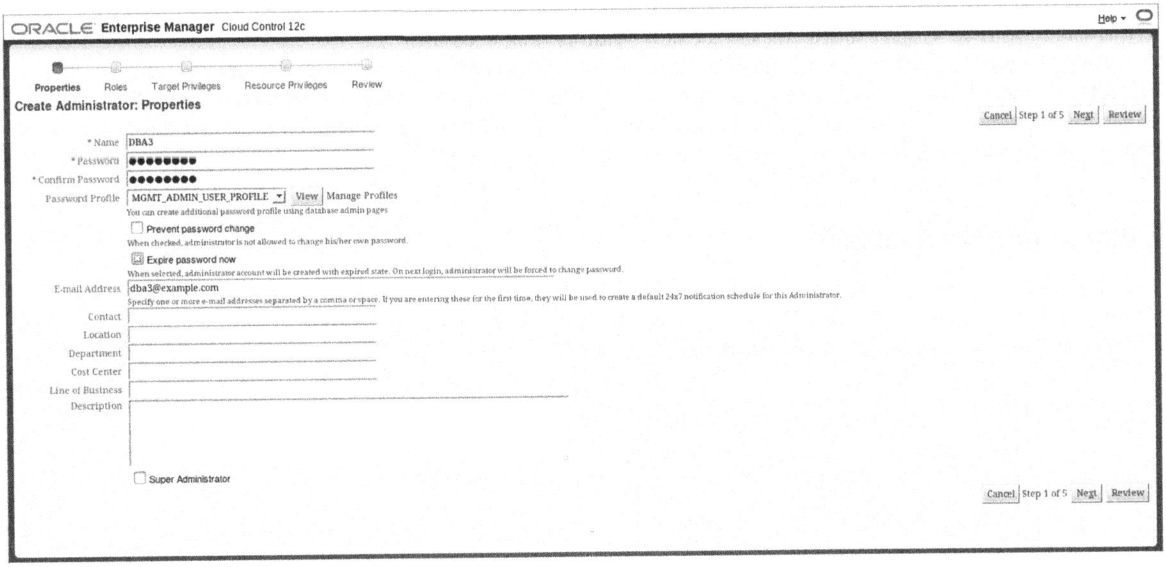

Figure 8-15. *The five-step process to create a new administrator*

Fields with an asterisk are mandatory in the screen. Name and password probably do not require an explanation. The password complexity rules are defined in the repository database's DBA_PROFILES password_verify_function. The database profiles available can be viewed, or new profiles can be added using the button and link next to the password profile drop down. For IT support staff you should consider adding the email address to allow Enterprise Manager to simplify sending out email notifications. Clicking "Next" takes you to the next screen where you assign roles to users. The screen is shown in Figure 8-16.

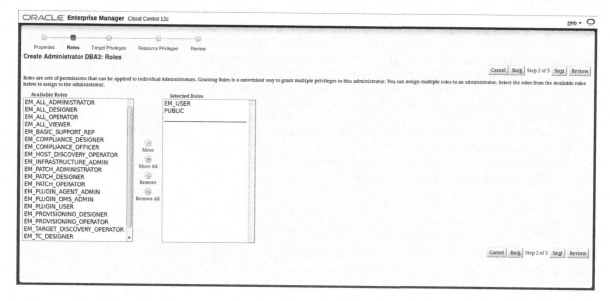

Figure 8-16. *Assigning roles to the user*

Review and Assign Roles

In this screen you can assign existing roles to the new administrator account.

Two roles are assigned by default. The EM_USER role is required for a user to connect to the EM Console. The PUBLIC role should contain the smallest common denominator of target and resource privileges. Add additional roles as you need, but do not remove the EM_USER and PUBLIC roles. Remember that all default roles are described in the Enterprise Manager documentation.

Manage Target Privileges

The next screen in Figure 8-17 requires a little more explanation. It has two parts—the first part in the upper half allows you to grant generic privileges that apply to all targets without having to name them explicitly. These privileges are quite powerful and should be used sporadically.

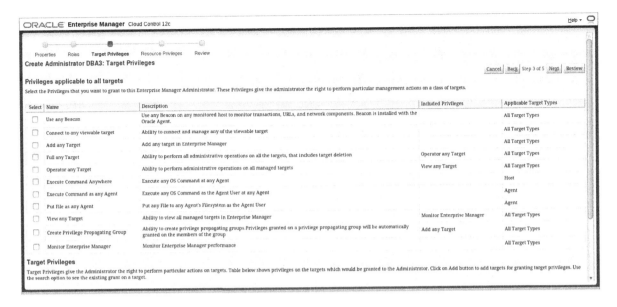

Figure 8-17. *Managing individual target privileges*

The lower half of the screen is dedicated to granting privileges to individual targets. Start by selecting the targets you want to grant privileges to. Clicking on "Add" opens a pop-up window which helps you find the targets you are after. Check the checkboxes next to the targets and click on the "Select" button to add the targets to the list. A pencil icon in the right-hand column named "Manage Target Privilege Grants". Click on it to manage individual privileges per target. For a large number of targets that can become quite tedious, luckily there is a quicker way to manage privilege. The first is to select a number of targets followed by a "Grant To Selected". Whichever privilege you select will automatically be assigned to all previously selected targets. The other way is to define privileges for one target, and then copying them to all others using the "Grant to All" button.

You find two fields labeled "Name" and "Type" right underneath the Target Privileges screen. They can be confusing at first. Their purpose is to control the chaos if you decided to add lots of different targets or target types. Remember to add target privileges by clicking on the "Add" button.

To ease the administrative burden of user maintenance it might be easier to grant privileges in this screen to a role rather than granting privileges individually. You create roles by navigating to Setup ➤ Security ➤ Roles, and the screens used for the role creation are almost identical to the ones just shown.

Manage Resource Privileges

The resource privileges allow you to grant or deny access to the various internal components of Enterprise Manager 12c Cloud control. The list of subsystems is long, and the exact layout of the screen depends on the plugins you have installed.

The intention of the privileges is to separate duties. Different members of the IT infrastructure team can have different tasks and therefore different access privileges. Consider this example: Enterprise Manager has functionality available for database backups. Members of the backup team should be granted these. If you have a quality assurance team they could be granted access to Application Replay for example and so on. With a freshly installed Enterprise Manager system you will see a similar screen to the one shown below in Figure 8-18.

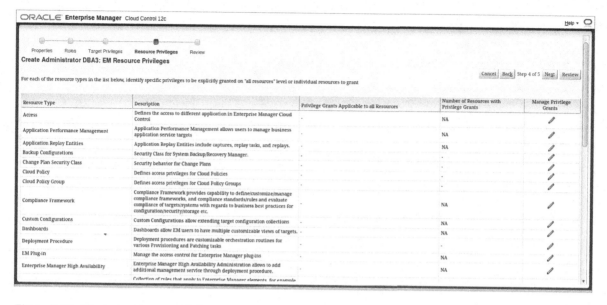

Figure 8-18. *Managing resource privileges*

Each resource type has one or more privilege grants available. To grant individual privileges you need to click on the pencil icon in the "Manage Privilege Grants" column. If you don't see "N/A" in the column labeled then you can further restrict a privilege to a target. For example, you could grant a backup administrator the ability to create a backup configuration plus the right to do so on specific targets only.

Managing resource privileges on an individual user account is a lot of maintenance work, especially with a large number of users to be created. It is easier to identify and group different tasks for users into roles. These roles can subsequently be granted to users. The added benefit of using roles is that there is less change needed when a privilege has to be revoked. Instead of changing each and every affected user account only a role has to change.

Review the Summary

The final step in the wizard shows you the summary of the last four screens you completed, and allows you to create the user. If you notice that a setting has been omitted or anything else does not look right to you then use the "Back" button to return to the view in question and correct or amend it.

If you are creating an account for an operational DBA, you should at least double-check the email address entered and that his or her account is not a super-administrator account. The "Finish" button creates the new administrator.

■ **Note**   You are definitely encouraged to read more about security and Enterprise Manager Cloud control in the official documentation. Especially look at Chapter 11 in the *Enterprise Manager Cloud Control Administrator's Guide*.

Managing Database Targets

Managing and monitoring databases is at the core of what Enterprise Manager really is made for. In the following section you will learn how to add a host to the Enterprise Manager configuration, and how to discover targets. The first step towards monitoring a target is to install an agent on a host. Using that agent you can then discover targets, either manually or using an automated process. Once the targets are added you can group them into administrative groups, allowing monitoring templates to be added automatically.

Deploying an Agent to a New Host

The agent deployment can be performed either via the OEM console, or alternatively from the command line. The command line installation is more suitable for a mass deployment of the agent, and it will be covered here. When installing the agent you will notice a slightly different directory structure than the previous versions of the agent. During the installation you need to define an agent base directory, which contains all agent related files. There are three directories of higher importance:

- The agent home directory

- The agent instance directory

- The plugins directory

The agent instance directory contains all configuration files, and especially the all-important sysman directory containing the log files for the agent. The instance home is not to be confused with the agent home directory, which is below $AGENT_BASE/core/*version*. The agent home contains the binaries used to run the agent on the server, but confusingly the emctl executable recommended for use with the agent is in the instance home. The plugins directory contains the plugins currently installed for the agent.

You can make use of the Enterprise Manager command line interface for mass-deploying the agent. Log in as the OMS software owner on an arbitrary management host. You then create a zip file with the agent software for a specific platform. If you wanted to create the deploy image for the Linux x86-64 agent, you should follow these steps:

```
[oracle@oem12oms1 ~]$ emcli login -username=sysman
Enter password

Login successful
```

Once logged in you can query the agents currently available on the management host:

```
[oracle@oem12oms1 ~]$ emcli get_supported_platforms
Getting list of platforms ...
Check the logs at /u01/app/oracle/oem12/gc_inst/em/EMGC_OMS1/sysman/emcli/↵
setup/.emcli/agent.log
About to access self-update code path to retrieve the platforms list..
Getting Platforms list  ...
-----------------------------------------------
Version = 12.1.0.2.0
 Platform = Linux x86-64
-----------------------------------------------
Platforms list displayed successfully.
```

Armed with that information it is possible to get the agent image and deploy it to the staging directory on the OMS as shown here:

```
[oracle@oem12oms1 ~]$ mkdir /u01/temp
[oracle@oem12oms1 ~]$ emcli get_agentimage -destination=/u01/temp \
> -platform="Linux x86-64"
Platform:Linux x86-64
Destination:/u01/temp
 === Partition Detail ===
Space free : 14 GB
Space required : 1 GB
Check the logs at /u01/app/oracle/oem12/gc_inst/em/EMGC_OMS1/sysman/emcli/setup/↵
.emcli/get_agentimage_2013-01-01_21-03-28-PM.log
Setting property ORACLE_HOME to:/u01/app/oracle/oem12/oms
calling pulloneoffs with arguments:/u01/app/oracle/oem12/oms/u01/app/oracle/oem12/oms/sysman/↵
agent/12.1.0.2.0_AgentCore_226.zip12.1.0.2.0linux_x64
Check this logs for more information: /u01/app/oracle/oem12/oms/sysman/prov/↵
agentpush/logs
```

The result of this process's execution is a deployable agent image for Linux x86-64. This process only needs to be completed once, the resulting zip file can be reused on as many hosts as you like. You could move the resulting zip file to a shared area to make it easier to deploy the zip file later. Whichever way you chose to make the image available, the newly created zip file needs to be accessible on the destination host. Most users decide to install the agent using the same user ID as they chose for the RDBMS binaries, as does this example. Once logged in as "oracle" on the destination host, prepare for the installation. If your host already has an Oracle database installed you should be fine with regards to the agent installation prerequisites. If not, you should review Table 6-1 in the Advanced Installation and Configuration Guide. Next you unzip the zip file to a convenient location, it is /tmp/agent12c in this example. Before the agent can be installed you need to provide a response file. An example response file is shown below, stripped of comments and empty lines:

```
[oracle@oem12db agent12c]$ sed -e '/^#/d' -e '/^$/d' agent.rsp
RESPONSEFILE_VERSION=2.2.1.0.0
OMS_HOST=oem12oms1.example.com
EM_UPLOAD_PORT=4900
AGENT_REGISTRATION_PASSWORD=<secretPassword>
b_startAgent=true
EM_INSTALL_TYPE="AGENT"
```

The full description of the response file parameters is listed in Table 6-3 in the Oracle® Enterprise Manager Cloud Control Advanced Installation and Configuration Guide. The above example is complete and can be used after changing it to match your environment. If you are unsure about the ports to be used, you can interrogate the OMS directly, using the command shown here:

```
[oracle@oem12oms1 ~]$ emctl status oms -details
Oracle Enterprise Manager Cloud Control 12c Release 2
Copyright (c) 1996, 2012 Oracle Corporation.  All rights reserved.
Enter Enterprise Manager Root (SYSMAN) Password :
Console Server Host       : oem12oms1.example.com
HTTP Console Port         : 7788
HTTPS Console Port        : 7799
HTTP Upload Port          : 4889
HTTPS Upload Port         : 4900
```

```
EM Instance Home            : /u01/app/oracle/oem12/gc_inst/em/EMGC_OMS1
OMS Log Directory Location : /u01/app/oracle/oem12/gc_inst/em/EMGC_OMS1/sysman/log
OMS is not configured with SLB or virtual hostname
Agent Upload is locked.
OMS Console is locked.
Active CA ID: 1
Console URL: https://oem12oms1.example.com:7799/em
Upload URL: https://oem12oms1.example.com:4900/empbs/upload

WLS Domain Information
Domain Name      : GCDomain
Admin Server Host: oem12oms1.example.com

Managed Server Information
Managed Server Instance Name: EMGC_OMS1
Managed Server Instance Host: oem12oms1.example.com
WebTier is Up
Oracle Management Server is Up
[oracle@oem12oms1 stage]$...
```

Supply the values shown in bold to the response file for the agent. The agent registration password is more difficult to recover. If you forgot your agent registration password you can create a new one in Setup ➤ Security ➤ Registration Passwords. Once you have completed the creation of the response file, begin with the installation of the agent. Change the agent base directory to match your directory standards.

```
[oracle@server1 agent12c]$ ./agentDeploy.sh AGENT_BASE_DIR=/u01/app/oracle/agent12c \
> RESPONSE_FILE=/tmp/agent12c/agent.rsp

Validating the OMS_HOST & EM_UPLOAD_PORT
Executing command : /u01/app/oracle/agent12c/core/12.1.0.2.0/jdk/bin/java -classpath ↵
/u01/app/oracle/agent12c/core/12.1.0.2.0/jlib/agentInstaller.jar:/u01/app/oracle/↵
agent12c/core/12.1.0.2.0/oui/jlib/OraInstaller.jar ↵
oracle.sysman.agent.installer.AgentInstaller /u01/app/oracle/agent12c/core/12.1.0.2.0
/tmp/agent12c /u01/app/oracle/agent12c -prereq

Validating oms host & port with url: http://192.168.1.223:4900/empbs/genwallet
Validating oms host & port with url: https://192.168.1.223:4900/empbs/genwallet
Return status:3
[...]
Agent Configuration completed successfully

The following configuration scripts need to be executed as the "root" user.
#!/bin/sh
#Root script to run
 /u01/app/oracle/agent12c/core/12.1.0.2.0/root.sh
To execute the configuration scripts:
1. Open a terminal window
2. Log in as "root"
3. Run the scripts
Agent Deployment Successful.
```

```
Agent deployment log location:
/u01/app/oracle/agent12c/core/12.1.0.2.0/cfgtoollogs/agentDeploy/agentDeploy_2013↵
-01-01_16-23-36-PM.log
Agent deployment completed successfully.
```

The agent deployment takes very little time, and at the end all you need to do is to execute the root.sh script from the agent home as shown here:

```
[root@server1 ~]# /u01/app/oracle/agent12c/core/12.1.0.2.0/root.sh
Finished product-specific root actions.
/etc exist

Creating /etc/oragchomelist file...
Finished product-specific root actions.
```

Congratulations, you just installed the Oracle agent. If for some reason the prerequisites for the agent installation are not met, the silent installation will fail. In such a case you should check the output of the log file to see which particular problem prevented the installer from completing its task. More information about the agent software prerequisites can be found in Chapter 3 of the "Enterprise Manager Cloud Control Basic Installation Guide", Table 3-2.

Before moving on to the next task you should quickly check if the agent can indeed communicate with the OMS. The command to use is shown here, together with the success message taken from a different machine:

```
[oracle@oem12oms1 ~]$ emctl status agent
Oracle Enterprise Manager Cloud Control 12c Release 2
Copyright (c) 1996, 2012 Oracle Corporation.  All rights reserved.
----------------------------------------------------------------
Agent Version      : 12.1.0.2.0
OMS Version        : 12.1.0.2.0
Protocol Version   : 12.1.0.1.0
Agent Home         : /u01/app/oracle/agent12c/agent_inst
Agent Binaries     : /u01/app/oracle/agent12c/core/12.1.0.2.0
Agent Process ID   : 3948
Parent Process ID  : 3902
Agent URL          : https://server1.example.com:3872/emd/main/
Repository URL     : https://oem12oms1.example.com:4900/empbs/upload
Started at         : 2013-01-20 20:24:30
Started by user    : oracle
Last Reload        : (none)
Last successful upload                       : 2013-01-20 21:45:46
Last attempted upload                        : 2013-01-20 21:45:46
Total Megabytes of XML files uploaded so far : 0.16
Number of XML files pending upload           : 0
Size of XML files pending upload(MB)         : 0
Available disk space on upload filesystem    : 66.09%
Collection Status                            : Collections enabled
Heartbeat Status                             : Ok
Last attempted heartbeat to OMS              : 2013-01-20 21:45:51
Last successful heartbeat to OMS             : 2013-01-20 21:45:51
Next scheduled heartbeat to OMS              : 2013-01-20 21:46:51


----------------------------------------------------------------
Agent is Running and Ready
```

If you like, you can add the agent home to the `oratab` file just as you would with a database:

```
agent:/u01/app/oracle/agent12c/core/12.1.0.2.0:N
```

You can then use the `oraenv` utility to switch back and forth Oracle homes as you do with the database. You do not need to worry about a start script, the agent installation creates such a script named /etc/init.d/gcstartup to automatically start and stop the agent when a runlevel changes.

The installation process can easily be scripted and packaged in the form of an RPM for example. All you need to do in order to fully automate the agent deployment is to:

- Provide a common, well-known location for the file.

- Configure the sudoers file to allow Oracle to execute the root.sh script as root.

- Make the zipfile available on the destination host for your platform.

- Provide the response file.

- Execute the agentDeploy.sh script as part of the post-install scriptlet in RPM.

- Change the sudoers file again and revoke the permission to execute root.sh.

In very security-conscious environments it might be difficult to get permissions to change the sudoers file. In these environments you need to ensure that a qualified system administrator with root access to the destination host is available to execute the final step in the installation procedure.

Getting Agent Software for Different Platforms

Unlike with Enterprise Manager 11.1 and before you cannot download the agent software from Oracle's OTN website anymore. This is quite startling at first, but the new process is very elegant and compensates you for the missing agents. You read earlier in this chapter that Enterprise Manager is built around a plugin infrastructure. As such only required functionality is deployed initially, updates and new functionality are available via Setup ➤ Extensibility ➤ Self Update. To use the Self-Update functionality you need to have configured access to My Oracle Support. Figure 8-19 shows the main interface to the Self-Update functionality.

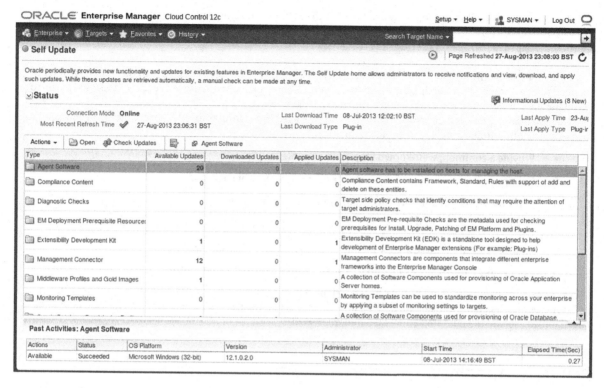

Figure 8-19. *The Self-Update portal*

The Self-Update is periodically refreshed via an Enterprise Manager job which executes daily. However if you are impatient you can always start a manual refresh by clicking on the "Check Updates" button. Information about the agents is shown in the "Agent Software" row. As you can see from the screen print there are 9 updates available, and the initial agent is installed ("Applied Updates" is 1). Clicking on the link "Agent Software" takes you to the detail screen. A value of "Available" in the Status column indicates that an agent is available, clicking on the "Download" button will trigger the agent download to the previously configured software library. A small dialog window prompts you for a time to download the agent. It might be a good idea to download the agent software at a quiet time instead of immediately. A job will be submitted to Enterprise Manager which will be in charge of downloading the agent software.

Once the status for the agent has changed to "Downloaded" you need to click on the "Apply" button to make the agent available for deployment. Another job will take care of the deployment, which should be completed in little to no time. A manual page refresh later the agent status has changed to "Applied". You can view the success of the operation by querying the supported platforms as you did during agent deployment. Remember that only the Linux x86-64 agent was initially available. Now the second agent has been made available as well:

```
[oracle@oem12oms1 ~]$ emcli get_supported_platforms
Getting list of platforms ...
Check the logs at /home/oracle/agent.log
About to access self-update code path to retrieve the platforms list..
Getting Platforms list  ...
-----------------------------------------------
Version = 12.1.0.2.0
 Platform = Linux x86-64
-----------------------------------------------
```

```
Version = 12.1.0.2.0
Platform = Linux x86
-----------------------------------------------
Platforms list displayed successfully.
```

Repeat these steps for any additional agent you need.

The Manual Target Discovery Process

After the agent has been deployed on the host you can start configuring the discovery process. There are two ways to discover targets using the Enterprise Manager console. The well-known, user-defined way of manually discovering targets in Grid Control is now called "Guided discovery" in Cloud Control. A second, more elegant way of target discovery is available as well, which makes a lot of sense in the consolidated environment. After a new host has been rolled out with an agent installed it makes sense to start a manual discovery of the components that have so far been installed. In most cases these components are the database home, a listener, and the ASM instance if applicable. Once these are registered one could define automatic target discovery to take the dynamic nature of the Database-As-A-Service environment into account.

Let's begin the discovery process by manually discovering targets. Navigate to Setup ➤Add Target ➤ Add Targets Manually. In the resulting screen you need to select the radio button "Add Non-Host Targets Using Guided Process (Also Adds Related Targets)". Select "Oracle Database, Listener and Automatic Storage Management" from the drop-down menu "Target Types". Click on the "Add using Guided Discovery" button to start the discovery process. Figure 8-20 shows this screen.

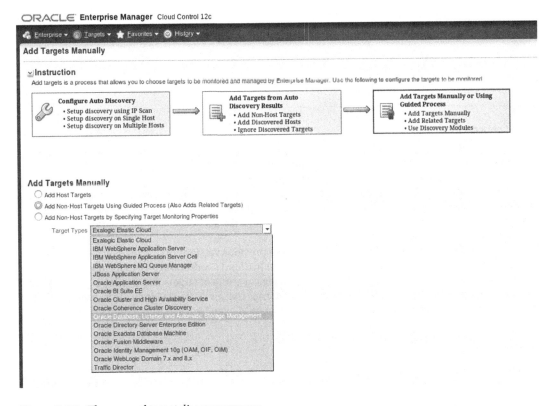

Figure 8-20. *The manual target discovery process*

On the next screen, titled "Add Database Instance Target: Specify Host" you need to select the host to which the target belongs using the magnifying glass or type the name in directly. If the host you want to add your target from does not exist in the list-of-values search you should investigate agent communication problems between the OMS and the host. Clicking on "Next" will initiate the target discovery process.

Once that process is completed you are presented with an overview of discovered targets as shown in Figure 8-21. The next step is to configure them by clicking on the wrench icon in the "configure" field.

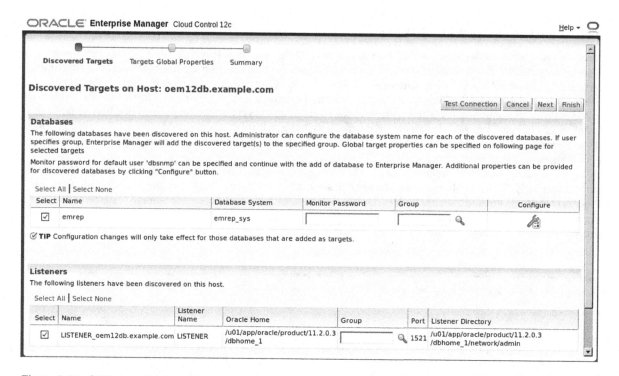

Figure 8-21. *OEM presents a list of discovered targets*

The target configuration screens are usually self-explanatory. For databases all you have to add is the dbsnmp password. Note that for newer database targets the dbsnmp is often locked and needs unlocking first. An additional screen allows you to define the Target Global Properties such as a contact, lifecycle status, and more. After saving the changes in the summary screen a new target becomes active after a slight delay. There is no need to panic if the target does not appear straight away or if there is a watch depicted as the status: the agent has to gather metric information about the target before it can be fully accessed.

If you look at Figure 8-21 closely you will notice a change from previous versions of Oracle Enterprise Manager. Instead of only adding the database instance, Enterprise Manager 12c Cloud Control will automatically create what it calls a *system* for a database. A system in OEM terminology is a logical group of targets that need to be up in order to support a given service. By default, the database system created uses the suffix "SYS" to indicate its function. You can view systems via Targets ➤Systems. A typical system created on ASM in an Oracle Restart configuration will have these members:

- ASM instance

- Listener

- The database instance

- The Oracle Restart (Grid Infrastructure) software home

- The RDBMS software home

This is very useful when it comes to patching these components as Enterprise Manager can also track the Oracle homes, including their patch levels. Click on the Finish button to finish the configuration of the newly discovered targets. You are presented a summary of all discovered targets to be added which you should acknowledge by clicking on the "Save" button. Enterprise Manager will then display a status page indicating it is saving the targets, and finally show the successful operation summary.

Automatic Target Discovery Process

In addition to the manual process Oracle Enterprise Manager Cloud control allows you to continuously monitor hosts which are already managed via an agent. The target discovery will be initiated automatically on a daily basis, however this interval can be configured. Navigate to Setup ➤ Add Target ➤ Configure Auto Discovery to configure options. The discovery module of choice is named "All Discovery Modules". Click on the wrench icon next to it to configure it. You can select the target type the agent should discover by clicking on a host in the list, as shown in Figure 8-22.

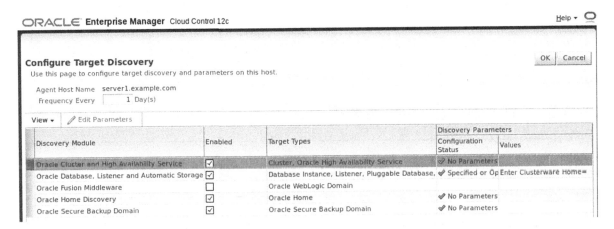

Figure 8-22. *Selecting discovery modules on a per host basis for single instance deployments without Oracle Restart*

Click on the "OK" button to save any changes made to the settings in Figure 8-22 to take you back to the previous screen. You can optionally wait until the discovery is automatically started on a daily basis, or if you are impatient run the discovery now by selecting the host and clicking on the "Run discovery now" button. A short prompt will appear asking if you are sure before the target discovery starts. At the end of it a pop up informs you of success or failure. If new targets have been discovered you will see a number in the discovered targets column for your host. If you click on the number you are taken to the auto discovery results screen, which is shown in Figure 8-23.

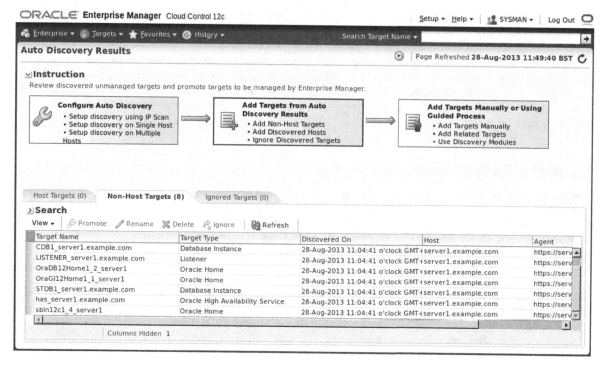

Figure 8-23. *Output of the automatic target discovery*

■ **Note**   You can get to the same screen after the routine discovery completed by navigating to Setup ➤ Add Target ➤ Auto Discovery Results

---

Here you can see all the targets discovered on `server1.example.com`. No manual target discovery has been performed: the tab "Host Targets" shows 0 managed targets, but there are 8 new targets found. You can now choose to either propagate the target to a managed target or ignore it. To promote a target, highlight it and click on the "Promote" icon. Depending on the target type you will have to add some more configuration information before promoting it. The configuration screens are the same for manual and automatic discovery, and almost all are self-explanatory. After the configuration information has been entered you have the option to promote the target to managed status. Some target types such as Oracle homes can be configured but not promoted, leaving that to a later stage. After a target has been promoted it will disappear from the list of non-host targets.

Support for Pluggable Databases

Unlike previous generations of the Enterprise Manager software OEM 12c has support for Pluggable Databases built in. You read earlier in the chapter that OEM functionality can be added and updated via plugins. The author's system used for this chapter was OEM 12c Release 2 or 12.1.0.2 with database plugin 12.1.0.3.0. Since then Enterprise Manager 12c Release 3 has been made available roughly at the same time as the database became generally available. The database plugin allows viewing the container database including the PDBs as you can see in Figure 8-24.

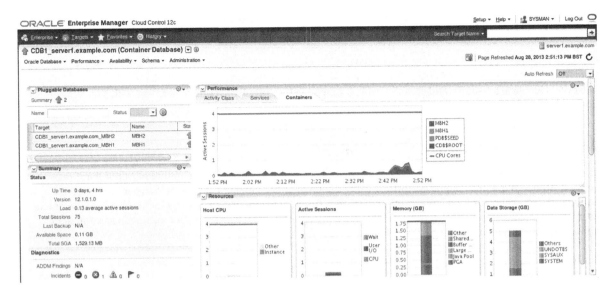

Figure 8-24. *Pluggable Databases monitored in Container Database CDB1*

The layout of the screen has been slightly modified. Normally you would see the summary in the top-left corner but for the sake of demonstration it has been moved up. Each PDB detected in the system has its own status as you can see. The performance panel allows you to view the load on the database broken down per container. You find the CDB$ROOT as well as each individual PDB. The rest of the screen is the same as for a non-CDB, you get to see the resources as well as a panel with statements for which you could invoke the SQL Monitor reports.

To drill down on a PDB simply click its name or select it from the drop-down list next to the database name. As you would expect a PDB behaves very much like a "regular" database from a management point of view. All the features and restrictions laid out for PDBs in the previous chapter still apply.

Standardized Monitoring

Enterprise Manager 12c has a very well thought-through feature named Administration Group. With Administration Groups it is possible to automatically group similar targets together based on a common attribute. OEM allows you to define attributes for targets, such as department, lifecycle status, location, and many more. Based on these attributes you can categorize targets. For example, you could put all production databases from Europe, Asia, and America into different groups. With the Administration Group created you can assign monitoring templates to every group, ensuring that members of a group are always consistently monitored. The beauty of Administration Groups lies in the fact that if you need to change the monitoring template, the change to the template is automatically propagated to all the targets it applies to, keeping the targets in sync with the monitoring requirements. With Administration Groups in place you need to worry less about newly deployed databases. As soon as they are classified by lifecycle status and location, they will be added to a group and monitored exactly as any other member of that group.

This sounds fairly abstract so let's use an example. Consider a number of databases in your estate, some of which are production; some are staging or user acceptance test environments plus all the inevitable test environments that you need to support. As soon as your database targets are registered in Enterprise Manager you can assign the appropriate lifecycle status to them. In a next step you define monitoring templates, which really are checks against the target to ensure that everything functions normally. A monitoring template for the listener for example could trawl the listener log file and check for occurrences of TNS-xxxx errors. If such an error is found the template can report that condition back to the Enterprise Manager console, where an incident will be created. Your monitoring templates can report normal execution, or alternatively warnings and critical states back. These are based on metrics you can collect. For example, if a tablespace is 75% full you might want to issue a warning. If the tablespace gets up to 85% you may want to report a critical condition back.

Administration Groups are not limited to a flat hierarchy. You can create arbitrarily complex group mappings based on multiple target properties. If you wanted different monitoring templates for production databases in EMEA from AMERICAS then you could create a hierarchy consisting of the lifecycle status and location. The basic principle however is identical for simple and complex setups, which is why you will only find a hierarchy with a maximum depth of one in this section.

Assign Extended Properties to a Database

The addition of properties to the database targets is a prerequisite for the implementation of Administration Groups. Although that task can be performed using the Enterprise Manager Console, it is easier to do it on the command line, especially for a large number of targets. Connect to one of your management servers as the oracle user, and then check which properties can be associated with the database target after logging in as sysman or another super administrator:

```
[oracle@oem12oms1 ~]$ emcli login -username=sysman
Enter password

Login successful
[oracle@oem12oms1 ~]$ emcli get_target_properties -target_type="oracle_database"
Comment
Contact
Cost Center
Customer Service Identifier
Department
LifeCycle Status
Line of Business
Location
Operating System
Platform
Target Version
Target properties fetched successfully
```

The property chosen for this example will be "LifeCycle Status". The syntax to set the Lifecycle Status for a database system "emrep_sys" is shown here:

```
[oracle@oem12oms1 ~]$ emcli set_target_property_value \
-property_records="emrep_sys:oracle_dbsys:LifeCycle Status:Production" \
-propagate_to_members
```

The following values are accepted for the LifeCycle Status property in descending order of priority:

- Mission Critical

- Production

- Staging

- Test

- Development

- None

Instead of setting these properties to each individual entity-database, listener, and so on you can benefit from an enhancement which allows you to propagate the properties to members. In other words, simply update the target properties for the members of your systems and specify the `-propagate_to_members` flag. Note that assigning a lifecycle status is optional; if you would like to exclude targets from the Administration Group then simply do not add any extra properties.

Create the Administration Group Hierarchy

Setting properties for targets as just explained is the first step towards creating an administration group. In the next step you will see how to complete the first task, the creation of the hierarchy. Even though there are only a few clicks to be made, the effect is far reaching: once created, it is impossible to change the hierarchy as such and it will have to be recreated if you realize later that it has not taken all factors into account. Begin the creation of the administration group by navigating to Targets ➤ Groups. From the "Create" button select "Administration Group" from the list of values in the drop-down menu. Note that if there is a group defined already it will take you there straight away. In other words the system only allows for one Administration Group.

Begin the definition of the hierarchy using the tab with the same name. There won't be a hierarchy initially, so click on the "Add" button on the left-hand side to create one. The initial—and only—hierarchy level in this example will be the lifecycle status. The different statuses are then displayed in the Hierarchy Nodes pane in the lower left of the screen. If you do not like the short names you can make use of the pencil icon to change them. The "Calculate Members" button is a convenient way to preview how many targets fall into a given category. This of course requires that you defined the extended attributes to the targets as discussed earlier.

You may want to add further levels to the hierarchy to represent your organization more accurately. Simply repeat the initial step for every additional level you want to add. When you are happy with the definition of your hierarchy, click on the "Create" button to save the configuration to the repository.

■ **Caution**   Do not switch tabs without saving the hierarchy or all changes will be lost.

Define Template Collections

Template collections group multiple monitoring templates together. Monitoring templates exist for each monitored target (agent, database, …) and are key to a centralized and standardized monitoring. With their use you define on a per-target type basis what should be monitored. Enterprise Manager comes with lots of templates out of the box, accessible via Enterprise ➤ Monitoring ➤ Monitoring Templates. If you would like to have a look at what they do, simply limit the target type to what you would like to monitor and then execute a search. To view the Oracle provided templates you need to check the box named "Display Oracle Certified templates".

Pick a template from the search result and click on the template name to view its definition. The tab named "Metric Thresholds" shows what the template monitors for. You will notice that a monitoring template is not limited to a single metric. Any metric gathered by the agent can be used in the monitoring template, it is up to the administrator to decide which metrics are important for his business area.

■ **Note**   The creation of metric templates is out of the scope of this chapter. Please refer to the official Enterprise Manager documentation "Cloud Control Administrators Guide" Chapter 7 "Using Monitoring Templates" for more information about creating and maintaining monitoring templates.

Once you are comfortable with the monitoring templates return to the Administration Group definition in the Targets ➤ Groups menu. You need to use the "Create ➤ Administration Group" menu item again to return the group's definition. Advance to the tab named "Template Collections". Using the "Create" button you can start the definition of a template collection. Since each template collection can be individually assigned to the hierarchy nodes, you should use a name that makes it easy to identify the collection's purpose. Once the name and description have been assigned, you can start adding monitoring templates by clicking on the green plus sign. Figure 8-25 shows that screen with two templates defined for production and test.

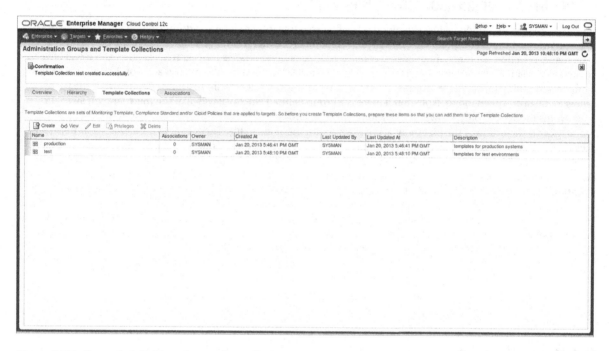

Figure 8-25. *Example definition of a template collection*

In the above example you can see a snapshot of the development of the administration group. In this figure two template collections have already been added, one for production systems and one for test environments. Remember, they have not been assigned to any target yet, this is done in the next step.

Associate Template Collections with Hierarchy Nodes

In the previous step you grouped monitoring templates for target types such as listeners, database instances, and others into monitoring templates. By adding the monitoring templates to the Administration Group you made those available for the next and final step in the wizard interface, accessible by clicking on the "Associations" tab.

On the following screen you are presented with the hierarchy from the first step. Highlight a node and click on "Associate Template Collection". A pop-up window will appear listing the template collection you have just defined. If you click on "Continue" you are once more shown the monitoring templates group to the template collection. You will also see how many targets are going to be affected. The node will reflect the association by showing the name of the template collection(s).

Repeat the association of template collections to hierarchy nodes for any remaining collection. When all template collections have been assigned you need to trigger their activation. The activation is governed by the "Synchronization Schedule" which needs to be configured first, use the "Synchronization Schedule" to do so. This was the last task to be performed in the Administration Group wizard. You can now switch to the group homepage and verify the status of its members. The great thing about the newly configured Administration Group is that targets join the group instantly when their extended properties are set. By joining the Administration Group the templates defined in the template collection will apply to the target, ensuring that monitoring is uniform and standardized. Assigning the target properties can be done at target provisioning time as part of the standard deployment scripts.

Incident Management

Incident management builds upon settings and configuration steps explained in previous sections. One almost imperative task is the creation of Administration Groups, and more specifically the definition of monitoring templates. After your important systems are properly configured for standardized monitoring then the next step is to define alerting. Elaborate workflows can be designed in Enterprise Manager, and if you like you can use OEM as your only incident management solution.

Oracle however knows that many organizations already have some kind of Trouble Ticket System (TTS) in place, and provides connectors for the most commonly used ones. Enterprise Manager collects metrics from targets. Lots of metrics are collected, such as CPU usage, database free space, and many more. In addition, OEM records when a target is down or a job did not execute successfully. The management agents also make extensive use of the Automatic Diagnostic Repository (ADR) to detect problems with a listener, ASM, or database instance. This section is about using Enterprise Manager 12c for the complete workflow. The workflow is based on notifications which you need to set up first.

Set up Notifications

Notifications—as their name implies—will inform you about events collected by the Enterprise Management infrastructure. The most common notification method in today's IT world is electronic mail, even though it has its flaws. Configuration of email notifications happens in two steps. The first is globally applicable and defines your email gateway.

Navigate to Setup ➤ Notifications ➤ Notification Methods. The screen is fairly self-explanatory. If you want to follow the example you need to specify the name of the outgoing mail server and connection details. If your Mail Transfer Agent supports encryption you should by all means make use of the TLS or SSL options. After supplying the required information you should click on the "Apply" button followed by a click to the "Test Mail Server" button.

■ **Note** There are many more configuration options to explore like the email format and a notification schedule. Please refer to Chapter 4 of the Cloud Control Administrator's Guide for all the detail about notifications, including notification beyond email.

Use Incident Management

To better understand the concept of incident management in Enterprise Manager it is important to understand some terminology first.

- *Event*: An event is raised by the management framework when something happens out of the ordinary. A metric violation can cause an event to be raised for example, or if a target goes down outside of a pre-defined maintenance window.

- *Incident*: Similar events are grouped together to form an incident. Although you can have some cases where a significant event causes an incident to be created. Enterprise Manager tries to reduce the number of notifications by aggregating related events into a single incident.

- *Problem*: A problem is purely an Oracle database issue reported in the Automatic Diagnostic Repository. A problem can be any error reported in the alert.log of the database, or a stuck archiver for example. If a problem does not lead to a situation affecting normal operations Enterprise Manager will not create an incident by default. Problems are comparatively easy to deal with since they can be packaged using the Support Workbench we know since Oracle 11.1 and sent to Oracle Support for investigation. If so desired a service request can automatically be created as part of the process.

- *Enterprise Rule Set*: An enterprise rule set defines criteria for raising events. Oracle supplies a basic set of rules out-of-the-box raising incidents for events requiring attention. You should however consider creating your own enterprise rule sets to better cater to your environment.

The aforementioned Enterprise Rule Sets define under which conditions events should be raised. Oracle allows a basic mode of operation out-of-the-box by defining rules to raise events for cases when you would expect the attention of an administrator. All events have an event type indicating the part of Enterprise Manager where the event was raised. In addition an event has a severity ranging from informational to fatal. The out-of-the box incident rules do not include escalation rules which you need to define yourself if they are needed in your environment.

Incidents are the entities you work on as an administrator. Enterprise Manager 12c uses the Incident Manager view to deal with events that occurred within the managed infrastructure. Figure 8-26 shows the Incident Manager's main screen which you can get to via Enterprise ➤ Monitoring ➤ Incident Manager. When an incident is raised it is placed into a queue with the status of "New" and not assigned to any user. An event is new until assigned, when its status changes to work in progress. Once the underlying problem has been resolved, the incident is resolved. The DBA manager can assign priorities to incidents. To ensure progress is made incidents can be escalated if they are not worked on for a defined period of time. Manual escalation is possible at any time by a manager. Escalation is possible in five different levels, giving you ample opportunity to alert even the VP of database operations if needed.

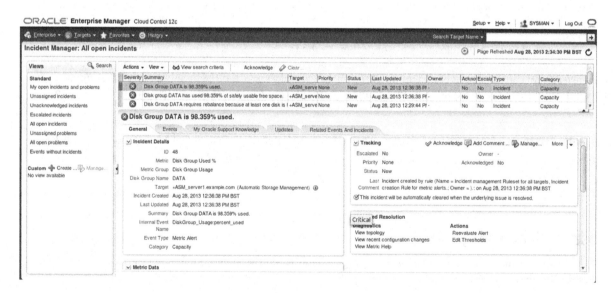

Figure 8-26. *Incident Manager with an incident selected*

Incident Manager will only display incidents belonging to targets you have access to in the top-right part of the screen. When selecting an incident as shown in Figure 8-26 more detail is provided. In this example disk group DATA has a few problems reported which needs to be investigated. The tracking pane is important from a manager's point of view. With it the database team leader can assign events to DBAs in his team, add comments and change the lifecycle. You can also see which rule set was responsible for creating the event. The "Guided Resolution" pane tries to be helpful by suggesting where to look for the root cause of the problem. The narrower the problem source the better the result but it cannot replace experience.

If multiple events are grouped by the incident then you will find those listed by clicking on the "Events" tab. The "My Oracle Support Knowledge" tab directs you to My Oracle Support if your OMS is on online mode. The Enterprise Manager tries to find MOS notes relevant to the problem at hand. The "Updates" tab shows what happened during the lifetime of the incident. The initial entry in the list is the incident creation. You will see who worked on the incident-acknowledgements, comments by the DBAs the incident was assigned to, and when the incident was resolved.

When a new incident is raised the DBA manager assigns it to a DBA, using the "manage" button shown in Figure 8-27.

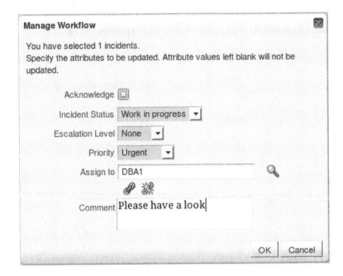

Figure 8-27. *Assigning an incident to a DBA*

Let's assume that the incident involves a crashed database. The DBA manager transfers the task of investigation to DBA1 with high priority, and sends a short message as well. DBA1 will then receive the new task in his queue, but still has to acknowledge it. This is useful for escalation: automatic escalation is based on incidents which have not been acknowledged after a user-definable amount of time has passed. The standard view "My open incidents and problems" shows each DBA which tasks remain to be dealt with. The database administrator can then acknowledge the problem to show he has taken ownership of it and begin working on the investigation or resolution after setting the status to "work in progress".

As it turned out the database has crashed due to an ORA-600 error but it could be restarted. After the error condition has cleared the incident was cleared as well.

Summary

Enterprise Manager is a feature-rich product, but like anything that has lots of features it is not trivial to operate. Installing Enterprise Manager is simple, but I hope the chapter made it clear that the deployment of the software is only half the job done. A lot of planning and coordination is necessary to get the sizing and eventually the deployment right. This is especially true if you are planning for business continuity and a disaster recovery site! If you do not already have a team of administrators focusing on Enterprise Manager you should seriously consider training a small team for the job. If OEM becomes an integral part of the monitoring infrastructure it is crucial that the administrators know how to deal with outages. A deployment that takes high availability into account is mandatory.

When the infrastructure has been put into place the hard configuration work begins. Agents need to be rolled out to managed hosts, and lots of targets need to be discovered. The next logical step is to define monitoring templates for the types of targets you would like to monitor before you create the Administration Groups. The necessary target properties can be retroactively added using the Enterprise Manager command line interface, newly deployed targets can include the call to emcli into the build scripts to ensure that new databases are adequately monitored.

As the activities begin you should think about creating the users and their associated privileges in OEM to allow users to work efficiently with the system. You should ensure that each user has an email address stored in the system to be notified if things go wrong. Oracle's predefined rule sets do not email by default. This and other factors imply that you need to create your own rule for notifications. The same is true if you need Enterprise Manager to raise a ticket in a supported third-party Trouble Ticket System.

CHAPTER 9

■ ■ ■

Learning About Data Guard

This chapter is dedicated to helping you make informed choices to protect your site from disaster. One cannot think of a hosting solution to be used by potentially hundreds or more databases without proper, standardized planning for what to do when disaster strikes. In order to be prepared for the disaster situation, practice and documentation are crucial to successful handling of the crisis situation. In the Oracle world there are broadly speaking two different ways to achieve the goal of ensuring that your business applications can continue if the lights on your primary data center go out. The first one is the more obvious one to the Oracle database professional: application level replication. The most common representative of this approach is Oracle Data Guard. The second option available is to use application-agnostic storage array replication. The latter is very popular with large organizations that have long-term relations with the established storage vendors. Please note that the chapter you are about to read deals with Data Guard only.

WHY YOU NEED A DISASTER RECOVERY STRATEGY

Most regulators, external and internal, will require your applications to be resilient to data center failures. That does not mean that your application has to be continuously available, although that could be specified too. Rather, it implies that your application must have some sort of standard operating procedure written down and practiced explaining the correct steps to undertake in case an application component irrevocably fails. Usually you will find service level agreements (SLA) with more or less strict obligations signed by the business continuity department and the hosting platform's product management. The intention of the SLA is to limit the time for unplanned outages. The most important aspects you will find covered are:

- The maximum amount of data lost, usually expressed in a time frame
- The maximum amount of time until the service must be restored

In the language of the business-continuity specialist, the first of the two is termed *Recovery Point Object* or RPO. The second bullet point is known as the *Recovery Time Object*, or RTO. Applications which are really critical for the survival of a company are often described as having an RPO and RTO of zero. In other words, there must be no data loss, and the service must be restored instantly. Such a configuration is very difficult and very expensive to implement.

It is not expected that a database hosted on the consolidation platform has these strict requirements. All services planned to be part of the consolidation platform should however have approval from the Business Continuity department from within your organization as a milestone on the project plan. The earlier you have involvement and sign-off from the right team the easier it is to implement your solution around the requirements. Before discussing your options to keep the light on in more detail let's have a look at the offering by Oracle: Data Guard.

An introduction to Oracle Data Guard

Oracle Data Guard is one of the primary means to protect the Oracle database from unplanned outages in the local data center. Unplanned data center outages, as their name implies, greatly affect the availability of the database service. Effective planning beforehand is required to minimize the impact of outages, and having a Data Guard configuration in place is usually great for peace of mind. You can refer to Table 9-1 for a better understanding of where in the Oracle product portfolio Data Guard is located with regards to protection from unplanned outages.

Table 9-1. *Protecting Oracle from Unplanned Outages*

Problem	Technology	Estimated recovery time
Database instance failure	Migration of the virtual machine	Depends on the technology used
	Active/passive clusters	Downtime for the duration of instance recovery on standby host
	Real Application Clusters	No downtime
LUN failure	Automatic Storage Management	No downtime when using ASM built-in mirroring for disk group
Human error	Flashback Database, Flashback Table, other Flashback technology	Duration of the Flashback Database command depends on amount of data changed.
		No downtime to recover from dropped tables if recycle bin is used
	Data Guard with delayed redo application	Very little downtime during failover operation. Certainly quicker than point-in-time recovery, but may incur data loss
Data corruption	Data Guard	Very little downtime during failover operation. Certainly quicker than point-in-time recovery, but may incur data loss
Site failure	Data Guard	Very little downtime during failover operation.

Data Guard allows the database administrator to maintain one or more standby databases, which are a copy of the production database. To be precise, a standby database starts its existence with the RMAN duplication of the primary database, the main difference between the standby database and production database is a flag in the standby database's controlfile indicating its role. Changes from the production database are automatically transmitted over a SQL*Net connection and are constantly applied to the standby database. Standby redo logs (SRL) on the disaster recovery site act as the counterpart to the primary database's online redo logs (ORL) and allow the remote site to receive redo more efficiently.

The standby database can either be identical with production down to the individual bit, or it can be a logical copy. The bitwise identical copy of production is more widespread as it guarantees better business continuity. The way changes from production are transmitted to the standby database—via an IP network—is an important differentiator to the storage replication mentioned in the introduction to this chapter which most commonly relies on the Fiber Channel protocol to keep the remote copies in sync.

Oracle automatically tries to stay in sync with the production database with the help of a set of background processes. One of these processes ensures that the standby database is constantly in the state of media recovery. A standby database can temporarily be opened for read-only access. Without the Active Data Guard option introduced in Oracle 11.1, there is a caveat you need to be aware of: while the database is opened in read-only mode, it doesn't apply changes received from the primary database.

While not a problem per se, the fact that changes are not being applied to the standby database when it is in read-only mode can extend the time needed for role transitions. This is because additional archived redo logs have to be applied first, unless you are willing to incur data loss. Without an Active Data Guard license the database has to be in mount state for managed recovery to work.

The standby database can be configured to be absolutely identical with the production database at any point in time. You could theoretically go so far as to instruct your production database to shut down in case it cannot get an acknowledgement from the standby database that a transaction has been committed. This is a little drastic though and could potentially impact the availability of your service! This is why you read "theoretical" earlier in the paragraph: very few sites operate Data Guard in this particular mode favoring protection over availability.

Processes related to Data Guard manage and monitor the standby database. Examples include shipping redo to the standby databases, the automatic request of missing redo information after a network glitch, the fully transparent addition of data files to the standby database and many more things we take for granted. You should compare how comfortable today's Data Guard is relative to its early days!

A comprehensive set of dictionary views allow the DBA and management frameworks such as Oracle Enterprise Manager to query the status of the Data Guard configuration and alert the DBA on shift should the standby database fall too far behind.

If the unthinkable happens, Data Guard allows you to perform a role transition. Effectively the roles of the primary and one of your standby databases are reversed during the process. The role transition can either be graceful or forced. If what you suffered was a transient failure such as a power-cut, then it is possible to recover from the situation without having to fully recreate the old primary. Sometimes however that cannot be avoided.

In addition to its primary function—preventing or shortening unplanned outages in your data center—Data Guard standby databases can be used for many other purposes. A commonly used feature is an RMAN backup using the standby database as a source. You read about the Active Data Guard option previously, it is very popular for users that have reporting requirements and want to offload them to a standby database. Other uses are less useful in the scope of database consolidation and will not be covered in this chapter, refer to the Data Guard Concepts and Administration Guide for more information.

■ **Note**   You can read more about backing up Oracle from a standby database in Chapter 11.

Standby databases: A historical perspective

When the standby feature was introduced in Oracle 7.3, maintaining a standby database was a highly manual process: the database administrator was in charge of transferring archived redo logs generated on the primary database to the standby site using utilities such as rcp, ftp, or rsync. This does not sound too bad, but bear in mind that the scripts written to that effect had to work out which archived online redo logs to fetch in the current invocation, compared to the last one. They also had to deal with network failures, low network bandwidth, needed to perform their own gap resolution involving archive log sequence numbers, and many other things. In short, they were prone to error; close monitoring was required and DBA intervention commonplace.

Once the logs were on the standby site, the standby database had to be placed in recovery mode via SQL*Plus (usually within a script). The only possible action the administrator could take was to activate the standby database in order for it to assume the primary role. This process, where the DBA was in charge of copying and applying archived redo logs, was referred to as *manual* recovery.

Beginning with Oracle 8*i*, the standby database uses *managed* recovery to stay in sync with the primary database. This was a great step forward in usability! Using Oracle SQL*Net communication, the primary database ships changes to the standby database, which are subsequently applied to the data files to keep the systems in sync. The application of changes can be delayed to protect the system from the aforementioned user errors. A standby database can also be used for reporting or backing up data; this removes some of the load from the primary database.

A further milestone was reached with Oracle 9*i*, which introduced the logical standby database and graceful switchover operations. The previously used standby databases were renamed to physical standby database. It was also in Oracle 9*i* that the standby database feature was renamed to Data Guard. Users of Data Guard were also given another choice for transmitting redo information to the standby. In addition to the archiver process, which traditionally shipped information to the standby database after an online redo log was archived, the log writer process could be used to perform the same task. Standby redo logs were introduced as the counterpart to the primary database's online redo logs. Instead of having to wait for a complete archived redo log to arrive, the redo stream could be written into a standby redo log, thus reducing the risk of data loss. Oracle Database 9*i* also introduced the Data Guard broker with support for Enterprise Manager, as well as a command-line tool to simplify the setup and management of standby databases.

Another noteworthy evolution came with Oracle 10g, when the Real Time Apply feature was integrated into the database kernel. Using standby redo logs on the standby database server, the redo stream arriving on the destination could be applied to the standby database immediately, without having to wait for the standby redo log to be archived and applied. This further reduces the possibility of data loss.

Oracle 11.1 refined the process. Redo could now be compressed for gap resolution, and there was limited support for heterogeneous Data Guard configurations involving Linux and Windows, and HP-UX. A new type of standby database has been added to the previously mentioned physical and logical standby databases called snapshot standby which is covered in more detail below. It was also in Oracle 11.1 that Active Data Guard was introduced.

Oracle 11.2 extended the number of standby database drastically: up to 30 standby databases are possible, and Active Data Guard has been enhanced to perform automatic block media recovery and the redo stream can also be compressed (if you have the necessary license).

Figure 9-1 illustrates the concept which applies since Oracle 11g: redo generated by user activity on the primary database is transported via the LNS*n* processes to the standby database's Remote File Server (RFS) process. Actually it is not the LNS process although it appears as such in v$managed_standby. The processes for sending redo are now named TT*nn* for if redo shipping is performed asynchronously. Synchronous redo transmission will see the LNS*n*/TT*nn* processes replaced by LGWR in v$managed_standby.

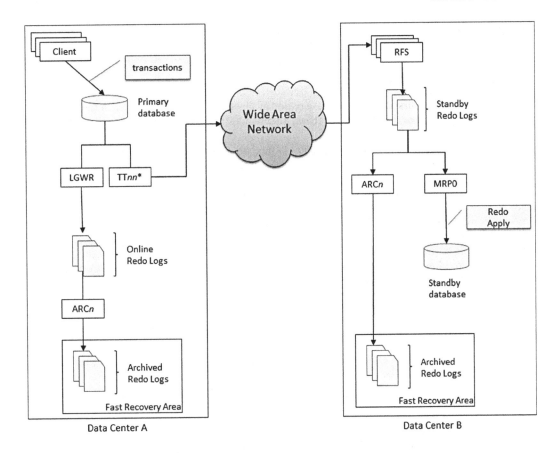

* Redo transport processes appear as LGWR and TT*nn* depending on configuration

Figure 9-1. *Overview of the main processes used in Data Guard with a single standby in sync with production using Real-Time-Apply and asynchronous redo transmission*

One of the RFS processes writes the redo stream into standby redo logs. The managed recovery process (MRP0) on the standby database applies the new information as soon as it arrives. Once filled, the standby redo log is archived by one of the standby database's archiver processes.

Before continuing the discussion let's review the various types of standby databases.

Types of standby databases

You can choose from the following five types of standby databases:

- Physical standby database

- Snapshot standby database

- Logical standby database

- Transient logical standby database

- Far Sync standby database

The first four of these will be covered in more detail in the subsections that follow. Far Sync Standby is a new feature in Oracle database 12c and will be covered in a little later in the section "New Data Guard Features in 12.1."

The physical standby database

The physical standby database was the first standby database option available. In all aspects, a physical standby database is an identical bit-for-bit copy of the primary database. All schema structures, database users, and segments are identical down to the block level.

A physical standby database is kept in sync with production through the application of redo (referred to as "redo apply"). The process employed is the same one that a database administrator would use to recover a live database after a media failure. Apart from disaster recovery scenarios, a standby database can be used for reporting and backup. With a little bit of manual effort, a physical standby database can also be used for testing hot fixes on production systems. You do this by activating it for read-write access after having taken it out of the Data Guard configuration. Once the testing of the hot fix on like-for-like production data is complete, the Flashback Database feature can be used to flash the database back to the point in time prior to its activation, followed by its conversion back to a physical standby. The downside to this procedure is that, while the database is open for read-write access, it won't receive any archived logs from the (real) primary database. This can cause a lot of network traffic once the database has been converted back to a physical standby. Since Oracle 11.1 this manual process is no longer necessary, and Oracle gave the database administrator a better option: the snapshot standby database discussed next.

The snapshot standby database

The snapshot standby database achieves the exact same result as the physical standby opened in read-write mode for testing as just described in the paragraph 'The physical standby database', but without requiring that the administrator worry about the details. The snapshot standby will continue to receive redo information from production, significantly reducing the overhead during gap resolution. However, the redo received from production is not applied until after the snapshot standby database has been converted back to a physical standby database, so the time it takes for the standby database to get back in sync with production is proportional to the amount of redo to be applied.

When upgrading a database with a standby database(s) in place, the redo transport mechanism will ensure that the dictionary changes are propagated to all destinations for as long as the catalog upgrade script is executing on the primary site. This is true for both physical and snapshot standby database configurations. All you need to do is ensure that the Oracle binaries on the standby servers exactly match the binaries on the primary database.

You can have both single-instance standby databases and multi-node RAC systems for your disaster recovery solution. However, bear in mind that your standby database must to be able to cope with the workload in a disaster recovery situation. You are well advised to use identical hardware for both production and standby environments. If you use identical hardware, and your standby database is a RAC database as well, then all instances can receive redo from the primary database, thereby spreading the load.

The logical standby database

A logical standby database differs from a physical standby database in that it is not an exact 1:1 copy of the live database. Every logical standby database starts its existence exactly like a physical standby database, but it is then converted for permanent read-write access. At this stage, the primary database and logical standby can deviate. Physical (and snapshot) standby databases stay synchronized through the application of redo information. However, a logical standby database stays synchronized by having it execute all the same SQL statements as the primary database. This mechanism is referred to as *SQL Apply* as opposed to *Redo Apply*.

Internally, SQL Apply uses the log miner functionality to extract SQL statements from the redo stream. It then applies SQL statements rather than redo to the standby database. Therefore, a logical standby database has the same data structure as the primary database, but the physical representation of the data in the database is likely to be different. There are also some restrictions as to which data types are supported on the primary database, and this list keeps growing from release to release.

Another big difference between a physical and logical standby database is the fact that a logical standby database is open read-write while it still receives and applies changes from production. A logical standby database is unlikely to be used for disaster recovery purposes. Its main purpose is to provide an environment in which reporting can be offloaded from production as changes from the live system are fed into the database. This provides a high degree of data accuracy. The fact that the logical standby database is open read-write means that additional data structures such as indexes and materialized views can be created to speed up queries that would otherwise be too expensive to maintain on the primary database.

Finally, logical standby databases can be used as part of the process to upgrade primary databases to newer releases or to apply patch sets to a system with almost no downtime. This little used technique is referred to as a *rolling upgrade* in the Oracle documentation. The transient logical standby database discussed in the next section is what you really want to use in cases where you want to apply a rolling upgrade in your own environment.

For operational reasons you would not expect a logical standby database to be part of the standard offering of a hosting service. The management of the logical standby is more complex, and it contradicts the ideas of saving cost and allowing lesser-skilled operators to manage the environment.

The transient logical standby database

Oracle has recognized that few businesses are willing to set up a logical standby database only for the rolling upgrade of an Oracle database. Setting up a logical standby database is not a trivial task, and maintaining a logical standby database requires close monitoring to check that all transactions have been applied. For this reason, Oracle 11g Release 1 provides the capability to transiently convert a physical standby database into a logical standby database for the duration of a rolling upgrade. After the upgrade, the logical standby database is converted back to its original role as a physical standby database.

This type of standby database is not listed under the name *transient logical standby* in the documentation; however, it is mentioned in the Maximum Availability Architecture (MAA) series of documents as well as in Chapter 13 of the Data Guard Concepts and Administration chapter, "Using SQL Apply to Upgrade the Oracle Database."

The use of a transient logical standby is not trivial and requires in-depth knowledge of the Oracle database as well as Flashback Database and general backup and recovery skills in addition to what you need to know and understand for the database upgrade. A transient logical standby database remains a logical standby database with its limitations towards unsupported data types and close monitoring requirements. For that reason (complexity!) it might not be the best choice for migrations on a hosted platform. This is even more relevant with the introduction of Pluggable Databases which can potentially be unplugged and plugged into databases with different patch levels

The Active Data Guard Option

The majority of standby databases are probably physical standby databases running in remote disaster recovery data centers waiting to be activated. Many users of such configurations have remarked that this isn't the best use of resources. While it is possible to use the standby database as a source for backups, the tapes must be shipped from the DR site to the primary site if something occurs. The other option, using the standby database for reporting and ad-hoc queries that couldn't possibly be executed on the primary database, also has a downside: while the database is open for read-only mode, no archived logs are applied, which causes the primary and the standby databases to go out of sync and the data to become stale.

Beginning with 11g Release 1, Oracle addressed these concerns with the Active Data Guard option, which needs to be licensed on top of Enterprise Edition. When purchased, this option offers the following benefits in Oracle 12c Enterprise Edition over and above what Data Guard already provides:

- Physical Standby databases in read-only mode can have managed recovery enabled. This allows users to offload their queries to current production data, thus combining the best of both worlds. Oracle refers to this feature as *Real Time Query*.

- This option also allows the use of block change tracking for faster incremental backups on the standby database

- Block corruption in a Data Guard environment can automatically be repaired

- The previously mentioned Far Sync Standby configuration about which you will read later in the chapter requires Active Data Guard. So do related technologies.

- There are other features that depend on Active Data Guard but they do not directly relate to this discussion.

- Please refer to the licensing guide for more information

Active Data Guard can also be used as a scalability tool for web-based content. Multiple standby databases opened read-only, with the Active Data Guard option enabled can provide real-time data access to web servers. This significantly scales data access. Updates to the data occur only on the primary database through a controlled user interface, and changes are immediately propagated to the reader farm through Real-Time Query.

Data protection modes

Data Guard offers three different data protection modes. Depending on the business requirements, Data Guard can be set up for maximum performance without affecting the operation of the primary database; alternatively, it can be set up to ensure zero data loss. There are advantages and disadvantages to all three options.

Maximum Protection Mode

This mode provides the highest level of protection from data loss, ensuring that there will be no data lost should the primary database experience an unplanned outage. To achieve this level of protection, the standby database has to acknowledge that the redo generated by a transaction on the primary has been written into its standby redo logs (this is of course in addition to the primary database's online redo logs) before the transaction can be committed on the primary. If the primary database can't write to the designated standby database's SRLs, it will shut down. If it didn't the configuration could not guarantee zero data loss. Obtaining this zero data loss guarantee comes at a price: the application's commit time can increase compared to a different protection mode proportionally to the network round trip time, and the primary database may shut down as a consequence of a network problem.

For exactly this reason the Maximum Protection Mode can potentially do more harm than good. Environments where an RPO of 0 is required usually need a protection mode similar to Maximum Protection, but as you read earlier these environments tend to have their own dedicated hardware and storage. If you are considering the use of Maximum Protection Mode you should have multiple standby databases as destinations for your redo on different networks each with its own hardware. Otherwise you run a high risk that the primary database shuts down! An implementation of Maximum Protection Mode is therefore out of the scope of this chapter.

Maximum Performance mode

This mode dictates that the performance and availability of the primary database are not affected by the standby database. The default protection mode, maximum performance, has no redo write dependency between the primary and standby databases; in other words, the primary database commits transactions independently of the standby database. Because of this, many businesses introduce regular, forced log switches on the primary database using the archive_lag_target initialization parameter.

Maximum Performance can still help you work towards a low Recovery Point Objective by employing Real Time Apply on the standby database. Using this protection mode your primary and standby database(s) usually are in an asynchronous configuration.

Maximum Availability mode

This is a hybrid mode that strikes a balance between the other two modes. For transactions to commit on the primary database, at least one synchronized standby database must have received the redo in its standby redo logs. If it's not possible to write the redo stream to at least one synchronized database, the primary will perform as if it were configured in maximum performance mode.

In this respect this protection mode seems most desirable. When using the Data Guard Broker as shown in the following example, you are well protected from rolling disasters. A rolling disaster not only affects your primary, but also your secondary site. In the default settings the Broker will configure Data Guard in a way that a transaction on the primary can only commit if the write is confirmed on the standby site.

Since Oracle 12.1 it is possible to configure the Maximum Availability mode so that it only acknowledges that redo has been received in memory with the log write initiated but not completed. It does not confirm that the redo has actually been written to a standby redo log. The slight performance benefit you get (not having to wait for the redo to be written to disk) comes at the cost of higher exposure to the rolling disaster: if both sides went down at the same time, you could have incurred data loss, since redo in the buffers may not have been written to disk yet.

Role transitions

Data Guard supports two types of role transitions: a *graceful switchover* and a *failover*. During a switchover operation, the primary database ensures that no data loss occurs by performing a log switch and waiting for the redo to be applied on all databases that form part the Data Guard configuration. Only then will it transform into a standby database itself. At this stage, *all* the databases forming part of the Data Guard configuration are physical standby databases. The administrator then chooses one of the other standby databases to assume the primary role.

A *switchover* is an elegant solution that helps to minimize time required for performing the following maintenance operations:

- Scheduled replacement of hardware

- Migration to another storage technology such as ASM

- Storage array migration when using traditional file systems for storage

- Data center migration

- Upgrading the version of Grid Infrastructure without upgrading the database at the same time

- Major operating system upgrades

- Changing the word size from 32 bit to 64 bit (although that is less common these days)

A switchover operation is not entirely free of downtime, but it provides a proven procedure and technology for such tasks.

A *failover* indicates a more severe situation in which the primary database is no longer available for a switchover, possibly because of a site failure or the loss of the storage backend. In such a situation, the administrator should try salvaging as many outstanding archived logs as possible. Since 11.2 it is even possible to flush unsent redo from the primary to the standby, potentially allowing a no-data-loss failover! The DBA should also minimize or, if at all possible, eliminate the gap to be resolved on the standby database before activating one of the standby databases for read-write access. Data loss may occur, depending on the protection mode the Data Guard configuration is using.

Prior to the introduction of the Flashback Database feature, activating a standby database always implied that the previous primary database had to be completely rebuilt by restoring it from a backup. Today, however, if the failed primary database has flashback database enabled, then the time and effort required for a reinstantiation of the database can be greatly reduced, assuming that it can be started up without problems. For example, once the failed database has been restarted after a complete data center power outage, it is possible to flash it back to the system change number that existed prior to the activation of the new primary. From there, the database can be converted to a physical standby with only a few commands. When the situation clears, the former primary database can then be the target of a graceful switchover to restore service to before the failover.

Role transitions are slightly different, depending on the type of standby database (logical or physical) to assume the primary role, and each database administrator should be familiar with the steps necessary to carry out the different role transitions. Regular disaster recovery tests should be performed to ensure that the standby database(s) and the entire dependent infrastructure, such as load balancers and application servers, can execute the workload in the disaster recovery center. Easily accessible documentation is important, helping the more junior team members perform this task and keep a cool head during a crisis.

An in-depth view on Data Guard terminology

You just read that Oracle Data Guard relies on redo to be shipped to the standby databases to keep the databases in sync. Certain operations on the primary database can be executed with the nologging clause, which has consequences for the standby database. Any nologging operation on the source does not generate sufficient redo to update the destination. If you were to switch over and there had been nologging operations on the primary you would end up with a corrupt database. If the database is in force-logging mode then it will ignore nologging statements, making redo generation and transport a lot more reliable. Note that it requires elevated privileges to change the force logging mode.

Standby redo logs (SRL) have briefly been discussed earlier. They are very important components of every database in the Data Guard configuration. In order to be prepared for role transitions you should not only create standby redo logs on the standby databases, but also on the primary. Data Guard Broker will complain if there are no standby redo logs! Additionally higher protection modes also require the existence of SRLs.

If SRLs are present they are used by Real Time Apply. In this apply mode, redo is applied from the standby redo logs as they are filled. Without Real Time Apply standby redo logs work exactly as Online Redo Logs do in the primary database. They are being written to in the circular fashion, and when full will be archived. The archived redo log is then applied to the standby database.

■ **Note**   It is strongly suggested that you use Standby Redo Logs in all Data Guard scenarios for primary and standby databases.

Data Guard allows you to have multiple copies of the same database in your configuration. This poses a challenge: if the databases are all identical, how can Data Guard work out who is who and what role is a database in? The solution to that problem is with the database unique name. Consider Figure 9-2.

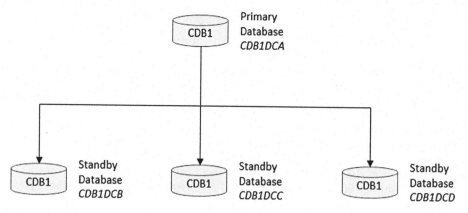

Figure 9-2. A Data Guard configuration with multiple standby databases using different database unique names (in italics)

In the above configuration you find three standby databases and a primary. The database name has to be consistent in the initialization file for all databases in the Data Guard configuration. The database name is defined in the db_name initialization parameter at the database creation time and cannot easily be changed. Each database however has its own *unique* name. The unique name often matches the Oracle SID and has a reference to the data center where the database is located. Refer to the section "Naming conventions" in the next chapter for an explanation of why this naming scheme has been chosen. The db_unique_name initialization parameter for each database (including the primary) is added when the standby database is created. In the absence of a db_unique_name initialization parameter the value defaults to the db_name. Setting the db_unique_name is often forgotten on the primary database.

All databases in a Data Guard Broker configuration are said to have a state associated with them. The state depends on the database role (primary, physical standby, etc.). The primary database can either be in state "transport-on", which means it ships redo to the destinations defined in the configuration, or it can be in state "transport-off" which has the opposite effect. Changing the state to "transport-off" is not allowed in higher protection modes. The standby databases in turn can be in state "apply-on" which starts managed recovery including Real Time Apply if there are standby redo logs. Alternatively managed recovery can be turned off by transitioning the standby database into the state "apply-off."

WHY DATA GUARD AND RAC ARE COMPLEMENTARY

Very often during user group meetings you meet participants confusing the Real Application Clusters option with a disaster recovery solution. A quote heard often is: "We use a stretch cluster-we do not need Data Guard." This confusion is not limited to user groups though, generally speaking, RAC and Data Guard can be the source of some controversy. The discussion can get quite heated, especially when extended distance clusters are mentioned. Why that confusion? Let's remember the following two simple points:

- Real Application Clusters are built to protect Oracle database instances from failure.

- Data Guard is designed to provide an additional copy of your production database.

The significance lies in the scope: remember that as per Table 9-1 the scope of RAC is the instance. To make this clearer, imagine a migration weekend, and the script turns out to have a bug corrupting the schema you are migrating. The consequence is logical corruption on the database level: you can start as many RAC instances now, the fundamental problem is that your schema is logically corrupt, no matter what. The common solutions are to either perform a Flashback Database operation if possible, or to do a point-in-time recovery.

A standby database on the other hand can be very beneficial in such a scenario. If the release procedure instructs the database administrator to either cancel or delay the redo application on the standby database you have a perfectly valid copy of the production database as it was when the release started. Remember that a standby database does not necessarily have to be in a remote data center! You could have situations where a primary database has a local and remote standby database. The local standby would be used in exactly the way just described and could be used to take over from production on very short notice. The remote standby database serves as the life insurance if the primary data center fails for whatever reason, and possibly to take backups and/or reporting.

To come full circle, Data Guard does not protect you from instance failure; remember the scope again. For this reason, RAC and Data Guard are complementary technologies. The existence of RAC or even stretched RAC does not make a Data Guard configuration redundant, and neither does Data Guard protect you from instance failure.

New Data Guard features in 12.1

As part of the new Oracle release there are some noteworthy changes to Data Guard as well. As with every new release it is a good idea to check the Data Guard Concepts and Administration Guide as well as the Data Guard Broker documentation for the section named "New features … in 12.1". The following sections explain what is new and useful from a Data Guard point of view with regards to consolidation and Database as a Service. In addition to the features you can read about in the next section there are development related changes as well, mainly geared towards enabling support for reporting applications to use sequences or temporary tables on the standby database. Although these new features are great steps forward in terms of technology they will not be discussed here. Please bear in mind that some of the new features require extra licenses on top of Enterprise Edition.

What will not be mentioned at this stage in the document is the support for Pluggable Databases. The remainder of the next chapter will deal specifically with these in mind. Since Data Guard operates at the database level, not at the PDB level, all operations shown below are executed at the CDB$ROOT level. It is not possible to limit the scope of redo transport to a single Pluggable Database. Also note that non-Container Databases are out of the scope of this chapter.

Better separation of duties for log shipping

You read in the Linux installation chapter that Oracle has expanded roles available to users. A frequent complaint in larger organizations was that Data Guard required the SYS account to transmit redo between the primary and standby database. The security departments rightfully remarked that the SYS role was too powerful, and a less powerful role should be used to transmit redo. With Oracle 12.1 this request has been implemented in the form of an initialization parameter.

A database account which has been granted the SYSOPER privilege can be defined to ship redo from the primary to the standby database. Interestingly at the time of this writing the SYSDG role did not allow you to ship redo to the standby databases. When granting the SYSOPER to a user please do not forget to synchronize the password files across all databases in the Data Guard configuration. You can easily check the contents of the file by querying v$pwfile_users. Remember that the redo transport user needs to be a common user in the CDB.

Better support for cascaded destinations

A cascaded standby database receives redo indirectly from the primary database via an intermediate hop. Although the ability to have cascaded standby databases allows the enterprise architect to develop interesting disaster recovery solutions, the main reason for cascading is to offload the redo burden from the primary database. The more redo destinations you define in the primary database the more work the host has to complete. Keep in mind that there has to be a log shipping process for every standby database. If there are lots of standby databases to be supplied with redo this can be a lot of extra work for the primary database and host.

Oracle 12.1 has improved support for cascading with physical standby databases. Consider a scenario as shown in Figure 9-3. Here a primary Redo arriving in data center B is cascaded to two standby databases in data center C.

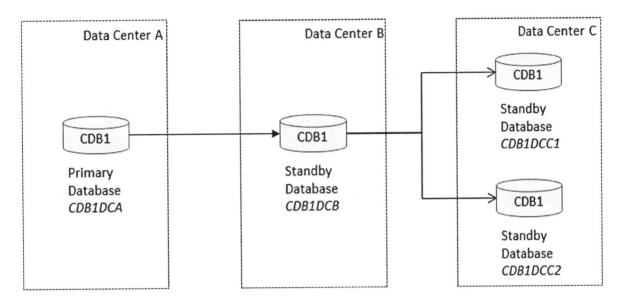

Figure 9-3. Example for cascaded standby databases.

In Oracle 12.1 the database CDB1DCB cascades redo as soon as it arrives in the standby redo logs. From a configuration point of view there are two pairs of configurations. The first pair is between CDB1DCA and CDB1DCB, and the second pair between CDB1DCB and CDB1DCC1 plus CDB1DCC2. As a result the database-in-the middle will be configured as the communication endpoint for CDB1DCA. Similarly the two standby databases in data center C will be the communication endpoint for CDB1DCB.

In previous releases Oracle did not pass redo on directly. Instead you had to wait until the standby redo log of the cascading database (CDB1DCB) had the log archived. The enhancement in Oracle 12c is named real-time-cascade and requires the Active Data Guard license. The old way is still available although you can cascade to a maximum of 10 databases that way. This limit does not exist for real-time cascade.

The use of cascaded standby database is not anticipated in the hosting services and therefore will not be covered in further detail here.

The Far Sync Standby Feature

The far sync standby is another approach to ease the burden of redo shipping to multiple standby databases, as shown in Figure 9-4. The benefit of the far sync standby is increased with every additional standby database in the configuration. The Far Sync standby is implemented as a cascaded destination. Despite the name, the far sync standby does not have to be far away, it could be geographically close and still help a lot with distributing redo.

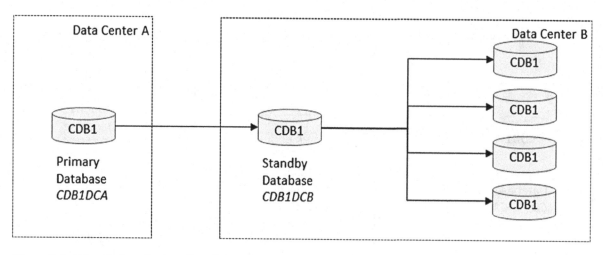

Figure 9-4. *Example for a Far Sync Standby configuration*

Unlike a "real" standby database, the Far Sync does not have any requirement for data files, significantly reducing the storage footprint. Apart from the data files all other physical structures of a database are present: control files, standby redo logs, archived (standby) redo logs, and the administrative files. Since there are no data files you cannot expect to open the database at all. Similarly you cannot switch over or fail over to a Far Sync Standby. In effect it really only serves as a relay for redo information. In addition to helping the primary database send redo, it could also be used to save bandwidth over long distances. If you considered Data Center A to be in North America, and Data Center B in the Far East, there is only one set of redo to be transported over the long-distance link, instead of potentially redundant information multiple times.

Ability to check for switchover readiness

The broker can now check for switchover readiness. In releases before Oracle 12.1 it has always been a manual process to find out whether a database was ready for a role change or not. This often included checking for potential archive log gaps, checking whether the network was ready and many more pre-checks. Luckily the Broker supports the DBA in this task. If everything is ok, you should see output similar to this:

```
DGMGRL> validate database "STDB1"

  Database Role:     Physical standby database
  Primary Database:  CDB1

  Ready for Switchover:  Yes
  Ready for Failover:    Yes (Primary Running)

  Current Log File Groups Configuration:
    Thread #  Online Redo Log Groups   Standby Redo Log Groups
              (CDB1)                   (STDB1)
    1         3                        2

  Future Log File Groups Configuration:
    Thread #  Online Redo Log Groups   Standby Redo Log Groups
              (STDB1)                  (CDB1)
    1         3                        2
```

In this example, managed recovery aborted due to a problem. The database is *not* ready for any role transition, as shown in the "Ready for Switchover" and "Ready for Failover" rows.

```
DGMGRL> validate database "STDB1"

  Database Role:     Physical standby database
  Primary Database:  CDB1

  Ready for Switchover:  No
  Ready for Failover:    No (Primary Running)

  Standby Apply-Related Information:
    Apply State:     Not Running
    Apply Lag:       505 days 18 hours 55 minutes 28 seconds
    Apply Delay:     0 minutes

  Current Log File Groups Configuration:
    Thread #  Online Redo Log Groups   Standby Redo Log Groups
              (CDB1)                    (STDB1)
    1         3                         2

  Future Log File Groups Configuration:
    Thread #  Online Redo Log Groups   Standby Redo Log Groups
              (STDB1)                   (CDB1)
    1         3                         2

  Automatic Diagnostic Repository Errors:
    Error                       CDB1     STDB1
    System data file missing    NO       YES
```

A crucial system data file is missing. Failing over at this stage would cause a lot of chaos.

Another example is shown here. The database is not ready for a switchover, because it is out of sync with the primary. Remember that a switchover is a no-data-loss operation, and only when all redo has been applied on the target standby will it switch over and reverse roles.

```
DGMGRL> validate database "STDB1"

  Database Role:     Physical standby database
  Primary Database:  CDB1
    Warning: primary database was not reachable

  Ready for Switchover:  No
  Ready for Failover:    Yes (Primary Not Running)

  Temporary Tablespace File Information:
    CDB1 TEMP Files:   Unknown
    STDB1 TEMP Files:  3

  Flashback Database Status:
    CDB1:   Unknown
    STDB1:  On
```

```
Data file Online Move in Progress:
   CDB1:   Unknown
   STDB1:  No

Transport-Related Information:
   Transport On:        No
   Gap Status:          Unknown
   Transport Lag:       1 hours 14 minutes 40 seconds
   Transport Status:    Success

Log Files Cleared:
   CDB1 Standby Redo Log Files:   Unknown
   STDB1 Online Redo Log Files:   Cleared
```

If you were desperate though you could initiate a failover operation at this point, but your data loss would be too high at 1 hour 14 minutes 40 seconds. For most applications this is too much to be accepted. In such a situation you need to double-check the monitoring to find out why the database could fall that far behind, and you should try and salvage any redo logs from the primary you can get hold of and apply them to minimize the data loss.

If your primary was still running you could try enabling the archive destination and/or switch a log file. This is normally enough to kick the log transport and apply mechanism back into gear after a transient failure.

Broker configuration can be renamed in place

Another nice feature is the ability to rename the configuration without having to drop it. If for example the name of your configuration does not match the standards, or if the standards change, then you can implement the change of name as shown in this example. Assume the configuration name is defined as "apress."

```
DGMGRL> show configuration

Configuration - apress

   Protection Mode: MaxPerformance
   Databases:
   CDB1  - Primary database
     STDB1 - Physical standby database

Fast-Start Failover: DISABLED

Configuration Status:
SUCCESS
```

Now change the configuration name to "DBAAS:"

```
DGMGRL> edit configuration rename to DBAAS;
Succeeded.
DGMGRL> show configuration
```

```
Configuration - dbaas

  Protection Mode: MaxPerformance
  Databases:
  CDB1  - Primary database
    STDB1 - Physical standby database

Fast-Start Failover: DISABLED

Configuration Status:
SUCCESS
```

It is as simple as that.

Managing and administering Data Guard

As with most Oracle technologies Data Guard can be managed in a number of ways, including command line and graphical user interface. The command line tools include SQL*Plus as well as dgmgrl, the Data Guard Manager Line Mode.

Managing using SQL*Plus

All Data Guard operations can be managed via SQL*Plus. Although the management of the configuration via SQL*Plus gives the administrator the greatest flexibility, it requires profound knowledge of the inner workings of Data Guard. The aim of this book is to simplify management and also deal with the fact that first- and second-level support may be outsourced. While it is still desirable for any database administrator to understand how Data Guard works in detail it should not be assumed that such knowledge is readily available. Depending on your organizational structure, troubleshooting Data Guard may be left to third-line support.

The remaining sections of this chapter therefore deal with a simplified yet very powerful interface to Data Guard-the Data Guard Broker.

Management using the Data Guard Broker

The Data Guard Broker is an integral part of the replication framework that lets you define Data Guard configurations, including support for all types of standby databases. The Broker is installed by default with the RDBMS binaries. Its architecture was added to Data Guard in Oracle 9i, and it is a mature but little-used feature. From a user's point of view, the Data Guard Broker simplifies the setup, maintenance, and monitoring of Data Guard configurations, as well as role transitions. The Broker fully supports Oracle RAC and RAC One Node as well. The tight integration into Enterprise Manager also allows the creation of a standby database through simple mouse movements and a few key strokes. The usability of the Enterprise Manager integrated Broker is higher than the command line interface via dgmgrl which is alternatively available to the administrator. Enterprise Manager is more feature rich but requires additional infrastructure, which your organization may already have in place anyway.

When used, Data Guard Broker will rely on its own binary configuration files and additional background processes to configure the relevant initialization parameters upon instance start; it will also monitor the databases in the configuration. In clustered environments the configuration files need to be on shared storage. ASM, raw devices, and cluster file systems are possible candidates to store the files; ASM really is the best choice. You do not have to replicate the configuration on each database. Rather, the broker will automatically preserve the single image view of your Data Guard configuration by replicating changes to all databases involved. You should not try to issue SQL commands through sqlplus to modify the Data Guard configuration because your changes are likely to be overwritten the next time the Data Guard broker starts: once the broker, always the broker; unless you remove or disable the Broker configuration.

Conceptually, the main objects the Data Guard Broker operates on are configurations, databases, instances, and properties. To begin, a configuration is created with the primary database only. Up to 30 standby databases can then be added since Oracle 11.2, along with their respective attributes. Data Guard Broker will automatically detect whether a database is made up of multiple instances and register them with their database. Once all databases are added in and the administrator is happy with the setup, the configuration can be enabled. From there, the Data Guard broker takes command over the Data Guard environment. Tailing the database's alert.log you can see how it manipulates the relevant initialization parameters and updates the configuration.

The database object has properties and state information associated with it. As noted earlier, you no longer set initialization parameters directly. Instead, you change the state of the database to enable/disable log shipping or enable/disable managed recovery. The list of database properties you can either read or modify has grown with the evolution of Data Guard and is based on the attributes of the log_archive_dest_*n* parameter. Important properties you can modify include the following (among other options):

- Synchronous or asynchronous sending of redo to the standby database

- The delay for the application of a redo to the standby database; this setting is useful for preventing data corruption caused by human error in a multi-standby database environment. You should ensure that you have another standby database that is using real-time-apply to stay as close to the primary database as possible

- Compression of the redo. Beginning with Oracle 11.1, archived logs could be compressed during gap resolution; Oracle 11g Release 2 introduces compression for the redo stream, but a license for the Advanced Compression option is required.

- Database file name conversion

- Log file name conversion

- Apply parallelism

- Standby file management which should set to auto. The default is manual standby file management

When using Enterprise Manager, you don't have to remember the property names. Instead, you use the graphical user interface (GUI) to manage your Data Guard configuration.

The Data Guard broker has built-in support to modify redo transport and apply services for RAC and single-instance installations. As an additional benefit, the Data Guard broker allows you to set up automatic failover for unsupervised Data Guard configurations. This is referred to as *Fast Start Failover*. With this feature, an observer process running on hardware separate from the database servers monitors the primary database, and it can be configured to automatically fail over to the standby based on user-definable conditions. Beginning with Oracle 11g Release 1, an API to control the Fast Start Failover option is available in form of the DBMS_DG package. After the failover is complete, the Data Guard broker will post a Fast Application Notification event indicating that the new primary database is ready for use. FAN uses the Oracle Notification Services process to post the event, so the database needs to either be a RAC database or single-instance database integrated with Oracle Restart.

Summary

Data Guard is a wonderful tool available to the database administrator to protect the primary database from more serious forms of unplanned (data center) outages. Data Guard has evolved over time to a very feature-rich option of the Oracle database. And unlike storage replication it firmly puts the DBA into a driving seat. Warnings issued by the database and sent to the central monitoring solution can be dealt with proactively, and potential problems should be fixed before they have a detrimental effect in the crisis situation.

The Data Guard toolkit gives the DBA a wealth of options to choose from. Many sites will likely use very few standby databases, if not just one. Given enough available storage however more than one standby database can be created. A physical standby in a data center a safe distance away is almost mandatory. In addition to the remote and true disaster recovery database local standby databases can be created to test hot fixes in a snapshot standby without compromising business continuity by taking the true DR database out of the configuration. Other Data Guard use cases for local standby databases are offloading backups or reporting.

Data Guard Broker is one of the most convenient tools to administer Data Guard configurations and is thoroughly recommended.

In the chapter that follows you can read in detail how to implement a Data Guard configuration, how to test it and how to perform role transitions. The creation of the standby database is equally important and will also be discussed in depth.

## CHAPTER 10

Implementing Data Guard

You were introduced to Data Guard terms and technology in depth in the previous chapter. Now it is time to put theory into practice. A Data Guard implementation always starts with the duplication of the primary database. This is easiest done using Recovery Manger, RMAN. The high-level steps are as follows:

1. Check if the primary database is in force-logging mode.

2. Optionally enable Flashback Database on the primary database.

3. Create standby redo logs on the primary database.

4. Create a backup of the primary database if there is not one already.

5. Make the backup of the primary database available on all standby servers.

6. Create a new init.ora file for each standby database to be created.

7. Duplicate the target database for use as a standby database.

8. Create the Data Guard configuration.

If you have enough network bandwidth, you can clone the database directly over the network without having to take a backup first. This becomes a true possibility with the wider adoption of 10GB Ethernet networks, except maybe when long distances are involved.

This chapter will guide you through the process of the standby database creation. There is a slight difference between using Oracle Managed Files (OMFs) on a file system or Oracle Automatic Storage Management and using the traditional file system approach. Both approaches will be covered in this chapter.

Naming considerations

Data Guard naming conventions are often the source of considerable controversy. When thinking of using Data Guard with a database you should consider its use right from the start, especially when using OMFs. The OMF directory structure follows the following naming convention in ASM:

```
+diskGroupName/db_unique_name/filetype/fileTypeTag.file#.incarnation
```

The database unique name is of importance here. If you create your database as PROD with a standby database unique name of STDBY for example, then the ASM files will be stored in +data/prod/datafile/... and +data/stdby/datafile/. Although there is nothing wrong with that, it can cause confusion when the PROD database had to perform a role change and subsequently is in a standby database role. If your naming standards are flexible enough you should consider naming the databases you create by location rather than initial role. The confusion about a database role can be greatly reduced in this case.

One possible approach would be as follows:

- Use a form of the application name as the db_name. This application name should be recognizable by the support staff, but does not necessarily have to be.

- Use a form of encoded location as the db_unique_name, even if you are not currently planning on using Data Guard but other storage replication.

- You could use the same ORACLE_SID as the db_unique_name to keep the naming scheme consistent.

Throughout the rest of the chapter you will find this principle applied. Figure 10-1 shows the configuration used from a high level.

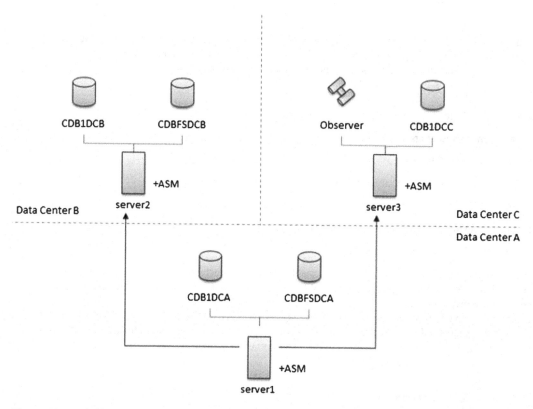

Figure 10-1. *The Data Guard configurations to be used in the following sections. The figure shows the initial configuration where the databases in data center A are in the primary role*

There are three different types of databases used:

- A Container Database as described in Chapter 7. The CDBs are numbered, starting with CDB1 to n. Container Databases use Oracle Managed Files and Automatic Storage Management by default. The database CDBFS is the only example where a CDB uses a XFS file system without OMF. Such an approach is often found in environments where block level replication is used or in Solaris zones.

- The ORACLE_SID reflects the data center where the databases are located. In the examples to follow you will notice data centers A to C. The SIDs therefore are named *databaseNAmeDataCenterName*. The standby database for database CDB1 in data center B is called CDB1DCB as a consequence.

- The db_unique_name is set to equal the ORACLE_SID

This naming scheme is only one out of a million possible combinations. Most often companies have naming schemes in use referring to continents, countries, cities, and so on. Regardless of how the naming scheme is implemented, it is important to make it consistent.

An observer process for lights-out management is started in data center c to observe the CDBFS databases.

Implementing Data Guard on a file system

The implementation of Data Guard using a traditional file system requires a little more thought, since the database administrator cannot rely on the OMF parameters db_create_file_dest and db_create_online_log_dest_n to perform the file name conversion if needed on the fly. As you read in Chapter 7, file name conversion with PDBs has to be taken care of. The same applies to a Data Guard environment, but on the CDB level. If you decided to use a different directory structure for your standby database (mount points for example), ensure that the relevant file name conversion parameters are set. Although you can specify the log file definition and a file name conversion pattern during the execution of the RMAN duplicate database command as well, it is often easier to have the conversion parameters in the initialization file of the standby database.

You begin the duplication process by copying the password file and a parameter file to the standby host. The steps will be shown in more detail in the next section. The files should be copied into the dbs directory of the RDBMS home. You should also add the new ORACLE_SID to the oratab file to make it easier to switch environments.

```
[oracle@server2 ~]$ echo "CDBFSDCB:/u01/app/oracle/product/12.1.0.1/dbhome_1:N:" >> /etc/oratab
```

The initialization file needs to be amended next. The stream editor sed is a great way to create an almost workable initialization file:

```
[oracle@server2 dbs]$ sed -e "s/${PRIMARY_SID}/${ORACLE_SID}/g" $PRIMARY_INIT_FILE_LOC \
> ${ORACLE_HOME}/dbs/init${ORACLE_SID}.ora
```

Edit the file with your favorite editor and ensure the following parameters are set correctly:

- db_name

- db_unique_name

- db_file_name_convert and log_file_name_convert

The diagnostic destination introduced with Oracle 11g is a great help in simplifying the creation of auxiliary directories. The only remaining directory required for Oracle is the audit_file_dest. This can be created in a small script:

```
[oracle@server2 dbs]$ ADUMP=`grep audit_file_dest init${ORACLE_SID}.ora \
> | cut -d= -f2 | tr -d "'"` ; mkdir -p $ADUMP
```

This example assumes that the directory structure is the same on the standby host with the exception of the top-level directory containing the database files. This directory is CDBFSDCB instead of CDBFSDCA. The directory structure to be put into place on the standby host to support the duplicate database command can easily be scripted on the primary database:

```
SQL> select distinct 'mkdir -p ' ||
  2  replace(substr(name,1,instr(name,'/',-1)),'DCA','DCB') cmd
  3  from v$datafile;

CMD
--------------------------------------------------------------------------------
mkdir -p /u01/oradata/CDBFSDCB/PDB1/
mkdir -p /u01/oradata/CDBFSDCB/pdbseed/
mkdir -p /u01/oradata/CDBFSDCB/
```

You can "union all" additional locations such as log file members, temp files, and so on should they not all be in the CDBFSDCA mount point. These commands are then to be executed on the standby host. If you are multiplexing the control files in the Fast Recovery Area (FRA) then the full path needs to be created too. The resulting initialization file for the standby database with the unique name "CDBFSDCB" is shown here:

```
*.audit_file_dest='/u01/app/oracle/admin/CDBFSDCB/adump'
*.audit_trail='db'
*.compatible='12.1.0.0.0'
*.control_files='/u01/oradata/CDBFSDCB/control01.ctl',
  '/u01/fast_recovery_area/CDBFSDCB/control02.ctl'
*.db_block_size=8192
*.db_domain=''
*.db_name='CDBFS'
*.db_unique_name='CDBFSDCB'
*.db_recovery_file_dest='/u01/fast_recovery_area'
*.db_recovery_file_dest_size=4800m
*.diagnostic_dest='/u01/app/oracle'
*.dispatchers='(PROTOCOL=TCP) (SERVICE=CDBFSDCBXDB)'
*.enable_pluggable_database=true
*.log_archive_format='%t_%s_%r.dbf'
*.open_cursors=300
*.pga_aggregate_target=512m
*.processes=300
*.remote_login_passwordfile='EXCLUSIVE'
*.sga_target=1024m
*.undo_tablespace='UNDOTBS1'
*.db_file_name_convert='/u01/oradata/CDBFSDCA','/u01/oradata/CDBFSDCB'
*.log_file_name_convert='/u01/oradata/CDBFSDCA','/u01/oradata/CDBFSDCB'
```

You should now add the service names to the tnsnames.ora file. The entries used for this example are shown here:

```
CDBFSDCA =
  (DESCRIPTION =
    (ADDRESS_LIST =
      (ADDRESS = (PROTOCOL = TCP)(HOST = server1.example.com)(PORT = 1521))
    )
    (CONNECT_DATA =
      (SERVER = DEDICATED)
      (SERVICE_NAME = CDBFSDCA)
    )
  )

CDBFSDCB =
  (DESCRIPTION =
    (ADDRESS_LIST =
      (ADDRESS = (PROTOCOL = TCP)(HOST = server2.example.com)(PORT = 1521))
    )
    (CONNECT_DATA =
      (SERVER = DEDICATED)
      (SERVICE_NAME = CDBFSDCB)
    )
  )
```

The following RMAN example will duplicate the database from the active database, in other words without an intermediate backup. For this to work the databases must be statically registered with the listeners on each host and for each database. A sample configuration necessary for the duplication ... from active database for the listener on server1 is shown here:

```
$ cat $ORACLE_HOME/network/admin/listener.ora
[...]

SID_LIST_LISTENER =
  (SID_LIST =
    (SID_DESC =
      (GLOBAL_DBNAME = CDBFSDCA)
      (ORACLE_HOME = /u01/app/oracle/product/12.1.0.1/dbhome_1)
      (SID_NAME = CDBFSDCA)
    )
  )

[...]

LISTENER =
  (DESCRIPTION_LIST =
    (DESCRIPTION =
      (ADDRESS = (PROTOCOL = IPC)(KEY = EXTPROC1521))
    )
    (DESCRIPTION =
      (ADDRESS = (PROTOCOL = TCP)(HOST = server1.example.com)(PORT = 1521))
    )
  )

[...]
```

Note that the listener.ora configuration file needs to be modified once more when implementing the Data Guard broker configuration. Make a corresponding similar change on server2's listener.ora file and reload both listeners before continuing. The duplicate ... from active database command will restart the auxiliary instance a number of times; without static listener registration this will certainly fail.

With all the supporting directories and other infrastructure in place you can now start the RMAN duplicate command. Since the example assumes an identical directory structure the following RMAN commands can be used:

```
[oracle@server1 ~]$ . oraenv
ORACLE_SID = [CDBFSDCA] ?
The Oracle base remains unchanged with value /u01/app/oracle
[oracle@server1 ~]$ rman target sys@cdbfsdca auxiliary sys@cdbfsdcb

Recovery Manager: Release 12.1.0.1.0 - Production on Sun Sep 15 19:48:19 2013

Copyright (c) 1982, 2013, Oracle and/or its affiliates.  All rights reserved.

target database Password:
connected to target database: CDBFSDCA (DBID=2052895639)
auxiliary database Password:
connected to auxiliary database (not started)

RMAN> startup clone nomount
[...]
RMAN> run {
allocate channel c1 device type disk;
allocate channel c2 device type disk;
allocate auxiliary channel a1 device type disk;
allocate auxiliary channel a2 device type disk;
duplicate target database for standby from active database;
}
RMAN> 2> 3> 4> 5> 6> 7>
allocated channel: c1
channel c1: SID=133 device type=DISK
[...]
input datafile copy RECID=10 STAMP=826229614 file name=/u01/oradata/CDBFSDCB/PDB1/sysaux01.dbf
datafile 10 switched to datafile copy
input datafile copy RECID=11 STAMP=826229615 file name=/u01/oradata/CDBFSDCB/PDB1/PDB1_users01.dbf
Finished Duplicate Db at 15.09.2013 20:13:37
released channel: c1
released channel: c2
released channel: a1
released channel: a2

RMAN>

Recovery Manager complete.
```

Don't forget to add standby redo logs on *all* databases in the configuration! You can query their location and size from the v$log and v$logfile views on the primary database. Please ensure that you create standby redo logs on all the databases in the Data Guard configuration. In the example, the following standby redo logs were created. The primary database used three online redo log groups, each with a size matching the online redo logs (they would be larger in a production environment).

```
SQL> alter database add standby logfile
  2  '/u01/oradata/CDBFSDCA/srl1.log' size 52428800;
```

Database altered.

Repeat the above command and create four groups of standby redo logs. Remember that you need n+1 SRL groups which is one more than online redo logs. If you are multiplexing your online redo logs, which is less and less common these days, then you only need one member in the standby redo log group. More information about standby redo logs are in the v$standby_log view.

You should double-check if the primary database has force logging enabled and enable it if needed. The query to use for this verification is "select force_logging from v$database."

You can read in the next section how to create a standby database when using ASM. Following that section the two streams will come together again and you will read more about creating a Data Guard broker configuration.

Configuring Data Guard with Oracle Managed Files

One of the easier configurations to implement with Data Guard is the use of Oracle Managed Files. Oracle Managed Files or OMF can be implemented as an option when using a file system, or the use is implicit when using Oracle ASM. With the number of Oracle hardware products and appliances using ASM underneath the covers increasing, there seems to be a benefit in using ASM throughout.

The creation of the standby database either begins with the backup of the primary database which needs to be made available on the standby system in exactly the same location as where it was taken on the primary. If you are using a tape library then this is not a problem, file system based backups however have to use the same directory structure. The alternative backup-less approach of using the "from active database clause" has already been demonstrated above and will again be used in this scenario.

Again, you should add the database name to the oratab file.

```
[oracle@server2 CDB1]$ echo "CDB1DCB:/u01/app/oracle/product/12.1.0.1/dbhome_1:N " \
> >> /etc/oratab
```

Next copy the password file and the parameter file to the standby host, and rename them to match the instance name. The standby database's parameter file does not need a lot of change. A careful search-and-replace operation could again be your starting point, but remember that the db_name parameter must be identical across all standby databases or you will receive errors. The most common changes for databases include:

- Changing the db_unique_name. but ensure that the db_name remains the same

- Ensuring that the audit_file_dest location is valid

- Changing the dispatchers parameter to match the $ORACLE_SID

- Remove the control_files parameter, it will be overwritten anyway

You also should review the OMF related parameters if your ASM diskgroups or mount points are named differently from production. As this is a standard deployment no such changes needed to be made. The data files are standardized to go into the +DATA disk group. The database has its Fast Recovery Area set to +RECO. Here is the final parameter file for use with the standby database using ASM:

```
*.audit_file_dest='/u01/app/oracle/admin/CDB1/adump'
*.audit_trail='db'
*.compatible='12.1.0.0.0'
*.db_block_size=8192
*.db_create_file_dest='+DATA'
```

```
*.db_domain=''
*.db_name='CDB1'
*.db_recovery_file_dest='+RECO'
*.db_recovery_file_dest_size=4800m
*.db_unique_name='CDB1DCB'
*.diagnostic_dest='/u01/app/oracle'
*.dispatchers='(PROTOCOL=TCP) (SERVICE=CDB1DCBXDB)'
*.enable_pluggable_database=true
*.open_cursors=300
*.pga_aggregate_target=384m
*.processes=300
*.remote_login_passwordfile='EXCLUSIVE'
*.sga_target=1152m
*.undo_tablespace='UNDOTBS1'
```

As it was the case earlier, you need to ensure that the directories referenced in the parameter file exist on disk. You should also update the tnsnames.ora file to include the new databases, please refer to the above section for an example.

With the infrastructure in place it is time to start the auxiliary and initiate the duplication. Luckily with Oracle Managed Files you do not need to worry about file name conversions! Consider this example where the primary database CDB1DCA is duplicated to the standby CDB1DCB:

```
[oracle@server1 dbs]$ rman target sys/xxx@cdb1dca auxiliary sys/xxx@cdb1dcb

Recovery Manager: Release 12.1.0.1.0 - Production on Sun Sep 15 21:43:19 2013

Copyright (c) 1982, 2013, Oracle and/or its affiliates.  All rights reserved.

connected to target database: CDB1 (DBID=799950173)
connected to auxiliary database: CDB1 (not mounted)

RMAN> duplicate target database for standby from active database;
Starting Duplicate Db at 15-SEP-13
using target database control file instead of recovery catalog
allocated channel: ORA_AUX_DISK_1
channel ORA_AUX_DISK_1: SID=123 device type=DISK
allocated channel: ORA_AUX_DISK_2
channel ORA_AUX_DISK_2: SID=242 device type=DISK
allocated channel: ORA_AUX_DISK_3
channel ORA_AUX_DISK_3: SID=362 device type=DISK

contents of Memory Script:
{
[...]
Finished Duplicate Db at 15-SEP-13
```

Please double-check if the database has standby redo logs, if not you should create them now. Since you do not need to specify absolute path names you can use a small PL/SQL anonymous block to create the files. Assuming again you have three online redo log groups you can create the four needed standby redo logs as shown:

```
SQL> begin
  2    for i in 1..4 loop
  3      execute immediate 'alter database add standby logfile size size';
  4    end loop;
  5  end;
  6  /

PL/SQL procedure successfully completed.
```

In case of Oracle Restart you should register your new standby database now with the framework. The srvctl command allows you to do this in a very elegant way. In the below example database CDB1 is registered with the unique name CDB1DCB as a physical standby database. The diskgroup option allows Oracle to mount the DATA and RECO disk groups as part of the database start procedure. The keyword automatic as an argument to the policy instructs Oracle Restart to start the database as part of the server boot process. The mount option ensures that the standby database is mounted, not opened read-only.

```
[oracle@server2 ~] srvctl add database -db CDB1DCB -oraclehome $ORACLE_HOME -spfile \
> /u01/app/oracle/product/12.1.0.1/dbhome_1/dbs/spfileCDB1DCB.ora \
> -role PHYSICAL_STANDBY -startoption mount -dbname CDB1 -diskgroup RECO,DATA
```

After the command has been executed, you can view the configuration as it is stored in Oracle Restart:

```
[oracle@server1 ~]$ srvctl config database -db $ORACLE_SID
Database unique name: CDB1DCB
Database name: CDB1
Oracle home: /u01/app/oracle/product/12.1.0.1/dbhome_1
Oracle user: oracle
Spfile: /u01/app/oracle/product/12.1.0.1/dbhome_1/dbs/spfileCDB1DCB.ora
Password file:
Domain:
Start options: mount
Stop options: immediate
Database role: PHYSICAL_STANDBY
Management policy: AUTOMATIC
Database instance: CDB1DCB
Disk Groups: RECO,DATA
Services:
```

In the next step you can start the database:

```
[oracle@server2 ~]$ srvctl start database -db $ORACLE_SID
[oracle@server2 ~]$ srvctl status database -db $ORACLE_SID
Database is running.
```

Congratulations, you have successfully created and registered a standby database in ASM!

CONSIDERATIONS FOR AUTOMATION

The above processes involve quite a few manual steps. Automating those could prove to be a difficult task. The situation looks a little brighter if you have Enterprise Manager, which allows you to create a standby database from an existing primary. The process is controlled via jobs in the Enterprise Manager repository.

To enable the creation of a standby database you need to use the graphical user interface, at the time of this writing there did not seem to be an option for emcli to automatically create a standby database.

Creating a Data Guard Broker configuration

After the standby databases have physically been created, they need to be aware of their primary database. While the following steps can all be performed on the SQL*Plus command line, this requires additional skill and knowledge. The Data Guard Broker puts an abstraction layer between the SQL commands necessary to modify the initialization parameters and the sequence of commands to be executed during role transitions. A switchover for example can be simplified to:

```
DGMGRL> switchover to standbydatabase;
```

There is an undeniable elegance in this approach. First- or second-line support should be able to execute the above statement after appropriate signoff. Should there be a problem during the switchover the operator can escalate to the level-two support to investigate.

If you intend to script the Broker configuration—maybe as part of the standard deploy mechanism—you could use the secure external password store to store credentials. This way the sensitive passwords do not need to be in the script. The following examples use the secure password store extensively. The wallets were created on each host in the Data Guard configuration. All wallets are created in /home/oracle/tns_admin. To ensure that the wallet works as expected, create a symbolic link for tnsnames.ora from $ORACLE_HOME/network/admin to ~/tns_admin and export the environment variable TNS_ADMIN to point to ~/tns_admin. Wallets can cause a security problem which is why you should create the wallet as explained in My Oracle Support note 1114500.1 using the -auto_login_local flag and orapki:

```
[oracle@server1 tns_admin]$ orapki wallet create -wallet . -auto_login_local
Oracle PKI Tool : Version 12.1.0.1
Copyright (c) 2004, 2012, Oracle and/or its affiliates. All rights reserved.

Enter password:
Enter password again:
```

Please note that the password must pass a simple validation. If the password does not satisfy these criteria an error is raised. Passwords must "have a minimum length of eight characters and contain alphabetic characters combined with numbers or special characters" as orapki will tell you.

```
[oracle@server1 tns_admin]$ mkstore -wrl . -createCredential tnsName sys sysPWD
Oracle Secret Store Tool : Version 12.1.0.1
Copyright (c) 2004, 2012, Oracle and/or its affiliates. All rights reserved.

Enter wallet password:
Create credential oracle.security.client.connect_string1
```

Repeat the call to mkstore for all databases in the configuration. In the next step you need to make Oracle aware of the wallet location. Edit the ~/tns_admin/sqlnet.ora file and add the following, changing the path to your wallet location.

```
SQLNET.WALLET_OVERRIDE = TRUE
WALLET_LOCATION =
  (SOURCE=
    (METHOD = FILE) (METHOD_DATA =
      (DIRECTORY=/home/oracle/tns_admin)
    )
  )
```

You can override the location where Oracle expects the net*8 configuration by setting the environment variable TNS_ADMIN, as in the following:

```
[oracle@server1 ~]$ export TNS_ADMIN=/home/oracle/tns_admin
[oracle@server1 ~]$ tnsping $ORACLE_SID

TNS Ping Utility for Linux: Version 12.1.0.1.0 - Production on 16-SEP-2013 00:23:55

Copyright (c) 1997, 2013, Oracle.  All rights reserved.

Used parameter files:
/home/oracle/tns_admin/sqlnet.ora
```

If all the databases in the configuration had their Broker services started by setting the initialization parameter dg_broker_start to true, then you should be able to create a new configuration. The command used by Data Guard Broker is called "create configuration." The syntax is not too complex:

```
CREATE CONFIGURATION <configuration name> AS
  PRIMARY DATABASE IS <database name>
  CONNECT IDENTIFIER IS <connect identifier>;
```

Following our example, the configuration is created using the following little snippet:

```
[oracle@server1 ~]$ dgmgrl /@cdb1dca
DGMGRL for Linux: Version 12.1.0.1.0 - 64bit Production

Copyright (c) 2000, 2012, Oracle. All rights reserved.

Welcome to DGMGRL, type "help" for information.
Connected as SYSDBA.

DGMGRL> create configuration apress as
> primary database is "CDB1DCA"
> connect identifier is "CDB1DCA";
Configuration "apress" created with primary database "CDB1DCA"
DGMGRL>
```

Translated into plain English the Broker was instructed to create a new configuration, named *apress* using the primary database CDB1DCA. The connection identifier should match an entry in tnsnames.ora. It will be used whenever the Broker connects to a database in the configuration to query or modify properties. In the next step the standby databases are added.

```
DGMGRL> add database "CDB1DCB"
> as connect identifier is "CDB1DCB"
> maintained as physical;
Database "CDB1DCB" added
DGMGRL> add database "CDB1DCC"
> as connect identifier is "CDB1DCC"
> maintained as physical;
Database "CDB1DCC" added
DGMGRL>
```

The Broker has been told to add two databases to the configuration as physical standby databases. If you had a logical standby database you could use the "maintained as logical" clause instead. Now review the configuration you just created:

```
DGMGRL> show configuration;

Configuration - apress

  Protection Mode: MaxPerformance
  Databases:
  CDB1DCA - Primary database
    CDB1DCB - Physical standby database
    CDB1DCC - Physical standby database

Fast-Start Failover: DISABLED

Configuration Status:
DISABLED
```

As you can see Oracle has correctly added our two standby databases into the configuration. Thankfully the configuration is not enabled by default, there is some more work to be done. Every database in the configuration can be queried and managed using the Broker interface. The databases have certain properties which are settable, some are read-only. Using the broker interface you control these; think of the Broker as another way of executing alter system statements.

■ **Caution** Do not try and modify Data Guard related parameters in the initialization files! You would only confuse the Broker. If you did anyway, you had to do a manual reconciliation of the Broker and database parameters.

Other parameters have a different scope and belong to the configuration as such. The best example for one of these is the protection mode.

To complete the Broker configuration, the following tasks need to be executed:

- Statically register the broker services with the listener

- Automate the management of standby database files

- Optionally define a delay for the application of redo to the standby database CDB1DCC. This is truly optional but allows you to have a safety net for human error. Detected quickly enough the trailing standby database can be activated in case of a catastrophic logical corruption

- Change the protection mode to maximum availability

The Broker syntax is not too daunting, but it is yet another tool to understand in addition to SQL and RMAN, which are quite common. The main verbs you need to be aware of in the next two sections are edit and show. Each verb is followed by an object such as the configuration or database. Add the database name as per the configuration and a property you would like to view or change. The following sections have all the examples you need to manage, modify, and otherwise maintain the broker configuration. There is also a very useful help function in dgmgrl that helps you remind yourself of the correct syntax.

Listener configuration

One of the greatest benefits of the Broker over the manual approach is that it fully automates the role transitions. During these, database restarts are required. As you know, a connection to a database which is shut down requires a static registration in the listener.ora file. Every listener for every host participating in the Data Guard configuration has to be amended. Remember that the listener is configured in the Grid home if you are using Oracle Restart. The Broker uses a database property, called StaticConnectIdentifier to address databases. It is populated by default and does not normally need to be changed. Using the broker, you can use the show database *databaseName* StaticConnectIdentifier command as demonstrated here:

```
DGMGRL> show database "CDB1DCA" staticConnectIdentifier
  StaticConnectIdentifier = '(DESCRIPTION=(ADDRESS=(PROTOCOL=TCP)(HOST=192.168.100.20)(PORT=1521)) ↵
(CONNECT_DATA=(SERVICE_NAME=CDB1DCA_DGMGRL)(INSTANCE_NAME=CDB1DCA) ↵
(SERVER=DEDICATED)))'
DGMGRL>
```

The service name is the one that has to be registered in the listener.ora file. To follow the example, here is the listener.ora for the current primary database.

```
[grid@server1 admin]$ nl listener.ora
    1  # listener.ora Network Configuration File: ↵
       /u01/app/grid/product/12.1.0.1/grid/network/admin/listener.ora
    2  # Generated by Oracle configuration tools.

    3  SID_LIST_LISTENER =
    4    (SID_LIST =
    5      (SID_DESC =
    6        (GLOBAL_DBNAME = CDB1DCA)
    7        (ORACLE_HOME = /u01/app/oracle/product/12.1.0.1/dbhome_1)
    8        (SID_NAME = CDB1DCA)
    9      )
   10      (SID_DESC =
   11        (GLOBAL_DBNAME = CDB1DCA_DGMGRL)
   12        (ORACLE_HOME = /u01/app/oracle/product/12.1.0.1/dbhome_1)
   13        (SID_NAME = CDB1DCA)
   14      )

[configuration information removed for clarity]

   25    )
   26  VALID_NODE_CHECKING_REGISTRATION_LISTENER = SUBNET
   27  LISTENER =
   28    (DESCRIPTION_LIST =
   29      (DESCRIPTION =
```

```
30          (ADDRESS = (PROTOCOL = IPC)(KEY = EXTPROC1521))
31        )
32        (DESCRIPTION =
33          (ADDRESS = (PROTOCOL = TCP)(HOST = server1.example.com)(PORT = 1521))
34        )
35      )
36    ADR_BASE_LISTENER = /u01/app/grid
37    ENABLE_GLOBAL_DYNAMIC_ENDPOINT_LISTENER = ON
[grid@server1 admin]$
```

The additional information to be added starts in line 3. Grid Infrastructure does not add database services statically by default. As you can see the global database name is set to the service name you got from the static connect identifier. If you are using a database domain (initialization parameter db_domain) then add the domain after the ${ORACLE_SID}_DGMGRL, for example CDB1DCA_DGMGRL.example.com. Do not forget to reload the listener for the changes to take effect. Careful though with instances that register dynamically with the listener: it could take a little while until they announce their presence again. You might want to run "alter system register" on these and/or perform the operation during a quieter period. Before you continue with the other listeners you should do a quick connection test. Launch sqlplus, then connect as sys@*staticConnectionIdentifier* as sysdba. If you are told you are connected, chances are high that the Broker can connect to the database as well.

Standby file management

The management of data files has to be automated. By default the DBA is responsible for managing data files on the standby databases which have previously been added to the primary database. The addition of a new file to the primary database generates redo as well. The same statement is then executed on the standby database, and thanks to Oracle Managed Files or the file name conversion parameters in the initialization file the file is created in the correct location with automatic standby file management.

Before you change the standby file management on all databases, primary and standby alike, you should quickly check if your file name conversion parameters are set.

■ **Note**   Skip this test if you are using Oracle Managed Files and your disk group names are identical.

The two file-system based databases used in the earlier example should have file name and log file name conversion parameters set in both directions. In the example the primary database did not have name conversion parameters set, which has been rectified:

```
DGMGRL> show database "CDBFSDCB" dbFileNameConvert
  DbFileNameConvert = '/u01/oradata/CDBFSDCA, /u01/oradata/CDBFSDCB'
DGMGRL> show database "CDBFSDCB" logFileNameConvert
  LogFileNameConvert = '/u01/oradata/CDBFSDCA, /u01/oradata/CDBFSDCB'
DGMGRL> edit database "CDBFSDCA" set property
> dbFileNameConvert = '/u01/oradata/CDBFSDCB, /u01/oradata/CDBFSDCA';
Warning: ORA-16675: database instance restart required for property value modification
to take effect
```

```
Property "dbfilenameconvert" updated
DGMGRL> edit database "CDBFSDCA" set property
> logFileNameConvert = '/u01/oradata/CDBFSDCB, /u01/oradata/CDBFSDCA';
Warning: ORA-16675: database instance restart required for property value modification
to take effect

Property "logfilenameconvert" updated
DGMGRL>
```

If your disk group names in ASM are the same across all databases in the configuration you do not need to set any file name conversion parameters. Now ensure that standby file management is set to auto:

```
DGMGRL> show database "CDBFSDCA" StandbyFileManagement
  StandbyFileManagement = 'MANUAL'
DGMGRL> edit database "CDBFSDCA" set property
> StandbyFileManagement = auto;
Property "standbyfilemanagement" updated
```

Repeat the edit command for all standby databases in the configuration.

Configuring redo application delay

Sometimes it is useful to have a third database lag a little behind the primary database to have more time to detect logical corruption. Humans are humans, and they make mistakes. Maybe someone starts a batch job at the end of the day with the wrong input parameters? Or someone executes a data cleaning operation that uses the wrong predicates in the where clause? There are many reasons your system could be in a bad state. If one of your standby databases trails behind for say 30 minutes then you have a little extra time before that, too, has to be recreated.

To enable the apply delay, you need to change the database property DelayMins as shown here, where a 30-minute delay is set.

```
DGMGRL> edit database "CDB1DCC" set property DelayMins = 30;
Property "delaymins" updated
DGMGRL>
```

Having one of the standby databases in the Data Guard configuration with an apply delay does not impact the ability to fail over to another standby database which is 100% in sync with production. Be aware though that a standby with an apply lag cannot be the target of a switchover operation.

Enabling the configuration

With all the above changes made, it is finally time to enable the configuration and to verify the setup. Enable the configuration while connected to the primary database in the Broker command line interface.

```
[oracle@server1 ~]$ dgmgrl /@cdb1dca
...
DGMGRL> enable configuration;
```

If everything went according to plan, you should get the prompt back a few seconds after issuing the statement. To see if there are any irregularities or other problems, execute the show configuration command again:

```
DGMGRL> show configuration

Configuration - apress

  Protection Mode: MaxPerformance
  Databases:
  CDB1DCA - Primary database
    CDB1DCB - Physical standby database
    CDB1DCC - Physical standby database
Fast-Start Failover: DISABLED
```

Configuration Status:
SUCCESS

The most commonly reported problems at this stage are missing server parameter files on either database, or missing standby redo logs. There should be no problems here at this stage if you followed the instructions in the chapter.

Changing the protection mode to maximum availability

You read in the previous chapter's section about protection modes that you need to set the log transfer mode to SYNC if you want any of the higher protection levels. With synchronous shipping of redo the speed at which a database's commit statement completes partially depends on the network latency as well. If it takes considerable time for a network packet to travel to a standby database the overall commit latency will suffer too. The advantage of the synchronous transfer mode though is a better protection from data loss.

The protection mode Maximum Availability seems to be the best compromise of data protection and continuity of service. To enable it, the databases in the Data Guard configuration need to be switched to ship redo synchronously. Connected to the Broker command line utility, you need to update the LogXptMode database property. You can see the example here:

```
DGMGRL> edit database "CDB1DCA" set property LogXptMode=Sync;
Property "logxptmode" updated
DGMGRL> edit database "CDB1DCB" set property LogXptMode=Sync;
Property "logxptmode"
```

You may have noticed that the third standby, which is configured to delay the application of redo for 30 minutes, has not had the log transport property changed. In a delayed configuration it does not matter much if the redo information is shipped asynchronously or synchronously.

As soon as the log ship property has been updated you can change the protection mode. The "edit configuration" command helps you do this. In the example the protection mode is upgraded from maximum performance to maximum availability. This upgrade does not require a restart of any database in the configuration.

```
DGMGRL> edit configuration set protection mode as maxAvailability;
Succeeded.
DGMGRL> show configuration

Configuration - apress
```

```
Protection Mode: MaxAvailability
Databases:
CDB1DCA - Primary database
  CDB1DCB - Physical standby database
  CDB1DCC - Physical standby database

Fast-Start Failover: DISABLED

Configuration Status:
SUCCESS
```

The configuration is now changed to maximum availability. You could read in the previous chapter that Data Guard redo can be shipped to the standby, which acknowledges that it received the redo in a memory buffer but has not written it to disk yet. This mode is only available in Maximum Availability and is called "fastsync". It corresponds to the options "SYNC NOAFFIRM" in the log_archive_dest_n initialization parameter. Before Oracle 12c you could only have ASYNC NOAFFIRM (logXptMode "async") or SYNC AFFIRM (logXptMode "sync"). Refer back to the previous chapter for a discussion of the fastsync transport mode.

Enabling Flashback on the standby

With the Broker active and managed recovery running you cannot add standby redo logs or enable flashback on the standby database. Trying to do so results in an error:

```
SQL> select flashback_on, open_mode from v$database;

FLASHBACK_ON        OPEN_MODE
------------------- --------------------
NO                  MOUNTED

SQL> alter database flashback on;
alter database flashback on
*
ERROR at line 1:
ORA-01153: an incompatible media recovery is active
```

Please do *not* issue the SQL command to stop managed recovery manually! All Data Guard related maintenance has to be performed via the Broker. Change the state of the standby database to "apply-off" using the Broker command line interface again. This will stop managed recovery.

```
DGMGRL> edit database "CDB1DCB" set state="apply-off";
Succeeded.
```

You can then enable the flashback database feature, and enable managed recovery again:

```
DGMGRL> edit database "CDB1DCB" set state="apply-on";
Succeeded.
```

Completely removing the Broker configuration

Sometimes it is necessary to completely remove a Data Guard Broker configuration. The main reason for having to remove the Broker configuration is a completely failed role transition paired with a network problem or some other hard-to-explain weirdness. In some rare circumstances the switchover succeeds, but the Broker is unaware that it did.

To remove the configuration you need to stop the Broker on each database in the broker configuration. If your configuration is not entirely broken then you might be lucky and query which databases are currently part of the configuration:

```
SQL> select DB_UNIQUE_NAME,PARENT_DBUN,DEST_ROLE from V$DATAGUARD_CONFIG;
```

DB_UNIQUE_NAME	PARENT_DBUN	DEST_ROLE
CDB1DCA	NONE	PRIMARY DATABASE
CDB1DCB	CDB1DCA	PHYSICAL STANDBY
CDB1DCC	CDB1DCA	PHYSICAL STANDBY

In our scenario, there are three databases in the configuration: CDB1DCA, CDB1DCB, and CDB1DCC. The first step in removing the broker configuration is to stop the Broker processes. On each database, issue this command:

```
SQL> alter system set dg_broker_start = false;
```

Then you need to remove the Broker configuration files. Their location is stored in the initialization parameters dg_broker_config_file1 and dg_broker_config_file2 respectively. After the Broker services are stopped, move these files to a different location. Now start the Broker on each database, the missing broker configuration files will be created as part of the process.

Performing a graceful switchover operation

Regular disaster recovery tests are essential in spreading confidence in the procedure and to detect changes to the setup that require either fixing or updating of the documentation. Very often it is not the database that causes problems—Data Guard is very reliable—but hard-coded connection strings in applications. These problems can easily be identified by regular switchover exercises.

With the Broker configuration in place it is very simple to perform the switchover. A first check should be the switchover readiness of the database you want to switch to. In a multi-standby scenario you should switch over to the database that is most in sync with production. Technically speaking there is nothing wrong with switching over to a database that is hours behind the primary, but to save time and nerves it is not recommended to send all that redo over to it before the switchover can actually occur. If you are unsure about transport and apply lags you can query the standby databases in your configuration as shown here:

```
[oracle@server2 ~]$ dgmgrl /@cdbfsdcb
DGMGRL for Linux: Version 12.1.0.1.0 - 64bit Production

Copyright (c) 2000, 2012, Oracle. All rights reserved.

Welcome to DGMGRL, type "help" for information.
Connected as SYSDBA.
DGMGRL> show database "CDBFSDCB"

Database - CDBFSDCB
```

```
   Role:                PHYSICAL STANDBY
   Intended State:      APPLY-ON
   Transport Lag:       0 seconds (computed 0 seconds ago)
   Apply Lag:           0 seconds (computed 0 seconds ago)
   Apply Rate:          1.22 MByte/s
   Real Time Query:     OFF
   Instance(s):
     CDBFSDCB

Database Status:
SUCCESS
```

The below example extends the file system scenario, and there are two databases in the configuration. Connect to the current primary database and query the state of the configuration:

```
DGMGRL> show configuration

Configuration - fsconfig

  Protection Mode: MaxPerformance
  Databases:
  CDBFSDCA - Primary database
    CDBFSDCB - Physical standby database

Fast-Start Failover: DISABLED

Configuration Status:
SUCCESS
```

The Data Guard broker returned success: there are no known problems that could prevent a switchover from succeeding. Just to be safe you can query the database for its readiness to switch roles:

```
DGMGRL> validate database "CDBFSDCB"

  Database Role:     Physical standby database
  Primary Database:  CDBFSDCA

  Ready for Switchover:  Yes
  Ready for Failover:    Yes (Primary Running)

  Flashback Database Status:
    CDBFSDCA:  Off
    CDBFSDCB:  Off

  Current Log File Groups Configuration:
    Thread #  Online Redo Log Groups   Standby Redo Log Groups
              (CDBFSDCA)                (CDBFSDCB)
    1         3                         2

  Future Log File Groups Configuration:
    Thread #  Online Redo Log Groups   Standby Redo Log Groups
              (CDBFSDCB)                (CDBFSDCA)
    1         3                         2
```

As you can see from the above output the database is ready for switchover, so let's try:

```
DGMGRL> switchover to "CDBFSDCB"
Performing switchover NOW, please wait...
New primary database "CDBFSDCB" is opening...
Operation requires startup of instance "CDBFSDCA" on database "CDBFSDCA"
Starting instance "CDBFSDCA"...
ORACLE instance started.
Database mounted.
Switchover succeeded, new primary is "CDBFSDCB"
DGMGRL>
```

Congratulations, you have successfully switched over to the standby database. Many DBAs worry what could happen during a switchover procedure, and the good news is: not too much. The worst case is a network problem right at the time the switchover has been initiated. As part of the switchover Oracle will send a special token over the network, indicating the last redo to be sent. This can be seen in the new primary database's alert.log.

```
2013-09-16 11:08:47.856000 +01:00
Media Recovery Log ↵
 /u01/fast_recovery_area/CDBFSDCB/archivelog/2013_09_16/o1_mf_1_14_93fp5h61_.arc
Resetting standby activation ID 2052880791 (0x7a5c7997)
Media Recovery End-Of-Redo indicator encountered
Media Recovery Continuing
Media Recovery Waiting for thread 1 sequence 15
SWITCHOVER: received request 'ALTER DTABASE COMMIT TO SWITCHOVER  TO PRIMARY'
from primary database.
ALTER DATABASE SWITCHOVER TO PRIMARY (CDBFSDCB)
[...]
SwitchOver after complete recovery through change 1842430
[...]
Standby became primary SCN: 1842428
2013-09-16 11:08:54.953000 +01:00
Switchover: Complete - Database mounted as primary
SWITCHOVER: completed request from primary database.
```

Only if all the redo information has been received the switchover will occur. Therefore you cannot incur data loss. As part of the switchover all databases in the Data Guard configuration will become standby databases (again, just a flag in the control file). If the switchover failed for any reason, the database can be converted back to a primary and resume normal operations.

If you made a mistake in statically configuring the DGMGRL services with the listeners you will get a message that in order to complete the switchover you have to manually start the old primary. This is not a problem, and once completed the Broker should return success when you check the status of the configuration. Verify that your configuration is what you expect it to be:

```
DGMGRL> show configuration

Configuration - fsconfig

  Protection Mode: MaxPerformance
  Databases:
  CDBFSDCB - Primary database
    CDBFSDCA - Physical standby database
```

```
Fast-Start Failover: DISABLED

Configuration Status:
SUCCESS
```

If you were using block change tracking on the primary before the switchover to facilitate faster level 1 backups of the database then please ensure you enable BCT again once the switchover completed, if you need it. By default the block change tracking file will not be created and enabled on the new primary. Be careful enabling BCT on the standby database because you need a license for Active Data Guard to do so. If your switchover operation is not part of a scheduled test then please test the connectivity with your backup solution and the database, the archive log deletion policy and other infrastructure tasks that you might regularly perform to be compliant with your standards and outside regulators. Also verify that the log file name and data file name conversion parameters are set on the new standby, and that it has standby redo logs. It always pays off to configure databases in a Data Guard environment for all roles. If you rely on Oracle Clusterware to start and stop databases, review the configuration to ensure that the standby database starts into the appropriate mode. Remember the license implications of having a standby database open read only while applying logs. You want the primary database to be open in read write mode.

Performing a failover operation

A failover operation is not usually something users are happy to test in a non-crisis situation. A decision for a failover has to be made by senior management for an application, and should have been practiced and documented to avoid mistakes when it happens. Coordination for a failover will be even more difficult in a DBaaS environment where all of the application owners have to agree. As with the switchover, the failover target should be selected in such way that data loss is minimized. The transport lag plays an important role, especially in protection mode Maximum Performance. Remember that the redo is sent directly to standby redo logs from where it is applied to the standby database with Real Time Apply. In the default settings for the maximum availability mode transactions commit on the primary only after the standby database confirmed that redo has been received and indeed written into the SRLs. The transport lag therefore is probably very small.

You could use the Broker command line interface to check the transport lag before a failover operation. Consider the following example, where database CDBFSDCB is the standby database for CDBFSDCA:

```
DGMGRL> show database "CDBFSDCB"

Database - CDBFSDCB

  Role:              PHYSICAL STANDBY
  Intended State:    APPLY-ON
  Transport Lag:     0 seconds (computed 0 seconds ago)
  Apply Lag:         0 seconds (computed 0 seconds ago)
  Apply Rate:        115.00 KByte/s
  Real Time Query:   OFF
  Instance(s):
    CDBFSDCB

Database Status:
SUCCESS
```

The conditions for a failover seem favorable. As with the graceful switchover operation you can check the destination database's role change readiness (the primary database has by now crashed):

```
DGMGRL> validate database "CDBFSDCB"

  Database Role:     Physical standby database
  Primary Database:  CDBFSDCA
    Warning: primary database was not reachable

  Ready for Switchover:  No
  Ready for Failover:    Yes (Primary Not Running)

  Temporary Tablespace File Information:
    CDBFSDCA TEMP Files:  Unknown
    CDBFSDCB TEMP Files:  3

  Flashback Database Status:
    CDBFSDCA:  Unknown
    CDBFSDCB:  On

  Data file Online Move in Progress:
    CDBFSDCA:  Unknown
    CDBFSDCB:  No

  Transport-Related Information:
    Transport On:      No
    Gap Status:        Unknown
    Transport Lag:     0 seconds
    Transport Status:  Success

  Log Files Cleared:
    CDBFSDCA Standby Redo Log Files:  Unknown
    CDBFSDCB Online Redo Log Files:   Cleared

DGMGRL>
```

The database is indeed ready for a failover, and you are informed that the primary database is not running. Unlike with a switchover, there are two possible ways to perform the failover: the preferred and strongly recommended complete failover and the emergency-not-to-be-used-if-at-all-possible immediate failover.

Performing an immediate failover

The immediate failover is the panic button. It is not recommended unless there is really no other way to fail over. You will almost certainly incur data loss! No additional redo is applied to the standby; if there is a transport lag, you will incur data loss which is proportional to the transport lag.

For the reasons shown in this section the immediate failover will not be discussed further. The only application one can think of is to allow a standby which is lagging behind by design to take over the primary role after a release went wrong or similar logical corruption occurred on the primary. Your monitoring tools should have picked that up.

■ **Caution** Always use the complete failover! The immediate failover is the last-resort-panic button to be avoided wherever possible.

Performing a complete failover

The complete failover, which Oracle recommends over the previously discussed immediate failover, is the default. During a complete failover Oracle will try to salvage as much redo from the primary as possible. This includes a new Oracle feature, which allows you to manually mount the old primary and flush previously unsent redo. At the time of this writing there was no Broker support to do so. This might allow for zero data loss, even though the Data Guard configuration is not set to such a protection mode. If the old primary cannot be mounted this operation cannot take place for obvious reasons.

The failover itself is executed very rapidly. Consider the below example:

```
DGMGRL> show configuration

Configuration - fsconfig

  Protection Mode: MaxAvailability
  Databases:
  CDBFSDCA - Primary database
    CDBFSDCB - Physical standby database

Fast-Start Failover: DISABLED

Configuration Status:
ORA-12543: TNS:destination host unreachable
ORA-16625: cannot reach database "CDBFSDCA"
DGM-17017: unable to determine configuration status
```

As you can see the primary database is inaccessible—the listener is down which implies a severe problem with the host. After a little further investigation it turned out that the whole rack has gone offline due to a problem with the power supply. After careful consideration and application of standard Business Continuity Plans the decision has been made to fail over to the standby database. The DBA then enters the failover command as demonstrated below. The connection to the Broker is initiated on the standby host to the standby database.

```
DGMGRL> help failover

Changes a standby database to be the primary database

Syntax:

  FAILOVER TO <standby database name> [IMMEDIATE];

DGMGRL> failover to "CDBFSDCB";
Performing failover NOW, please wait...
Failover succeeded, new primary is "CDBFSDCB"
```

The whole failover operation does not take long. The good news is that the operation did not involve data loss. The old primary database's alert.log reports:

```
Data Guard Broker: Beginning failover
ALTER DATABASE FAILOVER TO CDBFSDCB
[...log information about database recovery]
Terminal Recovery finished with No-Data-Loss
2013-09-16 12:05:57.922000 +01:00
Incomplete Recovery applied until change 1870588 time 09/16/2013 11:57:20
Media Recovery Complete (CDBFSDCB)
Terminal Recovery: successful completion
```

As part of the failover operation the protection mode is automatically downgraded, which is reflected in the output of the "show configuration" command.

```
DGMGRL> show configuration

Configuration - fsconfig

  Protection Mode: MaxAvailability
  Databases:
  CDBFSDCB - Primary database
    Warning: ORA-16629: database reports a different protection level from the protection mode

    CDBFSDCA - Physical standby database (disabled)
      ORA-16661: the standby database needs to be reinstated

Fast-Start Failover: DISABLED

Configuration Status:
WARNING
```

Two tasks are now remaining. The message that the database reports a different protection level from the protection mode refers to V$DATABASE.PROTECTION_MODE and PROTECTION_LEVEL. They are not identical since there is a network connectivity problem between the databases. Additionally the old primary database will not currently accept archived logs from the new primary: it still thinks it is the primary. Proceed with the reinstation of the failed primary.

Reinstating the old primary database

A failover operation always required a complete rebuild of the failed database up to Oracle 10g. Luckily this has changed with the introduction of the Flashback Database command. In addition to the recreation of the failed standby which still might be required you have the option to reinstate the failed database. Reinstating the database is a lot quicker than a recreation: it simply flashes the database back to the SCN before the standby became a primary (as per V$DATABASE.STANDBY_BECAME_PRIMARY_SCN on the old primary), and converts it to a standby database. If such an operation is possible the Broker will report the following message when you query the configuration status:

```
CDBFSDCA - Physical standby database (disabled)
  ORA-16661: the standby database needs to be reinstated
```

If the database cannot be reinstated, you will see the following message instead:

```
CDBFSDCA - Physical standby database (disabled)
  ORA-16795: the standby database needs to be re-created
```

If you had flashback database enabled and the required flashback and archived redo logs are present you can try to reinstate the database as shown here. The database can obviously be reinstated only if it can be brought online into the mount state, either manually or via the broker.

```
DGMGRL> reinstate database "CDBFSDCA"
Reinstating database "CDBFSDCA", please wait...
Reinstatement of database "CDBFSDCA" succeeded
```

Success! The database is now a fully functional member of the Broker configuration again:

```
DGMGRL> show configuration

Configuration - fsconfig

  Protection Mode: MaxAvailability
  Databases:
  CDBFSDCB - Primary database
    CDBFSDCA - Physical standby database

Fast-Start Failover: DISABLED

Configuration Status:
SUCCESS
```

The start of redo shipping after reinstating the failed database the protection_mode and protection_level columns in v$database will be both set to "MAXIMUM AVAILABILITY". You can begin raising a change request to reverse the roles during the next change window. Before doing so you should ensure that the broker does not complain; missing standby redo logs are a common cause for a warning. Block Change Tracking might need to be enabled, and Oracle Clusterware metadata for the databases should be reviewed and amended where needed.

Creating a lights-out configuration using the Broker

The Data Guard Broker can also be configured for a lights-out situation. Lights-out can be understood as an environment where the management of failover operations is delegated to software. In the case of Data Guard this software is called the Observer. The observer process, which should ideally be in a third site, has the task to monitor the primary database. Under certain conditions the failover operation can be initiated by the Observer, without human intervention at all. Refer back to Figure 10-1 for a description of the architecture. The Observer in this case is located in data center C, and the database configuration consists of the primary database in data center A and a single standby database in data center B. For this Broker configuration there is no third database, although it is possible to have many standby databases, even a mix of physical and logical.

The Fast Start Failover or FSFO configuration is always based on an existing Broker configuration such as the one shown here:

```
DGMGRL> show configuration verbose

Configuration - fsconfig
```

```
Protection Mode: MaxAvailability
Databases:
CDBFSDCB - Primary database
  CDBFSDCA - Physical standby database

Properties:
  FastStartFailoverThreshold      = '30'
  OperationTimeout                = '30'
  TraceLevel                      = 'USER'
  FastStartFailoverLagLimit       = '30'
  CommunicationTimeout            = '180'
  ObserverReconnect               = '0'
  FastStartFailoverAutoReinstate  = 'TRUE'
  FastStartFailoverPmyShutdown    = 'TRUE'
  BystandersFollowRoleChange      = 'ALL'
  ObserverOverride                = 'FALSE'

Fast-Start Failover: DISABLED

Configuration Status:
SUCCESS
```

Fast Start Failover (FSFO) is disabled as you can see. As a prerequisite to enabling FSFO you will need the primary and the target standby database to have Flashback Database enabled. Ideally the other databases in the configuration have flashback enabled as well, but this is not mandatory. It is possible to configure FSFO with a configuration using maximum performance—or asynchronous redo shipping—but that is not recommended for the risk of data loss. If you trust software to perform the failover operation then you would want to be in a position where no data loss is expected. The previously suggested maximum availability configuration is used in this example, and the Oracle documentation claims that it will ensure there is no data loss. In situations where you have multiple standby databases you need to define which standby database you would like the Observer to fail over to, and it can only fail over to that one database. Setting the database property "FastStartFailoverTarget" on the primary database triggers the Broker to update all other databases in the configuration. It needs to be set only if you have more than one standby database. Another parameter you need to set is the Fast Start Failover Threshold. This parameter which measures the maximum duration in seconds during which neither the standby nor the Observer have connectivity with the primary database. Automatic failover will be initiated by the Observer if no communication is possible with the primary for more than FastStartFailoverThreshold seconds. During the process the primary will shut down by default. As part of the failover procedure, the failed primary database is automatically reinstated by the Broker once it is entering mount state unless you configure it not to.

With the default configuration parameters in place you can enable FSFO, connected as SYS to the primary database:

```
DGMGRL> ENABLE FAST_START FAILOVER;
Enabled.
DGMGRL> show configuration

Configuration - fsconfig

  Protection Mode: MaxAvailability
  Databases:
  CDBFSDCB - Primary database
    Warning: ORA-16819: fast-start failover observer not started
```

```
CDBFSDCA - (*) Physical standby database
   Warning: ORA-16819: fast-start failover observer not started
```

Fast-Start Failover: ENABLED

```
Configuration Status:
WARNING
```

DGMGRL>

The little asterisk next to CDBFSDCB indicates that that standby database is the preferred failover target.

TROUBLESHOOTING USING THE BROKER LOGFILE

It is possible that the enable fast_start failover command fails. If it fails it is not immediately obvious why it does. The Broker commands "show configuration" and "show database" do not reveal the cause of the failure. In such cases you need to check the Broker log. The log file used by the Broker resides in the trace directory just like the text representation of the database's alert.log. If you are unsure where to find the directory on disk, simply query the database:

```
SQL> select value from v$diag_info
  2  where name = 'Diag Trace';
```

The Broker logfile is named drc${ORACLE_SID}.log. If you tail it just before you try to enable FSFO you hopefully get meaningful errors, like this one:

```
09/16/2013 15:25:14
ORA-16693, FSFO requires the target standby to be in flashback mode
```

The error message indicated the requirement for the database to have Flashback Database enabled.

In the next step you need to start the observer on the third site. The observer is simply an instance of the dgmgrl utility constantly checking the standby and primary database. As such it is sufficient to install the Oracle client for administrators or alternatively make use of an existing Broker in an RDBMS server installation. Note that the prompt will *not* return after you started the observer, making it advisable to start the broker in its own screen session. Screen is a little command line utility that should be installed by default on all machines in the author's opinion. Similar to VNC in principle it allows you to connect to a server and keep your session on the server. The connection is established using SSH however. Screen allows you to execute commands "in the background" using virtual sessions. The biggest benefit is that a loss of network connectivity does not impact your work. When reconnecting to the server you can re-attach to your screen session and resume where you left. When starting using "screen -L" it records all the output in a log file in the current directory. When you have started the observer as shown below you can detach from the screen session leaving the process to run. Refer to the manual page of screen for more information on how to use screen effectively.

Note that the observer is started from a host in data center C; none of the databases in the Broker configuration are located in this data center. The following example is executed from a screen session to allow the observer to execute even if the session to the database host is lost or disconnected:

```
[oracle@server3 ~]$ cd ~/tns_admin/
[oracle@server3 tns_admin]$ export TNS_ADMIN=$(pwd)
[oracle@server3 tns_admin]$ dgmgrl /@cdbfsdcb
DGMGRL for Linux: Version 12.1.0.1.0 - 64bit Production

Copyright (c) 2000, 2012, Oracle. All rights reserved.

Welcome to DGMGRL, type "help" for information.
Connected as SYSDBA.
DGMGRL> start observer
Observer started
[blinking cursor-command WILL not return]
```

After the Observer has been started the warnings in the Broker configuration disappear. You can query the FSFO configuration in two ways: showing the configuration as demonstrated before or by using the show fast_start failover command:

```
DGMGRL> show configuration verbose

Configuration - fsconfig

  Protection Mode: MaxAvailability
  Databases:
  CDBFSDCB - Primary database
    CDBFSDCA - (*) Physical standby database

  (*) Fast-Start Failover target

  Properties:
    FastStartFailoverThreshold      = '30'
    OperationTimeout                = '30'
    TraceLevel                      = 'USER'
    FastStartFailoverLagLimit       = '30'
    CommunicationTimeout            = '180'
    ObserverReconnect               = '0'
    FastStartFailoverAutoReinstate  = 'TRUE'
    FastStartFailoverPmyShutdown    = 'TRUE'
    BystandersFollowRoleChange      = 'ALL'
    ObserverOverride                = 'FALSE'

Fast-Start Failover: ENABLED

  Threshold:         30 seconds
  Target:            CDBFSDCA
  Observer:          server3.example.com
  Lag Limit:         30 seconds (not in use)
  Shutdown Primary:  TRUE
```

```
Auto-reinstate:       TRUE
Observer Reconnect: (none)
Observer Override:    FALSE
```

```
Configuration Status:
SUCCESS
```

The output of the Fast Start Failover configuration is shown next:

```
DGMGRL> show fast_start failover
```

```
Fast-Start Failover: ENABLED
```

```
    Threshold:          30 seconds
    Target:             CDBFSDCA
    Observer:           server3.example.com
    Lag Limit:          30 seconds (not in use)
    Shutdown Primary:   TRUE
    Auto-reinstate:     TRUE
    Observer Reconnect: (none)
    Observer Override:  FALSE
```

```
Configurable Failover Conditions
    Health Conditions:
        Corrupted Controlfile          YES
        Corrupted Dictionary           YES
        Inaccessible Logfile            NO
        Stuck Archiver                  NO
        Datafile Offline               YES
```

```
    Oracle Error Conditions:
        (none)
```

```
DGMGRL>
```

It summarizes the settings which trigger a failover, the ones shown here are the defaults. Note that a graceful shutdown of the primary will not automatically trigger a failover. Translated into English the FSFO process will be initiated if the observer and the standby database cannot "see" the primary database for more than 30 seconds. The lag limit which defines the maximum allowable time the standby is lagging behind the primary to be an eligible target for an automatic failover is not used in a Maximum Availability configuration. As part of the automated process the old primary will be shut down to ensure no one can connect to it. The old primary will also be reinstated. And finally, the observer will not reconnect to its targets. This is a property you should probably change. The value is in seconds; do not set it too low to incur the overhead of frequent connections but not too high either. Allowing the observer to reconnect gives you some more resilience over transient network glitches.

The section "configurable failover conditions" allow the administrator to fine-tune the failover conditions, and you can even add your own custom conditions using ORA-xxxxx error codes. If now for example your network connectivity from data center A to the rest of the world fails, the Broker will automatically fail over to the designated standby database. The output from the Observer process in data center C indicates that there has indeed been a problem:

```
DGMGRL> start observer
Observer started
```

```
17:55:11.81  Monday, September 16, 2013
Initiating Fast-Start Failover to database "CDBFSDCA"...
Performing failover NOW, please wait...
Failover succeeded, new primary is "CDBFSDCA"
17:55:37.00  Monday, September 16, 2013
```

The old primary is shut down at this stage, and the Broker logfile recorded more information as to what happened.

```
09/16/2013 17:55:12
FAILOVER TO CDBFSDCA
Beginning failover to database CDBFSDCA
Notifying Oracle Clusterware to prepare database for FAILOVER
09/16/2013 17:55:19
DMON: Old primary "CDBFSDCB" needs reinstatement
09/16/2013 17:55:33
Warning: Another process is opening pluggable databases
Waiting for open to complete.
Will retry in 15 seconds, maximim wait time is 15 minutes
09/16/2013 17:55:36
Protection mode set to MAXIMUM AVAILABILITY
09/16/2013 17:55:37
Deferring associated archivelog destinations of sites permanently disabled due to Failover
Notifying Oracle Clusterware to buildup primary database after failover
Posting DB_DOWN alert ...
        ... with reason Data Guard Fast-Start Failover - Primary Disconnected
```

Notice how it detected that a failover has likely taken place. As soon as the old primary is started again it will be reinstated:

```
18:01:19.41  Monday, September 16, 2013
Initiating reinstatement for database "CDBFSDCB"...
Reinstating database "CDBFSDCB", please wait...
Reinstatement of database "CDBFSDCB" succeeded
18:01:58.56  Monday, September 16, 2013
```

The configuration shows no more warnings, and you can switch over to the old primary during the next change window.

Maintaining archived logs

Maintaining archived redo logs in a Data Guard configuration is something that needs careful planning. A very common problem with standby databases falling out of sync with the primary is when the archive log destination fills up. Without space no additional redo can be applied on the standby, and a flurry of errors will be recorded in the alert log of both the primary database as well as the standby database that has run out of space. A fantastic way to deal with archived logs—but not only them—is the Fast Recovery Area ('FRA'). It has been introduced with Oracle 10g as the Flash Recovery Area, but was renamed to Fast Recovery Area in a later release; for all purposes the two are the same.

The goal of the FRA, as it is often abbreviated to, is to simplify management of files which need backing up. Files found to be stored in the FRA include

- A multiplexed copy of the control file

- A multiplexed copy of the online redo log

- Flashback logs

- Archived logs

- Database backupsets

The FRA is defined by two initialization parameters, and can be configured while the database is up and running, as shown here:

```
SQL> alter system set db_recovery_file_dest_size = 40G;

System altered.

SQL> alter system db_recovery_file_dest = '/u01/fast_recovery_area';

System altered.
```

Note that you have to define the size of the FRA before you can set the location. Oracle will then automatically create a directory /u01/fast_recovery_area/*instance_name* to store the contents pertaining to this database. For each file type, you will see an OMF-compliant structure. Archived logs are stored in ./archivelog/yyyy_mm_dd/ with an OMF file name, regardless of the log_archive_format you may have set. If you are on ASM then you set the FRA location to the ASM diskgroup, such as +RECO for example. Oracle will take care of the rest.

Now why is the FRA such a great help for the DBA? This has to do with the way the FRA handles space pressure. As soon as you are running very low on space, the FRA will automatically clear files that are no longer needed. It cannot work wonders though; if there is a guaranteed restore point, or if logs have not been applied to the standby then the files may not be deleted. The same is true for Streams or Golden Gate replication. The parameter to set for the automatic deletion of archived logs depends on the backup strategy. It is a RMAN setting, called ARCHIVELOG DELETION POLICY. In the context of Data Guard the policy can be set to either of these values:

- `applied on all standby`

- `shipped to all standby`

- `none`

- `backup up n times to device type [disk | sbt]`

▪ **Note**   Refer to Chapter 11 for more information about the Recovery Manager backup strategies available.

If you are implementing a backup strategy where you backup archived logs on the primary database, then you could set the deletion policy either to "none" or "backed up *n* times to device type sbt." Setting the policy to "none," which is the default, implies that archived logs in the FRA can still be deleted! However, to be deleted they have to meet all of the below:

- The archived log considered for deletion has been transferred to all required standby databases or other remote destinations.

- The archived log concerned has been backed up at least once.

- The archived log is considered obsolete according to the backup strategy, and is not needed for Flashback Database—either to satisfy the retention target or a guaranteed restorepoint.

You could use the "backed up *n* times" policy instead to get more control over the deletion process. An archived log will only be deleted if the specified *n* copies to the required medium-tape or disk.

The "applied to/shipped to standby" policies are very useful to manage space pressure. When selecting the "applied on all standby" policy archived logs will be deleted only if the archived redo logs have actually been applied on all standby databases. Conversely, the "shipped to all standby" policy will mark archived redo logs eligible for deletion after they have been transferred to the remote destination.

Oracle's recommendation with regard to these policies has been defined in the Maximum Availability Architecture as follows:

- If you are backing up archived logs on the primary, consider setting the log archive deletion policy to "none" or "backed up *n* times", depending on your company's backup standards. The same policies should be considered for a standby database if the standby is the source for backups.

- If not backing up on a particular standby database consider setting the log deletion policy to "applied on all standby."

The following example clarifies the point. The current space usage in the Fast Recovery Area can be queried from within a database:

```
SQL> select * from v$flash_recovery_area_usage;
```

FILE_TYPE	PERCENT_SPACE_USED	PERCENT_SPACE_RECLAIMABLE	NUMBER_OF_FILES	CON_ID
CONTROL FILE	.38	0	1	0
REDO LOG	71.44	0	7	0
ARCHIVED LOG	1.42	0	11	0
BACKUP PIECE	.38	0	1	0
IMAGE COPY	0	0	0	0
FLASHBACK LOG	0	0	0	0
FOREIGN ARCHIVED LOG	0	0	0	0
AUXILIARY DATAFILE COPY	0	0	0	0

```
8 rows selected.
```

You can see that the FRA—which had its size artificially reduced—has significant space pressure. In the next few minutes a few forced log switches on the primary increased this even further. But luckily the standby database is applying the logs in Real Time Apply, so the logs do not need to stay on disk for long. And indeed, thanks to the log deletion policy chosen—applied on all standby—the Oracle Managed Files are purged from the FRA as soon as they are no longer needed. This is reflected in the alert.log of the standby database:

```
[oracle@server1 trace]$ grep "Deleted Oracle managed" alert_CDB1DCA.log
Deleted Oracle managed file +RECO/CDB1DCA/ARCHIVELOG/2013_09_16/thread_1_seq_6.257.826281897
Deleted Oracle managed file +RECO/CDB1DCA/ARCHIVELOG/2013_09_16/thread_1_seq_7.264.826281945
Deleted Oracle managed file +RECO/CDB1DCA/ARCHIVELOG/2013_09_16/thread_1_seq_8.269.826300853
```

Querying the space usage again you see that the space used by the archived logs as well as the number of archived logs has changed.

```
SQL> select file_type,percent_space_used,percent_space_reclaimable,number_of_files
  2  from V$RECOVERY_AREA_USAGE;
```

FILE_TYPE	PERCENT_SPACE_USED	PERCENT_SPACE_RECLAIMABLE	NUMBER_OF_FILES
CONTROL FILE	3.6	0	1
REDO LOG	71.4	0	7
ARCHIVED LOG	3.4	.8	3
BACKUP PIECE	0	0	0
IMAGE COPY	0	0	0
FLASHBACK LOG	0	0	0
FOREIGN ARCHIVED LOG	0	0	0
AUXILIARY DATAFILE COPY	0	0	0

8 rows selected.

■ **Caution**　Oracle's documentation states that files that are required for Stream may be deleted from the FRA. Ensure you have backups of these files, for example by creating intra-day archivelog backups

---

The above usage of the Fast Recovery Area does not relieve you from the task of monitoring of the archive destination. It should however allow you to simplify the management of archived redo logs on systems where they are not constantly backed up and purged by RMAN.

Data Guard specifics for Pluggable Databases

Pluggable Databases are one of the most interesting new features of Oracle 12c and you can read a lot about them in Chapter 7. There are a few specifics when it comes to Data Guard and Pluggable Databases. No need to worry, all the previous examples have been using a Container Database (CDB). The following cases need closer examination:

- Creation of a new Pluggable Database on the primary database
- Plugging in a previously unknown PDB into the primary database
- Unplugging a PDB from the primary
- Dropping a PDB

As of this writing the scope of Data Guard is the Container Database, not the individual Pluggable Database. As you saw earlier in the chapter, role changes are performed for the Container. Following that logic you will notice that managed recovery is active for the CDB, not selectively for individual PDBs.

Using Data Guard with the Active Data Guard option greatly simplifies management of the standby databases. Without Active Data Guard the behavior is similar to that of transportable tablespaces in releases before 12c. When you plan to plug in a transportable tablespace set in the primary, it is your responsibility to make the same transportable tablespace data set available at the standby. The following examples will use the transparent solution with Active Data Guard in an effort not to extend the chapter even further. Be warned though that you need to be appropriately licensed to use the steps described here.

Creating a new Pluggable Database on the primary database

The creation of a new PDB is transparent to the end user. With Active Data Guard implemented the "create pluggable database" statement is executed on the standby database and the pluggable database is created. Any files that needed copying are then copied over the network. This copying is not very spectacular, since it simply works as the example will demonstrate. It does not matter if the new PDB is created from a clone of an existing PDB or as a clone of the seed PDB. The example assumes that you are familiar with creating a PDB from SQL*Plus, please refer back to Chapter 7 for a refresher on the syntax.

```
SQL> create pluggable database pdb4
  2  admin user PDB4_DBA identified by secretPassword
  3  file_name_convert=('/u01/oradata/CDBFSDCA/pdbseed','/u01/oradata/CDBFSDCA/PDB4');
```

The above example is the most basic example possible where the CDB resides on a file system. Prior to executing the above command you will need to ensure that the directories referenced in the file name conversion clause exist. In addition you will need to have db_file_name_convert defined on the standby database to translate the full path. The final parameter that comes to mind regarding data file creation is standby_file_management which should always be set to auto in any Data Guard configuration.

The standby database acknowledges the creation of the PDB in the alert.log:

```
2013-09-17 11:34:42.864000 +01:00
Recovery copied files for tablespace SYSTEM
Recovery successfully copied file /u01/oradata/CDBFSDCB/PDB4/system01.dbf from
/u01/oradata/CDBFSDCB/pdbseed/system01.dbf
Recovery created file /u01/oradata/CDBFSDCB/PDB4/system01.dbf
Datafile 21 added to flashback set
Successfully added datafile 21 to media recovery
Datafile #21: '/u01/oradata/CDBFSDCB/PDB4/system01.dbf'
2013-09-17 11:34:52.038000 +01:00
Recovery copied files for tablespace SYSAUX
Recovery successfully copied file /u01/oradata/CDBFSDCB/PDB4/sysaux01.dbf from
/u01/oradata/CDBFSDCB/pdbseed/sysaux01.dbf
Recovery created file /u01/oradata/CDBFSDCB/PDB4/sysaux01.dbf
Datafile 22 added to flashback set
Successfully added datafile 22 to media recovery
Datafile #22: '/u01/oradata/CDBFSDCB/PDB4/sysaux01.dbf'
```

Querying the V$PDBS view you can also see that it has been created.

The effect of plugging in PDBs into the primary

Plugging in a previously unknown PDB is very similar to plugging in a transportable tablespace data set into the primary database but easier. This Transportable Tablespace scenario is well known for quite some time and has been documented in the Data Guard Concepts and Administration Guide section 10.3.3 in the 12c documentation set.

The basic tasks for plugging in a PDB are almost the same. First you need to make the PDB files available to the primary and standby databases. In this example the DBA has been instructed to plug in PDB5 into the primary database CDBFSDCA for which there is a single standby database CDBFSDCB. The file system based case has deliberately been chosen over ASM and OMF as it requires a little more attention to detail. As part of the clone process the DBA has made the files available in the default location on the primary and standby database(s).

```
[oracle@server1 CDBFSDCA]$ ls -l PDB5
total 875548
-rw-r-----. 1 oracle asmadmin   5251072 Sep 17 12:12 PDB5_users01.dbf
-rw-r-----. 1 oracle asmadmin 618668032 Sep 17 12:12 sysaux01.dbf
-rw-r-----. 1 oracle asmadmin 272637952 Sep 17 12:12 system01.dbf
[oracle@server1 CDBFSDCA]$
```

```
[oracle@server2 CDBFSDCB]$ ls -l PDB5
total 875604
-rw-r-----. 1 oracle asmadmin   5251072 Sep 17 12:12 PDB5_users01.dbf
-rw-r-----. 1 oracle asmadmin 618668032 Sep 17 12:12 sysaux01.dbf
-rw-r-----. 1 oracle asmadmin 272637952 Sep 17 12:12 system01.dbf
-rw-r-----. 1 oracle asmadmin  20979712 Sep 17 01:12 temp01.dbf
[oracle@server2 CDBFSDCB]$
```

Remember from Chapter 7 that you need the XML file describing the PDB as well. Without the XML metadata you cannot plug the PDB into the CDB. The XML file resides in /home/oracle/PDB5.xml in the example. With this information it is possible to plug the PDB into the primary CDB:

```
SQL> create pluggable database PDB5
  2  using '/home/oracle/PDB5.xml'
  3    nocopy;

Pluggable database created.
```

The operation completes successfully on both primary and standby databases.

```
2013-09-17 12:20:07.834000 +01:00
Recovery created file /u01/oradata/CDBFSDCB/PDB5/system01.dbf
Datafile 23 added to flashback set
[...]
Successfully added datafile 25 to media recovery
Datafile #25: '/u01/oradata/CDBFSDCB/PDB5/PDB5_users01.dbf'
```

In scenarios where you have more than one standby database you need to make the PDB available to all standby databases.

Unplugging PDBs from the primary

In the next example pluggable database PDB3 is unplugged from the primary. Prior to this example PDB3 exists in the primary and standby database:

```
SQL> select name,guid from v$pdbs;

NAME                             GUID
-------------------------------- --------------------------------
PDB$SEED                         E6483A08FB7940D8E0431464A8C0318D
PDB1                             E6484B59FBEC4908E0431464A8C06F2E
PDB2                             E689AE04FAB41253E0431564A8C0354E
PDB3                             E689AE04FAB51253E0431564A8C0354E
```

To show you that it exists in the standby as well v$pdbs is queried against the GUID of PDB3:

```
SQL> select name,guid from v$pdbs
  2  where guid = 'E689AE04FAB51253E0431564A8C0354E';
```

```
NAME                          GUID
----------------------------  --------------------------------
PDB3                          E689AE04FAB51253E0431564A8C0354E
```

Now let's unplug the PDB:

```
SQL> alter pluggable database PDB3
  2  unplug into '/home/oracle/PDB3.xml';

Pluggable database altered.

SQL> select name,guid from v$pdbs
  2  where guid = 'E689AE04FAB51253E0431564A8C0354E';

NAME                          GUID
----------------------------  --------------------------------
PDB3                          E689AE04FAB51253E0431564A8C0354E

SQL> !ls -l /home/oracle/PDB3.xml
-rw-r--r--. 1 oracle asmadmin 3690 Sep 17 12:12 /home/oracle/PDB3.xml
```

The command completed without a problem. You will notice that it has no effect on the availability of the PDB to the CDB.

Dropping a PDB from the primary

Dropping the PDB from the primary is mentioned here only for the sake of completeness. The operation to drop a PDB from the primary is replicated as a DDL command and executed seamlessly. Consider the following example where PDB4 is dropped on the primary:

```
SQL> drop pluggable database pdb4 keep datafiles;

Pluggable database dropped.
```

The command is executed on the standby database as well:

```
2013-09-17 11:56:02.048000 +01:00
Recovery dropped temporary tablespace 'TEMP'
Recovery deleting file #22:'/u01/oradata/CDBFSDCB/PDB4/sysaux01.dbf' from controlfile.
Recovery dropped tablespace 'SYSAUX'
Recovery deleting file #21:'/u01/oradata/CDBFSDCB/PDB4/system01.dbf' from controlfile.
Recovery dropped tablespace 'SYSTEM'
2013-09-17 11:56:03.106000 +01:00
Recovery dropped pluggable database 'PDB4'
```

A quick check against v$pdbs on the primary and standby database reveals that the PDB is indeed gone.

Summary

Well thought-through naming conventions make the life of the database administrator a lot easier. With Data Guard a new dimension is added to the scope of the naming convention. Database instances in a Data Guard environment should probably not be named after their role, especially not in a consolidated environment. A location could be a good name, otherwise users might get confused when the database STANDBY1 is in the primary role.

Standby databases are easily created using the RMAN duplicate database command. You read about the two possible cases for database duplication: to file system or to ASM/OMF based storage.

Finally you read more about configuration a Data Guard environment. The large number of configuration options and choices are nicely hidden from view when using the Data Guard Broker interface. In addition to the Broker command line interface you can use Enterprise Manager. OEM will pick up any existing Broker configuration and allow you to manage the environment.

Recent versions of Enterprise Manager have had great support for Data Guard, and centrally managed monitoring templates make it easy to alert the database administrator on shift when there are problems. The Enterprise Manager Data Guard pages offer a great view of the various performance metrics in the Data Guard configuration, most notably the transport and delay lags. If you wanted you could even use Enterprise Manager to monitor and maintain Data Guard configurations, including the initial creation of a standby database.

Less experienced DBAs find role transitions intimidating and scary, but they need not be. Instead, practice, documentation, and training will make a switchover a standard procedure much like opening and closing a database. The "practice" aspect cannot be overrated in this context. If a failover situation occurs for some reason stress levels are guaranteed to rise. Good documentation and confidence will help getting the system up and running on the disaster recovery site more easily.

The Broker command line interface again is a great way of simplifying the role transitions, and the bet is that it will take longer to get approval for the role transition than it takes to carry it out. Despite the fact that the Oracle database is highly resilient to problems during a role transition one should not forget to regularly test if applications continue to function after a role reversal. Strict coding standards should prevent hard coded connection strings from entering production applications, but time pressure can lead to cutting corners, reinforcing the need to perform regular tests.

CHAPTER 11

■ ■ ■

Backup and Recovery

No database solution—hosted or in-house—would be complete without proper backup and recovery procedures. In fact the importance of getting a system back at any time within the limits of the service level agreements is of paramount importance. Backup and recovery complement the disaster recovery solution, which you read about in Chapters 9 and 10. In many ways you cannot have just the one solution—backups or a DR site—since large databases might take too long to be restored and rolled forward. It is important to keep in mind that the shared hosting platform is indeed shared, including the backup infrastructure. So if there is a separate tape library available to the shared platform, then you can almost certainly assume that there are going to be delays accessing it. Depending on your service level agreement it can be safer to invoke the standby database, and then rebuild the failed primary. For all other cases the restore and recovery are of course sufficient.

Despite existing standby databases which can be activated in literally no time, backups are essential. Assume for a moment that the regulator wants a copy of a specific database at a point in time, maybe weeks or months back. How would you be able to supply the regulator with the data in a straightforward way?

The chapter you are going to read will focus on the most important aspects of the backup infrastructure for a consolidated database environment. It will specifically focus on Pluggable Databases as explained in Chapter 7 as the focus of your attention. And again the solution to be put into place has to be simple and mostly automatic. Depending on your first line support the restore and recovery commands might need to be hidden in a shell script or similar abstraction layer. The importance of having skilled developers for these scripts cannot be overrated, since the tool will be rolled out globally. Any bugs in the abstraction layer can potentially mean data loss. The chapter is aimed at these developers, mainly to be found in engineering, explaining the tools and methods for creating a suitable abstraction layer for the operations team to use. The resulting script is left as an exercise to the reader.

The primary tool for taking Oracle backups is Recovery Manager, RMAN. While its appeal was little in the initial 8.x release, RMAN has become very mature and can care for literally any situation. RMAN hides a lot of the work to be done under the covers from the user. So-called user-managed backups or manual backups on the other hand are more difficult to take and require more knowledge of Oracle. The use of user-managed backups is strongly discouraged both for complexity and number of steps required. The more steps to be executed, the higher the probability of making mistakes.

An introduction to Backups

Backups are fundamental building blocks and the bread and butter for every database administrator. Without a working backup, or a database recovery based on it even the most prolific tuning expert would struggle to justify why he or she was there in the first place: if there is no database there is no need for tuning. Speaking more seriously there is a real need to be able to get your database back, and Oracle's own Recovery Manager is the foremost tool to address the needs of backup and recovery. After a complete, consistent backup of the database has been taken you are protected from many types of failures affecting your applications. The most common problems that require a restore of parts or the entire database are media failures and user errors. Oracle's inability to read or write to a physical file such as control files, data files, or online redo logs are called media failures. They can be caused by file malfunctioning host bus adapters or problems with a file system. Failing disks causing SAN storage to become unavailable are less common with enterprise storage arrays which use elaborate protection mechanisms internally. A media failure most often requires the database administrator to move the affected files off that particular mount point to another one.

Bugs in applications or errors caused by application changes implemented during maintenance windows can cause logical corruption. If that corruption cannot be corrected by rolling the changes back a restore operation is also often unavoidable. Not every change comes with a rollback script, and many rollback scripts have received little attention and testing.

Finally sometimes the Oracle database might discover corrupted blocks requiring block media recovery. In this case instead of restoring and recovering the whole data file only parts need to be restored and recovered. Again, a working backup strategy is required when you want to perform Block Media Recovery, or BMR for short. Block Media Recovery has changed very little since the last major release and therefore will not be covered here.

RMAN backups

Recovery Manager stores backups in two formats: image copies of data files or so-called backup sets. An image copy, as the name suggests, is a one-to-one copy of the source file. A backup set on the other hand is a RMAN specific format containing one or multiple backup pieces. A backup set can contain all files needed to restore a database, such as the server parameter file, control files, archived redo logs, and data files. Database administrators eyed the backup sets suspiciously at first since RMAN is the only tool to access them. Over time this suspicion has subsided. However, backup sets benefit from unused block compression and null block compression, potentially reducing the size of backup set. Additionally, you have the option to apply binary compression of backup sets.

Incremental vs. full backups

Two different kinds of backups exist in RMAN: incremental and full backups, the latter being the default. A full backup, as the name suggests, backs up every component of the database needed for restoring it. Since full backups always include everything needed for a complete restore, they can become real space hogs. Incremental backups are different: rather than backing up everything each time, they only back up what has changed since the last backup. Since there has to be a starting point, the initial incremental backup will—like a full backup—include all the physical structures required to restore the database. This backup is not called a full backup, it is referred to as an incremental backup of level 0, or base backup. Unfortunately a full backup as described earlier cannot be used as a level 0 backup. Subsequent backups will be of level 1, building on the foundation laid by the level 0 backup and include only what has changed since the level 0 backup has been taken. Incremental backups can further be divided into cumulative and differential backups, again with the latter as the default. The cumulative backup will back up all changes since the last level 0 backup. A differential incremental backup will only back up changes since the last backup, regardless whether it was level 0 or a previous level 1 backup. Cumulative backups are normally larger in size compared to a differential backup.

Cumulative backups can offer an advantage over differential backups. If your backup strategy consisted of a level 0 backup on the weekend and cumulative incremental backups on the weekdays, then your restore only required the application of the level 0 backup plus the latest cumulative backup. With differential backups you have to restore the level 0 backup followed by a restore of each differential backup. In summary you are trading recovery time against disk space. On the other hand, if a differential backup is small in size there is merit in using it instead.

The duration of incremental backup directly depends on the number of blocks that changed. Instead of reading every data file to ascertain which blocks have changed since the last backup, Oracle can be instructed to use a change tracking file instead. This so-called block-change tracking (BCT) file contains bitmaps that identify which blocks have changed since the last backup. There are a maximum of eight bitmaps maintained to cover the last eight backups. You should keep this in mind when designing your backup strategy; the eight bitmaps are usually sufficient for a week's worth of backups. After the eighth bitmap has been used Oracle will wrap around and start at the beginning of the change tracking file again, potentially degenerating the performance of the backup.

Online and offline backups

An online backup, which should really be the default, backs the database up while it is up and running. In order to take an online backup the database must be in archivelog mode. In other words, used online redo logs must be safely stored away by one of the archiver processes. An online backup by definition is inconsistent. This means that Oracle has to use the (backed up) archived logs to bring the database to a consistent state-a process called media recovery.

Offline backups, or RMAN backups taken while the database is in mount mode, are consistent if the database has been shut down cleanly. However the shut down and subsequent time to take the backup are a service outage; no user can access the database. For many scenarios this is hugely undesirable. The only upside to consistent backups is that no media recovery is required. Offline backups are usually taken only for databases which do not have archivelog mode enabled. And there should not be many of these anyway.

■ **Caution** Not using archivelog mode for a database is definitely a Big Problem for anything other than play databases! You are almost guaranteed to lose data operating in noarchivelog mode, the question is not whether or not to lose it but when.

Backup destinations

Another important aspect is the destination of the backup. Oracle offers two different destinations: either to disk, which is the default, or using a media manager. The media manager is accessed via a dedicated API Oracle makes available to third-party vendors. Using this API any third party can write software to interact with RMAN and storage libraries. Tape libraries and their virtual cousins are the most common source of longer-term backups. The beauty of this approach is that except for a short initialization section at the beginning of an RMAN session all commands are portable across any other environment.

The configuration of your Media Manager can be quite time consuming. The easiest way to deploy it is via your platform's package manager. If you are lucky and your vendor understands the platform well you get more than a simple installation script. Instead you get a package you can add as a dependency into your standard database server operating system build. The configuration options for tape backups are so many that they have not been included in the chapter. Very often however you can simply substitute the initialization of disk channels with tape channel (SBT-System Backup to Tape) to back up to tape instead.

Using a dedicated media manager usually involves extra cost for the software, which is why many environments perform a two staged Backup strategy:the RMAN database backup goes to a dedicated area on disk, from where it is backed up using a "normal" disk backup to tape. Disk in this respect can and maybe should be on a different host. In the UNIX world NFS seems to be a popular choice, and Oracle offers hardware solutions for this purpose. Most backups to disk are likely to complete as quick if not quicker than tape backups. If a low-enough storage tier is selected for them, then the cost advantage of tape drives can also partially be offset. The downside to the two-staged approach is that for a backup which is not on disk you first have to restore from tape to disk. Hopefully your backup area can take more than just one backup, otherwise you might have to remove the existing backup first. After the tape restore you have to initiate the RMAN restore and recover commands. All of these tasks will take time, and as with any critical operation should be documented well and practiced regularly. It is very important to stress that there is little worse during a restore than to find out that the a few crucial archived logs have not been restored from tape to disk.

Which approach you end up taking in the end will most likely depend on budget. If your organization has a favorable licensing deal with your backup vendor, then a direct integration of RMAN and the media manager is desirable. In most other cases you might end up with the more important databases being backed up to tape directly, whereas the lower tier databases probably will be backed up to disk first, then to tape.

Complete versus incomplete recovery

The scope of the recovery can either be full or partial. The latter is also known as incomplete recovery, or point in time recovery. A full recovery, as the name suggests, is applied when media failure has rendered a mount point unusable. The reasons for this are manifold, failure of a SAN switch or logical corruption on the file system level can cause a file system to be downgraded to "read-only" mode at best, or automatically dismounted at worst. In any case, the database will not be able to write to its files, causing it to crash.

If all information required for a full recovery is available you can restore the files on the lost mountpoint to another file system with sufficient free space and fully recover the database. A full recovery ends with the command to open the database, not specifying the resetlogs clause.

An incomplete recovery on the other hand is required in situations where for example a software release has gone badly wrong and the Flashback Database feature has not been enabled, rendering the feature unavailable. Another situation requiring a full recovery is the user error or a bug in the application using the database to store and retrieve data. In some circumstances it is impossible to create a fix for the logical corruption, and the database must be restored to a point in time prior to the failure.

The database incarnation

Whenever you open the database with the resetlogs option it creates a new incarnation. An incarnation as per the Oracle documentation is a separate version of the database. The original incarnation of each new database is incarnation 1, and others are added as and when needed. Using Recovery Manager it is possible to list the incarnations of a database:

```
RMAN> list incarnation;

List of Database Incarnations
DB Key  Inc Key DB Name  DB ID             STATUS  Reset SCN  Reset Time
------- ------- -------- ----------------- --- ---------- ----------
1       1       CDB2     573673282         PARENT  1720082    20.09.2013 09:39
2       2       CDB2     573673282         CURRENT 1764438    20.09.2013 10:24
```

The resetlogs system change number is tracked with every incarnation, as is the date. It is important to understand that the counter for the sequence numbers in Oracle online log files is reset with each incarnation. This posed a serious problem up to Oracle 10g when the new archived redo logs could potentially overwrite archivelogs with the same sequence number but from an earlier incarnation. Unless you decide otherwise Oracle will now include the resetlogs change number in the format for the archived redo logs, avoiding the problem. Also beginning with Oracle 10 it became possible to recover across the resetlogs statements, a feature which relied on the inclusion of the resetlogs change number in the archived log file name.

The Fast Recovery Area

The Fast Recovery Area or FRA is one of the greatest additions to the Oracle database over the last years. Although it started its existence as Flash Recovery Area Oracle renamed it in 11g to avoid further confusion with other technology using "flash" in its name. The recovery area is a central location for many backup related files, such as:

- Archived redo logs
- Backup piece
- Image copy
- Flashback log

Additionally you often find a multiplexed online redo log per thread and group as well as a multiplexed controlfile in it. The use of the FRA is so simple and the benefit of having a standard location for important backup files so big that there is actually no reason not to use it. All you need to do is define the size of the FRA and the location, shown here for ASM:

```
SQL> alter system set db_recovery_file_dest_size = 100G sid='*' scope='both';

System altered.

SQL> alter system set db_recovery_file_dest = '+RECO' sid='*' scope='both';

System altered.
```

For a FRA on a file system you simply point to the directory you set aside for it as shown here:

```
SQL> alter system set db_recovery_file_dest = '/u01/fast_recovery_area' scope='both';

System altered.
```

It is important that you do not include an identifier for the database. All files in the FRA are Oracle Managed Files, and a database identifier is appended automatically for you. Complaints from the system administrator that a common location or mount point for more than one database are a risk can be countered that every database has a set quota on that mount point. Unlike the diagnostic destination which—if shared—can become a problem if a single database suddenly fills the file system to 100% by core dumps or other unforeseen problems you specifically tell Oracle how much space is available. Querying the view shows the administrator explicitly how much space is used, and how much is reclaimable, leading to the next great feature of the FRA.

If your system experiences space pressure in the archive log destination and you are not using the FRA then there might be a point where there is no more space left, leaving the archiver stuck which is a common yet very undesirable situation. When using the FRA this problem can partly be mitigated by using the automatic space management features. To understand this feature it is important to understand the type of file in the FRA. Files which are part of the active database, such as online redo log members and a multiplexed controlfile are termed "permanent" files in the FRA. The other files in the FRA are called transient. Only transient files are eligible for automatic removal, and only under certain conditions. You need not worry that permanent files are deleted; they are not touched by the clean-up mechanism. When considering which files will be deleted, the retention policy plays a very important role. The RMAN retention policy defines the number of backups you need to keep or alternatively a time period over which backups are required before being purged.

■ **Note**   You can learn more about the retention policy later in this chapter.

Backups that are no longer needed may automatically be removed. Information about reclaimable space is managed in the v$flash_recovery_area_usage view, as shown here:

```
SYS@CDB$ROOT> select FILE_TYPE,PERCENT_SPACE_USED,PERCENT_SPACE_RECLAIMABLE
  2  from v$flash_recovery_area_usage
  3  where PERCENT_SPACE_RECLAIMABLE <> 0;

FILE_TYPE              PERCENT_SPACE_USED PERCENT_SPACE_RECLAIMABLE
---------------------- ------------------ -------------------------
ARCHIVED LOG                         4.86                      4.86
BACKUP PIECE                        10.37                       .42
```

In this example all of the archived redo logs have just been backed up, and there is a redundant backup piece as well leading to some reclaimable space. If needed, that space is freed automatically.

Flashback logs, which cannot be managed outside the Fast Recovery Area are always managed by Oracle. If space pressure occurs these logs are among the first to be reused or deleted, even if that means you cannot meet your flashback retention target. If you rely on flashback logs to rewind the database to a point in time, you need to set a guaranteed restore point. In this case you should ensure that there is actually enough space in the FRA to accommodate for all the required archived logs and flashback logs, otherwise you will run out of space and your database will pause until more space is provided.

When provisioning new databases you should strongly consider the use of the flash recovery area for the reasons just outlined. The extra work to enable it is marginal—setting two initialization parameters—and the maintenance benefit is enormous. As an additional plus point you have achieved standardization of your on-disk backup location.

Logical backups

In addition to using RMAN it is possible to take logical backups. These backups are taken using the expdp (Export Data Pump) utility. The biggest downside to taking logical backups is that you cannot perform a complete restore with them. In other words, restoring a Data Pump export file requires a database which is up and running. The effort to create a shell database and then to load the data into it is often too time consuming to be used in real life situations. Data Pump Exports however are ideally suited for developers to backup up changes to their own schemas in a development environment to keep reference of code before it was changed. Export Data Pump—unlike its predecessor—creates the dump file on the database server, and not on the client. Once a Data Pump export has been taken you should ensure that it is subsequently backed up to disk as well. It is advisable to choose unique file names, possibly with a time stamp in the name.

Taking a logical backup is quite simple, but needs a little bit of preparation during the database build. First, you need to have access to a directory object. The easiest way to create one is to do so during the build. If a directory has not been created, you can do so anytime as shown in the below code example.

```
SYSTEM@PDB1> create directory EXP_DIR as '/u01/oradata/CDB1/pdb1';

Directory created.
```

Note how the directory is created in the PDB. In the next step you can define which elements of the PDB you want to export. A convenient way to do so is to use a parameter file. This file contains name=value pairs and can be used to store the configuration for specific jobs. An example parameter file could have the following contents to export the whole metadata for a PDB:

```
content=metadata_only
directory=EXP_DIR
full=y
job_name=daily_metadata_export
```

The log file name and dump file name, which are mandatory for data pump exports have not been added to the parameter file on purpose. They can be passed dynamically at run time to avoid overwriting existing files. A purge job needs to be included in the daily export task to avoid the disk from filling up. The find command is a great tool to identify files with a creation timestamp of several days ago and can at the same time be instructed to remove the files it found.

```
[oracle@server1]$ expdp /@pdb1 parfile=exp_pdb1.par \
> dumpfile=exp_pdb1_$(date +%F).dmp logfile=exp_pdb1_$(date +%F).log
```

> ■ **Note** The funny looking connect string uses an Oracle Secure External Password Store. It allows you to store the connection credentials for a TNS alias in a securely encrypted file. Chapter 10 explains the password store in more detail.

What you will certainly learn to appreciate is that the file you get can be used for all sorts of transformations. Storage options can be skipped, owners can be replaced with the REMAP_DATA, REMAP_DATAFILE, REMAP_TABLESPACE, REMAP_SCHEMA, and REMAP_TABLE functions. More importantly you can get all DDL statement from the flat file if you specify the sqlfile option. Using the INCLUDE or EXCLUDE options you can limit yourself to individual objects. If you are interested in the table DDL for a specific schema, the following will work for you:

```
[oracle@server1 ~]$ impdp /@pdb1 dumpfile=exp_2013-10-04.dmp \
> logfile=imp_job001.log directory=exp_dir sqlfile=tables_user1.sql \
> include=table schemas=user1
```

The result is the same as you would get from the dbms_metada package. Like with the package you can further transform the output using the TRANSFORM clause in addition to the ones shown in the example. This way you could save the day for a developer who needs to revert back to last week's code he forgot to check into the version control system.

Additional technology available

Backup and recovery are all well and good. Sometimes however there is only a small problem and a full restore and media recovery would take just too long. Beginning with Oracle 10g further options are available to you to get out of a precarious situation. Most of these technologies are prefixed "flashback", which makes it quite confusing at first. In a backup and recovery scenario the following options can become useful, especially if the fault is discovered quickly.

- Flashback table
- Flashback database
- Storage snapshot

Flashback table is a very nice feature relying on UNDO information in the undo-tablespace to get information back to a table that has accidentally been changed. Note that the undo information actually has to be available in the undo tablespace for this to work. Furthermore, your table must have row movement enabled. Flashback table is demonstrated in the following code snippet. First, the table is created:

```
USER1@PDB1> create table fbtab1 enable row movement
  2  as select * from all_objects;

Table created.

USER1@PDB1> select count(1) from fbtab1;

  COUNT(1)
----------
     89646
```

The time was 16:12:35 when something bad (exemplified next) happened:

```
16:12:35 USER1@PDB1> delete from fbtab1 where object_id < 10000;

9645rows deleted.

USER1@PDB1> commit;

Commit complete.
```

Almost 10,000 rows have been deleted by accident, causing logical corruption. Luckily the user picked up the phone to the DBA on duty and reported his problem. Using the time and the useful timetamp_to_scn function the DBA could use the flashback table command to get the table back to what it was before the accident, and no damage was done.

```
DBA1@PDB1> flashback table user1.fbtab1 to scn 983544;

Flashback complete.

DBA1@PDB1> select count(1) from user1.fbtab1 where object_id < 10000;

  COUNT(1)
----------
      9645

DBA1@PDB1> select count(1) from fbtab1;

  COUNT(1)
----------
     89646
```

Flashback table can be extended to cater to dropped objects as well. Assume for a moment that instead of a delete the user issued a drop table command:

```
USER1@PDB1> drop table fbtab1;

Table dropped.
```

The user might be lucky if the 10g "recycle bin" feature was active at the time. If so, just like on your desktop operating system, you can move things out of the recycle bin and back into active service:

```
USER1@PDB1> select object_name,original_name,type from user_recyclebin;

OBJECT_NAME                      ORIGINAL_NAME                 TYPE
-------------------------------  ----------------------------  --------------------------
BIN$yZfeIpNmMcHgQwqYqMAW7Q==$0 FBTAB1                          TABLE
```

You or your DBA on duty can now restore the table to before the drop using a variation of the flashback table command:

```
DBA1@PDB1> flashback table user1.FBTAB1 to before drop;

Flashback complete.
```

Sometimes however it is not possible to correct a problem, and a point in time recovery is needed. This can become a time-consuming process as it involves a restore of the last level 0 backup followed by potential other incremental backup restore operations until finally you can apply media recovery. Flashback database, another new 10g feature can help in such situations since it merely "rewinds" the database instead. It requires the database to be in flashback mode. When flashback is enabled the database writes information into an additional set of log files, called flashback logs. Writing into flashback logs might have negative performance implications and should be tested first! Flashback database does not only rely on the flashback logs, the archived redo logs are equally required to perform the operation.

Flashback database is great prior to performing software releases as it allows you to get the database back to where it was before the release, saving you from having to apply rollback scripts which are usually poorly tested at best. Instead of having to memorize when the release started it is best to set a guaranteed restore point before starting to simplify the rollback operation. The guaranteed restore point prevents a situation whereby the information required to perform the flashback database call has been overwritten in a way similar to the infamous ORA-1555(snapshot too old) error. Create the guaranteed restore point before the release, as shown here. Remember that the restore point has to be set in the CDB root.

```
SYS@CDB$ROOT> create restore point pre_release guarantee flashback database;
```

Then proceed and deploy the release. If required you can perform a flashback database operation which is very straightforward, but it affects *all* PDBs in the CDB. If this is not possible or desirable refer to the PDB Point In Time Recovery later in this chapter.

```
SQL> shutdown abort
[...]
SQL> startup mount
[...]
SQL> flashback database to restore point 'pre-release';

Flashback complete.

SQL> alter database open resetlogs;

Database opened.
```

■ **Note**   Not every operation can be undone using flashback database, some tasks like dropping a data file or certain nologging operations cannot be undone and require a full point-in-time-recovery. In other words: test the flashback operation during a release in a non-production environment and read up on the feature's limitations in the documentation. In Data Guard configurations flashback database has additional consequences.

The final topic worth mentioning is similar to the flashback database feature just discussed. Rather than allowing Oracle to perform the rewind operation you could rely on the storage subsystem to perform this task for you. Your storage administrator can create snapshots on the array level before important operations, allowing the array to reset the database as it was before the release or batch-run. Whichever technique works best for you depends on the relationship of storage administrators and DBAs. If the DBAs like to be in control of the process to the greatest extent, then it makes a lot of sense to rely on Oracle's restore points and the flashback database feature.

Noteworthy new RMAN features in Oracle 12.1

New backup and recovery related features for Oracle 12.1 have deliberately not featured in the previous Chapter 2 to keep the information in context. After the introduction to Recovery Manager it is now time to provide more detail about some interesting new RMAN 12c features. The next section is a selection of new features by the author with regard to the consolidation and automation theme that you found throughout the book. There may be more interesting features for you to explore in the "What's new in Backup and Recovery" section of the Backup and Recovery User's Guide.

The SYSBACKUP role

Similar to the other roles that have been mentioned throughout the book the SYSBACKUP role addresses a security concern. The power of the SYSDBA role is indeed great, and the possibility to use it to see any data in the database can be seen as too much of a risk. And besides: why should the backup operator be able to see the data he or she is backing up? The solution is to use the SYSBACKUP role. You can find out whether it has been created by querying v$pwfile_users:

```
SYS@CDB$ROOT> select * from v$pwfile_users;

USERNAME                        SYSDB SYSOP SYSAS SYSBA SYSDG SYSKM     CON_ID
------------------------------- ----- ----- ----- ----- ----- ----- ----------
SYS                             TRUE  TRUE  FALSE FALSE FALSE FALSE          0
SYSDG                           FALSE FALSE FALSE FALSE TRUE  FALSE          1
SYSBACKUP                       FALSE FALSE FALSE TRUE  FALSE FALSE          1
SYSKM                           FALSE FALSE FALSE FALSE FALSE TRUE           1
```

As you can see all the different roles exist in the password file. You can use the existing SYSBACKUP user if you like. Nothing prevents you from choosing a different (common) user account, just grant it the SYSBACKUP role and you are ready to go.

First I would like to demonstrate that using the SYSBACKUP user has indeed been tightened up. Connecting to the database as SYSBACKUP shows fewer privileges compared to SYSDBA:

```
SQL> connect sysbackup as sysbackup
Enter password:
Connected.
SYSBACKUP@CDB$ROOT> select count(1) from session_privs;

  COUNT(1)
----------
        14

SYSBACKUP@CDB$ROOT> select count(1) from session_roles;

  COUNT(1)
----------
         2

SYSBACKUP@CDB$ROOT> select role from session_roles;

ROLE
------------------------------------------------------------
SELECT_CATALOG_ROLE
HS_ADMIN_SELECT_ROLE
```

In comparison SYSDBA has 233 different session privileges and no granted roles. As SYSBACKUP you cannot peek into user tables you do not have permissions for:

```
SQL> alter session set container=pdb1;

Session altered.

SQL> select * from user1.FBTAB1;
select * from user1.FBTAB1
                  *
ERROR at line 1:
ORA-01031: insufficient privileges
```

In case you need to know whether you are connected as SYSDBA or SYSBACKUP you can use the sys_context function:

```
SQL> select sys_context('userenv','authenticated_identity') from dual
  2  /

SYS_CONTEXT('USERENV','AUTHENTICATED_IDENTITY')
---------------------------------------------------------------------------
SYSBACKUP
```

A connection to the database must now be made with the "AS SYSBACKUP" clause. This is a slight deviation from the rule that the role did not have to be supplied in the target or auxiliary arguments to RMAN. To connect as SYSBACKUP the following works:

```
[oracle@server1 dbs]$ rman target '"sysbackup@cdb1 as sysbackup"'

Recovery Manager: Release 12.1.0.1.0 - Production on Fri Sep 20 20:57:23 2013

Copyright (c) 1982, 2013, Oracle and/or its affiliates.  All rights reserved.

target database Password:
connected to target database: CDB1 (DBID=800340993)

RMAN>
```

The placement of single and double quotes is important here. There is no syntax change if you would like to connect to the database as SYSDBA, which is still the default. Simply do not specify the "as sysdba" as you always did.

Ability to execute SQL directly in RMAN   •

RMAN has been improved significantly and you now can directly use it to enter SQL commands without having to switch back and forth to sql*plus. There were so many situations when a screen session was needed and CTRL-A-space was used simply too often to enter a command here or there. Worse, sometimes a restart of the database required you to reconnect. Those times are over! One of the operations more familiar to the author is to check for flashback mode in the database. This is no longer a problem at all:

```
RMAN> startup mount

connected to target database (not started)
Oracle instance started
database mounted
```

```
Total System Global Area      1603411968 bytes

Fixed Size                       2260920 bytes
Variable Size                  452984904 bytes
Database Buffers              1140850688 bytes
Redo Buffers                     7315456 bytes
starting full resync of recovery catalog
full resync complete

RMAN> select open_mode,log_mode,flashback_on from v$database;

OPEN_MODE             LOG_MODE        FLASHBACK_ON
-------------------   -------------   -------------------
MOUNTED               ARCHIVELOG      NO
```

This is one of the enhancements that put a large smile on the database administrator's face: nothing essential since we could check in sqlplus before, but such a convenience that you do not want to miss this.

Enhanced over-the-network features

The over-the-network capabilities existed before Oracle 12c in the form of the "from active database" clause in RMAN, but for a limited number of use cases. The duplication from the active database includes the copy of the source database over the network.

This functionality has been enhanced in 12c in that the auxiliary instance can use existing backup sets on the target database (host) to reduce the overhead of the network copy. If you would like to try this you should use the using (compressed) backupset or section size clause and allocate at least as many auxiliary channels as you have target channels.

Beginning with Oracle 12c you can also make use of backup sets created on the fly by the remote physical standby database to restore or recover another database. Backupsets are transparently transferred over the network to the destination host. But instead of using the "from active database" clause you use "from service" instead. The use of a TNS service name obviously requires a corresponding service name definition in the TNS_ADMIN directory. The main use case provided by the Oracle documentation is the recovery of a standby database using an incremental backup. The ease of use is demonstrated by the following example, issued while connected to the standby database. For this example to work the standby database CDB2 had media recovery stopped while the primary database—CDB1—was instructed not to transport redo. While the standby was effectively on hold, the primary performed log switches and a new tablespace "apress" has been created. The incremental backup is then initiated on the primary which in this case is the auxiliary database. Although the same end result could be achieved with Oracle 11.2 as well, it was a more complex process with room for error.

The first step is to connect to the databases in the correct way, that is, the standby database is your target while the primary is the auxiliary instance:

```
[oracle@server1 ~]$ rman target sys@cdb2 auxiliary sys@cdb1

Recovery Manager: Release 12.1.0.1.0 - Production on Fri Sep 20 22:01:34 2013

Copyright (c) 1982, 2013, Oracle and/or its affiliates.  All rights reserved.
```

```
target database Password:
connected to target database: CDB1 (DBID=800340993, not open)
auxiliary database Password:
connected to auxiliary database: CDB1 (DBID=800340993)

RMAN>
```

Once connected (remember to watch out for "reversed" primary and auxiliary) you can initiate the backup and recover operation:

```
RMAN> recover database from service cdb1 using compressed backupset;

Starting recover at 20.09.2013 22:01
using channel ORA_DISK_1
skipping datafile 5; already restored to SCN 1735864
skipping datafile 7; already restored to SCN 1735864
skipping datafile 8; already restored to SCN 1864611
skipping datafile 9; already restored to SCN 1864611
skipping datafile 10; already restored to SCN 1864611
skipping datafile 11; already restored to SCN 1864611
channel ORA_DISK_1: starting incremental datafile backup set restore
channel ORA_DISK_1: using compressed network backup set from service cdb1
destination for restore of datafile 00001: +DATA/CDB2/DATAFILE/system.290.826664973
channel ORA_DISK_1: restore complete, elapsed time: 00:00:07
channel ORA_DISK_1: starting incremental datafile backup set restore
channel ORA_DISK_1: using compressed network backup set from service cdb1
destination for restore of datafile 00003: +DATA/CDB2/DATAFILE/sysaux.269.826664973
channel ORA_DISK_1: restore complete, elapsed time: 00:00:07
channel ORA_DISK_1: starting incremental datafile backup set restore
channel ORA_DISK_1: using compressed network backup set from service cdb1
destination for restore of datafile 00004: +DATA/CDB2/DATAFILE/undotbs1.291.826664973
channel ORA_DISK_1: restore complete, elapsed time: 00:00:03
channel ORA_DISK_1: starting incremental datafile backup set restore
channel ORA_DISK_1: using compressed network backup set from service cdb1
destination for restore of datafile 00006: +DATA/CDB2/DATAFILE/users.288.826664993
channel ORA_DISK_1: restore complete, elapsed time: 00:00:01

starting media recovery

media recovery complete, elapsed time: 00:00:10
Finished recover at 20.09.2013 22:12
```

The code in bold font shows that the backup set is taken from the network. This new method is in stark contrast to the previous method where you needed to create an incremental backup from a specific SCN, transfer it to the standby database host and apply it. The option to compress the backupsets helps conserve bandwidth. Using multiple channels and the section size clause should make the restore a lot quicker.

Instead of recovering the whole database you can limit the scope to data files, tablespaces, and control files; both the "restore" and "recover" command have been enhanced to use the "from service" clause.

Another use case would be the restore of a lost data file on the primary. Connecting to the standby database you can restore the data file over the network. For the next example assume that the database crashed because of the loss of data file number 1. When the DBA tried to restart the instance after the crash he sees this error:

```
SYS@CDB$ROOT> startup
ORACLE instance started.

Total System Global Area 1603411968 bytes
Fixed Size                   2288872 bytes
Variable Size              520094488 bytes
Database Buffers          1073741824 bytes
Redo Buffers                 7286784 bytes
Database mounted.
ORA-01157: cannot identify/lock data file 1 - see DBWR trace file
ORA-01110: data file 1: '+DATA/CDB1/DATAFILE/system.265.826666055'
```

The logical next step to restore service is to restore the data file from a backup. This can be a lengthy process depending on how quickly the backup medium can be loaded. Another approach is to copy the file over the network. As before you have the option to use multiple channels and the section size clause to tune the recovery time. In the example the system tablespace is small and such optimizations were not needed. Connecting to the target database CDB1 (primary role) and auxiliary database CDB2 (physical standby) you simply transfer the file across and recover it at the same time:

```
[oracle@server1 ~]$ rman target sys@cdb1 auxiliary sys@cdb2

Recovery Manager: Release 12.1.0.1.0 - Production on Fri Sep 20 22:22:59 2013

Copyright (c) 1982, 2013, Oracle and/or its affiliates.  All rights reserved.

target database Password:
connected to target database: CDB1 (DBID=800340993)
auxiliary database Password:
connected to auxiliary database: CDB1 (DBID=800340993, not open)

RMAN> run {
2> restore datafile 1 from service cdb2;
3> recover datafile 1;
4> alter database open;
5> }

Starting restore at 20.09.2013 21:39
using target database control file instead of recovery catalog
allocated channel: ORA_DISK_1
channel ORA_DISK_1: SID=21 device type=DISK

channel ORA_DISK_1: starting datafile backup set restore
channel ORA_DISK_1: using network backup set from service cdb2
channel ORA_DISK_1: specifying datafile(s) to restore from backup set
channel ORA_DISK_1: restoring datafile 00001 to +DATA/CDB1/DATAFILE/system.265.826666055
channel ORA_DISK_1: restore complete, elapsed time: 00:00:07
Finished restore at 20.09.2013 21:39

Starting recover at 20.09.2013 21:39
using channel ORA_DISK_1
```

```
starting media recovery
media recovery complete, elapsed time: 00:00:01
```

Finished recover at 20.09.2013 21:39

Statement processed

Although the technology is not really new—you could achieve the same result in 11.2—the syntax is very straightforward and especially with OMF the switch to the new data file name is done automatically in the control file. Both of these commands you just read about are a huge convenience boost.

Point-in-Time Table Recovery

Despite all the great tools available to the database administrator to prevent "accidental" changes to a table or set of tables, mistakes do happen. Sometimes it is impossible to recover a table. This could be because a Flashback Version Query has run out of undo or a table has been dropped with the "purge" keyword. Or an over-eager DBA has issued a "purge dba_recyclebin" command to free up space... The list is long. In previous Oracle versions you almost always had to do a point-in-time recovery in this case. If your data was self-contained on a tablespace then you were lucky to be able to perform a Tablespace Point-in-Time Recovery or TSPITR. But sometimes objects were scattered across multiple tablespaces, making a TSPITR impossible. In that case you had to bite the bullet and perform a full point in time recovery. Not necessarily in your production environment! A restore of a backup from before the accident on a different host may enable your application developers to get enough data to produce a set of scripts and export dumps to rectify the situation.

The inevitable question this build-up of tension should provoke is: is there no other way to do this? With Oracle 12c there is indeed, and it is available in the form of an extension of the RMAN recover command. Luckily the designers thought of Pluggable Databases as well, which is what this section covers. Non-CDBs have this functionality available too.

The following example demonstrates the use of the "recover table" command. While connected to a PDB, additional tablespaces are created, which all will contain a table, plus a unique index. The scenario presents itself as follows:

```
USER1@PDB1> select table_name,tablespace_name from tabs;

TABLE_NAME                         TABLESPACE_NAME
----------------------------       ----------------------------
T_3                                PDB1_TBS_3
T_1                                PDB1_TBS_1
T_2                                PDB1_TBS_2
```

Each of these tables has been created using the "create table ... as command", using dba_objects as the source. To demonstrate the usefulness of the new feature a little chaos will be created, simulating an inexperienced operator. The current SCN of the database has been found to be 1993594.

```
USER1@PDB1> truncate table t_3;

Table truncated.

USER1@PDB1> truncate table t_2;

Table truncated.

USER1@PDB1> drop table t_1 purge;

Table dropped.
```

Will we be able to get the data back as it was before? One possible command to get the tables back is shown here. It will create an auxiliary database instance using existing RMAN backups and restore it up to the SCN specified. A Data Pump job will be started next to export the tables in the recover table clause and import it into the target database. To prevent an error message indicating that the tables to be recovered exist, the example used the remap table clause. Alternatively you could use the notableimport option instead which only creates the Data Pump export file without importing it into the target database.

```
RMAN> recover table user1.t_1, user1.t_2, user1.t_3
2> of pluggable database pdb1
3> until scn 1993594
4> auxiliary destination '+DATA'
5> datapump destination '+DATA'
6> dump file 'user1.restore.dmp'
7> remap table user1.t_1:t_1_restore,user1.t_2:t_2_restore,user1.t_3:t_3_restore;
```

The command to recover the tables has a few more options. If you are using a Fast Recovery Area for example then you do not need to specify the auxiliary destination; the temporary database files will be created in the FRA. You can optionally specify that the data pump export file containing the tables specified in the recover table command will not be imported in the live environment using the notableimport option.

You are not limited to recovering entire tables, if you need finer granularity then you can choose table partitions as well. In the above example the DBA has decided to allow the import the dump file into the tables t_{1,2,3}_restore, leaving the original tables untouched. Toward the end of the process you can clearly see the Data Pump activity:

```
Performing export of tables...
    EXPDP> Starting "SYS"."TSPITR_EXP_iafj_nopB":
    EXPDP> Estimate in progress using BLOCKS method...
    EXPDP> Processing object type TABLE_EXPORT/TABLE/TABLE_DATA
    EXPDP> Total estimation using BLOCKS method: 33 MB
    EXPDP> Processing object type TABLE_EXPORT/TABLE/TABLE
    EXPDP> Processing object type TABLE_EXPORT/TABLE/STATISTICS/TABLE_STATISTICS
    EXPDP> Processing object type TABLE_EXPORT/TABLE/STATISTICS/MARKER
    EXPDP> . . exported "USER1"."T_1"                         8.540 MB   73754 rows
    EXPDP> . . exported "USER1"."T_2"                         8.540 MB   73753 rows
    EXPDP> . . exported "USER1"."T_3"                         8.540 MB   73753 rows
    EXPDP> Master table "SYS"."TSPITR_EXP_iafj_nopB" successfully loaded/unloaded
    EXPDP> ************************************************************************
    EXPDP> Dump file set for SYS.TSPITR_EXP_iafj_nopB is:
    EXPDP>    +DATA/user1.restore.dmp
    EXPDP> Job "SYS"."TSPITR_EXP_iafj_nopB" successfully completed Sat Sep 21 22:41:23 2013
                    elapsed 0 00:00:33
Export completed
```

This dump file which was deliberately created in ASM is subsequently imported into the life environment and the auxiliary instance is removed. The end result is a success, as you can see for yourself:

```
USER1@PDB1> select count(1) from T_1_RESTORE union all
  2  select count(1) from T_2_RESTORE union all
  3  select count(1) from T_3_RESTORE union all
  4  select count(1) from t_2 union all
  5  select count(1) from t_3;
```

```
   COUNT(1)
----------
     73754
     73753
     73753
         0
         0

USER1@PDB1> select count(1) from t_1;
select count(1) from t_1
                    *
ERROR at line 1:
ORA-00942: table or view does not exist
```

After the import you can decide how you want to merge the contents of the restored tables with the live tables.

Taking RMAN backups

You read in the introduction that taking of backups is an essential part of the daily routine. It is equally important that the backup return code is reported back so that failed backups can be triggered manually if required and possible during the day. The backup frequency and the contents need to be defined by the owners of the database hosting service and presented to its users as a choice. There should not be too much choice so as not to confuse the users, and each option should be explained in simple terms understandable to the non-technical audience. The managers requesting a Pluggable Database most likely do not have a database background, nor do they need to have one. So instead of using cryptic-sounding technology terms such as "weekly level 0 backup on weekend, then differential incremental backups every evening" you could say "a full backup is taken on the weekend with additional backups during the week, capturing each day's changes individually" or similar. It is important for the person raising the request to understand the implications of different backup techniques. If you decide to offer a logical backup of the PDB as an option, it must be made clear that there will not be a point in time recovery, and a completely empty PDB has to be created first. The last thing the managers of the hosting service need are outages caused by improper documentation of the backup techniques! Transparency and openness will greatly help the service to gain acceptance.

Considerations for the Recovery Catalog

Backup information can either be stored in the database's control file or alternatively in a so-called catalog database. Although the use of a recovery catalog is not mandatory there are good reasons for using one. First of all, should you lose all controlfiles of a database due to a catastrophic failure there is a probability that you have lost the backup information with them. Recovery of the database is still perfectly possible but involves extra steps.

A Recovery Catalog is a schema in an Oracle database, which is initialized with data structures required for RMAN to store information related to backups. To create the catalog you first need to create a new user in a database, and then connect to it from within the RMAN executable to create the schema. It makes sense to dedicate a tablespace to the RMAN catalog in the database. The catalog database should be considered part of the infrastructure and not part of an operational database for obvious reasons. Depending on your organization's structure you could have a catalog database per region or multiple databases per region and/or tier. Whichever way you decide, your catalog schema has to be in a dedicated database. Please do not forget to back your catalog database up at regular intervals!

Note that when using RMAN in a Data Guard scenario and you intend to take the backups from your standby database to reduce load on the primary database then the use of a catalog database is mandatory if you want to use these backups to restore or recover the primary database. Otherwise, how could the primary "know" about the backups taken on the standby database? Remember that backup information is always stored in the controlfile unless the catalog is used, and controlfiles are local to each database.

While many organizations might have a non-CDB for the recovery catalog a CDB with multiple PDB sounds like an interesting alternative.

Creating the catalog owner

The catalog owner is an arbitrary user account in a non-CDB database. Before creating it you should ensure that the user has its own dedicated tablespace rather than using the database's default. The size of the tablespace depends on the number of database targets and the amount of archived redo logs they produce. The catalog keeps track of every archived log, and if you go through a lot then your catalog will grow larger. Obviously the more backups per database you keep in the catalog the larger the catalog.

To create the catalog owner, create the tablespace first, as shown in this example:

```
SQL> create tablespace rman_catalog_tbs datafile size 20G
  2   autoextend on next 1G maxsize 30G;

Tablespace created.
```

Next create the user, similar to this command:

```
SQL> create user rco identified by securePassword
  2   default tablespace rman_catalog_tbs
  3   temporary tablespace temp
  4   quota unlimited on rman_catalog_tbs;

User created.

SQL> grant recovery_catalog_owner to rco;

Grant succeeded.
```

This concludes the actions to be taken from a privileged account. The next step is to actually create the catalog.

Creating the catalog

The next step is the creation of the catalog itself. Exit sqlplus if you have not done so already and connect to rman using "catalog" option. It is assumed that a TNS-alias has already been defined for the recovery catalog database. The following example uses "rcat" as the TNS-name.

```
[oracle@server1 ~]$ rman catalog rco@rcat

Recovery Manager: Release 12.1.0.1.0 - Production on Sat Sep 21 23:20:40 2013

Copyright (c) 1982, 2013, Oracle and/or its affiliates.  All rights reserved.

recovery catalog database Password:
connected to recovery catalog database

RMAN>
```

Issue the "create catalog" command next to start the creation of the catalog which will take a short while to complete. Oracle 11g introduced a new feature, called a virtual private catalog. Such a virtual private catalog allows the main catalog owner-"rco" in the example-to grant access to specific objects in the basic catalog. The idea is to allow for stricter separation of duties. After all, in many enterprises dedicated teams are responsible for the operational support of databases, and do not necessarily include the task of managing backup and recovery. The virtual catalog allows the base catalog owner to logically subdivide the main catalog into smaller units. So instead of connecting as the base catalog owner each time, you can create additional accounts in the database, and grant them access to specific objects in the main catalog. The risk of these users to accidentally cause damage to the main catalog is reduced, and access to databases is granted on a need-to-have basis only. The following examples however do not use virtual catalogs, but instead focus on a base catalog instead which is probably the most widely used adoption of RMAN catalogs.

Registering databases in the catalog

When using the RMAN catalog database you should connect to the catalog database as well as the target database when taking backups. Before you can make use of the catalog however the target database(s) must be registered with it. Using the rman utility again connect to the target database as the catalog database to register the database as shown:

```
[oracle@server1 ~]$ rman catalog rco@rcat target sys@cdb1

Recovery Manager: Release 12.1.0.1.0 - Production on Sat Sep 21 23:22:18 2013

Copyright (c) 1982, 2013, Oracle and/or its affiliates.  All rights reserved.

target database Password:
connected to target database: CDB1 (DBID=800340993)
recovery catalog database Password:
connected to recovery catalog database

RMAN> register database;

database registered in recovery catalog
starting full resync of recovery catalog
full resync complete
```

The implicit resynchronization operation will ensure that existing backup information stored in the database's controlfile is transferred into the recovery catalog.

Keeping controlfile and catalog in sync

Typically when you are taking backups you are connected to the recovery catalog database as well as the target database. In certain circumstances however, it might not be possible to establish a connection to the recovery catalog database for all the reasons DBAs know. In other environments, you may find yourself generating lots and lots of redo log switches between backups. In both the foregoing cases it might be necessary to manually resynchronize the catalog. This operation is simple and can be performed quickly by issuing the following command when connected to the target database and catalog:

```
RMAN> resync catalog;
```

As soon as you start paying attention to the RMAN output when using the catalog you will see that the resynchronization happens fairly frequently.

Configuring the RMAN environment

Recovery Manager options can either be configured globally or at runtime. Options supplied at runtime take precedence over those defined globally. To view the configuration options, connect to the target database and catalog and type the "show all" command as shown in Listing 11-1.

Listing 11-1. Configuration options for Recovery Manager

```
RMAN> show all;

RMAN configuration parameters for database with db_unique_name CDB1 are:
CONFIGURE RETENTION POLICY TO RECOVERY WINDOW OF 8 DAYS;
CONFIGURE BACKUP OPTIMIZATION OFF; # default
CONFIGURE DEFAULT DEVICE TYPE TO DISK; # default
CONFIGURE CONTROLFILE AUTOBACKUP ON; # default
CONFIGURE CONTROLFILE AUTOBACKUP FORMAT FOR DEVICE TYPE DISK TO '%F'; # default
CONFIGURE DEVICE TYPE DISK PARALLELISM 4 BACKUP TYPE TO BACKUPSET;
CONFIGURE DATAFILE BACKUP COPIES FOR DEVICE TYPE DISK TO 1; # default
CONFIGURE ARCHIVELOG BACKUP COPIES FOR DEVICE TYPE DISK TO 1; # default
CONFIGURE MAXSETSIZE TO UNLIMITED; # default
CONFIGURE ENCRYPTION FOR DATABASE OFF; # default
CONFIGURE ENCRYPTION ALGORITHM 'AES128'; # default
CONFIGURE COMPRESSION ALGORITHM 'BASIC' AS OF RELEASE 'DEFAULT' OPTIMIZE FOR LOAD TRUE ; ↵
# default
CONFIGURE RMAN OUTPUT TO KEEP FOR 7 DAYS; # default
CONFIGURE ARCHIVELOG DELETION POLICY TO NONE; # default
CONFIGURE SNAPSHOT CONTROLFILE NAME TO ↵
    '/u01/app/oracle/product/12.1.0.1/dbhome_1/dbs/snapcf_CDB1.f'; # default
```

The following sections will explain the most important of these options.

Explaining the retention policy

The backup retention policy determines how backups are treated before they are considered obsolete by RMAN, and therefore eligible for removal. The first option is to keep a number of backups to satisfy a time window for recovery. The so-called recovery window is the window for which backups exist for a point in time recovery. A common case is to keep a week's worth of backups available. The aim is to be able to perform point in time recoveries anytime between the current time and seven days before that time. If your level 0 backup is created halfway in the 7 days—maybe at day 3—then it will be necessary to keep a previous backup. Otherwise you would not be able to restore a database at day 1. Although it is conceptually simple to understand a recovery window, it can become a headache to the backup and storage administrators since it is impossible to predict the backup volume. If, for example you decide to take additional backups from the backup strategy then the projected data volume increases proportionally to the number of additional-read: unplanned-backups taken.

The use of a recovery window is not the default. To enable it you have to issue the following statement in RMAN:

```
RMAN> configure retention policy to RECOVERY WINDOW OF X DAYS;
```

Simply substitute X with the number of days you need. You should match the value of the database's controlfile_record_keep_time with the recovery window, or have the initialization parameter greater than the RMAN policy.

For a more deterministic backup volume another option is available. Instead of specifying a time window for when you want to be able to perform a point-in-time-recovery you could specify the number of backups you want to keep. The default RMAN retention policy is to have one backup available, which is not very realistic. Depending on your company's requirements and enterprise Service Level Agreements you should increase the number of backups to a more sensible number. Your consolidation project's product manager is the best person to ask for advice. To increase the number of backups to be preserved you need to issue the following command:

```
RMAN> configure retention policy to REDUNDANCY X;
```

As a direct result, X backups will be preserved; backup X+1 is considered obsolete by RMAN. If you are using a Fast Recovery Area then the retention policy can help you when space pressure arises. Careful though: unplanned backups can cause a really important backup to be declared obsolete and removed!

If backups (or flashback logs for that matter) are considered obsolete by the retention policy they can automatically be purged from the FRA should it come under space pressure. This can be quite useful when you need space for additional archived redo logs. On the other hand, it is something to know about. You can see the impact if changing the retention policy quite clearly in the view v$recovery_area_usage, column percent_space_reclaimable.

If a backup falls outside the limits set by the retention policy then it will be considered *obsolete*. An obsolete backup can be removed by the media manager. In the context of RMAN it is important that the media manager lets RMAN manage the removal of backups. Removing backups outside of RMAN using operating system commands or—if stored on tape—letting the media manager remove them causes problems with RMAN as it does not know that a backup no longer exists. A backup that has been removed outside of RMAN is considered *expired*. Expired backups can become a problem when you need to rely on them to restore a database. Nothing is worse than being in the middle of a database restore operation when the backups you so desperately need are reported to be missing. The RMAN crosscheck command can be used at regular intervals to test if a backup is actually available. If it is not, it will be marked as expired in the catalog or control file.

Defining how and where backups should be stored by default

By default backups are stored on disk using the Fast Recovery Area if possible. The "CONFIGURE DEFAULT DEVICE TYPE TO DISK" setting in Listing 11-1 shows this. If you wish to change the default behavior and switch to tape backups, you can do so by issuing the "configure default device type to sbt" command. Bear in mind though that tape backups require additional configuration, both on the operating system as well as within Oracle. In most cases the system administrator will install the required software packages for interaction with the tape library. It often is the backup team's responsibility to configure the media manager to allow communication between the database server and the tape library. Finally the database administrator will be given the necessary information to be supplied for the channel allocation. A channel in Recovery Manager is responsible for reading data into the server process's PGA and writing it to the output device: disk or tape. Unlike in the first versions of RMAN you no longer have to explicitly allocate channels for a command to succeed. A well-balanced design however will require you to allocate channels to find a compromise between satisfying the backup window and throughput to the array or tape library. It is entirely possible to send more data down the pipe than the other end can digest!

Generally speaking multiple channels will back your database up quicker if you are not overwhelming the server and/or backup destination. During the initialization phase outstanding work is distributed to each channel. A great enhancement came with Oracle 11g, where RMAN can use multiple channels to work on a single file. Why is that useful? Using the default backup mode it was possible for a multi-channel backup channel to finish while the other one was still working on an enormous bigfile tablespace for quite a while. Using the then-new "section" keyword you can back up datafiles or the whole database using sections of a specific size. In the author's opinion this makes the most sense with databases made up of many very large bigfile tablespaces or any other system with a mix of small and comparatively large data files. Alternatively you could back up individual data files using the section size command as shown here. Two channels are manually allocated to back up datafile 1 in 250M chunks.

```
RMAN> run {
2> allocate channel ch1 device type disk;
3> allocate channel ch2 device type disk;
4> backup section size 250m datafile 1;
5> }
[...]
Starting backup at 21.09.2013 23:47
channel ch1: starting full datafile backup set
[...]
backing up blocks 1 through 25600 [...]
channel ch2: starting full datafile backup set
[...]
channel ch1: starting full datafile backup set
[...]
backing up blocks 25601 through 51200
[...]
channel ch2: starting full datafile backup set
[...]
backing up blocks 51201 through 76800 [...]
RMAN>
```

Oracle 12c introduced the ability to perform multi-section incremental backups which is very useful.

If you do not change the default option then backups will be taken as backup sets. Each backup set can comprise multiple backup pieces. Optionally you can chose to use binary compression of the backup sets. Depending on the content stored in the database using (binary) compressed backup sets can greatly decrease the backup size.

So-called image copies are an alternative to backup sets. An image copy is an exact copy of the source file. For obvious reasons an image copy is of the same size as a data file-an image copy of a completely empty 10G data file will require an additional 10G of disk space. Image copies can be useful in a scenario where you can afford a second copy of the database created as image copies in the FRA. The image copies can be rolled forward by applying incremental backups taken on the "live" data files. If the worst should happen, you can switch the database to the copy, apply the last remaining archived logs and open the database from within the FRA.

Backup optimization

Using backup optimization is a way to conserve space on the backup media by skipping files that have been backed up previously while adhering to the retention policy. Using the configure backup optimization on command in RMAN enables backup optimization for subsequent backups. For files to be skipped they must be identical and also be part of a valid backup as part of the retention policy. In practice you will find that read-only and offline tablespaces are most likely to be backed up only once in a recovery window. Assuming that the read-only tablespace TBS1 is already backed up on Monday in a recovery window of 7 days it will not be backed up on Tuesday and the following days unless it changes. It will however be backed up the following Monday again, allowing the media manager to expire the tape with the backup taken a week earlier.

For a retention policy requesting redundant backups to be available a read-only, offline tablespace or archived log will be excluded from the first additional redundant backup. If for example your retention policy is set to redundancy 5 and you execute the 6th backup of the database, identical files which have not changed will be skipped.

Archived redo logs can also be skipped from being backed up if they exist in a backup set. The retention policy does not play a role when backing up archived logs with backup optimization. During testing it turned out that with backup optimization enabled, Oracle will skip archive logs already backed up once in a backupset which is available if you back it up using the backup archivelog like or backup archivelog all commands. Assume for this example that backups exist for archived logs of thread 1, sequence 81 to 86. Additionally the archived logs have not been deleted from the FRA. Next you try to take another backup of these:

```
RMAN> backup archivelog all;

Starting backup at 22.09.2013 16:54
current log archived
using channel ORA_DISK_1
using channel ORA_DISK_2
skipping archived logs of thread 1 from sequence 81 to 86; already backed up
channel ORA_DISK_1: starting archived log backup set
[...]
```

You can see in bold that RMAN skips sequence numbers 81 to 86. If you specifically request a backup of archived logs they will still be taken. Continuing the previous example:

```
RMAN> backup archivelog sequence between 81 and 86;

Starting backup at 22.09.2013 16:58
channel c1: starting archived log backup set
channel c1: specifying archived log(s) in backup set
input archived log thread=1 sequence=81 RECID=89 STAMP=826760036
input archived log thread=1 sequence=82 RECID=90 STAMP=826821462
input archived log thread=1 sequence=83 RECID=91 STAMP=826822278
input archived log thread=1 sequence=84 RECID=92 STAMP=826822339
input archived log thread=1 sequence=85 RECID=93 STAMP=826822349
input archived log thread=1 sequence=86 RECID=94 STAMP=826822368
channel c1: starting piece 1 at 22.09.2013 16:58
channel c1: finished piece 1 at 22.09.2013 16:58
[...]
Finished backup at 22.09.2013 16:58
```

You can also use the "not backed up n times" clause limit the number of archivelog backups, or add the "force" keyword. If you used the "backup archivelog sequence between 81 and 86" command three more times you will end up with at least 4 backups of the same log, which might not be desirable.

Requesting automatic spfile and controlfile backups

For many situations it is very useful to have a recent copy of the controlfile or a server parameter file at hand. Luckily Oracle allows you to take automatic backups of the controlfile if you want. According to the documentation controlfile autobackups are taken by default in Container Databases. Instead of creating a little scriptlet and including the backup commands for server parameter file and controlfile each time, you can configure these to be backed up automatically using the following command:

```
RMAN> CONFIGURE CONTROLFILE AUTOBACKUP ON;
```

With this setting you will notice the following block after each Backup strategy:

```
Starting Control File and SPFILE Autobackup at 22.09.2013 16:58
piece handle=+RECO/CDB1/AUTOBACKUP/2013_09_22/s_826822683.260.826822683 comment=NONE
Finished Control File and SPFILE Autobackup at 22.09.2013 16:58
released channel: c1
```

Additionally Oracle will back up the control file after lots of structural changes have occurred, such as adding multiple tablespaces, online redo log groups, renaming files etc. In versions before Oracle 11.2 a line was added in the alert.log each time such a change occurred, and you ended up with lots of automatic controlfile backups taken immediately after the structural change happened. This proved to be inconvenient, especially if you consider massive releases to the database where data is reorganized and life cycle management starts. As a mitigating effect one of Oracle's MMON slave processes is responsible for the creation of the controlfile autobackups. Instead of creating the controlfile autobackup immediately after each change of the database structure during an application release, the creation of the backup is deferred by a few minutes after the event. You will not see entries about controlfile autobackups in the alert.log anymore, you need to check the trace directory within the database's Automatic Diagnostic Repository for files named *ORACLE_SID*_m000_*OSPID*.trc containing the information shown here:

```
*** 2013-09-22 17:46:06.432
*** SESSION ID:(10.23) 2013-09-22 17:46:06.432
*** CLIENT ID:() 2013-09-22 17:46:06.432
*** SERVICE NAME:(SYS$BACKGROUND) 2013-09-22 17:46:06.432
*** MODULE NAME:(MMON_SLAVE) 2013-09-22 17:46:06.432
*** ACTION NAME:(Autobackup Control File) 2013-09-22 17:46:06.432

Starting control autobackup

*** 2013-09-22 17:46:07.082
Control autobackup written to DISK device
        handle '/u01/fra/ORA12/autobackup/2013_09_22/o1_mf_n_826825566_93y7pgr3_.bkp'
```

In the above example lots of structural changes occurred in the time leading up to 17:46 but finished approximately at 17:40. So do not worry if you do not see a trace file immediately after those structural changes.

The Oracle database accesses and modifies the controlfile constantly. Therefore, a way has to be found to get a consistent copy of the controlfile. The simple solution is to create a read-consistent view of the controlfile, called a snapshot controlfile. This process is completely transparent, and in most cases you do not need to modify the location of the snapshot controlfile unless you use Real Application Clusters.

■ **Note**   The snapshot controlfile must be on shared storage for Real Application Clusters from 11.2.0.2 onwards.

If you are not on RAC and have to, use the "configure snapshot controlfile name to" command to define the snapshot controlfile location.

In addition to changing the snapshot controlfile location you can also define a non-default controlfile autobackup location. The implication of changing the controlfile autobackup location is that you need to specify the exact location when you restore it later. If you use a FRA the default location for the controlfile autobackup is your Fast Recovery Area. The restore of a controlfile autobackup is explained later in the chapter in the Restore and Recovery section.

Technical aspects around RMAN backups

Backing up the production database directly is a very common strategy. In quiet periods, usually over night for non 24 by 7 systems, a backup is initiated according to the backup schedule and internal Service Level Agreements. After the completion or failure, a notification is sent out to a central control system informing the database administrator of the outcome. In most cases the administrator is not interested in being paged about a successfully completed backup, a failure is more important and requires attention.

Recovery Manager allows you to take backups of all important components of the database, including data files, the control file, server parameter file etc. The Oracle binaries and log files such as the diagnostic destination, audit files, and Data Pump dump files are not backed up by RMAN. You need to request a standard file system backup for these files.

Recovery Manager has been enhanced to allow backups of individual Pluggable Databases, the root database and the whole CDB. In the author's opinion a PDB backup should not be part of a planned backup strategy but rather an ad-hoc backup prior to important tasks and immediately after the PDB creation. The simple rationale behind this is that a full recovery of a Container Database will require a restore/recovery of the CDB$ROOT followed by a restore/recovery of all Pluggable Databases. In the heat of the battle with the outage a multi-stage recovery strategy can easily turn out to be too complex and more importantly too time consuming. Instead the whole CDB should be backed up. This operation is not different from any other backup of a database you have issued before.

■ **Note** The following examples assume that your database is in ARCHIVELOG mode. Where specified the use of the Flashback Database feature will be required too. Please remember that activating the Flashback Database feature requires another background process to write additional data to the Flashback logs. This can have a negative effect on performance and should only be enabled after testing or where appropriate.

Backing up the whole CDB

As you read before, there are multiple ways to back up a Container Database. The most common of which is most likely the hot backup of the database, including a backup of the controlfile—automatic or manual—followed by a backup of archived logs. On sites with high redo-generation additional archived log backups are often scheduled. Archive log destinations can be multiplexed, either by using multiple different and distinct file system mount points or alternatively by sending files over the network using Redo Transport Services. A base backup for an incremental backup of the CDB is initiated as shown here:

```
RMAN> backup incremental level 0 database plus archivelog;
```

This is exactly the same command as you have used all these years to back up a database, there is no distinction between CDB and non-CDB when it comes to backing up everything. In the author's example the backup will go straight to the Fast Recovery Area on disk. Following this many sites opt to back the FRA up to tape, using the backup recovery area command in RMAN. Do not forget to review redo generation and schedule additional backups as and when needed.

Enhancements for Pluggable Databases

RMAN has seen many enhancements for Pluggable Databases, which was to be expected. This section covers the backup command, but numerous other commands have also been extended to take the PDBs into account. To backup up an individual PDB you need to issue the backup pluggable database command as shown in this example:

```
RMAN> backup pluggable database rcat_pdb;

Starting backup at 22.09.2013 17:34
allocated channel: ORA_DISK_1
channel ORA_DISK_1: SID=28 device type=DISK
[...]
channel ORA_DISK_1: starting full datafile backup set
channel ORA_DISK_1: specifying datafile(s) in backup set
input datafile file number=00017↵
[...]
```

```
input datafile file number=00018 ↵
  name=+DATA/CDB1/E6ED2028263F4B27E0436638A8C088A6/DATAFILE/rman_catalog_tbs.275.826759035
channel ORA_DISK_3: starting piece 1 at 22.09.2013 17:34
channel ORA_DISK_3: finished piece 1 at 22.09.2013 17:34
piece handle=↵
+RECO/CDB1/E6[...]A6/BACKUPSET/2013_09_22/nnndf0_tag20130922t173446_0.312.826824889
tag=TAG20130922T173446 comment=NONE
[...]

Starting Control File and SPFILE Autobackup at 22.09.2013 17:35
piece handle=+RECO/CDB1/AUTOBACKUP/2013_09_22/s_826824903.282.826824905 comment=NONE
Finished Control File and SPFILE Autobackup at 22.09.2013 17:35

RMAN>
```

You can back up multiple Pluggable Databases in a comma-separated list if you like. In a similar way it is possible to back up only the root, using the backup database root command. Again, a full backup of the whole CDB is likely to be more efficient in many cases.

Another command that can be used specifically with Pluggable Databases as well is backup validate. This will check for physical corruption of the files in the database, and can be instructed to check for logical corruption too. Physical corruption can be caused by write errors to disk or other otherwise hard to detect problems such as filesystem glitches if you are not using ASM anyway. The result can be seen immediately when the database wants to access a certain physically corrupt block, it will report an error. Checks for logical corruption can be made by adding the check logical clause to the backup validate command. An example check for Pluggable Database PDB1 is shown here:

```
RMAN> backup validate check logical pluggable database pdb1;

Starting backup at 22.09.2013 19:22
[...]
channel ORA_DISK_1: starting full datafile backup set
channel ORA_DISK_1: specifying datafile(s) in backup set
input datafile file number=00009 ↵
  name=+DATA/CDB1/DD7D8C1D4C234B38E04325AAE80AF577/DATAFILE/sysaux.261.826623815
[...]
List of Datafiles
=================
File Status Marked Corrupt Empty Blocks Blocks Examined High SCN
---- ------ ------------- ------------ --------------- ----------
9    OK      0             20027        80668           2130003
  File Name: +DATA/CDB1/DD7D8C1D4C234B38E04325AAE80AF577/DATAFILE/sysaux.261.826623815
  Block Type Blocks Failing Blocks Processed
  ---------- -------------- ----------------
  Data       0              14246
  Index      0              7448
  Other      0              38919
[...]

Finished backup at 22.09.2013 19:22

RMAN>
```

Backup validate will not generate any backup set files, and any findings will go into v$database_block_ corruption as well as the alert.log in addition to those that you see on screen. In the unfortunate event that more than one corruption is expected, you should set the tolerance towards detected corruption higher using the set maxcorrupt to a high number, indicating how many corruptions can be reported before the command aborts.

Restore and Recovery

The foundation of successful restores and recovery operations of a database are manifold. Well-trained staff, good written procedures, and the ability to keep a cool head all help the database administrator during the difficulties when restoring a database. With the previous section about backups the second essential success factor should have been covered as well.

There are many ways to restore a database—fully or parts—and recover it. The procedure chosen depends on the failure that has occurred. Oracle provides a system of identifying failures since version 11.1, called the Data Recovery Advisor. In some situations it can be sufficient to invoke it to get to a solution. If for example, a PDB "loses" a data file you will be informed by the database that a new failure has been detected. As soon as a user tries to access a data file, the failure becomes apparent. After the monitoring tool picked the missing file up, you can connect to RMAN and list the failures:

```
RMAN> list failure;

Database Role: PRIMARY

List of Database Failures
=========================

Failure ID Priority Status    Time Detected    Summary
---------- -------- --------- ---------------- -------
8          HIGH     OPEN      22.09.2013 19:30 One or more non-system datafiles are missing
```

The message leaves little for interpretation: a data file is missing. Now let's see what the advisor has to offer:

```
RMAN> advise failure 8;

Database Role: PRIMARY

List of Database Failures
=========================

Failure ID Priority Status    Time Detected    Summary
---------- -------- --------- ---------------- -------
8          HIGH     OPEN      22.09.2013 19:30 One or more non-system datafiles are missing

analyzing automatic repair options; this may take some time
using channel ORA_DISK_1
using channel ORA_DISK_2
using channel ORA_DISK_3
using channel ORA_DISK_4
analyzing automatic repair options complete

Mandatory Manual Actions
========================
no manual actions available
```

```
Optional Manual Actions
=======================
1. If file +DATA/CDB1/E6CDAD92377F667EE0436638A8C0DB6C/DATAFILE/pdb1_tbs_1.284.826754085
   was unintentionally renamed or moved, restore it
2. Automatic repairs may be available if you shutdown the database and restart it in mount mode

Automated Repair Options
========================
Option Repair Description
------ -----------------
1      Restore and recover datafile 13
   Strategy: The repair includes complete media recovery with no data loss
   Repair script: /u01/app/oracle/diag/rdbms/cdb1/CDB1/hm/reco_2181095021.hm

RMAN>
```

The repair script has the following contents:

```
# restore and recover datafile
sql 'PDB1' 'alter database datafile 13 offline';
restore ( datafile 13 );
recover datafile 13;
sql 'PDB1' 'alter database datafile 13 online';
```

In this particular case the suggested solution worked—but it was a trivial example. However, as with anything that is automated you are not freed from using common sense and experience to gauge the effectiveness of the solution. No machine logic is 100% free from error—admittedly the same can be said for human logic—but double-checking what the situation is and how it can be fixed is important. Some scenarios you will come across are too complex to be properly addressed by the recovery advisor, and it will not be able to present a solution.

The next sections deal with the recovery of a database from start to finish, detailing everything from the restore of the server parameter file all the way up to restoring data files. The next few sections will explain how to get the various parts of the database back into service.

Restoring the server parameter file

Having to restore the server parameter file is very straightforward provided you followed the advice outlined earlier in the chapter and configured the controlfile autobackup in RMAN. Do not be lazy and operate the database without controlfile autobackups: one day they could well save your career. A controlfile autobackup will automatically create spfile and controlfile autobackups after each backup and after structural changes as explained in the section above. Additionally you can make your life very easy by using a Fast Recovery Area. With such a setup, it is a walk in the park to restore the spfile. In this example the database is shut down. In preparation of the restore a tiny little parameter file helps a lot, releasing you from the need to have the database ID at hand. The file only needs to have the following minimal set of parameters, but yours may need more:

```
db_name=CDB1
db_recovery_file_dest     = '+RECO'
db_recovery_file_dest_size= 60g
cpu_count = 2
# not necessary but can help if the "dummy" instance won't start
# workarea_size_policy = auto
# pga_aggregate_target = 2G
# sga_target = 4G
```

Although strictly speaking you do not need an initialization file when starting the database for the restore of the spfile, you still may have to create one. Many Oracle parameters are calculated on-the-fly, and cpu_count is one of those many others are based on. With today's multi-core CPUs you can run into ORA-4031 errors if you are not setting the cpu_count to a low value as the default SGA size used by the dummy instance is too low for those servers. If you want to be on the safe side set the SGA and PGA parameters as well.

Armed with this file you can start the database. After the database instance has been started in nomount mode, you can restore the spfile:

```
RMAN> restore spfile from autobackup;

Starting restore at 22.09.2013 19:56

recovery area destination: +RECO
database name (or database unique name) used for search: CDB1
channel c1: AUTOBACKUP +RECO/CDB1/AUTOBACKUP/2013_09_22/s_826832795.297.826832795↵
  found in the recovery area
channel c1: looking for AUTOBACKUP on day: 20130922
channel c1: restoring spfile from AUTOBACKUP ↵
+RECO/CDB1/AUTOBACKUP/2013_09_22/s_826832795.297.826832795
channel c1: SPFILE restore from AUTOBACKUP complete
Finished restore at 22.09.2013 19:56
```

The file found by RMAN is indeed the latest spfile autobackup in the FRA. Be careful though the spfile could be restored in $ORACLE_HOME/dbs and not in ASM. If you are not using the Fast Recovery Area it is mandatory to set the dbid at the RMAN prompt, and you may have to specify the autobackup location as well in a run {} block. Such a block groups instructions together that are executed in the same context. The most common example is the incomplete recovery using a point in time. If the commands were not surrounded in the run {} block setting the time to recover up to would not have any effect. Restart the instance to make use of the restored spfile.

The easiest scenario for restoring the server parameter file is to use a recovery catalog. Since the database has not accessed the controlfile when in nomount mode it does not know about the backup information recorded in it. The recovery catalog however stores this information independently from the controlfile and is of great help. Start the database in nomount mode while connected to the target database and catalog. A stub-parameter file is not used in this example to show the alternative output:

```
[oracle@server1 ~]$ rman catalog rco@rcat_pdb target sys@cdb1

Recovery Manager: Release 12.1.0.1.0 - Production on Sun Sep 22 21:01:01 2013

Copyright (c) 1982, 2013, Oracle and/or its affiliates.  All rights reserved.

target database Password:
connected to target database (not started)
recovery catalog database Password:
connected to recovery catalog database

RMAN> startup nomount

startup failed: ORA-01078: failure in processing system parameters
LRM-00109: could not open parameter file ↵
'/u01/app/oracle/product/12.1.0.1/dbhome_1/dbs/initCDB1.ora'
```

```
starting Oracle instance without parameter file for retrieval of spfile
Oracle instance started

Total System Global Area     1068937216 bytes

Fixed Size                      2296576 bytes
Variable Size                 281019648 bytes
Database Buffers              780140544 bytes
Redo Buffers                    5480448 bytes

RMAN> run {
2> allocate channel c1 device type disk;
3> restore spfile;
4> }

allocated channel: c1
channel c1: SID=11 device type=DISK

Starting restore at 22.09.2013 21:01

channel c1: starting datafile backup set restore
channel c1: restoring SPFILE
output file name=/u01/app/oracle/product/12.1.0.1/dbhome_1/dbs/spfileCDB1.ora
channel c1: reading from backup piece ↵
  +RECO/CDB1/AUTOBACKUP/2013_09_22/s_826832795.297.826832795
channel c1: piece handle=+RECO/CDB1/AUTOBACKUP/2013_09_22/s_826832795.297.826832795 ↵
  tag=TAG20130922T194635
channel c1: restored backup piece 1
channel c1: restore complete, elapsed time: 00:00:05
Finished restore at 22.09.2013 21:01
released channel: c1

RMAN>
```

It does not get any easier than that. Should you be lucky enough to be on a database server with lots of CPUs then you might get an ORA-4031 error during the restore or channel allocation. In this case you have to create a minimalistic parameter file with a sufficiently sized SGA before starting the database as shown previously.

Restoring the control file

The loss of the controlfile(s) is an intrusive event, and unfortunate since a lot of useful information is contained in it. Thankfully the loss of a controlfile is no longer such a tragedy as it was in the 9i days thanks to the "catalog" command which has been introduced in Oracle 10g. It allows you to search directories for backups which are then cataloged in the controlfile, and therefore made available again for restore operations. The restore of the control file will still require you to open the database with the resetlogs option though! You may want to take a backup after the command completed.

Another great feature of recent Oracle versions is that the restore of the controlfile does not require editing the parameter or server parameter file anymore when using Oracle Managed Files. In older releases Oracle complained that it could not restore a controlfile with an OMF name. Instead, one had created a parameter file from the spfile, edit the parameter file (remove the *.control_files entry) and create a spfile from the pfile before starting the instance. These days are long over, and changes to the initialization parameters related to the control files are not normally necessary.

■ **Note**   One of the reasons to modify initialization parameters is media failure and the loss of a mount point. You can read more about this scenario in the next section.

The process for restoring the control file is very similar to the restoring of the server parameter file, the main difference being the command: instead of using "restore spfile from autobackup" you use "restore controlfile from autobackup". But before you start the restore process you should check if you do not have a multiplexed copy of the controlfile. The following query can help you find the other copy of the controlfile:

```
SYS@CDB$ROOT> select value from v$parameter where name = 'control_files';
```

Be careful not to copy the bad controlfile over the good one! If you are in a situation where the controlfile was not multiplexed you have to restore.

The example shown here assumes that all control files have been lost. Shut the database down if that has not yet happened to remedy the situation, and start it in nomount mode. If you are not using a catalog database, you may have to set the dbid and start into the nomount state, followed by the restore controlfile from autobackup command.

Users with a recovery catalog are luckier, the command sequence to restore the controlfile is shown here, with some of the RMAN output removed for clarity:

```
RMAN> startup nomount
[...]
RMAN> restore controlfile;

Starting restore at 22.09.2013 21:05
[...]
channel ORA_DISK_1: starting datafile backup set restore
channel ORA_DISK_1: restoring control file
channel ORA_DISK_1: reading from backup piece ↵
 +RECO/CDB1/AUTOBACKUP/2013_09_22/s_826832795.297.826832795
channel ORA_DISK_1: piece handle=+RECO/CDB1/AUTOBACKUP/2013_09_22/s_826832795.297.826832795↵
 tag=TAG20130922T194635
channel ORA_DISK_1: restored backup piece 1
channel ORA_DISK_1: restore complete, elapsed time: 00:00:02
output file name=+DATA/CDB1/CONTROLFILE/current.262.826623553
Finished restore at 22.09.2013 21:
```

The next steps are identical for both users without and with a recovery catalog database. You need to mount the database and recover it before opening it with the resetlogs option.

Restoring databases

Restoring database files is nothing to be afraid of, even though many production database administrators will likely get a little bit nervous when they are tasked with partial or full restore operations. This is completely understandable, especially if one is not all too familiar with the database having a problem. There are two complementary strategies for how to make the database administrator more comfortable with the restore/recovery situation. The first is to ensure that the procedures to be taken are well documented and more importantly: understood. The second option to be taken by management is to perform restore and recover exercises throughout the year and on a regular schedule. You can read a little more about this thought later in the chapter.

The following sections explain the general process of restoring database files for Container Databases and Pluggable Databases.

Restoring a Container Database

The restore operation of a Container Database is not very different from restoring a non-CDB. In any case, any Pluggable Database in the CDB is affected, especially if incomplete recovery has to be performed. As with every database-wide restore operation you need to bring the database into mount mode before you can initiate the restore, followed by the recover command. The following little command restores and recovers the CDB named "CDB1".

LET RMAN DO THE SYNTAX CHECKING FOR YOU!

If you are unsure if the syntax of your script is correct, you can use the checksyntax option in RMAN before trying the script in anger. Consider the following example of a script used for a full database restore and complete recovery:

```
[oracle@server1 (CDB1) ~]$ cat recover.rman
shutdown immediate;
startup mount;
restore database;
recover database;
alter database open;
```

You can check this script for correctness without having to execute it first and run into problems while a part is in progress:

```
[oracle@server1 ~]$ rman target / checksyntax @recover.rman

Recovery Manager: Release 12.1.0.1.0 - Production on Sun Sep 22 21:10:59 2013

Copyright (c) 1982, 2013, Oracle and/or its affiliates.  All rights reserved.

connected to target database: CDB1 (DBID=800340993)

RMAN> shutdown immediate;
2> startup mount;
3> restore database;
4> recover database;
5> alter database open;
6>
7>
The cmdfile has no syntax errors

Recovery Manager complete.
```

The example is of course oversimplified, but it gives you the idea. More complex scripts with multiple run {} blocks can easily fail at runtime, checking for syntax errors is a good idea.

Using the exact same script as in the sidebar you can restore and recover your database. The remainder of the section will walk you through the output. First the database must be shut down and started into mount state:

```
[oracle@server1 ~]$ rman target sys@cdb1 catalog rco@rcat_pdb @recover.rman
[...]
RMAN> shutdown immediate;
2> startup mount;
3> restore database;
4> recover database;
5> alter database open;

database closed
database dismounted
Oracle instance shut down

connected to target database (not started)
Oracle instance started
database mounted

Total System Global Area     1603411968 bytes

Fixed Size                      2288872 bytes
Variable Size                 520094488 bytes
Database Buffers             1073741824 bytes
Redo Buffers                    7286784 bytes
```

Once it is mounted, the restore part of the scripts is executed. In the example the global RMAN settings defined 4 parallel RMAN channels.

```
Starting restore at 22.09.2013 21:16
[...]
channel ORA_DISK_3: restored backup piece 1
channel ORA_DISK_3: restore complete, elapsed time: 00:01:06
Finished restore at 22.09.2013 21:17
```

Once the database has been restored, it will be recovered and opened:

```
Starting recover at 22.09.2013 21:17
using channel ORA_DISK_1
using channel ORA_DISK_2
[...]
media recovery complete, elapsed time: 00:00:07
Finished recover at 22.09.2013 21:17
```

Finally the database is opened and ready for service again.

An incomplete recovery of the database is possible as well, in which case you need to wrap your commands into a so-called "run block". The run block creates a context and the scope for operations to happen together. Consider the following example of an incomplete recovery of a CDB:

```
run {
        set until time="to_date('22.09.2013 21:00:00','dd.mm.yyyy hh24:mi:ss')";
        restore database;
```

```
       recover database;
       alter database open resetlogs;
}
```

Instead of relying on the defined NLS_DATE_FORMAT environment variable it has proved to be less ambiguous to use the to_date() function inside the set until clause. Instead of a human readable format you can also use the SCN or a sequence number instead if you have them documented. As you can also see, you need to open the database with the resetlogs option as with any incomplete recovery.

Restoring a Pluggable Database

One of the main contention points of the multi-schema/multi-tenancy approach in Oracle before 12c was the fact that it was very difficult from an operation point of view to perform a (point-in-time) restore of the Oracle database. Any such operation affected everyone in the database, and you can imagine how difficult it was to agree on a restore operation. Some database administrators tried to separate the different schemas as much as possible by creating dedicated tablespaces for each user, which in theory could have been recovered using Tablespace-Point-In-Time Recovery but even then this was a process that was difficult to coordinate.

Again, the notion of the Pluggable Database makes these tasks easier, allowing you to complete the recovery of individual PDBs without affecting others. Consider for example that a point in time recovery of PDB1 has been agreed between the product manager and all the other stakeholders. In this case you need to follow these steps to recover the PDB to a point in time. For any recovery operation-complete or incomplete, the PDB(s) in question must be in mount mode or closed in other words.

```
SYS@CDB$ROOT> select con_id,open_mode,name from v$pdbs;

    CON_ID OPEN_MODE  NAME
---------- ---------- ------------------------------
         2 READ ONLY  PDB$SEED
         3 MOUNTED    PDB1
```

Assume for the example that a user error has been identified at 10:00 AM, and all other means of fixing the problem have already been exhausted and all the approvers have given the database team the nod to restore the database to 09:00 AM at an SCN of 2188563 which has been obtained by using the timestamp_to_scn() function. Table t_1 in the schema USER1 contains a column ID. Someone accidentally inserted the value "10000" into it sometime after SCN 2188563. The contents of the table—simplified for readability—is shown here:

```
SQL> select * from user1.t_1;

        ID
----------
    100000
         3
         1
```

The PDB Point-in-Time recovery is initiated in RMAN using the familiar set until clause followed by the magic triple "restore-recover-open resetlogs":

```
RMAN> run {
2> set until scn = 2188563;
3> restore pluggable database pdb1;
4> recover pluggable database pdb1 auxiliary destination='xxx';
5> alter pluggable database pdb1 open resetlogs;
6> }
```

As you would have imagined the Point-In-Time-Restore of a PDB is not all too different from a Tablespace Point-In-Time-Recovery which has been with Oracle for a while. The RMAN script above can be divided into two major steps. The first is simple and is a restore of the PDB's data files to their respective locations. It is during the recover step where the similarity begins with the "Tablespace Point In Time Recovery". Although optional you should really specify a location where the auxiliary instance is going to be created. A file system location worked well even with ASM-it could be a NAS mount or similar. You will notice the creation of an auxiliary instance on the host for which you should ensure sufficient memory to be available. The instance name will be randomly chosen to avoid conflicts with existing Oracle instances, in the example above the auxiliary instance was named zgsF. You will see this output as part of the RMAN command output you entered.

```
Creating automatic instance, with SID='zgsF'

initialization parameters used for automatic instance:
db_name=CDB1
db_unique_name=mqol_pitr_pdb1_CDB1
compatible=12.1.0.0.0
db_block_size=8192
db_files=200
sga_target=1G
processes=80
diagnostic_dest=/u01/app/oracle
db_create_file_dest=/u01/temp
log_archive_dest_1='location=/u01/temp'
enable_pluggable_database=true
_clone_one_pdb_recovery=true
#No auxiliary parameter file used
```

Since a Fast Recovery Area was configured it has been used for the temporary destination for the restored files. At the end of the process the PDB was indeed restored to the SCN in question, and the table contained the correct values:

```
SQL> select * from user1.t_1;

        ID
----------
         1
         3
```

Full restore and recovery of a PDB is no different from restoring a non-CDB in principle. You connect to the CDB$ROOT before starting the commands. To restore a PDB you are required to add the "pluggable" keyword as shown here:

```
RMAN> select open_mode from v$pdbs where name = 'PDB1';

OPEN_MODE
----------
MOUNTED

RMAN> run {
2> allocate channel c1 device type disk;
3> restore pluggable database pdb1;
```

```
4> recover pluggable database pdb1;
5> alter pluggable database pdb1 open;
6> }
[...]
Starting restore at 23.09.2013 14:53
[...]
Finished restore at 23.09.2013 14:53
[...]
Starting recover at 23.09.2013 14:55
[...]
starting media recovery
[...]
media recovery complete, elapsed time: 00:01:01

Finished recover at 23.09.2013 14:56
```

You can also restore individual tablespaces and datafiles. The good news is that if you connect to the PDB directly you need not change your recovery scripts; almost everything works as before in the context of the PDB. There are a few commands that are not applicable in the context of the PDB, they are documented in the official "Backup and Recovery User's Guide", Chapter 4 in section "Restrictions when Connected to a PDB".

There are differences when you perform restore and recover operations from the context of the CDB. It is easier to explain using an example. You might remember the syntax from the introduction section about the Data Recovery Advisor. In this particular scenario tablespace TBS_1 of Pluggable Database PDB1 needs to be restored and recovered. In the example the user is connected directly to the PDB.

```
RMAN> run {
2> allocate channel c1 device type disk;
3> alter tablespace PDB1_TBS_2 offline;
4> restore tablespace PDB1_TBS_2;
5> recover tablespace PDB1_TBS_2;
6> alter tablespace PDB1_TBS_2 online;
7> }

allocated channel: c1
channel c1: SID=30 device type=DISK

Statement processed

Starting restore at 22.09.2013 22:08

channel c1: starting datafile backup set restore
channel c1: specifying datafile(s) to restore from backup set
[...]
Finished restore at 22.09.2013 22:08

Starting recover at 22.09.2013 22:08

starting media recovery

archived log for thread 1 with sequence 92 is already on disk as file ...
[...]
```

```
media recovery complete, elapsed time: 00:00:01
Finished recover at 22.09.2013 22:08

Statement processed
released channel: c1
```

The output above proves that existing tablespace recovery scripts should work more or less unmodified in Pluggable Databases—but please test your scripts for your environment. You can also restore and recover PDB related files from the CDB$ROOT, all you need to do is to add a prefix to the tablespace name. The exact same example just shown looks as follows if you are connected to the root:

```
run {
allocate channel c1 device type disk;
sql 'PDB1' 'alter tablespace PDB1_TBS_2 offline';
restore tablespace pdb1:PDB1_TBS_2;
recover tablespace pdb1:PDB1_TBS_2;
sql 'PDB1' 'alter tablespace PDB1_TBS_2 online';
}
```

This will take the tablespace offline. Note the PDB1 prefix in the SQL command! The next command is to restore the tablespace. Note how the PDB1 prefix is used to tell RMAN to which PDB the command is to be applied. The recover command behaves identically. The last step is to take the tablespace online again.

Restoring to a different location

Sometimes it is necessary to restore parts of the database—either individual files or whole tablespaces—to a different location on the file system. This could be due to planned maintenance such as the decommissioning of a tray in the storage array, or media failure associated with a mount point. In either case, you can definitely restore to a new location, and it is not difficult to do so. Assume for example that the datafile 11 of PDB "pdb1" needs to be restored to disk group FASTDATA residing on a higher tier of storage, and it currently is stored in the generic +DATA disk group.

The commands to restore the file while connected to the PDB instead of the CDB$ROOT are shown in this example:

```
run {
  set newname for datafile 11 to '+fastdata';
  alter database datafile 11 offline;
  restore datafile 11;
  switch datafile all;
  recover datafile 11;
  alter database datafile 11 online;
}
```

The little RMAN script "moved" the datafile to the new disk group.

```
RMAN> select name from v$datafile where file# = 11;

NAME
---------------------------------------------------------------------------
+FASTDATA/CDB1/E6CDAD92377F667EE0436638A8C0DB6C/DATAFILE/example.293.826875289
```

The process is identical for non-OMF/non ASM data files. In such a case you could set the new name of the datafile to the exact location where you want it to be restored.

The need for testing

With the basic steps of taking backups and restoring/recovering databases explained in the previous sections there is one more item close to the author's heart. Some sites appear to be happy to only take a backup and never try restoring it. Or not testing the backups rigorously enough. It is the author's firm belief that backup testing should be as automated as possible, and performed as often as possible. Setting aside a small quad-core system will be enough to restore random backups.

The benefit to this technique is that any faulty backups become apparent during a non-critical time. Many DBA have anecdotes to tell of corrupted backups, or backups that failed silently without being noticed until the Big Day when the backup was needed for recovery. Why not try and find out before the crisis if your backups do work? The idea is simple: a small dedicated host has to be set aside, connected in a secure way to the backup storage location. This setup permits that one random backup from the backup catalog can be restored on that host to attached SAN storage every day to see if the restore and recover completes successfully. There should be a log of activity and any failures should be escalated to the backup team straight away to allow them to take corrective measures before the next scheduled backup. Urgent cases might even require them to trigger a manual backup.

If a complete recovery testing is not possible then you should at least consider running the RMAN validate command against your backups to check for corruption. Although not the same as restoring the database from start to finish, it gives you a little more confidence that the media manager can find the backup pieces and did not introduce corruption.

Introduction to Querying RMAN metadata

Recovery Manager has a very useful set of commands allowing you to view metadata related to backups and the target database itself. The primary commands for interrogating RMAN are list and report. For example, if you want to know which file make up a database, you could use the following command, which should be known to Oracle administrators. Connected to the CDB$ROOT you could expect output similar to this:

```
RMAN> report schema;

using target database control file instead of recovery catalog
Report of database schema for database with db_unique_name CDB1

List of Permanent Datafiles
===========================
File Size(MB) Tablespace           RB segs Datafile Name
---- -------- -------------------- ------- ------------------------
1    790      SYSTEM               ***     +DATA/CDB1/DATAFILE/system.265.826666771
3    720      SYSAUX               ***     +DATA/CDB1/DATAFILE/sysaux.277.826623415
4    135      UNDOTBS1             ***     +DATA/CDB1/DATAFILE/undotbs1.263.826623523
5    250      PDB$SEED:SYSTEM      ***     +DATA/CDB1/DD7[...]403C/DATAFILE/system.[...]6623565
6    5        USERS                ***     +DATA/CDB1/DATAFILE/users.264.826623523
7    590      PDB$SEED:SYSAUX      ***     +DATA/CDB1/DD7[...]403C/DATAFILE/sysaux.[...]623565
8    270      PDB1:SYSTEM          ***     +DATA/CDB1/DD7[...]F577/DATAFILE/system.[....].826617
9    630      PDB1:SYSAUX          ***     +DATA/CDB1/DD7[...]F577/DATAFILE/sysaux.261.8266215
10   16       PDB1:USERS           ***     +DATA/CDB1/DD7[...]F577/DATAFILE/users.258.826623817
11   358      PDB1:EXAMPLE         ***     +RECO/CDB1/E6C[...]DB6C/DATAFILE/example[...]826875289
13   20       PDB1:PDB1_TBS_1      ***     +DATA/CDB1/E6C[...]DB6C/DATAFILE/pdb1_tbs_1.[...]32151
14   20       PDB1:PDB1_TBS_2      ***     +DATA/CDB1/E6C[...]DB6C/DATAFILE/pdb1_tbs_2.[....].82089
15   20       PDB1:PDB1_TBS_3      ***     +DATA/CDB1/E6C[...]DB6C/DATAFILE/pdb1_tbs_3.[...]75409
```

```
List of Temporary Files
=======================
File Size(MB) Tablespace          Maxsize(MB) Tempfile Name
---- -------- ------------------- ----------- --------------------
1    60       TEMP                32767       +DATA/CDB1/TEMPFILE/temp.270.826623561
2    20       PDB$SEED:TEMP       32767       +DATA/CDB1/DD[...]403/DATAFILE/pdbseed_temp01.dbf
3    20       PDB1:TEMP           32767       +DATA/CDB1/DD7[...]F577/DATAFILE/pdb1_temp01.dbf
```

Oracle enhanced the report schema command by showing you information about the container for the data file. In the figure above you can see data files from the root (CDB$ROOT), the seed database (PDB$SEED), and finally a user-PDB (PDB1).

If you are unsure if all files of the database have been backed up and satisfy the retention policy, then you can use the report need backup clause to view any file that needs backing up. Assume for example that a new data file has been added to a database during a change window. Consequently, before the nightly backup has run, RMAN will report the file as a candidate for backups:

```
RMAN> report need backup;

RMAN retention policy will be applied to the command
RMAN retention policy is set to recovery window of 7 days
Report of files that must be backed up to satisfy 7 days recovery window
File Days  Name
---- ----- --------------------------------------------------------
21   0     +DATA/CDB1/E6C[...]436638A8C0DB6C/DATAFILE/pdb1_tbs4.299.826877399
```

Another useful report is the check for existing backups. If you want to know which backups of datafile 1 exist, you can query the repository as shown in this example:

```
RMAN> list backup of datafile 1;

List of Backup Sets
===================

[some other output omitted]

BS Key  Type LV Size       Device Type Elapsed Time Completion Time
------- ---- -- ---------- ----------- ------------ ---------------
105     Incr 0  665.39M    DISK        00:00:11     23.09.2013 08:24
   List of Datafiles in backup set 105
   File LV Type Ckp SCN    Ckp Time         Name
   ---- -- ---- ---------- ---------------- ----
   1    0  Incr 2210065    23.09.2013 08:24 +DATA/CDB1/DATAFILE/system.265.826666771

   Backup Set Copy #1 of backup set 105
   Device Type Elapsed Time Completion Time  Compressed Tag
   ----------- ------------ ---------------- ---------- ---
   DISK        00:00:11     23.09.2013 08:24 NO         TAG20130923T082446
```

```
List of Backup Pieces for backup set 105 Copy #1
BP Key  Pc# Status      Piece Name
------- --- ----------- ----------
111     1   AVAILABLE   +RECO/CDB1/BACKUPSET/2013_09_23/nnndn0_tag201...46_0.345.826878287
113     2   AVAILABLE   +RECO/CDB1/BACKUPSET/2013_09_23/nnndn0_tag20130...6_0.346.826878291
114     3   AVAILABLE   +RECO/CDB1/BACKUPSET/2013_09_23/nnndn0_tag201...446_0.267.826878291
112     4   AVAILABLE   +RECO/CDB1/BACKUPSET/2013_09_23/nnndn0_tag20130...6_0.296.826878293
```

The output shown here is the result from a multi-section backup of the data file. Four channels were allocated to back up a 700 MB data file, resulting in 4 backup pieces generated under backup set 105. You can also see from the listing that the backup was an incremental level 0 backup and various other items of interest.

Refreshing an environment

Refreshing databases is part of the routine work database administrators have to go through. Once it is understood and a process is put into place a database refresh is not too exciting and a good candidate for a scripted approach. In recent years it has become more and more important to ensure that confidential information in the database-credit card data for example-is masked before a test environment is handed over. A scripted approach should make use of scrambling technology that has been developed with the business units. The effort in time this takes is proportional to the number of applications making use of the database to be duplicated. This fact will play a role when defining service level agreements with the business.

The RMAN "duplicate database" command has been available for a long time now and can be used for duplicating environments. The command can be employed for full database refreshes—test or UAT environments for example—or standby databases. The "from active database" option has been mentioned before in the introduction and the Data Guard Chapters 9 and 10. It allows the database administrator to duplicate a database even if RMAN does not have direct access to the source database backups on the destination host. Instead, the database will be copied over the network, or—new with 12c—remote backup sets can be transferred. This active database duplication is not always allowed on all sites as it poses an additional burden for the network. If possible, dedicated infrastructure should be used for active database duplication.

As you would expect, the RMAN duplicate command has been enhanced for Pluggable Databases as well. You can duplicate PDBs as well as CDBs. The use case for duplicating PDBs is interesting when it comes to cloning PDBs across hosts. You should be able to clone PDBs locally anyway, see chapter 7 for more information on how to do so. The RMAN duplicate command is one of the most complex RMAN commands, and the mastery of it requires training and experience. The learning curve is smoothed somewhat by keeping a log file of the RMAN activities. The command line parameter "log" can be used or a simple tail after output redirection. For interactive sessions the tee command can be very useful, unlike the "log" option it displays the commands on screen. Consider these two examples:

```
[oracle@server1 ~]$ rman @test.rman checksyntax log=rman.log
RMAN> 2> 3> 4> 5> 6> 7>
[oracle@server1 ~]$
```

Compared to using the output redirection and tee:

```
[oracle@server1 ~]$ rman @test.rman checksyntax 2>&1 | tee rman.log

Recovery Manager: Release 12.1.0.1.0 - Production on Mon Sep 23 07:23:21 2013

Copyright (c) 1982, 2013, Oracle and/or its affiliates.  All rights reserved.
```

```
RMAN> shutdown immediate;
2> startup mount;
3> restore database;
4> recover database;
5> alter database open;
6>
7>
The cmdfile has no syntax errors

Recovery Manager complete.
```

The log file contents are identical of course. As you just read the RMAN duplication can either be backup based or from the active database. Backup-based duplication requires that RMAN has access to the backups. The easiest way to achieve this is via tape backups or NAS storage. If the destination server is connected to the same tape library/network then the duplication is easier. Otherwise you have to transfer the backup to the destination host or NFS; export it should the firewall permit it.

The duplication from active database is easier to put into place logistically. All you need is a (good) Net*8 connection. But there are a few caveats to be aware of. First there will be additional network traffic. If you are not careful this can impact regular database connections. It would be nice if the backup/RMAN traffic was separate from user traffic, but again that might not be possible on all sites. But then not every product manager might feel comfortable about the intrusion to "his" production database. Technically speaking it helps to statically register the database services with their respective listeners. The clone will be shut down during the duplication, and if the service is not registered with the listener you will get a "listener does not currently know of service name ..." error when trying to start the database. It also proved helpful to use the same SYS password for both databases, or even copying the password file to the remote Oracle home. Once the listener.ora file has been changed the listener needs to be reloaded. If you are using Oracle Restart or Real Application Cluster then please edit the listener.ora file in the Grid home and use srvctl to communicate with the listener. When you are using Oracle Managed Files—either with ASM or on a file system—you need not worry about file name conversions. In other cases you should edit the clone's parameter file to include the db_file_name_convert and log_file_name_convert parameters. The initialization file of the target CDB must have "enable_pluggable_database" set to true. The actual duplication is simple if the prerequisites are met, and there are notes on My Oracle Support explaining how to recover from a failed duplication. You should connect to RMAN using service names and not the bequeath protocol as shown in the following code snippet:

```
[oracle@server1 ~]$ rman target sys@cdb1 auxiliary sys@cdb2

Recovery Manager: Release 12.1.0.1.0 - Production on Mon Sep 23 08:31:24 2013

Copyright (c) 1982, 2013, Oracle and/or its affiliates.  All rights reserved.

target database Password:
connected to target database: CDB1 (DBID=800340993)
auxiliary database Password:
connected to auxiliary database: CDB2 (not mounted)

RMAN> duplicate target database to CDB2;
[...]
```

The list of options to the RMAN duplicate command is very long and gives testimony to the flexibility of this great tool. Once the test has been complete "manually" and proven that it works you should put it into a script to make it repeatable. More information together with examples can be found in Chapter 10 in the context of standby database duplication.

Summary

Backup and Recovery are key elements of database operations. Nothing is as important as a backup and a proven and tested recovery strategy when it comes to a failure. And please remember that it is not a question of whether or not the failure occurs, but rather when it does so. Often the problem is not even related to your database. Even the most rigorously managed database with the best change control in the world is not immune to a bug in the storage controller's firmware writing garbage into data files. Being able to restore service at any required moment is paramount, and provides peace of mind.

Pluggable Databases have been covered in RMAN enhancements, and many scenarios with PDBs are possible. The enhancements of point in time recoveries with PDBs are especially welcome to database administrators since they make for a lot less coordination effort between stakeholders. Should it really be necessary to perform a point in time recovery the least number of people will be affected by the outage. Depending on the size of the database however it becomes impractical or too time consuming to restore a database and another option has to be chosen. The most common option to consider for the Oracle database is Data Guard which you read about in Chapters 9 and 10.

CHAPTER 12

■ ■ ■

Upgrading to Oracle 12c

The final chapter of this book will deal with the upgrade to Oracle 12c. It is unlikely that your Database as a Service (DBaaS) Platform or consolidation project starts on the green field, but if it does: congratulations! You probably waited just long enough to get started with the right technology for the task. This chapter, just like the rest of the book, is written specifically for Pluggable Databases (PDB) and consolidation in mind. However, since PDBs are a new feature you cannot migrate a database from a previous release straight into a PDB using the traditional upgrade path described here. There are of course other methods available to transfer your schemas from a pre 12c database into a PDB.

To convert your complete pre-12c database into a PDB you need to migrate the existing database to a 12c non-Container Database (CDB) first. In the next step you can use the techniques described in this chapter to convert the database to a PDB inside an existing CDB. Note that you need to be on the same platform for this to work-converting databases from one platform to another is a different problem.

Although the migration from a previous version to the current release using the DB Upgrade Assistant or manual approach seems the most applicable use case, you can also use the Data Pump utilities expdp and impdp to migrate databases or subsets of the database as well. Other means of transportation include the use of Transportable Tablespaces or replication technologies. This chapter gives you an overview about migrating from Oracle 11g Release 2 to Oracle 12c Release 1.Oracle 11g Release 2 is the only non 12c release at the time of writing which enjoyed premium support from Oracle and hence was the obvious candidate to be covered in this chapter.

The upgrade path to Oracle database 12c

As with previous Oracle releases you need to pay close attention to the upgrade prerequisites. One of the most important prerequisites, supported database versions, is found in the list of database releases supporting a direct upgrade. The distinction is important since the upgrade options for Oracle Restart are slightly different and will be covered in a later section in this chapter. The minimum database releases for a direct upgrade are listed in Figure 12-1 shown below.

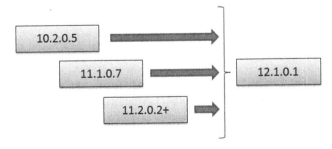

Figure 12-1. *Supported releases for a direct upgrade*

Any release lower than the ones listed require an intermediate upgrade before going to 12.1, or you can pursue an alternative strategy of some sort, such as to recreate the database and move the data from old to new. If you needed additional arguments why it is a good idea to stay reasonably current with your production environment, here is one. If you stayed on a release prior to let's say 10.2.0.5 for too long for example you have to perform one extra step before going to 12c, which will extend the time window required for the migration. The requirements however are moderate, and the application of a database patch set is not too much work, only time consuming. The functional risk is really all the regression testing, which for most applications is still not automated. Too large a "gap" however, might make it even more difficult to initiate a migration project, as the hurdles may be perceived to be too high.

Another important decision to be made is whether or not you want to perform a hardware refresh at the same time. Most companies use their hardware for a specific amount of time, and a migration project is often taken as an opportunity to get newer, faster hardware. Chapters 3 and 4 described hardware and software choices available for Oracle 12c in more detail.

If you go with a new server, you could install Oracle Restart and all other software homes in their respective version on the target server, and perform any configuration without time pressure you would certainly experience when performing the installation on the same host. Remember that you cannot install the 12c database binaries and continue to use the previous release's Oracle Restart at the same time. It has always been the case that Oracle Restart (and Clusterware for that matter) had to be a version number equal or higher than the Oracle database. But how would you get the database across to the new server? If you are staying within the restrictions set by Data Guard then it is the easiest technology to use for the hardware refresh/migration. Consider the following scenario:

As part of the migration you could perform a Data Guard switchover to the standby database on the new hardware. Emphasis should be put on the fact that the switchover does not change the Oracle version yet, but it does get you on newer better hardware! Although you are using Oracle Restart 12.1 on the target hardware you have an 11.2 RDBMS home as well-this is the home to use for the Data Guard configuration. The initial setup is shown in Figure 12-2 below.

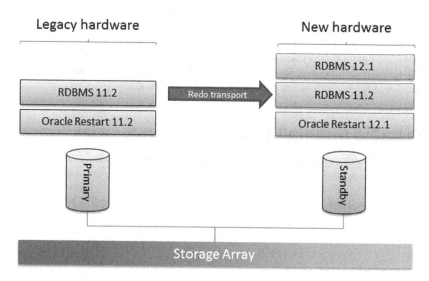

Figure 12-2. *Upgrade using a Data Guard switchover*

After the successful switchover you can upgrade the database just as you would without the Data Guard setup in the next step. This strategy gives you lots of freedom, and your back-out plan can be as elaborate as you like. One possibility is to use an Oracle 12c RDBMS home on the legacy hardware as shown in Figure 12-3 for a physical standby.

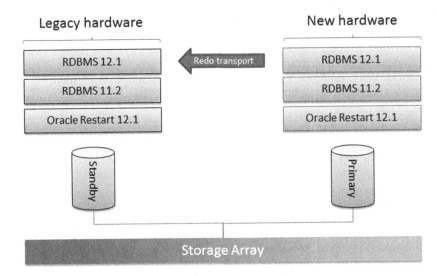

Legacy hardware   **New hardware**

Figure 12-3. Backout strategy with Data Guard in place

Using that approach you could downgrade the database to the previous release you migrated off and even switch back to the old hardware if that was required. Additionally you get the benefit of being able to implement separation of duties when installing the software on a different machine. An upgrade of Oracle Restart on the same server does not easily allow you to change the owner of the binaries. If you installed both Oracle Restart 11.2 and the Oracle database as the oracle account you tend to keep this configuration for version 12c.

In this chapter it is assumed that you are upgrading the database on the same host. Also note that the example assumes you are running a platform which is in premier support-at the time of this writing only Oracle 11.2 was in that support state. And since it is always good to be on the latest patchset to avoid the inevitable "apply the latest patchset" reply in a service request this is the case as well.

Before you upgrade production...

Performing a major release upgrade is anything but trivial depending on the application. The complexity increases with hardware and potentially associated platform change. The old rule that well-written, well-designed applications are easier to migrate still applies today. Complex applications written under a lot of time pressure are the most difficult to migrate. Hard-coded and undocumented connection strings buried deep within the application logic core are only the tip of the iceberg! You really need to ensure that you are working with all stakeholders, technical and functional, of your current product to ensure a smooth transition to Oracle 12c. This type of project definitely requires sufficient time for testing the application against the next database release. In the author's opinion there are two main areas to focus on during the testing period:

- *Functional.* Does the application perform as expected from a technical point of view? Does your regression test produce the same output on screen and in reports that you had previously? You are in a lucky position if your regression testing is automated, including the comparison of the application's output. If everything is the same: great! If not, you need to spend time investigating why. A prominent although somewhat older example includes the change from 9i to 10g when result sets were no longer implicitly ordered if the select statement did not have an "order by" clause. This is exactly the type of problem you want to catch before going live!

- *Technical.* Does the latest Oracle release produce the same results as the previous one? Did execution plans change? Do your important queries finish within the allowed time and Service Level Agreement? If not, why? Do you get any contention in the critical Oracle memory areas?

Both of the above mentioned areas are equally important, although the database administrator is more likely to be able to help with the second bullet point. For reasons outlined in chapter 1 it can be very difficult for an operational DBA to be reasonably familiar with the database he or she is about to upgrade. Changes from a technical point of view are easier visible to the technical staff. Comparing execution plans, response times and the general behavior between versions can be detected using the Automatic Workload Repository and other monitoring solutions. What's more difficult is to work out if the application does not show regressions under the new database release.

■ **Note** Ideally you are NOT changing the application code when migrating to a new release! Otherwise, how would you be able to attribute a problem post migration to the new database release or the new application release?

To address bullet point number two more forward-looking planning is necessary. Ideally an application support team has a set of end-to-end testing systems allowing (fully?) automated regression testing of the application. If the application features a graphical user interface then macro-recording software could be used to replay key transactions. Every Key Performance Indicator (KPI) of your software, especially if the KPI is under a Service Level Agreement, must be tested repeatedly and as automated as possible to prevent deviations due to human error. And let's face it-repeatedly testing the same processes is not the most entertaining activity in the world.

This section's nugget is that thorough testing using automated procedures would be ideal to prevent unpleasant surprises when going life in production with the next database release. This has been true for any major release change, not only Oracle 12c by the way. If automated testing is not available then the project manager should at least be available to identify key processes that the application team can test post the test migrations. In case of performance degradation theses users should contact the database team for further investigation. This could involve tracing specific end-user processes if possible or other "business as usual" troubleshooting processes. A migration to the next database release should not cause unexpected problems in the ideal world. In reality though all testing is limited to the ingenuity of the people involved, and sometimes it simply is not possible to plan for all eventualities. The more time you can spend on the migration, the more likely it is to capture problems beforehand. But please do not let the migration intimidate you too much: staying on a particular release for too long will make upgrades happening too late and even more daunting.

Upgrading Oracle Restart on the same server

If you are already using Oracle Restart in a version supporting a direct upgrade, the first step in the migration of your database is to upgrade Clusterware Since Oracle 11.2.0.2 all patches to Grid Infrastructure-clustered and unclustered-require an out-of-place upgrade. This means that you will need an additional, separate Grid Home for the base release, and each subsequent major patch. Oracle mandates the out-of-place upgrade to make it easier to revert to a previous version of the software. After sufficient testing has ensured that your environment is stable you can of course delete the old one, after a complete file system backup. As with every operation, the removal of the old, now unused, Grid Home must be tested first on an identical environment before performing this task in production, in addition to the file system backup you have taken! If possible you should draft a plan to create storage snapshots of the LUNs containing the Oracle binaries (all of them-not only the Grid home!) and if the storage admin is in good mood try to get the same service for your database LUNs as well. If storage snapshots are not possible then you must ensure alternative means of file system and database backups before starting any work. Snapshots based on the Logical Volume Manager (LVM) have proven to be useful in the world of Engineered Systems, and they might equally be useful for "regular" Oracle builds as well. You should perform a backup of the Oracle Local Registry manually just in case, before initiating the file system backup:

```
[root@server1 ~]# ocrconfig -local -manualbackup
```

Although the database is only indirectly affected you must have a backup of every single database using the ASM instance as well. Do not uniquely rely on the v$asm_client view for a list of databases making use of the ASM instance: if a database is stopped it will not be listed there!

Other places to look for hints of databases using the ASM instance are your company's configuration management database, parameter or server parameter files, the output of "srvctl config database" and database log directories in $ORACLE_BASE. Please do not continue until you have made sure that every component that could break has been backed up in a way that makes it possible to restore it.

Remember that all databases in an Oracle Restart environment are dependent on the ASM instance. In other words: you cannot patch the environment without incurring downtime. There is no way other than to stop the databases during the ASM upgrade unless you are using Real Application Clusters!

The upgrade path for Oracle Restart

As with the database, there are strict rules about which release can be upgraded. The releases eligible for direct migration are listed in the Grid Infrastructure Installation Guide for your platform. In case of Linux, the following versions are mentioned:

- 10.1.0.5

- 10.2.0.3

- 11.1.0.6

- 11.2

In reality you should not be concerned with any version other than 11.2 unless you are in extended support with Oracle. Bear in mind that there are additional restrictions for almost each of these releases, such as mandatory patches to be applied. In practice it makes a lot of sense to be on the latest available patchset and the terminal release for your release. For Oracle 11.2, which should be the main target for the migration, the following additional restriction has been identified: If you have applied the first patchset to 11g Release and are on 11.2.0.2.0 you must apply at least PSU 3. It does however seem more sensible to apply the *latest* PSU for 11.2.0.2 instead or better be on 11.2.0.3 which was the most current 11g Release patch set at the time of writing. When this book goes to print 11.2.0.4-the terminal release for 11g Release 2-will be out.

■ **Note** The requirements for upgrades might change while this book is out. Refer to the *Grid Infrastructure Installation Guide* for your platform, and refer to Appendix B in that guide for a complete list of current requirements.

Unsetting environment variables

If you have made your life easier by setting certain environment variables such as ORACLE_HOME and others then please ensure they are unset before starting Oracle Universal Installer. Candidates for unsetting are:

- ORACLE_HOME

- ORA_CRS_HOME

- ORACLE_SID

- LD_LIBRARY_PATH

- LD_PRELOAD

- ORACLE_BASE

Also ensure that neither of these environment variables are defined in /etc/profile, /etc/profile.local or your ~/.profile, ~/.bash_profile or ~/.bashrc files. Commands could be launched in shell sessions outside of yours inheriting the settings from the aforementioned files. Any variable found in a configuration file should be commented out or deleted as it could cause problems later.

Performing the Upgrade

The next step involves invoking Oracle Universal Installer from your staging location. You could read in chapter 1 that this could be a central build server with vetted binaries, or alternatively a temporary location where you downloaded the software from the web. In any way, unzip the software first before continuing. Do not place the zip files for the 11.2 and 12.1 software in the same directory-they both create a subdirectory "grid", and you do not want to mix and match versions.

The requirements for the installation of Oracle Restart have already been detailed in previous chapters and will not be repeated here. If you would like a refresher, please refer to chapter 6 for more information about the prerequisites.

■ **Caution**   Even though you are performing an out-of-place upgrade of Oracle Restart it is still a good idea to have a file system backup of the mount point(s) where *all* your Oracle software is installed. Better be safe than sorry.

With the prerequisites met it is time to start Oracle Universal Installer (OUI) from the command line. Please ensure that you select the radio button "Upgrade Grid Infrastructure or Oracle Automatic Storage Management" as shown in Figure 12-4.

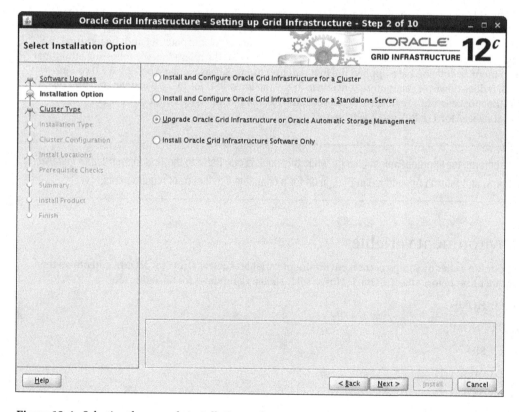

Figure 12-4. Selecting the upgrade installation path

All other screens from the installation are not very different from the "clean" installation of the software on a new server. When you initiate the upgrade then the following tasks are executed on your behalf:

- Prepared the dependent objects for the upgrade.

- Copied files to the new Oracle Restart home.

- Linked the binaries.

- Updated the repository.

The interesting events start to unfold when you are prompted to execute the upgrade script, which is shown in Figure 12-5:

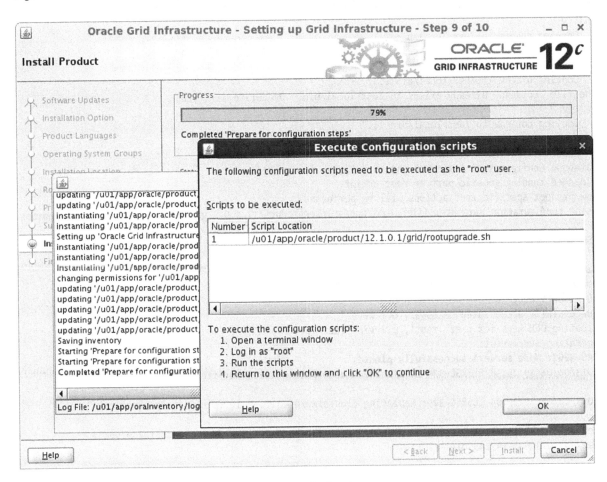

Figure 12-5. *The prompt for the execution of the rootupgrade.sh script*

As always with Oracle upgrades, execution of the root script is where it gets exciting. Either execute the command yourself, or have the sys admin execute it for you should you not have root access. Whichever is the case, you should double-check that no environment variables point to any Oracle home-neither the old nor new one. This could potentially confuse the upgrade scripts. A sample execution of the script is shown here. Note that existing files in the local bin directory (/usr/local/bin on Linux) have been overwritten with the 12c version. Some sites use the oratab file for customization in which case you need to preserve the original files first or choose not to overwrite them.

```
[root@server1 ~]# /u01/app/oracle/product/12.1.0.1/grid/rootupgrade.sh
Performing root user operation for Oracle 12c

The following environment variables are set as:
    ORACLE_OWNER= oracle
    ORACLE_HOME=  /u01/app/oracle/product/12.1.0.1/grid

Enter the full pathname of the local bin directory: [/usr/local/bin]:
The file "dbhome" already exists in /usr/local/bin.  Overwrite it? (y/n)
[n]: y
    Copying dbhome to /usr/local/bin ...
The file "oraenv" already exists in /usr/local/bin.  Overwrite it? (y/n)
[n]: y
    Copying oraenv to /usr/local/bin ...
The file "coraenv" already exists in /usr/local/bin.  Overwrite it? (y/n)
[n]: y
    Copying coraenv to /usr/local/bin ...

Entries will be added to the /etc/oratab file as needed by
Database Configuration Assistant when a database is created
Finished running generic part of root script.
Now product-specific root actions will be performed.
Using configuration parameter file: /u01/app/oracle/product/12.1.0.1/grid/crs/install/crsconfig_params

ASM Configuration upgraded successfully.

Creating OCR keys for user 'oracle', privgrp 'oinstall'..
Operation successful.
LOCAL ONLY MODE
Successfully accumulated necessary OCR keys.
Creating OCR keys for user 'root', privgrp 'root'..
Operation successful.
CRS-4664: Node server1 successfully pinned.
2013/08/04 19:25:36 CLSRSC-329: Replacing Clusterware entries in file 'oracle-ohasd.conf'

2013/08/04 19:29:04 CLSRSC-329: Replacing Clusterware entries in file 'oracle-ohasd.conf'

server1    2013/08/04 19:32:45      /u01/app/oracle/product/12.1.0.1/grid/cdata/server1/
backup_20130804_193245.olr

server1    2013/08/04 17:42:24      /u01/app/oracle/product/11.2.0.3/grid/cdata/server1/
backup_20130804_174224.olr
2013/08/04 19:33:34 CLSRSC-327: Successfully configured Oracle Grid Infrastructure
                              for a Standalone Server

[root@server1 ~]#
```

The all-important information is in the last line: the result of the operation was successful. If you are running into problems it is useful to raise a Service Request with Oracle Support straight away, in addition to your own troubleshooting efforts. It might take a little while for Oracle Support to develop new notes similar to the troubleshooting notes for rootupgrade.sh with version 11.2. In the meantime you should begin your investigation in the 12.1 Grid Home. You will find a directory name $GRID_HOME/cfgtoollogs/crsconfig/. Inside this directory you should have a file named roothas_*timestamp*.log. This log file is unusually detailed and useful. Have a look inside to find out where it went wrong. Additionally you can consult the files in $GRID_HOME/log/hostname/. Another useful starting point is the alerthostname.log file, which points you to the correct log file name in most situations.

After you have assured yourself that the installation has been successful close the "execute configuration scripts" window to proceed with the last remaining tasks. After those have completed and when you see the final screen, click on the "Close" button to exit Oracle Universal Installer. But how do you know if ASM has been upgraded? The easiest way is to connect to the ASM instance and query v$version:

```
SQL> select banner from v$version;
```

```
BANNER
--------------------------------------------------------------------------------
Oracle Database 12c Enterprise Edition Release 12.1.0.1.0 - 64bit Production
PL/SQL Release 12.1.0.1.0 - Production
CORE    12.1.0.1.0      Production
TNS for Linux: Version 12.1.0.1.0 - Production
NLSRTL Version 12.1.0.1.0 - Production
```

But if you carefully checked the output from the rootupgrade script you will have noticed the following:

```
ASM Configuration upgraded successfully.
```

This should take away any doubts. If you want more information about the migration process you can check the roothas-*timestamp*.log file in $GRID_HOME/cfgtoollogs/crsconfig/. With the Oracle Restart migration completed successfully you can either leave it as it is and complete your current change, or alternatively proceed with the database migration.

Performing additional post-migration validation

Your ASM installation has now been upgraded to version 12c. You should review any customizations you performed in the $GRID_HOME/network/admin directory, copy any wallets and files modified by you into the new home. At the same time it might be advisable to check the expiry date for your wallets to avoid them from being a show-stopper during the migration weekend. Additional things to check for are:

- Are the entries in the tnsnames.ora file correct?

- Is the (optional) sqlnet.ora file present, and with the correct contents? Are the paths referenced still valid?

- Are all the static registrations for the listener still correct? Remember the listener will be started from the 12c Grid Home.

- Have you used any wallets previously which need to be taken care of?

- Are there custom resources that need adapting?

You could also check if all the required components of the Oracle Restart stack are present. Is there a database missing? The minimalistic output for Oracle Restart could be similar to this one:

```
[oracle@server1 ~]$ crsctl stat res -t
--------------------------------------------------------------------------------
Name            Target  State        Server                   State details
--------------------------------------------------------------------------------
Local Resources
--------------------------------------------------------------------------------
ora.DATA.dg
                ONLINE  ONLINE       server1                  STABLE
ora.LISTENER.lsnr
                ONLINE  ONLINE       server1                  STABLE
ora.RECO.dg
                ONLINE  ONLINE       server1                  STABLE
ora.asm
                ONLINE  ONLINE       server1                  Started,STABLE
ora.ons
                OFFLINE OFFLINE      server1                  STABLE
--------------------------------------------------------------------------------
Cluster Resources
--------------------------------------------------------------------------------
ora.cssd
      1         ONLINE  ONLINE       server1                  STABLE
ora.diskmon
      1         OFFLINE OFFLINE                               STABLE
ora.evmd
      1         ONLINE  ONLINE       server1                  STABLE
ora.ora11.db
      1         ONLINE  ONLINE       server1                  Open,STABLE
--------------------------------------------------------------------------------
[oracle@server1 admin]$
```

Unless you specifically configured the Oracle Notification Server (ons) for sending Fast Application Notification events, this cluster resource will not be started by default. Until all databases on the server are migrated to 12.1 you need to use the local pre-12c ORACLE_HOME associated with the database to administer it:

```
[oracle@server1 ~]$ srvctl status database -d ora11
Database is running.
```

If unsure you can get the ORACLE_HOME from the resource profile (srvctl config database –d) or alternatively from the /proc file system in /proc/pid/environ. Can you start and stop the database resource using srvctl? Can you get the status of the database resource etc.-you get the idea. Please ensure that all your acceptance criteria are met before proceeding with the database migration.

Using Oracle Restart 12c and previous database releases in parallel

There is no strict dependency between the upgrade of Grid Infrastructure and the RDBMS instances on the same host. It is perfectly fine to keep pre 12c databases and 12c Grid Infrastructure for a period of time. As with 11.2 there are some known problems around such a configuration. These are documented in My Oracle Support note 1568834.1

"Pre 12.1 Database Issues in 12c Grid Infrastructure Environment." Bear in mind that the note is written for Real Application Clusters as well as Oracle Restart.

Most of the issues documented in the note can be solved if Oracle Restart is operating in a pre 12c friendly mode. In this mode, the server is said to be "pinned." When upgrading from a previous version of Oracle Restart the compatibility mode is always on. If you performed a fresh 12c Grid Infrastructure installation then you need to "pin" your node using crsctl. Please refer to the aforementioned MOS note for more information.

Another problem is that you cannot manage a pre 12c database when your ORACLE_HOME environment variable is set to the 12c Grid Home. Trying to interrogating the status of the database results in the following error message:

```
[grid@server1 crsconfig]$ srvctl config database -db ora11
PRCD-1027 : Failed to retrieve database ora11
PRCD-1229 : An attempt to access configuration of database ora11 was rejected because
its version 11.2.0.3.0 differs from the program version 12.1.0.1.0. Instead run the
program from /u01/app/oracle/product/11.2.0.3/dbhome_1.
```

This message is not new with 12c, it has been around for a while and the situation was exactly the same when using 11.2 Grid Infrastructure and pre 11.2 databases on the same host.

Upgrading the database

Compared to the migration of Oracle Restart which is mostly automatic, the migration of the database to the new release is where the real work lies. ASM has become a lot more sophisticated over time the databases acting as ASM clients did not necessarily take notice that a version change has occurred. Changes in the way the Oracle database operates internally however can make a version change a little more challenging. Luckily for you researchers have always scrutinized the behavior changes-mostly optimizer related-from release to release. Jonathan Lewis has published a lot on optimizer changes, and will surely continue to do so for the current release. Maria Colgan from Oracle is also a great source for information, she contributes to the Oracle blog related to the optimizer. And then there is too large a number of other reasearchers doing their own publications on how the current release is different from the previous one. Therefore you are going over multiple iterations until you understand the upgrade logic, then migrate the lower tiers until it is finally time to migrate production and the disaster recovery environment.

If there is a "magic" parameter that controls a lot within Oracle it is the initialization parameter named "compatible." It is rarely touched, and for good reason. Increasing the value for "compatible" makes it impossible to downgrade to a lower release unless you perform a restore from your backup medium. The message therefore has to be: do NOT touch the compatible initialization parameter unless you are absolutely sure that your application performs within the Service Level Agreements and there are no show stoppers that thorough, professional, regression testing have found.

From a process point of view the migration project can have multiple phases, not all of which are mandatory:

1. The engineering department reviews the new Oracle release and becomes familiar with it. In the absence of an engineering department dedicated members of the operational support team should test the new release.

2. An otherwise unused test environment with a clone of a database is created on separate hardware to allow database administrators to perform the migration without time pressure. So far the migration process was technology driven.

3. The development environments are migrated. Special emphasis should be on the development process. Can the development tools which are used still be used without limitations? Is the Continuous Integration process still working? Are you capable of performing unit tests? What about replication-Data Guard or other solutions? At this stage

some initial regression testing can be performed. Commercial packaged applications depending on the database for reporting or business intelligence might need upgrading too to support Oracle 12c. When migrating it is highly recommended to consider the full stack from top to bottom and carefully check product compatibility lists for all software involved.

4. The back-out plan is tested a few times to hone in the routine.

5. Upgrade of higher tiers, except production and disaster recovery ("DR"). This is the phase that requires most attention. Regression testing of the application, parallel runs, and much more are performed at this stage to ensure that the application continues to run within the required parameters. Anything external to the database should not be forgotten: feeds, web services, externally scheduled jobs, reporting software etc. fall into this category. Only if all stakeholders sign off can you proceed and migrate the life and DR environments.

6. As a last step of the upgrade project you upgrade production and the Disaster Recovery environments.

Once the immediate pressure of migrating to 12c is removed you can think of implementing the consolidation strategies. Non-Container Databases can be consolidated into Container Databases. You should consider implementing Resource Manager at the CDB and PDB level depending on the class of service the application is using. Refer back to Chapter 7 for more information about implementing Resource Manager with Pluggable Databases. This chapter will show you how to migrate a non-CDB into a CDB as part of the migration.

Let's have a look at the steps to be performed in more detail for a database migration.

High level steps

The individual database migration contains a number of steps that need to be performed sequentially. As one of the first tasks you need to become familiar with the new database release. This is why the author is hoping you are reading this book! Then you have to think about an upgrade strategy, which must include the worst case and a downgrade or a restore from backup if everything else fails. Like with every major task involving the Oracle database you must have a valid backup before commencing the work. Your upgrade plan should include phone numbers for escalation of calls to the backup team who will assist with the restore of the database if needed.

The test plan will be put to practice when you begin the migration of a fresh copy of production on a host clearly marked for development. It is possible that lots of developers depend on the machine you are testing on, if possible you should migrate an independent copy of the database, not an actual development database, space permitting. Although labeled development environment many of these systems are as important as the actual production database, especially for Independent Software Vendors (ISV). Imagine you had 50 developers sitting idle for a couple of days due to a database outage! Whichever way you choose, please ensure you have a strategy for backing out. This strategy must be tested and signed off as part of the process. RMAN backups can be used but any other reliable, supported, documented, tried and tested procedure will also be appropriate, if it has proven to revert back to the start without any issues.

Consider a cycle as show in Figure 12-6.

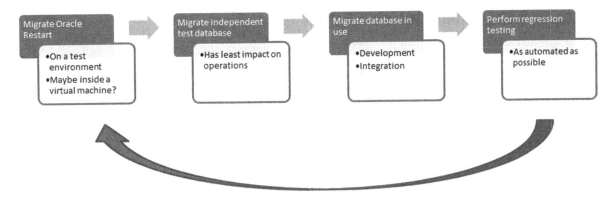

Figure 12-6. *The initial migration process for a development server*

Once the test migration has been completed, you need to point the application(s) to the newly created database and let the functional and regression testing begin. If you can you should adhere to the motto of changing only one thing at a time: planning on releasing new code to the application at the same time the database migration is scheduled for should be avoided. Otherwise it will be difficult to link cause and effect! Test the migrated database thoroughly with the application, just being able to get to the login screen is not good enough. The migration process needs to be tested as well, and ideally automated to a high degree. Once everyone is in agreement that all the tests were successful it is time to do it for real and upgrade the upper tiers up to production and disaster recovery. By now you need to have stakeholder agreements and valid test reports indicating that everyone is happy to go ahead with the production migration.

Finally the exciting week post go-live begins. Hopefully by then life should be normal, unless the testing phase was insufficient and you missed a lot of the detail which is now striking at you. The database is still running with an unchanged "compatible" setting. This phase of the migration could be referred to as "stable phase." The database runs out of the new RDBMS home. When appropriate testing has ascertained that changing the "compatible" parameter can be upgraded, you might opt to do so. There is no hard requirement to change the compatible parameter, but there will be a time when this should be done to prevent the software release and compatible value from drifting apart too much.

The steps in the following sections assume that you have taken note of all these warnings and good advice when upgrading. Refer to this section from time to time if you need words of caution. And finally: very few databases are the same. Just because something worked for one, does not necessarily imply it works for the other one too. It is ultimately the responsibility of the project management team to make the migration a success.

Performing a database software-only installation

The installation of the Oracle 12.1 binaries on the database host marks the true beginning of the database upgrade project. Depending on how strict your organization is the binary installation must be performed out of hours even for the development server where you test the migration initially. The installation of the database binaries has been described in great detail earlier in this book and will not be repeated here. Please revert back to chapter 6 for a more detail about performing a software-only installation of the Oracle 12c. In this example the software has been installed under the default location of /u01/app/oracle/product/12.1.0.1/dbhome_1. If it is different please adapt the path to your environment.

Running the pre-upgrade tool

Beginning with Oracle 12c the name of the pre-upgrade tool has changed to preupgrd.sql. It performs the necessary pre-upgrade checks. The Database Upgrade Assistant DBUA performs exactly the same checks by the way and invokes the script as well. The database to be migrated in this chapter has started its life as a "custom" database created with the Database Configuration Assistant dbca in version 11.2.0.3. It has a standard set of options registered in the server registry:

```
COMP_NAME                            VERSION
------------------------------------ ------------------------------
Oracle XML Database                  11.2.0.3.0
Oracle Expression Filter             11.2.0.3.0
Oracle Rules Manager                 11.2.0.3.0
Oracle Workspace Manager             11.2.0.3.0
Oracle Database Catalog Views        11.2.0.3.0
Oracle Database Packages and Types   11.2.0.3.0
JServer JAVA Virtual Machine         11.2.0.3.0
Oracle XDK                           11.2.0.3.0
Oracle Database Java Packages        11.2.0.3.0
```

Translating these to dbca options, only the installation of the Java Virtual Machine (JVM) and XML Database (XMLDB) options have been selected. The selection of these implicitly triggers the deployment of all those other components automatically. Note that beginning with Oracle 12.1 the use of XML Database is mandatory and XMLDB and its repository has to be present.

Following the example the file preupgrd.sql and the dependent script utluppkg.sql have been copied from the new Oracle 12.1 home to a temporary location and executed against the database ora11 running from the 11.2.0.3 Oracle Home. The script creates a log file and pre-/post upgrade "fixup" scripts. If an ORACLE_BASE was present-which should be the case with version 11.1 and later installations-then these files are in $ORACLE_BASE/cfgtoollogs/${ORACLE_SID}/. The resulting log file is broken down into various sections containing information about specific parts of the database to be upgraded.

> *Database information*: Including vital information such as the database release, setting of the compatible parameter as well as the timezone file version.

> *Renamed Parameters*: This section will highlight parameters which have been renamed in the new Oracle version.

> *Obsolete/deprecated parameters*: This section does not require an explanation. To avoid warnings when the Oracle database starts with such a parameter you should consider updating the initialization file.

> *Component List*: This section lists the components installed in the database. This output is very similar to what you saw earlier in this section. You should investigate why a component is invalid before upgrading.

> *Tablespaces*: Checks for sufficient space in the Oracle tablespaces SYSTEM, SYSAUX, UNDO, TEMP. A recommendation is offered to increase the size of these if they are too small for the migration.

- *PreUpgrade Checks*: Any potential problems which could arise with the migration are listed here. There is usually a description plus a solution offered. You should review the proposed change and act on them if needed.

- *PreUpgrade Recommendations*: Oracle will most likely recommend gathering of dictionary statistics.

- *Post Upgrade Recommendations*: Although not strictly speaking necessary Oracle might recommend upgrading the time zone file. This step is needed if your application makes use of named timezones (for example timestamp '2013-08-16 19:00:00 Europe/London BST' and the timezones you are storing changed recently. Remember to upgrade the server and all clients to the new timezone file!

- *Summary*: Presents a summary of the gathered information and lists any error that might prevent your upgrade from succeeding. Do not proceed until you fixed any potential error unless you want to practice restores under pressure!

In the demo system used for this chapter Oracle complained about too low a setting for the processes initialization parameter. In previous versions it was common to have this set to 150, especially for databases with fewer concurrent users. Oracle now insists on a value of 300 for the processes parameter. Note that if the tool finds the Enterprise Manager DBConsole repository in the database the preupgrade utility advises that the OEM repository will be removed as part of the upgrade. In order to save time it is therefore recommended by the utility to remove the repository prior to the upgrade. The final recommendation for the database was to gather dictionary statistics before starting the actual upgrade.

Before continuing you should get a list of objects currently invalid in the database. In an ideal world there are no invalid objects in a database after a global compilation using utlrp.sql for example has been started during a maintenance window. However the world is not perfect and there might be objects that do not compile. You should take note of them and compare the list with the list of invalid objects after the migration has completed. To do so, execute the script utluiobj.sql before and after the migration to get a list of invalid objects. The upgrade guide lists the following additional areas of interest before the upgrade:

- Access Control Lists (ACLs) which have been introduced with Oracle 11g for network related PL/SQL packages have been revised. The new database release 12c uses Real Application Security removing the dependency on XML DB.

- The way that database passwords for database links are stored has changed. If you plan on downgrading the database from 12c to your original release you should preserve the passwords before you upgrade.

- As with many Oracle migrations you need to upgrade the timezone files as part of the process. Be careful with the procedure-columns using TIMESTAMP WITH TIMEZONE could become corrupted if not treated correctly. Even if your application does not make use of this, the Oracle Scheduler does make intensive use of it!

- If your application or database makes use of materialized views, please ensure that all refresh operations have completed before migrating.

Additional information about pre-upgrade checks and prerequisites can be found in the official Database Upgrade Guide, section 2.5.

Making a database available for a first test migration

In the following step you need to make the database available to the new server for a first upgrade attempt. This can either be a clone of the database's LUNs or an RMAN-created clone. In any way you should try and get a database which has not been in use to ease the time pressure of having to succeed within a change window.

If you have been lucky and you storage administrator has given you a clone of the LUNs used for the test database, then you might have to rescan the SCSI bus and update the multipath configuration. The kpartx utility is a great way of making partitions on device-mapper multipathed devices known to the operating system without rebooting the server. If you are on an earlier version of RedHat or Oracle Linux and use ASMLib, then you might need to perform a scandisks operation to make the new LUNs available to Oracle ASM.

After adjusting any necessary parameters in the initialization file you can start the database. If the database was in ASM the new pfile is created very quickly: all you need is a pointer to the SPFILE as shown here:

```
[oracle@server1 ~]$ cat initora11.ora
SPFILE='+DATA/ORA11/spfileORA11.ora'          # line added by Agent
```

Before starting the database for the first time as shown below with the upgrade option you should create a pfile from the spfile and modify any parameters the pre-upgrade script recommended changing. Should the database fail to start then you most likely forgot to create the audit dump destination file or the diagnostic destination. You should not have set the background/user/core dump destination parameters in an 11g database, but if you are migrating from a 10.2 database then you might have to review these and change accordingly. If you are using a password file ensure that it is available in the new Oracle home's dbs directory. If you are not using Oracle Restart and previously had a SID_LIST in your listener.ora file ensure that this is available with the 12c listener, and that the listener is started.

In any case, create a new backup of the database using a proven and validated method before starting the actual migration of the test database. The backup should include the spfile and controlfile autobackup as well as all database files and necessary archivelogs.

Performing the upgrade

If not already done so, upgrade the /etc/oratab file (or /var/opt/oracle/oratab in Solaris) and create a new entry for the test database about to be migrated. In the next step you need to ensure your new environment has been sourced in to your session. The safest way to do so is to log out and log back in again. The environment variables should now point to the new Oracle home.

At this stage you need to be sure you have a tried and tested backup and recovery strategy in place in the event that the backup fails.

Navigate to the $ORACLE_HOME/rdbms/admin directory on the database server. Then start the database with the upgrade command:

```
[oracle@server1 admin]$ sqlplus / as sysdba
[...]

Connected to an idle instance.

SQL> startup upgrade
ORACLE instance started.

Total System Global Area 1068937216 bytes
Fixed Size                  2268624 bytes
Variable Size             314573360 bytes
Database Buffers          746586112 bytes
Redo Buffers                5509120 bytes
Database mounted.
Database opened

SQL> exit
```

Exit the SQL*Plus session and be amazed by one of the best new features from the author's point of view: the parallel dictionary upgrade. Instead of initiating the upgrade from within SQL*plus, you can launch a perl script to perform the task in parallel. The script is named catctl.pl and resides in $ORACLE_HOME/rdbms/admin as described earlier. It normally takes two parameters. The first one indicates the maximum degree of parallelism. It ranges from 1 to 8 with 4 being the default. The migration log files will be created in the current working directory but should rather be directed to a better location, possibly $ORACLE_BASE/admin/dbUniqueName/logs/. A sample session for the 11.2.0.3 database "ora11" is shown here:

```
[oracle@server1 admin]$ $ORACLE_HOME/perl/bin/perl catctl.pl -n 8 \
> -l $ORACLE_BASE/admin/$ORACLE_SID/logs catupgrd.sql

Analyzing file catupgrd.sql
14 scripts found in file catupgrd.sql
Next path: catalog.sql
32 scripts found in file catalog.sql
Next path: catproc.sql
37 scripts found in file catproc.sql
Next path: catptabs.sql
61 scripts found in file catptabs.sql
Next path: catpdbms.sql
205 scripts found in file catpdbms.sql
Next path: catpdeps.sql
77 scripts found in file catpdeps.sql
[...]
[Phase 53] type is 1 with 1 Files
cmpupend.sql

[Phase 54] type is 1 with 1 Files
catupend.sql

[Phase 55] type is 1 with 1 Files
catuppst.sql

[Phase 56] type is 1 with 1 Files
catshutdown.sql

Using 8 processes.
```

As you can see the migration is broken down into phases, and each phase has a number of scripts associated. After the analysis completed, the upgrade is started. The last few lines are shown here.

```
Analyzing file catupgrd.sql
Log files in /u01/app/oracle/admin/ora11/logs
Serial   Phase #: 0 Files: 1      Time: 77s
Serial   Phase #: 1 Files: 3      Time: 50s
[...]
Serial   Phase #:51 Files: 2      Time: 10s
Restart  Phase #:52 Files: 1      Time: 1s
Serial   Phase #:53 Files: 1      Time: 1s
Serial   Phase #:54 Files: 1      Time: 118s
Serial   Phase #:55 Files: 1      Time: 117s
Serial   Phase #:56 Files: 1      Time: 26s
Grand Total Time: 1169s
```

The parallel upgrade script was using a degree of parallelism of 8 as you can see by the line "using 8 processes."

■ **Note**   If you want you can still run the upgrade serially, by passing the –n 0 option to catctl.pl.

After the completion of the perl script you will notice that the database has already been shut down. The next mandatory step is to start it normally and run the post-upgrade script, utlu121s.sql after the database has been started normally. In the database which has just migrated, the following output was produced by the script:

```
SQL> @?/rdbms/admin/utlu121s
.
Oracle Database 12.1 Post-Upgrade Status Tool          08-13-2013 00:59:59
.
Component                      Current          Version   Elapsed Time
Name                           Status           Number    HH:MM:SS
.
Oracle Server
.                              UPGRADED         12.1.0.1.0 00:08:13
JServer JAVA Virtual Machine
.                              VALID            12.1.0.1.0 00:02:02
Oracle Workspace Manager
.                              VALID            12.1.0.1.0 00:00:58
Oracle XDK
.                              VALID            12.1.0.1.0 00:00:27
Oracle XML Database
.                              VALID            12.1.0.1.0 00:03:02
Oracle Database Java Packages
.                              VALID            12.1.0.1.0 00:00:10
Final Actions
.                                                         00:01:17
Total Upgrade Time: 00:16:23

PL/SQL procedure successfully completed.
```

Before handing the database over for testing you need to ensure that the catuppst.sql script in $ORACLE_HOME/rdbms/admin has been executed as part of the upgrade which it normally has unless the upgrade process has run into an error condition.

After that script has completed it is recommended to follow it up with the execution of the utlrp.sql script to recompile objects that have become invalid in the process. At the end of its execution you should not have additional objects in the dba_objects view with a status of "INVALID". Oracle provides a script to check for new invalid objects as a result of the migration named utluiobj.sql.

```
SQL> @?/rdbms/admin/utluiobj
.
Oracle Database 12.1 Post-Upgrade Invalid Objects Tool 08-13-2013 01:02:45
.
This tool lists post-upgrade invalid objects that were not invalid
prior to upgrade (it ignores pre-existing pre-upgrade invalid objects).
.
Owner                    Object Name              Object Type
.

PL/SQL procedure successfully completed.
```

Ideally the query against the dba_invalid_objects view returns zero rows. The final step when using Oracle Restart is to update the metadata configuration using srvctl upgrade database as shown in the example:

```
[oracle@server1 ~]$ srvctl upgrade database -d ora11 -o $ORACLE_HOME
```

This command does not seem to consider the oratab file which needs to be changed manually, replace the path to the pre-12c Oracle home with the installation path you chose if you have not done so already.

If the output of "srvctl status database -d <dbname>" complains that the database was not running but you clearly see that it is (for example, there are background processes) then you might need to stop the database using SQL*Plus and start it with srvctl. The environment for your Oracle processes should reflect the new Oracle home. Assuming that the UNIX process ID for the database's smon process was 10059, then the following little command taken from the proc(5) manual can help you get clarity about the ORACLE_HOME:

```
[root@server1 ~]# ( cat /proc/10059/environ; echo ) | tr '\000' '\n' | grep ORACLE_HOME
ORACLE_HOME=/u01/app/oracle/product/12.1.0.1/dbhome_1
```

A word of caution: your database is now migrated to the current release and should under no circumstances be started from the old ORACLE_HOME!

Performing necessary post-upgrade steps

Each new database upgrade guide lists a number of steps to be completed. Whether or not these steps are required depends on your configuration. Following are the steps to consider:

- Check your oratab file to ensure that the Oracle home for a given ORACLE_SID points to the 12.1 home, not the previous one. Do NOT start the 12.1 database instance from its old Oracle home!

- Ensure that your .bashrc, .bash_profile, /etc/profile or .profile scripts do not set environment variables pointing to an old Oracle home for your database.

- If you saved statistics using the DBMS_STATS.CREATE_STATS_TABLE procedure then these tables need to be updated using the UPGRADE_STAT_TABLE procedure in the DBMS_STATS package.

- Upgrade the RMAN catalog.

- If you want to make your XMLDB repository available for FTP and HTTP authentication then you may need to initialize the ports after the database migration.

- If the pre-upgrade tool recommended that you change the timezone file, you should do so. The log file lists a note on My Oracle Support which can be used for the process.

- Users of Application Express have to make changes to their configuration settings after the upgrade.

- If your IT security department has not created a compliance document then you should lock all Oracle supplied accounts except for SYS and SYSTEM. Use CDB_USERS.ORACLE_MAINTAINED column to define Oracle internal accounts and lock them if they are not already locked.

- You might want to recreate your orapw$ORACLE_SID file to the new 12c format or use the new INPUT_FILE parameter in orapwd to migrate it to the new format.

Each of these steps is explained in detail in chapter 4 of the official, *Upgrade Guide*. Consult that chapter for more information on any of the steps you wish to perform.

Upgrading the database with the Database Upgrade Assistant

After having experienced what happens during a database migration many database administrators might prefer to use a graphical tool for the same job for smaller, not quite as important databases. After all, the DBUA utility has been developed by Oracle to provide a means of upgrading databases repeatedly, in the same way without overlooking details. The code in DBUA will certainly be executed over and over, no matter if it is the first, second or tenth database you are upgrading.

Nevertheless the same precautions as described earlier in the context of the manual database migration have to be taken. Do not become lazy-there is nothing worse than a corrupt database that is stuck halfway between 11.2.0.3 and 12.1 and cannot be recovered.

It is recommended that the database you want to upgrade be running before DBUA is invoked. This ensures that the database has been started using the correct parameter files. Remember that DBUA will restart the database during the upgrade process using the default parameter files, so these need to be correctly configured. The interactive Database Upgrade Assistant requires an X server to connect to. Please refer back to chapter 5 for a refresher on how to provide an X-environment for a graphical Oracle utility if you are unsure how to proceed. The standard way of presenting X-applications to the database administrator in this book is vncserver. Using the vnc client to connect to the server in question you can start the DBUA in an X-terminal. Start the Upgrade Assistant from the 12.1 Oracle home. You will be surprised how flexible and useful the upgrade assistant has become! When started it will greet you as shown in Figure 12-7:

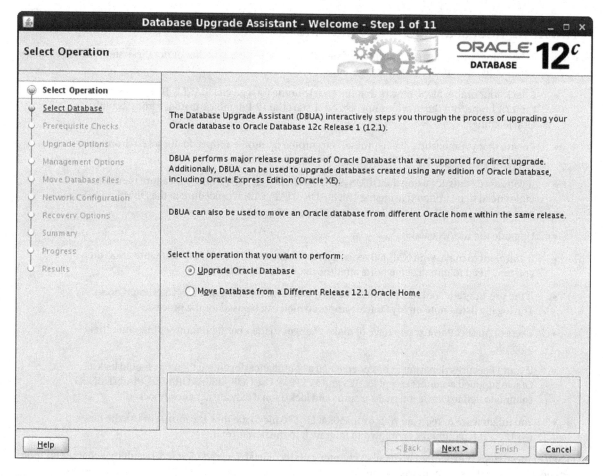

Figure 12-7. DBUA welcome screen

Select the "Upgrade Oracle Database" option to begin the upgrade process and click on the "Next" button to advance to step 2 shown in Figure 12-8.

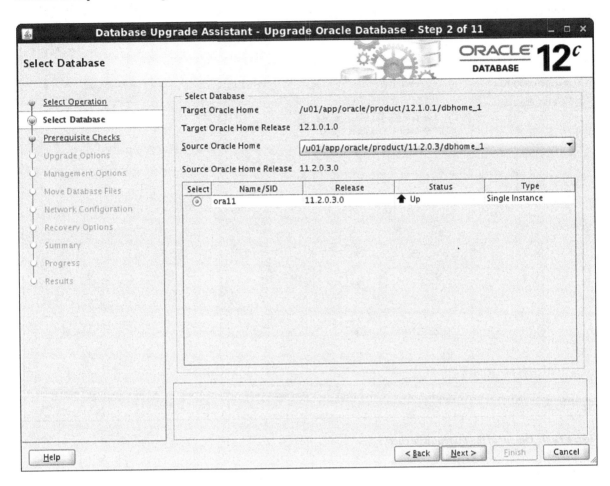

Figure 12-8. *The database selection screen*

In this screen you have the option to select the database you want to upgrade. In our case the only eligible database was named ORA11 and is created in an Oracle 11.2.0.3.x home. It is up, and it is a single instance database. The database instance name ORA11 has chosen for the sake of demonstrating the upgrade process only. In most production deployments it makes very little sense to create a database tied to a version. Version numbers inevitably increase causing the instance name to be out of sync with the database name. The workaround to the situation-using services-may add confusion to administrators looking after such an environment.

The target 12c RDBMS home is shown on the top of the screen and determined by the location of the DBUA executable on the file system. If you do not find the database you want to migrate you should check the source oracle home drop-down menu and chose the appropriate one. As per the recommendation above the database is started. Select the radio button next to it and click on "Next" to advance to step 3, shown in Figure 12-9:

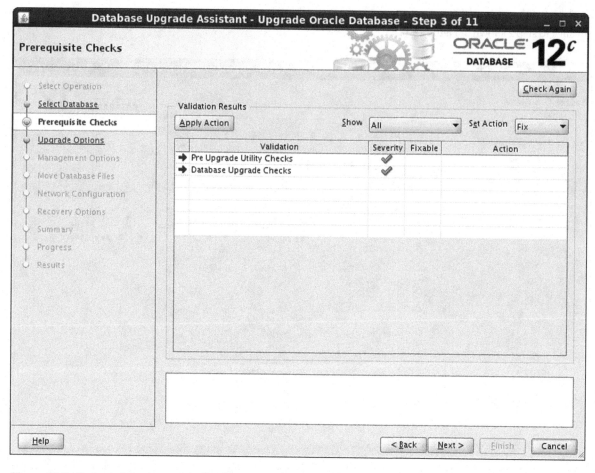

Figure 12-9. *Output of the prerequisite checks*

The database instance ORA11 has been created using the standard engineered build. With every database being designed and deployed in a same way bad surprises are less likely to happen. Since no severe exceptions were reported with the previously migrated database, the author was reasonably confident there were none with this database either. The checks performed by DBUA returned green light for a migration. If there were any problems you could click on the checks to expand a list of potential issues.

If problems had been detected then DBUA offers the option to fix those that can be fixed by a script. For each exception reported in the list which is "fixable" as per the column in the wizard you can apply the fix and check again if the problem has been solved. This again is very similar to the output of the pre-upgrade script you ran in SQL*Plus earlier: it too produced fixup scripts you could have executed in case of problems. Some issues reported by DBUA cannot automatically be fixed and require you to take a look at the Upgrade guide, My Oracle Support or your favorite search engine to find a solution to the problem. You should not continue until the Upgrade Assistant stops reporting warnings and/or errors.

In the above example none of that was necessary, a click on the "Next" button leads to the next screen, shown in Figure 12-10.

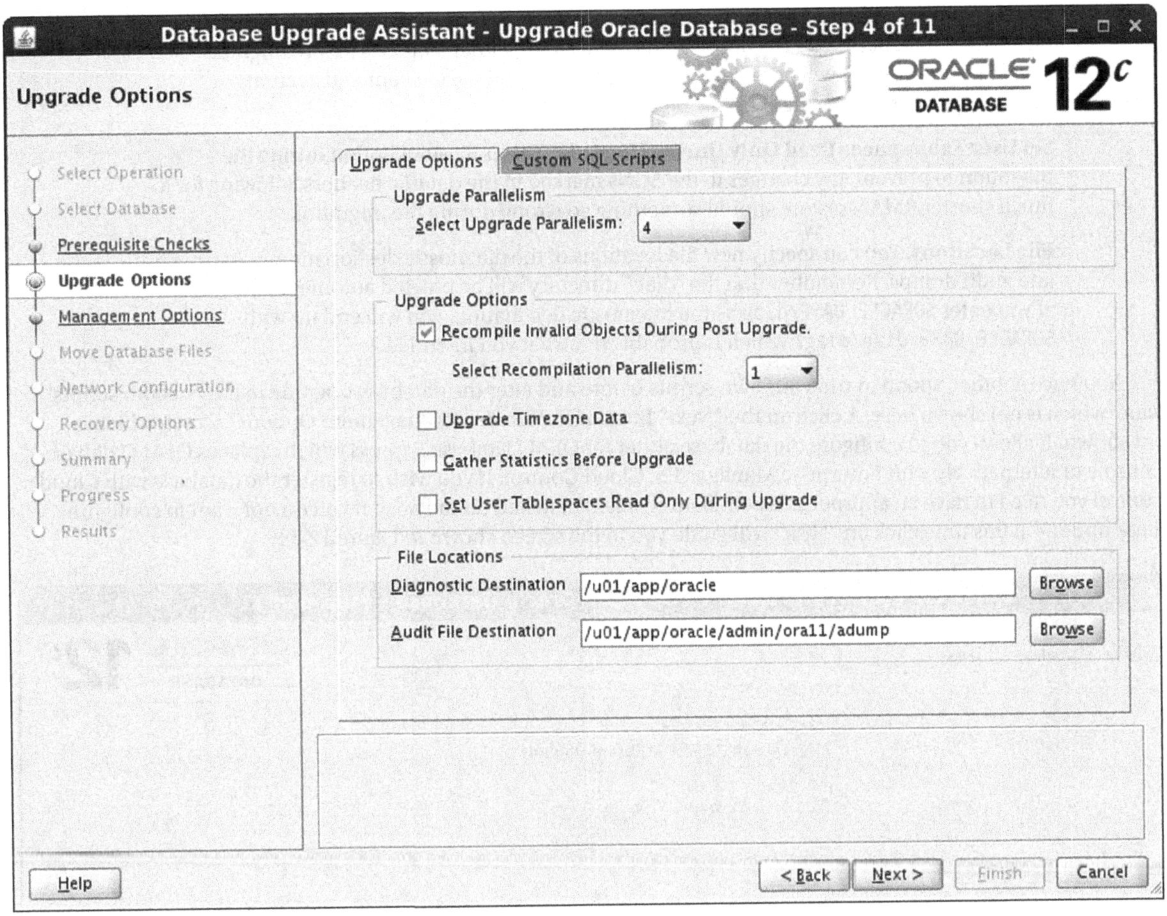

Figure 12-10. *Presenting the upgrade options*

In this part of the migration wizard you can fine tune which actions DBUA should perform for you. Amongst the options you can chose are:

> **Upgrade Parallelism.** Let's you select the degree of parallelism for the catctl.pl script. This script has been covered in more detail in the manual upgrade section earlier in the chapter.
>
> **Recompile Invalid Objects During Post Upgrade.** The Upgrade Assistant can recompile invalid options after the migration if you tick the relevant check-box. The degree of parallelism can be defined independently of the degree of parallelism the catctl.pl script uses.
>
> **Upgrade Timezone Data.** Choosing this option is a handy shortcut *if* you know that your database does not have timestamp with local time zone columns. If you are unsure you might want to review the relevant documentation in the Upgrade Guide and on My Oracle Support. Updating the timezone file is a not a trivial task and should better be performed by an experienced DBA. But please do not forget to work on the timezone file later!

Gather Statistics Before Upgrade. If your dictionary statistics are stale the migration can take longer than necessary to complete. If you tick the "gather statistics before upgrade" check box then DBUA will perform this step for you. If you have recent and accurate dictionary statistics this might not be needed.

Set User Tablespaces Read Only During Upgrade. This is a useful option during the migration to prevent any changes to the SCNs marked in the datafile headers, allowing for a much shorter RMAN restore should something go wrong during the migration.

File Locations. You can specify new file locations of the diagnostic destionation and audit dumps. Remember that the "diag" directory will be created automatically; if you enter $ORACLE_BASE/diag as the diagnostic destination, you will end up with $ORACLE_BASE/diag/diag/ which is probably not what you intended.

You have another option to run your own scripts before and after the database upgrade in the "custom scripts" pane, which is not shown here. A click on the "Next" Button leads to the "Management Options" screen which is not shown. It allows you to configure the database either for OEM Database Express which replaces OEM Database Console or alternatively with Enterprise Manager 12c Cloud Control. If you wish to register the database with Cloud Control you need to have an appropriately configured agent installed on the host. If you do not want to configure these options at this time click on "Next" will guide you to the screen shown in Figure 12-11:

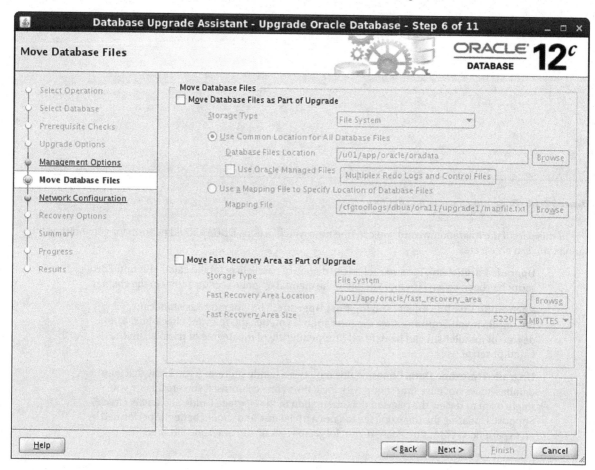

Figure 12-11. Move Database Files as part of the upgrade

The "move database files" screen allows you to move the database to a different location on the file system or alternatively into ASM if you so like. The screen is very similar to the one shown in the Database Configuration Assistant during the database creation. The question you need to ask yourself here is: where do you want the migrated database to be located? In this scenario, which is an "in-place" migration of a database which has been moved prior to the invocation of the Upgrade Assistant no action was necessary. Proceed to the next wizard screen, shown in Figure 12-12.

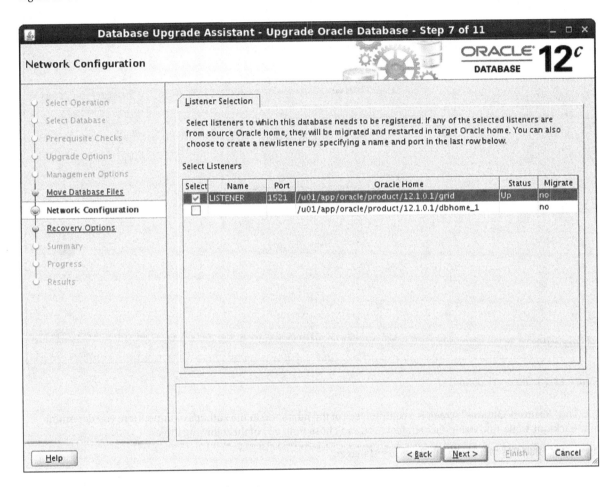

Figure 12-12. *Updating the network configuration*

If you had a listener operating out of the "old" Oracle home, such as from an 11.2 home, then you could opt to have DBUA to move it to the new database home. Since Oracle Restart is in use on this server, there is no listener in the database home. This screen is a very convenient way for systems not using ASM to have the listener moved as part of the migration. Another step less to perform post the migration! If you want to migrate the listener as well, select it before moving to the next screen shown in Figure 12-13.

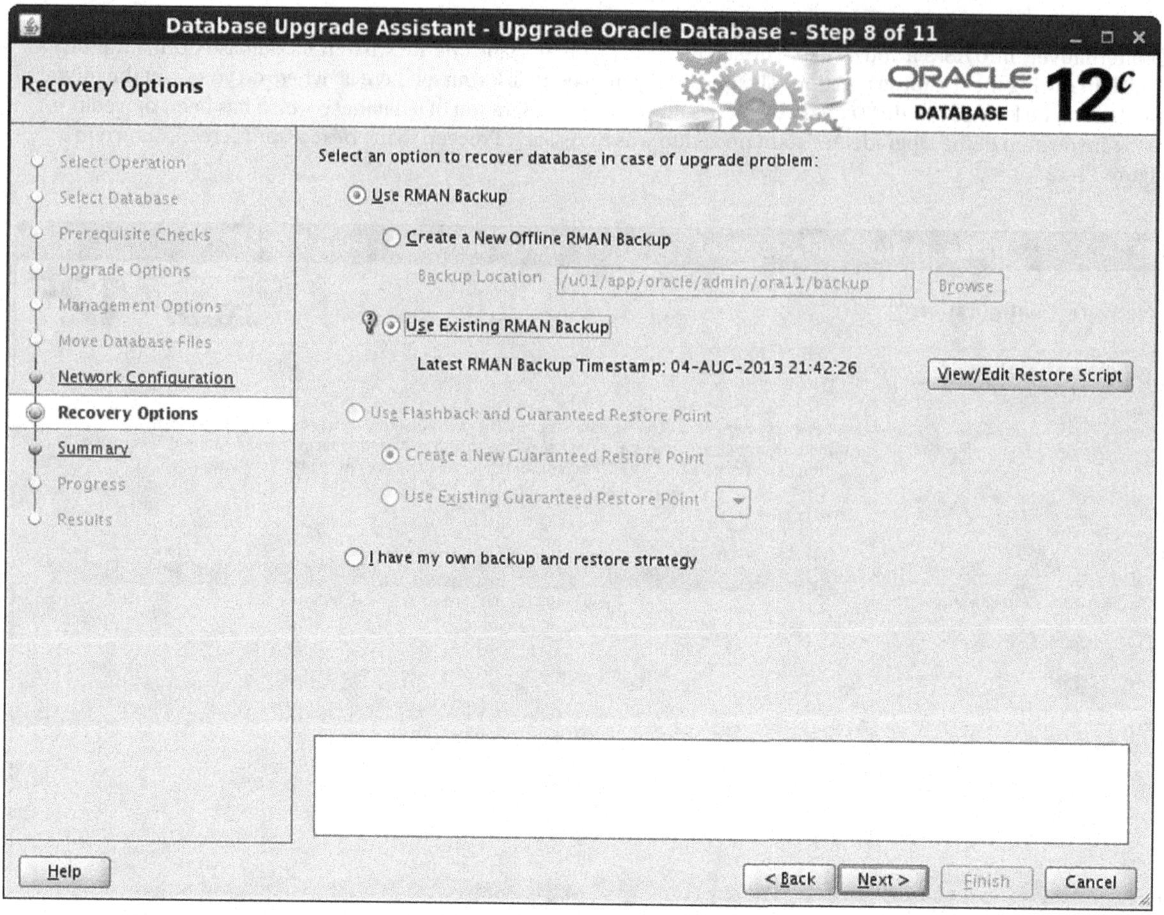

Figure 12-13. Recovery options

The "Recovery Options" screen is a central piece of the migration in the author's opinion. Here you determine your back-out-while-not-losing-face strategy. You can chose from any of the following three:

- Backups managed with Recovery Manager.

- Use of the Flashback Database feature for databases beginning with 11.1.0.7.

- Your own.

If you chose to use an existing backup then please make sure it is current and includes all relevant archived redo logs! You should also ensure that all the backup pieces are actually available if needed. If unsure, you could let RMAN create a backup for you. To use Flashback Database your source database must be 11.1.0.7 or later, and the Flashback Database feature must be enabled, otherwise you will see the option greyed out in in the screenshot. If you opt to use your own backup strategy, then please have one that is tested and valid. Choosing this option is like telling the Upgrade Assistant: "trust me, I know what I am doing". The backup and possibly restore operation will be your responsibility.

Finally it is time to start the actual migration! Another click on the "Next" Button will present you with a summary of operations shown in Figure 12-14 below.

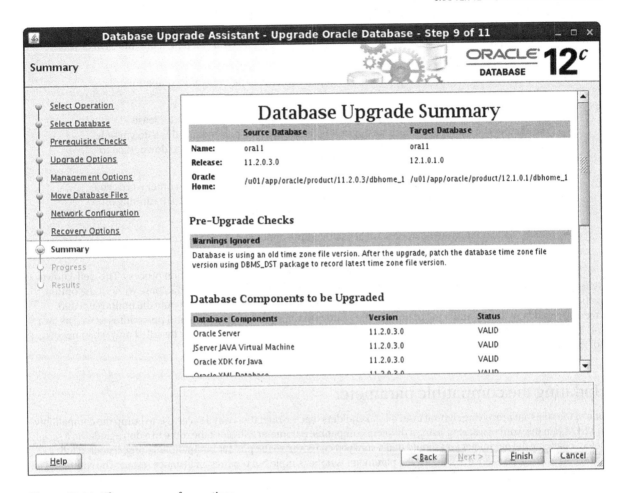

Figure 12-14. *The summary of operations*

The summary screen lists the options you have chosen and is the last time when you can change your mind. Carefully review the options, and when you are happy you need to click on "Finish" to begin the actual migration which might take a little while. Please note that the progress window is not shown here. After the migration completed, you are shown the results screen which again lists source and destination databases, any warnings and details. The most likely warning you are going to see is that your database uses an old timezone file. The upgrade of the timezone file is mandatory, and needs to be completed using the instructions provided on My Oracle Support.

Database Upgrade Assistant also supports silent migrations, which can come in handy when you do not have an X server available for security reasons.

Consolidating migrated databases

You read in chapter 7 that you could plug a non-Container Database (CDB) into a CDB. Transforming the freshly migrated database into a Pluggable Database (PDB) is a logical consequence of the idea described earlier and a further step to consolidation.

Here again it is beneficial to have a standard DBCA template or comparable method of creating databases identically. After the pre-12c database has been migrated to the new release you can plug it into the CDB of your choice, if the following prerequisites are met:

- The target CDB and the newly migrated database MUST use the same or a compatible character set *and* national character set.

- The compatible parameter of the pre-12c database must be advanced to 12.1. Please remember the warning of doing so: upgrading the compatible parameter rules a downgrade by script out. Advance the parameter *only* if you are sure you will not need to downgrade to the previous release.

- Both target CDB and migrated database must have the same endianness. In other words you cannot plug a database created on a popular RISC platform straight into a CDB running on Linux.

- Both CDB and migrated database must use the same options as shown in the DBA_SERVER_REGISTRY view.

The last bit can be a problem on sites where is little control over the database creation process. The well-known General_Purpose.dbc template seems to add every Oracle option under the sun to the database without the option to change it during the creation. "Custom" databases quite often-and rightly so-contain only the options needed. An engineered built ideally limits the options to the minimum required-catalog views and procedures as well as Java and XML DB. Spatial, InterMedia and Text are not standard components and should be installed only when needed, not the least to avoid license problems later!

Updating the compatible parameter

One of the steps after receiving sign-off from all stakeholders that the migration was a success is to bump the compatilibty to 12.1. Again the word of warning-using a different compatible parameter will block the route to a downgrade via a script. Before changing the parameter you should make sure you can revert to the pre-12c compatible setting. Usually a full RMAN backup will be needed. Changing the parameter is rather simple but requires an instance restart. The command to update the compatible settings is the usual alter system command:

```
SQL> show parameter compatible

NAME                                 TYPE        VALUE
------------------------------------ ----------- ------------------------------
compatible                           string      11.2.0.0.0

SQL> alter system set compatible='12.1.0' scope=spfile;

System altered.

SQL> shutdown immediate
Database closed.
[...]
Database mounted.
Database opened.
SQL> show parameter compatible
```

NAME	TYPE	VALUE
compatible	string	12.1.0

The corresponding information in the alert.log is shown here as well.

```
ALTER DATABASE   MOUNT
[...]
2013-08-14 18:56:15.100000 +01:00
ALERT: Compatibility of the database is changed from 11.2.0.0.0 to 12.1.0.0.0.
Increased the record size of controlfile section 12 to 96 bytes
Control file expanded from 614 blocks to 618 blocks
Increased the record size of controlfile section 13 to 780 bytes
Control file expanded from 618 blocks to 620 blocks
[...]
ALTER DATABASE OPEN
Switching redo format version from 11.2.0.0.0 to 12.1.0.0.0 at change 1106948
Thread 1 advanced to log sequence 87 (COMPATIBLE advance)
```

With that setting in place you can move on to the next task which is to check the compatibility of the database with the destination CDB. It allows you to check if the non-CDB can be plugged into a CDB.

Checking compatibility

The compatibility check is performed in two steps. In the first step you need to create an XML file describing the future PDB to be plugged in. It goes almost without saying that the aspiring PDB's data files are available to the CDB's host but this too is a requirement.

You create the XML file using the new DBMS_PDB package using the DESCRIBE function as shown here:

```
SQL> exec dbms_pdb.describe(-
>  pdb_descr_file => '/u01/app/oracle/admin/ora11/pdb/ora11.xml');

PL/SQL procedure successfully completed.
```

The database needs to be opened READ-ONLY or the execution of the procedure will fail with that error message. The file created-ora11.xml contains a logical description of the database to be plugged in. It specifically sets the pdbname to the database's unique name which will be important later. It also records further metadata such as the byte order ("endianness"), the database ID and others before it lists all the data files. Towards the end of the file you find the options in use in the database including their respective versions. Finally important initialization parameters are listed alongside their respective values. All the information in the XML file will next be used to assess the compatibility of the database with its future container.

Now switch to the CDB into which you want to plug the database and execute the compatibility check. This too is found in the DBMS_PDB package. Continuing the example here is the check:

```
SQL> declare
  2    is_compatible boolean;
  3  begin
  4    is_compatible := dbms_pdb.check_plug_compatibility(
  5      pdb_descr_file => '/u01/app/oracle/admin/ora11/pdb/ora11.xml'
```

```
6   );
7   end;
8   /
```

PL/SQL procedure successfully completed.

Now you need to query the new PDB_PLUG_IN_VIOLATIONS view since there will almost certainly be problems reported. In this case they were not severe though:

```
SQL> select message from pdb_plug_in_violations;

MESSAGE
--------------------------------------------------------------------------------
PDB plugged in is a non-CDB, requires noncdb_to_pdb.sql be run.
CDB parameter sga_target mismatch: Previous 4294967296 Current 8589934592
CDB parameter compatible mismatch: Previous 12.1.0 Current 12.1.0.0.0
CDB parameter pga_aggregate_target mismatch: Previous 1073741824 Current 2147483
648
```

Because the violations found are only parameters, they can easily be changed. After matching the parameters on ORA11 and creating a new XML file the execution of the compatibility check looked good:

```
SQL> select message from pdb_plug_in_violations;

MESSAGE
--------------------------------------------------------------------------------
PDB plugged in is a non-CDB, requires noncdb_to_pdb.sql be run.
```

This is the standard message indicating that a dictionary conversion script needs to be run after plugging a non-CDB into a CDB as a PDB. A common problem found during testing was that assigning a different "PDB" name causes issues when trying to plug the PDB into the CDB. The safest way was to keep the PDB name the same as the database name.

Different options in the non-CDB and CDB will result in messages similar to these:

```
MESSAGE
--------------------------------------------------------------------------------
PDB plugged in is a non-CDB, requires noncdb_to_pdb.sql be run.
Database option APS mismatch: PDB installed version NULL. CDB installed version 12.1.0.1.0.
Database option CONTEXT mismatch: PDB installed version NULL. CDB installed version 12.1.0.1.0.
Database option DV mismatch: PDB installed version NULL. CDB installed version 12.1.0.1.0.
```

The action column in the view indicates that the options should be installed where missing. Alternatively you could plug the non-CDB into a different CDB with matching options.

Plugging the non-CDB into the CDB

The remaining tasks are straight forward and involve the invocation of the "create pluggable database" command discussed in chapter 7. In the example the data files are already in the correct location and Oracle Managed Files are in use. These facts greatly simplify the plugging in of the database. Please refer back to chapter 7 for more information on how to plug in a database into a CDB including file name conversion and the decision to copy the data files or not.

Before you can try to plug in the database you need to shut it down safely. Following along the command to add the migrated database to the CDB is shown here:

```
SQL> create pluggable database ora11 as clone
  2  using '/u01/app/oracle/admin/ora11/pdb/ora11.xml'
  3  nocopy tempfile reuse;

Pluggable database created.
```

The operation is logged quite verbose in the alert.log as well:

```
2013-08-14 19:44:34.887000 +01:00
create pluggable database ora11
using '/u01/app/oracle/admin/ora11/pdb/ora11.xml'
nocopy tempfile reuse
*************************************************************
Pluggable Database ORA11 with pdb id - 4 is created as UNUSABLE.
If any errors are encountered before the pdb is marked as NEW,
then the pdb must be dropped
*************************************************************
Deleting old file#1 from file$
Deleting old file#2 from file$
Deleting old file#3 from file$
Deleting old file#4 from file$
Adding new file#13 to file$(old file#1)
Adding new file#14 to file$(old file#2)
Adding new file#15 to file$(old file#4)
Marking tablespace #2 invalid since it is not present in the describe file
2013-08-14 19:44:35.958000 +01:00
Successfully created internal service ora11 at open
ALTER SYSTEM: Flushing buffer cache inst=0 container=4 local
*************************************************************
Post plug operations are now complete.
Pluggable database ORA11 with pdb id - 4 is now marked as NEW.
*************************************************************
Completed: create pluggable database ora11
using '/u01/app/oracle/admin/ora11/pdb/ora11.xml'
nocopy tempfile reuse
```

Please resist the temptation to open the PDB straight away! Remember from the plug in violations view that you must run the noncdp_to_pdb script fist! This is done by switching to the new PDB and executing the script:

```
SQL> alter session set container = 'ORA11';

Session altered

SQL> @?/rdbms/admin/noncdb_to_pdb
```

After the script has completed it is safe to use the PDB as any other PDB in the Container Database.

447

Moving the database into ASM

If the decision has been made to consolidate databases in ASM, then it is a good idea to consider such move at time of the migration. Migrating a database from a file system into ASM is quite straight-forward since Oracle 11g. In summary you create an image copy of the database in ASM, and then switch to the database copy. This is very similar to the recovery strategy where a full copy of the database is stored in the Fast Recovery Area which can be the target of a (RMAN) switchover operation.

Before you are going to move the database into ASM you should first keep a log of where the files are located on the file system. Files eligible for a move into ASM are:

- Data files
- Temp files
- Control files
- Server parameter file

Some other file types such as certain Data Pump files can also be created in ASM, but many users keep those on a file system. If you are also moving an existing Flash Recovery Area into ASM then you need to drop all restore points and disable flashback database before doing so. This may have implications on existing back-out strategies for other changes, so better ensure there are no conflicts! Begin by checking your data and temp files. The below database has very few data and temp files but please be aware that the number of physical files in a database only extends the duration of the copy operation, otherwise a small database is moved into ASM using the same techniques as a large one.

```
SQL> select name from v$datafile union all
  2  select name from v$tempfile union all
  3  select value from v$parameter2
  4  where name in ('control_files','spfile') union all
  5  select member from v$logfile
  6  /

NAME
--------------------------------------------------------------------------------
/u01/oradata/CDB2/system01.dbf
/u01/oradata/CDB2/sysaux01.dbf
/u01/oradata/CDB2/undotbs01.dbf
/u01/oradata/CDB2/pdbseed/system01.dbf
/u01/oradata/CDB2/users01.dbf
/u01/oradata/CDB2/pdbseed/sysaux01.dbf
/u01/oradata/CDB2/MASTER/system01.dbf
/u01/oradata/CDB2/MASTER/sysaux01.dbf
/u01/oradata/CDB2/MASTER/MASTER_users01.dbf
/u01/oradata/CDB2/temp01.dbf
/u01/oradata/CDB2/pdbseed/pdbseed_temp01.dbf
/u01/oradata/CDB2/MASTER/temp01.dbf
/u01/app/oracle/product/12.1.0.1/dbhome_1/dbs/spfileCDB2.ora
/u01/oradata/CDB2/control01.ctl
/u01/fra/CDB2/control02.ctl
/u01/oradata/CDB2/redo03.log
```

```
/u01/oradata/CDB2/redo02.log
/u01/oradata/CDB2/redo01.log
```

18 rows selected.

The database CDB2 which is about to be migrated has block change tracking enabled as well as flashback database using a Fast Recovery Area in /u01/fra. Both of these must be disabled prior to the migration into ASM, and any restore points must be dropped. Before dropping these please ensure with the change approval board that these are not a life insurance for another change! During the next steps backups will be taken, creating image copies of the database's components in ASM. The disk groups to be used are RECO for the Fast Recovery Area and DATA for anything else. Begin by taking a backup of the database using RMAN.

```
RMAN> backup as copy incremental level 0 database
2> format '+DATA' tag 'CDB2_pre_migration';

Starting backup at 15.08.2013 17:53
using target database control file instead of recovery catalog
allocated channel: ORA_DISK_1
channel ORA_DISK_1: SID=10 device type=DISK
channel ORA_DISK_1: starting datafile copy
input datafile file number=00001 name=/u01/oradata/CDB2/system01.dbf
output file name=+DATA/CDB2/DATAFILE/system.288.823542809 tag=CDB2_PRE_MIGRATION↵
RECID=3 STAMP=823542819
[...]
input datafile file number=00010 name=/u01/oradata/CDB2/MASTER/MASTER_users01.dbf
output file name=+DATA/CDB2/E4002A8CC0102B3AE0436638A8C0D53A/DATAFILE/users.282.823542887↵
tag=CDB2_PRE_MIGRATION RECID=11 STAMP=823542888
channel ORA_DISK_1: datafile copy complete, elapsed time: 00:00:01
Finished backup at 15.08.2013 17:54

Starting Control File and SPFILE Autobackup at 15.08.2013 17:54
piece handle=/u01/fra/CDB2/autobackup/2013_08_15/o1_mf_s_823542889_90t1yso5_.bkp↵
comment=NONE
Finished Control File and SPFILE Autobackup at 15.08.2013 17:54

RMAN> alter system switch logfile

Statement processed
```

The process will copy all the files as image copies into the disk group specified and switches the archive log. So far so good! There are still components outside ASM which need to be moved as well, including the server parameter file (you can't have a parameter file in ASM), the control files as well as the online redo logs. The server parameter file can be backed up manually if you have not requested an automatic backup.

At this point the Oracle documentation recommends turning flashback off and drop all restore points if you are moving the Fast Recovery Area into ASM as well which you probably should do. Furthermore the Block Change Tracking feature must now be turned off if it was enabled as per the docs. With the initial preparations completed you need to perform a clean shutdown of the database. In most cases "shutdown transactional" or "shutdown immediate" will be sufficient. What remains to be done is the move of the server parameter file into ASM, followed by the control file, then the online redo logs at last. The previously taken backup of the server parameter file is the first to be migrated into ASM:

```
RMAN> startup mount;
[...]
RMAN> restore spfile to '+DATA/CDB2/spfileCDB2.ora';

Starting restore at 15.08.2013 18:01
allocated channel: ORA_DISK_1
channel ORA_DISK_1: SID=237 device type=DISK

channel ORA_DISK_1: starting datafile backup set restore
channel ORA_DISK_1: restoring SPFILE
output file name=+DATA/CDB2/spfileCDB2.ora
channel ORA_DISK_1: reading from backup piece⏎
/u01/fra/CDB2/autobackup/2013_08_15/o1_mf_s_823542889_90t1yso5_.bkp
channel ORA_DISK_1: piece handle=/u01/fra/CDB2/autobackup/2013_08_15/o1_mf_s_823542889_90t1yso5_.bkp⏎
tag=TAG20130815T175449
channel ORA_DISK_1: restored backup piece 1
channel ORA_DISK_1: restore complete, elapsed time: 00:00:01
Finished restore at 15.08.2013 18:01
```

To ensure that Oracle can make use of the spfile you should update the database definition in Oracle Restart to point to the spfile:

```
[oracle@server1 dbs]$ srvctl config database -db CDB2 | grep -i spfile
Spfile:
[oracle@server1 dbs]$ srvctl modify database -db CDB2 -spfile '+DATA/CDB2/spfileCDB2.ora'
[oracle@server1 dbs]$ srvctl config database -db CDB2 | grep -i spfile
Spfile: +DATA/CDB2/spfileCDB2.ora
```

The old server parameter file in the $ORACLE_HOME/dbs directory should be renamed-a server parameter file in the default location will most likely be chosen first when starting the database, and you want it to use the spfile in ASM.

Restart the instance to force the use of the new spfile. To instruct the database to use the ASM disk groups from now on rather than the file system, you need to update the following initialization parameters related to Oracle Managed Files:

- db_create_file_dest

- db_recovery_file_dest_size (if a FRA was not in use previously)

- db_recovery_file_dest

- db_create_online_log_dest_n (optional)

In addition the control file needs to be restored into ASM, so while you are setting the OMF parameters you might as well change "control_files." This can all be done in RMAN or SQL*Plus using the following examples:

```
RMAN> alter system set db_create_file_dest='+DATA';

Statement processed
```

```
RMAN> alter system set db_recovery_file_dest_size = 20G;

Statement processed

RMAN> alter system set db_recovery_file_dest = '+RECO';

Statement processed

RMAN> ALTER SYSTEM SET CONTROL_FILES='+DATA','+RECO' scope=spfile;

Statement processed
```

Now restart the instance once more in preparation of the restore of the control file, ensure you perform a "startup nomount." The restore command does not require a backup of the control file, you can simply pick one of the original ones. If unsure, refer to the file list generated before the migration. In the example, the copy in /u01/oradata was restored:

```
RMAN> restore controlfile from autobackup;

Starting restore at 15.08.2013 18:14
allocated channel: ORA_DISK_1
channel ORA_DISK_1: SID=13 device type=DISK

recovery area destination: /u01/fra
database name (or database unique name) used for search: CDB2
channel ORA_DISK_1: AUTOBACKUP /u01/fra/CDB2/autobackup/2013_08_15/o1_mf_s_823542889_90t1yso5_.bkp
found ↵
in the recovery area
channel ORA_DISK_1: looking for AUTOBACKUP on day: 20130815
channel ORA_DISK_1: restoring control file from AUTOBACKUP /u01/fra/CDB2/autobackup/2013_08_15/
o1_mf_s_823542889_90t1yso5_.bkp
channel ORA_DISK_1: control file restore from AUTOBACKUP complete
output file name=+DATA/CDB2/CONTROLFILE/current.278.823544041
Finished restore at 15.08.2013 18:14
```

Mount the database in preparation for the switchover operation. In the next step you perform the switchover and recovery:

```
RMAN> alter database mount;
[...]
RMAN> switch database to copy;

Starting implicit crosscheck backup at 15.08.2013 18:15
allocated channel: ORA_DISK_1
channel ORA_DISK_1: SID=13 device type=DISK
Finished implicit crosscheck backup at 15.08.2013 18:15
```

```
Starting implicit crosscheck copy at 15.08.2013 18:15
using channel ORA_DISK_1
Crosschecked 9 objects
Finished implicit crosscheck copy at 15.08.2013 18:15

searching for all files in the recovery area
cataloging files...
cataloging done

List of Cataloged Files
=========================
File Name: /u01/fra/CDB2/autobackup/2013_08_15/o1_mf_s_823542889_90t1yso5_.bkp

datafile 1 switched to datafile copy "+DATA/CDB2/DATAFILE/system.288.823542809"
datafile 3 switched to datafile copy "+DATA/CDB2/DATAFILE/sysaux.279.823542829"
datafile 4 switched to datafile copy "+DATA/CDB2/DATAFILE/undotbs1.284.823542885"
datafile 5 switched to datafile copy ↵
"+DATA/CDB2/E4002011F3732897E0436638A8C06C51/DATAFILE/system.285.823542883"
datafile 6 switched to datafile copy "+DATA/CDB2/DATAFILE/users.283.823542887"
datafile 7 switched to datafile copy ↵
"+DATA/CDB2/E4002011F3732897E0436638A8C06C51/DATAFILE/sysaux.280.823542845"
datafile 8 switched to datafile copy ↵
"+DATA/CDB2/E4002A8CC0102B3AE0436638A8C0D53A/DATAFILE/system.286.823542875"
datafile 9 switched to datafile copy ↵
"+DATA/CDB2/E4002A8CC0102B3AE0436638A8C0D53A/DATAFILE/sysaux.287.823542861"
datafile 10 switched to datafile copy ↵
"+DATA/CDB2/E4002A8CC0102B3AE0436638A8C0D53A/DATAFILE/users.282.823542887"
```

RMAN> recover database;

```
Starting recover at 15.08.2013 18:16
using channel ORA_DISK_1

starting media recovery

archived log for thread 1 with sequence 6 is already on disk as file↵
/u01/oradata/CDB2/redo03.log
archived log file name=/u01/oradata/CDB2/redo03.log thread=1 sequence=6
media recovery complete, elapsed time: 00:00:01
Finished recover at 15.08.2013 18:16
```

```
RMAN> alter database open;
```

If you used Flashback Database and/or Block Change Tracking, you should enable these now. You can use the "report schema" command to verify the status of the database.

```
RMAN> report schema;

Report of database schema for database with db_unique_name CDB2
```

```
List of Permanent Datafiles
===========================
File  Size(MB)  Tablespace          RB segs  Datafile Name
----  --------  ------------------  -------  ----------------------
1     770       SYSTEM              ***      +DATA/CDB2/DATAFILE/system.288.823542809
3     660       SYSAUX              ***      +DATA/CDB2/DATAFILE/sysaux.279.823542829
4     85        UNDOTBS1            ***      +DATA/CDB2/DATAFILE/undotbs1.284.823542885
5     250       PDB$SEED:SYSTEM     ***      +DATA/CDB2/E40..C51/DATAFILE/system.285.823542883
6     5         USERS               ***      +DATA/CDB2/DATAFILE/users.283.823542887
7     590       PDB$SEED:SYSAUX     ***      +DATA/CDB2/E40...C51/DATAFILE/sysaux.280.823542845
8     260       MASTER:SYSTEM       ***      +DATA/CDB2/E40...53A/DATAFILE/system.286.823542875
9     590       MASTER:SYSAUX       ***      +DATA/CDB2/E40...53A/DATAFILE/sysaux.287.823542861
10    5         MASTER:USERS        ***      +DATA/CDB2/E40...53A/DATAFILE/users.282.823542887

List of Temporary Files
=======================
File  Size(MB)  Tablespace          Maxsize(MB)  Tempfile Name
----  --------  ------------------  -----------  --------------------
1     60        TEMP                32767        /u01/oradata/CDB2/temp01.dbf
2     20        PDB$SEED:TEMP       32767        /u01/oradata/CDB2/pdbseed/pdbseed_temp01.dbf
3     20        MASTER:TEMP         32767        /u01/oradata/CDB2/MASTER/temp01.dbf

RMAN>
```

You can see that the permanent tablespaces have been switched, but not the temp files. This can be corrected by adding a new temp file to the tablespace TEMP and dropping the existing one. The last part of the database to be migrated are the online redo logs. The strategy to move those into ASM requires the creation of a new set of groups within ASM, and dropping the old ones. First you need to check the status of your current online redo logs, still on the file system.

```
SQL> select group#,thread#,sequence#,bytes,status
  2  from v$log;

    GROUP#     THREAD#  SEQUENCE#       BYTES STATUS
---------- ---------- ---------- ---------- ----------------
         1          1         13   52428800 INACTIVE
         2          1         14   52428800 CURRENT
         3          1         12   52428800 INACTIVE
```

A total number of three groups are required, which can be added using the alter database add logfile command. The difficult bit is dropping the existing groups. If the group is needed by Oracle you will not be able to drop it. Instead, you have to switch the logfile and try again.

When you are done with the migration, you should take a full backup of the database. In this context a full backup is either a level 0 or a "full" backup as per the RMAN terminology.

Being able to downgrade

One of the aspects rarely taken into consideration is the fact that there might be a point in time after the migration that your senior management decides that the upgrade-although technically a success-was a failure and you need to get back to square one from where you started. The most likely reason for this almost worst-case scenario is that a critical process has not been sufficiently tested.

Whatever the reason, for you to be able to downgrade to the previous release you must not have upgraded the "compatible" initialization parameter. As soon as you set this to the higher release you are in the world of point-in-time restores or "forward fixing" (and little sleep). Data that has been entered into the system is then lost, which is most likely not what you want. Downgrades to the previous release are possible, and most users will consider them for the database stack. Downgrades of Clusterware, including Oracle Restart are less common and often not needed. In most rollback-cases the rollback has to be performed as part of the migration weekend, not a number of business days earlier.

If a downgrade is a real possibility in your organization then it has to be tested with the same rigorous quality assurance as the upgrade. And since every upgrade and downgrade is different, you should test the process thoroughly, documenting anomalies and the expected outcome so that the DBA in charge during the day is able to see it through.

Summary

This chapter demonstrated possible methods to upgrade a database. Upgrading a database to version 12c is not very different from upgrading in previous releases. The chapter walked you through 2 different upgrade paths. The first one offered full control over the process using the manual method of upgrading. This method can potentially complete in less time compared to previous versions of the database thanks to the parallel execution of scripts during the upgrade process. Some database options such as Application Express extend this process significantly though, and not every step in the migration process can be executed in parallel.

The next upgrade method uses the wizard driven Database Upgrade Assistant. It can make the upgrade a much smoother process as it runs a lot of the checks prior to the upgrade entirely automatically and repeatedly. Once the database has been upgraded it is possible to plug the non-CDB into a CDB as part of the consolidation process after advancing the compatible parameter to 12c.

Index

■ P, Q

■ X, Y, Z

Get the eBook for only $10!

Now you can take the weightless companion with you anywhere, anytime. Your purchase of this book entitles you to 3 electronic versions for only $10.

This Apress title will prove so indispensible that you'll want to carry it with you everywhere, which is why we are offering the eBook in 3 formats for only $10 if you have already purchased the print book.

Convenient and fully searchable, the PDF version enables you to easily find and copy code—or perform examples by quickly toggling between instructions and applications. The MOBI format is ideal for your Kindle, while the ePUB can be utilized on a variety of mobile devices.

Go to www.apress.com/promo/tendollars to purchase your companion eBook.

Apress®
THE EXPERT'S VOICE™